MIDLOTHIAN
PUBLIC LIBRARY

Pursuit of Excellence **THE OLYMPIC STORY**

Pursuit of Excellence # THE OLYMPIC STORY

by

The Associated Press
and
Grolier

GROLIER ENTERPRISES INC.
Danbury, Connecticut

Grolier Incorporated

PRESIDENT AND CHIEF EXECUTIVE OFFICER: Robert B. Clarke

VICE PRESIDENT, EDITORIAL DIRECTOR: Bernard S. Cayne

EDITOR: James E. Churchill, Jr.

ASSOCIATE EDITORS: Jeff Hacker, Edward Humphrey

COPY EDITORS: Grace F. Buonocore, Sharon Wirt,
Melvin Wolfson

INDEXERS: Jill Schuler, Susan Deromedi

MANAGING EDITOR: Doris E. Lechner

PRODUCTION EDITOR: Diane G. Buch

PHOTO RESEARCHERS: Jane Carruth, Janet Filling,
Terri A. Tibbatts, Pat Zimmerman

DESIGN: Murray Fleminger

ART DIRECTOR: Eric E. Akerman

ARTIST: Richard D. Harvey

DIRECTOR OF MANUFACTURING: Harriet Ripinsky

SENIOR MANAGER, MAIL ORDER MANUFACTURING:
David Bonjour

PRODUCTION MANAGER: Valerie Plue

Grolier Enterprises Inc.

PRESIDENT AND PUBLISHER: Stephen E. Toman

SENIOR VICE PRESIDENT, ASSOCIATE PUBLISHER:
Henry J. Lefcort

The Associated Press

PROJECT DIRECTOR: Dan Perkes

EDITOR-IN-CHIEF: Ben Olan

ASSOCIATE EDITOR: Roy J. Silver

EDITORIAL ASSISTANT: Carl Reuter

CONTRIBUTING WRITERS: Hal Bock, Will Grimsley,
Mike Rathet

Grolier Enterprises Inc. offers a varied selection of both adult and children's book racks. For details on ordering, please write:

Grolier Enterprises Inc.
Sherman Turnpike
Danbury, CT 06816
Attn: Premium Department

Library of Congress Cataloging in Publication Data
Main entry under title:

Pursuit of excellence, the Olympic story.

Includes index.
1. Olympic games—History.   I. Associated Press.
II. Grolier Enterprises.   III. Title: Olympic story.
GV721.5.P87   1983   796.48'09   83-12681
ISBN 0-7172-8171-X

FOREWORD

If a smile is the worldwide sign of friendship, then sports must be the international language of goodwill. And in my estimation, the Olympic movement is a prime medium for communicating both friendship and goodwill. For if one thing can be gained from an Olympic experience, it is the virtue of communicating.

Having attended all but one of the Olympic Games since 1948, I have felt the friendship, goodwill, and affection of peoples throughout the world. As a shy, "green," small-town 17-year-old, I competed in London in 1948 before 70,000 roaring fans. I was amazed; the multitude said the same things I had heard in my hometown stadium in Tulare, California. From their cheers came the support, reassurance, and confidence I needed so desperately.

Four years later—from the children in the streets of Helsinki to the sports-loving fans in Olympic Stadium—the Finns treated me like a son. With the cold war at its height, even the Russians invited me to visit their enclave where they showed me every courtesy. When I tried to return the hospitality, they explained that it was against regulations for them to visit another nation's headquarters, but I saw the longing in their eyes. We understood each other. We communicated.

During the ensuing years, I had the honor of representing the United States at athletic and other conferences that took me to more than 50 nations. Throughout my travels, whether my hosts spoke English or not, we understood without difficulty.

As the Olympics face the future, I am hopeful that the Games will be left to their rightful guardians, the youth of the world. If politics, the nemesis of past Games, can be notable for its absence, I am confident that the language of sports will be heard loud and clear. I look forward to this articulation.

Bob Mathias

BOB MATHIAS
Decathlon Gold Medalist, 1948 and 1952

CONTENTS

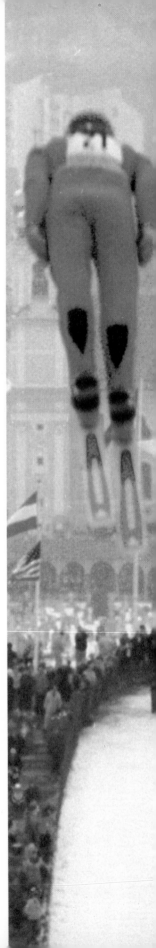

Swifter, Higher,

A study in poise and concentration, he draws three deep breaths and takes his practice swings at the back of the circle. Then, dipping his shoulder and bending his knees, he begins the first pivot. Gathering momentum as he turns, he gradually extends to full height and hurls the flat disc with maximum leverage and force. The release is accompanied by a loud grunt that breaks the morning stillness. As the discus arcs across the field he trudges toward its landing spot, measuring the distance and considering how to improve his technique. With the retrieved discus he goes back to the circle to try again. And when he is not throwing the discus he is running, exercising, or lifting weights to build his muscles and increase his agility. Not a day passes that he can't be found in the gym or on the practice field.

Five o'clock in the morning. Other than the two people entering the ice rink the streets are deserted. In a few minutes the teenage girl, wearing skates, limbers up on the deserted ice. The man waits. Then he calls for a figure and the practice begins.

Over and over she repeats compulsory figures, refining control and accuracy, while the coach's eye is quick to spot the smallest flaw. As long as the session lasts she concentrates on the complex movements she has done hundreds of times before, while the voice from the side lines criticizes timing, or posture, or even the expression on her face. Sometimes nothing seems to go right, and she wants to stamp off the ice and out of range of that insistent voice forever. But other times they both know she has a detail perfect—fatigue is forgotten and the goal that has brought them to work at this dead time of the morning seems reachable.

Stronger

From the first snowfall, the woods, roads, and fields witness the fleeting passage of the lithe young man on skis who seems to thrust himself at the rises—all poling arms and shushing skis—straining to maintain an even pace, responding to some interior timepiece. Before sunup and after it sets, whenever the snow permits, he can be found at the muscle-punishing effort that absorbs him.

Hour after hour she has been practicing the same routine—mounting the narrow beam, dancing, spinning, leaping, tumbling, and then dismounting in spectacular flying somersaults never before seen in gymnastics competition. Miraculously, she lands on her feet. But the lissome young acrobat, at 13 a relentless self-critic, is dissatisfied. She runs to the corner of the gym and buries her face in a towel. Her coach, who has seen this before, comes to her side to offer advice and encouragement. Finally, composure restored, the girl rubs some chalk on the bottoms of her feet and marches back to the balance beam for another routine.

What's got into them, these four isolated youths? Unknown to each other or to the hundreds of others who are similarly engaged, they are under the spell of a great dream. To realize that dream they have committed the major part of their lives to practicing a sport at which they have unusual talent. If they succeed in their effort, if they hone innate skill as close to perfection as possible, they may be chosen to compete in the next Olympic Games.

Once that ambition possesses them the dedicated know no letup. Every day is practice day, every practice session is another self-stretching test, every chance to compete with other athletes, an all-important comparison—right up to the moment when a selection committee picks the lucky few who will represent the nation in the Games.

The excitement and nervous tension of the athletes who make it to the Games can scarcely be measured. True, they have the confidence that comes with being selected to represent the nation. But what about the champions from other nations? When they face the final test, when they are all together in that massive arena, the focus of that awesome crowd, with only the judges' eyes, the stopwatch, and the measuring tape to gauge greatness, will they prove worthy of the confidence put in them? Can they expect to do as well in the actual Games as they did in the qualifying competition? What about the chance of stage fright, there under the gaze of those assessing thousands?

> "I had goose bumps from my Achilles tendons to my forehead," said swimmer Gary Hall, U.S. flagbearer in Montreal in 1976. "When we came out of the tunnel into the lights and the crowd began to echo, I started trembling. I hope people didn't notice the flag was shaking."

His sensations have no doubt been experienced by contestants as far back as the earliest Games of ancient Greece. The moving ceremony which Hall was remembering and the pageantry of the Olympic meets are modern manifestations of a tradition that is rich in symbolism, memorable for drama and excitement, occasionally lightened by comic interludes and colorful personalities.

The Games themselves have always been more than ceremony or lists of records or tallies of medals won. They are the legacy of a civilization that valued athletic prowess and physical perfection as among the noblest human attributes. In spite of national controversies and the tendency to equate numbers of medals with national prestige, the Olympics remain a stirring reaffirmation of high ideals.

The spirit of camaraderie and understanding among the amateur athletes of contrasting backgrounds and cultures transcends narrow nationalism or personal glory. The contestants are bound together by the shared experience of rigorous training and dedication to a universal standard of excellence.

> "The greatest thing I got out of the Olympics," said Bill Toomey after the 1968 meet in Mexico City, "was that I was able to go on that field and participate with guys from every country in the world. I didn't care how they got there. They were personally involved, physically involved, and intellectually involved."

Whenever and wherever the Games have taken place, they have provided a common ground for the display of maximum strength, skill, and grace. The cheers for Jesse Owens in 1936 in Berlin, the swapping of gifts by U.S. and Soviet oarsmen in 1952, the tumultuous joy for Rosi Mittermaier among the rival skiers in 1976 exemplify the selfless good sportsmanship and mutual respect which the Olympics are meant to foster.

The ceremonial opening of a modern Olympic meet is a thrilling spectacle. First, an official of the host nation proclaims the opening of the Games. Then the parade of the athletes begins, led by the bearer of the white Olympic flag with the familiar design of five colored rings, blue, yellow, black, green, and red, linked together to represent the sporting friendship of all the peoples of the world. After the official flag, the athletes of Greece, where it all began, enter the stadium. They are followed by the athletes of the participating countries in the alphabetical order of the host-country's language, except for the representatives of the host country. They come last.

Each team of athletes follows one of their number whom they have selected to carry their country's flag. The teams wear costumes that suggest a particular native dress. They parade the complete circuit of the stadium, to the applause of the crowd in the stands. Soon several thousand white doves are freed above the stadium, their flight symbolizing a spirit of peace and freedom and recalling the agreement, made more than 2,800 years ago by the kings of Elis and Sparta, that the territory devoted to the Games should be neutral ground.

No part of the opening pageantry is more memorable than the recitation of the Olympic oath by an athlete of the host nation, on behalf of all the participants:

> "In the name of all competitors I promise that we will take part in these Olympic Games, respecting and abiding by the rules which govern them, in the true spirit of sportsmanship, for the glory of the sport and the honor of our teams."

The final and most inspiring ritual is the solemn carrying in of the Olympic Flame. The earliest Games, held to honor Zeus, took place near the temple dedicated to him in which a sacred flame was kept burning. The flame borne into the stadium in the opening ceremony symbolizes the continuity between the ancient and modern Games. The ceremony we see now, of bringing in the flame carried from Greece, started in 1936. A torch, lighted by the sun's rays near Zeus' temple in ancient Olympia, is carried by a relay of runners, and by ships or planes when necessary, to the site of the newest Games. The final relay runner enters the stadium, torch carried high. He circles the track. The watching throng is hushed as he reaches a point below a giant dish fixed to the rim of the arena and, still running, mounts to the dish. The whole sky seems to catch fire. The crowd erupts in transports: the new Games have begun!

The Games have established a tradition of friendly competition among nations. Nevertheless, the compelling drama of every Olympics is the individual athletic performance. It is the strength of the weightlifter, shot putter, or wrestler; the speed of a sprinter or downhill skier; the grace of a gymnast or figure skater; the steadiness of a marksman; and the coordinated play of a soccer, basketball, or ice hockey team. It is the effortless artistry of skater Peggy Fleming and gymnast Nadia Comaneci; and the unorthodox technique—flailing arms and rolling head—of runner Emil Zátopek. It is Bob Beamon seeming to walk in air to a world record in the long jump; and it is relentlessly driving Dorando Pietri collapsing 300 meters from the marathon finish line.

The code by which they all live was summarized in 1895 by Father Henri-Martin Didon, a French educator and sports enthusiast. Three Latin words engraved on the lintel of his school's doorway—''Citius, Altius, Fortius''—have been adapted as the Olympic Motto—Swifter, Higher, Stronger. Whether a teenage swimmer or an aging long distance walker, the athlete governed by that code has forsaken other interests to stretch for new pinnacles in athletic skills.

Proving to be best in an Olympic event is the sports amateur's dream. Just as in ancient Greece the laurel wreath was the highest honor that could be bestowed upon an athlete, so an Olympic medal

The arrival of the Olympic torch, brought from Olympia by a relay of runners, is the highlight of the opening ceremonies. For the first time, a young girl and boy carried the torch in Montreal in 1976. They later married.

Innsbruck, 1964: Speed skater Lidia Skoblikova proudly displays her four golds. An Olympic medal is the most cherished prize in amateur athletics.

The Olympic torch is used to light the Olympic flame, "which shall not be extinguished until the close of the Games."

is the most treasured prize in modern nonprofessional sports. Its presentation is a forever-bright climax. All the pain, the sacrifice, and the lonely preparation are repaid by that small disc and ribbon. Purely and simply, its recipients stand above the heads of all others.

"If you don't try to win," said Jesse Owens, America's running star at the 1936 Games in Berlin, "you might as well hold the Olympics in somebody's back yard. The thrill of competing carries with it the thrill of a gold medal. One wants to prove himself the best."

But even where no gold or silver or bronze medal is awarded, the years of hard training and competing have their own reward for the true amateurs of sports. Those who did not win know that they contended *with* the world's best and that they lost *to* the best. There can be only honor in that. Pierre de Coubertin, working to revive the ancient Games, said that for him "the most important thing in the Olympic Games is not to win but to take part, just as the most important thing in life is not the triumph but the struggle. The essential thing is not to have conquered but to have fought well."

The Ancient Games

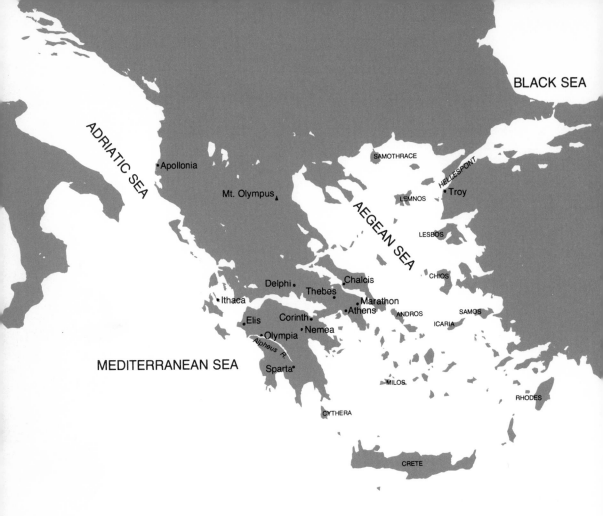

The map shows the Aegean region with the following labeled locations:

BLACK SEA

ADRIATIC SEA

- Apollonia
- Mt. Olympus
- SAMOTHRACE
- HELLESPONT
- Troy
- LEMNOS
- AEGEAN SEA
- LESBOS
- Delphi
- Chalcis
- Thebes
- CHIOS
- Ithaca
- Marathon
- Athens
- ANDROS
- SAMOS
- Elis
- Corinth
- Nemea
- ICARIA
- Olympia
- Alpheus R.
- MEDITERRANEAN SEA
- Sparta
- MILOS
- RHODES
- CYTHERA
- CRETE

The isles of Greece, the isles of
Greece!
Where burning Sappho
loved and sung,
Where grew the arts of war
and peace,
Where Delos rose, and
Phoebus sprung!
Eternal summer gilds them yet,
But all, except their sun,
is set.

—LORD BYRON

Photo pages 14–15: An ancient altar near the stadium at Delphi bears five interlocking rings. It is supposed to represent the five concentric rings on the discus hung in the temple of Hera at Olympia. In 1920 the rings became the Olympic symbol.

Reporting today's Olympic Games is a technological masterpiece. It encompasses everything from worldwide television relayed by space satellites to electronic high-speed computers, tallying the results of each event and delivering them around the globe within seconds after athletes have completed their competition.

Electric timers measure performances and scoreboards flash instantaneous results to the assembled fans, who gather each four years to watch this celebration of sport.

Each event is carefully recorded with a sense of history by the organizers of the modern Olympics. But there was no such concern for records or history when the Games began in ancient Greece. If there had been, the recording of winners would have been much easier for the ancient Greeks than it is for the organizers of today's brief Olympic festivals, despite our advanced technology.

The reason? Simple. From all that historians can determine, there was only one event in the earliest meet at Olympia and it lasted no longer, perhaps, than 30 seconds!

The first recorded champion at Olympia was a sprinter, Coroebus, a cook from the nearby Greek city of Elis. Running naked on a sanded course he sped across the finish line under the gaze of thousands of Greeks to win a foot race that was approximately 630 feet long—or one stade—from which the word stadium was derived. His feat won him a wreath of olive leaves.

That was in 776 B.C. The year became important for later Greek historians. Starting in about 300 B.C. they dated everything by the Olympiads—the periods of 4 years between Games—that began with that first recorded foot race.

As far back as we can trace the civilization of ancient Greece, there was a reverence of the athlete. The Greeks believed that the body of man has a glory, as well as his mind, that both mind and body need discipline, and that by such discipline men best honored Zeus. From time to time they held great ceremonies of Games, named for the areas in which they took place—Pythian, Isthmian, Nemean, and above all, Olympian. The Olympian Games go back to the time of the first people to live in the valley of the Alpheus River. There, at Elis in the western Peloponnesus, was Olympia, "the fairest spot of Greece." In the spacious and charming valley from which snow-covered distant mountains can be seen, was one of the most famous sanctuaries of ancient Greece. The religious role of the sanctuary began thousands of years ago, long before the Games held there every four years to honor Zeus.

As it happens we know a good deal about Olympia. It was brought to light, beginning in 1875, by German archeologists. The most important of the ruins they uncovered are those of a temple of Zeus that was in use about 2,500 years ago, and a temple of his wife, Hera, that is even older—about 2,900 years. The world-famous statue of Hermes by the sculptor Praxiteles, now in the nearby museum, was found in the Temple of Hera. The Temple of Zeus contained one of the Seven Wonders of the World—a statue, larger than a two-story house, of Zeus on his throne, made by Phidias of ivory and gold.

Above: Praxiteles' statue of Hermes is on display in Olympia's museum. The patron deity of young men and athletes is delivering the baby Dionysus to the protecting nymphs in Nysa. At left: the remains of a secret entrance to the stadium from the sacred grove of Olympia in which the temples of Zeus and Hera were located.

The Ancient Games   17

Foot racers using the full arm swing are depicted on a 6th century B.C. Greek vase.

The great desire of the cities near the temple of Zeus was to win the favor of the god by their show of reverence. So, by 500 B.C., Sparta, Elis, Athens, and Syracuse rivaled each other in the magnificence of their offerings to the temple.

Whatever the earliest religious ritual at Olympia may have been, over the years it evolved into a festival of the state. To it, to enter themselves in the festival Games, went candidates from all parts of Greece. They were tested in the gymnasium at Elis before they were allowed to compete at Olympia. The ten-month training at Elis was considered the most valuable preparation athletes could undergo. They lived in the gymnasium (from the word for naked) and practiced all day, every day, under the eyes of professional trainers. Officials of Elis decided who could compete and, later, who should get the prizes.

Athletes from Elis won the first 13 Olympic races. Only the Doric peoples of the Peloponnesus participated originally. Other Greek tribes joined in later; then came the peoples from Crete, Rhodes, Sicily, Egypt, and Asia Minor. The Games served as a common link in the Hellenic world.

Nothing was more important to the Greeks than the Games, and nothing was permitted to interfere with them—not even wars. During the month of the festival of religious rites and sporting events called the Hieromenia, trade ceased and a truce was declared in the constant bickering that existed between the Greek city-states. This Olympic peace was called the Ekecheiria. For as long as the Games lasted, no one under arms could enter Olympia. It was sacred ground.

Just how much the Games meant to the ancient Greeks can be gathered from one event. In 480 B.C. the festival of the Games was in process when a Spartan army had to defend Thermopylae, and with it all Greece, against Persian King Xerxes and his invaders. Although the very fate of their country was at stake, thousands of Greeks showed up at the stadium at Olympia to watch the championship round of the boxing competition.

Where and when did this business begin? The fables of ancient Greece offer many explanations. Greek poets told of a great duel between Zeus and his father, Kronos, one of the Titans, for mastery of the world. Zeus won, and to honor him, a temple was raised in the valley of the sacred river Alpheus, below the mountain—the Kronion—where the titanic duel was fought.

An archtectural model of Olympia (c. 150 A.D.) shows the columned Temple of Zeus in the center of the sacred grove, the Temple of Hera (center, rear), the ceremonial reception hall (left, front), the house of priests (left, center), and the palaestra (left, rear).

The Ancient Games   19

Or there is the tale of Pelops and his duel of wits with King Oenomaus of Pisatis, the son of Ares, God of War. Oenomaus had a beautiful daughter named Hippodameia. The king had offered her hand in marriage to any suitor who could take the girl from her home by chariot and then outspeed Oenomaus when he pursued them.

Winning the race was vital because it was the custom of Oenomaus to execute the losers to prevent the fulfillment of an oracle's prophecy that he would die at the hands of his son-in-law. Thirteen suitors raced off with Hippodameia and each lost his life because the king had the fastest steeds.

Pelops studied the tactics of the losers and decided he needed help. So he made Myrtilos, the king's charioteer, an offer he couldn't refuse—half the kingdom if his master was defeated.

When the chase began Oenomaus was confident that Pelops would end on a spear like all the other suitors. However, what he didn't know was that Myrtilos had damaged an axle on the regal chariot. As the king closed in on Pelops, the axle gave way and Oenomaus broke his royal neck in the crash, fulfilling the prophecy. So proud was Pelops of his cunning victory over Oenomaus that he instituted the contests as a memorial, and held them near Olympia in the fertile valley where he and others had chased for the hand of his bride, Hippodameia.

While its origins are shrouded in myth and mystery, the festival at which Coroebus won his wreath in 776 B.C. was repeated at 4-year intervals for the next 1,200 years.

The first contestants at Olympia, who gathered in the autumn, were sprinters. The lone race was run on a straight track. Twenty athletes could take positions at the starting line, marked by grooved limestone blocks. A bugle blast was their signal to start.

As Olympiad followed Olympiad, the contests increased in number and variety. The first expansion of the Games occurred in the XIV Olympiad, when a race covering two lengths of the stadium was added. Four years later a race of about three miles became part of the program. In 708 B.C. the five-event pentathlon was introduced. It was designed to provide the ultimate in well-coordinated athletes. Contestants first competed in a jumping event, with the best finishers advancing to the spear (javelin) throw. The four best in that competition advanced to the sprint race, where another athlete was eliminated. That left three for the discus. The two best of them wrestled for the pentathlon championship.

The discus was a Greek favorite. The man who could throw it farthest was regarded as the greatest athlete. It was on a bronze discus, which Aristotle saw in the Temple of Hera, that the traditional laws governing the festival at Olympia were inscribed.

Following the first Games in 776 B.C., Olympia, an area of beautiful, hilly countryside lying about 14 miles from the sea in Elis, became a center of Greek civilization. Citizens from all parts of the Hellenic world flocked to the area to honor Zeus and revere the athletes. The sacred hill where Zeus battled Kronos is the treed area (upper right); the end of the race track is at its base.

Boxing was part of the competition by 688 B.C. Boxers wore only straps with metal rings around their fists, and metal knuckles. The match continued until a contestant announced that he was defeated. The palaestra in Olympia (ruins, below) was the place of exercise for wrestlers and boxers. It was located directly outside the west wall of the sacred grove.

By 688 B.C. there were boxing contests in which the competitors at first tied leather straps around their fists. Later they would fit metal rings on the straps and then metal knuckles. Four-horse chariot races, first run in 680 B.C., were open to men rich enough to afford chariots and horses. From the beginning they were a spectacular and popular event very different from the older contests, which were mainly athletic or military in nature. Horse races were part of the festival in 648 B.C. They were run in a separate hippodrome next to the stadium. These horse races were the only events in which bondsmen or slaves were permitted to participate. A winning owner received the olive wreath, while his victorious servant was given a cotton headband.

It was in 648 B.C., too, that the contest called pancration (from the Greek words for "all strength") was introduced. It was a cruel combination of wrestling and boxing, and no holds were barred. Each match went to the finish with no rest periods. Only when one contestant lay unconscious or raised his hand as a sign of defeat did the event end.

The victory of Arrachion of Phigalia gives us an idea of the character of the pancration. Arrachion, it is said, was being strangled by his opponent, a perfectly legal maneuver according to the rules. As he was losing consciousness, Arrachion in desperation twisted his foe's leg. He inflicted such pain that the opponent lifted his hand to signal defeat. But as the judges declared Arrachion the winner, he lay dead before them, ultimate loser in the pancration.

Over and above these exercises of physical strength and agility, the celebrations included contests in music, poetry, and eloquence. The festivals gave musicians, poets, and authors the best possible chance to present their work to the public. The fame of those whose efforts were rewarded with the olive wreath spread far and wide.

The stadium to the east of the sacred grove was one stade (630 feet) long. Some 45,000 spectators could witness the contests from the slopes at the sides and far end of the running track.

Winners of Olympic events were revered as heroes; their exertion and sacrifice could result in rich rewards. Their triumphs became part of the record kept in the altis, or sacred grove. Three-time winners had statues erected in their likeness and received various gifts and honors, including exemption from taxation.

Often a winner would return to his home and be escorted through an opening in the wall surrounding his city—an opening created by the citizens to show the world that a city with an Olympic champion need fear no enemy.

Among the legendary heroes of the ancient Games were Milo of Croton, who won six wrestling competitions during the sixth century B.C., and Polydamas of Thessaly, victor in the pancration in the XCIII Olympiad (408 B.C.).

Milo supposedly developed his brute strength by carrying a calf on his shoulders every day of his life until it was a full grown bull. Polydamas is said to have killed a lion with his bare hands and stopped a chariot by grabbing the back of it with one hand.

Theagenes of Thasos possessed several skills. He competed in boxing, sprinting, and the pancration, winning the wreath no fewer than 1,400 times!

At the stadium, grooved limestone blocks (above) served as the starting point for the barefooted runners. Running in full armor—helmets and shields—(below and page 25) was a particular favorite among the Greeks. The olive branches given to the winners were the most desired prize.

By the fifth century B.C., Olympia was the holiest place of ancient Greece and its ceremonial Games were at their height. They lasted five days; religious rituals occupied much of the time. At the opening of the Games a pig was sacrificed to Zeus and a black ram to Pelops. When an athlete won an event he was supposed to give public thanks to the deities.

Set above the multitude by their championships, Olympic victors expected esteem. Occasionally, Olympic champions returning home did not receive the welcome they felt they deserved. Thus, when Oebotas returned to Achaia following a victory and was virtually ignored, he put a curse on his city. During the next 74 Olympiads, no citizen of Achaia won an event. The Oracle at Delphi told the people of Achaia to honor the memory of Oebotas with a statue. When they did Sostratas of Achaia won the foot race for boys in the next Olympiad.

Women were barred from the early Games, both as spectators and competitors, because the Olympics were regarded as primarily religious ceremonies. Those women who let curiosity get the better of them were put to death if they were caught.

However, in 396 B.C. a woman from Rhodes escaped that fate. Kallipateira dressed in men's clothes so she could watch her son compete in boxing in the XCVI Olympiad. When he won, Kallipateira ran to shower him with kisses, and so gave herself away. Because her father was Diagoras, the boxing champion of the LXXIX Olympiad in 464 B.C. and one of the most celebrated of all ancient athletes, the penalty of death was waived.

The ancient Games reached their zenith in the so-called Golden Age of Greece. With the emergence of the mighty Roman Empire, the sun began to set on Greece. Then the glory of the Olympic Games began to dim. Contests among amateur sportsmen gradually changed. The high ideals of the earlier years were lost sight of. Interest in striving to be perfect, just for the satisfaction of doing one's best, gave way to emphasis on the rewards. Winning became the only concern. Foreign athletes of known prowess were given Greek citizenship so they could enter the Games. Rich men who could not themselves hope to compete began to hire professionals so that they might be sure of winning the bets wagered on the contests.

As the original purpose of the Games was forgotten Olympia itself began to decline, even though Romans, who had conquered Greece, continued the Games and added to the riches of the temple of Zeus.

Perhaps the low point was reached in 67 A.D. when Nero appeared at the CCXI Olympiad with a retinue of 5,000, whose primary function was to applaud him. No opponent dared face Nero in the chariot race. When he fell from his chariot, fawning officials put him back, but he could not finish the race. Yet the jury declared him champion. It had been ordered to do so.

The Games continued for some three centuries after Nero's sham, but the days of splendor had passed. The long list of ancient Olympic champions ends with the boxer Varazdetes or Varastad, an Armenian. In 393 A.D. Roman Emperor Theodosius I, a convert to Christianity who considered the Games pagan, ordered them to be abolished because they had become a public nuisance. The immense statue of Zeus was taken from the temple and carried away to Constantinople, where it was lost in a huge fire. A few years later, in the reign of Theodosius II, the marvelous temples of Zeus and Hera were dismantled. Successive earthquakes and floods ruined the site and gradually Olympia was completely buried. So it would remain, lost from sight and half-forgotten, through century after century, until 1875.

The Games Revived

For 15 centuries the world went along without the Olympic Games. And it probably would have continued to do without them except for an energetic Frenchman, Baron Pierre de Coubertin. Coubertin is credited with almost single-handedly bringing about the revival of the Olympic festival.

He was born on January 1, 1863, in Paris into a family with wealth and aristocratic position. His older brother was enrolled at St. Cyr, the traditional training school for military career officers. Pierre considered following suit, but at barely 5′ 3″, he hardly possessed a commanding stature. He turned his attention first to political science, and then to the field of public education.

It was in the latter area that he found fulfillment. He traveled widely, studying the education offered in Europe and the United States.

Everywhere he went Coubertin was fascinated by the way education seemed to be intertwined with sports. Everywhere, that is, except in his native France, where tradition kept the two separated. He went to work to change that practice.

About this same time, a team of German archaeologists were engaged in digging up and restoring the ruins of ancient Olympia. News of their work attracted visitors to Greece from around the world, Baron de Coubertin among them.

As he toured the site where once Coroebus had raced and Milo had wrestled, Coubertin was enthralled.

What great good might not accrue, he wondered, if the Games that celebrated perfection in amateur sports could be reintroduced into a world that already was blighted by an international trend toward commercialism in sports. Just *how* commercial they had become and how restricted the definition of amateur had grown he had learned when he tried to send French rowers to compete at Henley. The money prizes that were given winning rowers in France made their recipients professionals in the eyes of the Henley officials.

Now a man with a mission, Coubertin set out to achieve the goal of an Olympic revival. He worked slowly, attracting widespread attention through the publication of dozens of books (published at his own expense) that dealt with educational theory and his efforts to modernize the French system of studies. Tirelessly, he gave dinners, wrote articles, gathered meetings to publicize and gain support for his ideas. In 1888 he helped to found the Athletic Sports

Union, an organization which sought to increase physical education in French schools and universities.

A year later, he began to publish a monthly newspaper designed to stimulate an interest in sports through France. That same year the French government commissioned him to study physical culture on a worldwide scale.

By 1892, he had a proposal to make. Using a November 25 meeting of the Athletic Sports Union in Paris for his forum, he called for an international gathering of athletes in all sports for the purpose of friendship, fellowship, athletics and, most importantly, peace:

> "Let us export oarsmen, runners, fencers; there is the free trade of the future—and on that day when it shall take place among the customs of Europe the cause of peace will have received a new and powerful support."

The first reactions to the proposal were less than enthusiastic: Coubertin was a dreamer. But he persisted, pressing the idea with athletic organizations throughout the world.

One year after he first broached the Olympic idea, Coubertin was host to an international gathering of sportsmen, together with the Athletic Sports Union, at the Sorbonne. That meeting greatly encouraged him.

On June 16, 1894, he assembled another athletic congress with delegates from nine nations, including Russia and the United States, to study the questions of amateurism. Seven items were on the published agenda but on his own Coubertin added an eighth—the possibility of reviving the Olympic Games.

It was his moment. He spoke with such conviction that when he finished he had won the support of all delegates. On June 23, 1894, the congress unanimously voted to revive the Olympics and, to Coubertin's surprise, decided to speed up by four years his own timetable for the first games of the Modern Olympiad.

Coubertin originally hoped to have the renewal of the Games coincide with the Paris International Exposition of 1900 and the start of the twentieth century. But the enthusiasm of the delegates could not be denied; they voted to hold the revived Games in 1896 in Athens, Greece.

It was a charming idea, returning the Olympics to the land of their ancient origin, but problems began to spring up like mushrooms. The most troubling was the lack of a suitable stadium in which to hold the Games. The Greek government, facing serious economic difficulties even before the Games were dropped in its lap, nevertheless embarked on an ambitious fund-raising campaign to generate income. Their efforts included the issuance of commemorative stamps, a device still in use today.

Despite public contributions and income raised from the sale of stamps, there was an enormous shortage until an approach was made to George Averoff, a wealthy Greek merchant living in Alexandria. Averoff was fascinated by the idea of an Olympic revival and agreed to pay the entire cost of restoring Athens' once magnificent stadium of Herodes Atticus. It had originally been constructed in 143 B.C. by Tiberius Claudius Herodes Atticus, an administrator of the Emperor Hadrian. Averoff's extraordinary philanthrophy made it possible to hold the Games on schedule.

George Avyheris (1814–1899) made a fortune in Russia. Thereafter, he was called Averoff. He used his great wealth to benefit his native Greece, restoring ancient monuments and helping to finance the redesigned capital city. In 1896, grateful Athenians erected a statue of him near the stadium he restored for the revival of the Olympic Games.

The first Modern Olympic Games were just the beginning of Coubertin's connection with the Games. For a period of years, during which sports became more generally practiced and physical education more firmly integrated in public education systems, Coubertin did not enjoy a proportionate renown, as might have been expected. However, after the very successful Stockholm Games in 1912 he was generally recognized as the driving force behind the Games' revival. He managed personally to preside over the International Olympic Committee until 1925, assuming the greatest part of the financial and administrative duties by himself. He created the Olympic Charter and Protocol and the Athlete's Oath, as well as the format of the opening and closing ceremonies. He fought off all attempts to immobilize the Games in some permanent location (Switzerland and Sweden were often suggested), and he successfully persisted in opening the Games to any qualified amateur, without regard to social class.

In 1918 he moved permanently from France to Switzerland. For the remainder of his life he continued to devote his energies and his dwindling funds to his great idea, but with less and less effect. As his control and personal influence diminished, he became embittered and angry. When he died, in Geneva on September 2, 1937, he had been left behind by the International Olympic Committee.

Except for his heart, he was buried in Lausanne. His heart was taken to Olympia, to be buried in the sacred grove there.

Of the Games that had been so great a part of his life's work, he wrote:

A simple monument of marble, its plinth surrounded by wild flowers, was erected in Olympia to mark the spot where the ancient Games were held to honor Zeus. The god's head, circled by a victor's chaplet, is carved above the inscription. Coubertin's heart was buried here. Of Olympia he wrote ". . . that ground belongs to me."

My friends and I have not worked to bring back the Olympic Games in order that they may be turned into a museum or cinema piece, or so that they may be exploited by commercial or political powers. Our desire has been in reviving an institution which goes back 25 centuries, that you may once again become followers of the religion of sport as it was conceived by our glorious ancestors. In this modern world, full of great possibilities but which is at the same time threatened by a perilously decadent trend, the Olympic Movement can become a school not only of physical endurance and energy, but also of moral nobility and purity. This, however, can only be achieved if you strive continually to raise your standards of honor and your conception of impartial sport to the same height as that of your physical achievement. The future lies in your hands.

Peace would be furthered by the Olympic Games, but peace could be the product only of a better world; a better world could be brought about only by individuals; and better individuals could be developed only by the give and take, the buffeting and battering, the stress and strain of fierce competition.

First of all, it is necessary to maintain in sport the noble and chivalrous character which distinguished it in the past, so that it shall continue to be part of the education of present day peoples, in the same way that sport served so wonderfully in the times of ancient Greece. The public has a tendency to transform the Olympic athlete into the paid gladiator. These two attitudes are not compatible.

The Olympic Organization

The agency that must deal with the problems of organizing and running the modern Games is the International Olympic Committee (IOC). It was created by the Congress of Paris, on June 23, 1894, to be "the final authority on all questions concerning the Olympic movement." It is a permanent organization whose headquarters are the Château de Vidy in Lausanne, Switzerland. It retains all rights to both the Games of the Olympiad, the proper name of the summer events, and to the Olympic Winter Games, the proper name for the winter events.

Organization and Meetings. The IOC selects such persons as it considers qualified to be its members. They must speak French or English and be citizens of and reside in a country possessing an IOC-recognized National Olympic Committee (NOC). Only nations that have hosted the Olympics or those extremely active in the Olympic movement may have two IOC representatives; other nations have one. IOC members were elected originally for life, but any representative elected after 1965 must retire at the age of 72. An IOC member "may be expelled by resolution of the IOC."

The IOC president is elected by members of the committee by an absolute majority of those present. The term of office is eight years, and reelection for successive four-year terms is permitted. Three vice presidents are chosen for four-year terms. The president, three vice presidents, and five additional IOC members form the Executive Board. The basic duties of the board, which meets when convened by the president, are to ensure that the rules are rigidly enforced; to propose the agenda for IOC sessions; to recommend persons for possible election to the IOC; to manage IOC finances; to appoint the IOC directors; to be responsible for the administration and organization plan; and to maintain IOC records.

A session, a general meeting of IOC members, is held at least once a year at a place fixed by the IOC. An extraordinary session is also possible. The NOC of the host city bears the cost of a session. The Olympic Congress, composed of the members and the honorary members of the IOC, the delegates of the International Sports Federations (IFs) and NOCs, and representatives of

Amid carefully staged pageantry, the athletes take the oath.

other organizations invited by the IOC, is convened by the IOC president.

Languages and Finances. French and English are the official languages of the IOC. In the case of discrepancy, the French text prevails. The IOC is permitted to accept financial gifts and to seek funds from other sources to fulfill its functions. Cities selected to organize the Games must pay the IOC the sum requested. All funds coming from an Olympic or Winter Games celebration belong to the IOC. Portions of such sums may be granted or allocated by the IOC to the Organizing Committee of the Olympic Games (OCOG), the IFs, and the NOCs.

National Olympic Committees. In order to further the Olympic movement, the IOC recognizes NOCs. The primary duty of the NOCs is to guarantee the "development and safety of the Olympic movement and sport." In addition, NOCs are solely responsible for the representation of their respective countries at the Olympics and must make the necessary organizational arrangements when their countries are hosts. NOCs must remain completely autonomous.

Eligibility and Regulations. To be eligible for Olympic competition, an athlete must observe IOC and IF rules and must not have received financial rewards or material benefits in connection with sport participation. Those competitors who have "been registered as professional athletes or professional coaches in any sport; signed a contract as a professional athlete or professional coach in any sport before the official closing of the Olympic Games; accepted without the knowledge of their IF, national federation, or NOC, material advantages for their preparation or participation in sports competition; allowed their person, name, picture, or sports performances to be used for advertising, except when their IF, NOC, or national federation has entered into a contract for sponsorship or equipment . . . ; carried advertising material on their person or clothing in the Olympic Games and Games under the patronage of the IOC, other than trademarks on technical equipment or clothing as agreed by the IOC with the IFs; in the practice of sport and in the opinion of the IOC, manifestly contravened the spirit of fair play in the exercise of sport, particularly by the use of doping or violence" may not participate in the Olympic Games.

The IOC does not stipulate an age limitation for competitors. With IOC approval and according to IF rules, women are permitted to participate. A medical code lists prohibited drugs and makes competitors liable to medical control and examination.

Administration and Organization. The Olympic Games must take place during the first year of the Olympiad (a period of four successive years which follows the Games) that they are to celebrate. They may not be postponed to another year. The Games of the Olympiad may not exceed 16 days. The Winter Games must be limited to 12 days. If there is no competition on Sundays or holidays, the time span may be extended accordingly.

The IOC selects the city in which the Games are to occur. The OCOG is responsible for all "problems of organization." The OCOG must provide an Olympic village for men and another for women.

Exhibitions and demonstrations of national art are to be arranged by the OCOG, subject to IOC approval.

White doves, symbolizing the spirit of peace and freedom, are released during the opening ceremonies. The act is traditional, not part of the official program.

The IOC recognizes the following sports federations: International Amateur Athletic Federation (IAAF), International Rowing Federation (FISA), International Amateur Basketball Federation (FIBA), International Bobsleigh and Tobogganing Federation (FIBT), International Amateur Boxing Association (AIBA), International Canoe Federation (ICF), International Amateur Cycling Federation (FIAC), International Equestrian Federation (FEI), International Fencing Federation (FIE), International Association Football Federation (FIFA), International Gymnastics Federation (FIG), International Weightlifting Federation (IWF), International Handball Federation (IHF), International Hockey Federation (FIH), International Ice Hockey Federation (IIHF), International Judo Federation (IJF), International Luge Federation (FIL), International Amateur Wrestling Federation (FILA), International Amateur Swimming Federation (FINA), International Skating Union (ISU), International Modern Pentathlon and Biathlon Union (UIPMB), International Skiing Federation (FIS), International Tennis Federation (ITF), International Table Tennis Federation (ITTF), International Shooting Union (UIT), International Archery Federation (FITA), International Volleyball Federation (FIVB), and the International Yacht Racing Union (IYRU).

Athletes from Saudia Arabia enter the stadium. "Each delegation dressed in its official uniform must be preceded by a name board bearing the name of the country under which it is recognized and must be accompanied by its flag."

Once the IOC decides to include a sport on the Olympic program, it becomes an Olympic sport and must comply with the rule requirements. Only sports widely practiced by men in at least 50 countries and 3 continents and by women in at least 35 countries and 3 continents may be part of the program. "An event is a competition included in a sport or in one of its disciplines, resulting in ranking and medal awards." Only events practiced in at least 25 countries and 3 continents may be included.

The program of the Games of the Olympiad is to include at least 15 Olympic sports. There is no minimum number of sports required for the Olympic Winter Games. The IOC in consultation with the IFs fixes the number of entries. The number of entries for individual events may not exceed three per country; some winter sports may be exceptions. The number of teams is not to exceed 20 in those team sports in which men and women participate. The number of teams is not to exceed 12 for team sports in which only one of the sexes participates; in football (soccer), there are 16 teams.

With IOC approval, the OCOG may choose not more than two recognized sports as demonstrations during the Games.

The technical officials (referees, judges, umpires, timekeepers, inspectors, and a jury for each sport) shall be appointed by the appropriate IF. The official and jury members cannot have been professionals in sport. The jury decides technical questions.

Mass Media, Publications, Copyrights. Steps must be taken to guarantee that representatives of the different mass media can attend the competitions and ceremonies. The IOC's Executive Board oversees media accreditation. The IOC may, subject to payment, grant the right to broadcast/distribute coverage. All agreements with radio-television networks must be negotiated by the IOC and the OCOG. Each Olympic and Winter Games shall be filmed for historic posterity.

An explanatory pamphlet for each sport, outlining the program and arrangements, shall be printed in French and English

Judges oversee the 1964 Games in Tokyo. The appropriate international sport federation appoints the necessary technical officials who promise to officiate "with complete impartiality, respecting and abiding by the rules which govern them, in the true spirit of sportsmanship."

and in the language of the host country. It must be distributed by the OCOG to the IOC, to the IF concerned, and to all NOCs not less than one year before the Games open. The OCOG also distributes the medical brochure. A complete report must be prepared for the IOC within two years of the completion of the Games. No advertising material is permitted in official Olympic literature.

All demonstrations—including political, religious, and racial propaganda—are forbidden in the Olympic areas. Commercial installations and advertising signs are forbidden inside the sports arenas. Nothing, except the Olympic flag or the emblem of the NOC or OCOG, may be worn on the uniforms of contestants or officials.

Publicity regarding the Games should not be released before the conclusion of the preceding Olympics.

Patronage and Recognition. With instructions from the IOC, the OCOG must forward invitations to participate in the Games to the recognized NOC of each nation. Such invitations are to be sent simultaneously by registered airmail and not through diplomatic channels.

The OCOG makes available the Olympic identity card.

In the Olympic city the Olympic flag must be flown freely where other flags are flown. A large Olympic flag is to fly from a flag pole in a central position in the middle of the stadium throughout the Games.

The OCOG is responsible for bringing the Olympic flame from Olympia to the stadium. The flame—there is to be only one except by special permission of the IOC—must be in a prominent position and clearly visible from within the main stadium.

Regarding the opening ceremonies, the sovereign or head of state who has been invited to open the Games is received at the stadium entrance and is escorted to the official box. The national anthem of the official's country is played.

The parade of the participants follows. Each delegation dressed in its official uniform must be preceded by a name-board bearing its name and must be accompanied by its flag. No participant in the parade is permitted to carry cameras, flags, or banners. The contingent parades in alphabetical order according to the language of the country organizing the Olympic Games, except that Greece leads the parade and the organizing country brings up the rear. Only those who are competing in the Olympic Games, and no more than four noncompetitors in each delegation, parade.

The delegations salute the sovereign or head of state of the country by turning their heads toward his or her box, with no other demonstration. The flags of the participating delegations, as well as the name-boards and their bearers, are furnished by the OCOG and are of equal size. Each contingent, after completing its march around the stadium, lines up in the center of the field.

The president of the OCOG, with the president of the IOC, proceeds to the rostrum and introduces the president of the IOC to the crowd. The IOC president then delivers a brief speech of welcome and introduces the sovereign or head of government. The latter then says: "I declare open the Games of . . . (name of city) celebrating the . . . Olympiad of the modern era (or the . . . Olympic Winter Games)."

Immediately a fanfare of trumpets is sounded and, to the strains of the Olympic anthem, the Olympic flag is slowly raised on the flagpole erected in the arena. The mayor of the city then joins the IOC president on the rostrum. A representative of the city where the previous Games of the Olympiad were held delivers the official Olympic flag to the president of the IOC who hands it over to the mayor. For the Winter Games there is another flag, presented in 1952 by the city of Oslo.

A release of pigeons precedes the arrival of the Olympic flame, brought from Olympia by a relay of runners, the last of whom, after circling the track, lights the sacred Olympic fire which is not extinguished until the close of the Olympic Games.

The solemn Olympic oath is then taken in the following ceremony: The flag bearers of all countries advance and form a semicircle around the rostrum; an athlete of the country where the Olympic Games are taking place then advances to the rostrum accompanied by the flag bearer of his country; he mounts the rostrum and, holding a corner of the flag in his left hand, and removing his hat, raises his right hand and takes the oath on behalf of all the athletes: "In the name of all the competitors I promise that we shall take part in these Olympic Games, respecting and abiding by the rules which govern them, in the true spirit of sportsmanship, for the glory of sport and the honor of our teams."

Immediately after, a judge of the host country advances to the rostrum and similarly takes the oath on behalf of all the judges and officials: "In the name of all the judges and officials, I promise that we shall officiate in these Olympic Games with complete impartiality, respecting and abiding by the rules which govern them, in the true spirit of sportsmanship."

The anthem of the organizing country is then played or sung. The participants then leave the arena by the shortest route. The official ceremony comes to an end. Only then may any artistic program and the competitions take place.

In the case of an opening ceremony being authorized by the IOC to be held at a secondary Olympic venue, the OCOG must submit details of the ceremony in advance to the IOC.

The OCOG provides the medals and diplomas.

In individual events the first prize is a silver-gilt medal and a diploma, the second prize a silver medal and a diploma, and the third prize a bronze medal and a diploma. The medals must bear the name of the sport concerned and be fastened to a detachable chain or ribbon to be hung around the neck of the athlete. Diplomas but not medals also are awarded for the fourth, fifth, sixth, seventh, and eighth places, if any. Participants in a tie for first, second, and third places are entitled to a medal and a diploma.

In team sports and in team events included in other sports, except those of an "artificial" nature (i.e., those in which placings are determined by position of the contestant in the individual competition), each member of a winning team participating in at least one match or competition is awarded a silver-gilt medal and a diploma, each member of the second team a silver medal and a diploma, and each member of the third team a bronze medal and a diploma. The other members of these teams are awarded diplomas but no medals. In "artificial" team events only one medal shall be given to the team and its members shall receive diplomas

Queen Elizabeth II and Prince Philip view the 1976 Games in Montreal. The sovereign or head of state and his or her retinue are conducted to a "box in the stand of honor where he or she shall be greeted with the national anthem of his or her country."

only. Members of teams placed fourth, fifth, sixth, seventh, and eighth, if any, are awarded diplomas.

All competitors and officials in the Olympic Games receive a diploma and a commemorative medal.

The names of all winners are inscribed upon the walls of the main stadium where the Olympic Games have taken place.

Diplomas and commemorative medals shall be given to all noncompetitors who are attached officially to Olympic teams and are recognized by the NOC of their country.

The members of the IOC, the presidents and secretaries general of the IFs recognized by the IOC and of the NOCs who are present at the Olympic Games, and the judges, referees, timekeepers, inspectors, and umpires officiating at the Olympic Games and officially appointed by the IOC also are given diplomas and commemorative medals according to scales fixed by the IOC.

The medals and diplomas distributed on the occasion of the Winter Games must be different from those of the Games of the Olympiad.

The medals are presented during the Olympic Games by the president of the IOC (or a member selected by him), accompanied by the president (or his deputy) of the IF concerned, if possible immediately after the event at the place where the competition was held. "The competitors who have been judged first, second, and third take their places, in their official uniform, on a stand in the stadium facing the stand of honor, with the winner slightly above the second who is on his right and the third who is on his left." The flag of the winner's delegation is hoisted on the central flagpole and those of the second and third on adjoining flagpoles on the right and on the left, as they face the arena. Meanwhile the anthem (abbreviated) of the winner's delegation is played.

The closing ceremony occurs at the stadium at the conclusion of the last event. The flag bearers and bearers of the name boards march into the arena and take their positions in the center of the field. Six competitors of each delegation march eight or ten abreast united not by nationality but "only by the friendly bonds of Olympic sport." The flag bearers form a semicircle around the rostrum and the IOC president proceeds to the foot of the rostrum. The Greek national anthem is played as the Greek flag is hoisted on a flag pole to the right of the central flag pole. The national anthem of the host country is then played as the flag of the host nation is hoisted on the central flag pole, and then the national flag of the city selected to organize the next Games is hoisted on the left-hand flag pole, and the anthem of the next host nation is played. The IOC president then closes the Games: "I declare the Games of the . . . Olympiad (or the . . . Olympic Winter Games) closed and, in accordance with tradition, I call upon the youth of all countries to assemble four years from now at . . . there to celebrate with us the Games of the . . . ."

A fanfare is sounded and the Olympic flame is extinguished, and to the strains of the Olympic anthem, the Olympic flag is slowly lowered from the flagpole and carried horizontally from the arena by a group of eight men in uniform. A salute of five guns follows, the choir sings, and the standard and flagbearers and the competitors march out to the sound of music.

Source: *Olympic Charter 1983*

Ethiopia's Abebe Bikila, the 1964 marathon winner, receives his gold. The president of the International Olympic Committee or his representative presents the medal "if possible immediately after the event at the place where the competition was held."

The Modern Games

1896

Athens, Greece

The first meeting of the revived Olympics was well this side of dazzling. Twelve nations besides Greece—Australia, Austria, Bulgaria, Chile, Denmark, France, Germany, Great Britain, Hungary, Sweden, Switzerland, and the United States—succeeded in fielding athletes. The largest group came from the United States. European nations now renowned in Olympic meets were not prominent in Athens. The Dutch, who distrusted Coubertin, and the Belgians, who condemned the projected International Games, sent no athletes. Sweden was represented by a weightlifter, France by two cyclists, some fencers, and a runner, Germany by three track and field athletes and ten turners (practitioners of special exercises, called turning, originally devised to promote physical fitness). The sole Italian, who walked from Milan to Athens, was disqualified as not an amateur.

Their testing ground—the refurbished stadium of Herodes Atticus—bore little resemblance to the elaborate facilities that are constructed for the Games today. Instead of a 400-meter track, it presented a 333.33-meter course whose sharp, unbanked turns caused slow running times and forced the elimination of the 200-meter dash. Moreover, the racers were expected to go in a clockwise direction, the opposite of their custom.

Nowhere was there much knowledge of or information about the meeting. The situation in the United States is an example. There was no organization to serve as coordinator. There were no ready-to-hand teams to represent the nation in the Games. There were no funds which could be

Restoration work on Athens'
Panathenaic Stadium (photo, page
35) was begun in 1895 and
was completed in time for the first
modern Games. Some 80,000
persons (left) attended the opening.

used to pay the expenses of athletes who might be qualified to compete in Athens.

Nevertheless, there were a few individuals from various sections of the United States who knew about the meet and were eager to take part in it. From Princeton University, shot-putter Robert Garrett, captain of the track team, and three of his teammates—sprinter Francis Lane, pole vaulter Albert Tyler, and middle distance runner Herbert Jameson—headed for Greece. There were reports, never confirmed, that Garrett paid all of the expenses.

The Boston Athletic Association raised funds and sent five athletes—sprinter Tom Burke, the lone national champion of the first United States Olympic team; hurdler Thomas Curtis; jumper Ellery Clark; pole vaulter William Hoyt; and distance runner Arthur Blake. But the New York Athletic Club chose to ignore the Games, which was a serious loss, because most American national champions were affiliated with the NYAC.

The remainder of the first American Olympic team was composed of jumper James B. Connolly; swimmer Gardner Williams, a non-finisher; and the Paine brothers, John and Sumner, both captains in the United States Army, who were to become Olympic revolver champions.

The squad of 13 Americans set out for Athens aboard a tramp steamer on March 20, 1896. They were under the assumption the Olympics would begin April 18. The ship arrived in Naples, Italy about April 1, and only then did the Yanks learn that the Games were scheduled to open April 6. With fewer than five days to get from Naples to Athens the athletes hurried on, arriving shortly before the opening ceremonies, weary and out of shape.

On April 6, the 75th anniversary of Greek independence from Turkey, King George I proclaimed the opening of the modern Games before 80,000 spectators.

In addition to track and field, competition in the first Modern Olympiad included swimming, wrestling, weightlifting, cycling, fencing, gymnastics, shooting, and lawn tennis.

The first final to be held in the 1896 Olympics was the triple jump (hop-step-and-jump). Connolly, a college freshman who had been refused a leave of absence from Harvard to compete in the Games, quit school. He traveled to Athens at his own expense, and made his college proud of him by winning the event. His effort of an even 45 feet made him an easy winner and the first modern Olympic champion, successor to the long line that had ended with the ancient boxer Varastad.

Connolly's victory was saluted by the playing of the "Star Spangled Banner" and the raising of the American flag, practices that have been a part of the Olympic ceremonies ever since.

Next on the track program was the discus, an event unfamiliar to most Americans, who did not add it to their national championships until 1897. Garrett had heard of the event and had practiced with a homemade steel model which he thought approximated the regulation discus. And it did, except for one major difference.

Garrett's practice discus was considerably heavier than the Greek model and so, when he reached Athens, he was really ready. His final throw of 95' 7½" was more than 7 inches better than the distance reached by the Greek champion, Panagiotis Paraskevopoulos, who had been expected to win an event that was considered a Greek specialty.

To the delight of Greek royalty and of a partisan Athens crowd, Spyridon Louis, from the town of Marousi, won the 1896 marathon. Dressed in traditional costume, still worn by elite evzone infantry, he holds his awards.

Connolly and Garrett touched off an American blitz in the track and field competition. There were 12 events on the program and the United States put at least one man in 10 of them, winning nine championships.

Burke took the 100 meters in 12.0 seconds and the 400 meters in 54.2. Curtis captured the 100-meter hurdles (changed to 110-meters in 1900) in 17.6. Hoyt won the pole vault at 10′ 9¾″. Clark scored a double, taking the long jump at 20′ 9¾″, and the high jump at 5′ 11¼″. Garrett, with a toss of 36′ 9¾″, added the shot-put to his discus title.

No activity in Athens was more remote from present-day Olympic practice than the swimming. Of tempered water in regulation pools, marked lanes, and firm starting blocks there was not even the imagination. The swimmers were taken by launch off the shore of the Bay of Zéa, to the approximate distance of a given race. Swimmers plunged into Mediterranean water that, in April, was still icy cold. Whatever stroke propelled them fastest to the beach was what was used.

Perhaps the most dramatic victory of the 1896 Games came in the marathon, a 26-mile race added to the Olympic program to commemorate the feat of an anonymous runner who, in 490 B.C., ran that distance from the plains of Marathon to Athens to announce the Greek victory over the invading Persians—and then fell dead.

It was with a burst of national pride that Greece recorded the victory in the 1896 marathon of Spyridon Louis, a native of the little town of Marousi, who has been called both a shepherd boy and a post office messenger, but about whom very little is known with certainty.

Whether or not he spent the night before the marathon in prayerful vigil, as has been asserted, he remained far behind the front runners until about the 23rd mile. Then, on the long incline before entering Athens, he inched by the front runners and into the stadium. His was the only Greek victory in the 1896 track and field program.

For royalty and simple citizen alike, Louis' accomplishment had a kind of mystical significance. It was estimated that 100,000 people watched the marathon, a huge crowd by any standard, but the more remarkable when it is remembered that the total population of Athens in 1896 was 135,000. As he reached the entrance of the stadium for his final lap, Louis was joined by Prince George and Prince Constantine, and the trio circled the track to the roar of the multitudes.

As the Games drew to a close there was a surge of fellowship among the competitors. Their performances were mediocre by today's standards but the enthusiasm of both athletes and spectators was enormous. That was as Coubertin had wished.

A total of 311 athletes competed in the first Modern Olympics—the size of a single major nation's contingent in today's Games. In the ancient Games, only the victors were acknowledged. In 1896, the first and second place finishers in each event were honored. A first place winner received a diploma, silver medal (gold, it was thought, smacked of vulgar commerce), and a crown of olive branches. The prizes for a second place consisted of a diploma, a bronze medal, and a laurel crown. All prizes were awarded by King George I on April 15, the final day of the Games.

FINAL MEDAL STANDINGS			
Nation	G	S	B
United States	11	7	1
Greece	10	19	17
Germany	6½	5	2
France	5	4	2
Great Britain	2½	3	1
Hungary	2	1	2
Austria	2	–	3
Australia	2	–	–
Denmark	1	2	4
Switzerland	1	2	–

Fencing, a mode of combat in use perhaps as early as 3000 B.C., was a fading art when it was reintroduced as an event in the 1896 Games. The artist has here caught foil fencers, one left- and one right-handed, in a parry of sixte. They are minus the face masks that began to be used in the 18th century. The basic fencing weapons, foils are 43" overall. The foil target is the trunk, which is protected by a padded vest. For electric recording of hits, the vest now incorporates a wire mesh lining.

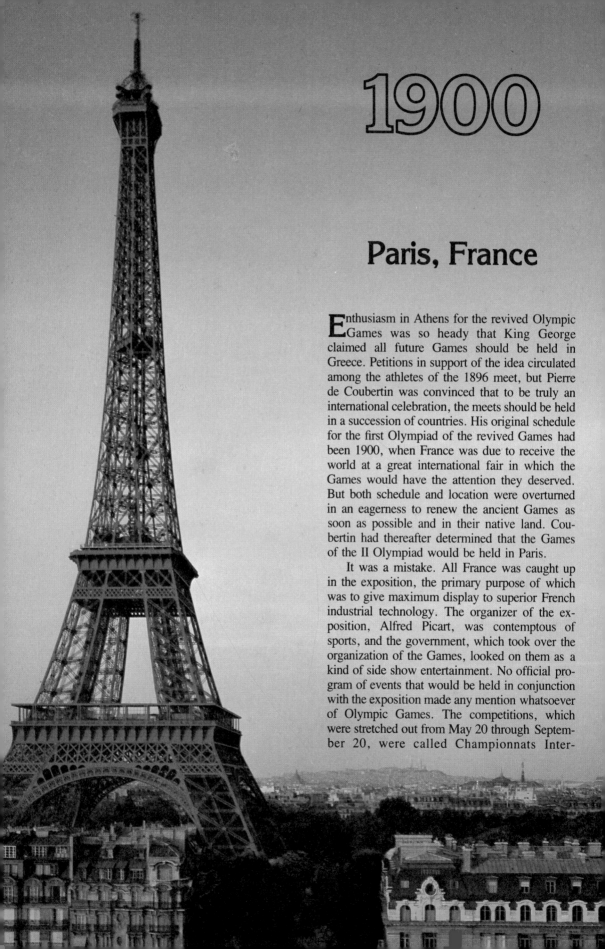

1900

Paris, France

Enthusiasm in Athens for the revived Olympic Games was so heady that King George claimed all future Games should be held in Greece. Petitions in support of the idea circulated among the athletes of the 1896 meet, but Pierre de Coubertin was convinced that to be truly an international celebration, the meets should be held in a succession of countries. His original schedule for the first Olympiad of the revived Games had been 1900, when France was due to receive the world at a great international fair in which the Games would have the attention they deserved. But both schedule and location were overturned in an eagerness to renew the ancient Games as soon as possible and in their native land. Coubertin had thereafter determined that the Games of the II Olympiad would be held in Paris.

It was a mistake. All France was caught up in the exposition, the primary purpose of which was to give maximum display to superior French industrial technology. The organizer of the exposition, Alfred Picart, was contemptous of sports, and the government, which took over the organization of the Games, looked on them as a kind of side show entertainment. No official program of events that would be held in conjunction with the exposition made any mention whatsoever of Olympic Games. The competitions, which were stretched out from May 20 through September 20, were called Championnats Internationaux—International Championships. So swamped were the Games in the commotion of the exposition that many participating athletes believed their contests were part of the fair.

Small wonder. Scoffing off Coubertin's proposal that the Games be gathered in a reconstructed stadium complex, Picart spread the competitions through the 16 sections, classified according to industry, of the vast exposition. Thus, sports societies were put with social welfare; ice skating was to be seen where cutlery was displayed; sailing was part of the life saving exhibits. Adding to the confusion, Olympic contests were mixed up with matches between professionals, and with competitions that were open to professionals and amateurs.

Coubertin made an eleventh hour attempt to salvage the Games by organizing a separate international competition, and when that effort failed, to draw some unmistakable distinction between Games and exposition. The momentum of the exposition was too great, however. As serious contests to prove the world's best athletes, the Games were slated for fiasco. Athletes of quality were not lacking: facilities were.

Consider the track and field competition. It was held at the Racing Club de France, in the Bois de Boulogne at the western edge of Paris. It is a beautiful location, but not for Olympic contests.

There was no track. The grass field was uneven and in many areas it sloped. Discus and hammer throwers watched as their efforts invariably landed in trees that surround the field. French officials, lukewarm at best about the Games, never even considered removing the trees or destroying the grass in order to make a cinder track. They contented themselves with marking off various racing distances on the green turf of the little open field known as Pré Catalan.

The 500-meter oval was not even level. The only pits the jumpers had were the ones they dug for themselves. The hurdles—some were nothing more than broken telephone poles—had been hastily constructed over bumpy, bush-covered ground.

In spite of everything the Paris Games achieved wider international acceptance than the Athens revival had been able to generate. To Athens in 1896, 13 countries had sent 311 athletes. Paris had 1,330 athletes from 22 countries.

Of the 55 American contestants in Paris, many were from colleges and universities. Princeton, proud of the performances of its men in the 1896 Games, sent a contingent. So did the University of Pennsylvania, alma mater of many of the nation's finest track and field athletes. At the University of Chicago, Amos Alonzo Stagg, who was to leave his mark on American collegiate football, borrowed $2,500 to finance a five-man team. Yale, Georgetown, Michigan, and Syracuse were represented.

The New York Athletic Club, which had shrugged aside the 1896 Games, changed its mind and sent athletes to Paris. Among the NYAC group was Ray Clarence Ewry, "The Rubber Man," one of the most remarkable athletes in all Olympic history.

As a child in his native Lafayette, Indiana, he had been so frail he was confined to a wheelchair. After he survived a polio attack a doctor suggested that he try to build up his body with a series of exercises and calisthenics. He did as directed and was able, eventually, to add jumping to his daily regimen.

Ewry was 26 and a graduate of Purdue University when he made his way to the 1900 Games. There, one day was sufficient to dem-

Britain's Doherty brothers were highly visible on the Paris tennis courts. Hugh Lawrence (above) won the men's singles; Reginald Frank got the singles bronze. They won the men's doubles. Frank and Charlotte Cooper (Great Britain) had the mixed doubles gold, in which event Lawrence and Marion Jones (USA) were the bronze medalists.

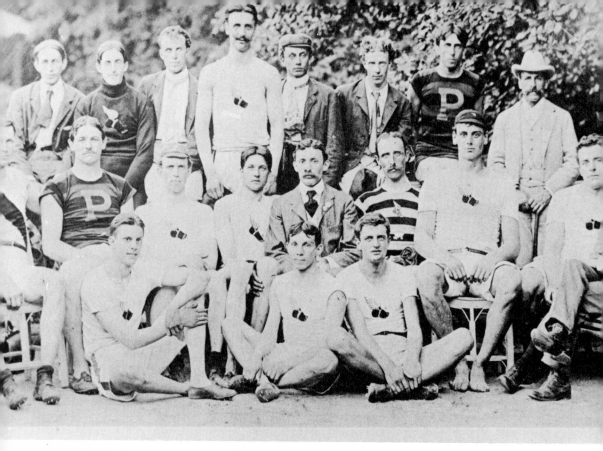

The 1900 U.S. Olympic team won a total of 50 medals—20 gold, 14½ silver, and 15½ bronze. A representative group of the "team" shows how much a gathering of individuals they were. They proudly wore the insignia of their college or athletic club affiliations.

onstrate to what good purpose he had performed his exercises. He entered three jumping events (which are no longer in the Games): the standing high jump, the standing long jump, and the standing triple jump. The trio of events was held on Monday, July 16, and Ewry swept them. That started his all-time record string of 10 consecutive Olympic championships stretching through 1908. The lanky Hoosier, whose childhood had looked so bleak, never lost any Olympic contest he entered.

The scheduling of events entangled the members of the U.S. team in disputes with French officials, and with their own teammates. The Americans found several finals scheduled for Sunday, July 15. They protested, pointing out that Sunday contests would violate the Sabbath observance for many athletes. The Americans proposed advancing the schedule by a day to Saturday, July 14. But French officials observed in their turn that that was Bastille Day, sacred to all Frenchmen, and the celebration of the national holiday would keep spectators away from any competitions. Debate raged over the issue until, it was thought, the French yielded.

But on Sunday, the finals took place. The Americans were disarrayed by the switch. Athletes from Yale, Princeton, Syracuse, Chicago, and Michigan refused to compete. The officials of the teams from Georgetown and the NYAC left the decision to the individual athletes, some of whom chose to compete while others refused. To the general muddle characteristic of the Games all together, particular confusion was now added.

On Saturday, July 14, in the preliminary competition, Myer Prinstein, a long jumper from Syracuse, cleared 23′ 6½″. He was capable of more, as the Penn Relays in 1900 had shown. There he had set a world record of 24′ 7¼″, shattering the mark of his principal rival, Alvin Kraenzlein of Penn.

Although an oil tycoon transported them to France on a tanker, and they paid their own expenses in Paris, the Syracuse students took their orders from university officials. When those officials ordered Syracuse athletes to boycott Sunday competitions, Prinstein obeyed.

Kraenzlein, however, took advantage of the option that Penn offered its men, and he went on to jump Sunday, July 15, posting a 23' 6⅞" distance—⅜" better than Prinstein's mark of the previous day. Kraenzlein took the gold medal. When Prinstein learned what had happened, he challenged Kraenzlein to a Monday jumpoff. But the Penn star refused, and Prinstein was so angry that he went after Kraenzlein with his fists.

Peace was restored in time for Kraenzlein to win three other events in the 1900 Games, and to become the first athlete to collect four individual gold medals in a single Olympics. He captured the 60-meter dash, the 110-meter hurdles, and the 200-meter hurdles, the last in world record time and while running on grass!

Kraenzlein's hurdling style was revolutionary. He was the first competitor who chose to clear the hurdles with one leg extended instead of having both tucked up under him as others did. He "sprinted" rather than "sailed" over the hurdles.

At Penn, Kraenzlein shared an apartment with two other athletes, John Walter B. Tewksbury and Irving Baxter. Both men enjoyed success at the Paris Games, also. Tewksbury won the gold medals

Hurdling is essentially a combination of sprinting and jumping. Alvin Kraenzlein's innovation was to bring the two actions closer together. The artist has caught his way of taking hurdles with one leg extended. Hurdlers nowadays use an open-scissors technique. A dentist who never practiced, Kraenzlein was once considered the greatest all-around athlete in America. Germany appointed him, a German-American, to prepare its athletes for the 1916 Berlin Games that never took place.

for the 200-meter dash and 400-meter hurdles, silver medals for the 60-meter dash and the 100-meter dash, and a bronze for the 200-meter hurdles. Baxter took the gold medals for the running high jump and the pole vault, and silver medals for the standing high jump, standing broad jump, and standing triple jump.

To the silver medal for the long jump, Prinstein added the gold medal in the triple jump, beating the defending champion, James B. Connolly, with a world record.

The lack of accord about Sunday competition affected others besides Prinstein and Kraenzlein. Fred Moloney of Michigan and Dixon Boardman of the NYAC both qualified for the 400-meter final on Saturday but refused to run on Sunday. Maxey Long, another NYAC athlete, who had had the fastest qualifying time, did compete, and he won the event. In the running high jump, W.P. Remington of Penn and Princeton's W.C. Carroll qualified on Saturday but sat out Sunday's final, in which Baxter did participate and win the gold medal.

Bascom Johnson of the NYAC, who had won the pole vault in a competition in England en route to the Paris Games, showed up for the final on Sunday with another vaulter, Charley Dvorak of

J.W.B. Tewksbury (above) was a talented sprinter with stamina. He placed in the 200-meter dash (gold) and the 200-meter hurdles (bronze) on one day, and the 60-meter dash (silver) and 400-meter hurdles (gold) on another. Ray Ewry (right), a daddy longlegs, had no equal in the standing high, standing long, and standing triple jumps. He competed in 1900, 1904, 1906, and 1908 and won 10 medals, all gold. In that, too, he has had no equal.

Michigan. The two men were told the final had been postponed, so they left the grounds. Later in the day French officials reversed themselves and went ahead with the vault. Baxter was still nearby, learned about the change in plan, and competed. He won the event. M. B. Colkett (USA) won the silver medal.

Despite the split over whether to take part in the Sunday finals, Americans dominated the track and field competition, capturing 17 of the 23 events on the program. Other American winners included Frank Jarvis of Princeton, who took the 100-meter dash when the favorite, Arthur Duffy of Georgetown, collapsed with a strained tendon halfway through the race; and George Orton of Penn, a bronze medalist in the 400-meter hurdles, won the 2,500-meter steeplechase, surviving the test of hedges, walls, and water jumps. John Flanagan won the hammer throw, to start a streak of victories in that event by Irish-Americans.

As the first host nation had, France won the marathon race, its lone track and field victory. The race as originally announced was to go from Versailles to Paris. After the runners of various countries had studied the route, French officials switched to a course that looped the Racing Club track four times and then trailed around Paris. The winner was Michel Theato, a baker's delivery boy whose knowledge of the narrow back streets and paths of Paris enriched his chances of winning. In fact, some foreign observers suggested that Theato might have taken one or more shortcuts en route to his victory.

Archery may have the longest history of any sport, although it was no game for most of its time. The reflex bow, pictured here, the type used when archery was made part of the Olympics, is essentially the same as those to be seen in prehistoric cave paintings. The artist has stopped the bowman just before his full draw, as he brings the taut string and its arrow up to his cheek.

FINAL MEDAL STANDINGS			
Nation	**G**	**S**	**B**
France	26	36	33
United States	20	14½	15½
Great Britain	17	7½	12
Belgium	5	6	3
Switzerland	5	3	1
Germany	4	2	2
Australia	2	–	4
Italy	2	2	–
Denmark	1½	3	2
Hungary	1	2	2
The Netherlands	1	1	3
Canada	1	–	1
Cuba	1	1	–
Sweden	½	–	1
Austria	–	3	3
Norway	–	2	3
Czechoslovakia	–	1	1½
India	–	2	–

Rudolf Bauer of Hungary won the discus throw, and British athletes took the golds in the 800-meter race (Alfred E. Tysoe); 1,500-meter race (Charles Bennett); 4,000-meter steeplechase (John Rimmer); and 5,000-meter team race.

Swimmer John Jarvis of Great Britain won gold medals in the 1,000-meter freestyle and 4,000-meter contests; Australia's Frederick C.V. Lane won the 200-meter freestyle race and the 200-meter obstacle event; and Ernst Hoppenberg of Germany won the 200-meter backstroke contest. Germany also won the swimming relay.

The gold medal in cycling went to Georges Taillandier and the gold for best gymnast to Gustave Sandras, both Frenchmen. E. Coste exceeded with foils and Georges de la Falaise with sabre for France, but the épée fencing gold went to Ramón Fonst of Cuba.

Paris saw the first women contestants in Olympic Games. Charlotte Cooper of Great Britain became the first female gold medalist by winning the lawn tennis singles. She took a second in mixed doubles with Reginald Doherty. The Dohertys, Reginald and Lawrence, won the men's doubles, and Lawrence took the men's singles.

In other events France took firsts in shooting (2), yachting, croquet, the plunge, and rowing (3); Great Britain won gold medals in water polo, soccer football, shooting, and yachting; Switzerland took its gold in yachting and in shooting (4), and shooting gave Australia, Canada, and Denmark each a gold medal. Charles Sands and Margaret Abbot (the first American female gold medalist) won the golf events for the United States. France took 3 and Belgium 2 of the archery golds.

In planning the Paris exposition, the French intention was to create an unmatchable world's fair—bigger, brighter, bolder. Toward that end they made room not only for the athletic contests we associate with the word Olympics, but also for such pastimes as require neither much physical movement nor strength. Although no awards were given, there were billiard and checkers matches, open to all, and even competitions in still-fishing in the Seine.

Olympic rowing events were held for the first time in 1900. One reporter described the rowing participants as "coarse fellows, noisy, rowdy, who under the name of boatmen spread terror among the peaceful riverside inhabitants."

1904

St. Louis, Missouri

Only 12 countries and 625 athletes took part in the Games of the III Olympiad, the first to bear the official designation of Olympics. IOC President Pierre de Coubertin himself was not there. The location in a midwestern city of the United States made the Games too distant and too expensive to reach for many European athletes. Although there had been some talk of an American ship going to fetch the European teams, nothing had come of it. Moreover, many in Europe were anxiously preoccupied by the news from the Far East. On February 8, 1904, the Japanese navy had, with apparent ease, destroyed or immobilized in Port Arthur the Russian imperial fleet. It was widely seen as a portent. Neither Great Britain, strong in track and field, nor France sent any teams.

In St. Louis, where the Games were finally located, there was no time for anxiety. The centenary of the Louisiana Purchase was being celebrated with an international exposition. President Theodore Roosevelt recognized that for America it was only in St. Louis and its fair, as the Judy Garland song puts it, that the lights were shining. So when it was known that the IOC had reluctantly settled on Chicago for the 1904 Games,

Fred Winters won a silver in the 1904 dumbbell competition.

OLYMPIC STADIUM – ST. LOUIS, 1904

which Coubertin had failed to interest New York in hosting, the president intervened. He used his position as honorary president of the first official United States Olympic Committee to persuade the IOC to move the Games to St. Louis. During his travels in the United States in 1889 Coubertin had met Theodore Roosevelt, who thereafter was for him a lifelong hero. When the president expressed his concern lest rival attractions in two midwestern cities hurt both, the IOC—which in the main meant Coubertin—acceded. St. Louis and its exposition did not suffer. The Games did. For the second time they became a kind of side-show to a fair.

In St. Louis, to be sure, there was no Picart organizing the Games out of recognizability. The "World's Fair" simply engulfed them. In the hustle of too much else, no one took time to prepare for them in advance. Besides an avenue called "Olympian Way," tucked off in the northeastern corner of the fair, there was no other hint of any Olympic facilities. As in Paris, there was no stadium in which to center the competitions. Most of the contests were held on the campus of Washington University of St. Louis, where the running track, an oval, was 536.45 meters, or three laps to the mile.

The swimming events were held in an artificial lake built near the Exposition. Dr. Ferenc Mezo, a member of the IOC and an Olympic historian, later wrote: "A makeshift raft was used for a starting platform but it could not bear the weight of six to eight men and sank so deep that competitors stood in water up to their ankles. The raft slid back in the movement of the plunge and the competitors

Fifty swimmers from four nations entered the 1904 swimming events. A makeshift raft was used as the starting point. Moored to the unstable raft, in the artificial lake, was a life-saving boat.

practically fell flat. The floating turn badly affected the time results.''

The 1904 Olympics officially extended from July 1 through October 15 but competition, demonstrations, and exhibitions were conducted long afterward. The official events numbered 67, although ''local'' competitions enabled the winners of 390 events to claim the title of Olympic champion when the Games were over.

The program omitted several previously held contests and added others. Boxing was included for the first time, lacrosse was played, and the new events included a variety of croquet, called roque. Women did not compete in the events that had marked their initial appearance in Paris. According to James E. Sullivan, the main organizer of the 1904 Games, archery shoots were part of the ''Olympic Championships.'' The Cincinnati Athletic Club and Potomac Archers of Washington, D.C., were represented by women. In the women's Double National Round, W.C. Howell, H.C. Pollock, and E.C. Cooke placed 1-2-3, and in the Double Columbia Round the order of placement was Howell, Cooke, and Pollock. All told, 8 women participated in 1904.

Submerged by an exposition, as they had been in Paris, even the most exciting events in the St. Louis Games failed to attract more than 2,000 spectators. Moreover, the third modern Olympics were, in a sense, little more than an intra-American meet; in some sports, teams from the United States competed against ''international'' squads composed of other Americans and some foreign athletes.

Bare-knuckle boxing won such esteem for Varazdetes, the last champion of the ancient Games, that he was made king of Armenia. Boxing officially joined the modern Olympics in 1904. Although the Queensbury Rules of 1867 required gloves, world championship fights were bare-knuckle until Jim Corbett defeated John L. Sullivan in 1892. The painting depicts a boxer posed outside the ring in a favorite bare-knuckle fighting stance.

A demonstration of the American-spawned sport of basketball was won by the Buffalo-German YMCA team. Canada also won its sport—lacrosse—but that victory was worth a gold medal, one of four captured by Canadians.

The Galt Football Club of Ontario won the two-nation soccer competition (called Association Football), with two United States teams, Christian Brothers College and a local club from St. Louis, placing second and third.

George Seymour Lyon won the golf title although he had never handled a club before he was 38, and a Montreal policeman, Etienne Desmarteau, won the gold medal in the 56-pound-weight throw. Desmarteau had been fired from the police force because he had taken time off, against orders, to compete in St. Louis. But two weeks later, when he was a champion, his dismissal papers were "lost."

Cuba won all five gold medals for fencing. Ramón Fonst, a star performer in Paris, was again in St. Louis. Greece won the two-arm lifting. Germany and Hungary combined for six gold medals in the swimming and diving, two more than the United States took. But in this most lopsided of Olympics virtually every event in every other sport went to Americans.

So complete was their domination that all the gold medals in boxing, lawn tennis, roque, water polo, archery, tug-of-war, and wrestling went to Yanks. The United States won 10 gymnastic gold medals, with Anton Heida capturing four individual golds and one team gold medal, as well as an individual silver medal. The United States swept up every rowing medal except the silver in the eight-oar race, which went to Canada. America took the gold in dumbbell competition.

The first Olympic heavyweight boxing champion of modern times was Samuel Berger. The division weight for the 1904 Games was over 158 pounds. Berger, a member of the same San Francisco Olympic Club that produced James J. Corbett, was a 6-foot-2, 200-pounder. He turned professional soon after his Olympic victory, had a brief career in the ring, and before he opened a clothing store in San Francisco took a turn as one of Jim Jeffries' managers.

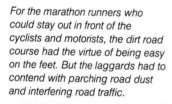

For the marathon runners who could stay out in front of the cyclists and motorists, the dirt road course had the virtue of being easy on the feet. But the laggards had to contend with parching road dust and interfering road traffic.

Thomas Hicks, the designated winner of the marathon, and the judge for the event use a car as the setting for a victory photograph. J.D. Lightbody (below), a sprinter from the Chicago Athletic Club, won the 800- and 1,500-meter runs and the 2,500-meter steeplechase.

The host-nation victory in the marathon that was started by a Greek in Athens and repeated by a Frenchman in Paris carried over to St. Louis, where an American won the 40,000-meter race. Although Fred Lorz was the first man to cross the finish line, Thomas Hicks, another United States runner, was the real winner, leading a 1-2-3 American sweep.

Among the 31 starters in the marathon was Felix Carvajal, a tiny Cuban mailman who was the hit of the 1904 Games. He financed his trip to St. Louis through contributions from his countrymen. Carvajal's itinerary from Havana took him through New Orleans, where he was parted from much of his money in a friendly dice game. Undaunted, he hitchhiked most of the way to St. Louis, subsisting on handouts. He was half-starved and wholly exhausted when he got to the Games.

Carvajal was immediately adopted by a group of American athletes who were amused by his grit. Marathon day, August 30, was sweltering in heat and high humidity. The Cuban appeared at the starting line dressed in a long-sleeved shirt, long pants and heavy boots. His American friends persuaded him to let them cut off his shirtsleeves, and his trousers at the knees. They also lent him a pair of low-cut shoes for the run through the streets of St. Louis.

The marathon course was mass confusion. Besides the watching crowds and the runners, there were trainers on bicycles who rode along shouting encouragement, and medical personnel, who kept pace in automobiles. The runners were choked by the billowing dust of the "helpers."

Nine miles into the race Lorz developed cramps and dropped out. He waved to other runners from the side of the road as they passed him. Eventually he got a ride in a motor vehicle, but that broke down about four and one-half miles from the finish line. By then over his cramps, Lorz started to run again. He crossed the finish line first and was hailed as the winner, although he was in remarkably good shape, considering the heat and humidity, and he was not covered with marathoner's dust. He did not disclaim the victory.

Archie Hahn, nicknamed the "Milwaukee Meteor," crossed the finish line first in the 60-, 100-, and 200-meter events.

Several explanations have been offered for Lorz' action: he was headed to the finish point, intending to collect his clothes and watch the end of the race; or, he played along with the mistake as a joke.

In any case, the flim-flam was exposed when the next man across the finish line wobbled in. It was Hicks, covered with dirt and grime, and obviously played out.

Lorz, amused at the misunderstanding, then explained how he had managed to arrive first. The officials were not amused, especially since Lorz had been about to receive the first place award from Alice Roosevelt, daughter of the president, when Hicks appeared.

The Amateur Athletic Union expelled Lorz from the United States team and suspended him for life. However, the AAU lifted the suspension later. In 1905 Lorz proved his worth when he won the Boston Marathon.

Hicks' marathon victory also was clouded by what may have been the first doping episode of the modern Games. With seven miles remaining in the race, Hicks was exhausted and ready to quit. But his handlers refused to let him. They were alleged to have doped him with strychnine so that with his pain dulled by the chemical he was able to complete the race.

Carvajal, the plucky Cuban, had a most adventurous marathon. With no formal training, with no knowledge of pace or timing, with nothing but pride for his spur, he ran in a style best described as "impromptu." Unlike his competitors, he chatted with bystanders along the way, just as he might while delivering the mail back home in Havana.

It was hunger that doomed Carvajal's chance for Olympic glory. He detoured off the course into an orchard, ate several green apples, and developed cramps that forced him to take a lengthy rest. Even so, he managed to come in fourth, behind the trained Americans, Albert Corey and Arthur Newton. (Newton, the fifth-place finisher of the Paris marathon, got the bronze in the 1904 1,500-meter race.)

Of the 25 track and field events, many of them no longer contested, the United States won 23. In 20 of the events, U.S. athletes took all three medals. Only the gold medals in the 56-pound weight throw and the decathlon did not go to an American.

The St. Louis decathlon was different from the 10-event competition, introduced in 1912, which is the current Olympic decathlon. The 10 events in 1904 were the 100-yard dash, one-mile run, 120-yard hurdles, 880-yard walk, high jump, long jump, pole vault, shot put, hammer throw, and 56-pound weight throw. It was won by Tom Kiely, an Irishman representing Great Britain, with Adam Gunn and Truxton Hare of the United States finishing second and third.

The most prominent trackmen of the host nation were Ray Ewry, Archie Hahn, Harry Hillman, and Jim Lightbody. Each left St. Louis with three gold medals.

Ewry repeated his 1900 triple, winning the standing high jump, standing long jump, and standing triple jump.

Hahn, a master of the fast start, justified his "Milwaukee Meteor" nickname by capturing the 60-, 100-, and 200-meter events. He won the 200 by two meters with a time of 21.6, a mark that remained the Olympic record until 1932!

Lightbody, originally a sprinter, clicked in the middle distances. He won the 800- and 1,500-meter runs, as well as the 2,500-meter

BROAD JUMP

Under the watchful eye of the judges, Myer Prinstein takes part in the long (broad) jump, for which he was awarded a gold. Charles Dvorak (below) established the first Olympic record in the pole vault.

steeplechase. Hillman took the 200- and 400-meter hurdles and the 400-meter run.

It was in the 400-meter hurdles race that Wisconsin's George Poage finished third, thereby becoming the first black man to win an Olympic medal. He also won a bronze medal in the 200-meter hurdles and he finished sixth in the 400-meter run.

The St. Louis Olympics gave two athletes—Myer Prinstein and Charles Dvorak—a chance to prove their talents. Deprived of gold medal opportunities by the Sunday schedule conflict in Paris, both won their specialties in 1904. Prinstein was so versatile that he took the long jump, added a second gold medal in the triple jump, and placed fifth in the 400-meter run. Dvorak won the pole vault, setting an Olympic record.

Two days in August, called Anthropology Days, were embarrassing. Regular Olympic events were parodied as African Pygmies, Japanese Ainus, Moros from the Philippines, American Indians, and even Patagonians went through the motions of the contests, to which they added pole climbing and mud fights.

When news of the undignified occurrence in St. Louis reached him, Coubertin dismissed it as an "outrageous charade" that would, he predicted, "of course lose its appeal when black men, red men, and yellow men learn to run, jump, and throw and leave the white men behind them."

The St. Louis Games were, on the whole, worthwhile. In one respect they were a significant advance over the earlier meets. The Ivy League colleges that had sent athletes to Paris ignored the St. Louis meet. But the athletes who did attend, while not college stars were, as members of athletic clubs across the country, much closer to a national representation than had been true in the Athens or Paris Games. As such, they were moving in the direction of Coubertin's desire. Many prior Olympic records were bettered in the course of the 1904 Games. But there was no gainsaying the fact that they were far from the ideal of an international meet. When the final contests and demonstrations were over, November 25, none of the departing participants were sorry to be finished with a diet that had offered buffalo meat all too frequently.

FINAL MEDAL STANDINGS			
Nation	G	S	B
United States	70	75	64
Cuba	5	2	3
Germany	4	4	5
Canada	4	1	–
Hungary	2	1	1
Austria	1	1	1
Great Britain	1	1	–
Switzerland	1	–	1
Greece	1	–	1

1906

Athens

If the high hopes raised in 1896 by the renewal of the Games were not to be dashed, something had to be done, and fast. The poorly organized and worse attended Games of 1900 and 1904 had not only not advanced the cause of an international sports festival, they had set it back.

The Greeks' intense satisfaction with the 1896 Games had led to their desire to keep the Olympics in Athens. Coubertin opposed that idea, urging that the Games would gain in international character if they were staged in different locations. The Greeks clung to their desire, but war with Turkey in 1897 and its consequences kept them from acting upon it in either 1900 or 1904. In 1906 they were able to convene new competitions. Their desire and Coubertin's need to re-orient the revived Games were both served by the international sports competitions held in 1906, again in Athens' great stadium of Herodes Atticus. What was proposed was to have a program in Athens every four years, midway of the modern Olympiads. The "Interim" or "Athenian" Games would keep up interest in sports. Coubertin and the IOC committee would not treat them as official Olympics, but they would support them.

In other areas of the world, 1906 would be remembered as a disastrous year. One of the strongest earthquakes on record would shatter San Francisco and start a nearly consuming fire. Some 6,000 people on Taiwan would die in another earthquake, and 1,500 or more Chileans would not survive a third quake. But Greece was unhurt, and joyous.

The Greeks outdid themselves in their effort to assure the success of the 1906 interim games. What international amateur sports needed most was a well-managed, well-attended set of events. Athens provided just that. From April 22 to May 2, the stadium and its surrounding hills were filled

Paul Pilgrim won the 400-meter race in Athens in 1906.

with large and enthusiastic crowds. The opening ceremonies were lavish and colorful, and the competitions were smoothly run.

Unfortunately, it was the last chance for the Greeks. Four years later political unrest forced the cancellation of the ''interim games,'' and they were never resumed.

Because the 1906 Games were a one-time affair and were not held in an official Olympic year, they are not included in the formal records of the International Olympic Committee. Yet they saw important new developments and were an important step forward in the pursuit of the Olympic ideal.

Several new events were introduced in 1906. The pentathlon, which bore no resemblance to the one staged in 1912 and thereafter, consisted of the standing long jump, the Greek-style discus throw, the javelin throw, a one-lap (192-meter) race around the track, and Greco-Roman wrestling. The winner was determined on the basis of a point system. Hjalmar Mellander of Sweden won the event with 24 points.

Javelin throwing, part of the pentathlon of the ancient Games, had two objectives for the early Greeks. Because it was a war weapon, accuracy of throw was as important as distance. The ancient javelin was thrown by hooking a finger into a leather thong, called an amentum. It added distance by lengthening the thrower's arm and improved accuracy by giving the javelin a spin. As the painting shows, the modern javelin is gripped about midway of its shaft. It is thrown for distance only.

A photo of Ray Ewry in repose shows the unusually strong legs he developed by dedicated exercise to recover from childhood paralysis. George Bonhag (below) of the United States edged out Donald Linden of Canada and Konstantin Spetsiotis of Greece in the 1,500-meter walk—an event held only in 1906.

Erik Lemming, Mellander's teammate, finished third in the pentathlon and won the javelin throw, another new event. Sweden recorded a 1-2-3 sweep in the 1906 javelin throw, and Lemming went on to win three consecutive gold medals in that event.

The 1,500-meter walk, the first walking event in Olympic history, was won by George Bonhag, a U.S. long distance runner. "Serious George" had been a favorite in the five-mile run but finished a disappointing fourth. He finished sixth in the 1,500-meter run after setting the pace for his teammate, James Lightbody, who won the gold. Determined to bring home a medal, Bonhag entered the 1,500-meter walk even though he had never before competed in a walking race. He received some last-minute pointers on heal-and-toe technique from a Canadian walker and outlasted the eight other entrants, several of whom were disqualified for using an illegal step.

In Paris and St. Louis there had been three sprint races and three hurdles races on the track and field program. The only sprint held in 1906, the 100-meters, was won by Archie Hahn of the United States. His teammate, R.G. Leavitt, won the only hurdles event, the 110-meters.

The interim Games attracted 884 athletes representing 20 countries. In addition to those awarded in the 22 track and field events, the total of 77 gold medals awarded were won in fencing, soccer, weightlifting, cycling, wrestling, rowing, shooting, swimming, tennis, and gymnastics. Although the United States won 11 of the track and field competitions and 12 gold medals in all, France was the overall winner with 15.

Egypt and Finland made their Olympic debuts in these non-official Games. Egypt did not win any medals, but the Finnish team went home with three. Werner Järvinen, nicknamed "The Big Finn," won the bronze medal in the discus throw and the gold medal in the ancient Greek-style discus throw. Verner Weckman won a second gold medal for Finland in the middleweight division of Greco-Roman wrestling.

The 1906 Games were noteworthy for the United States because for the first time they sent an "official" team. Until then, U.S. Olympic representation was fragmented. The athletes competed independently and were sent to the Games by colleges or private clubs. But this time a unified team of 35 athletes was selected by the United States Olympic Committee (with President Theodore Roosevelt as its honorary chairman). They trained as a unit and wore an official U.S. Olympic uniform. Their trip to Greece was financed by public contributions to a special fund.

The journey to Athens proved even a greater test of their strength and endurance than the Games themselves. Sailing from New York on the *SS Barbarossa*, they were hit on the second day at sea by

Martin Sheridan won a gold in the discus after a throw-off with Ralph Rose. The Irish-American, who took the event in 1904, repeated in 1908. He received nine medals overall in the three Games.

His old fedora and his shamrock identified William John Sherring in the pack of marathoners. He took the prize from the favorites with almost insolent ease.

FINAL MEDAL STANDINGS			
Nation	G	S	B
France	15	9	16
United States	12	6	5
Greece	8	13	13
Great Britain	8	11	6
Italy	7	6	3
Switzerland	5	4	2
Germany	4	6	4
Norway	4	1	–
Austria	3	3	2
Sweden	2	5	7
Hungary	2	5	3
Belgium	2	2	3
Denmark	2	2	1
Finland	2	–	1
Canada	1	1	–
The Netherlands	–	1	2
Australia	–	–	3
Czechoslovakia	–	–	2
South Africa	–	–	1

a huge wave washing over the deck. Six athletes were injured, and one of them, Jim Mitchell, dislocated a shoulder in keeping a team-mate from being sluiced overboard, and had to miss the competition. He had been favored to win the fourteen-pound stone throw (held for the first and only time in 1906). When the team finally arrived in Italy, they had to forage for food, which a succession of earth-quakes and volcanic eruptions had prevented from reaching the markets. They crossed Italy by train, took a steamship to Greece and another train to Athens, arriving a few days before the opening of the Games.

One aspect of the U.S. participation that did not change in 1906 was the way athletes were chosen. There were no competitive tryouts. Athletes were picked on the basis of reputation. The practice almost cost the Americans dearly. Paul Pilgrim, a runner unknown outside the New York Athletic Club, originally had been left off the team. He was added to the squad at the last moment and became the hero of the Games by winning both the 400-meter and the 800-meter races. Not until 1976 would another athlete win both those events.

A notable all-around performer on the U.S. team was Martin Sheridan, a New York policeman. Sheridan won gold medals in the shot put and free-style discus throw, and placed second in the stand-ing high jump, standing long jump, and fourteen-pound stone throw.

The standing triple jump (hop, step, and jump) was eliminated from the program, but Ray Ewry, who had won one of his three gold medals in that event in St. Louis, again won the standing high jump and standing long jump. Myer Prinstein, in his third set of Games, won the running long jump. Peter O'Connor, an Irishman representing Great Britain, placed second to Prinstein in the running long jump and won the running triple jump. Another Irishman, Con Leahy, took the running high jump and placed behind O'Connor in the hop, step, and jump.

The marathon, which had been won by a runner of the host country in each of the first three modern Olympic Games, was a highlight again in 1906. The Greeks hoped, of course, that the pattern would continue. The people of Athens offered such prizes as a statue, a loaf of bread every day for life, and a free weekly lunch for one year to any victorious Greek marathoner. Of the 75 or so runners who began the race at the village of Marathon, about one-half were native Greeks. Approximately half way to Athens a skinny Canadian runner named William John Sherring closed on the leading runner, the American Billy Frank. With a light-hearted "Good bye, Billy," he forged ahead. When he entered the stadium in Athens, Prince George joined him in the final lap to the finish line. Sweden's John Svanberg won the silver medal, and Billy Frank finished third. Although no Greek could finish better than fifth, the crowd cheered the foreign runners in the best Olympic spirit.

During the Games the Italians announced that the 1908 Games could not be held in Rome as planned. The earthquakes and eruptions had hurt too much of their country, physically and economically. Great Britain was invited to take over the 1908 Games, and they accepted.

The Athenian Games of 1906 took place without IOC official patronage. It is a nice irony that they showed the world that Coub-ertin's ideal was attainable. In 1908 it was London's turn to reach for it.

1908

London, England

Once London put its shoulder to the wheel, arrangements were soon made. In less than two years a 68,000-seat stadium was constructed at Shepherd's Bush, a district of Hammersmith at the western edge of Greater London. Among the facilities provided was a swimming pool, built within the stadium. Between April 27 and October 31 the panorama of the 1908 Games entertained an avid public and made copy for a sometimes pontifical press.

The opinion expressed by *The Olympic Handbook of the Association of Track and Field Statisticians* was that the London track and field events provided "the first truly international championships in Olympic history."

Elsewhere, however, the 1908 Olympics have been given another character. Bad weather spoiled some of the events, but it was not weather that marred the Games. It was partisanship. The division between the representatives of the United States and Great Britain grew so sharp that the 1908 Games were named "The Battle of Shepherd's Bush."

The first dispute erupted during the opening ceremonies. The stadium was decorated with the flags of several of the competing nations, but the U.S. team was indignant to find that its banner was missing. The pat British explanation was that they could not find one. The Americans were well supplied with flags for the opening parade of 2,035 athletes. It was expected that each of the 22 participating nations' flag bearers would dip his flag as the delegation marched past King Edward VII. The Americans, however, refused to dip theirs. Discus thrower Martin Sheridan, an Irish-American who needed no encouragement when it came to balking the English, asserted "this flag dips to no earthly king." He started a U.S. tradition that continues even today.

Sweden also was angry because, like the United States, its flag did not hang in the stadium. Finland refused to carry a flag in the opening parade after being informed that it would have to carry the banner of Czarist Russia.

Although there were smaller crowds at the Shepherd's Bush stadium than had been expected, the marathon drew like a magnet. As the racers walked to the assembly point, where Queen Alexandra waited to give the starting signal, they passed through ranks of spectators, among whom a camerawoman (center) made a picture record.

The organizers of the Games had decreed that Irish athletes would compete as members of Great Britain's teams. The Irish who did not thereupon refuse to take part were in the uncomfortable position of aiding the English, as likely as not against their own kith from America.

The tumult of the opening ceremonies suggested what was to come. The events themselves would prove rancorous and, on occasion, would end in plain enmity. In the aftermath, British official judges were said to have cheered and coached their countrymen in the competitions. They held drawings for qualifying heats in private, which raised the suspicion that the organizers were rigging some events. Members of the American Olympic committee, whose protests were perhaps the loudest, were barred from the field. James Sullivan, secretary of that organization, led the attack on the British. "They were unfair to the Americans," he charged. "They were unfair to every athlete except the British, but their real aim was to beat the Americans. Their conduct was cruel and unsportsmanlike and absolutely unfair."

Perhaps the most controversial and bitterly contested decision was made by British officials in the 400-meter run. The final was held July 23, with four runners competing. Three were American—W.C. Robbins of Harvard, J.C. Carpenter of Cornell, and J.B. Taylor of the Irish-American A.C. The fourth finalist was Lieut. Wyndham Halswell of Great Britain, who had set an Olympic record in the semifinals. Newspapers warned that the U.S. runners would

After he had fallen five times, Dorando Pietri was helped across the marathon finish line. The artist shows the moment when, urged by the crowds, the chief track official (left) and the attending doctor extended their helping hands. That help caused Pietri to be disqualified, although the spectators plainly wished otherwise. Inevitably, perhaps, the frail Italian recalled to mind the first marathon runner, who ran himself to death.

conspire against Halswell. The American coach, Mike Murphy, urged his athletes not to interfere.

Taylor, the top American threat, got off to a bad start and the race quickly turned into a three-man battle. As they came into the homestretch, Robbins held a narrow lead and Halswell and Carpenter moved out to pass him. Carpenter succeeded in doing so, but supposedly ran in such a way that Halswell had no chance to pass on the outside. At that moment, officials at the turn signaled "foul" and judges at the finish line broke the tape.

Carpenter finished first, Robbins second, and Halswell third, but the result was voided. Carpenter was disqualified for interfering with Halswell. The British charged that Carpenter had run diagonally across Halswell's path and that the disqualification had been justified. Carpenter laughed off the accusation saying, "Halswell had lots of room to pass me on either side. We just raced him off his feet. He couldn't stand the pace." A rerun was ordered for July 25, but the Americans, enraged at the decision, refused to participate. This left Halswell to amble around the track and be declared the winner of the gold medal. It was the only "walkover" in Olympic history.

Another squabble between the Americans and the British occurred in the tug-of-war. The rules stated that competitors could not wear "prepared boots or shoes," only everyday footwear. When the Americans faced the Liverpool police team in an elimination match, the bobbies wore their regulation steel-rimmed boots. The U.S. team protested, but the boots were ruled legal. The Americans withdrew and British teams gathered up all three medals.

The 1908 marathon, one of the most dramatic and celebrated races in Olympic history, also was decided by a controversial ruling. The now standard distance of 26 miles, 385 yards (42,195 m) was run for the first time in the London Games. The race was begun on the lawn of Windsor Castle so that it could be watched by the royal grandchildren. The finish line was at the Royal Box at the Olympic stadium at Shepherd's Bush. The final 385 yards were the distance the runners had to cover after entering the stadium. Without those 385 yards, Dorando Pietri, a confectioner from Capri, Italy, would have been the Olympic champion. Because of them, John Joseph Hayes of the United States received the gold medal.

The runners set out at 2:30 P.M. on one of the hottest and most humid days of the English summer. Pietri, who had won the 1907 Paris Marathon, and Hayes, a 22-year-old New Yorker, were considered long shots in a field that included Thomas P. Morrissey of the United States, who had won the 1908 Boston Marathon, and Tom Longboat, a Canadian Indian with a reputation for silence and stamina, whom the U.S. runners accused of being a professional.

One by one the favorites dropped out of the race, victims of the intense heat. After 20 miles, South Africa's Charles Hefferon had a lead of almost four minutes over Pietri. By the 25-mile mark Pietri had passed Hefferon and Hayes was closing fast. But Pietri's spurt apparently took too much out of him. Although he was the first runner to reach the stadium, Pietri clearly was disoriented. He turned in the wrong direction and collapsed on the track.

Doctors and track officials swarmed around the fallen Italian, who reportedly had been given a shot of strychnine during the race. They helped him to his feet and pointed him in the right direction. He tottered forward, no longer in control of his body. He fell to the ground and then got up, only to fall again, and then again. British

John Flanagan, shown here in his athletic club uniform, threw the 16-pound hammer to Olympic record distances in 1900, 1904, and 1908. He took a silver medal in 1904 in the 56-pound weight throw.

officials put an end to the pleadings of the crowd by seizing Pietri by the arms and dragging him across the finish line. His time for the entire distance was 2 hours, 54 minutes, 46 seconds. Johnny Hayes, little bothered by the heat, breezed across the finish line 32 seconds later.

Unconscious after his ordeal, Pietri was rushed to the hospital, leaving officials to battle over the bizarre ending to the race. Who had won? At first it appeared that Pietri would be considered the winner; the Italian flag went up the pole. U.S. officials howled in protest, saying that anyone with even a minimum of fairness knew that Pietri had to be disqualified: he'd been unable to finish the race without assistance. Hayes remained calm. ''I knew it was going to be all right,'' he said afterward. ''They *had* to disqualify Dorando.''

Eventually they did. Several hours late, Hayes was declared the official winner. The next day, recovered from his near fatal ordeal, Pietri complained about the decision. ''If the doctor had not ordered the attendants to pick me up, I believe I could have finished unaided,'' he said. Although he was not awarded an Olympic medal, Pietri had won the sympathies of the British public. They were much gratified when Queen Alexandra presented to Dorando an enormous gold cup for his effort.

The dramatic race caused a surge of interest and participation in marathon running in subsequent years. It also inspired a young American songwriter, Irving Berlin, to write his first hit tune—''Dorando.''

Other complaints were lodged by the French and the Canadians in the cycling events, and by the Swedish Greco-Roman wrestling team. The general bitterness eventually prompted the British to publish a 60-page book entitled *Replies to Criticism of the Olympic Games*. The disputes, in particular those over the 400-meters and the marathon, put an end to the practice of the host nation supplying the judges of Olympic events. In succeeding Games, control and direction of the competition would be given to impartial members of international governing bodies for each sport.

The Battle of Shepherd's Bush generated almost as much con-

With a Bible in hand, Forrest Smithson was first in the 110-meter hurdles in 1908. Two other Americans—John Garrels and Arthur Shaw—took the silver and bronze.

One hundred and twenty-one American athletes participated in the 1908 Games. For the first time, they were selected on the basis of tryouts, and as this track and field group shows, they had a uniform and a badge.

Mel Sheppard (USA) was number one in the 800- and 1,500-meter races and the winning anchorman on the first Olympic track relay team.

fusion as resentment. The schedule was expanded to 22 sports, with more than 100 gold medals awarded. Track and field, cycling, swimming, fencing, gymnastics, and wrestling all were held in the Olympic stadium, often at the same time.

The 1908 Games represented a major step forward in women's Olympic competition. The number of female participants increased from 7 in 1906 to 36 in 1908. Women took part in a gymnastics demonstration (to the distress of Pope Pius X), as well as in the lawn tennis events. The London program also saw the first winter sport in the Olympics—figure skating. Four separate competitions were held: men, women, pairs, and the special figures event.

Great Britain accumulated the most gold medals, 56, with the United States a distant second at 23. The British dominated the boxing competition, winning all the gold medals and all the silver medals except one. They won 11 of 15 medals in freestyle wrestling, and also scored heavily in rowing, yachting, cycling, and tennis. The hosts won seven gold in track and field, including Halswell's 400-meter walkover and victories by George E. Larner in the 3,500-meter and 10-mile walks. Henry Taylor of Great Britain was the swimming star of 1908, capturing the 400- and 1,500-meter freestyle races and anchoring the championship 800-meter freestyle relay team.

The United States team, 121 strong, was for the first time selected on the basis of tryouts. The Americans came away from Shepherd's Bush with a total of 15 gold medals in track and field competition, four more than all the other nations combined. Among the U.S. gold medal winners were Johnny Hayes in the marathon; Mel Sheppard in the 800- and 1,500-meters; Harry Porter, running high jump; Francis Irons, running broad jump; and Ralph Rose, shotput. Edward Cooke tied for first in the pole vault with A.C. Gilbert, who later founded the A.C. Gilbert toy company and created the Erector Set. Forrest Smithson, a divinity student, won the 110-meter hurdles with a Bible in hand, as a protest against Sunday competitions. Mel Sheppard also won a gold medal as anchorman in the first track relay race in the Olympics—the 1,600-meter. The race was run as a medley, with two 200-meter legs, one 400-meter leg, and a final 800-meter leg. Martin Sheridan again won both discus events, giving him a total of five gold medals, three silver, and one bronze in the 1904, 1906, and 1908 Games. Swimmer Charles Daniels closed out his Olympic career with a world record in the 100-meter freestyle and a bronze medal in the 800-meter relay. John Flanagan, who in 1908 won the hammer throw for the third consecutive time, also retired after the London Games. Victories in the standing high jump and standing broad jump gave Ray Ewry the ninth and tenth gold medals of his career, the most ever.

George Mehnert won the bantamweight freestyle wrestling, thereby becoming one of America's two double gold medalists. In 1904 he had taken the light flyweight title. (The other double gold medalist was Oliver Kirk, who in 1904 had won both the bantam and featherweight boxing titles.)

U.S. domination of the sprint races came to an end in 1908 as Reginald Walker, a young South African, won the 100-meter dash and Robert Kerr, a Canadian, won the 200-meters. Russia, which had appeared in the 1900 and 1906 Games, won its first medals in 1908—a pair of silvers to Aleksandr Petrov and Nikoly Orlov in Greco-Roman wrestling. France and Hungary excelled in fencing.

FINAL MEDAL STANDINGS			
Nation	G	S	B
Great Britain	56	48	37
United States	23	12	11
Sweden	7	5	10
France	5	5	9
Canada	3	3	8
Hungary	3	4	2
Germany	2	4	4
Norway	2	3	3
Italy	2	2	–
Belgium	1	5	2
Finland	1	1	3
Australia	1	2	1
South Africa	1	1	–
Denmark	–	2	3
Greece	–	3	1
Russia	–	2	–
Czechoslovakia	–	–	2
Austria	–	–	1
The Netherlands	–	–	1
New Zealand	–	–	1

1912

Stockholm, Sweden

An Olympics can be made memorable by a single athlete or a single event. The 1912 Games in Stockholm, Sweden, were fortunate to have featured both in duplicate. There were two outstanding individuals in track and field—Hannes Kolehmainen, the first of the "Flying Finns," and Jim Thorpe, the star-crossed, Oklahoma-born Sac and Fox Indian. And there were two extraordinary races—the 800- and the 5,000-meters. Each played a part in helping to establish the Olympics as an international event of major importance.

Sweden, which had made rapid strides in physical education, was the perfect host, organizing and conducting a smoothly run set of Games from May 5 through July 22. Twenty-eight nations and 2,547 athletes participated. Daily attendance averaged between 20,000 and 30,000. Facilities were the best yet for track and field. The running track was 383 meters in circumference. For the first time the 400-meter race was run in lanes. Timing to the tenth-second, instead of the fifth-second, was introduced. (It was dropped after the Games, but returned in 1932.) Most nonwinning track times were made available for the first time.

The 22-year-old Kolehmainen, a vegetarian who ran his first marathon at 17, was the youngest brother and the most gifted in a family of runners. His brother Willie, a professional distance runner who toured the United States, and brother Tatu (David), who ran in Stockholm, were fast. But the always smiling Hannes was faster, and in 1912 he emerged as one of the world's great distance runners. Kolehmainen won gold medals in the 5,000- and 10,000-meter events (both new to the program in the 1912 Olympics) and in the cross-country run. He also won a silver medal in the three-man, 3,000-meter cross-country race. In the team race on July 12, Kolehmainen set a world record of 8 minutes 36.9 seconds. But his Finnish teammates were in a slower class and Sweden captured the gold medal.

Hannes Kolehmainen captured the individual cross-country event by 33.2 seconds. He won heats in the 10,000-meters on July 7 and the final the following day. He took the lead on the second lap and widened his margin throughout. Brother Tatu quit at 5,000-meters, when he was fifth. Kolehmainen ran away from the 11-man field in the closing stage of the race and finished 45.8 seconds ahead of Louis Tewanima, an American Indian in his 40's, who would become a high priest of the Hopi tribe. Like Thorpe, Tewanima was a product of the Carlisle Institute for Indians.

Kolehmainen had all he could handle from France's Jean Bouin in the 5,000-meter final on July 10, a day after both won heats. Bouin was a handsome, 23-year-old from Marseilles and, like Hannes, the idol of his country. He always raced with a toothpick in his mouth. The two made the 5,000 final a personal duel. Kolehmainen took an early lead and then he and Bouin ran away from the pack, with the Frenchman in front most of the way. On the last lap, Bouin began to sprint, but Kolehmainen hung on. As the cheers of the crowd reverberated through the stadium, the two reached the final straightaway. Then, with just 20 meters left, Kolehmainen drew even with his rival and went on to win in 14 minutes, 36.6 seconds—a world record. Bouin, one step behind, clocked 14:36.7. The third-place finisher, Britain's George Hutson, was 31 seconds behind the Finn (15:07.6). The world record had been 15:01.2. It would not be lowered again until 1924.

Despite his victories, Kolehmainen was unhappy because of the intrusion of politics. Four years earlier Finland had been barred from flying its own flag because it was part of the Russian Empire. The same was true in 1912, and when Kolehmainen watched the Russian standard raised to celebrate his 5,000-meter triumph, he shook his head. "I would almost rather not have won, than see that flag up there," he said. But the politics of the moment could not diminish the brilliance of the Kolehmainen-Bouin duel. The two got along well, and after the 5,000, the Frenchman presented his colors to the Finn. Kolehmainen would return to a later set of Games, but the Frenchman would die in 1914 on the Western Front during World War I.

Duke Paoa Kahanamoku of Hawaii was the most sensational swimming star to emerge at the 1912 Games. The son of Princess Ruth won the 100-meter freestyle and was a member of the runner-up team in the 800-meter freestyle relay.

The 800 produced the same exciting, record-breaking finish as the 5,000-meter race. Eight men qualified for the final on July 8. Six of them were Americans, including Mel Sheppard, the defending champion, and James "Ted" Meredith, a Pennsylvania schoolboy. Hanns Braun of Germany, the bronze medalist in London, also was in the field. Italy's Emilio Lunghi, the 1908 silver medalist, had been eliminated in the heats. The main threat to Sheppard was expected to come from Braun, a fast finisher. The American plan was to burn out the German early with a blistering pace set by young Meredith. But when the race started it was Sheppard who took the lead. He flew over the first 400 meters in an incredibly fast 52.4 seconds. Meredith followed. Braun and the other Americans were bunched behind him. When the field turned for home, Meredith had closed on Sheppard. Braun was sandwiched and had to swing outside. For a few seconds it seemed as if Braun would join the front-runners. But he dropped back. Ira Davenport of the United States moved into contention. He closed fast on the pole, but Meredith, running on the outside, caught and passed Sheppard for the victory. His time was 1 minute 51.9 seconds, a world record. Sheppard and Davenport took the silver and bronze medals. Both clocked the identical time of 1:52.0 for 800 meters, also breaking the world record. Braun was fourth in 1:52.2. Only eight tenths of a second separated the first six finishers in a classic 800-meter race.

Meredith, Sheppard, Edward Lindberg, and Charles Reidpath were gold-medal-winning members of America's 1,600-meter relay team. Reidpath won the gold medal in the 400-meter run in which Germany's Braun placed second and Meredith fourth. The British team of David Jacobs, Harold Macintosh, Victor d'Arcy, and William Applegarth captured the 400-meter relay, a newly introduced event.

Yet the athlete whose name overshadows all others associated with the 1912 Olympics is Jim Thorpe. The 24-year-old Indian was hailed as the world's greatest athlete after he captured two of the most demanding Olympic tests—the 5-event pentathlon and the 10-event decathlon. The 15 events required a diversity of skills. Thorpe excelled in most of them. He won the pentathlon long jump, discus, 200-meter dash, and 1,500-meter run, and finished third in the javelin. He was first in the decathlon high jump, 120-meter hurdles, shot put, and 1,500-meter run. He even tied for fourth in the individual high jump.

No one else has won a decathlon-pentathlon double. Yet Thorpe's name was removed from the list of Olympic champions. All his honors were erased because it was discovered that Thorpe had received money for playing professional baseball before the Stockholm Games. The action by the International Olympic Committee, meeting in Lausanne, Switzerland, on May 26, 1913, wounded Thorpe. He was fiercely proud of what he had accomplished in Stockholm. "I did not play for the money," Thorpe said of his baseball playing. "I did it because I liked to play ball. I was not very wise in the ways of the world. . . ."

Following a prolonged campaign to undo the IOC's action against Thorpe, his medals were returned and his name was reinstated in the Olympic records in January 1983. Until then, the man listed as winner of the 1912 Olympic decathlon was Hugo Wieslander of Sweden. The pentathlon winner was recorded as

Ralph Craig of the University of Michigan captured both the 100- and 200-meter races.

Jim Thorpe

You, sir, are the greatest athlete in the world.

—KING GUSTAV V OF SWEDEN

As the 1912 Olympics drew to a close in Stockholm, Jim Thorpe was ushered to the victory podium to receive gold medals for winning the decathlon and pentathlon, a staggering double victory involving 15 events. With the medals, King Gustav V presented to Thorpe a bronze bust in the King's likeness for his decathlon victory and a jeweled model of a Viking ship for his pentathlon triumph.

"You, sir," proclaimed the king, "are the greatest athlete in the world."

Jim Thorpe is said to have replied: "Thanks, King." There has been considerable debate over whether Thorpe was that glib. But there never has been any debate about what the king said.

Just one year later, as a result of a controversy over his amateur standing, Jim Thorpe was forced to return the two gold medals, the bronze bust, and the ship model. But no one could take away what the king had said. And no one could change what Thorpe had done. In the years since, Jim Thorpe has remained "the world's greatest athlete."

Ironically, while there seldom has been any debate about Thorpe's skills, the controversy persisted into the 1980's. Periodic campaigns were mounted to have Thorpe's Olympic honors restored. In 1975—63 years after Thorpe's achievements in Stockholm and 22 years after his death—President Gerald Ford appealed to Lord Killanin, president of the International Olympic Committee (IOC), in Thorpe's behalf. "The name of Jim Thorpe," Ford wrote, "has represented excellence, dedication, pride, and com-

petitive zeal. As one of the greatest athletes the world has ever known, he has become a legend in this country." The appeal failed, but the campaign did not die. Finally, in October 1982, the IOC voted to return the medals and reinstate Thorpe's Olympic accomplishments in its archives. Earlier the U.S. Amateur Athletic Union and the International Amateur Athletic Federation had agreed to restore Thorpe's amateur status. William E. Simon, president of the U.S. Olympic Committee, was a prime force behind the successful plea. New gold medals—the original were given in 1913 to the second-place finishers—were presented to two Thorpe children on January 18, 1983, in Los Angeles. At the ceremony his daughter Charlotte said that she was "overwhelmed" and "thrilled to death." "We are really full circle."

James Francis Thorpe was born in a one-room cabin near Prague, Okla., on May 22, 1887. (His twin brother, Charles, died in 1896.) His mother was three-fourths Indian and one-fourth French; his father was half Indian and half Irish. In the community of the Sac and the Fox Indians, Thorpe was named Wa-tho-huck, meaning Bright Path. And no one went up the path quicker. But when he was young, Thorpe had doubts about his athletic abilities. "When I was a kid, I didn't ever expect to get very far in sports," he said. "I wasn't big enough for one thing. And the way we lived—way off from everything—made it hard to learn. We didn't have a coach and most of the time we played barefoot. We made our own balls out of whatever was handy, used sticks for bats, flat rocks for bases, and made up our own rules," he explained.

The Jim Thorpe story might never have unfolded if the Carlisle Institute, a government-operated school for Indians in Carlisle, Pa., had not included Jim among the students recruited for the 1904 school year. The school operated on a half school—half work principle. Thorpe, only 16, went to work as a tailor.

Two years later he competed in organized athletics for the first time. He played guard on the tailors' football team in the Shop League. The tailors won the school title, and in 1907 Thorpe was elevated to Carlisle's varsity scrubs. One afternoon during the spring of 1907, Thorpe had to clean up the field after the track team completed practice. The high jump bar had been left at 5' 8", the best effort for the team's best jumpers. Thorpe muttered, "That don't seem very high." "Ever high jump?" he was asked. "Not over a bar," Thorpe said. "But, if a horse can do it, I can do it." Thorpe hauled up his overalls, took off his shoes, and easily cleared the bar. Among those who had been watching was Glenn "Pop" Warner, the track and football coach who would provide the teaching that would exploit Thorpe's natural abilities.

Thorpe was all set to return to Oklahoma to take it easy following the 1909 track season when he made the error that cost him his Olympic medals. "A couple of Carlisle baseball players named Jesse Young Deer and Joe Libby were going to North Carolina that summer to play ball," Thorpe explained, "so I tagged along just for the trip. Libby and Young Deer were fair outfielders, and they caught on with the Rocky Mount club. I got short of money, so when the manager offered me $15 a week to play third base, I took it. I didn't even think about doing anything wrong, because there were a lot of other college boys playing there." Thorpe played professional baseball in 1909 and 1910, returning to Carlisle in 1911.

Pop Warner was unaware of Thorpe's baseball playing, assuming he preferred Oklahoma to school. In the summer of 1911, Warner wrote to him. "If you will come back to Carlisle," Warner said, "I think you have a chance to make the United States Olympic team next year."

Several weeks later, without prior notice, Thorpe appeared at Carlisle. "Where've you been?" Warner asked. "Playing ball," Thorpe said without elaboration. Warner did not realize it was professional baseball and began to prepare Thorpe for the Olympics.

When the U.S. team sailed for Stockholm on the liner *Finland,* Thorpe was aboard. He would attempt a unique double—the decathlon and pentathlon. In 1912, a new 10-event decathlon and a new five-event pentathlon, each encompassing a series of track and field events, were on the program. (Since 1924, only the decathlon has been contested by men.)

Thorpe was the first and only athlete to win both. He did it with such ease that his accomplishments astonished everyone. Thorpe was first in four pentathlon events—the long jump, discus, 200-meter dash, and 1,500-meter run. He finished third in the javelin.

Thorpe won the high jump, high hurdles, shot put, and 1,500-meter run in the decathlon, which was spaced over three days instead of two. He completely outdistanced the field and finished with 8,412.995 points to 7,724.495 for the run-

ner-up, Hugo Wieslander of Sweden. His 1912 decathlon finishes, with three events held on July 13, four on July 14, and three on the third day, were as follows: 100 meters—11.2 seconds; long jump—22'3¼"; shot put—42' 3½"; high jump—6' 1¾"; 400-meter run—52.2 seconds; 110-meter hurdles—15.6 seconds; discus—121' 4"; pole vault—10' 8"; javelin—149' 11"; and 4 minutes, 40.1 seconds in the 1,500.

Thorpe returned to the United States a hero. President William Howard Taft hailed him as "the highest type of citizen." He rode through the streets of New York City before large crowds reveling in his achievements. He was honored at

banquets in New York, Philadelphia, and Carlisle. Back at school, Thorpe played football.

Then in 1913 he was accused of having been a professional athlete when he competed in the Olympics. The revelation came from the typewriter of Roy Johnson of the *Worcester* (Mass.) *Telegram*. Thorpe later met Johnson and said: "He seemed like a pretty nice guy—he was just doing his job."

With that same laconic manner, Thorpe answered the charges against him, never once trying to avoid them. "I did not play for the money . . . but because I liked to play ball," he said.

Pop Warner also felt that Thorpe had been naive. "Thorpe was a fellow who always laid his cards on the table face up," Warner said. "Many other(s) were playing (in) the same league, but they were careful and wise enough to play under assumed names. Thorpe played under his regular name, probably never thinking he would participate in any amateur sports after that. In a way, the boys at the Indian school were children mentally and did not understand the fine distinctions between amateurism and professionalism. Thorpe saw no harm in playing baseball and earning a little honest money in the summer. He did not understand why that would prevent him from participating in the Olympic Games on the other side of the world," Warner explained.

The International Olympic Committee showed as much understanding of the situation as Thorpe had of the rules. Thorpe was judged guilty as charged. He was ordered to return his medals and his gifts. He was banned from amateur competition, and his name was stricken from the record books.

Thorpe obviously was hurt, but he seemed to cope with it as long as he played professional sports. But when his baseball and pro football careers were over, he floundered emotionally and financially. Thorpe worked for $4 a day digging ditches. He was an extra in Hollywood movies, a guard in an automobile plant, and a deckhand on a freighter. He even managed a girls' softball team. When the 1932 Olympics were held in Los Angeles, he could not afford the price of a ticket to watch the events he loved most.

"In the twilight of my life," he said, "the one thing I dream of constantly is that the American people will try to get back for me the Olympic trophies I won in 1912. I'd be the happiest man in the world if I could just get my medals back."

"Jim wants to be vindicated as an honest athlete before he goes to his happy hunting ground," said his wife, Patricia. It did not happen. Jim died of cancer on March 28, 1953, in their modest trailer in Lomita, Calif., a suburb of Los Angeles. He was buried in Shawnee, Okla. When the state of Oklahoma refused to allot $25,000 for a memorial and the towns of Mauch Chunk and East Chunk in Pennsylvania, 75 miles from Carlisle, decided to merge and to be named thereafter Thorpe, Pa., Thorpe's wife had his body moved there.

At the time Thorpe was re-entombed in a red marble mausoleum, soil from Mauch Chunk, from Shawnee, Okla., and from the Polo Grounds, where Thorpe played baseball for the Giants, was sprinkled at three corners of his coffin. A packet of earth from the stadium in Stockholm where Thorpe performed his extraordinary feats was sprinkled in the fourth corner. It was sent by the King of Sweden.

In a 1950 poll, conducted by The Associated Press, Jim Thorpe was voted the "greatest male athlete" of the first 50 years of the 20th century. Not only was the 6' 1", 185-pounder an outstanding track star, he was also a fine professional football and baseball player. As a football player, he was first team back in 1911 and 1912 and led the nation in scoring with 198 points in 1912. After his Carlisle team defeated Army in a game in 1912, a young Army halfback named Dwight D. Eisenhower called Thorpe "the greatest football player I have ever seen." In fact, Thorpe was elected to both the college and professional football halls of fame.

As a major league baseball player, Thorpe appeared in 289 games during a six-year career with the New York Giants, Cincinnati Reds, and Boston Braves. Although a drinking problem interfered with Thorpe's last years as a baseball star, he batted .327 for the Braves in his final season and ended his career with a .252 lifetime average.

There probably is no better illustration of Thorpe's unparalleled athletic abilities than a track and field meet in 1912 between Carlisle and Lafayette. Lafayette had 48 men on its unbeaten squad and, when Carlisle appeared for the meet, there was immediate snickering. Legend says that only Thorpe and coach Pop Warner arrived at Lafayette to be greeted by its coach, Harold Bruce. "Where's the team?" inquired Bruce. "Here it is," said Warner, pointing to Thorpe. The story is not true. Carlisle came with a larger squad. It may have included as many as six athletes. Thorpe could have won by himself.

Ferdinand Bie of Norway. Both had finished second to Thorpe in their respective events. However at the insistence of Juan Antonio Samaranch, president of the IOC, Thorpe was listed as cowinner of the decathlon and pentathlon. Samaranch felt that too much time had elapsed not to include Wieslander and Bie as winners too.

American medal sweeps were scored in the 100- and 800-meter races, the 110-meter hurdles, pole vault, and shot put. Abel Kiviat and Norman Taber finished 2-3 in the 1,500-meter run, both one tenth of a second behind British winner Arnold Jackson. Sweden swept the triple jump and decathlon (with Thorpe eliminated). South Africa's Ken MacArthur and Chris Gitsham finished 1-2 in the 40.2-kilometer marathon, with Gaston Strobino of the United States third.

Obviously, the United States had done something right in preparing for the Games. A cork track had been installed on the liner *Finland* that carried the American team to Stockholm and that served as the squad's quarters during the Games. The cork track enabled the athletes to work out at their convenience on the trip across the Atlantic and during their stay in Sweden. The practice paid off for Ralph Craig of the University of Michigan, who won both the 100- and 200-meter races. There were seven false starts in the 100 final and in one of them Craig ran the entire distance before returning to the starting line!

Craig returned to the Olympics 36 years later in 1948. That time he sailed in the Dragon class yachting championship. However, the longevity record for an Olympic competitor belongs to Ivan Osiier of Denmark, who won a silver medal in individual épée in 1912. He also competed in the Games of 1908, 1920, 1924, 1928, 1932, and 1948.

Show jumping was one of three equestrian events introduced in 1912. The riders, all male through World War II, were often cavalrymen on cavalry mounts. South African Ken MacArthur (below) won the marathon.

Ladies hit the Olympic waters for the first time in 1912. Australia's Fanny Durack and Wilhelmina Wylie (left and center) and Great Britain's Jennie Fletcher (right) completed the 100-meter freestyle in the first, second, and third positions, respectively.

Women's swimming and diving were introduced in the 1912 Olympics. Fanny Durack and Wilhelmina Wylie of Australia finished 1-2 in the 100-meter freestyle swim. Greta Johansson and Lisa Regnell of Sweden won the gold and silver medals, respectively, in the highboard diving. But the most sensational performer to emerge in the Games was Duke Paoa Kahanamoku of Hawaii. Kahanamoku was of Hawaiian royal blood. He was born in the Honolulu palace of Princess Ruth in 1890 during a visit of the Duke of Edinburgh, the second son of Queen Victoria. His father christened him Duke to celebrate the occasion. Kahanamoku was swimming's first charismatic personality. He was big and handsome and planed through the surface of the water as no man his size ever had. He won one of the two gold medals credited to the United States in 1912 swimming events. Kahanamoku took the 100-meter freestyle, breaking the world record in the semifinals, and a silver medal in the 800-meter freestyle relay, won by a team from Australasia (composed of athletes from Australia and New Zealand). Kahanamoku, who later played an island king in many Hollywood films, would swim in four Olympics. He missed a fifth because of war.

Canada's 18-year-old George Ritchie Hodgson was a double gold medalist in the 400- and 1,500-meter freestyle events, the only swimming gold medals won by a Canadian man or woman through the 1976 Olympics. Russians, who would not appear again in the Olympics for another 40 years, numbered 169 athletes in 12 sports.

For Russia, the Estonian Martin Klein won a silver medal in middleweight Greco-Roman wrestling. In team shooting at 30 meters (no longer contested) Russian marksmen edged out Great Britain for the silver medals, thanks to more bull's eyes. Harry Blau won a bronze in clay pigeon shooting. Mikhail Kusik tied with Canada's Everard Butler for third place in single sculls, and Russia's "Gallia II" took a bronze in the 10-meter class yachting races.

Only one American, a lieutenant from West Point, competed in the modern pentathlon—a five-event competition new to the Olympics. The program, which was geared to the hazards a military man might face in combat, consisted of shooting, swimming, fencing, horseback riding, and a cross-country run. The event was swept by Sweden. Lt. George Smith Patton, Jr., finished fifth, placing 27-7-4-6-3 in the five events.

Stockholm also inaugurated competition in five branches of the arts—architecture, painting, sculpture, music, and literature—held in conjunction with the Games. Gold medals were awarded in literature to Georg Hohrod and M. Eschbach of Germany for their "Ode to Sport." The names were pseudonyms. Olympic historians assert that the work was actually written by Baron de Coubertin. Dr. Ferenc Mezo wrote: "I have a feeling that Coubertin, in choosing a German and French pseudonym, wanted to symbolize that the Olympic idea created a rapprochement even between conflicting states."

At the closing ceremonies of the Games of the V Olympiad, Coubertin saluted the athletes and nations who had helped make the Games what he called "an enchantment." The memory of those efficiently organized and conducted Games was vital to the Olympic movement because war clouds were gathering. Stockholm proved how well the Olympics could work and that was an important recollection. The 1916 Games, scheduled for Berlin, were canceled. Berlin and most of Europe were otherwise occupied.

FINAL MEDAL STANDINGS			
Nation	G	S	B
Sweden	24	24	17
United States	24	19	19
Great Britain	10	15	16
Finland	9	8	9
France	8	5	3
Germany	5	13	7
Italy	5	1	2
Norway	4	1	5
South Africa	4	2	–
Hungary	3	2	3
Canada	3	2	3
Australia	2	2	2
Belgium	2	1	3
Denmark	1	6	5
Greece	1	–	1
Switzerland	1	–	–
Russia	–	2	3
Austria	–	2	2
The Netherlands	–	–	3
New Zealand	–	–	1

At the conclusion of the Games, the Swedish security force was crowned with laurels for its efforts in keeping order during the events.

1916

Berlin, Germany
(canceled)

Berlin, Budapest, and Alexandria were the prime candidates for the 1916 Games. However, as 1912 passed, the temper of Europe was altering. Political turmoil was general, German militarism was increasing, and war was a real possibility. President Coubertin and other IOC members banked on their conviction that if Berlin were selected as the site for the 1916 Games war could be avoided. Coubertin, enjoying the euphoria of the 1912 Games, believed that holding the Games in Berlin would divert the interests of the Germans away from war and would strengthen the hands of the German populace that desired peace.

After Jules de Muzsa, the IOC member from Hungary, withdrew his demand that the Games be held in Budapest, Berlin was selected unanimously as the site. The German government, sure that any war would be a short one, continued to prepare for the 1916 Games and declined to withdraw as host. Coubertin, clinging to his faith in the spirit of the games, would not hear of other arrangements for the events as long as Berlin remained the officially designated site. The guns of August 1914 proved both Coubertin and Germany wrong. The first World War forced the cancellation of the VI Olympiad. Without the 1916 Games and with certain forces urging that Germany be punished for its bellicose actions, the years between 1912 and 1920 were bleak ones for the Olympic movement.

1920

Antwerp, Belgium

Jazz set the pace for the twenties. Its heady sounds and insistent rhythms were the perfect tonic for people sick of the years from 1914-1918 and eager to end restrictions and deprivations. The world had been made safe for democracy; now the great need was to forget the war and get on with living. New, and always renewing, jazz expressed the impulse to change.

In the United States, undamaged by war, it was easy for the prosperous to indulge themselves to excess. Privileged young people—the Smart Set—lugged around long raccoon coats, made a point of owning a hip flask, and would soon welcome the roadster with rumble seat as the climax of the auto makers' art. The pre-war ankle-length hemline climbed and climbed, until exposed knees labeled a girl a flapper. Tight-lipped traditionalists railed away about sin, but the great majority had no more energy for crusades. The sooner the bad old days were forgotten, the better.

In Europe there was an even stronger wish to forge a new life, but not so much opportunity to do so. The continent had been devastated by the long war. In large measure, a generation had been blotted out by the struggle. Ruin was everywhere, hunger and poverty were the general lot, and many were afflicted by a nagging restlessness. The war had wrenched society out of its accepted forms. Everything familiar was either vanished or altered. Not only had the towns and cities to be reconstructed; the way people lived had to be reestablished, as well.

Pierre de Coubertin's circumstances were a case in point. A Parisian, man and boy, for 55 years, he had become so impoverished at war's end that it was necessary in 1918 to uproot himself and family, thereafter to live in reduced circumstances in Switzerland. A lifetime of devoted work seemed to have had little effect. His painstaking plans for the 1916 Berlin Games had been wasted, but what was worse, he'd seen how little such international festivals could do for peace when militarists took charge. For a time he considered retiring from the presidency of the IOC.

Eventually, the balm of peace once more restored his spirits and energies, and he got to work. The VII Olympiad would fall in 1920. It was not to be missed. Belgium had been as brutally hurt by the war as any part of Europe, and staggered in economic misery by the war's end. Yet somehow Antwerp summoned the wherewithal to receive and be host to the 1920 Games. The principal Belgian organizer was Count Henri de Baillet-Latour, who in 1925 would succeed Coubertin as IOC president. With the recollected success of the Stockholm Games for inspiration, the organizers determined to make the Antwerp Games the best yet. They brought together 2,606 athletes from 29 nations, including a New Zealand team for the first time not attached to Australia's. Germany and Austria, the recent enemies, were excluded.

Two of the most electrifying performers of the 1920 Olympics had worn their nation's military uniforms until a year before the Games. One was "The Flying Finn," also known as "The Phantom Finn" and "The Abo Antelope," whose idol was Hannes Kolehmainen. The other was a Texas-born sprinter with a unique leap to the tape, who had won his first international races in the 1919 Inter-Allied Games in Pershing Stadium in Paris.

When they and the other athletes reached Antwerp, there was a 30,000-seat stadium in readiness, a huge undertaking under the circumstances. But building it proved easier than filling it for the contests scheduled for April 20 through September 12. For the average Belgian, struggling to acquire the bare essentials, the general admission—about 30 cents—was too high. The stadium was almost empty through many events until it was thrown open, free of charge, to school children.

Ugo Frigerio joyously crosses the finish line in the 10,000-meter walk. The Italian also won the 3,000-meter walk in 1920 and repeated his victory performance in the 10,000-meter walk in 1924.

The 1920 Games added several pages to Olympic history. It was at Antwerp that the Olympic flag, with its five interlocking, multi-colored rings was unfurled for the first time.

It was at Antwerp that the Olympic oath was introduced. Belgian fencer Victor Bion, a silver medalist in team épée that year, was the first to take the oath on behalf of all the competitors.

And it was at Antwerp that one of the greatest runners made his Olympic debut. Paavo Nurmi launched a career during the Antwerp Games that made his name internationally famous. His feats became the yardstick against which distance runners afterward would be measured.

During the course of three Olympics "The Flying Finn" won nine gold medals and three silver medals!

Nurmi's 1920 commencement resembled that of his idol, Kolehmainen, in 1912. Nurmi won the 10,000-meters, with France's 5-foot-3 Joseph Guillemot second; then the Frenchman beat Nurmi in the 5,000-meters. It was a replay of the French-Finnish rivalry between Jean Bouin and Kolehmainen.

The remarkable thing about Guillemot's performance was that he was able to run at all. He had fought in the war and been poisoned with mustard gas. He was told that his lungs were so badly damaged that he would never run again. But in the 1920 Olympics, Guillemot proved the doctors wrong.

On August 17, Nurmi broke in front in the 5,000-meters and led most of the way. The Frenchman was content to stay a few strides behind on the slow 400-meter track that was made slower by rain that fell during most of the track competition.

Midway through the final turn, Guillemot shifted speeds. With a sudden spurt, he bolted past Nurmi and won by more than four seconds.

Although the Winter Games did not become a separate entity until 1924, ice hockey was part of the Olympic competition in 1920. Canada began a stretch of four consecutive championships. Considered the world's fastest game, ice hockey had originated in Canada during the mid-nineteenth century. As the artist accurately depicts, heavy woolen stockings (sometimes shin guards), thick gloves, and tightly-laced skates were part of the uniform.

The 23-year-old Nurmi was a student of racing tactics. Three days later, in the 10,000-meter race, he faced Guillemot again. Instead of leading, Nurmi hung back and let Guillemot set the pace. Then, on the final lap, Nurmi began his kick and won the race in exactly the same fashion as the Frenchman had in the 5,000.

The two faced each other once more in the 10,000-meter cross country run. But a showdown never developed. Guillemot had to withdraw during the race after he suffered an injury. Nurmi ran easily and captured a second gold medal. He won a third gold medal in the team cross country race, finishing first in the field.

After the Olympics, Nurmi reviewed his losing effort in the 5,000 and determined that faulty judgement of pace had cost him a fourth gold medal. Thereafter he always carried a stopwatch with him when he ran—in practice and during competition.

Among other multiple track and field double winners in the 1920 Games were Albert Hill, a Britisher who, in his Olympic debut at the age of 36, captured the 800- and 1,500-meter races; and Ugo Frigerio of Italy, who won the 3,000- and 10,000-meter walks, neither of which is contested today.

In the 800, Hill ran down Earl Eby of the United States and South African Bevil Rudd, to win by a yard. Two days later he took the 1,500 meters, which had been expected to go either to America's Joie Ray, a Chicago taxi driver, or to Sweden's John Zander, the world record holder. Zander, attempting a comeback after retiring in 1918, was never a factor and did not finish. Ray, who was bothered by a sore tendon, placed eighth after leading most of the way. Another Englishman, Philip Baker, who as Philip Noel-Baker would receive the Nobel Peace Prize in 1959, finished second behind Hill. Larry Shields of the United States was third. Hill also won a silver medal in the 3,000-meter team race.

Rudd captured the gold medal in the 400-meter run and a silver in the 1,600-meter relay won by Great Britain.

Charley Paddock (USA), "The World's Fastest Human," habitually threw himself at the tape (above). At Antwerp he took the 100-meter race (right).

But it was Charley Paddock of the United States who was as electrifying in his way as Nurmi. Paddock was among the first to be named "The World's Fastest Human." He won the 100-meter dash, a most unusual race. Loren Murchison of the United States, one of the fastest starters in sprint history, was left at the start.

According to *The Olympic Handbook of the Association of Track and Field Statisticians* " . . . the clerk of the course cautioned Paddock not to put his hands over the mark, just as the men were about to start.

"Murchison, accustomed to the methods of American starters in similar instances, expected an order to 'stand up' and proceeded to rise just as the others were off. Naturally, he was never in the race and finished a distant last."

At the half mark the lineup was Jackson Scholz (USA), Harry Edward (Gt. Britain), Morris Kirksey (USA), and Paddock. Kirksey and Paddock passed the other two and then Paddock used his characteristic "jump" finish to beat. With approximately 12 feet left in a race, Paddock literally threw himself at the tape in a "jump" that was meant to attract attention of race officials at the finish line.

Paddock was favored to double in the 200 meters, but had to settle for the silver medal. He finished behind Allen Woodring of the United States. Woodring was a last-minute addition to the

Pole vaulting was part of the Irish Tailtean Games as long ago as 1829 B.C. Solid hardwood poles, which limited achievable heights, were changed after 1904. Bamboo put Frank Foss (above) over the bar at a record 13' 5".

American team. He was not expected to last past the preliminaries. He did, but with his only pair of track shoes ruined. Woodring borrowed a pair for the final.

The shoes had longer spikes than those he usually wore. He thought they would slow him down but because the track was muddy the longer spikes gave him better traction and helped him to win the gold medal. Paddock was second, Edward third, and Murchison fourth.

Paddock, Scholz, Murchison, and Kirksey won the gold medal in the 400-meter relay, introduced in Stockholm, in world record time.

Paddock would compete in three Olympics. He died in World War II as a Marine Corps captain. A United States ship was named in his honor.

Scholz had the distinction of appearing in sprint finals in three successive Olympics.

The Antwerp Games also marked the return of Hannes Kolehmainen with his familiar white headcloth to the Olympics. He won the gold medal in the 42,750-meter marathon. His brother Tatu finished 10th.

Hannes' marathon victory was one of eleven track and field gold medals won by Finland. That tied the United States. American

Yale's Dick Landon (above) set an Olympic record in the high jump. Patrick Ryan (USA) received the gold in the hammer throw.

victors included Dick Landon of Yale in the high jump; Frank Loomis, who set a world record of 54.0 seconds in the 400-meter hurdles; Patrick Ryan in the hammer throw, and pole vaulter Frank Foss, who set a world record of 13 feet, 5 inches—an incredible 15 inches better than Danish silver medalist Henry Petersen.

The United States was represented in women's swimming for the first time and swept all the events. Ethelda Bleibtrey won the 100- and 300-meter freestyle races, both with world records, and added a third gold medal in the 400-meter freestyle relay.

Gen. John Pershing personally congratulated Norman Ross, following pre-olympic field-day competitions. At Antwerp the American captured the 400- and 1,500-meter freestyle swimming races and was on the gold-winning 800-meter relay team.

Duke Kahanamoku was on hand to win gold medals in the 100-meter freestyle and in the 800-meter freestyle relay. He also played water polo for the United States team that placed fourth in the event won by the British.

The 100-meter swim was unique in Olympic history. Kahanamoku won it in 1:00.4, a world record. Although the time was ratified the Olympic final had to be swum again.

François Oppenheim, in his *The History of Swimming,* wrote: "The Australian, (William) Herald, who came in fourth, had lodged a protest against third place winner Norman Ross, who had impeded him. At the same time there were no lane dividers in the pool, so the rules provided for just such a situation.

"The jury, of the opinion that Ross had in fact jeopardized Herald's chances of gaining a medal, ordered the race to be swum over, the victor again being Kahanamoku in 1:01.4."

Ross did not compete in the second final, but before he left Antwerp he had 3 gold medals, for the 400- and 1,500-meter freestyle races and the 800-meter relay.

Despite the lack of lane dividers, Olympic swimming had made major advances since Hungary's Alfréd Hajós won a 100-meter—1,200-meter freestyle double in 1896, swimming in open water in the Bay of Zéa.

The races in Paris in 1900 had taken place with the current in the River Seine. Competition in 1904 was in the still water of an artificial lake, part of the setting of the St. Louis World's Fair. London in 1908 had a pool which was specially constructed for swimming events, but in 1912 they were held in salt water once again, though within a sheltered harbor.

It would be another four years before a stadium would be built for swimming events, with a pool containing floating markers and divisions into lanes.

The U.S. team's travel across the Atlantic left about everything to ask. Their transportation was to have been on a liner, but when it broke down they were shunted to an old freighter doing service as a funeral ship. It had just unloaded the bodies of 1,800 war dead, whose caskets lined the dock as the team boarded.

The women contestants had upper deck accommodation, but the men were not so lucky. Olympic official Dan Ferris later described the setting: "The athletes were quartered down in the hold. The smell of formaldehyde was dreadful. What a black hole that was for them! The athletes had to sleep in tripledecker bunks that hung on chains. The place was infested with rats. The athletes used to throw bottles at the rats. It was terrible, but we had to go this way because we had no money. No money at all."

The provisions in Antwerp posed their difficulties, too. The cots in the old schoolhouse that housed male athletes were so small that they could not be used by three huge American weight throwers—Matt McGrath, Pat McDonald, and Pat Ryan. The trio received permission to move into a local inn. Dan Ahearn, a triple jumper, without permission joined his teammates because he also couldn't fit his frame to the little schoolhouse cots. When he was thereafter found to have missed curfew, the U.S. Olympic Committee suspended him from the team.

Their action precipitated a confrontation of athletes and officials. Many of his teammates rushed to Ahearn's defense. They signed a petition demanding that he be reinstated and threatened not to

Aileen Riggin led an American sweep of the springboard diving and set a 32-year pattern.

compete if the Olympic Committee refused to accede to their demand. The athletes won their point. Ahearn was reinstated. He placed sixth behind the winning Finn, Vilho Tuulos.

Two of the swimming team are of special interest. Both were divers—Alice Lord and Aileen Riggin. Lord won no medals at Antwerp but she did win a husband. On the long boat trip that carried the athletes to the Games, she became friendly with Dick Landon, who was to win the high jump gold medal. After the Games the two athletes were married, culminating what was probably the first Olympic romance.

Romance did not concern Riggin, who won the springboard diving title. She had just turned 14—the youngest Olympian at the Games.

Ethelda Bleibtrey won the 100- and 400-meter freestyle races in world record times. On a public beach, her fame drew crowds and her thin, one-piece tank suit comparisons. "Decent" attire still meant heavy "bathing costumes" that included high-laced shoes, stockings, foundation garments, hats, and, for both men and women, a kind of apron called a "modesty skirt."

FINAL MEDAL STANDINGS			
Nation	**G**	**S**	**B**
United States	41	26	27
Sweden	17	19	26
Belgium	16	12	13
Great Britain	15	16	12
Finland	14	10	8
Italy	14	6	5
Norway	13	8	8
France	9	20	13
The Netherlands	4	2	5
Denmark	3	9	1
South Africa	3	4	3
Canada	2	3	3
Switzerland	2	2	7
Estonia	1	2	–
Brazil	1	1	1
Australia	–	2	1
Japan	–	2	–
Spain	–	2	–
Greece	–	1	–
Luxembourg	–	1	–
Czechoslovakia	–	–	1
New Zealand	–	–	1

John Kelly, who had not been permitted to race in Britain's Henley Royal Regatta earlier in 1920 because as a part-time bricklayer he was considered a professional, won the single sculls in rowing. He then teamed with his cousin, Paul Costello, to capture the double sculls.

Kelly fathered two children who were to become famous. One was John, Jr., who would win the single sculls at Henley and the 1947 Sullivan Award, and would become president of the Amateur Athletic Union. The other child became a film star and later Princess Grace of Monaco.

The United States also won rowing's eight-oared race.

A winter sport, ice hockey, was introduced in the 1920 Games. Canada beat out the United States for the gold medal. Figure skating reappeared for the first time since 1908. Gillis Grafström of Sweden won the men's championship. His countrywoman, Magda Julin Mauroy, took the women's title. The gold medal in pairs went to Finland's Ludowika and Walter Jakobsson-Eilers.

Suzanne Lenglen of France won the tennis gold medal in women's singles. She was a six-time Wimbledon singles champion.

The United States was shut out in Greco-Roman wrestling, but won five medals, including one gold, in the freestyle competition. The heavyweight silver medalist was Nat Pendleton, who became a Hollywood film actor.

Two Americans won gold medals in boxing—Sammy Mosberg in the lightweight division and Eddie Eagan in the light-heavyweight class.

Eagan made Olympic history in 1932 by winning a gold medal in the four-man bobsled event. He is the only athlete to win gold medals in both Summer and Winter Games.

The United States also excelled in shooting in Antwerp. Willis Lee won five gold medals, one silver medal, and one bronze. Lloyd Spooner collected four gold, one silver and two bronze medals.

Despite many difficulties the Antwerp Games went a long way toward uniting nations in sports again. It was a good omen for the future. In 1924 the Games would take a new direction and add an important dimension.

John Kelly of the famous Philadelphia family won the single sculls rowing event.

1924

Winter Games
Chamonix, France

When figure skating and an ice hockey tournament appeared on the program of the 1920 Games, it was only a question of time before winter sports in general would become regular events. Figure skating had been included in the London events of 1908, when the women's title went to Madge Syers-Cave of Great Britain and the men's top honor went to Sweden's Ulrich Salchow, who gave his name to the Salchow jump. Pairs skating was seen in London, too. Anna Hubler and Heinrich Burger of Germany took the top prize, delighting the audience with the lifts they introduced to ''artistic'' skating. The runners up were two Britons, Phyllis and James Johnson, who inspired shadow skating.

So there was precedent building for winter sports competitions within the Olympics. In 1924 in Chamonix, France, winter events were accepted as part of the VIII Olympiad.

But not without a struggle. From the start, the Scandinavians were opposed. They had their own Nordic Games in Sweden, and in Norway the Holmenkollen competition. It was suggested that Coubertin himself agreed with the Scandinavians because he felt a separate meet for winter events would weaken the Olympic movement.

His *Mémoires Olympiques* shows that the opposite was so. ''Not only had winter sports become so widespread in a large number of other countries,'' Coubertin wrote, ''but there was such a genuine amateur character and sporting dignity attached to these events that to press for their exclusion from the Olympic program was an argument of doubtful validity.''

After considerable debate, a compromise agreement was devised by J. Sigfrid Edström of Sweden and the Marquis Melchior de Polignac of France.

It called for winter sports competitions to be

held as a prelude to the Summer Games. They would be Nordic events and would be administered by the IOC. Competition would be conducted in the same country that hosted the Summer Games. And the Games would not be called Olympics; at least not at the start.

The 1924 Summer Games were scheduled for Paris in tribute to Baron de Coubertin, who retired as IOC president the following year. In keeping with the compromise, France was obliged to host the Winter Games which were called The International Winter Sports Week. The community selected was Chamonix near Mont Blanc, about 60 miles northeast of Grenoble.

Competition was held from January 25 through February 4. Sixteen nations—Austria, Belgium, Canada, Czechoslovakia, Finland, France, Great Britain, Hungary, Italy, Latvia, Norway, Poland, Sweden, Switzerland, the United States, and Yugoslavia—sent 293 athletes, including 13 women, to participate. Estonia participated in the opening ceremony, but entered no athletes in the competition. Japan readied a team, but was unable to send it because of the great earthquake in the Kwanto plain that destroyed all of Yokohama and half of Tokyo, and killed 95,000 people.

Chamonix presented a pattern of weather problems that would become all too well known in the future Winter Games. When the skating rink was just ready for use, it was buried under a 3-½ foot snowfall. It had to be cleared by men with shovels.

A week before the start of competition the same rink was turned into a lake by a rainstorm. Only a sudden frost saved the opening ceremony from catastrophe.

The opening of the first Winter Games in Chamonix, France, Jan. 25, 1924, was a momentous occasion for the Olympic movement.

Charles Jewtraw (left) of Lake Placid, N.Y., who won the 500-meter speed skating, was not so conscious of streamlining as later racers. He wore no hat and kept both arms in motion. Thorleif Haug (below) a superb skier, took home to Norway three gold medals from the only Olympics he entered.

The athlete's oath was repeated this time by a member of each of the participating delegations. Staff Sgt. C. Manndrillon, a skier, recited the oath for the host French and carried his nation's flag.

Hockey player Clarence "Taffy" Abel took the oath for the United States team. The Games were officially declared open by Gaston Vidal, French Under Secretary for Physical Education.

And once again, as happened during the rebirth of the Modern Games in Athens in 1896, an American won the first event. Charles Jewtraw of Lake Placid, New York, won the 500-meter speed skating race by two tenths of a second from Oscar Olsen of Norway. There were 27 competitors in the event. Other United States finishers were Joseph Moore, tied for eighth; Harry Kaskey, 12th; and William Steinmetz, 14th.

Jewtraw's victory over the more experienced Scandinavians was the biggest surprise of the Games. He beat them in European-style racing, which paired skaters against the clock, rather than American-style, in which all contestants started at the same time.

Only Jewtraw prevented a Finnish-Norwegian sweep of every medal in the speed skating events. Finland's Clas Thunberg and Julius Skutnabb, as well as Norway's Roald Larsen, were multiple medalists. Thunberg, who tied with Larsen for the 500-meter bronze medal, won the 1,500-, 5,000-meter, and the combined event, the only time it appeared in the Winter Games. He also won a silver medal in the 10,000 meters. Skutnabb captured the 10,000, won a silver medal in the 5,000 meters, and a bronze in the combined. Larsen was second in the 1,500 meters and the combined, and the bronze medalist in the 5,000- and 10,000-meters.

Norway, which had been the most vocal in opposition to Winter Games, was the most successful participant in Chamonix. Its star was 29-year-old Thorleif Haug, whose victory in the 18-kilometer cross-country race gave him the first skiing gold medal of the Games.

Haug made it a triple by winning the 50-kilometer race and the Nordic combined (skiing and jumping). A statue was unveiled in his honor in Kongsberg, Norway, during his lifetime.

Only the bronze medal won by Finland's Tipani Niku in the 18 kilometers prevented Norwegians from sweeping every medal in events won by Haug.

Thoralf Stroemstad won a pair of silver medals in the 50 kilometers and the Nordic combined. Johan Gröttumsbraaten collected a silver in the 18 kilometers, and a pair of bronze medals in the 50 kilometers and Nordic combined.

Jacob Tullin-Thams, Narve Bonna, and Haug led Norway to a sweep in the ski jumping events. Anders Haugen of the United States placed fourth and was later awarded Haug's bronze when it was announced that his scores were totaled incorrectly.

Tullin-Thams introduced the ''aerodynamic style'' of ski jumping. He bent forward from the waist instead of remaining in an upright position during the jump.

Sweden's Gillis Grafström won the men's figure skating championships for the second time in a row. ''His name sounds poetic and he was in fact a poet and lived like a poet,'' French Olympic historians noted about Grafström.

A four-man bobsled race was part of the program at the first Winter Games. The painting shows a 4-man bob on one of the less dangerous parts of a run. The extremely expensive modern run is a precision-engineered construction of concrete with built-in refrigeration. The bob, rather like an open sports car, with the crew seated one behind another, hurtles along at 80-odd miles an hour through curves that require 20-foot-high banking walls.

Willy Bockl of Austria and George Gautschi of Switzerland placed 2–3 behind Sweden in Chamonix. Nathaniel Niles of the United States was sixth, duplicating his 1920 finish.

Niles and all American figure skaters owe a debt to Irving Brokaw, a sixth place finisher in the 1908 competition. When Brokaw returned home to New York after finishing his studies in Europe, he worked tirelessly to improve the caliber of American skating. It was Brokaw who organized the first United States championships in 1914, which served as a springboard for future American successes.

The 1924 women's figure skating gold medal went to Herma Planck-Szabo of Austria. Beatrix Loughran of the United States was second. Ethel Muckelt of Great Britain placed third and Theresa Weld-Blanchard of the United States, a bronze medalist in 1920, finished fourth.

Eighth and last was the 11-year-old Norwegian champion, who would become the world's most famous figure skater. Her name was Sonja Henie.

The pairs title went to Helene Engelmann and Alfred Berger of Austria. Finland's Ludowicka and Walter Jakobsson-Eilers—gold medalists in Antwerp—finished second. They were 39 and 42 years old, respectively. They would place fifth in 1928.

Andrée Joly and Pierre Brunet of France claimed the bronze medal. The American tandem of Weld-Blanchard and Niles was sixth.

The United States was not represented in the only bobsledding event contested in Chamonix. Eduard Scherrer drove Switzerland's four-man sled to victory ahead of Great Britain and Belgium.

Canada and the United States repeated their one-two ice hockey finish of 1920, with Great Britain, instead of Czechoslovakia, third this time. But unlike the contests in Antwerp, where teams played with seven men, Chamonix watched 6-man teams.

Canada and the United States had too much power for the rest of the field. The Granites of Toronto, representing Canada, outscored their rivals 30–0, 22–0, 33–0 and 19–2. The Americans won 19–0, 22–0, 11–0 and 20–0, heading into the final against the Granites.

But Canada won the gold medal with 6–1 victory. Harry Watson, the Canadian player-coach who scored 13 goals in a 30–0 romp over Czechoslovakia, scored three against the United States. He later was elected to Hockey's Hall of Fame.

American defenseman Taffy Abel finished as the second highest scorer in the competition with 15 goals. He subsequently played eight years in the National Hockey League with the New York Rangers and the Chicago Black Hawks.

During the International Winter Sports Week the International Skiing Federation (FIS) was founded in Chamonix. The date was February 2, 1924.

The following year the IOC Congress met in Prague. Baron de Coubertin, in his *Mémoires Olympiques* said: "The Winter Games had been a complete victory, our Scandinavian colleagues have been won over to our point of view entirely, and this made me most happy, as I had always wished to see this winter extension duly approved and endorsed."

Two years after the Chamonix competition, the IOC finally accorded it the title of First Winter Games. The new set of Olympics was established.

Figure skaters Sonja Henie and Gillis Grafström, her coach. Miss Henie made her Olympic debut in 1924; Sweden's Grafström received a second consecutive gold medal.

FINAL MEDAL STANDINGS			
Nation	G	S	B
Norway	4	6	6
Finland	3	3	2
Austria	2	1	–
United States	1	–	2
Switzerland	1	2	–
Canada	1	–	–
Sweden	1	–	–
Great Britain	–	1	2
Belgium	–	–	1
France	–	–	1

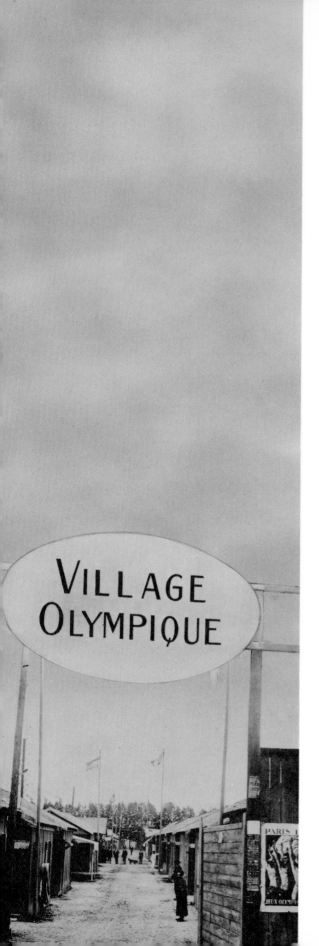

1924

Summer Games
Paris, France

Coubertin's long presidency of the IOC was nearing its end in 1924. In deference to him, the committee agreed to shift to Paris the Summer Games that had been scheduled for Amsterdam. With the benefit of what had been learned since 1900 Coubertin was confident that the inadequacies of the first Paris Games would be avoided. He wanted the association of "Paris" and "Olympic Games" in the popular mind to be respectful.

But for months it appeared that the IOC decision had been a mistake. France had made great strides in recovering from World War I—80% of the destroyed houses had been rebuilt, 88% of the factories were back in operation, 80% of the trenches used by the troops of both armies had been filled in—but at a huge outlay. The fall in foreign exchange had resulted in an alarming increase in the cost of living. The necessity for the government to retrench in the interest of sound finances was clear. Because the reparations expected from Germany were not forthcoming, the proposal was for a 20 percent increase of nearly all taxes. Railway fares were to be advanced, post and telegraph rates increased, and heavy penalties imposed for tax evasion. Unhappiness was general, and vociferous.

To add to the discontent of the winter of 1923 the Seine extensively overflowed its banks, flooding much of the city on either side. The available sports facilities were inadequate, and making them right meant more money to be spent. In a low moment Los Angeles was picked as an alternate city.

However, Paris overcame all problems and staged a successful Olympics from May 4 through July 27.

A total of 44 nations was represented by 3,092 athletes. The number of spectators who viewed the Games was 625,821.

Ireland was represented under its own colors for the first time. Germany again was not invited to participate. But Austria and Hungary, who had also fought against the Allies during World War I, returned to the Olympic fold.

The 1924 Olympics marked an important change in the Games. The responsibility for conducting the competitions was turned over to the individual international federations that governed each sport.

The Games had previously been controlled, although loosely, by the IOC. Events had appeared on the Olympic program at the whim of the host nation. But that changed in 1924 when the Modern Games were "modernized."

The 1924 Paris Olympics also provided the first collective housing for athletes. It was not at all suggestive of a contemporary Olympic Village. The simple huts surrounding Colombes Stadium look to us now rather like a collection of tool sheds or fisherman's shacks. But their simplicity and closeness, like the tents of a bivouac, gave the athletes access to their fellows, and encouraged the international intermingling that had been so strong an argument for the revival of the Olympics.

The stadium of Colombes, with its 500-meter running track, was more of an oven than a pleasure arena during the Games. Competition was conducted during a punishing heat wave that sent temperatures soaring as high as 113 degrees!

That was about where the thermometer was when Finland's Paavo Nurmi started and won the grueling 10,000-meter cross-country race. Nurmi also won the 1,500- and 5,000-meters and picked up gold medals in the team cross-country and in the 3,000-meter team race.

The organizers of the 1924 Summer Olympics provided the athletes with collective housing for the first time. Although rudimentary in design, the shelters offered the Games' participants an opportunity to become better acquainted.

From the sidelines, passersby watched the running of the marathon, won by Finland's Albin Stenroos.

During one remarkable day, July 10, Nurmi won the 1,500 meters, then after resting for less than an hour, captured the 5,000 meters, both with Olympic records. His five gold medals from Paris were the largest track and field haul in a single Olympics.

Nurmi was not the only Finn to draw raves during the 1924 track competition. So did Ville Ritola, who lived in the United States, but retained citizenship in his native land. Ritola spent seven days in Paris. He ran a long distance race each day, a total of 39,000 meters. His efforts earned him four gold medals. He won the 10,000 meters in world record time and the 3,000-meter steeplechase with an Olympic record. Nurmi did not enter either race.

Ritola also won gold medals in the team cross-country and the 3,000-meter team races and silver medals behind Nurmi in the 5,000 meters and in the individual cross-country race.

Finland completed a sweep of the long distance races. Albin Stenroos, a 40-year-old sewing machine salesman from Helsinki, won the marathon, the length of which had been made standard at 26 miles, 385 yards.

Stenroos had finished third to Hannes Kolehmainen in the 10,000 meters in Stockholm in 1912. He then retired from running after breaking a leg in a cross-country race. But in his Olympic comeback in Paris, he beat runner-up Romeo Bertini of Italy by almost six minutes. Clarence DeMar of the United States was third.

Great Britain dominated the shorter races, winning three of the four events against favored Americans.

Harold Abrahams of Cambridge University won the 100-meter dash. Abrahams had failed at his first try, in Antwerp, in 1920. But this time he equaled the Olympic record of 10.6 seconds in two heats and in the final. Jackson Scholz of the United States was a tenth of a second behind him, and Arthur Porritt of New Zealand a tenth of a second behind Scholz. Charley Paddock, "the world's fastest human," had been expected to win. He came in fifth.

Abrahams, who also won a silver medal as a member of Britain's 400-meter relay team which finished behind the United States, had outrun the fastest human, but the *Times* of London broke out no flags: "In the final, H. M. Abrahams, who won, could do no more than equal the Olympic record."

Looking back from the vantage point of nearly 50 years, Abrahams remembered the absence of fuss in the days before the Olympics became a worldwide enterprise. He could recall no victory ceremony. "In fact," he said, "I don't believe there was a flag raising at all in Paris." When did he get his medal? "About a month later. I was home in London. It came by post."

Paddock hoped to salvage a gold medal in the 200 meters. He took the lead late in the race but made the mistake of glancing around to measure his advantage. Scholz bolted past him to capture the event. Eric Liddell of Britain, the 400-meter winner, was third. Abrahams was sixth.

Douglas Lowe of Britain won the 800 meters. Daniel Kinsey regained for the United States the 110-meter hurdles title won in world record time in 1920 by Earl Thomson, an American-trained Canadian. Thomson returned to the United States to coach at his alma mater, Dartmouth. Thereafter, he spent 37 years as track coach at the United States Naval Academy.

The U.S. team, which included (above, from left) Con Cochrane, William Stevenson, Oliver McDonald, and Alan Helffrich, won the 1,600-meter relay in world record time. Following a jump-off Glen Graham (left) was runner-up to his American teammate Lee Barnes in the pole vault.

Paavo Nurmi

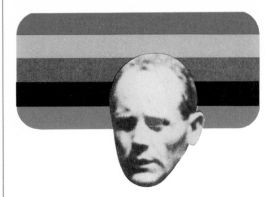

I ran for myself, not Finland.

—PAAVO NURMI

Silhouetted against the sky, on the path that leads up to the Olympic Stadium in Helsinki, Finland, stands a bronze statue of a runner in action. It was sculpted in 1925 to honor the achievements of the great athlete known as "The Flying Finn."

It is Paavo Nurmi. And, it is not Paavo Nurmi.

But that is probably as it should be; it always has been difficult to separate the man from the myth. The statue was sculpted after Nurmi's amazing series of triumphs in the 1924 Olympics, and everyone knows it is supposed to be Paavo Nurmi there on the pedestal. But the sculptor, exercising artistic license, fashioned a classic runner, and that is not Nurmi as he really was.

Nurmi was not the long-striding, muscle-rippling runner of the sculptor's mold. He was barrel-chested, ran upright with head erect, and periodically glanced down at the stopwatch he always carried during practices and races.

The pattern never varied until the final lap when, certain he had kept to the predetermined pace he was sure would win the race, Nurmi ignored the stopwatch and sped to the tape.

Running against time rather than men, Nurmi set world records in the astonishing total of 16 individual events. He ran faster than then existing world records at least 35 times. And he won 12 Olympic medals during the decade in which he dominated long-distance running.

The carefully noted triumphs tell us so much about Nurmi's medals, his running times, and his array of records that it is easy to think of him as a kind of running machine powered by some kind of clockwork.

In fact the figure of a running machine is ap-propriate. From his earliest years Paavo wanted to be an athlete and showed his ability to train himself.

He was born on June 13, 1897, in Turku, a seaport in southwest Finland called Abo by Sweden. He was the eldest of five children.

Time to play boys' games he did not have, but from the age of 9, when he had seen a track meet, he knew he wanted to be an athlete. As a member of a youth club he got his first taste of running. The satisfaction of it would grow into the great passion of his life, a passion that would make him as famous a Finn as Jean Sibelius and Marshal Carl von Mannerheim.

When Finland's Hannes Kolehmainen won three gold medals in the 1912 Olympics, Nurmi was one of thousands of Finnish boys who idolized him. If Nurmi needed an inspiration, Kolehmainen provided it. The teenager dedicated himself to becoming just such a world-class runner, and began to follow a strict program of training. To develop speed and stamina he chased an early morning mail train in Turku. Later, when World War I forced him to become a soldier, he kept up his daily training by getting up before reveille and running mile after mile before the rest of the camp was awake.

When the war was ended Nurmi began to execute his plans for a scientific conquest of long-distance running, with time, not men, his chosen opponent. Whatever he tried in the way of diet, pacing, breathing he carefully recorded, together with his performance.

He was 23 when he went to Antwerp for the first Olympics held after the war. In a physical sense he was ready, but he was relatively unexperienced in competition and in his first race, the 5,000 meters, the fact probably cost him the victory. He let someone else dictate pace for the last time.

Following that inaugural silver medal performance, Nurmi would win nine gold and two more silver medals in three different Olympics. He won his first gold medal in the 10,000 meters in Antwerp, plus two more golds in the cross country race, one in the individual event and the other as a member of the winning team.

Four years later, in Paris, there was not much reason to expect any very remarkable running performances. The city had not experienced a more wilting July. The temperature went to 113°F.

Nurmi himself had had an unpromising spring. On Easter he had fallen on an icy road and injured his knee. He didn't walk then for two weeks, and for another two couldn't run. When he had resumed training his times were depressingly slow.

As for his events, it appeared that the Olympic

organizers had effectively stacked the deck against him by placing the 1,500- and the 5,000-meter finals just 55 minutes apart. A runner contending in both of them, let alone winning both, was not taken seriously—until July 10, 1924.

The 1,500 came first. It was a shorter distance than he usually raced. But that did not alter his approach, which was to run each race evenly, which meant each quarter in even time. To that end he always wore a stopwatch. For this race he had trained to do 1,000 meters in 2 minutes 30 seconds. His actual performance was 2:30.1—a poor show by his exacting standards.

But when he looked over his shoulder on the final lap, he knew he would win. His time was an Olympic record 3:53.6—1.4 seconds faster than runner-up Willy Scherer of Switzerland. He continued running right into the locker room and, obviously refreshed, emerged 45 minutes later for the 5,000.

Nurmi, countryman Ville Ritola, and Edvin Wide of Sweden ran together for the first half of the race. Then Nurmi took a look at his stopwatch and flashed ahead.

When he finished, he had another Olympic record in 14 minutes, 31.2 seconds. Ritola had kept pace and finished in 14:31.4. In his usual manner, without breaking stride, Nurmi picked up his sweatsuit and continued running to the locker room.

He was a superman, in the sense that he exceeded his competitors, but not in the sense of superhuman. He was totally immersed in what he was doing, which was part of his strength. But beyond that he had to an unusual degree what the Finnish call *sisu*, a combination of will-power and endurance. With his clockwork precision, in spite of the heat, he added three more gold medals to his trove before he left Paris. They were for winning the individual cross country run, and for the team cross country and 3,000-meter team race victories.

In 1928, at age 31, Nurmi added what would be his final gold medal by winning the 10,000 meters in Amsterdam. He also won silver medals in the 5,000 meters and in the steeplechase there.

He wanted to run in one more event he had not entered, the marathon, and he set his sights on the 1932 Olympics.

But it was not to be. Just prior to the Games in Los Angeles, the IOC barred the greatest runner, as a professional. He had been charged with demanding and accepting excessive expense money three years earlier in Germany.

By nature a solitary man, he grew more removed as the years advanced. He had been mar-

ried, and sired a son, but the marriage ended after about a year.

In 1952, when the Games took place in Helsinki, Nurmi was awarded one more Olympic honor. He was asked to carry the Olympic flame into the stadium. The flourish of trumpets as he appeared, and the throbbing cheers and applause of the crowd left no doubt of the esteem felt for the runner.

Nurmi died in Helsinki on October 2, 1973. He was given a state funeral. His lifelong preoccupation with understanding the body of a runner guided the disposition of his estate. He arranged to leave it to a foundation supporting heart research. When he announced that fact, he agreed to an interview:

"When you ran Finland onto the map of the world," one reporter asked, "did you feel you were doing it to bring fame to a nation unknown by others?"

"No," said Nurmi, "I ran for myself, not Finland."

Thomas Woodson (above) was
among the entrants in the high
jump competition. Clarence "Bud"
Houser of the United States was
awarded two golds—shot put
(right) and discus.

The runner-up to Kinsey in Paris was Sidney Atkinson of South Africa. He would be the gold medalist four years later.

F. Morgan Taylor retained American domination in the 400-meter hurdles. But his time of 52.6 seconds was not accepted as a world or Olympic record because he knocked down the last hurdle. That was prohibited for record consideration under the then existing rule. The Olympic record of 53.8 seconds thus went to Erik Vilén of Finland, who finished third. Vilén was given the silver medal after America's Charles Brookins, who finished second, was disqualified for running out of his lane.

The United States breezed to a world record in the 1,600-meter relay ahead of Sweden and Britain.

Italian walker Ugo Frigerio, a double gold medalist in Antwerp, won the 10,000 meters. He is the only man in Olympic history to walk to three gold medals. (Frigerio would also win a bronze medal in the 50 kilometers in 1932.)

The world long jump record also was shattered but it didn't happen in the Olympic long jump competition. Robert LeGendre of the United States leaped 25 feet, 5¾ inches on July 7 while finishing third behind two-time gold medalist Eero Lehtonen of Finland in the pentathlon. LeGendre was not entered in the individual long jump.

The next day he watched his American teammate and fellow black, William DeHart Hubbard of the University of Michigan, win the Olympic long jump with a mark of 24 feet, 5⅛ inches, thereby becoming the first black American to win an Olympic gold medal.

Harold Osborn of the United States won a double in the decathlon and high jump. He is the only man in Olympic history to win the decathlon plus an individual event. Clarence "Bud" Houser, another American, captured the shot put and discus.

Loren Murchison (above) ran third man in the U.S. world-record-setting 400-meter relay in both 1920 and 1924. He finished fourth in the 200 meters in 1920 (shown here) and sixth in the 100 meters in 1924, and only ⁴/₁₀ths of a second behind the gold. Harold Osborn (left) was the first Olympic athlete to win the decathlon and an individual event, the high jump.

Although lawn tennis made its final Olympic appearance in 1924, an all-star cast was featured. Helen Wills (left) and Hazel Wightman teamed to take the women's doubles.

Seventeen-year-old Lee Barnes of the United States won the gold medal in the pole vault after a jumpoff with 18-year-old teammate Glen Graham.

Lawn tennis bowed out of the Olympics in 1924 with a Hall of Fame cast and a United States sweep of all five events.

Vincent (Vinnie) Richards won the men's gold medal, finishing ahead of Henri Cochet of France. Richards and Frank Hunter took the doubles while France's Four Musketeers combined to finish second and third. Jacques Brugnon and Cochet won the silver medal. Jean Borotra and René Lacoste won the bronze.

The women's singles went to Helen Wills. Miss Wills teamed with Hazel Wightman, for whom the tennis Cup is named, to win the doubles. Then Miss Wightman and R. Norris Williams captured the mixed doubles.

American and British boxers found they had problems with the way the matches were conducted in Paris. They were unfamiliar with the custom, followed in many European nations, of the referee being seated outside of the ring. Many times, the fighters were unable to hear instructions shouted into the ring by the referees. Nevertheless, Britain's Harry Mallin and Harry Mitchell won the middleweight and light heavyweight gold medals, respectively, and

Fidel La Barba took the flyweight, and John (Jackie) Fields the featherweight, golds back to the United States. Fields was sent to the Olympic Games as an alternate. He defeated Joey Salas, the American amateur featherweight king in the final.

Fidel LaBarba followed 1920 winner and fellow New Yorker Frankie Genaro into the pro ranks, where both became world champions in this division. And featherweight gold medalist Jackie Fields became the world pro welterweight titleholder.

South America flexed its muscle in Olympic soccer for the first time. Uruguay won the gold medal, finishing ahead of Switzerland and Sweden. Uruguay returned to defend its championship successfully four years later with Argentina second and Italy third.

Kindly Parisians had turned cooling water hoses on the marathoners of 1900, but in 1924 the race was more formally conducted. In wilting heat American Clarence De Mar (above), who finished 7 minutes after Stenroos, the winner, won the bronze. He continued to run marathons until age 68. Fidel La Barba (left) shows the form that won him the flyweight boxing gold.

*The team of Gertrude Ederle,
Euphrasia Donnelly, Ethel Lackie,
and Mariechen Wehselau set a
world record in winning the
400-meter relay.*

The United States placed second behind Argentina in polo. The American team included Tommy Hitchcock and Rodney Wanamaker. On the five occasions that polo appeared on the Olympic program—1900, 1908, 1920, 1924, 1936—Great Britain won three championships and Argentina two.

The United States earned four of the seven gold medals in free-style wrestling. Robin Reed and Chester Newton placed one-two in the featherweight division. Russell Vis, John Spellman, and Harry Steele took the lightweight, light heavyweight, and heavyweight titles, respectively.

Finland won three of the six Greco-Roman wrestling gold medals, with Oskari Friman taking the lightweight class. Four years earlier, in Antwerp, he had won the featherweight championship.

Five divisions were contested in the weightlifting competition. Italy won three and France two.

For the first time since the St. Louis Olympics in 1904 an American won a gymnastics medal. Frank Kriz took the gold in the long horse vault. Yugoslav Leon Stukelj won the horizontal bar and the individual men's combined exercises. Italy triumphed in the men's combined team exercises. The gold for parallel bars went to August Güttinger of Sweden; that for individual pommelled horse to Swiss Josef Wilhelm; individual rings to Franco Martin of Italy; rope climbing to Bedrich Supcik of Czechoslovakia; and the side-horse vault to France's Albert Séguin.

Roger Ducret helped France to a good showing in fencing. He was runner-up to Belgian Charles Delporte in individual épée and to Hungarian Sandor Posta in individual sabre, but came away from the team épée with gold.

Women's fencing appeared in the Olympics for the first time. Ellen Osiier of Denmark won the individual foil event. She was married to Dr. Ivan Osiier, the fencer who holds the Olympic competitive longevity record of 40 years.

The 1924 Olympics brought an end to the swimming reign of Duke Kahanamoku in the 100-meter freestyle. His successor was Johnny Weissmuller, who swam the event in Olympic record time. Kahanamoku was second, finishing ahead of his brother, Sam.

Weissmuller set another Olympic record in winning the 400-meter freestyle. Then he anchored the United States' 800-meter freestyle team to a world record for his third gold medal.

Three other Americans enjoyed success in the pool. Albert White swept both springboard and high diving championships. Warren Kealoha retained his 100-meter backstroke title, setting a new Olympic record time, and Robert Skelton won the 200-meter breaststroke event.

In winning the 1,500-meter freestyle swimming event, Australia's Andrew "Boy" Charlton posted a world record. When he went home from his first Olympics—he would be back in 1928 and 1932—he took along the bronze medal for the 400-meter freestyle and a silver for the 800-meter relay.

Arne Borg of Sweden had made his Olympic debut in Antwerp. A durable athlete—he participated in the 1928 and 1932 Games—and a free spirit who set 32 world records, Borg's range was enormous. He swam every freestyle distance at one time or another. He was the silver medalist in the 1,500-meter freestyle. He earned a second silver medal in the 400-meter freestyle. He placed fourth in the 100. And he was a bronze medalist in the 800-meter relay. His twin brother Åke swam the 400- and 1,500-meter freestyle events, in which he finished 4th and 6th, respectively, and the 800-meter relay, in which he won a bronze.

The 1924 Olympics marked the first time that one man coached the winners of both the men's and women's 100-meter freestyle events. Ethel Lackie joined Weissmuller as a gold medalist. Both were coached by William Bachrach of Chicago's Illinois Athletic Club. No coach duplicated that feat until 1956. Lackie took another gold, as part of the 400-meter relay team that set a world record.

Martha Norelius, with a world record, led Helen Wainwright and Gertrude Ederle to an American sweep in the 400-meter freestyle. Ederle, who became the first woman to swim across the English Channel, in 1926, also won a gold in the 400-meter relay and a bronze medal in the 100-meter freestyle.

Other United States winners included Sybil Bauer in the 100-meter backstroke, Elizabeth Becker in springboard diving and Caroline Smith in the highboard diving. (Becker took the highboard silver medal as well.)

Great Britain's Lucy Morton established an Olympic record in the 200-meter breaststroke.

Aileen Riggin, 1920 springboard diving champion, returned to take a silver medal in her specialty and a bronze medal in the 100-meter backstroke. She did not compete in the highboard finals, as she had in Antwerp.

Besides Weissmuller, there was another 1924 American gold medalist whose fame in another field would outshine his Olympic

Johnny Weissmuller was gifted with extraordinary buoyancy. He swam so high in the water that his back showed above the surface almost to the waist.

L. De B. HANDLEY
FORMER OLYMPIC COACH

Martha Norelius of New York City set a world record in the 400-meter freestyle swim.

Johnny Weissmuller

You'd think the kids wouldn't know Tarzan the way their parents and grandparents did. But, thanks to television showing my old movies, I'm still Tarzan to them.

—JOHNNY WEISSMULLER

The moving picture spread his fame. The cathode ray tube perpetuated it.

It was a career he had not planned. He was representing a swimsuit manufacturer when he was invited to take an MGM screen test for the role of Tarzan, the vine-swinging hero of Edgar Rice Burroughs' jungle stories.

Weissmuller said no, but after being promised he would meet Greta Garbo and lunch with Clark Gable, he agreed. He was one of 150 men testing for the role first created on the silent screen by Elmo Lincoln in 1918. After his test he went back to his job, not really interested in making movies.

But he won the role, and kept his own name—after the sports-ignorant producer, who wanted to shorten it for motion pictures, learned about Weissmuller's background.

"Tarzan the Ape Man," starring Weissmuller, appeared in 1932.

Tarzan was the ideal of masculine energy and daring. Tall, bronzed, his muscular body free of restraints except for a loincloth, Tarzan fearlessly protected the hunted from the hunter in his African kingdom.

Other actors would eventually follow in the role, but they were only stand-ins. His image never faded. Johnny Weissmuller was Tarzan. Tarzan was Johnny Weissmuller.

The fiction was so powerful that it tended to obliterate fact. But the facts about Johnny Weissmuller were just as amazing as the fiction. Before

he was Tarzan of the Apes, he was the Tarzan of swimmers. During 10 years of world-class amateur swimming competition, Weissmuller reputedly was never beaten in races from 50 to 880 yards.

Weissmuller set 24 world records. He won 33 individual national indoor and outdoor titles, and was a member of 10 national indoor and outdoor championship relay teams.

He churned to three gold medals in the 1924 Olympics and two gold medals in the 1928 Games. He also won a bronze medal as a member of the United States team in 1924.

Weissmuller was the first man in history to break one minute for the 100-meter freestyle and five minutes for the 400-meter freestyle.

He set his first world records in the 300-yard and 300-meter freestyle events when he was 17. He had his third world record in the 150-yard backstroke 26 days later.

Johnny Weissmuller had had a long way to travel before he crossed his first Olympic finish line. He was born June 2, 1904, in the coal town of Windber, Pennsylvania. His immigrant parents, Peter and Elizabeth, were on their way from Austria to Chicago when their money ran out, forcing the senior Weissmuller to work in the mines.

The family reached Chicago, where Johnny's father unsuccessfully tried saloonkeeping. Straitened circumstances made the home and family life far from happy.

Johnny found his escape in swimming. He started when he was eight. Mrs. Weissmuller took her children to Fullerton Beach on Chicago's side of Lake Michigan. Immediately Johnny was at home in the water; he could swim about as soon as he got wet.

Fullerton Beach became a retreat for Johnny and his younger brother, Peter. Both soon challenged "the rocks," a dangerous breakwater of boulders over which the unpredictable lake waves crashed and sucked away.

"Swimming came natural to us," said Johnny, "and like all kids, we yearned for adventure. If our mother had known, we'd have been lashed with a belt. It was dangerous, but it was exciting. Youngsters need excitement."

Life sobered for the youth when his father died and Johnny went to work to help support his family. He started as an errand boy and later became a bellhop and elevator operator at the Chicago Plaza Hotel. It was a dreary existence.

At 16, he was beginning to have self doubts, when he bumped into a childhood friend, Hooks Miller. Miller was a member of the Illinois Athletic

Club swimming team. He couldn't stop talking about his coach, "Big Bill."

Big was what William Bachrach was—a 350-pound hulk of a man with a cigar clenched in his teeth. Weissmuller showed what he could do in the pool. He could swim, all right, but his form was all wrong. Big Bill offered a challenge.

"Swear to me that you'll work a year with me, without questions, and I'll take you on," Bachrach said. "I want you to change your stroke and do everything I say, to the letter. And no excuses.

"You won't swim against anybody. You'll be a slave and you'll hate my guts. But in the end you might break every record there is."

Bachrach obviously had seen something more than a teenager who could stay afloat. Somewhere within the large-chested, 6-foot-3 youngster he suspected a champion. A year was not too long to work to find him.

No lesson Bachrach taught Weissmuller was more valuable than the secret of relaxing. Years after the formal training was over, Johnny emphasized his ability to take it easy.

Bachrach's chief problem with Weissmuller was the age-old one between coach and athlete—how to avoid romantic distractions.

He took his swimmer to Hawaii for a series of exhibitions against Duke Kahanamoku, the two-time Olympic champion. Kahanamoku was a great athlete and a smart competitor. When he learned a swimming session was scheduled for Weissmuller, Duke "discovered" other pressing business.

However, the head-to-head confrontation between the reigning champion and the future champion could not be avoided forever. Both qualified for the 1924 Olympics in Paris.

The first event for Weissmuller was the 100-meter freestyle. He faced Duke, Duke's younger brother, Sam, Arne Borg of Sweden, and Katsuo Takaishi of Japan.

When the gun sounded, Weissmuller was off, flanked by the Kahanamoku brothers. Legs kicking, arms flashing, he pulled ahead at 75 meters and finished in a dazzling 59 seconds flat—the first time the one-minute barrier had been broken in the Olympics. Duke finished second, Sam third, Borg fourth, and Takaishi fifth.

The 400-meter freestyle again brought together Weissmuller and fellow Illinois Athletic Club member Borg, whose world record of 5 minutes, 11.8 seconds had been chewed down to 4:57.0 by Johnny in two bites. Johnny won the gold medal in Olympic record time, 5:04.2, and scored a convincing victory over Borg.

Weissmuller anchored the American 800-meter freestyle relay team to a gold medal in 9:53.4—another Olympic record. And, lest it be missed in the golden hoard, he took home a bronze medal as a member of the United States water polo team.

Weissmuller returned to the Olympics in Amsterdam four years later. After carrying the stars and stripes in the opening ceremony, he added to his gold medals by lowering his Olympic 100-meter record to 58.6 seconds. He also anchored another 800-meter relay team to a 9:36.2 Olympic record.

With a living to make, Weissmuller retired from amateur competition and became a pro. A $500-a-week job promoting swimsuits took him to Hollywood and fame as "Me, Tarzan."

When The Associated Press voted Johnny Weissmuller the outstanding swimmer of the first half century, many of his movie fans learned for the first time that he also had achieved fame, not only in jungle rivers, but in Olympic pools.

Johnny Weissmuller is Tarzan; Johnny Sheffield, Boy.

FINAL MEDAL STANDINGS			
Nation	G	S	B
United States	45	27	27
France	14	15	12
Finland	14	13	10
Great Britain	9	14	12
Italy	8	3	5
Switzerland	7	8	10
Norway	5	2	3
Sweden	4	13	12
The Netherlands	4	1	6
Belgium	3	7	3
Australia	3	1	2
Denmark	2	6	3
Hungary	2	4	4
Yugoslavia	2	–	–
Czechoslovakia	1	4	5
Argentina	1	3	2
Estonia	1	1	4
South Africa	1	1	1
Luxembourg	1	1	–
Greece	1	–	–
Uruguay	1	–	–
Austria	–	3	1
Canada	–	3	1
Ireland	–	1	1
Poland	–	1	1
Haiti	–	–	1
Japan	–	–	1
Monaco	–	–	1
New Zealand	–	–	1
Portugal	–	–	1
Rumania	–	–	1

Fred Etchen, member, U.S. clay pigeon shooting team.

accomplishment. His Yale crew represented the United States in the rowing eights and, at number seven oar, he was an obscure competitor. But at his life's work Benjamin Spock was to become a world-renowned authority on the care of infants.

John Kelly of the United States, who had won the single sculls in 1920, became the first triple gold medalist in Olympic rowing. He combined with his cousin, Paul Costello, to repeat the double-sculls victory they had enjoyed first in 1920. Four years later, with another partner, Costello would become the second of only four triple Olympic rowing gold medalists when he captured his third straight double sculls title.

Great Britain's Jack Beresford, Jr. had an unusually long-lasting Olympic career. In 1920 he had won the single sculls silver; in 1924, though at a slower pace, he got the gold. He took another gold as a member of the winning coxswainless fours in 1932, and in 1936 his third gold medal was won, in double sculls with Leslie Southwood.

Russia's Vyacheslav Ivanov completed the quartet of triple gold medal winners with consecutive single sculls victories starting in 1956.

Sweden took the first four places in the modern pentathlon. Top man Bo Lindman would reappear, in second place, in 1928 and 1932.

France cleaned up the field in cycling, taking individual (188-kilometer), 1,000-meter sprint, 2,000-meter tandem, and road race, and coming in behind Italy in the 4,000-meter team pursuit.

Except for Sloan Doak of the United States team, who placed third in the 3-day event, the equestrian successes were exclusively European in composition.

The shooting competition in the 1924 Olympics was memorable. The Olympic record for the most gold medals won in the sport is five. Three men, each of whom had competed in previous Olympic Games, reached that total in Paris.

Two were Americans—Carl Osburn and Morris Fisher. The third was Norway's Ole Andreas Lilloe-Olsen. Of the three, Osburn retired from Olympic competition with the most impressive record. He also won four silver and two bronze for a total of 11 Olympic shooting medals.

The 1924 Games also were notable for the final appearance of a member of the remarkable Swahn family of Sweden. Alfred Swahn captured a bronze medal in shooting to close out an Olympic career that started in 1908. During that period, he won three gold, three silver, and three bronze medals. Swahn's father, Oscar, had participated in the 1908, 1912, and 1920 Games. When he won a silver medal in 1920, he was 72 years, 280 days old, the oldest person ever to win an Olympic medal. He qualified for the 1924 Games, but was unable to compete because of illness. During his Olympic career, Oscar Swahn won three gold, one silver, and two bronze medals. The total of 15 medals by members of a single family is unmatched in Olympic history.

The 1924 Olympic art competitions added to the two gold medals Alfred Hajós had won in 1896 swimming events. For his plan of an Olympic stadium he received the silver medal.

Oliver St. John Gogarty, the Irish surgeon-poet-playwright of legendary wit, was awarded a bronze medal for his ''Ode to the Tailtean Games'' (Ireland's ancient games).

1928

Winter Games
St. Moritz, Switzerland

The Second Olympic Winter Games were marked by near-tragedy and controversy. And when the 1928 Games were over three athletes—Jacob Tullin-Thams and Sonja Henie of Norway, and Irving Jaffee of the United States—would be discussed for many years. In fact, Sonja Henie was the Olympics' first "golden girl" from the world of ice and snow. These Games were held in St. Moritz, Switzerland, from February 11 through February 19. The dictum that a single nation must host both the Summer and Winter Games in the same year was abandoned. (Amsterdam, The Netherlands, had been selected as the site of the 1928 Summer Games.) A total of 491 athletes representing 25 nations participated at St. Moritz. Bobsledder Godfrey Dewey carried the Stars and Stripes and took the athlete's oath in the opening ceremony. Swiss President Edmund Schulthess officially opened the Games.

Tullin-Thams, defending the ski jumping championship, was too good for his own good and almost lost his life. On a hill designed for leaps of 65 meters (213 feet, 3 inches), the Norwegian soared 73 meters (239 feet, 6 inches). He was badly injured. However, eight years later Tullin-Thams returned to win an Olympic silver medal in yachting.

His countrymen, Alf Andersen and Sigmund Ruud, finished one-two in the 1928 ski jumping event. Despite an ailing knee, Rolf Monsen of the United States placed sixth. Anders Haugen, third at Chamonix in 1924, was 18th, while another American, Charles Proctor, was 14th.

Johan Gröttumsbraaten won the 18-kilometer cross-country race and the Nordic combined to lead Norwegian sweeps in both events. Per Erik Hedlund paced Sweden to a 1–2–3 finish in the 50-kilometer race.

The U.S. team of William Fiske,
Nion Tocker, Charles Mason,
Clifford Gray, and Richard Parke
won the bobsled contest. In 1928
the event was for five-man teams,
not the usual four-man teams.

Although St. Moritz is at a much higher altitude than Chamonix, site of the 1924 Games, the 1928 Games were troubled by sudden changes of temperature and by rain. During the morning of the 50-kilometer race, for example, athletes waxed their skis at zero degrees Fahrenheit. But when the race was over that afternoon the thermometer read 77 degrees! As a result, Hedlund's winning time was more than an hour slower than that which earned Norway's Thorleif Haug the gold medal in 1924.

The United States did not participate in ice hockey. Canada, represented by the Toronto Varsity Grads, won the gold medal for the third consecutive time. The Canadians posted three lopsided shutout victories en route to the championship. Sweden and Switzerland placed second and third. Richard "Bibi" Torriani was a member of the Swiss bronze medal team. He would earn a second bronze medal in hockey 20 years later.

The bobsled race was for five-man teams instead of four. And only two runs, instead of the usual four, were held because of thawing ice. The United States took the gold and silver medals, with Germany third. The winning sled was driven by William Fiske, the youngest American ever to win a Winter Olympics gold medal. He was 16 years and 3 months old at the time. The silver medal United States sled was driven by John Heaton, whose brother Jennison was a member of his team. Jennison and John Heaton were one-two in the skeleton competition.

During the speed skating in St. Moritz, among the most unusual ever held, a future star named Irving Jaffee made his Olympic debut. Five medals were awarded in the 500-meter speed skating competition. Clas Thunberg of Finland and Bernt Evensen of Norway tied

Prior to the competition, the women figure skaters gathered for a photo session. Skirts were generally short, but there was nothing, as yet, about skating dress that was very different from street dress.

Sonja Henie

I am sure that my introduction of dance pattern into my free-skating program had a great deal to do with my winning.

—SONJA HENIE

She was born on April 8, 1912 during an out-of-season blizzard—the worst that ever struck Oslo, Norway. Before she died of leukemia aboard an ambulance plane en route from Paris to Oslo on October 12, 1969, she had revolutionized the way people thought about ice skating. Her name was Sonja Henie and more than anyone else, she helped to popularize the sport of figure skating.

She first competed in the Olympics at the age of 11. And she made $1 million a year many years before such salaries became common for athletes. After winning three consecutive Olympic figure skating gold medals, she became the No. 3 movie box-office attraction, surpassed only by Shirley Temple and Clark Gable. It is as the charming, whirling dervish of the movies that she is best remembered. However, Sonja Henie would have preferred to be remembered for her athletic achievements. For she was the unmatched queen of figure skating through the 1920's and 1930's. When she turned professional after the 1936 Paris world championships, her trophy room contained 257 medals, cups, plates, and bowls. They commemorated an athletic career in which she reached unparalleled heights with 10 consecutive world titles (1927–1936), six European championships (1931–1936), and an unprecedented string of three women's Olympic championships (1928, 1932, and 1936).

In addition, she and her third husband, Niels Onstad, amassed an impressive art collection. An art museum and cultural center was donated by the couple to the Norwegian nation in 1968.

When someone suggested that her life be made into a film, Sonja rejected the idea. "Who would believe it?" she asked. To those who later watched Henie skate in Hollywood films or in person, she tried to explain her feelings. "I could try to tell you by saying it's a feeling of ice miles running under your blades, the wind splitting open to let you through, the world whirling around you at the touch of your toe, and speed lifting you off the ice far from all things that can hold you down," she said. "It's a sense of power, of command over distance and gravity, and an illusion of no longer having to move because movement is carrying you."

Sonja could ski before she could skate. Her father, Wilhelm, a well-to-do wholesale fur merchant and former champion cyclist, was credited with giving Sonja her competitive zeal. Her parents took her and her older brother, Leif, to the family hunting lodge at Geilo, a Norwegian mountain village. She began going to the popular resort at the age of four as soon as the first snow fell. No one walked in Geilo. They skied. "Out of this early start on skis," Sonja said, "I gained a good feeling for balance and rhythm in movement. These gave me a head start later as a novice on skates."

An early interest in ballet also aided her skating career. "I absorbed so much that it has marked everything I have done since," she said. "Dancing, like skating in the years after, was far from forced on me. The ballet was my first love, skating my second, chronologically speaking. . . . I wanted to bring dancing into skating, to transport the ballet onto ice."

Sonja received her first pair of skates at age six after a long argument with her parents, who said she was too young. They offered double runners; she held out for skates—and won. Sonja had never been on skates before and learned by watching her brother. Soon she skated with him. At 6½ she skated alone. Before she was seven, a member of a private club was impressed with her and invited her as a guest. There Sonja was given lessons. When she was seven, she entered her first competition and won. Her prize was a small silver paper cutter with a mother-of-pearl handle.

At eight, Sonja entered and won the higher Junior Class C competition. The following year, she jumped to the Norwegian national championships. And, at the age of nine, Sonja Henie was the women's figure skating champion of Norway.

She also began taking professional skating and ballet lessons. She went to London to study ballet under a woman associated with Russian ballerina Anna Pavlova.

When she was 10, the Henie family took Sonja to St. Moritz and Chamonix to improve her skating. She met the Swedish champion, Gillis Grafström, who himself won three consecutive Olympic championships (1920, 1924, and 1928). Grafström became Sonja's coach.

Not yet 12, she "entered the 1924 Olympic Games for the experience. That was just what I got. No honors but a vivid introduction to just how bright the constellation of the world's skating stars was and a heady anticipation of what I might be taking real part in some day," she later said. Henie finished eighth and last in the field. But one of the seven judges gave her the highest score in free skating. "I don't like to think what might have happened if I had become Olympic champion at that age," she said. "It might have gone to my head and surely would have robbed me of the fun and fine training of four years' work toward that goal."

Studying ballet and practicing seven hours a day were part of the formula for accomplishing the goal. After seeing Pavlova perform in London, Sonja decided that the ballerina's movements could be adapted to figure skating. She then incorporated the "Dying Swan" sequence from *Swan Lake* into her repertoire.

Because she was so young, she wore short skirts that more mature skaters would have considered immodest. It was an attractive innovation. The shorter skirts enabled her to develop faster spins and higher jumps. She also was the first one to break away from black boots and stockings. She wore a variety of colors such as gray, beige, and white.

When she reached St. Moritz for the 1928 Olympics the 15-year-old Norwegian with the stunning blonde hair and sparkling brown eyes was a one-woman skating revolution. With eye-catching costumes swirling above her knees, Sonja exhibited brilliant free skating maneuvers. The crowd and judges gasped as she spun and glided across the ice, blending ballet and skating to perfection. The championship came as a matter of course. "Until then, skating had been rather stiff and pedantic in form," Henie wrote in her autobiography.

She was again the Olympic champion in 1932 at Lake Placid, N.Y. Although the United States was going through a depression, scalpers asked $50 a ticket to watch her skate. After her victory, her parents thought she might be ready to quit. But Sonja Henie had her sights set higher. "I want to win 3 Olympics and 10 world championships," she said. "After that, I shall go into the movies."

Rumors of an impending professional career surrounded her when she arrived in Garmisch-Partenkirchen, Germany, for the 1936 Games. But she was spinning on the ice faster than the rumors were spinning off it. She was 5'-2", weighed 110 pounds, and was at her athletic peak. She had developed 19 separate types of spins and, on some of them, she whirled around as many as 80 times at speeds that frightened some observers. She enthralled the crowd. German Chancellor Adolf Hitler was so captivated that he presented her with an enormous autographed picture of himself after the Games.

By the time Hitler invaded her homeland in 1940, Sonja Henie had moved on, as she said she would. She gave skating exhibitions in the United States, had tea with President and Mrs. Franklin D. Roosevelt, and embarked on a screen career. Her first feature-length film about figure skating, *One in a Million,* was released in 1937.

Through her films and numerous skating exhibitions, Sonja created an immense interest in the sport she made to appear so enjoyable and effortless. Skating rinks opened throughout the United States. Skating clubs were formed in many cities. Little American girls, who had never taken an interest in sports, began to skate. They pretended that they were Sonja Henie.

for first place. Bronze medals went to Johnny Farrell of the United States, Roald Larsen of Norway, and Jaakko Friman of Finland who tied with the second fastest time. No silver medal was awarded. Jaffee, new to European-style paired-skating, tied for 11th, one place behind teammate Ed Murphy.

Next on the program came the 5,000-meter race. Norway's Ivar Ballangrud won the gold medal, trailed by Julius Skutnabb of Finland and Bernt Evensen of Norway. Jaffee, from the streets of New York and with a background of skating on artificial ice, came within three-tenths of a second of beating out Evensen, for the bronze medal.

On February 14, Thunberg, Evensen, and Ballangrud placed one-two-three in the 1,500 meters. Jaffee was seventh. It was Thunberg's last Olympic medal. He closed out his career with an Olympic men's speed skating record of five gold, one silver, and one bronze medal. Ballangrud also earned a total of seven medals before he retired in 1936. He accumulated four gold, two silver, and one bronze medal.

The 10,000 meter competition in 1928 triggered a major controversy. After six races had been run off, involving the fastest men in the field, Jaffee had the best time—18 minutes 36.5 seconds. Evensen was one-tenth second behind. Austria's Otto Polaczek had the third fastest time, but he was unable to break 20 minutes. Only those who seemingly had no possible chance of bettering the top three times were left to compete when the weather suddenly turned warm and the ice began to melt. The competition was halted. Without precedent, the Norwegian referee annulled the 10,000-meter results. The event, the final one on the speed skating program, was canceled.

Jaffee had expected to receive the gold medal because he had posted the fastest time. He protested, but the referee refused to reverse his decision. That night a group of skaters from several nations gathered in front of the hotel in which the Norwegian referee was staying. The skaters included Evensen, Norway's 1927 world

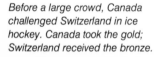

Before a large crowd, Canada challenged Switzerland in ice hockey. Canada took the gold; Switzerland received the bronze.

champion. They demanded that Jaffee be declared the winner. The referee stood firm. Jaffee left St. Moritz as the uncrowned king of the 10,000 meters. He had no gold, only a goal: to do better the next time.

St. Moritz marked the second appearance of a doughty Frenchman named Léon Quaglia. In two Olympics he competed in seven speed skating events and in seven hockey games. His only reward was the exercise.

Gillis Grafström of Sweden won his third straight men's figure skating title. Austria's Willy Böckl was runner-up for the second straight time.

The gold medal in the women's figure skating event went to 15-year-old Sonja Henie. Fritzie Berger of Austria was second, while Beatrix Loughran and Maribel Vinson of the United States placed third and fourth.

Henie wrote in her autobiography: "The American champion Vinson was competing for the first time. She was one of the new guard of skaters, many from Canada and the United States. There was a new approach, new life, and a stiffer challenge in the field than there had been at Chamonix in my dismal 1924.

"Unhappily for me, Mme. Planck-Szabó, the 1924 Olympic champion whom I had hoped to meet again at St. Moritz, did not appear to defend her title, and so I could not feel that I had tested my 1928 ability against her."

But others knew the moment the Norwegian teenager stepped on the ice for her free-skating program that she was superior to any skater in the world. Henie adapted the "Dying Swan" sequence from Tschaikovsky's *Swan Lake* ballet and her routine amazed the audience. Ulrich Salchow, president of the International Skating Union, who had won the men's gold medal in 1908, was among those who viewed the most unmistakable virtuoso performance of the St. Moritz Olympics.

In his classic *Ice Skating—A History*, Nigel Brown said: "(Henie) introduced pattern into her free programs. Until now the highest interpretation of individual skating was expressed by little more than variations of school figures linked with simple stunt movements. Sonja Henie sought 'to tell a story.' She planned her program on a dance choreography and gave form to the whole. Jumps and spins no longer were stunt movements isolated between Rockers or Counters. She gave flow to the sequences of different figures and meaning to the program."

Figure skating was never the same after Henie's gold medal performance. And the Winter Games had not only its first golden girl, but an ice queen who would reign through 1936.

Pierre Brunet of France and his future bride, Andrée Joly, won the pairs gold medal. They eventually went to the United States, where Brunet coached many outstanding skaters, including Olympic champion Carol Heiss.

Before the closing ceremony of the 1928 Winter Olympics, an historic meeting was held in St. Moritz by the International Skiing Federation. FIS agreed to include downhill and slalom races, on a test basis, in international competition. The vote was taken on a proposal made by Sir Arnold Lunn of Great Britain, whose father, Henry, is generally credited with inventing the slalom. The word means "turning" in Norwegian. However, Alpine skiing did not appear on the Olympic program until 1936.

For Maribel Vinson, figure skating was a lifelong delight. She finished fourth in 1928, but from the 1932 Games she went home with the bronze medal. In time, her daughters Maribel and Laurence became contenders of promise. A plane crash in 1961 killed all three.

FINAL MEDAL STANDINGS			
Nation	G	S	B
Norway	6	4	5
Sweden	2	2	1
Finland	2	1	1
United States	1	1	2
Canada	1	–	–
France	1	–	–
Austria	–	3	1
Belgium	–	–	1
Czechoslovakia	–	–	1
Germany	–	–	1
Switzerland	–	–	1

1928

Summer Games

Amsterdam, The Netherlands

Prior to the 1928 Summer Games, a dispute arose between the Vatican and members of the International Olympic Committee. After the IOC voted to include women's track and field in the 1928 Games, Pope Pius XI condemned the decision. And he had an articulate ally—the retired president of the International Olympic Committee and founder of the Modern Games, Pierre de Coubertin. Coubertin cited ancient Greek prohibitions against women athletes and said: "It is against my wishes that they have been admitted to an increasing number of events."

The argument centered on the 800-meter track race. Those in opposition insisted it was too strenuous for women. Coubertin's position on the subject was known as early as 1912, when he opposed the addition of women's swimming to the program in Stockholm. He said then: "We feel that the Olympic Games must be reserved for men. . . ." And shortly before his death in 1937, when his cause had been lost, Coubertin said: "Let women participate in all sports if they wish, but let them not exhibit themselves in doing so."

When the 1928 Summer Olympics were held in Amsterdam, The Netherlands, from May 17 through August 12, there were five events on the women's track and field program. They produced five world records.

Germany, readmitted to the Olympic family following its exclusion due to World War I, produced the women's 800-meter champion. Running on a 400-meter track, which became the Olympic standard, 25-year-old Lina Radke won in 2 minutes 16.8 seconds. Kinuye Hitomi of Japan was second, Inga Gentzel of Sweden third.

In a 50-year retrospect to the initial inclusion of women's track and field, *Olympic Review,* the

IOC publication, noted: "The event (800 meters) was so dramatic and grueling that it was abandoned for 32 years, not to reappear until the 1960 Olympic Games in Rome." For in 1928, several women had collapsed during the event. The *Olympic Review* also paid tribute "to the lithe, harmonious, and fresh image" that women's track and field contributed to sport. It added that the appearance of women "left its mark of beauty and grace in competitions where previously only male ruggedness could have been imagined."

The first women's track and field event held in the 1928 Olympics was the 100-meter dash. Seventeen-year-old Elizabeth Robinson of the United States won the gold medal in 12.2 seconds in a disputed finish after Canada's 18-year-old Myrtle Cook and Germany's Leni Schmidt were disqualified for making two false starts. Two Canadians, the 23-year-old Rosenfeld and 21-year-old Ethel Smith, clocked an identical 12.3. Rosenfeld was awarded the silver medal and Smith the bronze. The finish between Robinson and Rosenfeld was so close that judges picking first and second disagreed. When the decision went to Robinson, whom Rosenfeld had beaten in the semifinal, Canada protested. It was to no avail.

Although Canada was one of the nations that voted against inclusion of women's track and field events in the Olympics, Canadians performed well in the program in 1928. In addition to the medals won by Rosenfeld and Smith, Ethel Catherwood won the high jump at 5' 3". (Carolina Gisolf of The Netherlands and Mildred Wiley of the United States finished 2-3.) Canada also won the gold medal in the 400-meter relay. Rosenfeld, Smith, 19-year-old Florence Bell, and Cook, running in that order, posted a combined time of 48.4 seconds. That was four-tenths of a second faster than the United States team anchored by Robinson. Germany took the bronze medal.

Women's track and field competition joined the Olympic program in 1928. Five events were held, and five world records were produced. Canada finished first in the 400-meter relay (below).

In the 400-meter hurdles (right), Britain's David Burghley won in Olympic record setting time. Kinuye Hitomi (below) of Japan, sensibly costumed, although perhaps not to please the ultra conservative of the time, strove to win the 800. She was eight tenths of a second too slow, and got the silver.

Poland's Halina Konopacka took the discus with a toss of 129'3". Lillian Copeland of the United States and Ruth Svedberg of Sweden were second and third.

The American men's track team, which expected to enjoy as much success as the women, fell far short of what was anticipated. Yet, in his official report at the conclusion of the 1928 Summer Games, Gen. Douglas MacArthur, president of the U.S. Olympic Committee, was enthusiastic. Never one to hide his patriotism and nationalistic spirit, MacArthur had predicted a standout performance for the United States before the contestants ever left for the Olympics. He saluted their "superb condition" for the "great test," and promised that "Americans can rest serene and assured," of the team's ultimate success.

When the Games were over, MacArthur's report said "Nothing is more synonymous of our national success than is our national success in athletics. The team proved itself a worthy successor of its brilliant predecessors. The American team worthily represented the best traditions of American sportsmanship and chivalry. Imperturbable in defeat, modest in victory, its conduct typified fair play, courtesy, and courage. It was worthy in victory, it was supreme in defeat. . . ."

If one compared the report with the results of the Amsterdam Games, it seemed that the General had watched another Olympiad. His praise could not have been directed toward an American men's team that suffered through its most dismal performance in track events since the revival of the Games.

Prior to 1928, the United States had lost only one event in hurdles competition—to Earl Thomson of Canada in the 110-meter race in 1920. Non-Americans won both the 110-meter and the 400-meter hurdles races in Amsterdam. South Africa's Sidney Atkinson and Stephen Anderson of the United States clocked an identical 14.8 seconds in the 110-meter hurdles. But the decision went to Atkinson by a few centimeters. John Collier of the United States was third. Britain's David Burghley ended the string of American victories in the 400-meter hurdles. The man who would become an IOC member, and as Lord Burghley would chair the British Olympic Committee in its hectic preparations for the 1948 Summer Olympics, set an Olympic record of 53.4 seconds. Americans—Frank Cuhel and 1924 gold medalist F. Morgan Taylor—placed second and third.

There were 11 individual men's track races in Amsterdam. The only gold medal won by an American went to Ray Barbuti, a Syracuse football player, who took the 400 meters. Barbuti captured the race with a lunge that broke the tape two tenths of a second ahead of Canadian James Ball. "I was going to send the Stars and Stripes up the victory pole if I had to pull it up myself," he said. "I don't remember anything of the last 100 meters except a mad desire to get to that tape. It seemed a mile off." Barbuti also anchored the United States' world record victory over Germany and Canada in the 1,600-meter relay.

In the eight other races—the 100-, 200-, 800-, 1,500-, 5,000-, 10,000-meter races; the marathon; and the steeplechase—no American was a medalist. The shocking United States performance delighted other nations. There were many explanations for what went wrong with the U.S. team. The most commonly accepted reason was that the team was victimized by various excesses. The explanations ranged from too much coaching to overeating by the participants. There were 1 head coach and 10 assistant coaches, plus 1 head manager and 3 assistant managers solely for the track team. Instruction came from all sides. Occasionally, advices conflicted. Some athletes became confused. Racing tactics suffered.

The training table was another point of criticism. Sailing to Amsterdam aboard the *S.S. President Roosevelt*, the American squad of 250 men and women—more than one third of them track and field athletes—consumed 580 steaks during one meal. The ship was loaded with enough ice cream to last for the round trip but the dessert was devoured before the Games began.

Additionally, American athletes may have been made more than complacent by MacArthur's pre-Olympic assertion of their near-invincibility. They learned, however, that they could be beaten and beaten often. It was a lesson taught them during the track competition by such heroes as sprinter Percy Williams, a 19-year-old Canadian who had worked his way across the country to try out for

F. Morgan Taylor had won the 400-meter hurdles in 1924, but in 1928 he was a full second slower, and finished third. Canada's Percy Williams (left), shown working out in Los Angeles, won both the 100- and 200-meter sprints.

Jackson Scholz, one of the great sprinters of his day, retired after his third Olympics in 1928. He became a successful writer of sports stories for young readers. Mohamed El Ouafi (right), a former member of the French Foreign Legion, took the marathon crown from favorite Martti Marttelin.

his nation's team and who won the 100- and 200-meter races; marathon winner Mohamed El Ouafi of France, a former member of the French Foreign Legion; and Harri Larva, a watchmaker from Paavo Nurmi's hometown of Turku, Finland, who took the 1,500-meter race.

Percy Williams traveled from Vancouver to Toronto for the Canadian Olympic trials. He hitchhiked part of the way, and completed the journey by working as a waiter in a railroad dining car. He was determined to get to the trials because his high school coach, Bob Granger, convinced him he could become an Olympic champion. Williams was an unlikely-looking athlete. He weighed 126 pounds. At age 15, he was told to restrict his physical activities because he had rheumatic fever. Nevertheless, five years later, he scored an Olympic sprint double. The slender Canadian teenager equaled the Olympic 100-meter record of 10.6 seconds in a heat and then won the final with a 10.8 clocking. He finished ahead of second place Jack London of Great Britain and Georg Lammers of Germany, who had identical 10.9 times.

Williams fought hard to survive in the 200 meters. He advanced to the final and won the championship in 21.8 seconds. Walter Rangeley of Great Britain was the silver medalist. Helmut Körnig of Germany and the defending champion from the United States,

Jackson Scholz, were bracketed in third place. Rangeley, Körnig, and Scholz all clocked 21.9. When officials tried to break the tie for third place by suggesting a match race, Scholz declined. The bronze medal thus went to Körnig.

The marathon was one of the most fascinating races of the Games. The favorite was Finland's Martti Marttelin. Chicago taxi driver Joie Ray and a pair of Japanese runners, Kanematsu Yamada and Seiichiro Tsuda, also were considered to be top contenders. Form held for 20 miles. Then, the Algerian-born El Ouafi, who worked in a Paris automobile factory, made his move. He was followed by Miguel Plaza, a newsboy from Chile. They had been running together during the race. And they crossed the finish line with El Ouafi the gold medalist and Plaza in second place. Marttelin was third, Yamada fourth, Ray fifth, and Tsuda sixth.

Britain's Douglas Lowe repeated as the 800-meter gold medalist with an Olympic record of 1 minute 51.8 seconds. Lloyd Hahn of the United States was fifth.

Finland's Harri Larva succeeded Nurmi as the 1,500-meter winner. Nurmi had decided not to defend his 1,500-meter title. Larva chopped four tenths of a second off Nurmi's Olympic record, beating favored Jules Ladoumègue of France.

Nurmi and compatriot Ville Ritola resumed their rivalry. Nurmi won the 10,000 meters in Olympic record time, with Ritola second. Ritola defeated Nurmi in the 5,000 meters. Another Finn, Toivo Loukola, captured the 3,000 meter steeplechase and cut the Olympic record by almost 12 seconds. Nurmi was second. His final appearance in the Summer Games earned him one gold and a pair of silver medals.

Frank Wykoff anchored the United States to a gold medal in the 400-meter relay. Germany and Great Britain placed second and third.

The United States won five gold medals in field events. That helped to overcome U.S. frustrations in the flat races. Stanford's

Robert King led the high jumpers. Defending champion Harold Osborn placed fifth. Edward Hamm of Georgia Tech captured the long jump. Defending champion William De Hart Hubbard tied for 11th.

Sabin Carr, who was the first to reach 14 feet, led an American sweep in the pole vault with an Olympic record. Lee Barnes, the 1924 winner, could do no better than fifth.

Of the Americans returning to defend their titles, only discus thrower Clarence "Bud" Houser was able to retain his crown. The California dentist did it with an Olympic record, winning with his best mark from the qualifying round. Houser did not defend his shot put title but it stayed in American hands. John Kuck set a world record to win the gold. The silver medal went to Herman Brix, who became motion picture actor Bruce Bennett.

Finland placed 1-2 in the decathlon, with Ken Doherty of the United States third. Gold medalist Paavo Yrjölä set a world record. Sweden's Erik Lundkvist threw the javelin to an Olympic record.

The United States lost the hammer throw for the first time when the event went to Patrick O'Callaghan of County Cork, Ireland. O'Callaghan, who became a veterinarian, had begun specializing in the ball and chain in 1927. Edmund Black earned a bronze medal for the United States behind Ossian Skiöld of Sweden.

Japan, which made its Olympic debut in Stockholm in 1912, finally struck gold in Amsterdam. Mikio Oda, sixth in 1924, won the gold medal in the triple jump, finishing ahead of Levi Casey of the United States.

American swimmers fared considerably better than their track and field counterparts. The men won five of eight events; the women captured five of seven. Johnny Weissmuller retained his 100-meter freestyle championship, bettering his 1924 Olympic record time. The 400-meter freestyle went to Alberto Zorilla of Argentina, followed by Australia's Andrew "Boy" Charlton and Sweden's Arne Borg. Borg won the gold in the 1,500-meter freestyle with Charlton second. The bronze medalist was Clarence "Buster" Crabbe, who would star as the movies' Flash Gordon. Missing as bronze medalist was Frank Beaurepaire of Australia. He had finished third in 1908,

California dentist Clarence "Bud" Houser repeated as discus champion. Edward Hamm (right) of Georgia Tech captured the long jump.

1920, and 1924. He also was a silver medalist in the 1908 400-meter freestyle and in the 1920 and 1924 800-meter freestyle relays. Beaurepaire, lord mayor of Melbourne from October 1940 through August 1942, was knighted in 1942. He died six months before the 1956 Games opened in Melbourne.

Japan won its second medal of the Games when Yoshiyuki Tsuruta took the 200-meter breaststroke. George Kojac led a United States sweep in the 100-meter backstroke. Kojac then joined Weissmuller, Austin Clapp, and Walter Laufer on the victorious American 800-meter freestyle relay team that finished ahead of Japan and Canada.

Peter Desjardins, the silver medalist in 1924, beat fellow American Michael Galitzen to win the springboard diving title. Egyptian-born, American-trained Farid Simaika was third. Desjardins won the highboard diving, with Simaika second and Galitzen third.

Desjardins was awarded the gold in the high dive after a mixup. Later, Desjardins recalled, "They declared Simaika the winner and me second. They started playing the Egyptian national anthem and everything. Then they had to interrupt it. I had gone to the boat to shave, thinking I was second, when this girl came running up the gangplank yelling, 'Pete won, Pete won!' They had to lower the Egyptian flag and apologize to Simaika. They'd made a mistake. He won in total points, but I won first place from four of the five judges, so I got the gold and he didn't."

The United States placed 1-2 in the women's 100-meter freestyle. Albina Osipowich beat out Eleonor Garatti for the gold medal. Martha Norelius successfully defended her 400-meter freestyle title for the United States in world record time.

Hilde Schrader of Germany succeeded Britain's Lucy Morton as the 200-meter breaststroke champion. The 100-meter backstroke went to Maria Johanna Braun of The Netherlands. She also took a silver medal in the 400-meter freestyle. Eleanor Holm of the United States tied for fifth in the 100-meter backstroke. Adelaide Lambert combined with Garatti, Osipowich, and Norelius to give the United States the 400-meter freestyle relay gold medal in world record time. Great Britain was second, followed by South Africa.

Herman Brix (later Hollywood actor Bruce Bennett) was runner-up in the shot put. George Kojac and other swimmers practiced aboard the SS President Roosevelt, en route to Amsterdam. Kojac led an American sweep of the 100-meter backstroke and was a member of the gold-winning 800-meter freestyle relay team.

The United States took both ladies' diving events. Helen Meany led an American sweep of the springboard. The silver medalist was Dorothy Poynton, who was two weeks past her 13th birthday. Elizabeth Pinkston-Becker, a silver medalist in 1924, won the high dive. She was coached by her husband, Clarence Pinkston, who had collected one gold, one silver, and two bronze medals in the 1920 and 1924 diving events. Both are now members of the Swimming Hall of Fame. Germany captured the water polo championship, finishing ahead of Hungary and France, the 1924 gold medalist.

Uruguay retained the soccer championship. India started a string of six consecutive field hockey championships, posting shutouts in all five games it played in Amsterdam. Germany and The Netherlands both did well in equestrian events. The dressage team event was held for the first time and taken by Germany.

George Calnan won a bronze medal in men's épée. It was the first fencing medal won by an American in individual competition since 1904. Lucien Gaudin of France won a rare double, capturing both the épée and foil championships. Germany's Helene Mayer won the women's foil.

The United States, represented by the University of California crew, retained the eight-oar championship on a course that was less than 50 yards wide. There were countless heats. The American shell was forced to win five separate races before beating Britain by one-half length for the gold medal. There was also a royal winner on the water. Crown Prince Olav of Norway skippered his 6-meter yacht to a championship.

In gymnastic events, Georges Miez of Switzerland took the men's individual combined exercises and the horizontal bar, and led his nation to victory in the team combined exercises. Miez' countrymen Eugen Mack and Hermann Hänggi were victorious in the long horse vault and the pommelled horse respectively; and Ladislav Vácha of Czechoslovakia won the men's parallel bars competition. Ladies gymnastic events were introduced in the 1928 Games. Holland won the team combined exercises. Italy and Great Britain were awarded silver and bronze medals.

Denmark's Henry Hansen returned home from Amsterdam with a gold for the individual road race cycling event. Italy took the 4,000-meter team pursuit and the team road race. René Beaufrand won the 1,000-meter sprint, and the host nation captured a gold in the 2,000-meter tandem.

Argentinians, Britons, and Italians dominated in boxing competition for the most part. Kurt Leucht of Germany won the bantamweight gold medal in greco-roman wrestling. Estonian Voldemar Väli earned the featherweight gold, Hungary's Lajos Keresztes the lightweight, Vaino Kokkinen of Finland the middleweight, Egyptian Ibrahim Moustafa the light heavyweight, and Sweden's Rudolf Svensson the heavyweight. The freestyle wrestling golds were widely scattered: Finland won the bantam- and welter-weight, Sweden the light heavy- and heavy-weight, United States the feather-, Estonia the light-, and Switzerland the middle-weight.

A total of 3,014 athletes representing 46 nations participated in the 1928 Summer Games. Haiti was represented by only two athletes. Of them, long jumper Silvio Cator won a silver medal. A month after the Olympics, Cator went to Paris. There, on September 9, the former captain of the Haitian national soccer team became the world's first long jumper to achieve 26 feet.

FINAL MEDAL STANDINGS			
Nation	**G**	**S**	**B**
United States	22	18	16
Germany	11	9	19
The Netherlands	8	10	5
Finland	8	8	9
France	7	12	6
Sweden	7	6	12
Italy	7	6	7
Switzerland	7	6	4
Hungary	5	5	–
Great Britain	4	11	7
Canada	4	4	7
Argentina	3	3	1
Denmark	3	2	4
Austria	3	–	1
Czechoslovakia	2	5	2
Japan	2	2	1
Poland	2	1	4
Estonia	2	1	2
Egypt	2	1	1
Australia	1	2	1
Norway	1	2	1
Yugoslavia	1	1	3
South Africa	1	–	2
India	1	–	–
Ireland	1	–	–
Luxembourg	1	–	–
New Zealand	1	–	–
Spain	1	–	–
Uruguay	1	–	–
Belgium	–	1	2
Chile	–	1	–
Haiti	–	1	–
Portugal	–	–	1
The Philippines	–	–	1

1932

Winter Games

Lake Placid, New York

Between 1923, when the International Olympic Committee decided that Los Angeles would be the host of the X Olympiad, and the opening ceremonies of the Winter Games in Lake Placid, New York, the world sustained a bone-jarring shock. Surging prosperity had seemed a permanent fact after World War I. In 1928, Herbert Hoover, campaigning for the United States presidency, observed that "our peoples have more to eat, better things to wear, better homes" than ever. Times were so good, he told a complacent public, that "we have been forced to find a new definition of poverty."

Little more than a year later the bottom dropped out of the stock market and what would be remembered as the Great Depression gripped the industrial nations. The American economy, which had been one of the strongest, was shattered. Where there had been perhaps 2 million unemployed at the time of Hoover's confident speech, at the start of the Olympic year there were a million in New York City alone who could find no work.

On its beam ends, the nation felt its self-confidence seeping away. It was becoming clear that everything was not for the best, in the best of all possible worlds. Between the holding of the Winter and Summer Games, the nation would be jolted anew by riot in Washington, D.C., where the 20,000-man Bonus Expeditionary Force of World War I veterans, camped in the capital, were attacked (against Hoover's orders) by troops led by willful Gen. Douglas MacArthur and with gas, sword, and fire, driven out of town.

Anxiety was pervasive; everywhere people were preoccupied with the daily struggle to make ends meet. Conventional wisdom suggested that in such circumstances the Games might better be postponed; they would attract only the frivolous.

Conventional wisdom erred. The millions with enforced leisure and the eager, young broadcasting industry found they were made for each other. For anyone within earshot of a receiver, the airwaves were bristling with free entertainment. Between 1930 and 1940 the number of receivers in American homes quadrupled to 40 million. As nothing before it had done, radio would homogenize the nation in terms of its entertainment, its symbols, its dreams. Radio characters like Amos and Andy, Fibber McGee and Molly, Jack Benny, and One Man's Family became weekly living room guests. After the Culbertsons broadcast a tournament of contract bridge games, some ten million people set themselves to learn the Culbertson point system.

Lake Placid was a new and little-known resort when it became the site of the 1932 Winter Games. Two weeks later, thanks to radio, it was familiar to the whole country. The National Broadcasting Company's pioneer Olympic broadcast crew—George Hicks, Ben Grauer, and Ed Thorgersen—under the direction of Pulitzer Prize-winning reporter William Burke Miller, in providing the radio public with a running description of the sports events, had effectively transported the listeners, however remote, to rink- and course-side. At Lake Placid America discovered downhill skiing and figure skating, and in pursuit of those sports started a national craze which cheap rail fares fostered.

The broadcasts couldn't have come at a better time for the American audiences. There was a dramatic change in the pattern of the Winter Games. For the first time United States athletes won more medals than those from any other nation—a total of 6 golds, 3 silvers, and 2 bronzes.

Sixty-five countries had been invited to compete in Lake Placid, but only 17 nations and 307 athletes participated when the Games took place between February 4 and February 13.

The British flag was carried in the opening ceremonies by a woman—an Olympic first. Bobsledder William Fiske carried the American flag. Speed skater Jack Shea of Lake Placid took the oath for all participating athletes. In the absence of the head of state, the Games were officially declared open by Governor Franklin D. Roosevelt, who had not hesitated to accept the invitation of the Lake Placid organizing committee. Mrs. Roosevelt accompanied him and, to the consternation of officials charged with her safety, buckled on a helmet and whisked down the bobsled run.

Scandinavians again swept the Nordic skiing events. Sweden's Sven Utterstroem and Axel Wikstroem placed 1-2 in the 18-kilometer cross-country race. Finland's Veli Saarinen was third. Olle Zetterstrom, in 23rd place, was the best American finisher.

Three days later, on a course left bare in many places by a thaw, Saarinen won the 50-kilometer cross country. The course had been shortened to 48.2 kilometers because of the poor weather. Saarinen upset his Finnish compatriot, Vaino Liikanen, the favorite. Arne Rustadstuen of Norway came in third. Utterstroem, the 18-kilometer gold medalist, was the first Swede to finish. When he placed sixth Sweden considered it a national disgrace.

Johan Gröttumsbraaten was 35 years old when he retained the Nordic combined and led Norway to a sweep of the event. Ole Stenen and Hans Vinjarengen won the silver and bronze medals.

Norway recorded a second sweep in the ski jump, Birger Ruud, Hans Beck, and Kaare Wahlberg finishing in that order.

Canada, which won its fourth consecutive gold in ice hockey in 1932, defeated Germany (dark shirts), 4-1, in tournament play.

The figure skating competition was conducted in an indoor rink for the first time. Norway's Sonja Henie easily won the women's title. She captured her second straight gold medal, garnering first place votes from all seven judges. Fritzi Burger of Austria again was the silver medalist. America's Maribel Vinson was third. Britain's Cecilia Colledge, who finished eighth, is believed to be the youngest athlete ever to appear in the Winter Olympics. She was 11 years and 2 months old at the time.

The men's figure skating competition found Sweden's three-time gold medalist Gillis Grafström locked in a duel with Karl Schäfer of Austria. The antagonism between the two was such that they refused to speak to each other. Schäfer emerged the winner, and Grafström added a silver medal to his collection of three consecutive golds. Montgomery Wilson of Canada captured the bronze medal.

Pierre Brunet and Andrée Joly of France retained their pairs championship, this time as man and wife. Beatrix Loughran and Sherwin Badger of the United States won the silver medals. At the time Badger was the president of the United States Figure Skating Association. Hungary's Emilie Rotter and Laszlo Szollas took the bronze.

Joseph Savage of the United States, who paired with Gertrude Meredith was, at 53, the oldest man ever to appear in the Winter Olympics. Savage and Meredith finished seventh.

Four of the six bobsled medals went to the United States. Bobsled enthusiasts and critics who had protested that American representatives had not been chosen in trials, were quieted by acquisition of two gold, a silver, and a bronze medal.

One of the reasons for the success of the United States in bobsledding was its development and use of iron V-shaped runners. The runners increased the speed of the sleds as they roared down Lake Placid's Mt. Van Hoevenberg run, the only bob run in North America to this day.

The United States placed 1-3 in a new event—the two-man bobsled. The Stevens brothers, J. Hubert and Curtis, won the gold medal. Hubert was 42 at the time. He remains the oldest American Winter Games gold medalist. A Swiss team placed second in the boblet. The bronze medal went to John Heaton and Robert Minton.

A blizzard forced the boblet competition to be shifted from February 8-9 to February 9-10, and a thaw caused the four-man bobsled competition to be held February 14-15—after the closing ceremonies—and just before another blizzard hit Lake Placid!

Behind driver William Fiske on the championship United States four-man sled, was boxer Eddie Egan. Until three weeks before the Games, the 1920 Olympic light-heavyweight gold medalist had never been on a bobsled. As part of Fiske's victorious team, Eagan became the only athlete to win gold medals in different sports, one in Summer Games and one in Winter.

Fiske lost his life flying for Britain during World War II. A trophy bearing his name is the top prize in the National AAU four-man bobsled championship.

Henry Homburger drove a second American sled to the silver medal in the four-man competition. Germany finished third. Among several accidents on the bob run, the German *Deutschland II* came to grief. It was replaced by an American sled and crewed by Germans living in the United States who were not thoroughly trained. That sled placed seventh.

Speed skating gold medalist Jack Shea (USA) and bronze medalist William Logan (Canada) looked on as Godfrey Dewey, president of the Organizing Committee of the 1932 Winter Games, presented a silver medal to Canada's Alex Hurd. The event was the 1,500-meter race.

Irving Jaffee

They called me the "Hothouse Champion" because my background in skating was on artificial ice.

—IRVING JAFFEE

When his Olympic career was over, Irving Jaffee was a celebrity in Europe and relatively unknown in the United States. He was a champion in a sport that Americans did not consider major.

In a sport dominated by Europeans, Irving Jaffee was the fastest skater in the disputed 10,000-meter race in the 1928 Olympics at St. Moritz, Switzerland. Then he won a 5,000–10,000 double at Lake Placid in 1932.

Irving Jaffee was born on September 15, 1906, in New York City. He grew up on roller skates. He skated to complete his newspaper route quickly. He first stepped on ice at age 14 in skates that were four sizes too big. Jaffee dropped out of high school during his freshman year after learning that he couldn't make the baseball team. He devoted himself to speed skating and made his competitive debut on an indoor rink. Jaffee lost 22 straight races before Norval Baptie, an outstanding all-around skater, made him his protégé.

Progress was slow. It wasn't until Jaffee's third Silver Skates appearance in 1926 that he won a major race. He set a world record for five miles the following year, and in 1928 he was selected to represent the United States at St. Moritz. However, he wasn't certified for Olympic competition because team officials felt that he was no match for the experienced Scandinavians. Jaffee was crestfallen. But 24 hours before the American team left for Europe, he was told that he could go.

At St. Moritz he placed fourth in the Olympic 5,000 meters, two tenths of a second behind the bronze medalist. It was the best performance in the distances by an American, especially one not familiar with European-style racing. Ice races in the United States were run like track races—all competitors started at the same time. The European practice was to start skaters two at a time; the skater with the fastest time was the winner. Skaters with the fastest times then started first.

Jaffee had posted the fastest time in the 1928 Olympic 10,000 meters when the ice began to thaw. The competition was called off and ruled no contest; no medals were awarded.

Jaffee now had only one target—the 1932 gold. He had to "prove I wasn't a fluke champion." In Lake Placid there was no mushy ice to contend with. Instead, there were his teammates.

"I was an outsider, an outcast," Jaffee said. "They didn't like the idea of a New Yorker—an upstart—like me showing 'em up. They did everything possible to keep me from winning." In addition to his rigorous daily skating practice, Jaffee put in two hours of hiking and trotting. "Taylor (coach Bill Taylor) and the rest of the team claimed I was a show-off because I worked so hard," Jaffee said.

Jaffee's victory in the Olympic 5,000 meters was a tremendous boost for the United States. Jack Shea had won the 500 and 1,500. A first in the 10,000 would give the United States a clean sweep of all four speed-skating events.

The race was 25 times around a 400-meter course. As the contestants rocketed into the final lap, Ivar Ballangrud, the Olympic 5,000-meter champion in 1928 and 1936, was on the pole. Jaffee was alongside. Then Jaffee stepped up the pace and displayed his unrivaled sprinting ability. He outraced the Norwegian to the final turn, zoomed into the straightaway still out front, and, in the last 100 meters, increased his lead to five yards. He lunged with such force at the red worsted strip strung across the finish line that he lost his balance and took a nosedive.

Following the 1932 Olympics, Jaffee retained his interest in ice skating, serving as director of a Manhattan skating rink and conducting exhibitions and promotional events. In a 1976 interview, he said that he did not have his 1932 gold medals. In the depth of the Depression, he needed money and was forced to pawn them. "By the time I was ready to redeem them, the pawnbroker was out of business." However, he kept looking for the medals until his death in San Diego, California, on March 20, 1981.

Irving Jaffee was elected to the U.S. Skating Hall of Fame in 1940.

The medalists in the 5,000-meter speed skating competition were: Edward Murphy (USA), silver; Irving Jaffee (USA), gold; and William Logan (Canada), bronze.

After the Olympics, V-shaped runners were prohibited because they cut into the course. Only arched runners with specified diameters were permitted.

Canada won its fourth straight ice hockey championship in Lake Placid. The Canadians beat the American team, 2-1, in overtime in the game that opened the hockey tournament. Then, in the final games, the United States led 2-1 in the third period until N. Romeo Rivers tied it at 14:10. The game remained tied, at the end of regulation time. After three scoreless overtime periods, the contest was halted. Canada, with 11 points, won the gold medal. The United States, with 9, took the silver. Germany was third.

To the dismay of European skaters and their fans, the United States swept all four speed skating races. The Europeans claimed that the Americans won because the races were run according to United States rules, which started all competitors at the same time. The Europeans paired skaters two at a time, and the skater with the fastest time at the conclusion of the competition was the winner. The American rules kept Clas Thunberg, who in 1924 and 1928 won a total of 4 golds, home in Finland.

Two finals were held on February 4. Jack Shea won the 500 meters. Bernt Evensen of Norway finished second, ahead of Alexander Hurd of Canada.

Irving Jaffee, frustrated not to have been awarded the 10,000-meter gold medal in St. Moritz in 1928, finally struck gold in the 5,000 meters. His American teammate, Edward Murphy, won the silver medal, while William Logan of Canada placed third.

But the 10,000-meter competition was the one Jaffee felt he had to win. Between the 1928 and '32 Olympics, Jaffee had worked for the Curb Exchange, a New York firm that sponsored a skating team. It was there that Jaffee came under the wing of Emil Mosbacher.

"Emil was a broker and the boy wonder of Wall Street," Jaffee said. "He was like a second father to me. He and several friends took an interest in me and sent me up to Lake Placid to train."

It paid off. After Shea completed a double by winning the 1,500 meters on February 5, it was time for Jaffee to meet the 10,000-meter test.

Jaffee and Norway's Ivar Ballangrud matched stride for stride into the last lap. Then, skating into a 40-mile per hour wind, the American put some daylight between himself and the Norwegian in the final turn.

As he sped to the finish line, Jaffee lunged forward and threw himself across it. He was taking no chances with the gold medal he thought he had won four years earlier. Ballangrud finished ahead of bronze medalist Frank Stack of Canada. Evensen was sixth.

The spectators in Lake Placid were entertained by a demonstration dog sled race, won by Canadian Emile St. Goddard. A second demonstration, with implications for future winter games, was women's speed skating. The contests were won by Jean Wilson of Canada (500 meters), Elizabeth Dubois and Catherine Klein of the United States, who took the 1,000-meter and 1,500-meter honors, respectively.

Recalling the 1932 Winter Olympics some years later, broadcaster Ben Grauer said, "Generally, as a new breed of broadcast reporters, we were treated with great respect. With one exception. We invited Sonja Henie out with us for a beer. She came along. But so did her daddy!"

FINAL MEDAL STANDINGS			
Nation	G	S	B
United States	6	3	2
Norway	3	4	3
Canada	1	1	5
Sweden	1	2	–
Finland	1	1	1
Austria	1	1	–
France	1	–	–
Germany	–	–	2
Hungary	–	–	1
Switzerland	–	1	–

1932

Summer Games
Los Angeles, California

In 1932 Hollywood, which liked to call itself the movie capital of the world, was unsurpassed in the making of "spectaculars." Busby Berkeley, the Broadway dance director who had gone to Hollywood in 1930, gave free rein to flair and imagination to dazzle audiences with elaborate costumes and extravagant sets.

About a dozen miles away, in Los Angeles, another sort of extravaganza, the result of some nine years' labor, went on view for two summer weeks of 1932. Its director was William May Garland, a Maine man who had made his fortune in the booming West Coast real estate business of the turn of the century. He had become president of the California Chamber of Commerce and a leading booster of Los Angeles. His show was the Summer Games, and in a very real sense it was his. He had begun in 1920 to secure the Olympics for his adopted city. He appeared before the International Olympic Committee in Antwerp in 1920, empowered by the Los Angeles mayor to seek the 1924 or the 1928 games. The IOC preferred Paris and Amsterdam for these years. They turned down Garland's request, but not Garland: they elected the persistent man to their committee and sent him home with the possibility of Los Angeles for 1932. The possibility was confirmed three years later.

When the time came, the prospect was grim. Economic depression had wiped across the land, affecting everyone. Frightened people stood in soup and bread lines, driven by hunger to swallow their shame at taking handouts. Games, Olympic or otherwise, were a long way down the list of priorities. Money was not at hand in many nations to send athletes to the far coast of America.

Against all the odds, William May Garland, head of the Los Angeles organizing committee and as stubborn as he was enthusiastic, insisted that the Games would take place. The Community Development Association, an adjunct of the Los Angeles organizing committee, persevered. The state voted a million dollars to help with the expenses and Los Angeles floated a $1.5 million city bond. When the athletes of the 37 participating nations reached the coast they found facilities undreamed of before. They included the Los Angeles Coliseum, now enlarged and named Olympic Stadium, with seats for more than 100,000 spectators and a revolutionary new track of crushed peat; an auditorium with 10,000 seats for boxing and wrestling events; a swimming arena, with a 12,000 seat capacity; tennis courts; rifle range; bowling green; and a rowing course with seats for 17,000 viewers.

But of all the provisions made, none was more gratifying to the male athletes than the Olympic Village of 550 cottages and other buildings laid out on a spacious tract of land overlooking the Pacific Ocean. The quarters were strikingly simple and pleasant. Each unit contained two rooms connected by a shower and wardrobe. Larger buildings housed meeting halls, lounges, library, dining rooms, hospital, fire department, and post office. Skeptics who had ridiculed the plans as impossible to carry out without going into deficit had to eat their words. The housing units were erected, as planned, for $165 each, and when the Games were over, the bulk of that investment was recouped when the units were sold to automobile courts and construction companies.

Babe Didrikson, already the gold medalist in the javelin event, has been caught by the painter as she sped over the 80-meter hurdles. She won the gold medal and lowered the world mark to 11.7 seconds.

In his *All That Glitters Is Not Gold* William Oscar Johnson quotes Zack Farmer, chairman of the Los Angeles local planning committee on the question, raised before Olympic Village was seen, of privacy for the athletes: "Oh, we got privacy for those athletes, all right. We fenced it all in and put cowboys on riding the fences. Those Europeans used to love to watch those cowboys lassoing any who tried to climb over the fence. That village was the marvel of the Games."

It was exclusively for the male athletes. The 127 women athletes who took part in the Los Angeles competitions were accommodated in more luxury in hotel rooms.

Garland and his committee held to their other promises, too. To financially embarrassed national committees abroad the pledge was made, in 1930, that each athlete would be maintained for $2 a day in Los Angeles.

The curtain rose on Garland's production on Saturday, July 30, when Vice President Charles Curtis proclaimed the Games open in the name of the president. Mr. Hoover, too busy trying to keep Franklin Roosevelt out of the White House to go to Los Angeles, had originally asked Cal Coolidge to pinch hit for him, but the home-loving former president declined.

The serious competitions began on Sunday. On that day, the capacity crowd saw in action a girl they had been reading about for two weeks, one of the most remarkable stars in the sports firmament. She was Mildred Didrikson, an 18-year-old from Beaumont, Texas, where she was known as "Babe" because she hit a baseball just like Babe Ruth. At Northwestern University in July the United States women's track and field championship had been won by the slight Texan, who took first place in shot-put, javelin throw, broad jump, baseball throw, and 80-meter hurdles, tied for first in the high jump, and placed fourth in the discus throw.

In the Los Angeles Games she was limited to three track and field events. In the javelin throw and 80-meter hurdles she took the gold medals. She had been expected to have the gold for the high jump, too, but the "western roll" that she was accustomed to use, literally diving head first over the bar, was ruled out of order. Babe was awarded the silver medal, and the gold went to her teammate, Jean Shiley.

There were five individual events on the women's track and field program. Didrikson broke world records in three of them. However, the 1932 Games were Didrikson's only Olympics. She was declared a professional shortly after the Games because her picture appeared in an automobile advertisement. Babe turned to golf and during one stretch, won a remarkable 17 straight tournaments.

Didrikson was not the only American woman to win a track and field event. Lillian Copeland came from behind on her final throw of the discus to beat teammate Ruth Osborn. The United States' 400-meter relay team of Mary Carew, Evelyn Furtsch, Annette Rogers, and Wilhelmina Von Bremen won the gold medal in a close race with Canada. Both nations were timed in 47 seconds, a world record. Great Britain was third, with a time of 47.6 seconds.

The only non-American winner in the women's competition was Poland's Stanislawa Walasiewicz, who beat Canada's Hilde Strike in the 100-meter dash. Both clocked 11.9 seconds, a world record. Walasiewicz, who grew up in the United States but represented her native country, became better known as Stella Walsh.

Stella Walsh, running for her native Poland, set a new world record in the 100-meter dash.

Babe Didrikson

My goal was to be the greatest athlete who ever lived.

—"BABE" DIDRIKSON

In the opinion of sportswriter Paul Gallico, Mildred Ella "Babe" Didrikson was "probably the most talented athlete, male or female, ever developed" in the United States. Another journalist held Babe "capable of winning everything except the Kentucky Derby."

She was born on June 26, 1914, in Port Arthur, Texas, the daughter of poor Norwegian immigrants. "Before I was in my teens," she wrote in her autobiography, "my goal was to be the greatest athlete who ever lived."

When she marched into Olympic Stadium in Los Angeles as a member of the United States team Babe was already familiar to sports-conscious people. She had twice been selected All-American basketball forward, she had set three national track and field records, and she was ranked in *Famous American Athletes of Today* as the world's greatest female athlete.

Babe didn't confine herself to the things young women usually did. She had never worn stockings and found they were the most uncomfortable things she had ever put on. She was an exuberant tomboy whose life was athletics. She ran, she threw, she swam, she jumped. She played baseball, basketball, football, tennis, lacrosse, handball. She boxed, bowled, fenced, skated, golfed, shot, cycled.

Within the Didrikson family she was close to her father, a ship's carpenter who was frequently at sea. Ole Didrikson was obsessed with physical fitness. He required each of his seven children to exercise. Mildred, the second youngest in a brood that included four boys, was the most responsive.

"When I got to be a sports champion," Babe said, "Poppa would kid around and say, 'well, she must get it from me.' But I think that as far as athletics are concerned, I probably took after my mother. I understand she was considered the finest woman ice skater and skier around her part of Norway."

She was always outside, where she could challenge neighborhood boys to athletic contests. Youngsters who pitched to her said she hit a ball like Babe Ruth. Before long they called her Babe, too. She also had a strong arm, as she would one day prove by throwing a baseball a tape-measured 296 feet to win a national AAU championship.

But Babe was more than a tomboy and a one-dimensional sports freak. "I was also interested in the woman's things around the house, like cooking and sewing and decorating," she said. "I loved all the pretty things." And she would prove it by winning first prize at the 1931 Texas State Fair with a sport dress she designed.

Her path to the Olympics began in Beaumont High School. She joined the basketball team as a junior and began to score as many as 30 points a game—the total scored by opposing teams. Babe was such a sensation that she was offered a job by the Employers Casualty Company of Dallas—an insurance firm that sponsored athletic teams.

Babe earned $75 a month as a clerk and typist. She starred on the company basketball team and became an AAU All-America player. She persuaded Employers Casualty to start a track team. She was determined to try every event.

The track team held two-hour afternoon practice sessions. But that wasn't enough for Babe. She would practice alone at night. By now Babe's body had matured. She was 5'4" and 105 pounds. She was a jut-jawed, raw-boned girl with the muscles of an athlete, not pretty, but not unattractive.

Babe won two events in the 1930 National AAU championships. She won three events the following year. And then, in 1932, came the National AAU Championships and Olympic tryouts, combined into one meet at Northwestern University in Evanston, Illinois.

There were more than 200 contestants. The Illinois Women's Athletic Club entered a team of 22. But when the scores were in the Employers Casualty Company of Dallas had won the team title with 30 points to 22 for the Illinois A.C. The "team" from Dallas was Babe Didrikson! She entered 8 of the 10 events on the program. Within 2½ hours she was shut out in only one—the 100-meter dash. She won five events—the shot put, baseball throw, long jump, 80-meter hurdles, and the javelin throw.

Babe set a world record of 11.9 seconds in a hurdles heat and added a second world mark of 139′3″ with the javelin. She tied for first place in the high jump with Jean Shiley in a world record 5′3³⁄₁₆″. She finished fourth in the discus.

On the first day of Olympic competition she won the gold medal in the javelin on her first toss—143′4″—breaking her own world record. She didn't try hard on her next attempts because she tore a cartilage in her right shoulder.

Three days later, after equaling her world record in a heat, Babe went after another gold medal in the 80-meter hurdles. She jumped the gun. When the finalists regrouped, Babe was cautioned by the starter that a second false start would cause her elimination. She made certain this time. She was last off her mark and was unable to catch up until the fifth hurdle. Then she drew even with Evelyne Hall of Chicago and the two matched strides the rest of the way. As they neared the finish, both leaned forward. Babe pushed her left shoulder across the tape just before Hall. Both clocked the same time—11.7 seconds—another world record! There was a short debate about the winner, and then Babe had her second gold medal.

The high jump matched Babe against Shiley, with whom she had tied in the Olympic Trials. This time they again matched each other height for height. Both cleared 5′5″ and broke the world record they shared by almost two inches. Then the bar was placed at 5′5¾″, for a jump-off to break the tie. But Babe and Shiley missed their lone attempts at that height. Under existing rules, the bar was lowered. Shiley jumped first and cleared it. So did Babe, flying over the bar head first.

Officials ruled Babe's leap illegal. They said that diving over the bar was not permitted. Shiley was awarded the gold medal. Babe received the silver. She was crushed. She pointed out that she had used the same technique throughout the competition. But her argument was rejected by an official. The height was not ratified as a world record because it was set in an event decided by a jump-off.

Still, nothing could minimize Babe's achievements or the accolades she earned in the Olympics. She won the first of her five Woman Athlete of the Year awards from The Associated Press. (She would eventually be voted the top woman athlete of the first half of the 20th Century.)

When the Amateur Athletic Union suspended her because her name was used to advertise an automobile, she decided to become a professional. Too late, the AAU offered to reinstate her. People wanted to see Babe, and she obliged.

Babe became the only woman member of the bearded House of David baseball team. She pitched for the St. Louis Cardinals in an exhibition game against the Philadelphia Athletics. She played a match against tennis champion Vinnie Richards. She played basketball with the Babe Didrikson All-Americans, the only girl on the team. She appeared in a vaudeville act. The money she received she shared with her family.

In 1934, she turned full-time to golf. She was the medalist in the first tournament she entered. She shot a 77—an indication that she would become one of the greatest woman golfers of all time. Babe won the United States National Amateur championship and the British Women's Amateur title—the first American to do so. She became a professional golfer in 1948. As a professional she captured the United States Open three times and was a founder of the Ladies Professional Golf Association.

Between her second and third Open championships, Babe contracted cancer. In 1953 she had to undergo surgery, but she was back on the course in only three and a half months. She won her third Open by 12 strokes on May 16, 1954.

In 1938 Babe had married George Zaharias, a 285-pound wrestler called the "Crying Greek from Cripple Creek." It was an idyllic relationship. With him she set up a fund for cancer research.

She was only 42 when cancer downed her on September 27, 1956.

Lillian Copeland, silver medalist with the discus in 1928, was the recipient of the gold four years later. Other members of the American discus team in 1932 (below) were: Ruth Osborn (left), silver medalist, and Margaret Jenkins.

With Shiley's high jump gold, Von Bremen's bronze in the 100 and Evelyne Hall's silver behind Didrikson in the 80-meter hurdles, American women won nine of the possible 18 medals in track and field.

In the men's 5,000-meter run a dispute between Finland's Lauri Lehtinen and Ralph Hill of the United States almost caused an international incident. From the days of Paavo Nurmi and Ville Ritola, Finland had dominated the distance races. But in 1932, Nurmi was an Olympic spectator, barred from amateur competition for alleged expense account irregularities. Ritola, having announced his professional status, was no longer a contestant. Thus, Lehtinen, who held the world record, was the man to watch in the 5,000 meters.

Lehtinen was running easily in the lead during the late stages of the race. As the two turned into the homestretch, Lehtinen led by a stride. Then Hill made his move. He swung outside in an effort to pass the Finn. But Lehtinen also went wide, blocking the American's path. Hill returned to the inside and, mirroring the move, Lehtinen did the same thing, checking Hill for the second time. Thrown off stride, Hill made one last try but he could not catch Lehtinen, and the Finn broke the tape inches ahead of him. But both men had the identical time—14 minutes, 30.0 seconds, an Olympic record. Lauri Virtanen of Finland finished third.

Spectators howled in protest. They demanded that Lehtinen be disqualified for illegally blocking Hill. Public address announcer Bill Henry finally calmed the crowd. "Remember, please," he urged, "these people are our guests."

The judges debated before deciding that the alleged infraction had been unintentional. Lehtinen's triumph was confirmed by Chief Judge Gustavus T. Kirby of the United States. Lehtinen apologized, saying that it was a coincidence that he and Hill had twice changed direction at precisely the same time. During the medal ceremony, he tried to pull Hill up to the victory stand alongside him. When Hill refused, Lehtinen pinned a small Finnish flag to his opponent's sweater. It was an act of sportsmanship that delighted the crowd.

The victory pedestal upon which Lehtinen and Hill stood—with the gold medalist higher than the flanking silver and bronze medalists—was introduced in the Los Angeles Games. So was photoelectric timing, which, as a backstop for the official hand timing, showed its value in settling close contests.

Chunky Eddie Toland of the University of Michigan and big, brawny Ralph Metcalfe of Marquette finished in a virtual dead heat in the 100 meters. Both clocked 10.3 seconds to equal the world record. Arthur Jonath of Germany was third. Two watches caught Tolan in 10.3 and the third in 10.4. Metcalfe was timed in 10.3 on all three watches. But judges declared Tolan the winner after examining photos of the finish. Tolan's margin of victory was one inch. Canada's Percy Williams, the world record co-holder and defending Olympic champion, was eliminated in the heats.

There was no doubt about the outcome in the 200 meters. Tolan beat George Simpson of Ohio State by seven feet. Metcalfe completed an American sweep, but the Games were a disappointment for him, because he had won both events in the Olympic Trials.

Even more disappointed was the "Bronze Man"—Phil Edwards, a New York University star middle-distance man from Canada. Edwards placed third in the 800- and 1,500-meter events and was a member of Canada's third place 1,600-meter relay team. He finished his Olympic career in 1936 with a total of five medals—all bronze!

It was Bill Carr of Pennsylvania against Ben Eastman of Stanford for the gold medal in the 400-meter run. Carr had won two previous

In an intercollegiate meet prior to the 1932 Olympics, William Carr upset Stanford's Ben Eastman in the quarter-mile dash. The Pennsylvanian repeated his victory performance over Eastman in the 400-meter run at the Los Angeles Games.

races between the two. Eastman set a blistering pace in the Olympics. He ran 21.7 seconds for the first 200 meters, only half a second slower than Tolan's winning time in the individual event. But Carr stayed with Eastman and slowly cut down his lead. With 80 meters remaining Carr drew even and then he crossed the finish line with a world record of 46.2 seconds. Eastman was two tenths of a second behind. Alex Wilson of Canada placed third.

Eight months after his Olympic victory, Carr, whose effortless, flowing style had marked him as a rising track star, broke his legs in an automobile accident and never raced again.

Thomas Hampson, a thin, bespectacled British schoolteacher not considered any great threat before the Games, pulled away from Canada's Wilson in the last few meters to win the gold medal in the 800 meters. Hampson's time was 1 minute, 49.7 seconds—a world record. Wilson finished in 1:49.9. It was the first time in history the 1:50.0 barrier was broken.

Hampson was a member of the British 1,600-meter relay team that finished second to the world record-setting American quartet anchored by Carr.

Italy's Luigi Beccali won the 1,500 meters in one of the surprises of the Games. Springing, as it seemed, from nowhere in the final two laps, Beccali led John F. Cernes, captain of Oxford University's track team, and Phil Edwards to the tape.

Janusz Kusocinski of Poland won the gold medal in the 10,000 meters, breaking a string of Finnish victories that dated back to Hannes Kolehmainen in 1912. But Finns Volmari Iso-Hollo and Lauri Virtanen won the silver and bronze medals.

Iso-Hollo won the 3,000-meter steeplechase that was marred by the lap scorer's failure to count correctly. The field ran an extra lap of 460 meters. Thomas Evenson of Great Britain was second and Joe McCluskey of the United States was third.

Italy's Luigi Beccali (above) and Finland's Volmari Iso-Hollo were number one in the 1,500 meters and the 3,000-meter steeplechase, respectively. Steeplechase is derived from the old custom of using church steeples as landmarks to guide the riders.

Frank Wykoff anchored the United States to a world record in the 400-meter relay, ahead of Germany and Italy.

George Saling and Percy Beard of the United States finished 1-2 in the 110-meter hurdles, ahead of Donald Finlay of Great Britain, in a race that is remembered for the fact that every contestant knocked over at least one hurdle.

In the 400-meter hurdles Robert Tisdall of Ireland won the event despite hitting a hurdle. Glenn Hardin and F. Morgan Taylor placed second and third for the United States, ahead of Britain's David Burghley, the defending champion.

Four men tied for the gold medal in the high jump—Canada's Duncan McNaughton, Philippine Simeon Teribio, and Cornelius Johnson and Robert Van Osdel of the United States. The awards were decided in a jump-off: McNaughton, gold, Van Osdel, silver, and Teribio, bronze.

In the 400-meter hurdles, Ireland's Robert Tisdall knocked down a hurdle but still won.

The 1,600-meter relay trials: Britain's David Burghley hands off to Thomas Hampson. The British team finished runner-up to the Americans.

The world record-holder in the long jump, Chuhei Nambu of Japan, disappointed expectations when his distance was measured at 7.45 meters. It got him the bronze medal. U.S. jumpers Edward Gordon and Charles Lambert Redd jumped 7.64 meters and 7.60 meters, respectively, and went home with the gold and silver medals.

In the triple jump, Nambu shone, however. His 15.72-meter distance set a world record and won the gold medal. Sweden's Erik Svensson took the silver and Japanese Kenkichi Oshima the bronze.

Leo Sexton's winning heave of the shot put, the first contest of the track and field events, set an Olympic record of 16.005 meters. The 22-year-old giant from New York and his runner-up, Californian Harlow Rothert, surpassed Czech Frantisek Douda, the bronze medalist, and astonished those who expected one of the European record holders to walk off with the honors.

Until his final cast Patrick O'Callaghan of Ireland, winner of the hammer throw in Amsterdam, looked like second best to Finland's Ville Pörhölä. But with his last effort popular Pat landed the hammer five feet beyond the Finn's best distance.

For the third set of games in a row an American won the discus throw. John Anderson established a new Olympic record with his victory. Moreover, the silver medalist, Henri Jean Laborde, a Stanford University student, and France's Paul Winter, the bronze medalist, both broke the former Olympic record with their throws.

From 1906, the name Järvinen had been a familiar one in Olympic circles. In that year, Werner Järvinen had won for Finland her first Olympic honors when he took ancient discus throw, was third in modern discus, and fifth in throwing the javelin. Two years later, he had finished third in ancient discus throwing. In 1932 the Games brought three Järvinen sons to Los Angeles. Kaarlo did not place, but Matti set a new Olympic record with his javelin throw, leading a Finnish sweep of that event, and Akilles won the silver medal in the decathlon, as he had in Amsterdam four years earlier. He was bested by James A. Bausch of the United States, whose total score of points established a new world record.

Attendance at the Games had routed the nay sayers, starting on opening day. Upwards of 75,000 spectators were a frequent occurrence. For the pole vault, it was estimated that 80,000 people watched as William Miller of the United States and Shuhei Nishida of Japan pitted their strength against the rising bar. With the bar at 4.315 meters, both grazed it. As Nishida hit the pit, so did the bar. Miller's luck held: the bar jiggled but remained on the pins. Miller's gold-winning height was a new Olympic record.

Patrick O'Callaghan of Ireland repeated as hammer throw champion. Hammer throwing requires long training, but once the ability is learned, the thrower can continue for years. The original hammer was a sledge. Burly King Henry VIII enjoyed throwing a sledgehammer.

Japanese youngsters were overpowering in the men's swimming competition. Kusuo Kitamura (extreme right), aged 14, and Shozo Makino, 16, were gold and silver medalists in the 1,500-meter freestyle. Sixteen-year-old Yasuji Miyazaki (below) was the victor in the 100-meter freestyle swim.

The 50,000-meter walk was a Los Angeles first, staged through the streets of the city. Four hours, fifty minutes, and ten seconds from its commencement, Great Britain's Thomas Green walked in to claim the gold medal. Some seven minutes behind was Latvian Janis Dalinsch and, a couple of minutes later, Italy's veteran Olympic figure, Ugo Frigerio, who had won the first of his three gold medals in 1920.

Since the days of the ancient Greeks, the event most closely coupled in the popular mind with Olympic striving has always been the marathon, whose winner is wreathed with laurel. In 1932 this final event of the track and field program was won by Juan Carlos Zabala of Argentina. The 20-year-old who promised he would win set such a fast pace throughout the race that he established an Olympic record and led the two nearest contestants—Samuel Ferris of Great Britain and Armas Toivonen of Finland—to break the record, established by Hannes Kolehmainen in Antwerp in 1920, along with him.

The American rebound from a poor 1928 showing in track and field was not repeated in the men's swimming events. There, Japan was overwhelming, winning five of the six events. In the 800-meter freestyle relay the Japanese smashed the world record and broke the Olympic mark by a remarkable 38 seconds.

Yoshiyuki Tsuruta repeated his 1928 gold medal performance in the 200-meter breaststroke. The three other Japanese champions were 14-year-old Kusuo Kitamura, first in the 1,500-meter freestyle, 15-year-old Masaji Kiyokawa, winner of the 100-meter backstroke, and 16-year-old Yasuji Miyazaki, who took the 100-meter freestyle event. In all, Japan won 11 of the 18 available medals.

Gold medals went to Eleanor Holm (100-meter backstroke) and Buster Crabbe (400-meter freestyle). Both later had show business careers, she as a swimmer and he as the movies' Flash Gordon and Buck Rogers. Masaji Kiyokawa (below), part of the youthful Japanese swimming blitz, won the 100-meter backstroke.

The lone American to take a swimming first was Clarence "Buster" Crabbe, who set an Olympic record in the 400-meter freestyle.

The United States swept the springboard diving with Michael Galitzen, Harold Smith, and Richard Degener.

Galitzen and Smith had placed second and fourth in Amsterdam springboard diving, and Galitzen, who took the bronze in the 1928 highboard event moved up to silver in that activity in Los Angeles. Highboard gold went to Harold Smith in 1932, and the bronze to Frank Kurtz.

American women won four of five swimming events. Helene Madison captured the 100- and 400-meter freestyle events, setting an Olympic record in the first and a world record in the second. She also anchored the gold medal 400-meter freestyle relay team to a second successive world record. Eleanor Holm emerged as the 100-meter backstroke champion. The only non-American gold medalist was Australia's Claire Dennis, who set an Olympic record in the 200-meter breaststroke.

The United States swept both diving events. Georgia Coleman, Katherine Rawls, and Jane Fauntz finished 1-2-3 in the springboard. Dorothy Poynton won the gold medal in the high dive. Coleman repeated her 1928 capture of the silver medal, and Marion Roper was the bronze medalist.

Hungary won the water polo, with Germany second and the United States third. Brazil was disqualified after its team insulted the Hungarian referee.

Flyweight boxers from Hungary, France, and Italy took the honors in that order. Canadian Horace Gwynne was the bantamweight victor. The featherweight winner was Argentine Carmelo Robledo. South Africa's Lawrence Stevens won the lightweight contest. Edward Flynn became the first American welterweight gold medalist since Albert Young in 1904. The middleweight gold won by Carmen Barth had likewise not been in United States hands since 1904. South African David Carstens got the gold in light heavyweight boxing. Heavyweight Santiago Lovell went back to Buenos Aires with the gold medal, and straight to jail, on complaint of the captain of the ship that took home the Argentine team, quarreling and fighting among themselves.

France carried away the golds for weightlifting in the featherweight, lightweight, and light heavyweight contests. Germany won the middleweight and Czechoslovakia the heavyweight.

In Greco-Roman wrestling, Swedish contestants took four of the seven gold medals. Carl Westergren won the heavyweight event and became the first of three men to acquire three wrestling gold medals. He had been 1920 middleweight victor and 1924 light heavyweight champion.

Freestyle wrestling gave Sweden two more golds, for middleweight and heavyweight categories. The United States won the bantamweight (Robert Pearce), welterweight (Jack Van Bebber), and light heavyweight (Peter Mehringer) golds.

Italian fencers won the individual foil and épée honors, and French fencers proved the best teams. Hungary, always strong in sabre fencing, took the sabre golds. For the first time an American fencer took a medal for foils (Joseph Levis won the silver) and for the first time a U.S. team got a fencing medal, for épée fencing. The ladies foil champion was Ellen Preis of Austria. She was beginning an Olympic career that would span 24 years and make her the woman with the longest competitive span in Olympic history.

The modern pentathlon was a Swedish triumph in both gold and silver ranks. Bo Lindman, the silver medalist, had taken the gold in 1924 and in 1928 the silver.

In rowing the United States won the double sculls, coxed pairs and eights. Great Britain took the uncoxed pairs and fours, Australia the single sculls, and Germany the coxed fours.

Star class yachting was a new event in 1932, which the United States won. Holland won the gold for dinghy, Sweden for 6-meter yachting, and the United States for 8-meter yachting.

Italy garnered the gold medals in cycling for the road race, the 4,000-meter team pursuit, and the team road race. Edgar Gray of Australia set an Olympic record in the 1,000-meter time trial. Holland won the 1,000-meter sprint and France the 2,000-meter tandem.

Holland retained the three-day equestrian crown. France was best in individual and team dressage, Japan in jumping, and the United States in the 3-day team event.

There were only two shooting contests. Sweden was best in the small-bore prone firing and Italy in the rapid pistol event.

The gymnastic star of Los Angeles was Italy's Romeo Neri, who acquired gold medals for combined individual exercises, combined team, and parallel bars, and a silver medal in floor exercises. United States athletes Dallas Bixler won the horizontal bar and George Gulack the rings.

India's field hockey team trounced the Japanese team 11-1 and the United States team 24-1, the highest number of goals in international competition.

FINAL MEDAL STANDINGS			
Nation	G	S	B
United States	44	36	30
Italy	12	12	12
France	11	5	4
Sweden	10	5	9
Japan	7	7	4
Hungary	6	5	5
Germany	5	12	7
Finland	5	8	12
Great Britain	5	7	5
Poland	3	2	4
Australia	3	1	1
Argentina	3	1	–
Canada	2	5	9
The Netherlands	2	5	1
South Africa	2	–	3
Ireland	2	–	–
Czechoslovakia	1	3	2
Austria	1	1	3
India	1	–	–
Denmark	–	5	3
Mexico	–	2	–
Latvia	–	1	–
New Zealand	–	1	–
Switzerland	–	1	–
The Philippines	–	–	3
Belgium	–	–	1
Spain	–	–	1
Uruguay	–	–	1

Germany
1936

Forty years after he won the first marathon race of the modern Games Spyridon Louis appeared in the Olympic Stadium in Berlin. Under the eyes of 110,000 spectators, accompanied by an orchestra under the baton of composer Richard Strauss, Louis walked slowly toward the principal spectator's box. To its brown-shirted occupant Louis handed an olive branch brought from Olympia, in Greece. It was August 1, 1936 and the recipient of the symbol of peace was Chancellor Adolf Hitler.

Greater irony would be hard to contrive. The swastika-emblazoned head of Nazi Germany was a military dictator whose "solutions" of his country's economic problems promised war. In January 1936, defying the Versailles Treaty and the Locarno Pact of 1925, he had signaled that fact by remilitarizing the Rhineland.

Hitler was by no means alone in contemning peace. On May 9, the Italian dictator, Benito Mussolini, proclaimed a new Italian Empire incorporating conquered Ethiopia. In July Spanish troops in Morocco rebelled against the Republican government of Spain; led by Francisco Franco, they began its overthrow. The Games were hardly over in Berlin before the Spanish civil war became international. Italian and German forces were soon engaged in helping Franco, while Soviet, Mexican, and American fighters of the Lincoln Brigade went to the aid of the Republicans.

Peace within Germany, moreover, was ebbing fast. The Nuremberg Laws promulgated in 1935 had stripped German Jews of citizenship and civil rights. Anti-Semitism had been made national policy; preparations were already underway to effect the "final solution" of the non-Aryan people now labeled enemies of the state.

Road to War was a bestseller in 1935. Its author, Walter Millis, an editorial writer for the influential New York *Herald-Tribune*, blamed the first World War on "the ceaseless, intricate, and insane game of European diplomacy," and charged that the United States had been duped by U.S. banking interests as much as by allied propagandists into taking part. The majority to whom Millis directed his conclusions might deplore events in Europe in general and Germany in particular, but their strongest desire was to keep clear of any additional international entanglements.

There was a minority, of course, that saw the implications of Hitler's National Socialism. As the Berlin Games came closer, voices were raised against the idea of sending a United States team to Berlin. Various sports, educational, labor, and political groups protested against participation. The national organizations of the major religious faiths throughout the United States vehemently expressed their opposition.

A resolution seeking an American boycott of the Games was introduced in the U.S. House of Representatives. A Committee on Fair Play in Sports was organized in July 1935 in a move to thwart United States participation. Judge Jeremiah T. Mahoney, president of the Amateur Athletic Union and the Committee on Fair Play in Sports, was among those most opposed to sending teams to Germany.

But when the AAU held its 1935 convention, Mahoney withdrew his candidacy for reelection as president. He was succeeded by Avery Brundage. Mahoney also resigned from the United States Olympic Committee, of which Brundage was president. That AAU convention had before it a petition bearing 500,000 names and resolutions from organizations totaling 1,500,000 members. All demanded nonparticipation because of Germany's discrimination against Jews.

The United States Olympic Committee, incensed to be questioned about what it considered to be its private affairs, would brook no opposition to its plans. In rejecting all protest, USOC members shamed the Olympic ideal. USOC President Avery Brundage, in an official statement, coolly advanced the outrageous argument that persecuting minority peoples is as old as history and "the customs of other nations are not our business." The secretary of the USOC, Frederick W. Rubien, claimed that Jews were eliminated in the German tryouts because they were not good enough athletes, and asserted that "there are not a dozen Jews in the world of Olympic caliber." Neither Brundage nor Rubien, however, matched the immorality of General Charles Sherrill. That sterling member of both USOC and IOC declared that it did not concern him one bit the way the German Jews were treated, any more than did "the lynchings in the South of our own country."

Within Germany, for quite opposite reasons, there had been strident objections raised against having the Games there at all. Some were opposed on the grounds that visitors would see and be repelled by the authoritarian rule, and Germany would thereby lose friends. Heinrich Himmler, head of the SS security force, urged against having the Games, but propaganda chief Joseph Goebbels countered him, arguing that it was a chance to impress a watching world favorably. After nine months of such pulling and hauling, Hitler came down on Goebbels' side and ordered preparations to proceed in Garmisch-Partenkirchen and Berlin. No expense was to be spared.

Belgium's Henri de Baillet-Latour, the fourth president of the IOC, managed the politically sensitive 1936 Games with a firm hand.

1936

Winter Games
Garmisch-Partenkirchen

When Count Henri de Baillet-Latour of Belgium, president of the IOC, drove to Garmisch-Partenkirchen for the start of the 1936 Winter Games, he was angered by numerous anti-Semitic signs along the road. He demanded to see Hitler. The two argued vehemently. Baillet-Latour threatened cancellation of both the Winter and Summer Olympics unless the signs were removed. Hitler complied.

In another conciliatory move, Germany persuaded Rudi Ball, a Jew, to return from a self-imposed exile in France to play for the German ice hockey team. Ball was the best player on the 1932 bronze medal German team.

Once the competition began, the hockey tournament caused a major uproar. The dispute involved Great Britain's 13-man squad, which included 11 Canadian-born players. All qualified to play for Britain under the residency rules of the international hockey federation. Canada, the defending champion, protested. It felt that Canadian-born players belonged on the Canadian team. But when the protest was turned down and then withdrawn, the players were allowed to compete for Britain. A British threat to withdraw from all the Olympic events unless the 11 players were certified undoubtedly helped to determine the decision.

One of the 11 players, Jimmy Foster was among the best goalies in the world. Almost singlehandedly he secured the title for Britain and ended Canada's string of four consecutive championships. Foster allowed only three goals in seven games. He posted shutout victories over Sweden, Japan, and Czechoslovakia and again did not give up a goal as Britain and the United States played to a scoreless overtime tie.

Later, a 2-1 loss to Canada in the final round cost the Americans a chance to win the gold

Maxie Herber tests the ice at the new stadium built especially for the 1936 Winter Olympics. The fifteen-year-old German teamed with Ernst Baier to win the pairs figure skating championship.

medal. Canada took the silver medal and the United States finished third. Even with Ball in its lineup, Germany failed to qualify for the final round in the 15-nation tournament.

Three Scandinavian nations shared the medals in the 18-kilometer cross-country race. The gold went to Erik-August Larsson of Sweden. The silver was won by Oddbjorn Hagen of Norway. Pekka Niemi of Finland took the bronze. The first American finisher was Karl Magnus Satre, who placed 34th.

Sweden swept the first four places in the 50-kilometer Nordic cross-country skiing event, after being shut out in 1932. The medal winners, in order, were Elis Viklund, Axel Wikstrom, and Nils-Joel Englund. Rolf Monsen, who carried the American flag in the opening ceremonies, injured his ankle before the race and was forced to withdraw.

Oddbjorn Hagen won a double, leading Norway to a sweep in the Nordic combined. Olaf Hoffsbakken was second and Sverre Brodahl third.

Birger Ruud of Norway successfully defended his Nordic ski jumping title. When they invaded Norway a few years later, the Nazis put Ruud and his two ski-jumping brothers in a concentration camp. Sweden's Sven Eriksson and Norway's Reidar Andersen were 2-3 behind Ruud in the jump.

Three new events appeared on the Winter Olympic program in Garmisch-Partenkirchen. They were a 40-kilometer Nordic cross-country relay and an Alpine combined for both men and women.

The 40-kilometer relay went to Finland. Anchorman Kalle Jalkanen started 1 minute 22 seconds behind Norway's Bjarne Iversen and brought his team home in front by six tenths of a second! Sweden won the bronze medal.

Germany took the first two places in the women's Alpine combined which, like the men's event, consisted of a downhill and slalom race. Christl Cranz and Kathe Grasegger were the gold and silver medalists. The bronze went to 16-year-old Laila Schou-Nielsen of Norway. At the time, the Norwegian teenager held the women's world speed-skating records from 500 to 5,000 meters.

Franz Pfnur and Gustav Lantschner gave Germany another 1-2 finish in the men's Alpine combined. Emile Allais of France was third. Birger Ruud, the jumping champion, placed fourth, although he posted the fastest downhill time.

The United States repeated its 1-3 finish of 1932 in the two-man bobsled. The team of Ivan Brown and Alan Washbond won the gold medal. Gilbert Colgate and Richard Lawrence took the bronze medal. The second place finisher was a Swiss sled driven by Fritz Feierabend.

Switzerland won gold and silver medals in the four-man bobsled races, with Great Britain third. Pierre Musy piloted the winning bob. Reto Capadrutt drove the silver-medal sled. He had been a silver medalist on the two-man team in 1932.

Ivar Ballangrud of Norway dominated the competition when speed skating returned to European-style paired races against time in Garmisch, instead of following the 1932 Lake Placid plan of massed starts. Ballangrud won gold medals in the 500, 5,000, and 10,000 meters. He missed a sweep of the four events by exactly one second. Countryman Charles Mathisen beat him by that margin in the 1,500 meters.

Christl Cranz, in sweater and ski pants, and with a simple band around her hair, skied to first place in the Alpine combined. Ivar Ballangrud (left) was supreme in men's speed skating—taking golds in the 500-, 5,000-, and 10,000-meter competitions and the silver in the 1,500 event.

FINAL MEDAL STANDINGS			
Nation	G	S	B
Norway	7	5	2
Germany	3	3	–
Sweden	2	2	3
Finland	1	2	3
Austria	1	1	2
Switzerland	1	2	–
Great Britain	1	1	1
United States	1	–	3
Canada	–	1	–
Denmark	–	–	1
France	–	–	1
Hungary	–	–	1

Anywhere but in a contest with Ballangrud, Birger Vasenius would have been a gold medalist. Before being harnessed with a horse-sized wreath he had finished the 10,000 meters less than 4 seconds behind the winner.

Photo page 147:
German Chancellor Adolf Hitler and an aide personally inspected the 1936 Olympic Village, which was dedicated "to the youth of the world."

The only speed skating multiple winner besides Ballangrud was Finland's Birger Vasenius. He won silver medals in the 5,000 and 10,000 and a bronze medal in the 1,500 meters.

Other medalists included Georg Krog of Norway and Leo Freisinger of the United States, 2-3 in the 500; Antero Ojala of Finland, third in the 5,000; and Max Stiepl of Austria, third in the 10,000 meters.

Despite Ballangrud's success, the Norwegian athlete who attracted the most attention in Garmisch was Sonja Henie, who won her third straight women's figure skating gold medal. Henie, who had matured from child skating prodigy into a beautiful woman, found herself challenged by 15-year-old Cecelia Colledge of Great Britain. However, Henie proved she was still figure skating's high priestess. Hitler was delighted by the victory of Henie, with whom he had been smitten. Vivi-Anne Hultén of Sweden won the bronze.

Karl Schäfer of Austria easily retained his men's figure skating championship. The silver medal went to Ernst Baier of Germany. Felix Kaspar of Austria won the bronze medal.

Baier then combined with Maxie Herber, who was only 15 years and 4 months old, to win the pairs championship for Germany with a brilliant display of shadow skating. Ilse and Erich Pausin of Austria won the silver medal, while Hungary's Emilie Rotter and Laszlo Szollás repeated their third place finish of 1932. Maribel Vinson and George Hill of the United States were fifth. The fourth Winter Olympic Games attracted 756 athletes from 28 countries.

Undoubtedly, United States Olympic officials were impressed by Germany's hospitality and efficiency. "The Germans gave several banquets and entertainments, including a farewell dinner for all of the contestants at Munich," the USOC report on the Winter Games noted. "Each competitor received an elaborate invitation, a ticket to the ball, and a book of coupons which entitled him to a ride to Munich on a special train met by a brass band, and a dinner including a delightful souvenir. The farewell ball was a delightful affair with 2,000 in attendance."

William L. Shirer and Westbrook Pegler were among the most perceptive correspondents who covered the 1936 Winter Olympics. In his *Berlin Diary* Shirer, who was based in Berlin, wrote: ". . . too many SS troops and military about. . . . On the whole the Nazis have done a wonderful propaganda job. They've greatly impressed most of the visiting foreigners with the lavish but smooth way in which they've run the Games and with their kind manners, which to us who came from Berlin of course seemed staged."

Pegler, a sportswriter for the Scripps-Howard newspapers, wrote the day after the closing ceremonies: "Everything is said to happen for the best, and whatever anyone may think of the propriety of our taking part in the political, military, and sporting activities here in Garmisch, Thursday's experience should show a net profit to the United States. . . . The Olympics were of secondary importance, if any. This was the Dictator's day, and it's a good thing for the Americans present that this was so, because they have nothing important to learn from the athletes but much to learn about absolute authority in government."

Pegler concluded: "Well, I'm glad I was here for this particular day and I insist that as matters turned out it was a good thing to send an American team. If they didn't learn their lessons this afternoon they're beyond teaching."

1936

Summer Games
Berlin

Hitler had ordered that all sports were to be organized and conducted by the Nazi party. There would be no participation in championship sports events by the non-Aryans, and after 1935, Jews were forbidden even to use public sports facilities. Among the despised, Jews might be confused with the master race (and so must wear identifying badges), but blacks could neither lower their visibility nor raise their acceptability.

The United States 66-person track and field team included 10 blacks who exposed the stupidity of the Third Reich's vaunted claim of Aryan supremacy. The athletes, who were not to be acknowledged as equal to the master race in any way, were called "Black Auxiliaries" by the German press.

They were not equal. They were better, and eight gold, three silver, and two bronze medals proved it. They took every flat race from 100 through 800 meters and outscored every national team, including their 56 white teammates.

The most impressive showing was that of James Cleveland "Jesse" Owens, who won four gold medals. His powerful legs carried him to victories in the 100- and 200-meter dashes and the long jump. His 200 meter time—20.7—set an Olympic record. He also ran the leadoff leg on the world record 400-meter relay team. His teammate, Frank Wykoff, won his third gold medal in that race.

The toughest tests for Owens were the 100-meter dash and the long jump. He beat black teammate Ralph Metcalfe in the 100, and he defeated another black American, Matthew Robinson, in the 200 meters. Martinus Osendarp of The Netherlands was the bronze medalist in both races.

Owens' most memorable moment in Berlin came in the long jump. Although he was the world record holder, Owens did not qualify for the final in his first two of three jumps. Then Luz Long, a German jumper, suggested that he mark the ground behind the takeoff line and jump from there. Owens took Long's advice and qualified on his final attempt.

Long and Owens dueled head-to-head in the final. Owens soared 26' 5-5/16" on his final jump. He became the first jumper in Olympic history to reach 26 feet, and established an Olympic record that lasted until 1960. The first man to congratulate him was Long, as the two walked around the infield together.

Owens was drawn into a controversy that surrounded the victorious 400-meter relay team. Owens and Foy Draper were last minute substitutes for Marty Glickman and Sam Stoller; they ran with Metcalfe and Wykoff. Marty Glickman, later a noted sports announcer, and Sam Stoller were the only Jewish members of the United States track team. They were also the only members of the team who did not compete in Berlin, to their bitter disappointment. In *All That Glitters Is Not Gold* William O. Johnson, Jr. affirms that Stoller, who kept a diary, noted two days before the relay that the head coach, Lawson Robertson had promised he would run. His note twelve days later is that Draper had pressed the assistant coach, Dean Cromwell, Draper's coach at USC, to let *him* run. The August 22 entry states that Cromwell disclaimed the responsibility for excluding Stoller and Glickman, and says it was Robertson's decision

Throughout the XI Olympics crowds overflowed the sidewalks before the ticket hall in Berlin's Mauerstrasse, eager to buy admission to the events. Among the most memorable events was the long jump. The medalists (right) were: Japan's Naoto Tajima (bronze), America's Jesse Owens (gold), and Germany's Luz Long (silver). Long, who gave the Nazi salute during the award ceremonies, had the courage to befriend Owens in the presence of Hitler.

entirely, and that Cromwell said he himself had wanted an all-white team. Afterward, Glickman, who held Cromwell to be as sympathetic to the Nazis as Brundage—and Brundage had been the principal speaker at a Madison Square Garden rally of the pro-Nazi German-American Bund—was certain that their religion had been the reason for sidelining Stoller and him. Metcalfe and Wykoff agreed. Jesse Owens doubted it. In view of their qualifications, the exclusion of Stoller and Glickman remains a puzzle.

The master race continued to be embarrassed by the triumphs of the American blacks. The first black champion of the Berlin Olympics was Cornelius Johnson. On the first day of competition he won the high jump gold medal at 6' 7-15/16", establishing a new Olympic record.

Other black medalists included John Woodruff, a University of Pittsburgh freshman who gave America its first victory in the 800 meters in 24 years; Californians Archie Williams and James LuValle, who ran 1-3 in the 400 meters; Frederick Douglas ''Fritz'' Pollard, son of the Brown University All-America football player, who took a bronze medal in the 110-meter high hurdles; and David Albritton and Delos Thurber, who completed an American sweep in the high jump.

Woodruff ran an exceptional 800-meter race. He got off to a bad start and was boxed on the pole. He slowed down to a virtual

Jesse Owens (above, left) and Ralph Metcalfe were the recipients of the gold and silver medals in the 100-meter dash. The future congressman lost to the Buckeye Bullet by one tenth of a second. John Woodruff (left) defeated Italy's Mario Lanzi and Canada's Phil Edwards in the 800-meter race.

Jesse Owens

We had nothing to do but run. We couldn't afford any kind of equipment, so we ran and ran and ran.

—JESSE OWENS

Jesse Owens always remembered the moment when Adolf Hitler entered the Olympic stadium in Berlin in 1936.

"I remember seeing Hitler coming in with his entourage and the storm troopers standing shoulder to shoulder like an iron fence. Then came the roar of 'Heil Hitler!' from 100,000 throats. And all those arms outstretched. It was eerie and frightening."

A favorite Nazi propaganda slogan was "Heute haben wir Deutschland, Morgen die ganze Welt." (Today we have Germany, tomorrow the whole world.) The Nazi leadership that had transformed Germany was ready to do as much for the world.

Berlin in 1936 was to be the stage and the Olympic Games were to be the vehicle for showing the Aryans' superiority. Their prowess would overwhelm all inferiors, including the "Black Auxiliaries" from America. Particularly the blacks, said Dr. Julius Streicher, founder of the obscene newspaper *Der Stürmer*, since "they are little more than trained baboons."

But James Cleveland "Jesse" Owens, born September 12, 1913, in Oakville, Alabama, a grandson of slaves, gave the lie to that and all the other foolishness about master race.

Owens was awesome as he put himself through one contest after another. He won gold medals in the 100- and 200-meter dashes, the long jump, and the 400-meter relay, in which his team set a new world record.

There is no doubt that Owens stunned Hitler. His star performance alone wrenched the carefully staged Olympics out of the direction they had been expected to take. It was a black man who took most of the bows.

For his part, Owens' concentration was on other things altogether. "When I competed, I never looked toward the box where Hitler and his entourage sat. Ideology meant nothing to me. I wasn't politically oriented. None of us was. I only know I was thrilled when the crowd kept yelling 'Yes-sa, Yes-sa, Yes-sa Ov-enns,' " he said.

Jesse was one of seven children who grew up in a cotton-growing community. His earliest memories were of the cotton fields, where even the youngsters put in long hours "blacking a strip"— picking all the white cotton bolls. Progress was measured in the number of pounds picked in a day.

"There were no towns to go to and the nearest cotton-gin was 10 miles away," Owens said. "I learned to read and write in a one-room school where I could go only when it wasn't cotton-picking time."

When Owens was nine, his family moved to Cleveland. Life wasn't much easier financially, but there were fewer deprivations, and Jesse began to find an outlet for his energies in running.

"We had nothing to do but run," he said. "We couldn't afford any kind of equipment, so we ran and ran and ran."

Owens displayed his athletic prowess when he was 15. He ran 100 yards in 9.9 seconds, high-jumped 6'2¼" and long-jumped an even 23 feet. At 19, he clocked 9.4 seconds for the 100, tying the world record, 20.7 seconds for the 220 yards on a straightaway, and long-jumped 24' 11¼" for Cleveland East Technical High School.

His performances earned him a scholarship to Ohio State University, where he became known as the Buckeye Bullet.

On May 25, 1935, during a meet in Ann Arbor, Michigan, Owens accomplished what is regarded as the greatest single afternoon's work in the history of track and field. In the space of 45 minutes, he broke five world records and tied one!

Owens equaled the 9.4 second world record in the 100-yard dash. He set a world record in the long jump of 26'8½"—a mark that was not surpassed for 25 years. He followed with world records in the 220-yard dash (20.3) and 220-yard low hurdles (22.6) on a straightaway. The times were automatically recognized as world records for the slightly shorter 200-meter distances.

When he stepped to the line for the start of the 100-meter final in Berlin, Owens got off with the gun and had a seven-yard lead at the halfway mark.

His teammate, Ralph Metcalfe, later a U.S. congressman (D.–Ill.), started poorly, but he closed the gap and finished a tenth second behind Owens' 10.3, which equaled the world record.

The long jump the following day was a stiffer test. According to the official 1936 American Olympic committee report, "Owens apparently had more difficulty reaching the qualifying standard of 23'5½" . . . than in winning the event.

"He was not aware that the competition had started and ran through the pit to warm up, which was charged as one of his three trials. On his second effort, he fouled, but he managed to qualify on his last jump with a leap of 23'5⁹⁄₁₆"."

"I kicked at the dirt," Owens later said. " 'Did I come 3,000 miles for this?' I thought bitterly. Suddenly, I felt a hand on my shoulder. I turned to look into the friendly blue eyes of a tall German long jumper. He offered me a firm handshake. 'I'm Luz Long,' he said, and he offered me advice that helped me qualify for the final later in the day."

A stiff breeze enabled six men to exceed 25 feet. The USOC report said: "In the final, Long, on his second try, equaled Owens' best effort of 25'9¾", but Owens took the lead a second later with a leap of 26'1½". In his final effort, Owens hurled himself almost five inches beyond his best previous performance."

The first three finishers represented three different races. Owens took the gold with an Olympic record jump of 26'5⁵⁄₁₆". Long, in second place, posted a mark of 25'9¹³⁄₁₆", and bronze medalist Naoto Tajima of Japan, who won the triple jump two days later, leaped 25'4¹¹⁄₁₆".

After Owens won, he remembered "Luz Long was at my side, congratulating me. It wasn't a fake smile, either," Owens said.

The friends did not see each other again. Long fought in the German army during World War II and was killed in Sicily. Owens never forgot the man who befriended him, and after the war he met Long's family. "Luz was a wonderful guy," Owens said. "It took a lot of courage for him to befriend me in front of Hitler."

After winning the 100-meter dash and the long jump, Owens took the 200-meters in an Olympic record 20.7 seconds. He finished ahead of teammate Mack Robinson, the brother of Jackie Robinson. Then Owens helped the United States to the 400-meter relay gold medal.

On the opening day of competition, German winners were taken to Hitler's box to receive congratulations. Then IOC president Baillet-Latour told the dictator that he was a guest of honor and had no business congratulating winners. Hitler didn't have much opportunity after that to congratulate the German track and field team. Jesse Owens had beaten the German men's track team by himself, four events to three.

Subsequently, Owens turned his hand to a variety of business ventures, some more successful than others. Wherever he might be, the soft-spoken man devoted a large part of his time to efforts that keep youngsters active in sports.

Honors accumulated over the years. In 1974 Owens received the NCAA Theodore Roosevelt Award, given to prominent Americans for whom athletics have been important in shaping a distinguished career of national significance. President Gerald Ford gave Owens the Presidential Medal of Freedom in 1976. In 1979 President Jimmy Carter, presenting the Living Legacy Awards, said of Owens, "A young man who possibly didn't even realize the superb nature of his own capabilities went to the Olympics and performed in a way I don't believe has ever been equaled. . . . And since this superb achievement, he has continued in his own dedicated but modest way to inspire others to reach for greatness."

Jesse Owens died of lung cancer in Tucson, Arizona, on March 31, 1980.

UCLA's Jimmy LuValle finished a close third in the 400 meters.

walk to permit the field to pass him. Then Woodruff ran past everybody on the outside. He took the lead shortly after the midway mark of the race and beat Italy's Mario Lanzi and Canada's Phil Edwards.

The United States won 12 of 23 men's track and field events. Hitler, who attended almost every track and field competition won by black Americans, was so passive that he was reported to be snubbing the victors, especially Owens. If that was the intent, Owens was the wrong man for it. "People kept writing that Hitler snubbed me," he said afterward. "If he did, I never noticed."

On the same day that Owens won the high jump, shot putter Hans Woellke won Germany's first gold medal in the Games. Hitler rose to congratulate him—and brought down the wrath of IOC president Count Henri de Baillet-Latour. Pointedly, Baillet-Latour reminded Hitler that his only role in the Games was in the opening and closing ceremonies. The dictator was not to congratulate *any* medal winners. He complied publicly, but reportedly he congratulated German winners in the course of lavish private receptions.

The receptions weren't the only lavish aspect of the 1936 Summer Olympics. Germany spent an unprecedented $30 million to create a setting more splendid than any prior Games had seen. There were a Reichssportfeld which contained four stadiums, a 20,000-seat swimming facility, a polo field, a gymnasium, and basketball courts. The complex covered 325 acres. Owners of property in the vicinity had been ordered to paint and clean their properties, and decorate their windows with flowers. A huge 140-acre Olympic Village was constructed, considerably more luxurious than the pioneer housing provided for the athletes in the 1932 Games. To underline the contrast the Germans acquired one of the Los Angeles Olympic Village bungalows and installed it in their own village. The German village was converted to military barracks after the Games.

During the opening ceremony the magnificent airship *Hindenberg* bore the swastika flag over the stadium. For the first time, the Olympic flame was carried from Olympia, Greece, by relays of 3,300 runners through seven countries, finally to ignite the flame that burned throughout the Berlin Games. The relay was the idea of Dr. Karl Diehm, of the German Organizing Committee.

In his biography, *Adolf Hitler*, John Toland wrote that during the parade of nations the Austrian delegation modified the stiff right-arm Olympic salute to make it a Nazi salute, while the Bulgarians went them one better and added a smart goose step. The 250-member French team, whose salute was more Roman than Olympian, won great applause, but the British, in straw hats, by merely executing an 'eyes right', offended numerous onlookers. The Americans also turned eyes right as they passed the Tribune of Honor, but as usual would not dip their flag. That set off some foot stamping by irritated spectators.

The shadows thrown over the Berlin Games did not dim the luster of individual achievement. Owens' triumphs were a case in point. The 1,500-meter race was lifted out of the ordinary by a field that included the top five finishers in the 1932 Olympic race. Luigi Beccali of Italy, who had won the gold medal in Los Angeles, returned along with John Cornes of Great Britain, Phil Edwards of Canada, America's Glenn Cunningham and Eric Ny of Sweden. Also in the field were Archie San Romani of the United States, Jack Lovelock, a New Zealander who was studying medicine in Great Britain, and German champion Fritz Schaumburg.

Cornes, the silver medalist in Los Angeles, took the early lead, with Beccali close behind. But at 400 meters Cunningham was in front, with Ny, Schaumburg, Lovelock, and Beccali trailing in that order. With 400 meters remaining, Lovelock took the lead and held it to win the race. He chopped a full second off the world record with a time of 3 minutes, 47.8 seconds. Cunningham, who trailed Lovelock, also broke the world record.

The next three finishers—Beccali, San Romani, and Edwards—all broke the Olympic mark of 3:51.2. After the race, Lovelock returned to his studies at St. Mary's Hospital in London. (Interestingly, almost 18 years later another St. Mary's doctor-to-be would make track history by running the world's first sub-four minute mile. His name: Roger Bannister.)

German men won only three gold medals in track and field. In addition to Woellke, Karl Hein set an Olympic record with his hammer throw, and Gerhard Stöck was best with the javelin.

America's Ken Carpenter won the discus with an Olympic record throw, while Germany's world record holder, Willy Schröder, finished fifth. Earle Meadows, another American, beat Shuhei Nishida of Japan with a pole vault of 14' 3-¼". Nishida was the 1932 silver medalist. Glenn Morris set a world record in leading a United States sweep in the decathlon.

Finland, as usual, dominated the distance races. Volmari Iso-Hollo was the only Finn from the 1932 Games to defend a championship successfully. He won the 3,000-meter steeplechase. He also took a bronze medal in the 10,000 meters, swept by his countrymen Ilmari Salminen (gold) and Arvo Askola (silver). Gunnar Höckert took the 5,000, beating 1932 titleholder Lauri Lehtinen.

Glenn Morris (above) established a world record in the decathlon, while another American, Ken Carpenter (left), threw the discus for a new Olympic record.

Juan Carlos Zabala of Argentina, the defending marathon champ, went to Germany to train six months before the Games. Zabala held the lead in the race for 17 miles, when he collapsed. He got up, resumed running, but collapsed again after two additional miles, and dropped out of the race. At that point, Kitei Son, a Korean-born Japanese student, took the lead and went on to win the race by more than two minutes. In second place was Ernest Harper of Great Britain. Shoryu Nan of Japan finished third. Son's time was the fastest ever recorded for the 26-mile, 385-yard distance. He was clocked in at 2 hours, 29 minutes, 19.2 seconds.

Naoto Tajima and Masao Harada of Japan finished 1-2 in the triple jump, with Tajima setting a world record of 52' 5-⅞". His best performance prior to the Berlin Games had been 50' 6-¼".

The United States won both hurdles races. Forrest "Spec" Towns equaled his own world record of 14.1 seconds in a heat of the 110-meter hurdles and then won the final in 14.2 seconds. Glenn Hardin, the 1932 silver medalist, struck gold in the 400-meter hurdles.

Great Britain won the 1,600-meter relay. The United States did not run its best team, and took a silver medal. Williams and LuValle, American medalists in the 400-meter run, did not compete because of the close scheduling of the two relays. In addition, head coach Lawson Robertson chose not to use Woodruff and Hardin, although both were available.

Great Britain got the gold in the 50-kilometer walk. Harold Whitlock established an Olympic record of 4 hours, 30 minutes, 41.4 seconds. It would hold until 1952.

German women won two of the six track and field events. Tilly Fleischer was best with the javelin and Gisela Mauermayer with the discus; both set Olympic records. The outstanding American woman was Helen Stephens. She beat Stella Walsh, the defending cham-

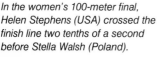

In the women's 100-meter final, Helen Stephens (USA) crossed the finish line two tenths of a second before Stella Walsh (Poland).

pion, for the 100-meter gold medal, and anchored the victorious United States 400-meter relay team.

Germany, which set a world record in a heat, was leading the relay race by 10 yards when Ilse Dörffeldt dropped the baton at the last hand-off. The Germans were disqualified.

Hungary's Ibolya Csak won the gold medal in the high jump. She beat Britain's Dorothy Odam and Elfriede Kaun of Germany in a jump-off after all three tied at 5′ 3″. Tied for sixth place was Francina Koen, who would emerge 12 years later as the world's outstanding female track and field athlete.

Trebisonda Valla and Claudia Testoni of Italy, Anna Steuer of Germany, and Elizabeth Taylor of Canada all clocked 11.7 in the 80-meter hurdles. Only after photofinish pictures were examined could the awards be made: Valla (gold), Steuer (silver), and Taylor (bronze).

A Jewish ice hockey player, Rudi Ball, had been invited back to support the German team in the Winter Games. For the Summer Games, there was a parallel token Jew on the German team. She was fencer Helene Mayer, who had won a gold medal in the 1928 Olympics and had taken part in the 1932 Games. She was living in Los Angeles. Under pressure from the IOC, Germany admitted Mayer to its team. American Jews tried to dissuade her from competing, especially after Germany declared her an "Aryan" despite

Germany spent $30 million on the 1936 Games. The Olympic complex included four stadiums, a 20,000-seat swimming arena, and an Olympic Village on 140 acres.

1936 Summer   155

Fencer Helene Mayer (325) returned to her native Germany and won the silver medal in the individual foil.

her mixed parentage. But Mayer, eager to visit her mother and two brothers, who still were living in Germany, and apparently fearing reprisals against them, accepted the invitation.

Mayer placed second in the individual foil event. Another Jew, Ilona Elek of Hungary, won the gold medal.

Giulio Gaudini of Italy won the individual foil, led the victorious Italian épée team, took a silver medal in the team sabre, which Hungary won, and placed sixth with the individual sabre, which Hungarian Endre Kabos won. In 1928 and 1932 Gaudini had taken bronze medals for individual foil, gold and silver for team foil, and silver for individual and team sabre.

On the Italian team that won the épée gold was Edoardo Mangiarotti. Before his Olympic career was ended in 1960, Mangiarotti would accumulate 6 gold, 5 silver, and 2 bronze medals in fencing events—the record.

Sweden's Ivar Johansson joined countryman Carl Westergren as a three-time wrestling gold medalist. He had won the freestyle middleweight and the Greco-Roman welterweight championships in 1932. He topped off in Berlin with a gold medal in the Greco-Roman middleweight division.

Sweden took 3 golds in Greco-Roman wrestling; Hungary, Turkey, Finland, and Estonia one each. Kristjan Palusalu, the Estonian, also won the gold in freestyle heavyweight wrestling. Hungarian wrestlers won 2 freestyle events, and one each went to Finland, France, Sweden, and the United States.

Germany won five of the eight gymnastics events, with Karl Schwarzmann and Konrad Frey each winning three gold medals. Frey took a silver and two bronzes in addition, and Schwarzmann got two bronzes.

Georges Miez of Switzerland added the individual floor exercises championship to the three gold medals he had won in 1928. Between 1924 and 1936 he received 4 golds, 3 silvers, and a bronze.

Germany took the gold medals for all six equestrian events. Ludwig Stubbendorf, the winner of the three-day event, rode a horse named Nurmi to the gold medal.

On the water Germans were dominant, taking the gold medals for single sculls, coxed and coxless pairs and fours in rowing, and the star and 8-meter categories in yachting. It was the last time the 8-meter yachting event was held. Great Britain took the gold for double sculls. For the fifth consecutive time a U.S. team was first in rowing eights, and for the second time in a row an Italian team was runner-up. No member of the 1932 American team competed in 1936.

Canoe and kayak events, seen as demonstrations in 1924 in Paris, were part of the 1936 program for the first time. Interestingly, only the Canadian 1,000-meter single canoe event was won by a Canadian. Czech canoers took the 1,000-meter pairs and the

Although canoeing was one of man's earliest forms of transportation, it did not join the Olympic program until 1936. A total of nine events was held, in both single-bladed (Canadian) and double-bladed (Kayak) categories. Only men competed in 1936; women canoeists first entered the Olympics twelve years later. As is apparent from the artist's drawing below, the position and paddling technique of the canoeist are of prime importance.

10,000-meter pairs. Austria won the kayak 1,000-meter singles and pairs, and also the 10,000-meter singles in folding kayak. Germany won both the 10,000-meter kayak singles and pairs, and the 2,000-meter kayak relay. Sweden paddled to victory in the 10,000-meter folding kayak pairs event.

Basketball also made its official Olympic debut. It had appeared as a demonstration sport in 1904 and, in a Dutch variation, in 1928. The United States won the gold medal, launching a 63-game winning streak. Canada took the silver medal and Mexico the bronze. Dr. James Naismith, originator of the game, was present at the opening of the tournament. The United States won the gold medal with a 19-8 victory over Canada in a game played in a heavy rainstorm on an outdoor court. The team included Joe Fortenberry and Willard Schmidt, both 6 feet, 8 inches tall, and Sam Balter, who later became the first American sports commentator to have a regularly scheduled nationwide radio show.

No one who attended the Berlin Games was likely to forget their spectacle. The drama inherent in torchlight processions or vast floodlit spaces surrounded by dark bleachers was well understood by the German organizers. Thousands of youths—there are more than 2,000 here—dressed alike and moving in pattern, with the Olympic flame set off against the night sky, were billed as the Festival of Olympic Youth.

Jack Medica, who trained at the University of Washington, won the 400-meter freestyle. American swimmers (left to right) Eleanor Holm, Olive McKean, and Dorothy Hill-Poynton enjoyed the cruise to Europe. Miss Holm was dismissed from the U.S. team; Miss McKean was a member of the bronze-winning 400-meter relay team; and Mrs. Hill-Poynton repeated as highboard gold medalist and took a bronze medal in the springboard event.

Robert Charpentier of France won three cycling gold medals in 1936, in the 100-kilometer, 4,000-meter pursuit and team road races. The Netherlands won the 1,000-meter time event, and Germany the 1,000-meter sprint and 2,000-meter tandem. In a decision unique in Olympic history, the judges gave Toni Merkens of Germany the gold for his sprint, but fined him 100 gold francs for going off course.

Anthony Terlazzo, a featherweight, was the only American among the five gold medal winners in weightlifting. Egypt took first place in the lightweight and middleweight divisions. Louis Hostin of France retained the light heavyweight title he had won in 1932. Germany's Josef Manger was heavyweight gold medalist.

Gotthard Handrick of Germany won the gold medal in the modern pentathlon. Charles Leonard, who placed second, performed better than any previous American in the event. The 1928 gold medalist, Sven Thofelt of Sweden, finished fourth, as he had in 1932.

Soccer, not played in Los Angeles, was back and for the first time Italy went home with the gold medal. Austria was second, and Norway third.

Field handball made its first appearance on the program (and would not appear again until 1972, under the title indoor handball). Germany, Austria, and Switzerland were the medalists, in descending order, having bested Hungary, Rumania, and the United States.

For the third Olympics in a row India was victorious on the hockey field, ranking Germany and The Netherlands. About a third of the Indian team had had prior Olympic success.

Of the eight boxing competitions in the Berlin Games Germany won the flyweight and heavyweight; Italy the bantamweight; Argentina the featherweight; Hungary the lightweight; Finland the welterweight; and France the middle- and light heavyweight.

In the men's swimming the Japanese won three events, were second in two, and third in three. Noboru Terada took the 1,500-meter freestyle, with Jack Medica less than 21 seconds behind him. Tetsuo Hamuro won the 200-meter breaststroke, setting an Olympic record, and for the second consecutive Olympics the Japanese 800-meter freestyle relay team set a world record, finishing ahead of the United States and Hungary.

The American winners were Jack Medica in the 400-meter freestyle and Adolf Kiefer in the 100-meter backstroke.

The United States took five of the six men's diving medals. Richard Degener, Marshall Wayne, and Al Greene finished 1-2-3 in the springboard. Wayne and Elbert Root were the gold and silver medalists in the highboard.

The American women's swimming team was at a disadvantage in Berlin. It had lost Eleanor Holm, the defending 100-meter backstroke champion, before the Games began. She was dismissed from the team by American Olympic committee officials after disobeying rules—playing dice with newsmen, drinking champagne, ignoring curfew—on the ship carrying United States athletes to Europe. The punishment, considered by many to be an over-reaction by the USOC, had the effect of turning the swimmer into a star attraction.

Dina Senff of The Netherlands succeeded Holm as the women's 100-meter backstroke champion. Her teammate, Hendrika Mastenbroek, the silver medalist, struck gold in the 100- and 400-meter freestyle events, and anchored the gold medal Dutch 400-meter freestyle relay team. Germany and the United States placed second and third. The 200-meter breaststroke was won by Japan.

Like their male teammates, the American women captured five of the six diving medals. Dorothy Hill-Poynton repeated her 1932 success as highboard gold medalist, with Velma Dunn second. Marjorie Gestring, Katherine Rawls, and Mrs. Hill-Poynton placed 1-2-3 in the springboard event.

Gestring was 13 years and nine months old. She is the youngest girl ever to win an Olympic gold medal, although not the youngest gold medalist. A French boy, whose name is not known to Olympic historians, was between 7 and 10 years of age in 1900 when he coxed The Netherlands' pairs, substituting for heavy Hermanus Brockmann, who had coxed the heats.

The 1936 Berlin Games closed on August 16; they were the last held during the lifetime of Coubertin. They had brought together 4,066 athletes from 49 countries, a proof of interest and commitment that should have gratified the prime mover of the revival in Athens in 1896, with its 311 athletes from 13 countries.

Thirty-five years after their end, IOC President Avery Brundage, who considered his opinions to be definitive, looked back on the Berlin Games as the zenith of the international meets.

"The Berlin Games were the finest in modern history," he declared. "I will accept no dispute over that fact."

FINAL MEDAL STANDINGS			
Nation	G	S	B
Germany	38	31	32
United States	24	21	12
Hungary	10	1	5
Italy	9	13	5
Finland	8	6	6
France	7	6	6
Sweden	6	5	10
Japan	6	4	10
The Netherlands	6	4	7
Austria	5	7	5
Great Britain	4	7	3
Czechoslovakia	3	5	1
Switzerland	2	9	5
Argentina	2	2	3
Estonia	2	2	3
Egypt	2	1	2
Canada	1	3	5
Norway	1	3	2
Turkey	1	–	1
India	1	–	–
New Zealand	1	–	–
Poland	–	4	5
Denmark	–	2	3
Latvia	–	1	1
Rumania	–	1	–
South Africa	–	1	–
Yugoslavia	–	1	–
Belgium	–	–	3
Mexico	–	–	3
Australia	–	–	1
Philippines	–	–	1
Portugal	–	–	1

1940 1944

(canceled)

The decision to mark the XII Olympiad in Japan—the Winter Games in Sapporo and the Summer Games in Tokyo—was met with great enthusiasm. Olympic officials felt strongly that holding the Games in an Asian nation—a land still mysterious and romantic in the minds of many—would do much to enhance the Olympic ideal. The Japanese Olympic Committee also welcomed the decision and began preparations immediately. However, after the second Sino-Japanese war broke out in July 1937, the Japanese government forced the Japanese Olympic Committee to resign as host.

The International Olympic Committee then moved the Winter Games to St. Moritz, Switzerland. But after the Swiss, in opposition to the IOC, supported the International Skiing Federation's stance that skiing instructors should be considered amateurs, the IOC switched the Winter events to Garmisch-Partenkirchen, Germany. Helsinki, Finland, was chosen as the locale for the Summer Games. World War II intervened, however, and forced the cancellation of the Games.

Although Cortina d'Ampezzo, Italy, and London were officially designated as the sites of the 1944 Games, the continued fighting in Europe, which lasted until VE-Day (May 8, 1945), prevented their taking place.

1948

Winter Games
St. Moritz, Switzerland

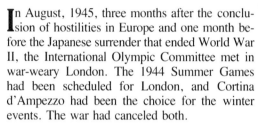

In August, 1945, three months after the conclusion of hostilities in Europe and one month before the Japanese surrender that ended World War II, the International Olympic Committee met in war-weary London. The 1944 Summer Games had been scheduled for London, and Cortina d'Ampezzo had been the choice for the winter events. The war had canceled both.

St. Moritz in neutral Switzerland was untouched by war. As a long-established playground of the privileged, it was well supplied with hotels and restaurants, and equally important, it had the habit of taking care of strangers smoothly, on short notice. It was as commonsense a determination to shift to serene St. Moritz for the Winter Games, as staying with the choice of London, ravaged by the war, was felt to be quixotic.

Germany and Japan, the Axis aggressors, were barred from St. Moritz; 28 other nations sent 713 athletes to the Games. Like the non-Swiss spectators there to watch the contests, the athletes lived in hotels near the sites of the events. That was the origin of the name given the 1948 Winter Games—the Hotel Olympics.

Alpine ski events were introduced in 1948, and figure skating was once again revolutionized. In both fields North Americans moved into the front ranks.

The period of the Games, January 30 through February 8, was not notable for postwar peacefulness and goodwill. There was a dispute over United States representation in the ice hockey tournament. Fists flew freely in a hockey game between Canada and Sweden, after which the Canadians were denounced as "unsportsmanlike." The American bobsleds were sabotaged, and one American sledder complained bitterly when officials canceled his run after he had posted the fastest time.

The Americans had no more than arrived when they were reported to have trouble of a different sort. ''We were advised,'' reported the United States Olympic Committee's J. Lyman Bingham, ''that a national radio broadcast in the United States had announced that our teams were stranded in Switzerland without funds. This false information proved to be of considerable embarrassment to us and necessitated a great many explanations to the press.''

Haste and its consequences were evident. The U.S. entries were not presented to the organizing committee until the team arrived in St. Moritz. They had been prepared on the ship that took the team to Europe. After arrival the Americans had to have additional time for tryouts to select bobsled and ski teams. While there were two masseurs with the team, there were no trainers. Nevertheless, the U.S. team made its best overseas showing to date.

The introduction of individual Alpine events would have surprised the planners of the first Winter Games. Their expectation was that Nordic events would be more numerous and popular than Alpine. In St. Moritz the new men's downhill race attracted 102 entrants, the Alpine combined had 67, and the slalom 66. By contrast, the most popular Nordic event, the 18-kilometer cross-country race, had 83 entrants. The Nordic combined had 26 and the 50-kilometer race only 20.

Henri Oreiller of France took the gold medals in both the downhill and combined Alpine competitions. Austrian Franz Gabl was the silver medalist in the downhill, and Karl Molitor and Rolf Olinger, both Swiss, tied for the bronze.

At St. Moritz in 1948, Barbara Ann Scott of Canada (page 162) won the gold for women's figure skating. In the Alpine downhill, the gold and silver medalists were France's Henri Oreiller (below, left) and Austria's Franz Gabl. The Frenchman also placed first in the combined Alpine.

The slalom gold went to Edy Reinalter of Switzerland. James Couttet of France won the silver, and Oreiller got the bronze.

Gretchen Fraser, a 28-year-old housewife from Vancouver, Washington, was the star of the women's skiing events. Her performance in the slalom and the combined Alpine took the European women by surprise.

Her slalom race was dramatic. The 39-gate course had been designed by Marc Hodler, head of the International Skiing Federation, to be a stiff challenge to the contestants. Fraser was the first down the hill for the first run, and she posted the fastest time. That gave her the right to the first start on the second run. As she stood at the top, and got ready to break the cord that would start the clock ticking against her, the telephone connection between the top and the foot of the run was broken.

On her nerve ends, she waited in position for seventeen minutes before the signal came to start. Fraser shot down the hill in 1:57.2. The next best time was 1:57.7, achieved by Switzerland's Antoinette Meyer. Erika Mahringer of Austria was third.

The women's downhill was another close contest. Hedy Schlunegger of Switzerland ran it in 2:28.3. Resi Hammerer of Austria, with the slowest time of the medalists, clocked 2:30.2. The silver was won by Austrian Trude Beiser in 2:29.1.

Beiser won the gold in the combined Alpine, Fraser the silver, and Mahringer another bronze.

Hidden among the contestants in all three races was Andrea Mead, a 15-year-old American girl, who placed 35th in the downhill, 8th in the slalom, and 21st in the combined Alpine, not a record to suggest that in 1952 she would carry off gold.

The Nordic events continued to be the private preserve of the Scandinavians. Swedish Martin Lundstroem, Nils Oestensson, and Gunnar Eriksson swept the three ranks in the 18-kilometer cross-country race, with only a little over two minutes' spread between the gold and bronze times.

Nils Karlsson and Harald Eriksson of Sweden placed 1-2 in the 50 kilometers, and Finland's Benjamin Vanninen was third.

Sweden won a third gold medal in the 40-kilometer relay, beating Finland and Norway in that order.

Norway's string of four victories in the Nordic combined was ended by Finland, whose Heikki Hasu and Martti Huhtala placed 1-2. Sven Israelsson of Sweden was the bronze medalist.

However, Petter Hugsted preserved the unbroken Norwegian winning streak in ski jumping, in which he led a sweep. The sentimental favorite was middle-aged Birger Ruud, survivor of a Nazi concentration camp. Sixteen years after his first Olympic gold medal in the event, Ruud won the silver. Thorleif Schjelderup placed third for Norway.

A bitter struggle for control of amateur hockey in the United States was the cause of two different ice hockey teams appearing in St. Moritz, each claiming to be *the* U.S. team. One was under the auspices of the Amateur Hockey Association of the United States (AHA). The other arrived as the official delegation of the United States Olympic Committee. That team had the blessing of the Amateur Athletic Union (AAU), which represented amateur hockey in the councils of the USOC. The AHA was not affiliated with the USOC, but held United States membership in the International Hockey Federation (IHF).

In St. Moritz both teams claimed to be the official U.S. team and demanded certification as such.

The USOC had warned less than two months before the start of the Winter Games that it would withdraw the entire United States Olympic team from the St. Moritz competition if the AHA squad were allowed to compete. Nevertheless, the Swiss organizers accepted the AHA representatives and turned their backs on the team backed by the USOC. They did so because they faced a much worse threat: the IHF warning that it would withdraw hockey altogether from the program if its AHA affiliate were excluded. The Swiss relied heavily on receipts from the hockey tournament to help carry the financial burden of the Games.

At this point, annoyed by the bizarre turn of events, the International Olympic Committee (IOC) added a comic opera touch: it barred both American teams.

However they might be confused by the conflicting claims of legitimacy on the part of the two teams, the Swiss organizers were crystal clear where money was involved. They agreed with the IHF that the AHA team would be allowed to compete.

The IOC then decided to go along with that decision, but decreed that the hockey tournament would not be official. More IHF balking. More IOC pondering. Finally, jibbing again, the IOC ruled that the hockey contests would be official, but that all games played by the AHA team would be regarded as exhibitions. With the august IOC thus firmly on the fence the competitions took place.

After all the to-do, the AHA team lost to all three medalist teams—12-3 to Canada, 4-3 to Czechoslovakia, and 5-4 to Switzerland. Nevertheless, they played. The only satisfaction for the USOC team, however, was being allowed to march in the opening procession of teams, from which ceremony the AHA group was barred.

Canada, represented by the Royal Canadian Air Force Flyers, and Czechoslovakia deadlocked for first place. Each had 15 points and they had played a scoreless tie. On the basis of goals scored, Canada regained the championship it lost to Britain in 1936.

The United States v. Canada in ice hockey: Fred Pearson (AHA-USA) tries a shot. Murray Dowey is Canada's goalie. The Canadians won both the game and the gold medal.

Dick Button

I skate because I love it . . .

—DICK BUTTON

Richard Totten Button received his first pair of figure skates for Christmas in 1941. "This is so you'll practice the piano more often," Evelyn Button told her 12-year-old son.

Although the boy's after-school hours were occupied at the piano, his Saturday afternoons were spent at a skating rink near his Englewood, N.J., home. Dick's father provided lessons to go along with the skates, and the boy was a serious and enthusiastic student. Still, his first teacher was less than optimistic. "He'll never be a skater, not in a million years. He's too fat and lacks coordination," the instructor said.

But Dick Button grew to a trim 5'11", 165 pounds, and his many hours at the piano were put to good use. Combining strength, rhythm, and precise timing, Button won Olympic gold medals in 1948 and 1952. He won the world championship five years in a row and in 1949 became the first skater to hold the five major men's titles—North American, U.S. National, European, World, and Olympic. His acrobatic leaps and spins added a totally new dimension to the sport.

Beyond even his athletic and musical abilities, Button's greatest assets were his patience, determination, and love of the sport. These were the qualities that impressed Swiss-born Gustave Lussi, a former ski jumper from Lake Placid, N.Y., whom Dick's father hired during the summer of 1942 to be the boy's coach. "In all the years I was his teacher," Lussi said later, "he never raised a question. I tell you, it was fantastic."

Dick skated as many as 7½ hours a day to slim his body and perfect his technique. "I'm all set to be carried to bed about 8:30 at night," he said. "I never let myself get too satisfied because you can always do better. If you're satisfied you may as well hang up your skates."

In planning a routine, Button first chose the music and played it on the piano to get accustomed to the rhythm. Only then would he and Lussi work out the order and timing of the moves. The goal was a jump or spin every 10 seconds during a five-minute exercise.

By the time he reached St. Moritz, Button had perfected a routine that no one believed possible. While other skaters performed the one-revolution Axel-Paulsen, Lutz, or Salchow jump, Button made two full turns before landing gracefully on one skate. He remained airborne seemingly forever, and his rapid-fire spins from one skate to the other left spectators in awe. Button became the first American figure skater to come home from the Olympics with a gold medal.

Showmen urged him to turn professional. Offers went as high as $100,000, but Dick refused. Now a student at Harvard University, he was determined to finish his education and defend his Olympic title in 1952.

"It's hard to convince people that finishing my studies at Harvard and winning the Olympics again mean much more to me than professional propositions. I skate because I love it, and I'm afraid if skating became work I wouldn't enjoy it anymore."

Others tried to master his jumps, but Button always remained one "revolution" ahead. When others finally conquered the double, Button did the double-double (two in succession). His next goal was the triple Axel—taking off on one foot while skating backward, doing three full turns, and landing on the same skate. On Feb. 21, 1952, at Oslo's Bislett Stadium, Button executed the first triple in major competition. It helped him earn another Olympic gold medal.

Button graduated from Harvard Law School in 1955 and was admitted to the bar in Washington, D.C. He also skated in professional ice shows and became known for his expert television commentary of major figure skating competitions. He is the author of the book *Instant Skating*.

His pure love of the sport was reflected in a comment made 31 years after winning his first gold medal. "The thing I remember most, the moment that mattered," he recalled, "was the day before the Olympics when I went through a clean double Axel. No one else in the world had done one and I had worked it into my routine. That is what you remember. That is what has the meaning."

A member of the Czech team that won the silver medal was Jaraslov Drobny. Six years later, he won the Wimbledon men's singles tennis championship. Switzerland's team won the bronze medal. Playing for them was Richard "Bibi" Torriani, who took the oath for all athletes in 1948, 20 years after winning his first bronze medal.

Barbara Ann Scott, a beautiful 20-year-old figure skater from Ottawa, Ontario, almost didn't make it to the Games because of the enthusiasm of her hometown supporters. A year before the Games, after she had won the world championship in Stockholm, the city of Ottawa decided to present to Barbara Ann a canary yellow convertible automobile to honor her skating achievements. When Avery Brundage, the untiring watchdog of amateurism, learned about the plan, he notified Scott that her acceptance of such a gift would endanger her amateur standing and eligibility for the Olympics.

Barbara Ann tearfully complied with the ruling by Brundage, and refused the car. With her amateur status preserved, she went to St. Moritz, to win the Olympic gold medal. Eva Pawlik of Austria and Jeanette Altwegg of Great Britain were the silver and bronze medalists. Three months after the Winter Olympics, Barbara Ann Scott bid farewell to amateurism and accepted the car.

The star of the men's figure skating was an 18-year-old Harvard freshman, Richard Button. He was a revelation to watch. After his display in St. Moritz, figure skating would never again be mainly an artistic expression. Sonja Henie had revolutionized figure skating by her introduction of ballet. Button changed it utterly by incorporating athletics in the form of high jumps. He was not a weaver of graceful patterns on the ice, he was an athlete using the speed provided by the ice to escape into the air, where he could perform movements not possible elsewhere—double jumps, spins, combinations of jumps and spins. The exact opposite of serene gliding, it was a demonstration of strength and athletic control. It was breathtaking, and it staggered the viewers. He was the first American to win an Olympic figure skating competition.

Thirty-odd years after his St. Moritz triumph Button recalled, "The thing I remember most, the moment that mattered, was the day before the Olympics when I went through a clean double Axel. No one else in the world had done one and I had worked it into my routine. That is what you remember. That is what has the meaning."

Shut out by North Americans in the individual events, Europeans

The United States was first and third in the four-man bobsled racing. The gold-winning team was (front to rear), Francis Tyler, Patrick Martin, Edward Rimkus, and William d'Amico.

placed 1-2 in the pairs skating. Micheline Lannoy and Pierre Baugniet of Belgium took the title. Hungary's Andrea Kekessy and Ede Kiraly were the runners-up. Suzanne Morrow and Wallace Diestelmeyer of Canada won the bronze medal.

Scandinavians won all four speed-skating events. Finn Helgesen of Norway took the 500 meters in an Olympic record 43.1 seconds. That was one tenth of a second faster than both his countryman, Thomas Byberg, and America's Robert Fitzgerald and Ken Bartholomew. All received silver medals. No bronze medal was awarded.

Sverre Farstad of Norway took the 1,500 meters with an Olympic record of 2 minutes, 17.6 seconds. Ake Seyffarth of Sweden was second and Odd Lundberg of Norway was third.

Reidar Liaklev won Norway's third gold medal in the 5,000 meters, with teammate Lundberg second. Gothe Hedlund of Sweden was third.

Seyffarth took the 10,000 meters. Finland's Lauri Parkkinen and Penti Lammio placed 2-3.

On the morning of the start of the two-man bobsled races the United States discovered that several of its boblets and four-man sleds had been sabotaged. Some had their steering mechanisms damaged. Another had a pusher broken off and the cowling jammed in. Fortunately, the runners on all sleds remained intact and the sleds could be repaired in time to race. The person or persons responsible for the damage were not apprehended.

Swiss boblets placed 1-2, with Felix Endrich and Fritz Feierabend the drivers. The bronze-medal United States team was Fred Fortune and Schuyler Carron.

The four-man bobsled event, in which the United States won the gold and bronze medals, also was not without incident. After the first of four runs, Feierabend's sled was in front. An American bob, piloted by Francis Tyler, and three other sleds were less than a second behind the leader.

Tyler's sled was the first down the course in the second run. After eight sleds had gone down the hill, the run was called off because a broken water pipe had damaged the track. Tyler's time had been the fastest, but among the seven sleds that did not race were some of the swiftest bobs in the first run. That meant three runs had to be scheduled for the second day.

Additional complications developed when snow fell during the night and continued throughout the next day. When competition resumed, Tyler posted the fastest time on his second run despite starting in first place, a position not considered advantageous because the course had been grooved. Tyler's sled went on to win the gold medal after a last-place start on the final run. No American sled has won the event since that time.

A Belgian sled driven by Max Houben, competing in his fourth Olympics, placed second. James Bickford, who would also be a four-time Olympian, was the pilot of the bronze-medal U.S. crew.

The return to St. Moritz also meant a return of the one-man skeleton bobsled event. In it Italy's Nino Bibbia won his country its first Winter Olympics gold medal. John Heaton, who carried the Stars and Stripes during the opening ceremony, repeated his silver medal performance of 1928. John Crammond of Britain was third.

The Swiss organizers sighed with relief at the closing ceremonies when the Olympic flag was lowered. It was the third flag flown during the 1948 Winter Games. The other two had been stolen.

FINAL MEDAL STANDINGS			
Nation	G	S	B
Sweden	4	3	3
Norway	4	2	4
Switzerland	3	2	2
United States	3	2	2
France	2	1	1
Canada	2	–	1
Finland	1	3	2
Belgium	1	1	–
Italy	1	–	–
Austria	–	3	2
Czechoslovakia	–	1	–
Hungary	–	1	–
Great Britain	–	–	1

1948

Summer Games
London, England

London's second hosting of the Olympics was a contrast with the first. The devastation of World War II was still visible, in spite of energetic rebuilding. The organizers had to operate within a budget whose restrictions allowed no expensive new stadium or housing constructions. Wembley Stadium, in use for 24 years, was the principal site, and converted Royal Air Force barracks were the housing for the athletes. There was none of the lavish display of the Berlin Games, but neither was there any of the acrimony that was remembered from the London Games of 40 years earlier. To participate in the XIV Olympiad 59 nations entered 4,099 athletes—the greatest numbers to that time, and more than double the 1908 figures. Before a crowd of 82,000 King George pronounced the Games open on July 29. The pageant of activities between then and August 14 was distinguished by the display of the sportsmanlike spirit in which the revivers of the 1896 Games conceived them.

Attendance was so large at many of the events that Wembley Stadium was packed. An estimated million and a half people paid admissions, which totaled something like $2 million, more than had ever before been paid to see the contests. Over and above the stadium spectators, it was estimated that half a million Britons made use of the 80,000 television receivers then in operation. It was the first time that that medium had been part of the reporting of the Games. In North America the coverage was mainly by radio and newspaper, there still being no comparable television networks.

The track in Wembley presented a succession of stars: Fanny Blankers-Koen, Bob Mathias, Harrison Dillard, Emil Zátopek, Arthur Wint.

Fanny—Francina—Blankers-Koen might better be called a superstar. She went home to The Netherlands with four gold medals in track—for the 100- and 200-meter races, the 80-meter hurdles, and the 400-meter relay—a feat which no woman before her had accomplished. The 200 meters was a new event. In the hurdles race, the lean Dutch housewife was slow off the mark, but she poured on speed and won in 11.2 seconds, an Olympic record. The silver medalist, British Maureen Gardner, clocked the same time.

The Netherlands team was in fourth place when Fanny got the baton on the anchor leg of the 400-meter relay. She brought her team home in first place in 47.5 seconds, one tenth of a second in front of second-place Australia, and three tenths swifter than Canada's bronze-medal team.

The London Games launched the Olympic career of Australia's Shirley Strickland. She won a silver medal in the 400-meter relay and bronze medals in the 100-meter dash and the 80-meter hurdles. As Shirley de la Hunty-Strickland she participated in 1952 and 1956 and became the Olympic record holder for the most medals won by a woman in track and field. Her total was seven medals—three gold, one silver, and three bronze.

Strickland deserved a fourth bronze medal. A photo finish picture discovered a quarter of a century later showed that she finished third in the 1948 200-meter dash instead of fourth, her official placing.

Although Fanny Blankers-Koen (692) and Britain's Maureen Gardner clocked the same Olympic record time in the 80-meter hurdles, the 30-year-old Dutch housewife was awarded the gold medal.

Fanny Blankers-Koen

All I've done is run fast. I don't quite see why people should make so much fuss about that.

—FANNY BLANKERS-KOEN

The women's competition at the 1948 Summer Olympics in London was a one-woman assault. Francina "Fanny" Blankers-Koen, the "marvelous mama of The Netherlands," won three individual events and a total of four gold medals.

When Fanny Blankers-Koen returned to The Netherlands from London, thousands of Dutch men and women staged a reception for her in Amsterdam, where she was born in April 1918. Fanny rode with her husband, Jan, and their two children from the railroad station to the town hall in an open coach drawn by four white horses. Fanny didn't understand why the usually reserved Dutch made such a display over her because she had done what she had been doing since childhood. "My father," she recalled, "said I never could walk when I was a child—just run."

Fanny Koen first set her sights on Olympic gold when she was 17 years old, but she was undecided which sport to make the means to that end. Advised that the Dutch had many outstanding swimmers, Fanny turned to track and field. Her coach was Jan Blankers. Fanny was good enough to compete in the Olympics in 1936. She tied for sixth placed in the high jump.

Fanny Koen left Berlin determined to become an Olympic champion. But it was 12 years before she realized her ambition, years during which life changed for Fanny. She married Jan Blankers and they had two children. Domestic life appealed to her. "My wife is a real housewife," Jan Blankers said with pride during the 1948 Olympics. "She cooks, cleans, and takes care of our children. She sews and knits their clothes."

She continued to harbor her gold-medal dream and when World War II ended, she resumed training.

It was not an easy task for a woman with two children—Jan, born in 1941, and Fanny, born in 1945.

"The trouble (with most women athletes) is that they do not want to train hard enough," she said. "One must practice every day." And, every day when Fanny practiced, the people of Amsterdam could watch her wheel a baby carriage to the stadium. She parked the child and carriage alongside the track and then proceeded through a schedule of rigorous workouts. Even during competition, she often was seen knitting between heats of races.

Although there were those who suspected that at 30, and with two children, Fanny Blankers-Koen might just be over the athletic hill, the indomitable 5' 10", 145-pounder was ready for the 1948 Games.

Not only did Fanny win an unprecedented number of gold medals, but she got them despite the fact that she did not compete in her two best events—the long jump and the high jump—in which she was the world record holder. Limited to three individual events, Fanny entered the 100-meter dash, the 80-meter hurdles, and the 200-meter dash (on the women's program for the first time). She won the 100-meter dash in 11.9 seconds. She took the hurdles in an Olympic record 11.2 and the 200 in 24.4, becoming the first triple winner in history. The long-legged blond was a hurdler and sprinter of perfect form, so superior her competitors looked like novices.

Fanny put a punctuation mark on her achievement by anchoring the gold medal Dutch team in the 400-meter relay.

Fanny's career could have ended in London, but it didn't. At 34, Fanny went to Helsinki in 1952 with her eyes again on a gold medal harvest. However, blood poisoning, an upset stomach, and a boil on her leg forced her to withdraw from three events. She entered only the 80-meter hurdles.

Fanny was given penicillin the night before the race and early the next morning. But she tripped on the second hurdle, lunged forward a few wobbly steps, then stopped as the field sped away toward the finish line. Fanny walked dejectedly off the track.

When she refused to quit even after her Helinski disappointment, the subject of her retirement became a matter of Dutch national concern. A newspaper issued "An Appeal to Fanny":

"Put away your spikes for good. The same Holland that demanded successes of you wants to keep the best memory. Render the sport this last service."

Gallant Fanny Blankers-Koen didn't understand the fuss, but she listened.

Bob Mathias (USA) and Peter Mullins (left) were neck and neck in a heat of the 100-meter run of the decathlon. The young Californian went on to win the gold in the ten-event competition; the Australian finished sixth. The women's long jump was added to the Olympic program in 1948. Hungary's Olga Gyarmati (below) won the event; Noëmi Simonetto De Portela (Argentina) and Ann-Britt Leyman (Sweden) were runners-up.

Another multiple track and field medalist in 1948 was France's Micheline Ostermeyer, who won gold medals in the shot put, a new event, and in the discus, and a bronze medal in the high jump.

Alice Coachman of the United States and Dorothy Tyler-Odam of Britain, the Berlin silver medalist, in the high jump tied for first with an Olympic record 5′ 6¼″. Coachman was awarded the gold medal on the basis of fewer misses, the only gold won by an American woman in track and field.

The long jump was new in 1948. Olga Gyarmati of Hungary won it with a leap of 18′ 8¼″—almost two feet short of the world record held by Blankers-Koen, who did not compete in the event.

Herma Bauma of Austria set an Olympic record of 149′ 6″ in winning the javelin throw.

The youngest American ever to win an Olympic gold medal was seventeen-year-old Bob Mathias, competing in only his third decathlon. In punishing contests with older and more experienced athletes, and in spite of two seemingly endless days of miserable weather, he carried off the laurels for the demanding 10 events with a score of 7,139 points. Ignace Heinrich of France was second, with 6,974. Floyd Simmons of the United States took the bronze medal with 6,950.

The biggest upset of the Games was the victory by Harrison Dillard in the 100-meter dash, an event he qualified for before missing out on his specialty, the 110-meter hurdles. Dillard won the gold medal in a photo finish in 10.3 seconds. He edged fellow American Norwood "Barney" Ewell and Panama's Lloyd LaBeach, co-holders of the world record. Another American, Mel Patton, owner of the world record at 100 yards, placed fifth.

Patton recovered to win the 200-meter dash. He defeated Ewell, LaBeach, and Jamaican Herb McKenley, who finished in that order. McKenley's specialty was the 400-meter run. He was the world record holder in the 400 meters and 440 yards, and was considered unbeatable at those distances.

The Olympic 400-meter field in London included Mal Whitfield of the United States and Arthur Wint, an old rival of McKenley's. They ran for the same high school in Jamaica.

McKenley led by four meters as the race entered the homestretch. With 20 meters remaining, the giant-striding Wint drew even with McKenley, and then pulled away to win in 46.2 seconds. Officially, McKenley was timed in 46.4 and Whitfield, the bronze medalist, in 46.9.

The 800 had preceded the 400 meters on the program. In it Whitfield set an Olympic record of 1:49.2, defeating Wint (1:49.5) and Marcel Hansenne of France (1:49.8).

Sweden placed 1-2 in the 1,500 meters, thanks to Henry Eriksson and Lennart Strand. Willem Slijkhuis of The Netherlands was third. Eriksson's time was 3:49.8.

The long distance races, long dominated by Finland, turned up a new hero in Zátopek, the 27-year-old Czech Army lieutenant. He was entered in the 5,000- and 10,000-meter races. World record holder Viljo Heine of Finland took the early lead in the 10,000, which was run first, while Zátopek lagged behind. Halfway through the race, the Czech "Choo Choo" sprinted into the lead. At 7,000 meters, the world record holder had enough, and dropped out of the race.

Harrison Dillard (left) of Cleveland, Ohio, was the first to cross the finish line in the 100-meter dash. Britain's Emmanuel McDonald Bailey (35) and Alistair McCorquodale (36) and Panama's Lloyd LaBeach were sixth, fourth, and third, respectively.

Bob Mathias

I never worked so long and so hard for anything in my life.

—BOB MATHIAS

Robert Bruce Mathias was born in Tulare, Calif., on Nov. 17, 1930. His interest in sports was kindled by his father, a physician and surgeon who had starred in football at the University of Oklahoma. At age six, Bob demanded that he be allowed to play baseball with his older brother and the latter's friends. At age 12, he used the backyard as a track and field, practicing the high jump all day long. But young Bob Mathias was anemic; for years he had to live on special diets and take iron pills.

In high school, the by-now hefty teenager starred on the football and basketball teams, and was a regular in the winners' circle at scholastic track meets. For a new challenge his coach, Virgil Jackson, suggested in the spring of 1948 that Bob try the decathlon event in the forthcoming Southern Pacific AAU Games in Los Angeles. Bob agreed, but was shocked to learn that he had only three weeks to prepare for the ten events. Mathias had never pole-vaulted, long jumped, thrown the javelin, or run a distance race. For three weeks, Mathias and Jackson worked together. Mathias learned quickly. But there were bleak moments, too. At the start, the future champion couldn't clear 8 feet in the pole vault.

However, when they traveled to Pasadena, Calif., for the two-day meet, Mathias won the decathlon. Then it was cross country to Bloomfield, N.J., for the combined National AAU championships and Olympic Trials on June 26–27. Mathias became the youngest ever to make the United States Olympic track team when he beat Irving "Moon" Mondschein by 123 points. It seemed inconceivable that a 17-year-old, appearing in only his third decathlon competition, could beat the world's best in the Olympics.

There were so many athletes—28 from 20 nations—in the Olympic decathlon field that it was split into two groups. Mathias drew the second section—a handicap because the second group would finish last, late in the evening.

After three events on August 5th, Mathias was third, behind Enrique Kistenmacher of Argentina and Ignace Heinrich of France. The fourth event was the high jump, and Mathias needed a leap of at least 6 feet to stay close to the leaders. He missed his first two chances at 5' 10". Mathias then cleared 6' 1¼" and finished the first day's events in third place with 3,848 points. Kistenmacher, the leader, had 3,897 points.

Rain pelted Wembley Stadium the next day. Mathias was on the field for almost 12 hours. He huddled under a blanket when he wasn't running, jumping, or throwing. Day turned into afternoon and afternoon into night and the crowd of more than 70,000 began to dwindle.

Mathias had to pole-vault in half-light with a wet, slippery pole. Officials held flashlights so he could see the take-off line for the javelin throw. When he ran the 1,500, the only light available came from the stands. But by that time, Mathias was ahead of the field. He had taken the lead after winning the discus. All Bob had to do was perform reasonably well in the 1,500 meters to win the decathlon and become the youngest athlete ever to get an Olympic track and field gold medal. He did better than well.

Mathias looked forward to Helsinki and the 1952 Games. No one had ever won the decathlon twice. In the four years since 1948 Mathias had captured the Sullivan Award as the nation's outstanding amateur athlete and had become an outstanding fullback at Stanford. Now 21, he was 6' 3" and 205 pounds.

The weather was better in Helsinki than in London, and so was the performance by Mathias. When he beat his career bests in the javelin and 1,500-meter run during the second day of competition, he had his second consecutive gold medal in the decathlon. Mathias had been the only competitor to exceed 7,000 points (7,139) in 1948. He bettered his world record with 7,887 in 1952, where he finished more than 900 points ahead of Milton Campbell (USA)—the largest victory margin in Olympic decathlon history.

As he had in 1948, Mathias said in 1952 he would not do it again. This time he meant it.

After graduation from Stanford and time in the Marine Corps, the California Republican served in the U.S. House of Representatives (1967–75).

Zátopek crossed the finish line to become the first gold medalist of the Summer Games; he set an Olympic mark of 29 minutes, 59.6 seconds. Alain Mimoun of France was second and Bertil Albertsson of Sweden placed third.

Zátopek came within two tenths of a second of winning another gold medal in the 5,000 meters. He led for nine laps before Gaston Reiff of Belgium took the lead. Reiff gradually increased his margin to 20 meters over Willem Slijkhuis, with Zátopek another 20 meters back in third place. At that point, Zátopek made his move. He passed Slijkhuis and cut down Reiff's lead. It seemed that Zátopek would catch Reiff in the homestretch, but the cheers of the spectators for the challenger spurred on the Belgian and he crossed the finish line first. His time was an Olympic record 14 minutes, 17.6 seconds. Zátopek was clocked in 14:17.8.

Etienne Gailly, another Belgian, was the first runner into Wembley Stadium in the marathon. He had taken the lead with a little more than a mile to go, but he was exhausted by the time he started to run around the stadium track. On the final lap Delfo Cabrera of Argentina overtook Gailly and became the gold medalist. Britain's Thomas Richards also passed Gailly, to finish second. Gailly placed third. Forty-two seconds separated the first and third finishers.

William Porter, with an Olympic record 13.9 seconds, led Clyde Scott and Craig Dixon to a United States sweep in the 110-meter hurdles. America's Roy Cochran won the 400-meter hurdles with another Olympic record—51.1 seconds. He was seven tenths of a second faster than Duncan White of Ceylon.

Emil Zátopek was one of the most popular of Olympic stars. He delighted the crowds with a face contorted by simulated anguish as he ran long distance races. For his "pains," which are clearly portrayed here, the fans named him Emil the Terrible. To other trackmen he was terrible in another sense, beating them with withering bursts of speed when they were all in. Zátopek was said to have trained himself in endurance by holding his breath while he walked until he fell in a faint.

Belgium's Gaston Reiff completed the 5,000 meters two tenths of a second ahead of the Czech "Choo Choo," Emil Zátopek. Below, Wright (arms folded) and Dillard, members of the U.S. 400-meter relay, met with officials following the team's disqualification.

Sweden took all three medals in the 3,000-meter steeplechase, with Thore Sjöstrand, Erik Elmsäter, and Göte Magström placing in that order.

The United States team, with Roy Cochran and Mal Whitfield running the third and fourth legs, won the 1,600-meter relay, with France second and Sweden third. Jamaica, which was given an excellent chance of winning the gold, abandoned the race when Arthur Wint pulled a muscle while running the third leg. Italy did not finish.

In the 400-meter relay the U.S. team of Norwood Ewell, Lorenzo Wright, Harrison Dillard, and Melvin Patton clocked a time of 40.6, seven tenths of a second ahead of Great Britain, but it was judged to have passed a baton outside the legal zone, and so was disqualified. That gave the gold to Britain, the silver to Italy, the bronze to Hungary. Great Britain was jubilant, having won no track and field event up to then. The U.S. team was sure it was within bounds, and questioned the decision. When careful study of the films of the relay showed the baton hand-on was legal, the British made the finest show of the Olympic spirit, relinquishing the gold medals, while the crowds cheered the U.S. team.

Britain's two-time hold on the 50-kilometer walk honors was ended by Sweden, whose John Ljunggren won, although not in any record time. Switzerland took silver, as it had done in 1936, and Great Britain was third.

Arthur Wint (122) and Herb McKenley, former classmates and close rivals from the island of Jamaica, raced to the wire in the 400 meters. Wint won by two tenths of a second. The United States' Mel Patton (below), a favorite but fifth-place finisher in the 100 meters, took the 200 meters.

United States athletes had considerable success in the field events. Wilbur Thompson put the shot an Olympic record 56′ 2″. Francis Delaney and Jim Fuchs, his teammates, were the silver and bronze medalists.

Willie Steele and Herb Douglas placed first and third in the long jump, with Australian Thomas Bruce in the silver slot between them.

Australia's John Winter took the high jump. Björn Paulson of Norway, George Stanich and Dwight Eddleman of the United States, and Georges Damitio of France all jumped the same height. Paulson and Stanich were the silver and bronze winners. Arne Åhman of Sweden captured the triple jump, besting Australian George Avery and Turkish Ruhi Sarialp.

The pole vault first and third winners were Americans—Guinn Smith and Robert Richards. Richards vaulted as high as the silver medalist, Erkki Kataja of Finland. Richards would be first in 1952 and 1956, by which time metal poles would be used.

Tapio Rautavaara (Finland), Steve Seymour (USA), and Jozsef Varszegi (Hungary) won the javelin prizes, although none of their throws approached the world record.

Italian Adolfo Consolini and Giuseppe Tosi outdistanced the favored American discus thrower, Fortune Gordien, who would go medalless from the 1952 meet, but take silver on his third try in 1956. Consolini's gold-bearing throw of 173′ 2″ was an Olympic record.

Harrison Dillard

I had set my heart on it so long ago. I wanted that hurdles championship.

—HARRISON DILLARD

Recalling a parade held in Cleveland in 1936 in honor of Olympic hero Jesse Owens, Harrison "Bones" Dillard said:

"Jesse was waving at everybody and they were pretty wild over it all. That's when I made up my mind to go to the Olympics."

The future star was born in Cleveland on July 8, 1923. Two years after the Owens parade, Dillard was running in organized competition in a Cleveland playground when Jesse dropped by to encourage the youngsters. Owens had grown up in the neighborhood and frequently visited the playground. "He gave me a pair of track shoes," Dillard said, "and told me to stick with it." Owens also gave Dillard some advice. Owens thought hurdling, not sprinting, suited Harrison better.

Dillard used Owens' shoes for three years. He also listened to the advice. Three years later, Dillard won the state high school hurdles championship for East Technical, the same school Owens had attended.

Shortly after Harrison began his college career at Baldwin-Wallace, World War II intervened. Dillard served as an infantryman in Italy. When that interruption was past, he began to revolutionize hurdling.

Nicknamed Bones because he carried only 152 pounds on a 5′ 10″ frame, he didn't have the strength of many other hurdlers. Consequently he changed his form in clearing hurdles. Eddie Finnigan, his coach at Baldwin-Wallace, said Harrison "drives over a hurdle—the others jump over." The result was that Dillard cleared 13 feet—seven feet in front of the hurdle and six beyond—while making his leap, approximately two feet more than other hurdlers. It was such an advantage that Dillard set world records and won 82 consecutive hurdles and sprint races before the string was snapped by William Porter prior to the 1948 Olympic Trials.

Nevertheless, Dillard said, "in the Olympic Games in London, I want to clean up the way Jesse Owens did in Berlin." But it didn't appear possible initially, because Dillard qualified for the Olympics only by finishing third in the 100-meter dash in 10.4 seconds. Then Dillard came apart in the 110-meter hurdles final, won by Porter.

There were 68 sprinters in the Olympic 100-meter dash final in London, among them Dillard and America's two main hopes—Barney Ewell and Mel Patton.

There was one false start. Patton got off to a slow start and was never in contention. Ewell broke well in the final and pounded down the track. Straining to beat Panama's Lloyd LaBeach, he lunged toward the tape just ahead of the Panamanian. "Well, I guess I took that one," Ewell said.

"I'm not so sure," Dillard replied.

The judges reached a decision only after viewing photo finish pictures of the race. At the victory platform, Dillard was the man flanked by the runners-up, Ewell and LaBeach. Not only had Harrison made up for the lost chance to win the hurdles gold medal, he had tied the Olympic record (10.3) shared by Owens and Eddie Toland (1932).

"There was a great deal of criticism when I let Dillard compete in the dash in the Olympic Trials," said Finnigan. "Critics said it cost him the hurdling championship. We all know Dillard is the best hurdler in the world. Now we know he is also the best sprinter. We all feel vindicated now."

But neither the gold medal in the dash nor an additional gold he won as a member of the United States 400-meter relay team could really overcome the disappointment of not being the Olympic hurdles champion. Four years later, in Helsinki, he was in the 100-meter hurdles final.

Dillard cleared the ninth hurdle cleanly while his chief rival, John Davis (USA), nicked it and landed flat-footed. That was all Dillard needed to finish inches in front. Each clocked an Olympic record 13.7 seconds.

Dillard obviously was pleased. "This was the big one," he said. "But I waited so long for it, it's just a little bit anticlimactic."

Dillard was the first athlete to win the dash in one Olympics and the hurdles in another. When he also won a gold medal on the United States 400-meter relay team in 1952, his career gold medal total equaled Jesse Owens'.

Imre Nemeth of Hungary threw the hammer 183′11″, the best distance of the contest. Yugoslav Ivan Gubijan was next, with 178′ ½″, and Robert Bennett (USA) placed third with a throw of 176′ 3½″. Nemeth would compete again four years later and win a bronze medal.

There were eight men's swimming and diving events on the program. The United States won them all.

Walter Ris set an Olympic record of 57.3 seconds in winning the 100-meter freestyle, with teammate Alan Ford second and Hungary's Géza Kádas third. William Smith and James McLane placed 1-2 in the 400-meter freestyle, with the winner establishing an Olympic record of 4 minutes, 41.0 seconds. Australia's John Marshall was third.

McLane captured the 1,500-meter freestyle, Marshall came in second, and Hungarian Gyorgy Mitro was third. Allen Stack and Robert Cowell were the gold and silver medalists in the 100-meter backstroke; Georges Vallerey (France) got the bronze. Joe Verdeur, Keith Carter, and Robert Sohl completed a sweep of the 200-meter breaststroke. Verdeur set an Olympic record of 2 minutes, 39.3 seconds. Ris, McLane, Wallace Wolf, and Smith swam the 800-meter freestyle relay in a world record 8 minutes, 46.0 seconds. Hungary and France placed second and third.

Bruce Harlan, Miller Anderson, and Samuel Lee placed 1-2-3 in springboard diving. Lee and Harlan finished 1-2 in highboard diving, with Mexico's Joaquin Capilla Pérez the bronze medalist.

Ann Curtis was the star of the American women's swimming squad. She anchored the gold medal 400-meter relay team which set an Olympic record of 4 minutes, 29.2 seconds. She won the 400-meter freestyle, setting an Olympic mark of 5 minutes, 17.8 seconds, and finished second in the 100-meter freestyle won by Greta Andersen of Denmark. Andersen later turned to long distance swimming and was one of many conquerors of the English Channel.

Sammy Lee, 28-year-old medical doctor in the U.S. Army, was first in highboard diving and third in springboard.

Mrs. Victoria Draves of the Lyle Draves squad at the Athens Club in Oakland, California, was the first woman to capture both diving events in the same Games.

One of her Danish teammates, Karen-Margrete Harup, took the 100-meter backstroke and was the runner-up in the 400-meter freestyle. Petronella van Vliet of The Netherlands placed first in the 200-meter breaststroke, followed by Australian Beatrice Lyons and Hungarian Eva Szekely.

Victoria Manola Draves of the United States became the first woman in Olympic history to win both diving gold medals in the same Games. She led Zoe Ann Olsen and Patricia Elsener to an American sweep in the springboard. After Miss Olsen married baseball's Jackie Jensen she competed under the name Jensen-Olsen in the 1952 Games. Elsener took the silver medal in the highboard dive, and Birte Christoffersen (Denmark) was bronze medalist.

After winning the gold in 1932 and 1936, Hungary was upset by Italy in water polo. The Netherlands was third. The Hungarian team included only one man from the victorious 1936 squad, whereas that group had had five veterans from the gold medal 1932 team.

Led by 7-foot Bob Kurland, the United States won its second consecutive basketball championship, romping to a 65-21 victory over France in the final. Brazil was the bronze medalist. Alex Groza and Ray Lumpp each scored 11 points in the championship game. Groza was the tournament's top scorer with 76 points and Kurland was the runner-up with 65. The team also included Wally "Wah Wah" Jones, Vince Boryla, and Ralph Beard.

The United States won four of the six weightlifting gold medals, with Egypt taking the other two. Every category established a new record. Joe De Pietro captured the bantamweight title, setting a world record. His competition were Julian Creus (Great Britain), the silver medalist, and Richard Tom (USA), the bronze.

The featherweight contest belonged to Mahmoud Fayad of Egypt, who set a new world record, Rodney Wilkes (Trinidad), and Jaffar Salmassi (Iran).

Ibrahim Hassan Shams, the bronze featherweight lifter in 1936, became the gold lightweight champion with an Olympic record lift. His countryman Attia Hamouda lifted the same weight as Shams, but on the basis of greater body weight was given the silver. James Halliday of Great Britain took the bronze.

In the middleweight range Frank Spellman and Peter George of the United States placed 1-2. Spellman set an Olympic record. Korean Sung-Jip Kim won the bronze.

Gold and silver in the light heavyweight class were awarded to Americans Stanley Stanczyk (who established an Olympic record) and Harold Sakata. Runner-up was Gösta Magnusson of Sweden.

Heavyweight John Davis (USA) won a gold medal with an Olympic record lift, a feat he would repeat four years later. Norbert Schemansky (USA), second to Davis, was started toward an Olympic record of four medals in weightlifting. He would compete in three more meets and gather up one gold and two bronze medals.

The Greco-Roman wrestling was dominated by Sweden, whose wrestlers took five golds and two silvers. Turks won two golds, two silvers, and a bronze. One gold went to Italy, for the flyweight class which was new in 1948, as well as two bronze medals. Finnish, Egyptian, Hungarian, Danish, and Norwegian wrestlers shared the remaining nine medals.

Freestyle wrestling included the flyweight class, absent since 1904, when it was a USA sweep. Finnish Lennart Vitala won the championship. Turkish Halit Balamir was the runner-up, one of six medals taken by Turks: Nasuh Akar was the bantamweight champ, Gazanfur Bilge the featherweight, Celal Atik the lightweight, Yasar Dogu the welterweight. Akil Candemir got the silver medal in the middleweight class, in which Glen Brand (USA) was the gold medalist. American Henry Wittenberg earned the light heavyweight gold, and the heavyweight victor was Hungarian Gyula Bobis. After the Games, Wittenberg, a New York City policeman, declined a $60,000 offer to turn professional. In 1952 he competed again, and won a silver medal to add to his gold.

The boxing laurels were well spread around. Argentina won the flyweight and heavyweight golds; South Africa the lightweight and light heavyweight; Italy the featherweight; Czechoslovakia the welterweight; and Hungary the bantam- and middle-weight. Southpaw Laszlo Papp, the middleweight victor, would win the light middleweight titles in both 1952 and 1956, the only Olympic boxer to win three gold medals.

French fencers Jehan Buhan and Christian d'Oriola were the gold and silver medalists with individual foils, and gold medalists as part of the winning foils team. The team included René Bougnol, who had won gold in 1932 and silver in 1936.

Italy took the first and third awards in individual épée, with Switzerland in the silver position, but in team épée was second to France. Hungary's sabre men won gold and bronze medals in the individual competition (Italy got the silver) and held on to the uninterrupted team championship won in 1928. The Hungarian team was remarkable. Four of its six members had won gold medals in 1936. The careers of several would be notable: Aladar Gerevich in 6 Olympics, earning 7 golds, 1 silver, and 2 bronze medals; Pál Kovács in 5 meets, winning 6 gold and 1 bronze medal; Rudolf Kárpáti in 4 Olympics, with 6 gold medals; Laszlo Rajcsanyi in 3 Olympics, with 3 gold medals to show.

The women's individual foils placed Ilona Elek (Hungary), Karen Lachmann (Denmark), and Ellen Müller-Preis in 1-2-3 order. All three were former Olympic fencers.

Members of the U.S. basketball squad (left to right), Vince Boryla, Alex Groza, Wallace Jones, Jesse Renick, Robert Kurland, and Lou Beck enjoyed a midnight snack after defeating France in the finals.

*Renovated barracks of the Royal
Air Force in the Richmond Park
suburb of London served to house
the athletes at the 1948 Summer
Games.*

Sweden's William Grut retrieved the modern pentathlon gold
that had been taken by Germany in 1936, the one time that Sweden
had not been victor since the event was started in 1912. Grut's score
for the five days' events was the best recorded up to that time.

The six equestrian events were won by riders of six different
nations. France got the gold for the 3-day individual; the United
States for the 3-day team. Switzerland won the dressage and, by a
wide margin, Sweden the team dressage. Mexico was champion in
individual jumping, and Great Britain in team jumping.

One year after the Olympics, the International Equestrian Federation disqualified the Swedes because Gehnäll Persson, a member
of its three-man team, was entered in the Games as an Army officer
when, in fact, he was a non-commissioned officer. The disqualification advanced France to the gold standing and moved the United
States up to silver.

Discrimination against non-commissioned officers was eliminated before the next Summer Olympics and Persson returned to
help Sweden win the gold medals in the event in 1952 and 1956.

Gert Fredriksson took home to Sweden the gold medals for the
1,000-meter kayak singles races. Swedish canoers had the golds as
well in the 1,000-meter and 10,000-meter doubles contest. Czech
paddlers won the 1,000-meter Canadian singles and pairs. In the
new 10,000-meter singles event Czech Frantisek Capek was the
victor, followed by Frank Havens (USA) and Norman Lane (Canada). The Canadian 10,000-meter doubles was taken by Stephen
Lysack and Stephan Macknowski (USA).

The ladies 500-meter kayak race was new in 1948. Karen Hoff
(Denmark) bested Alida van der Anker-Doedans (The Netherlands)
by nine tenths of a second and Fritzi Schwingl (Austria) by a second.

Australia won the single sculls event, Great Britain the double
sculls and coxless pairs. Denmark took the gold for coxed pairs,
and Italy for coxless fours. The United States was winner of the
coxed fours race and, maintaining an unbroken record begun in
1924, of the rowing eights.

Paul Elvström of Denmark won the dinghy race, the first of what would be a 4-time string. United States yachts came home first in the Star and 6-meter class races. The new class of Dragon yachting gave Norway a gold medal.

French cyclists proved best in three contests: the individual road race, 1,000-meter time trial, and 4,000-meter team pursuit. Italy claimed the gold for the 1,000-meter sprint and the 2,000-meter tandem race. The team road race was Belgium's show.

Swiss Emil Grünig set an Olympic record in the free rifle shooting. Arthur Cook (USA) gained a gold medal in the small bore (prone) contest, and with the free pistol Edwin Cam of Peru won *his* gold. In the rapid-fire contest Hungary's Kárply Takács was the popular favorite. He had been European champion in his sport before World War II. During the conflict he lost his right hand in a grenade explosion. He trained himself anew to shoot left-handed, winning gold medals in 1948 and again four years later.

Men's gymnastics gave Finland's Veikko Huhtanen the chance to win gold medals in individual combined exercises, team exercises, and pommeled horse, silver on the parallel bars, and bronze on the horizontal bar. His teammate, Paavo Aaltonen won the gold for the long horse vault, a matching gold for pommeled horse, and a gold for team exercises. A third Finn, Heikki Savolainen, whose effort matched his countrymen's on the pommeled horse, took a gold there, and a second in the team exercises. Switzerland's Michael Reusch won the parallel bars, Joseph Stalder the horizontal bar, and Karl Frei the rings. Individual floor exercises honors went to Hungarian Ferenc Pataki.

The women's combined team exercises were won by Czechoslovakia.

Soccer matches ended with Sweden the victor, followed by Yugoslavia and Denmark.

For the fourth Olympics in a row India walked away with the field hockey gold, ahead of Great Britain and The Netherlands.

FINAL MEDAL STANDINGS			
Nation	G	S	B
United States	38	27	19
Sweden	17	11	18
France	11	6	15
Finland	10	8	6
Hungary	10	5	13
Italy	9	13	11
Turkey	6	4	2
Czechoslovakia	6	2	3
Switzerland	5	12	6
Denmark	5	8	9
The Netherlands	5	2	9
Great Britain	4	16	7
Argentina	3	3	1
Australia	2	6	5
Austria	2	2	4
Belgium	2	2	3
South Africa	2	2	2
Egypt	2	2	1
Mexico	2	1	2
Norway	1	3	3
Jamaica	1	2	–
Poland	1	–	1
India	1	–	–
Peru	1	–	–
Canada	–	2	2
Yugoslavia	–	2	–
Portugal	–	1	1
Uruguay	–	1	1
Ceylon	–	1	–
Cuba	–	1	–
Spain	–	1	–
Trinidad and Tobago	–	1	–
Korea	–	–	2
Panama	–	–	2
Brazil	–	–	1
Iran	–	–	1
Ireland	–	–	1
Puerto Rico	–	–	1

Wembley Stadium, London, August 14, 1948: the flame was extinguished, the flag was lowered, and the XIV Olympiad was history.

1952

Winter Games
Oslo, Norway

The Cold War was at its peak. Although peace had officially come to Japan, the conflict in Korea continued. Twenty years of a Democrat in the White House were about to end as "I Like Ike" buttons showed the popular preference. The Robert Schuman plan for uniting Europe got started, and Farouk left the throne of Egypt. For entertainment, people were reading Hemingway's *The Old Man and the Sea* and beginning to enjoy situation comedies on television. The year was 1952—the "midway point of a century of continuing challenge."

Oslo, the capital of Norway and the cradle of winter sports, was the site of VI Winter Olympics. From February 14 through February 25, 1952, mammoth crowds attended every sports event held in that city and its surrounding areas—an unusual development for the Winter Games. Athletes from 30 nations participated in the Games.

A crowd of 150,000 stood in the snow at Holmenkollen to see the ski jumping. Spectators pressed shoulder to shoulder through the woods watching the cross-country races which had been held in virtual isolation in past Olympics. Tens of thousands flocked to the Alpine events. Skating and hockey events could have been sold out many times over. It was a striking change from previous Winter Olympics and gave winter sports, and the Games in particular, a vast new prestige.

There was one somber note. On the day of the opening cermony, the funeral of King George VI of Great Britain took place. Athletes from Britain and the Commonwealth nations wore black armbands in tribute to their king.

There were several changes in the Olympic program. The Alpine combined and skeleton events were eliminated. A giant slalom for men and women, and a women's 10-kilometer cross country race were added. For the first time, the

Olympic flame did not come from Greece. It was brought 138 miles by relay from Morgedal, Norway, home of Sondre Nordheim, the father of modern skiing. It was in Morgedal that fasteners were first used on skis, making competition possible in jumping and Alpine events.

The Games were plagued by a lack of snow for the Alpine events. Norefjell, where the men's and women's giant slalom and downhill events were held, was so bare that Norwegian soldiers laid a foundation of straw on the courses. Then they brought snow by shovel from nearby gullies and packed it down. The snow was packed five feet deep in some places on the course. At Rodkleiva, where the slalom events were held, soldiers hauled in the equivalent of 100 boxcars of snow and foot packed it onto the slope. Weather conditions forced the women's giant slalom and the two-man bobsled events to be held the day before the official ceremony opening the Games.

The 1952 Games marked the return of Germany and Japan to Olympic competition. At Oslo, Germans were the recipients of three golds, two silvers, and two bronzes.

Andrea Mead Lawrence, a 19-year-old Vermont housewife, got the United States off to a gold medal start in the women's giant slalom. Mrs. Lawrence outraced Austrian movie star Dagmar Rom and Germany's Annemarie Buchner, who took the silver and bronze medals.

Austria's Trude Jochum-Beiser, the 1948 Alpine combined gold medalist, finished first in the downhill. She beat Buchner and Giuliana Chenal-Minuzzo of Italy, who placed third. All three American entrants fell.

Lawrence became the first American to win an Alpine double when she captured the slalom. She won it despite a fall during her first run which left her in fourth place behind leader Ossi Reichert of Germany, the eventual silver medalist. Buchner finished third. She collected a medal in each of the women's races.

After completing her double, Lawrence said, "I think my advantage lay in my nature. The pressure on Olympic competitors is just awful, which is why there are so many upsets. Someone who doesn't think she will win is a bit more relaxed than the favorite. She just goes all out to take a shot at it and sometimes surprises even herself."

Norway's Stein Eriksen, whose father Marius had built the first "toe irons" to be placed on top of skis, won the men's giant slalom. Austrians Christian Pravda and Toni Spiess placed second and third.

The downhill went to 33-year-old Zeno Colo, an Italian mountaineer from Tuscany, who placed fourth in both the giant slalom and the slalom. Othmar Schneider of Austria finished second, ahead of his teammate, Pravda.

Schneider won the slalom, with Eriksen second and Guttorm Berge of Norway third. A Greek racer fell 18 times during the early part of the slalom. Then he sat down and descended the hill backward.

During the Games, the 22-year-old Eriksen was romantically linked with America's Catherine Rodolph. This caused Rodolph and an American teammate, Nordic skier Alvin Paul Wegman, to reveal that they were secretly married. The marriage had not been announced because Wegman was in the Naval Aviation Cadet program in Pensacola, Florida, which accepted only single men.

The men's giant slalom was a new race on the Winter program in 1952. Medalists in the event were: Norway's Stein Eriksen (center), and Austria's Christian Pravda and Toni Spiess (right).

One of the major surprises of the Games was the failure of Sweden to win a gold in Nordic skiing events, a development that delighted Norwegians. For the first time in Olympic history, women competed in a Nordic event—the 10-kilometer cross-country race. It was swept by Finland. Lydia Wideman led Mirja Hietamis and Siiri Rantanen across the finish line. The fourth place finisher, Marta Norberg of Sweden, was beaten for the bronze medal by only three seconds after the 6-mile, 376-yard race.

There was an upset in the men's 18-kilometer race. Hallgeir Brenden of Norway, a 1,500-meter runner when he wasn't competing in winter sports, took the gold medal. Two Finns, Tapio Mäkelä and Paavo Lonkila, won the silver and bronze medals. Another Finn, Heikki Hasu, the 1948 Nordic combined champion, placed fourth.

Twenty-seven-year-old Veikko Hakulinen of Finland won the gold medal in the 50-kilometer race, finishing ahead of countryman Eero Kolehmainen. Hakulinen almost missed the Games. He injured a finger, then cut his leg with an axe while chopping wood, but recovered in time to compete. He won the race by almost five minutes. Norwegians placed third and fourth. The bronze medal went to Magnar Estenstad. Olav Okern, 42 years old, was fourth. He was 13th in the 18-kilometer race in 1948. Okern had been captured by the Germans and sent to a Nazi concentration camp in 1941. He weighed 88 pounds when he was released in 1945.

A Finnish team, which included Hasu, Lonkila, and Mäkelä, won the 40-kilometer relay. Norway and Sweden took the silver and bronze medals. The United States was last among the 12 finishers, 33 minutes and 12 seconds behind Finland. Bulgaria started the race, but abandoned it.

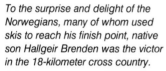

To the surprise and delight of the Norwegians, many of whom used skis to reach his finish point, native son Hallgeir Brenden was the victor in the 18-kilometer cross country.

Andrea Mead Lawrence

I race for fun. It's not worthwhile unless you enjoy it.

—ANDREA MEAD LAWRENCE

At the 1952 Winter Games in Oslo, Norway, Andrea Mead Lawrence became the first American to win two gold medals in Olympic skiing. The skier credited her husband David with her success at Oslo. "David waits at the end of the course for me. When I start, I know he'll be waiting with open arms, so I speed like the devil."

Mrs. Lawrence added, "I think maybe the fact that I enjoy it helps me to win. I'm hardly ever nervous before a race. And I absolutely do not feel bad when I lose. Everybody wants to win. But honestly, I don't. I'd just like to do my best."

Andy's parents, Bradford and Janet Mead, were winter sports enthusiasts who had the financial ability to ski in the Swiss Alps and to establish their own resort in 1938 at Pico Peak near Rutland, Vermont, where Andrea had been born on April 19, 1932.

"People often speak of Andy's poise," Janet Mead later said. "I believe it comes in part from the simplicity of her childhood. Brad and I had ideas that some people call foolhardy. We built our home on a wooded hill. We never gave our children silly toys; they played with what they found along our brook.

"We showed them all the things we loved in the woods and then took them on little hiking trips, where they learned along the way. We weren't hermits, but we didn't take either of the children (they also had a son Peter) to the city of Rutland until Andy was four."

The training of Andy Mead as a skier began when she was six. Her teacher was Carl Acker, a Swiss pro lured to Pico Peak by her parents. However, Andy does not remember receiving formal lessons. She watched Acker and her parents and imitated them.

At 11, she was competing against adults. When she was 14, she qualified for the Olympic tryouts, and when she was 15, she was in the 1948 Olympics.

A year later, the 5'7", 130-pound Andy Mead met a blond Dartmouth skier, David Lawrence, at Whitefish, Montana. Two years later, they were married in Davos, Switzerland.

At the Oslo Olympics, Andy began with the giant slalom at the Norefjell course, twisting in and out of the 59 gates over the two-thirds-of-a-mile course in 2 minutes, 6.8 seconds—3.0 seconds better than the runner-up.

Andy fell in the first of the two heats of the slalom near the top of the Rodkleiva course. But she bounced back and finished the heat in fourth place. Her time was 1 minute, 7.2 seconds.

Ossi Reichert of Germany was the leader in 1 minute, 6.0 seconds. On her second run, Lawrence swept flawlessly down the 508-yard course which dropped 196 yards from its peak. Her time was 1 minute, 3.4 seconds for a combined time of 2:10.6. She defeated Reichert, the silver medalist, by eight tenths of a second.

"Mainly, I just want to do well—which is why when I fell I didn't give up," Andy said. "I didn't want to look bad. I didn't think I *would* win, but I thought I *could.* I just threw caution to the winds. Instead of breaking my neck I got gold medals to hang around it. You work a long time and dream a lot about such a moment.

"Winning once in the Olympics is staggering, but winning more is unbelievable."

Andrea and David, who had finished 35th in the men's giant slalom at Oslo, returned to the United States, settled on a ranch in Colorado, and began to raise a family. They had three children, the last just four months before the opening of the 1956 Winter Olympics in Cortina d'Ampezzo, Italy.

Andy wanted one more shot at the Olympics— just for the fun of it. On the eve of the competition, after only a month of training, she said, "I don't think my children have interfered with my skiing. Actually they've probably helped. They kept me off skis some of the time. You can over-train. . . ."

Andy finished in a tie for fourth in the giant slalom, only one tenth of a second behind the bronze medalist. She fell during both her slalom runs and placed 25th. Then she closed out her career by placing 30th in the downhill.

"That's it," she said. "No more skiing. My family comes first."

Figure skater Dick Button (USA) repeated as a gold medalist. Speed skater Ken Henry of Chicago was an unexpected winner in the 500.

Simon Slättvik of Norway won the gold medal in the Nordic combined. Defending champion Heikki Hasu of Finland took the silver medal after placing first in the 18-kilometer portion of the event and fifth in the jumping. Another Norwegian, Sverre Stenersen, won the bronze medal. Theodore Farwell finished 11th—an unusually impressive showing for an American.

Norway captured its sixth straight championship in the special jumping event and put four of its competitors in the first six places. The gold medal went to Arnfinn Bergmann. Countryman Torbjörn Falkanger, who recited the oath for all athletes during the opening ceremony, took the silver medal. The bronze went to Sweden's Karl Holmström. In a field of 44, the American jumpers were 12th (Keith Wegeman), 15th (Art Devlin), 18th (Art Tokle), and 22nd (Willis Olson).

The United States made a better showing in figure skating than in any previous Olympics. Every member of the American team finished in the top six. Dick Button repeated his gold medal victory of 1948 with a brilliant performance that included a triple jump, a maneuver never before seen in major competition. After a near fall, he was asked if it was due to a flaw in the ice. "The ice is never bad," he said with utter candor. "Only the skater is."

The proficiency of Hellmut Seibt in the compulsory figures enabled the Austrian to edge 20-year-old James Grogan of the United States for the silver medal. Another American, 18-year-old Hayes Alan Jenkins, was fourth. Alain Giletti, a 12-year-old from France, placed seventh.

Britain's Jeanette Altwegg, the 1948 bronze medalist, struck gold in the women's figure skating. Tenley Albright, a 16-year-old from the United States, placed second, ahead of Jacqueline du Bief of France, who was 16th four years earlier. Immediately after the Games, Altwegg retired from the sport and helped run a children's village in Switzerland.

A German couple, Ria and Paul Falk, won the gold medal in the pairs. They defeated Karol and Peter Kennedy of the United States. Hungary's Marianne and Laszlo Nagy took the bronze medal.

A 29-year-old truck driver, Hjalmar Andersen of Norway, was a worthy successor to his countryman Ivar Ballangrud in speed skating. He won three gold medals just as Ballangrud did in 1936. Andersen won the 5,000 meters in the Olympic record time of 8 minutes, 10.6 seconds. He took the 1,500 meters the next day and captured the 10,000 meters the day after with an Olympic record time of 16 minutes, 45.8 seconds.

The 500-meter race was dominated by Americans. Ken Henry won the gold medal, Donald McDermott took the silver, and Arne Johansen of Norway captured third place. Norway's Finn Helgesen, the defending champion, placed fifth. Frank Stack of Canada, the bronze medalist in the 1932 Olympic 10,000-meter race, was 12th.

Kees Broekman of The Netherlands placed behind winner Andersen in both the 5,000- and 10,000-meter races. Sverre Haugli of Norway was the bronze medalist in the 5,000. Willem van der Voort of The Netherlands and Roald Aas of Norway finished second and third in the 1,500 meters. Carl-Erik Asplund of Sweden was the bronze medalist in the 10,000.

The ice hockey competition was held in an enclosed arena without a roof. During snowstorms, players often lost sight of the pucks. Nevertheless, the Canadians, represented by the Edmonton Mercuries, were able to win their second consecutive gold medal. The victory marked the sixth time in seven tournaments that Canada had captured the leading ice hockey prize.

The U.S. hockey team placed second. Prior to the opening of the Games, the U.S. Olympic Committee and the U.S. Amateur Hockey Association had agreed to sponsor a new and independent U.S. Hockey Committee that selected and organized the American team sent to Oslo. The action prevented a repetition of the 1948 quarrel which caused two American teams to be sent to the Winter Games.

The United States opened the tournament with a 3-2 victory over Norway. The Americans then scored victories by identical 8-2 scores over Germany, Finland, and Switzerland. Jim Yackel scored three

On three successive days, Norwegian speed skater Hjalmar Andersen captured three gold medals and established two Olympic records.

The German gold-winning boblet team of Andreas Ostler and Lorenz Nieberl held a commanding lead from the very beginning.

goals against Germany, Bob Rompre netted four against Finland, and Andre Gambucci had three against the Swiss. Then the United States was upset by Sweden, 4-2, but came back to defeat Poland, 5-3, and Czechoslovakia, 6-3.

As the United States headed into its final game against Canada, it faced these possibilities: a loss meant a fourth place finish; a tie meant a silver medal; a victory would tie the Canadians for first place, necessitating a play-off for the championship the following day. With three minutes to play, James Sedin scored to give the United States a 3-3 tie, and second place in the tournament.

Sweden, which led Canada 2-0 before losing 3-2, tied with Czechoslovakia for third place. In a play-off for the bronze medal and the unofficial championship of Europe, the Swedes beat the Czechs, 5-3, after trailing 3-0.

The Americans engaged in a number of fights and were characterized by spectators and the European press as "rowdies," a reputation that the Canadians bore four years earlier. The Russians, who had declined an invitation to participate in the Winter Games, were among the harshest critics of the American team. Some Russian journalists even charged that the tie in the final game between the two North American nations was the result of collusion, and was devised to prevent Communist Czechoslovakia from finishing higher.

Andreas Ostler drove German sleds to bobsledding gold medal victories in the two-man and four-man events. The American boblet crew of Stan Benham and Pat Martin placed second, ahead of a Swiss sled driven by Fritz Feierabend, the silver medalist in 1948. Felix Endrich, who drove the gold medal boblet four years earlier, placed fourth for Switzerland. Fred Fortune drove the second American sled to a seventh-place finish.

Unusual strategy by the Germans in the four-man race enabled them to capture the gold medal. It was the reason that the International Bobsled Federation altered its rules after the Games. The Germans, aware that American and Swiss sleds had faster practice times, decided to sacrifice their number two team. They took the heaviest members from both of their sleds and placed them on sled number one. The number one team averaged over 240 pounds! Rules limiting the weights of two- and four-man sleds were introduced later that year in an effort to equalize competition.

The United States Olympic Committee's official report noted, "This added weight seemed to be the deciding factor in the race. In each slide, Stan Benham (USA) would have the best time at the intermediate point. But the Germans' greater weight caused a pickup and they would have the best time on the last half of the run."

The sled driven by Benham, with crew members Pat Martin, Howard Crossitt, and James Atkinson, placed second—ahead of Swiss sleds driven by bronze medalist Feierabend and fourth-place finisher Endrich. The second American sled, driven by James Bickford, who carried the American flag in the opening ceremonies, placed ninth.

"Benham and his crew had a great chance of winning," said the USOC report. "But eight sleds before they were to leave in the last heat, it started to snow hard and this made a very wet snow track. Benham said the snow stuck to his goggles with the result that he couldn't see. At this time all the other better teams had already had their last run."

FINAL MEDAL STANDINGS			
Nation	G	S	B
Norway	7	3	6
United States	4	6	1
Finland	3	4	2
Germany	3	2	2
Austria	2	4	2
Italy	1	–	1
Canada	1	–	–
Great Britain	1	–	–
The Netherlands	–	3	–
Sweden	–	–	4
Switzerland	–	–	2
France	–	–	1
Hungary	–	–	1

1952

Summer Games
Helsinki, Finland

It had been 40 years since Czar Nicholas dispatched a Russian team to the 1912 Olympic Games in Stockholm. After one revolution and two world wars, Russians, representing the Soviet Union, rejoined the international sports community at the Helsinki Summer Olympics in 1952.

Invited to participate in the 1948 Olympics, the Russians sent only coaches and trainers. Their job was to observe world class athletes and their techniques. They took more notes than some of the journalists assigned to report on the Games.

An unfortunate side effect of the Cold War that had divided the world by ideology was that the Olympics began to be treated as some sort of athletic showdown in which the relative strengths of participating nations would be exposed and assessed.

The result was that in 1952, for the first time in Olympic history, the athletes were segregated on political lines. Instead of one Olympic village housing the athletes of all nations, the Soviets insisted on quartering their athletes and those of the other countries east of what Winston Churchill had named the Iron Curtain—Bulgaria, Czechoslovakia, Hungary, Poland, and Rumania—in their own village. It was near a Soviet naval base, and guarded. Why the International Olympic Committee allowed such an infraction of one of its basic rules is unexplained to this day.

For whatever reasons the Soviets insisted on segregated quarters and the IOC permitted them, when the athletes of the two camps came together, in training before the Games opened and in the contests themselves, they mingled without incident. In fact, the 1952 Helsinki Games are remembered as the best of all Olympics.

Helsinki's Olympic Stadium, site of the 1952 Summer Games, was built for the canceled 1940 Games.

Paavo Nurmi, "The Flying Finn," was still, for his countrymen, the brightest Olympic star as he carried the torch around the Helsinki track in 1952. Grantland Rice described him most succinctly in the phrase: Superman of the track.

Helsinki, with a population of about 400,000, was the smallest city to have staged the Olympics, and one quite unknown except to Scandinavians. Finland itself was in large measure a mystery, a tiny country that had earned admiration as a staunch David in conflict with the Russian Goliath in World War II. What the visitors found were superb facilities, hosts who were models of efficiency and courtesy, and exciting contests memorable for their dramatic moments.

The Olympic flame carried from Greece had made one of its longest journeys, as a result of the refusal of the Soviets to allow it to be carried across their territory. When it arrived in Helsinki for the opening ceremonies on July 19, the crowd of 73,000 waiting in the stadium was thrilled. The runner bearing the torch was Paavo Nurmi, at 55 still effortless as he circled the stadium and then ignited the great dish at the side of the track. The booming cheers of the crowd were a delayed reply to the International Amateur Athletic Federation, which had prevented their great runner from taking part in the Los Angeles Games.

Adding delight to delight, Nurmi passed the torch to Finland's second track hero, Hannes Kolehmainen, whose swift passage to the top of the stadium, where he lighted a second flame, made his 62 years scarcely believable.

The following day the outstanding track man of the 1952 Games made his first appearance. Emil Zátopek, the Czech whose facial contortions gave a quite untrue impression of intense suffering and earned him the affectionate name of Emil the Terrible, defended his 1948 championship in the 10,000-meter race. He broke his own Olympic record, and so did the two runners-up. Zátopek's time was

29.17, a new Olympic record. Alain Mimoun of France was the silver medalist, as he had been in 1948. The bronze went to Aleksandr Anufriyev. It was the first medal won in track and field by either Russian or Soviet.

"I am disappointed," said suffering Emil afterward. "I was not fast. I was bad, very bad. I will try to do better in the 5,000-meter run."

Not since Kolehmainen in 1912 had anyone captured the 5,000-10,000 double. Entering the backstretch on the final lap of the 5,000, Zátopek was second to Britain's Chris Chataway, with Mimoun and Germany's Herbert Schade not far behind. On the last turn, the runners bunched and Chataway tripped and fell. Zátopek swung outside and beat Mimoun, the runner-up, by eight tenths of a second. He was timed in an Olympic record 14:06.6. Schade placed third. Once again, all three medalists had bettered the Olympic record set in 1948. Gastson Reiff of Belgium, who had beaten Zátopek for the gold in 1948, failed to finish.

Less than an hour after Zátopek completed his double, his wife made it a family double. Dana Zátopková established an Olympic record in the women's javelin throw, beating the favored Soviets. It was the first time in Olympic history that a husband and wife won gold medals in the same Games.

(At the end of the Summer Games another couple would return home with his and her gold medals. Dezsö Gyarmati was a member of Hungary's winning water polo team. His wife of a year, Eva Székely, won the women's 200-meter breaststroke with an Olympic record time of 2 minutes, 51.7 seconds.)

Zátopek concluded his demonstration of long distance running excellence, unmatched in Olympic history, by winning his first marathon. His time was an Olympic record 2 hours, 23 minutes, 3.2 seconds. He finished more than 2 minutes in front of runner-up Reinaldo Gorno of Argentina. Gustaf Jansson of Sweden placed third. Delfo Cabrera of Argentina, the defending champion, was sixth. His losing time was more than eight minutes faster than his gold medal performance in London in 1948.

The 3,000-meter steeplechase was the one long-distance race that Zátopek did not enter. The favorite was Vladimir Kazantsev, who had beaten Zátopek at 5,000 meters prior to the Games. Kazantsev's 8 minutes, 48.6 seconds was the fastest time ever posted for the steeplechase and his 8:58.0 in the first qualifying heat established an Olympic record. But an American, FBI agent Horace Ashenfelter, lowered that figure to 8:51.0 in his heat.

The Soviet and the American stayed close to each other during the race. The event was decided at the last water jump, its most difficult hazard. Kazantsev stumbled as he landed and Ashenfelter sprinted into the lead. The Soviet never recovered and the American won in a record 8:45.4, the first time since 1908 that an American had won an Olympic race longer than 800 meters. Kazantsev placed second in 8:51.6, two tenths of a second ahead of fast-closing John Disley of Britain. All three had beaten the old Olympic record.

The triumph of Josef Barthel of Luxembourg in the 1,500 meters was also a major upset. The field of 12 included Werner Lueg of Germany, co-holder of the world record, and British medical student Roger Bannister, who would make history in 1954 by being first to run the mile in less than 4 minutes.

To the delight of their fans, Emil Zátopek, still wearing his track number, rushed to congratulate his wife, Dana, on winning the javelin throw. In her joy, she had just done cartwheels.

Emil Zátopek

After all those dark days of the war, the bombing, the killing, the starvation, the revival of the Olympics was as if the sun had come out.

—EMIL ZÁTOPEK

From July 20 through July 27, 1952, Emil Zátopek of Czechoslovakia entered three Olympic races, won three races, and set records in three races. By winning the 5,000- and 10,000-meter events and the marathon, he established himself as the greatest distance runner of all time. Britain's Roger Bannister, the first miler to break four minutes, called Zátopek "the greatest athlete of the postwar (World War II) world."

Emil Zátopek was born in Koprivnice, Northern Moravia, on September 19, 1922, the son of a poor carpenter. He was considered a bookworm as a youth. It wasn't until 1941, when he was 19 and working as an apprentice in a shoe factory, that he was introduced to running.

"One day the factory sports coach, who was very strict, pointed at four boys. including me, and ordered us to run in a race," Zátopek said. "I protested that I was weak and not fit to run, but the coach sent me for a physical examination and the doctor said I was perfectly well.

"So I had to run, and when I got started I felt I wanted to win. But I only came in second. That is the way it started."

When the Germans began their withdrawal from his homeland in 1945, Zátopek was drafted into the Czech army. It is probable that, because he was a runner, he found immediate favor with the officers and became a career military man. That enabled Zátopek to follow a disciplined routine every day of his competitive years. He arose at 6 in the morning, exercised, and ran at least 10 miles. He alternated between jogging and sprinting. He sometimes ran in heavy army boots to push himself harder. "I just keep on running," he said. "There is no secret about what makes Zátopek tick. It is just that."

Zátopek was 25 when the Olympics resumed in London in 1948. "I went into the Olympic Village and suddenly there were no more frontiers, no more barriers. Just the people meeting together. It was wonderfully warm. Men and women who had just lost five years of life were back again," he said.

He won the 10,000 meters in Olympic record time and took the silver medal in the 5,000, losing a close race to Gaston Reiff of Belgium.

Then, it was 1952. Spectators at Helsinki included Finland's two great runners—Paavo Nurmi and Hannes Kolehmainen. The first race was the 10,000 meters on July 20. His winning time was 29 minutes, 17.0 seconds—42.6 seconds faster than his 1948 Olympic record.

The strong field for the 5,000 meters on July 24 included Reiff, the defending champion; Herbert Schade of Germany, who set an Olympic record in winning his heat; Chris Chataway of Great Britain; and Alain Mimoun, Algerian-born Frenchman who took the silver in the 10,000 meters in 1948 and 1952.

Zátopek finished ahead of Mimoun, with Schade in third place. His time of 14 minutes, 6.6 seconds bettered the Olympic record. On the same day Dana Zátopková, his wife, threw the javelin an Olympic record 165' 7". It was the first time a husband and wife had won gold medals.

Although he had covered the 26-mile, 385-yard distance of the marathon many times during his training sessions, Zátopek ran in his first marathon in Helsinki. To the surprise of many, the Czech "Choo Choo" won the marathon with a time of 2 hours, 23 minutes, 3.2 seconds. Subsequently he called the marathon "a very boring race."

Zátopek's face always looked agonized, but his legs moved effortlessly in short strides.

The Czech completed his Olympic career in Melbourne, Australia, in 1956 with an unsuccessful attempt to retain his marathon gold. He finished sixth. He retired as a runner two years later.

Zátopek's rise in the Czech army paralleled his success on the running track. In 1968, Zátopek signed his name to a 2,000-word anti-Soviet manifesto calling for the liberalization of the Czech government. After the rebellion, led by Alexander Dubcek, was quelled, Zátopek was expelled from the Communist Party, and stripped of his rank in the Army. The greatest distance runner became a garbage collector. But admiring people along his route insisted on helping with the garbage collection, to the embarrassment of the authorities. Predictably, he lost his job. Eventually he recanted, and was given employment as an oil-deposit researcher.

Lueg led going into the last lap. On the final curve, his margin was 12 feet. Coming off the turn he was overtaken by Barthel. Bob McMillen of the United States, who had been back in the pack, also began to challenge. Barthel crossed the finish line in 3 minutes, 45.1 seconds for an Olympic record and won the first gold medal ever for Luxembourg. McMillen, with a 56-second final 400 meters, finished one tenth of a second behind Barthel and bettered his personal best by 4.1 seconds. Lueg placed third, just ahead of Bannister.

Barthel's time was officially rounded off to 3:45.2, since the 1,500-meter races were then timed to a fifth of a second. There had been a panic among the organizers until the music for Luxembourg's anthem was located. As Barthel stood on the victory platform listening to the Olympic orchestra play his national anthem, tears streamed down his face.

The closest race in the 1952 Summer Games was the 100-meter final. The first four finishers—Lindy Remigino and Dean Smith of the United States, Herb McKenley of Jamaica, and Emmanuel McDonald Bailey of Great Britain—were timed in 10.4 seconds. It took a photo finish picture to determine the winner. Remigino made a last-second lunge and his margin of victory over McKenley, the runner-up, was one inch. McDonald Bailey, who was another three inches back, won the bronze medal. Smith was fourth.

"I thought Herb won," said Remigino. "Another yard and he would have beat me."

McKenley thought he had won, too. "I feel certain I won," he said. "Yes, even after studying the picture of the photo finish until my eyeballs nearly fell out."

McKenley's disappointment increased when he lost the 400-meter run by a foot to countryman George Rhoden. Both clocked an identical Olympic record 45.9 seconds. Ollie Matson of the United States, who became an outstanding pro football player, was third in 46.8. The defending champion, Arthur Wint of Jamaica, was fifth.

Sim Iness put both the defending champion, Adolfo Consolini, and the U.S. favorite, Fortune Gordien, to rout with his throw of the discus. The schoolmate of Bob Mathias tossed 180' 6½".

A portrait of Soviet leader Joseph Stalin and the official emblem of the Soviet nation were hung at the separate headquarters for athletes from the CCCP (USSR) and other Iron Curtain countries.

An over-zealous official and Horace Ashenfelter, the unexpected winner of the 3,000-meter steeplechase, just avoided a collision at the finish.

Sixth and last in the 400 meters was the 1948 bronze medalist, Sgt. Mal Whitfield of the United States. Whitfield won his second straight 800-meter championship, tying his own Olympic record of 1 minute, 49.2 seconds. Wint repeated as the silver medalist, with Heinz Ulzheimer of Germany third.

Andy Stanfield led Thane Baker and James Gathers, who clocked identical times, to a United States sweep in the 200 meters. Stanfield's time of 20.7 seconds equaled the Olympic record.

There was another American sweep in the 110-meter hurdles. Harrison Dillard, the 1948 100-meter dash champion, finally won his specialty with an Olympic record of 13.7 seconds. Jack Davis clocked the same time for the silver medal, while Art Barnard finished third.

The favored Charles Moore of the United States won the 400-meter hurdles in 50.8 seconds, an Olympic record. He finished five tenths of a second ahead of Soviet Yury Lituyev. John Holland of New Zealand was the bronze medalist.

The United States won its seventh consecutive 400-meter relay. The team of Smith, Dillard, Remigino, and Stanfield finished two tenths of a second in front of the Soviet team and four tenths of a second ahead of the Hungarians.

The 1,600-meter relay was also closely contested between the defending champion United States and Jamaica, which had had to abandon the 1948 race when Wint was injured. In Helsinki, with the same team that was to have run in 1948—Wint, Leslie Laing, McKenley, and Rhoden—Jamaica set a world record of 3 minutes, 3.9 seconds. The United States team of Matson, Gerald Cole, Moore, and Whitfield finished one tenth of a second behind, also breaking the world record. Third-place Germany, which clocked 3:06.6, established a European record.

Wint became a physician and eventually served as Jamaica's ambassador to Great Britain. Whitfield devoted his time to teaching young athletes from the newly-emerging African nations the techniques of track and field.

Bob Mathias had so totally mastered those techniques that by 1952 he won his second decathlon and racked up a world record in the process. Mathias accumulated a total of 7,887 points. He was voted The Associated Press male athlete of the year. His teammates Milton Campbell and Floyd Simmons placed second and third. Ignace Heinrich of France, the silver medalist in 1948, withdrew after six of the ten events because of an injury.

Giuseppe Dordoni of Italy walked 50 kilometers in Olympic record time: 4 hours, 28 minutes and 7.8 seconds. His nearest rival, Josef Dolezal of Czechoslovakia, was 2.1 minutes behind him. Antal Róka was 3.19 minutes later than Dordoni.

Walter Davis, a polio victim at the age of eight, won the high jump with an Olympic record 6' 8⅜". Kenneth Wiesner (USA) was second and José Telles da Conceicão of Brazil was the bronze winner. The Rev. Robert Richards, nicknamed "The Vaulting Vicar," who had been the bronze medalist in 1948, won the pole vault at 14' 11¼", an Olympic record. Except for 1906 that gold medal had been consistently in American hands. Until his final jump Richards had been deadlocked with his teammate, Donald Laz, who took the silver with 14' 9¼". Ragnar Lundberg of Sweden was third. Richards, at 5' 9½", was small for a vaulter. He won the unfeigned admiration of a huge Russian vaulter, who swept up Richards in a congratulating bear hug.

Jerome Biffle and Meredith Gourdine of the United States placed 1-2 in the long jump, with Ödön Földessy of Hungary third, and Americans Parry O'Brien, Darrow Hooper, and James Fuchs were 1-2-3 in the shot put. O'Brien established an Olympic record of 57' 1½". He later became the first to reach 60 feet in the event.

Sim Iness (USA) shattered the Olympic mark on each of his six throws of the discus and won the gold medal with 180' 6½". Adolfo Consolini of Italy, the 1948 gold medalist, was second, followed by James Dillon (USA). Fortune Gordien, the world record holder who had taken the bronze for the United States in 1948, placed fourth.

Cy Young celebrated his 24th birthday by becoming the first American to win a javelin gold medal. With the exception of 1936 it had been a Scandinavian event. Young set an Olympic mark of 242' 0½", eclipsing the record set by Finland's Matti Järvinen in 1932.

Adhemar Ferreira Da Silva of Brazil shattered the world record in the triple jump in four of his six tries. His gold medal performance was 53' 2½", the first time anyone from South America had taken the event. Soviet Leonid Schtscherbakov was the silver medalist and Venezuelan Arnoldo Devonish won the bronze.

József Csermák of Hungary set a world mark in the hammer throw with a toss of 197' 11½". With 193' 1" 30-year-old Karl Storch placed second, ahead of Hungary's Imre Németh, the former world record holder and 1948 gold medalist.

Cy Young of the Los Angeles Athletic Club was the first American to win the javelin throw. Another American, William Miller, was runner-up.

Josef Barthel (406) captured Luxembourg's first gold medal, defeating Bob McMillen of the United States in the 1,500-meter run.

American men won 14 track and field events; Soviet men took four silver and one bronze. In the women's events, however, the tables were turned.

The Soviet entrants captured a total of 11 medals, including golds by Galina Zybina, who set a world record in the shot put, and Nina Romaschkova, who led a Russian sweep in the discus and established an Olympic record with her throw of 168' 8½".

Aleksandra Tschudina won silver medals in the javelin and long jump and took a bronze in the high jump.

The single medal—a gold—won by American women was for the 400-meter relay. The team of Mae Faggs, Barbara Jones, Janet Moreau, and Catherine Hardy defeated a German quartet although both clocked a world record of 45.9 seconds. The American girls were so surprised and delighted by their success they joined hands and danced ring-around-a-rosy.

Australia's Marjorie Jackson won a sprint double, setting a world record of 11.5 seconds in the 100 meters, and then taking the 200 meters. Her teammate, Shirley de la Hunty-Strickland, in the second of her three Olympics, established a world record of 10.9 seconds in capturing the 80-meter hurdles. She had won the bronze medal in 1948, when Fanny Blankers-Koen took the gold. In Helinski, Fanny started the race, but did not finish.

Esther Brand, a 34-year-old South African, was the surprise winner in the high jump. Yvette Williams of New Zealand was the long jump gold medalist, setting an Olympic record of 20' 5½".

Olympic records were broken in 5 of the 6 swimming events. United States swimmers took the gold medals in the 100-meter freestyle (Clarke Scholes), 1,500-meter freestyle (Ford Konno), 100-meter backstroke (Yoshinobu Oyakawa), and 800-meter relay (Wayne Moore, William Woolsey, Konno, James McLane). John Davies of Australia outswam Bowen Stassforth (USA) and Herbert Klein (Germany) in the 200 meter breaststroke, and Jean Boiteux of France took the 400-meter freestyle, establishing an Olympic record and becoming the first French swimmer to win a gold medal. Jubilant Gaston Boiteux endeared himself to the spectators when he jumped into the pool with all his clothes on to embrace his victorious son.

There were no Soviet swimmers in the men's events, and only one representative in the two diving contests. In the springboard diving, Roman Brener placed fifth. The three medals were taken by American divers: David "Skip" Browning, Miller Anderson, and Robert Clotworthy. The highboard made 5' 1¼" Samuel Lee, the Korean-American Army doctor, look inconsequential. He was anything but. He outdid his nearest rival, Joaquin Capilla Pérez of Mexico, by better than 11 points, and won his second championship, the first highboard man to retain his Olympic title.

Hungarian women bore off the top honors in four of the five swimming events. Katalin Szöke and Judit Temes were 1-3 in the 100-meter freestyle; Valéria Gyenge and Eva Novák were 1-2 in the 400-meter freestyle; Eva Székely and Eva Novák were 1-2 in the 200-meter breaststroke (in which the sole Soviet swimmer appeared); and with Ilona Novák, Temes, Szöke, and Eva Novák won the 400-meter relay, setting a world record in the doing. Both Gyenge and Szöke set Olympic records in their individual gold performances.

The one event not dominated by Hungarians—the 100-meter backstroke—was taken by Joan Harrison of South Africa. Geertje

Wielema of The Netherlands and Jean Stewart of New Zealand were the second and third placers.

In the diving Patricia McCormick repeated the feat of Victoria Draves in 1948; she won both the springboard and highboard titles. And she did it by wide margins in both events. The springboard silver went to Mady Moreau (France) and the bronze to Zoe Ann Jensen-Olsen (USA). Fourth was Ninel Krutova (USSR).

The highboard was an American sweep, with Paula Jean Myers in second place and Juno Irwin-Stover third.

Hungary won the water polo, besting Yugoslavia and Italy. Three of the Italian team had taken gold medals in London in 1948, where about half the Hungarian group had won silver.

Although the Russians were years behind in swimming they were the clear masters in other sports. Gymnastics was their cup. Among the gymnasts Viktor Tschukarin came on like a storm. In his first Olympics he entered 6 events and won gold medals in 4 and silvers in 2. He was first in the individual combined exercises, followed by his teammate, Grant Schaginyan. Josef Stalder of Switzerland was third. The Soviets took the team gold, ahead of the Swiss and the Finnish teams.

On the parallel bars Hans Eugster of Switzerland won the gold medal and his teammate Stalder took the bronze. Tschukarin had the silver, as he did on the rings, where Eugster was third and Schaginyan the gold medalist.

The long horse vault and the pommeled horse earned Tschukarin two more gold medals. The pommeled horse was a Soviet sweep, with Yevgeny Korolkov in the silver slot and Schaginyan the bronze. Japan's Masao Takemoto and Takashi Ono were the runners-up in the longhorse vault.

The floor exercises medals went to William Thoresson (Sweden), Tadao Uesako (Japan), and Jerzy Jokiel (Poland).

Jack Günthard took the horizontal bar championship from his fellow Swiss, Josef Stalder, the 1948 Olympian. In third position once again was Alfred Schwartzmann of Germany, who contested in Berlin in 1936.

The women's events were very much a repeat story. There were two new events in Helsinki, the horse vault and the balance beam. Soviet gymnast Nina Botscharova won the balance beam gold, teammate Maria Gorokhovskaya the silver, and Hungary's Margit Korondi the bronze.

Korondi had the gold for her asymmetrical bars performance. Gorokhovskaya was second to her, and Hungary's Agnes Keleti third. Keleti took the floor exercises gold, and her teammate, Margit Korondi the bronze. Gorokhovskaya was once more the silver medalist. So, too, was she in the horse vault, which was a Soviet sweep. Yekaterina Kalintschuk won the gold and Galina Minaitscheva the bronze.

The team combined exercises ranked Soviet, Hungarian, and Czech teams in that order.

Soviet wrestlers were best in four of the eight Greco-Roman classes, won a silver in another, and bronzes in two others. The welterweight class was taken by Miklós Szilvási of Hungary, with Gösta Andersson of Sweden as silver runner-up. In 1948 their positions had been the reverse. Axel Grönberg, the Swedish middleweight champion of 1948 was the only wrestler to retain his gold standing. Kaelpo Gröndahl of Finland moved up from silver in 1948

Patricia McCormick, a 22-year-old American who greatly admired the 1948 star, Vicki Draves, easily won both diving crowns.

Horace Ashenfelter

Horace has taken second so many times I wondered why he didn't give up running.

—MRS. HORACE ASHENFELTER, SR.

On July 27, 1952, there was unusual excitement on a small farm on Black Rock Road near Collegeville, Pa. It was caused by the news that Horace Ashenfelter, Jr., had won the 3,000-meter steeplechase in the Helsinki Summer Olympics.

No one had given Horace Ashenfelter much of a chance. In fact, he wasn't even expected to finish in the top three. The steeplechase wasn't his specialty. As Brutus Hamilton, the U.S. Olympic track and field coach, pointed out, the Russians had a fellow named Vladimir Kazantsev who had the fastest time ever posted in the event—8 minutes, 48.6 seconds.

Prior to Helsinki, Ashenfelter ran the steeplechase—a race of just under two miles sprinkled with hurdles and a water jump—only seven times. His best time for the event was 9 minutes, 06.4 seconds. More to the point, there was unusual pressure on the Americans because of the participation of the Russians for the first time in 40 years. Not since Hitler's 1936 Berlin Olympics had the Games had such political overtones. To many, the Olympics were not just an international sports festival, but a contest between East and West—communism against capitalism.

"Nip" Ashenfelter, a 29-year-old FBI agent and the unmistakable underdog who weighed just 145 pounds, won the gold medal. He captured it with the best time recorded in the steeplechase up to that point, 8 minutes, 45.4 seconds—18 seconds better than the Olympic record. Ashenfelter's achievement should be considered against this background: no American ever had won the Olympic steeplechase, an event rarely run in major U.S. track meets; no American since 1908 had won an

Olympic race longer than 800 meters. For such distances Americans used cars, went the joke.

Horace Ashenfelter Jr., was born in Collegeville on January 23, 1923 and was graduated from Penn State.

"On our first farm, between Collegeville and Phoenixville," his mother said, "we had a half-mile dirt road. I recall Horace running every day on that road. He ran in a small race in Collegeville but it didn't amount to anything. It wasn't until he entered Penn State that we heard he went out for track."

His Penn State coach, Charles "Chick" Werner, didn't seem surprised at Nip's success. "Ash can do anything he sets out to do," he said. "Ash ran a little as a freshman, but then went to war. And he married before he returned to the campus again in 1946."

When he returned, Gerry Karver and Curt Stone were the mainstays of Penn State's team. At Werner's insistence, Ashenfelter remained on the track team. He became proficient at two and three miles. He qualified for the 1952 U.S. Olympic team in the 10,000-meter event.

But when he arrived in Helsinki he was given so little chance in the 10,000 meters that American coaches determined his best chance was the steeplechase. Ashenfelter "had no notions of giving up" before setting foot on the track. "I did well in training—and I spent considerable time studying the water jumps and other hazards," he said. He determined the water jump was the key. And the key to the water jump, he discovered, was held by the Finns. Finnish steeplechasers took the water jump by hitting the top of the barrier with one foot and then leaping over the water. It saved time and energy. Others hurdled the fence and risked a dip in the water.

Eight runners beat the Olympic record time in the heats at Helsinki. Obviously, the final was going to be a real race. Ashenfelter took the lead on the third lap, followed closely by Vladimir Kazantsev. They ran abreast until the final lap. Then, leaving the backstretch, Kazantsev, as expected, moved past the American.

Kazantsev had trouble at the water jump. Ashenfelter, employing the Finns' technique, took the jump with less difficulty, recovered quickly, and passed the startled Russian. He finished 6.2 seconds ahead of Kazantsev.

Ashenfelter attempted to repeat his gold medal performance in 1956. But he never reached the final. The 33-year-old said: "It's progress, I guess. The old guys fade away and new ones take their places."

to gold in the light heavyweight category, bumping the 1948 champion, Karl-Erik Nilsson (Sweden), down to third place.

The freestyle medals were more widely distributed. Turkish Hasan Gemici took the flyweight gold, and his countryman Bayram Sit won the featherweight. Japan's Shohachi Ishii was the bantamweight champion, and William Smith of the United States was welterweight gold medalist. Swedes prevailed in the lightweight (Olle Anderberg) and light heavyweight (Wiking Palm) classes, and Soviet wrestlers took the middleweight (David Tsimakuridze) and heavyweight (Arsen Mekokischvili) classes. Iranian wrestlers earned two silver and four bronze wrestling medals.

The weightlifting gold medals went to either USA (4) or USSR (3) contestants. Ivan Udodov took the bantamweight, Rafael Tschimischkyan the featherweight, and Trofim Lomakin the light heavyweight. The lightweight went to Thomas Kono, who would be seen among the lifters in 1956 as a light heavyweight and in 1960 as a middle heavyweight. Peter George won the middleweight, with Canadian Gérard Gratton as runner-up. Norbert Schemansky moved up from his 1948 silver in heavyweight to the middle heavyweight gold, and John Davis defended his 1948 heavyweight championship. Other faces seen in earlier Games included Mahmoud Namdjou of Iran, who won the bantamweight silver, Rodney Wilkes of Trinidad, the featherweight bronze medalist, and Korean Sung-Jip Kim, who added another bronze in middleweight lifting to the one he acquired in 1948.

One of the youngest champions in the Games was 17-year-old George Genereux, who gave Canada its only gold medal of this Olympics and its first since 1936. After finishing second in the world trapshooting championships, Genereux was asked what score he thought would win in the Olympics. He said 192 out of 200. That is precisely what he shot in winning the gold medal. The event had not been part of the Games since 1924.

The shooting scores in the six events were remarkably close. In the rapid-fire pistol Károly Takács (Hungary) was one point ahead of the silver (teammate Szilárd Kun) and bronze (Gheorghe Lichiar-

The medal that Herb McKenley holds—the silver—was what Lindy Remigino thought he had won, until photos of the finish showed he had taken the gold. At the left, Viktor Tschukarin (USSR) is presented with a gold medal for the individual long horse vault gymnastic event. Japan's Masao Takemoto (left) and Takashi Ono were recipients of the silver and bronze.

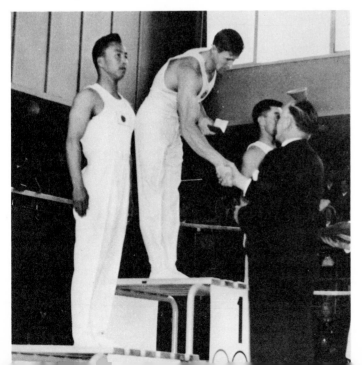

Nate Brooks (USA) takes a punch from a Rumanian competitor en route to the championship in the Olympic flyweight division.

dopol of Rumania), who shot identical scores. In winning the free rifle gold, Soviet Anatoly Bogdanov established an Olympic record. World records were set by Iosif Sirbu of Rumania and Soviet Boris Andreyev, whose scores were the same in the small bore, prone, rifle event. Huelet Benner (USA) beat Spain's Angel León de Gozalo and Hungarian Ambrus Balogh in free pistol shooting.

Three-position firing of small bore rifles was a new event. Norway's Erling Kongshaug won it, but Vilho Ylönen of Finland matched his score, and Boris Andreyev was only a point behind.

The American basketball team won the championship with a 36-25 victory over runner-up Soviet Union. The United States squad included Bob Kurland, who had played on the championship team in 1948, and Clyde Lovellette.

Floyd Patterson, who was to become a two-time professional heavyweight titleholder, took the Olympic middleweight boxing crown in 1952. Four other Americans won titles—flyweight Nathan Brooks, light welterweight Charles Adkins, light heavyweight Norvel Lee, and heavyweight Ed Sanders.

The title bout between Sanders and Ingemar Johansson was stopped in the second round. The Swede was disqualified because he was not aggressive. Johansson was not awarded the silver medal although he had cinched second place in the division. Johansson knocked out Patterson in the third round in June 1959 to win the world heavyweight crown, but the American regained it a year later. The IOC restored the silver to Johansson in 1981.

Both the light welterweight and light middleweight classes were new in 1952. László Papp of Hungary added the light middleweight gold to the gold he took in 1948 in the middleweight class. The bantamweight victor was Pentti Hämäläinen of Finland. Featherweight gold went to Czech Jan Zachara, the lightweight to Italy's Aureliano Bolognesi, and the welterweight to Zygmunt Chychia of Poland.

Hungary was a knockout in soccer, the first time its team had placed among the top four teams. India, which had taken the field hockey event continuously from 1928, kept the title secure with a 6-1 success over the Netherlands.

Great Britain won the bronze medal. Half of India's victorious team had been on the 1948 team.

The 3-day individual equestrian event ranked Swedish, French, and German horsemen in that order. Sweden was the first in the individual and team dressage and in the 3-day team riding. Individual jumping put France first, and team jumping was Great Britain's gold-medal event. Women riders were part of the German and United States dressage teams.

Italian cyclists racked up the best cycling performance—2 gold, 1 silver, 1 bronze. Australians took 2 golds and 1 silver. Russel Mockridge set an Olympic record in winning the 1,000-meter time race.

The six men's fencing events were won by fencers of three nations: France took the foils, single and team; Italy the épée, and Hungary the sabre. Outstanding was Edoardo Mangiarotti, who took golds in individual and team épée, and silvers in both foils events.

Irene Camber of Italy won the women's foil contest. The silver went to Ilona Elek who had been champion in 1936 and 1948. Bronze medalist Karen Lachmann of Denmark was participating in the third of her four Olympics.

Sweden's Lars Hall won the modern pentathlon individual event. His runners-up, Hungarians Gábor Benedek and István Szondy, were two thirds of the victorious group in the new team event, in which Swedish men were second and Finns third.

The youngest gold medal winner of the Games was Bernard Malivoire, a 12-year-old who coxed the French pairs to championship in rowing. The United States won the coxless pairs and the eight-oared race in which Russia placed second. Soviet Yury Tyukalov won a gold medal in the single sculls contest. Argentina took the double sculls. Sweden won the 1,000-meter single kayak event. Finnish boaters won the 10,000-meter kayak singles, and 1,000- and 10,000-meter pairs (Kurt Wires and Yrjö Hietanen in both events), and the 500-meter women's singles. Czechs took the 1,000-meter Canadian singles and the coxed fours. Denmark had the 1,000-meter Canadian pairs and the dinghy race; in the latter Paul Elvström repeated his 1948 success. Frank Havens (USA) won the 10,000-meter Canadian singles, and Georges Turlier and Jean Laudet (France) took the doubles. Yugoslavs took the coxless fours.

Italian yachtsmen won the Star class and Norwegians the Dragon class. In the new 5.5-meter class Americans proved triumphant, and the gold for the final running of the 6-meter race went to United States yachtsmen, as well.

The XV Olympiad closed on August 3. The Games had marked the Olympic debut of nine nations besides the Soviet Union: Dutch Antilles, Ghana, Hong Kong, Indonesia, Israel, Jamaica, Nigeria, Thailand, and Vietnam.

The leading political powers of the world—the United States and the Soviet Union—had met each other in the Olympic arena for the first time. The pre-Games worries had been for nothing. Jesse Abramson, sports correspondent for the *New York Herald Tribune*, wrote: "Except for the segregation of her athletes, Russia showed up very well. The behavior of her athletes was impeccably correct. She sent a full team, took her defeats gracefully, got involved in no disputes or what we have come to call 'rhubarbs,' vetoed no official decisions and demonstrated overall strength in the Games second only to that of the United States."

FINAL MEDAL STANDINGS			
Nation	G	S	B
United States	40	19	17
Soviet Union	22	30	19
Hungary	16	10	16
Sweden	12	12	10
Italy	8	9	4
Czechoslovakia	7	3	3
France	6	6	6
Finland	6	3	13
Australia	6	2	3
Norway	3	2	–
Switzerland	2	6	6
South Africa	2	4	4
Jamaica	2	3	–
Belgium	2	2	–
Denmark	2	1	3
Turkey	2	–	1
Japan	1	6	2
Great Britain	1	2	8
Argentina	1	2	2
Poland	1	2	1
Canada	1	2	–
Yugoslavia	1	2	–
Rumania	1	1	2
Brazil	1	–	2
New Zealand	1	–	2
India	1	–	1
Luxembourg	1	–	–
Germany	–	7	17
The Netherlands	–	5	–
Iran	–	3	4
Chile	–	2	–
Austria	–	1	1
Lebanon	–	1	1
Ireland	–	1	–
Mexico	–	1	–
Spain	–	1	–
Korea	–	–	2
Trinidad and Tobago	–	–	2
Uruguay	–	–	2
Bulgaria	–	–	1
Egypt	–	–	1
Portugal	–	–	1
Venezuela	–	–	1

1956

Winter Games
Cortina D'Ampezzo, Italy

The ideally situated health and winter sports resort of Cortina D'Ampezzo in northeastern Italy was selected to host the 1956 Winter Games. Located in the province of Belluno in the center of the Dolomites, the town is surrounded by pastures and pinewoods that sweep up to magnificent peaks of the eastern Alps. The population of the beautiful tourist spot tripled during the period of the Games, January 26 through February 5, and countless other people in Europe witnessed the competition in their homes. The Winter Games were televised for the first time in 1956.

Guiliana Chenal-Minuzzo of Italy, the 1952 downhill skiing bronze medalist, became the first woman to recite the Olympic oath for all athletes. Forest Ranger James Bickford carried the U.S. flag during the opening ceremonies for the second consecutive time.

The presence of television was a real embarrassment for Guido Caroli, the Italian speed skating champion who was selected to light the Olympic flame. With the flame in hand, Caroli skated to the dignitaries' box and prepared to salute Italy's President Giovanni Gronchi. However, the skater tripped and fell over microphone wire in front of the president's box. Caroli, who kept his composure, later pointed out proudly, ''I didn't let the flame go out.''

The Cortina Games marked the debut of the Soviet Union in Winter Olympics competition. Speed skater Yevgeni Grishin and the Soviet ice hockey team were particularly outstanding. The USSR emerged from the Games as the leading nation in number of gold medals won. Other brilliant performances were turned in by Sweden's Nordic racer Sixten Jernberg, the U.S. figure skaters, and Austria's Alpine skiing rocket, Toni Sailer.

Anton ''Toni'' Sailer of Kitzbühel, Austria,

put on an Alpine skiing exhibition without precedent. He won all three races, as dazzling a display of stamina as Emil Zátopek's three distance events in Helsinki in 1952 had been. The skiers faced unusually hazardous conditions. In the days just before the Games, Olympic officials looked hopefully to the heavens and saw mostly blue skies. Snow had been carried down from the higher slopes of the Dolomites and packed on the ski runs. But that created uneven, treacherous surfaces. The Olympic infirmary was half full of injured skiers before the Games began. Maurice Martel, a French official, warned, "The Olympic downhill ski competition will be a race to death if it doesn't snow soon." It did snow, a welcome 14 inches, promptly melted in a sudden thaw, and then as quickly froze, leaving the runs glistening with ice. Skates, many thought, were more appropriate equipment than skis. Not Toni Sailer. The 20-year-old glazier's son did not wait for any particular kind of snow; all he asked was that the runs be covered.

The 1952 double victory of Christian Pravda, his Kitzbühel townsman, inspired young Sailer to practice in the hope that he might equal Pravda's achievement. Toni Sailer exceeded it. In fact, at Cortina he became the fourth athlete to win three gold medals in a single Winter Olympics. The previous three-time gold medalists were Scandinavians—Nordic skier Thorleif Haug (1924) and speed skaters Ivar Ballangrud (1936) and Hjalmar Andersen (1952).

Sailer's assault on the slopes began with the giant slalom. He finished an incredible 6.2 seconds ahead of runner-up Anderl Molterer, also a Kitzbühel neighbor. Walter Schuster, the bronze medalist, gave Austria a sweep in the event.

An indication of Sailer's superiority was the fact that while his margin of victory was more than six seconds, only 2.3 seconds separated Molterer from the seventh-place finisher, Hanspeter Lanig of Germany. The official report of the British Olympic Committee noted that Sailer "seemed to make no effort, and was not unduly daring, seeming rather to perform a matter-of-fact rhythmical dance down the tremendous slopes."

Sailer won his second gold medal in the two-run slalom. He finished exactly four seconds ahead of Chiharu "Chick" Igaya of Japan, a Dartmouth student who placed second. Stig Sollander of Sweden was third, 5½ seconds behind Sailer. Brooks Dodge placed fourth, the best finish to this point by an American Alpine skier. The standings were queried by Swedish and American officials who claimed that Igaya missed a gate during one of his runs. They sought to have the Japanese disqualified. That would have given Sollander the silver medal and Dodge the bronze. The gate judge said there had been no infraction by Igaya. The protesters were given two weeks to produce film evidence of an infraction. They did not and Igaya became the first Japanese medalist in the Winter Olympics.

Only the challenging downhill remained for Sailer. He was undeterred by Martel's pre-Games pronouncement on the dangers of the course, which the Japanese called "a hara-kiri with a run-on." But even Sailer looked at one point as if he might fail. One of the icy bumps in the course bounced him into the air. His skis flew apart and he looked out of control. "It was murderous," he said afterward. "I have never known such hazards." Only 47 of the 85 starters finished the course. Igaya was not among them. The fastest was Sailer, by 3.5 seconds. Raymond Fellay of Switzerland was next, and Molterer was third.

Toni Sailer, a 20-year-old Austrian plumber, completed his Alpine triple by winning the downhill, his favorite kind of race.

Giant slalom entrants Ossi Reichert, a Berlin cafeteria manager, and Josefine Frandl (right) of Austria were proud to display their gold and silver medals.

Following his grand-slam success, Sailer's hip-waggling style began to be copied. With it Austrian skiers enjoyed skiing supremacy for a number of years. The man who had shown how successful it could be later became the director of the Austrian national ski team.

Only one woman Alpine medalist from 1952 captured a medal in Cortina. She was Ossi Reichert of Germany, the Oslo slalom silver medalist, who won the giant slalom. Josefine Frandl and Dorothea Hochleitner of Austria placed second and third. America's Andrea Mead Lawrence, the defending champion, and Madeleine Berthod of Switzerland tied for fourth, one tenth of a second behind the bronze medalist. The competition was held on a substitute course at Tofana because the slope at Faloria was unfit for racing.

Berthod was favored in the slalom. However, she took many risks and tumbles and placed 17th. The winner was another Swiss, Renée Colliard, a pharmaceutical student from Geneva. Regina Schopf of Austria was second. But the biggest surprise was provided by Russia's Yevgeniya Sidorowa, who won a bronze medal. Sidorowa was one tenth of a second faster than Italy's Chenal-Minuzzo.

Berthod took the downhill by 4.7 seconds over Frieda Danzer, another Swiss. Lucile Wheeler of Canada finished ahead of Chenal-Minuzzo, who repeated her fourth-place finish. The American team suffered from the loss of Jill Kinmont. The U.S. slalom champion had been permanently paralyzed as a result of a fall during the Olympic Trials.

A number of changes in Nordic skiing had been effected since the previous Winter Games. The men's 18-kilometer cross country race was shortened to 15 kilometers (9.3 miles). The 18-kilometer portion of the Nordic combined also was reduced to 15 kilometers. A 30-kilometer individual men's race and a women's 15-kilometer relay race, involving three athletes per team, were added to the program.

The standout of the Nordic competition was Sixten Jernberg of Sweden. His 4 medals, including 3 individuals, were the most won in the Games. He captured 1 gold, 2 silvers, and 1 bronze. Before his Olympic career ended in 1964, Jernberg won a record number of men's Nordic gold medals—4, including one in a relay. His total also included 3 silver and 2 bronze for a total of 9 medals.

Jernberg's only gold medal in Cortina came in the 50-kilometer race. Defending champion Veikko Hakulinen of Finland was second. Hakulinen's time for the first 30 kilometers was only 2½ minutes slower than his time in winning the new 30-kilometer individual race. Russia's Fyedor Terentjev finished third in the 50-kilometers, ahead of Finland's 1952 silver medalist, Eero Kolehmainen. There were no American entries in the 50-kilometer event.

Jernberg won silver medals in the 15- and 30-kilometer races. He also anchored Sweden to a bronze medal in the 40-kilometer relay in which the Soviet Union was the winner, followed by Finland. The relay was Russia's only championship in the men's Nordic events.

Hallgeir Brenden of Norway successfully defended his 15-kilometer title. Pavel Koltschin of the Soviet Union was third. He also was a bronze medalist in the 30-kilometer race.

Finland ended Norway's string of six ski jumping gold medals. Antti Hyvärinen and Aulis Kallakorpi placed 1-2 ahead of Germany's Harry Glass. United States entries were so far out of the

Toni Sailer

What can compare to sweeping all of your events in a single Olympics, to winning three gold medals, to knowing you do your thing better than anyone else in the world?

—TONI SAILER

A poll was taken in 1958 to determine which Austrian had done the most for his country. Anton "Toni" Sailer placed fifth, just behind Mozart. That a skier should be regarded almost as highly as one of history's greatest musical composers astonished many Austrians. However, at the 1956 Winter Olympics at Cortina d'Ampezzo, Italy, Toni Sailer had accomplished the unprecedented feat of winning the Alpine slalom, giant slalom, and downhill races.

Toni Sailer, born on November 17, 1935, in the Tyrolean village of Kitzbühel, first heard the call of the ski slopes at an early age. The handsome Sailer later recalled his first experience on skis.

"My father bundled me and a pair of tiny skis and poles and we went to a test hill behind our home in Kitzbühel. There, he put us together and, after a countdown that included fixing of diapers, he shoved me down the hill. I soon found myself sitting on my behind. I had made the mistake every beginner makes. I leaned back and lost my balance. After a dozen falls I completed my first run. Kids aren't scared on skis. They just let go."

Sailer called skiing the "superlative" of all sports. "It's the most thrilling, yet most relaxing, and the healthiest," he said. "It combines the open air pleasure of golfing or mountain climbing, the powerful precision of tennis, and the elegance of figure skating.

"Yet it's easier than any of them because you don't have to learn any difficult rules or systems. You don't ski by the book, you ski by instinct. Skiing is more than just a sport, it's a way of life, an addiction. Even in a crowd of skiers, you feel you are the only one in the world," he said.

Sailer was not the only proficient skier in Kitzbühel. Anderl Molterer and Hias Leitner battled him for the top ranking in the community. The competition forced all to excel.

The 6-foot, 185-pound Sailer developed a somewhat high and straight style. It suited his physique which was unusually large for a champion skier. His heavier weight increased his speed.

When Sailer arrived in Cortina d'Ampezzo in 1956, he was called "The Blitz from Kitz." A broken leg had prevented him from competing in the 1952 Games. Although the 1956 Olympic field was strong, the Austrian was favored to win at least one gold.

The first of the 1956 Olympic Alpine events was the giant slalom on January 26. Sailer faced his boyhood rival, Molterer, and an even sterner foe—the course which stretched almost 2,660 meters, with a 623-meter vertical drop and 71 gates.

Molterer was the sixth skier down the course. He posted a fast time of 3 minutes, 6.3 seconds. Many believed no one could beat him. Eleven skiers followed, but Molterer retained first place. Then it was Sailer's turn. He rocketed between gates so quickly that he posted a time of 3 minutes, 0.1 second—a lead of more than six seconds—and won the gold medal.

The slalom event on January 28 consisted of two runs, the first with 79 gates and the second with 92. Sailer again outclassed the field. He had the fastest time down both courses and finished with a combined time of 3 minutes, 14.7 seconds. That put him precisely four seconds ahead of Chiharu Igaya, a Dartmouth student from Japan.

The final event on January 31 was the downhill. "I like downhill racing the best because, in the slalom, you have to brake," Sailer said. "I like to run free. The secret of downhill is really the ability to think ahead."

The 1956 Olympic downhill course was more than 3,641 meters long, with a drop of 902 meters, and the route was laced with ice. But there was no stopping Sailer. He completed the run in 2 minutes, 52.2 seconds, approximately 3½ seconds faster than silver medalist Raymond Fellay of Switzerland. Molterer was third.

Austria reveled in Sailer's achievements. The government awarded him its most coveted honor—The Golden Cross of Merit. Subsequently, the Olympic champion had a brief career in motion pictures.

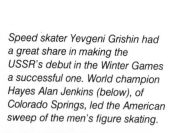

Speed skater Yevgeni Grishin had a great share in making the USSR's debut in the Winter Games a successful one. World champion Hayes Alan Jenkins (below), of Colorado Springs, led the American sweep of the men's figure skating.

medal contest that the American officials were criticized for selecting the jumping team the season before the Games.

Sweden took the first two positions in the Nordic combined. Sverre Stenersen, the bronze medalist in Oslo, captured the gold medal. The silver went to Bengt Eriksson. Franciszek Gron-Gasienica of Poland captured the bronze and became the first non-Scandinavian to win a medal in the event.

Soviet women won three of the six medals in the Nordic events. Ljubovj Kozyreva and Radya Jeroschina were first and second in the 10-kilometer cross country. Sonja Edström of Sweden was third. Twelve seconds separated the first- and third-place finishers.

Finland was the victor in the initial 15-kilometer relay, trailed by the USSR and Sweden. The United States entered no women in the Nordic events.

In individual figure skating there was no stopping the United States. Americans received five of the six medals. Hayes Alan Jenkins, who had been fourth in the 1952 finals, succeeded Dick Button as the men's champion. Ronald Robertson was second, followed by David Jenkins, the younger brother of Hayes. It was the third straight United States gold medal in the event and marked the first time since 1908 that a nation had swept the men's figure skating. Hayes Jenkins was superb in the compulsory figures. His lead over Robertson was commanding and earned him the gold medal, overcoming Robertson's superior free skating performance that included a triple jump in the Dick Button tradition.

The women's gold medalist was Tenley Albright, the Oslo silver medalist. The Radcliffe pre-medical student was the pre-Games favorite until she tripped and sliced her right ankle during a training session. The wound had not healed completely when the competition began. Albright built a fractional lead in the compulsory figures over her American teammate, Carol Heiss. A pretty 16-year-old who was the crowd favorite, Carol had grown up skating with the Jenkins brothers in Colorado Springs, Colorado. She had an outstanding free skating performance. But Albright, who had polio at the age of 11 and who would follow in her father's footsteps and become a surgeon, accumulated sufficient points to edge Miss Heiss for the title. Tenley was the first American to become Olympic women's figure skating champion. Ingrid Wendl of Austria was third.

A couple from Vienna, Elisabeth Schwarz and Kurt Oppelt, captured the pairs gold medal. Frances Dafoe and Norris Bowden of Canada were second. For the second consecutive time, Marianne and Laszlo Nagy of Hungary placed third. The audience insisted that the German duo of Marika Kilius and Franz Nigel were clearly superior to the Hungarians and should have been awarded the bronze. The press termed the crowd's opposition to the decision "a disgusting spectacle."

The Soviets ended Scandinavian—especially Norwegian—supremacy in speed skating. Norway, winner of 12 of 23 gold medals in previous Olympic skating events, managed to win only one silver and one bronze medal in Cortina. Soviet skaters won three golds. The fourth went to a Swede. American speed skaters went home without a medal.

Races were held on Lake Misurina at an altitude of 5,758 feet. The Soviets brought with them special scientific devices for measuring the speed and quality of the ice. This prompted one speed skating official to say, "Russian sports science has replaced Norwegian tradition." The altitude of the lake and its fast surface helped to produce a series of new records. Six skaters broke or equaled world records. Olympic records were shattered 73 times! A total of 41 national marks was established, including American records in the 500, 1,500, and 5,000 meters.

The caliber of the competition was so extraordinary that Ken Henry, America's defending gold medalist in the 500 meters, skated four tenths of a second faster than his 1952 winning time in Cortina but only tied for 17th place. Forty-three skaters, including four Americans, beat the 1,500-meter winning time that Oslo's triple gold medalist Hjalmar Andersen posted in 1952. And Andersen's winning time in the 5,000 four years earlier was bettered by 16 skaters in Cortina.

The star of the speed skating competition in Cortina was Yevgeni Grishin, a nonmedal-winning cyclist in the 1952 Summer Olympics. Grishin, a Moscow engineer, won the 500 meters with a world

Tenley Albright, women's Olympic figure skating champion. The gold-winning Soviet hockey team (dark uniform) defeated the Canadians, 2-0.

On Italy's gold-winning boblet team, Lamberto Dalla Costa (left) was the driver and Giacomo Conti was the brakeman.

record of 40.2 seconds. His teammate, Rafael Gratsch, was second, with Norway's Alv Gjestvang the bronze medalist.

John Werket of the United States tied for 11th. Another American, Donald McDermott, the Oslo silver medalist in the 500, and Canada's Gordon Audley, who was declared fourth in the 500 in 1952, tied for 25th. Both were only a tenth of a second slower than the former Olympic record.

The Soviets outskated everyone in ice hockey and were the surprise winners of the gold medal. Although they had been playing international hockey only since the end of World War II, they swept through their competition with a 5-0-0 record, outscoring their opponents, 25-5. They shut out the second-place United States team, 4-0, and Canada, the bronze medalist, 2-0.

The American team, coached by Johnny Mariucci, a former Chicago Black Hawk defenseman, had been picked by a special committee of representatives from the Amateur Hockey Association of the United States, the National Collegiate Athletic Association, and the Amateur Athletic Union.

Canada, represented by the Kitchener-Waterloo Dutchmen, was the favorite. The Canadians were not only blanked by the Soviets but were also upset by the Americans, 4-1. It was the first United States victory over Canada in Olympic competition. Johnny Mayasich scored three goals and Weldon Olson had one for the winners. Wendell Anderson, who served as governor of Minnesota (1971–77) and as a U.S. senator (1977–79), was on the American team.

The Americans trailed the Soviets by only 1-0 late in the third period of their game. Then, the Soviets scored three times in the final 3½ minutes, to hand the United States its lone setback of the tournament. The Soviet starting team consisted of Nikolai Pushkov, the goalie, Nikolai Sologubov, Ivan Tregubov, Yevgeni Babich, Viktor Shuvalov, and Vsevolod Bobrov.

Italy and Switzerland shared the two bobsledding gold medals. The host Italians won their only championship of the Cortina Games when Lamberto Dalla Costa drove a two-man sled to victory ahead of a boblet piloted by his countryman, Eugenio Monti, a former Alpine skier. Switzerland edged Spain for the bronze medal by 14/100ths of a second after four runs. The driver of the Spanish sled was the Marquis Alfonso DePortago, playboy and Grand Prix auto racing driver who was making his international debut in bobsledding.

The United States was favored to win the four-man event after turning in the fastest practice runs. However, the best the Americans could do was a bronze. The sled driven by Art Tyler, a physicist from Rochester, New York, finished 29/100ths of a second behind the silver medal sled driven by Italy's Monti, who was beginning an Olympic career in which he would win a record 6 bobsled medals (2 golds, 2 silvers, and 2 bronzes). A Swiss sled, piloted by Franz Kapus, won the gold. Kapus is the oldest gold medalist in Winter Olympic history. He was 46 years and 10 months old when he won in Cortina. A Swiss compatriot, Albert Madorin, was 46 years and 11 months old when he was a member of the bronze medal four-man sled in 1952.

At the conclusion of the Games, Nikolai Romanov, the Soviet minister of sports, commented on Soviet success. "We came here expecting triumphs in our strong events and expecting to gain experience in the others," he said. "We did both and we're going to win in Melbourne, too."

FINAL MEDAL STANDINGS			
Nation	G	S	B
Soviet Union	7	3	6
Austria	4	3	4
Finland	3	3	1
Switzerland	3	2	1
Sweden	2	4	4
United States	2	3	2
Norway	2	1	1
Italy	1	2	–
Germany	1	–	1
Canada	–	1	2
Japan	–	1	–
Hungary	–	–	1
Poland	–	–	1

1956

Summer Games
Melbourne, Australia

The 1956 Summer Olympics in Melbourne, Australia, were held in the autumn, from November 22 through December 8.

The decision to award the Games to Australia—the first time they were held in the Southern Hemisphere—caused a change in training schedules for most of the 3,184 athletes who competed. Because of the reverse of the seasons in the Southern Hemisphere, a majority of the athletes had to be at peak performance at a time when they are not normally competing.

As the opening date drew closer, the sluggish preparation for the Games by the Australian Organizing Committee gave rise to general apprehensions. Serious doubt about Melbourne's ability to host the Games was not new. The International Olympic Committee had awarded them to Melbourne in 1949 by the margin of only a single vote. When Avery Brundage, the American president of the IOC, announced in 1953 that he planned to make a personal inspection of the facilities, he was advised not to come as there would be nothing for him to see.

Australia confounded the doubters, and had all the necessary facilities in readiness when they were wanted—with one exception. The Australian requirement of a six-month quarantine before horses could be admitted to the country put the IOC into a quandary: cancel the equestrian events, or hold them elsewhere. Reluctant though they were to act in violation of the Olympic charter, which mandates that all Olympic events must be held in the same country, they were more reluctant to cancel an event. They determined that the equestrian events would be held from June 10 through June 17 in Sweden—more than five months before the opening of the Summer Games.

A Melbourne park features a beautiful floral clock. The Australian city was host for the 1956 Summer Games.

To Stockholm, site of the 1912 Olympic Games, 29 nations sent 158 athletes for the equestrian competition. The host Swedes won 3 of the 6 gold medals—the individual three-day event, the dressage, and the team dressage, Great Britain was first in the team three-day contest, and Germany took both the individual and team jumping honors.

Before the month of June was finished, the worry about Melbourne's readiness was displaced by the soberer worry over the possible collapse of plans. Egyptian discontent over the Suez Canal reached a pitch in June. Egypt seized the canal; Israel marched into the Gaza Strip, aided by Great Britain and France, the Canal's "legitimate owners." Egypt, Lebanon, and Iraq notified the Melbourne organizing committee that they were withdrawing.

In the autumn, the Hungarians who hoped to escape from Soviet control were given a lesson—to be noted by their neighbors—in what it cost to alarm the rulers of the Soviet Union. As the Games were about to open in Melbourne the stone-throwing Hungarian "Freedom Fighters" were being crushed by the wave of military tanks sent crashing into Budapest. In protest, Spain, The Netherlands, and Switzerland withdrew their athletes from the Melbourne Games. And as though those crises were not enough, the People's Republic of China had its own, the cause of its leaving the Games: someone raised the flag of Taiwan in the Olympic Village, which was taken as an intolerable "scheme of artificially splitting China." Avery Brundage, contemplating the prospects for Melbourne, observed that "in ancient days, nations stopped wars to compete in the Games; nowadays we stop our Olympics to continue our wars."

Hungarians and Soviets found themselves in a mini-war during the Melbourne Games. Part of the Hungarian team was aboard a Soviet vessel en route to Australia when their countrymen began their revolution. The balance of the team was in Prague, ready to go by air. They didn't know whether to go or not, but finally did. In Australia they refused to compete under the Communist banner and flew the flag of Free Hungary in the Olympic Village. When the Communist flag was ordered restored by officials, two Hungarian athletes climbed the flagpole and tore it down.

Hungarian athletes, who wore black mourning arm bands for the people killed during the uprising, were understandably distracted. Swimmer Eva Székely and her husband, Dezsö Gyarmati, captain of the Hungarian water polo team, were typical.

"We left Hungary to go to Australia," Székely said, "during the first few days of the revolt, when it looked as if Hungary would be free. When we arrived in Melbourne we learned that the Russians had come into power. From that time, until the conclusion of the Olympics four weeks later, we had no word of our two-year-old daughter, or my parents. I didn't get any real sleep for a week before I was due to race, and lost over 12 pounds. My husband was also extremely worried, of course," she said.

Székely, the defending champion in the 200-meter breaststroke, was 3.1 seconds off her 1952 time, placing second in Melbourne between Germany's Ursula Happe and Eva Maria Ten Elsen. However, her husband led Hungary to its second consecutive gold medal in water polo. During a career that began in 1948 and ended in 1964, Gyarmati won 3 gold medals, 1 silver, and 1 bronze.

When the Duke of Edinburgh opened the Games, there were 67 countries represented. During the ceremony, in which Australian miler Ron Clarke suffered minor burns while lighting the Olympic cauldron, the scoreboard in Melbourne's Olympic Stadium said, "Classification by points on a national basis is not recognized."

Official recognition or not, the struggles in the political world intruded, inevitably, and the moment competition began the compilation of point totals began. In general, it was East versus West, and in particular, the USSR versus the USA. No matter what method of scoring was used, the USSR came out the winner, 37 gold medals to 32 for the USA. European sportswriters unofficially gave 622 points to the USSR, 497 to the USA. The American scorekeepers figured the USSR won by 722 points to the USA's 593.

Points and medals did not—never do—tell it all. In track and field, the heart of the Games, the Soviets bettered their 1952 performance, but American athletes dominated the competition—15 gold medals to the Soviets' 3.

Bobby Morrow, a 21-year-old from Abilene Christian College, won a sprint double, set an Olympic record in one, and anchored the United States 400-meter relay team to a world record of 39.5 seconds. His relay teammates were Ira Murchison, Leamon King, and Thane Baker. The Soviet team finished second, as it had in 1952, and the German team third.

Morrow and Baker, the runner-up, had the identical time of 10.5 seconds in the 100 meters. Hector Hogan of Australia was 1/10th second slower. Morrow set an Olympic record of 20.6 seconds in the 200 meters, 1/10th of a second faster than countryman Andy Stanfield. Baker was the bronze medalist.

After two victories by Jamaican runners, Charlie Jenkins brought the 400-meter title back to the United States. His margin of victory was 1/10th of a second over Karl-Friedrich Haas of Germany, who bested Voitto Hellsten (Finland) by 2/10ths of a second.

Bobby Morrow (55) of the United States, who established an Olympic record in the 200 meters, defeated Poland's Edward Schmidt (40) in the ninth heat.

The USSR's Vladimir Kuts (200) won both distance track events in 1956. Britain's Gordon Pirie (189) posed a major challenge throughout much of the 10,000-meter race.

Another 1/10th of a second triumph was recorded by Tom Courtney, who gave the United States its fourth successive 800-meter championship. His time of 1 minute, 47.7 seconds was an Olympic record. Derek Johnson of Great Britain was second and Audun Boyson of Norway was third.

"When Johnson got a yard ahead of me—I guess it must have been about 50 yards from the finish—I thought the race was all over," Courtney said. "I thought I had lost. I don't even remember what happened after that." Courtney was so exhausted that the medal ceremony had to be delayed for an hour.

The 1,500-meter race also had an American flavor. A Villanova University student running for Ireland, 21-year-old Ron Delany, started the last lap in 10th place in the 12-man field. An unofficial 53.8-second clocking in the final 400 meters earned Delany the gold medal with an Olympic record time of 3 minutes, 41.2 seconds. Klaus Richtzenhain of Germany was second and John Landy, the world's second sub-four-minute miler, was third, although both clocked identical times of 3:42.0. All together, eight men bettered the former Olympic mark.

Vladimir Kuts, a 29-year-old sailor, gave the USSR a gold medal double in the distance events, winning the 5,000- and 10,000-meter races. He demolished the Olympic records set four years earlier by Emil Zátopek of Czechoslovakia.

Kuts won the 10,000 meters on November 23 in 28 minutes, 45.6 seconds, clipping 31.4 seconds off Zátopek's mark. He ran a 61.2 second opening lap and his time for the first 5,000 meters was just 4/10ths of a second slower than Zátopek's time in winning the 5,000 in Helsinki. Britain's Gordon Pirie was in the lead on the 20th lap, but he faltered and finished eighth. Hungary's Jozsef Kovacs was second in 28:52.4. Allan Lawrence of Australia won the bronze medal in 28:53.6.

The Aussies did a magnificent job after early difficulties.

ARTHUR DALEY
The New York Times

Kuts took 27 seconds off Zátopek's 1952 Olympic record in the 5,000 on November 28. At 4,000 meters, Kuts ran away from Pirie, the world record holder, and romped to victory in 13 minutes, 39.6 seconds. Pirie was 11 seconds behind, followed by another Briton, Derek Ibbotson. Kuts' iron-man performance won great admiration all around. With his tremendous finishing spurts he simply ran the competition into the ground.

The marathon went to Alain Mimoun, the Frenchman who collected three silver medals while chasing Zátopek in 1948 and 1952. This time it was the Czech's turn to do the chasing. He finished sixth.

"I was sure Emil was there at my heels," said the 36-year-old Mimoun after running his first competitive marathon. Instead of accepting congratulations, he wheeled and waited at the stadium tunnel for Zátopek. "I was hoping Emil would be second," he said. "I was waiting for him. Then, I thought, well, he will be third—it would be nice to stand with him on the podium again."

When the exhausted Zátopek reached the stadium, he seemed to be in a daze. Then, when he realized that his longtime rival, Mimoun, was the winner he embraced the Frenchman. "For me," Mimoun said, "that was better than the gold medal." On the podium were Franjo Mihalič of Yugoslavia, the silver medalist, and Veikko Karvonen (Finland).

America's Horace Ashenfelter returned to defend his 3,000-meter steeplechase. He ran 8 minutes, 51.0 seconds, duplicating his 1952 qualifying time. But it put him in sixth place in his heat, not fast enough to qualify for the final.

Britain's Christopher Brasher won the event in 8 minutes, 41.2 seconds, an Olympic record. Sándor Rozsnyói of Hungary placed second, ahead of Norway's Ernst Larsen. Brasher survived a disqualification for allegedly impeding Larsen. The decision was reversed by the Jury of Appeals.

Marathon medalists (left to right) Veikko Karvonen of Finland (bronze), Alain Mimoun of France (gold), and Franjo Mihalič of Yugoslavia enjoyed the camaraderie of the award ceremony.

Americans won all six medals in the hurdles races. Lee Calhoun took the 110-meter high hurdles in an Olympic record 13.5 seconds, beating world record holder Jack Davis, who clocked the same time. Joel Shankle was third. Glenn Davis, Eddie Southern, and Josh Culbreath ran 1-2-3 in the 400-meter hurdles. The winner's time was an Olympic record 50.1 seconds.

The winner of the 1,600-meter relay was the United States with Lou Jones, Jesse Mashburn, Charlie Jenkins, and Tom Courtney. They finished ahead of Australia and Great Britain.

There was a Soviet sweep in the 20-kilometer walk—a new event. The winner was Leonid Spirin. Just over 35 seconds behind him were Antanas Mikenas (silver) and Bruno Yunk (bronze).

Norman Read became the first contestant from "down under" to place in the 50-meter walking competition. The New Zealander's 4:30:42.8 time was 2 minutes, 14.2 seconds better than Soviet Yevgeny Maskinskov's.

Americans won six of the eight field events. The Reverend Bob Richards successfully defended his pole vault title, but not without difficulty. He missed twice at 13′ 1½″ before qualifying at that height in his final attempt. He went on to establish an Olympic record of 14′ 11½″ and became the first repeat winner in the event. Teammate Bob Gutowski won the silver medal and Georgios Roubanis of Greece got the bronze.

Charles Dumas of the United States, the first ever to reach seven feet in the high jump, cleared 6′ 11½″ for an Olympic record on his final try. Runner-up Charles Porter of Australia was second at 6′ 10⅝″, and Soviet Igor Kaschkarov was third.

The United States placed 1-2 in the long jump with Gregory Bell and John Bennett; Jorma Valkama of Finland was the bronze winner. Brazil's Adhemar Ferreira Da Silva retained his triple jump championship with an Olympic record 53′ 7¾″. Vilhjalmar Einarsson, who won the silver, was the first Icelandic to place in this event. He bettered Da Silva's 1952 Olympic record. Vitold Kreyer of the Soviet Union was third.

With the javelin, Norway's Egil Danielson wrote a new world record. He threw a distance of 281′ 2½″, 18′ 10″ farther than Poland's Janusz Sidlo and 20′ 4½″ beyond Soviet Viktor Tsybulenko's best toss.

Americans Parry O'Brien, the defending champion, and Bill Nieder finished 1-2 in the shot put. O'Brien broke his Olympic record six times en route to the winning toss of 60′ 11¼″. Czech Jiři Skobla won the bronze medal.

A University of Kansas sophomore, Al Oerter, won the discus throw, beating teammate and world record holder Fortune Gordien with a throw of 184′ 10½″, an Olympic record. Desmond Koch, the bronze medalist, gave the United States a sweep in the event. Italy's 39-year-old Adolfo Consolini, the 1948 gold and 1952 silver medalist, was sixth.

Two school teachers, Harold Connolly of Boston and Soviet Mikhail Krivonosov, had taken turns in shattering the world hammer throw record before the Games. Melbourne was their first head-to-head encounter. Krivonosov held the lead until the next-to-last round. Then Connolly broke the Olympic record with a toss of 207′ 3½″, to win the showdown. His margin of victory was six inches. Anatoly Samotsvyetov of the Soviet Union won the bronze. Hungary's defending champion, Jószef Csermák, placed fifth.

An Olympic romance: Hammer throw gold medalist Harold Connolly of the United States and women's discus throw gold medalist Olga Fikotová of Czechoslovakia were married in Prague in March 1957. They were attended by Dana (left) and Emil Zátopek.

Al Oerter

There is no job, no amount of power, no money to approach the Olympic experience.

—AL OERTER

Alfred Oerter's place in Olympic history is as secure as any athlete's who ever competed. There are others with more medals and a few with longer careers in the Olympic Games but no one has quite the record of coming from behind, four Games in a row, to win the top rank in one of the most strenuous of the classic field events.

Al Oerter was never the favorite discus thrower in any of the Games in which he competed. But he was in love with what he was doing. "I like the beauty, the grace, and the movement. I can feel myself through the throw and can feel the discus in flight." It flew 184' 10½" in 1956 in Melbourne; 194' 2" in 1960 in Rome; 200' 1½" in Tokyo in 1964; and 212' 6½" in 1968 in Mexico City. Each was an Olympic record, achieved without the help of the best wind conditions with which world records usually are made. (In large stadiums, the wind usually comes from all directions.)

Oerter, born September 19, 1936, in Astoria, New York, was 32 when he won in Mexico City. His reason for putting himself through the preparation to climb sports' highest mountain four different times underscored the ideals of the Olympics.

"I don't chase world records," he said. "If they come during the competition, fine. But the competition is first."

Oerter set a national high school discus record in 1954. That enabled him to gain a scholarship from the University of Kansas. Two years later, as a Jayhawk sophomore, he was on the way to the Melbourne Olympics. Oerter was America's No. 2 man in the discus, behind Fortune Gordien, the world record holder.

His first toss on November 27 in Melbourne, 4' 4" better than the Olympic record set in 1952 by Sim Iness of the United States, was an unhappy surprise to the favorite, Gordien. Gordien could not come closer than five feet to it.

Rome four years later was not the relaxed affair Melbourne had been. For one thing, Melbourne was the last set of Games without the intensifying eye of television. For another, Oerter had had plenty of time to think about the Games, what they mean, and what doing less than his best would mean to him. Tension, he said later, was like a pain, so great that he could barely throw. It took him five throws to beat his teammate, Richard "Rink" Babka, holder of the world record. Then his toss was 3' 10" better than Babka could do.

Oerter became the first ever to exceed 200 feet in the event on May 18, 1962. But he injured his neck later that season and had to compete while wearing a surgical collar. The neck injury was only one of his problems in the 1964 Tokyo Olympics. Six days before the final, Oerter tore the cartilage in his rib cage.

"I had to use novocaine. I was wrapped up in bandages like a mummy," he said. "But the pain was still fierce, and I was popping ammonia capsules to clear my head. I was thinking of dropping out. Then the competition began and the adrenaline started flowing."

On his fifth attempt, Oerter threw 200' 1½", "even though it felt like somebody was trying to tear out my ribs."

When he headed for Mexico City in 1968, the gentle giant (6' 4", 290 pounds) still had neck problems, and a week before the discus event, he pulled a muscle in his right thigh, with the result that he could not make an involuntary left turn —the worst thing that can happen to a discus thrower. Again he declined to quit.

Oerter had a poor first throw and fouled on his second. He ripped off his neck brace, he stepped back into the circle, and threw 212' 6½". It was 5' 7" better than the best throw by runner-up Lother Milde of East Germany. Oerter had discarded the neck brace to give himself a "boost of confidence and to worry the opposition." Obviously, the dramatic tactic was most successful.

He retired from the Olympic competitions after 1968, but he continued to keep in trim physical condition. And while he said of himself that he is not the type of person to go home and look at his medals, much less shine them, he also said, "There is no job, no amount of power, no money to approach the Olympic experience."

A gold medal wasn't all that Connolly won in Melbourne. He won the heart of Olga Fikotová, the discus gold medalist and Olympic record setter from Czechoslovakia. The two became inseparable during the Olympics. After the Games, they wrote to each other. With aid from the United States State Department, Connolly went to Czechoslovakia in 1957, and married her in Prague. Zátopek acted as Connolly's best man at the wedding. The Connollys competed for the American team in the next Summer Games.

World record holder Rafer Johnson, hampered by an injured knee, finished second in the decathlon. The event was won by his teammate, Milton Campbell, who set an Olympic mark. Campbell had been runner-up to Mathias in 1952. Vassily Kuznyetsov (USSR), with 122 points less than Johnson, ranked third.

The outstanding woman track and field athlete was Betty Cuthbert, an 18-year-old Australian. She won a sprint double and anchored the winning 400-meter relay team to a world record of 44.5 seconds. A United States team that included Mae Faggs, Margaret Matthews, 16-year-old Wilma Rudolph, and Isabelle Daniels placed third behind silver medalist Britons Anne Pashley, Jean Scrivens, June Paul-Foulds, and Heather Armitage.

Cuthbert finished ahead of Christa Stubnick of Germany and Marlene Matthews of Australia in both the 100 and 200 meters.

One of Cuthbert's relay teammates was Shirley de la Hunty-Strickland, who successfully defended her 80-meter hurdles championship with an Olympic record 10.7 seconds. The two medals brought Strickland's career total to a record seven.

"I did it because I was self-testing," the 31-year-old Strickland said. "I did it because I regarded my body merely as a piece of machinery. I wanted to see if I could make my machinery work better than others'."

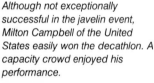
Although not exceptionally successful in the javelin event, Milton Campbell of the United States easily won the decathlon. A capacity crowd enjoyed his performance.

Australia captured four gold medals in women's track at Melbourne. Betty Cuthbert (468) put on the steam to take the 100 meters. Shirley de la Hunty-Strickland repeated in the 80-meter hurdles.

United States women won only one gold medal in the field events. The victor was Mildred McDaniel, who established a world record of 5′ 9¼″ in the high jump. The next five contestants jumped the same 5′ 5¾″. Two—Maria Pissaryeva (USSR) and Thelma Hopkins (Great Britain)—were awarded silver medals. No bronze was given.

The Soviets won two events, each with Olympic records. Tamara Tyschkevitsch put the shot 54′ 5″ to beat teammate Galina Zybina, the defending gold medalist. (Germany's Marianne Werner, the 1952 silver winner, took the bronze.) Inese Yaunzeme threw the javelin 176′ 8½″ to take the gold medal. The defending title-holder, Dana Zátopková, placed fourth.

Poland's Elzbieta Krzesinska set a world record of 20′ 10″ in the long jump, finishing almost one foot ahead of Willye White of the United States, the silver medalist, and nearly two feet ahead of Soviet Nadyeschda Dvalischvili.

The host Australians captured 8 of 13 gold medals in swimming, sweeping all the men's and women's freestyle events. It was the first such achievement since 1920. The Australians won 5 of the 7 men's events and 3 of the 6 women's.

Australia took all six medals in the men's and women's 100-meter freestyle races, with Jon Henricks and Dawn Fraser the gold medalists. Both were coached by Harry Gallagher. Fraser set a world record of 1 minute, 2 seconds in placing ahead of Lorraine Crapp and Faith Leech. It was the first of Fraser's three victories in the event.

Henricks posted an Olympic record of 55.4 seconds in finishing in front of John Devitt and Gary Chapman.

Murray Rose, 17-year-old English-born Australian, led Tsuyoshi Yamanaka (Japan) and George Breen (USA) across the finish line in both the 400-meter and 1,500-meter freestyles. Rose set an Olympic record of 4 minutes, 27.3 seconds in the 400. He became the first male swimmer since Johnny Weissmuller in 1924 to win two freestyle championships in the same Olympics.

Rose's individual gold medal total matched that of United States swimmers. The American victories were scored by William Yorzik in the 200-meter men's butterfly and by Shelley Mann in the women's 100-meter butterfly. Both events were new to the Olympic program.

Pat McCormick

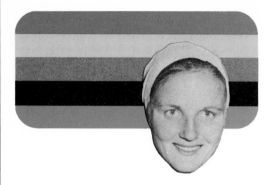

The money would have bought a house, but so many kids look up to you as an amateur.

—PAT MCCORMICK

Mrs. Pat Keller McCormick is the only Olympian to win both the springboard and highboard (platform) diving events in successive games. Pat McCormick accomplished her "double double" by winning both events as a 22-year-old in the 1952 Helsinki Olympics and then repeating—just months after giving birth to her first child—in the 1956 Melbourne Olympics. As a result she was named in 1956 The Associated Press Woman Athlete of the Year and the winner of the Sullivan Award as America's outstanding amateur athlete.

Obviously many of those who voted for Pat understood what most of the general public do not—that diving can be as grueling as the decathlon. Diving is not considered to be a contact sport. But hitting the water in the attempt to conquer the intricate maneuvers required from the 3- and 10-meter heights can be dangerous. There is documentation of the physical hazards Pat McCormick encountered. During a 1950 physical examination her doctor jotted down the following: a six inch, healed-over scalp wound; several scars above the base of the spine; welts across the collarbone; lacerations of the feet and elbows; a healed cracked rib and broken finger; a loose jaw and chipped upper front teeth.

"I've seen worse casualty cases, but only where a building caved in," Pat McCormick remembers the doctor saying.

Pat McCormick was born on May 12, 1930, in Seal Beach, California, near Santa Monica. She rode the waves as a child and swimming was part of her daily existence.

"I started diving when I was a sophomore in high school because I was a great admirer of Vicki Draves," McCormick said. "So, I just drifted into diving competition."

Pat was still drifting when she met her future husband at pool side in 1947. They were married a year later and, under Glenn's guidance, she emerged as one of the nation's foremost women divers. He provided the stability she needed. He was older and had experience as a diving coach.

"I can't dive well at all when he isn't around," she said. Pat Keller was an unsuccessful diver, who began to win titles after she became Mrs. McCormick. She completed an unprecedented grand slam in 1951 by winning all U.S. indoor and outdoor championships. A year later, she was the diving star of the Helsinki Olympics. Her husband was in the stands when Pat went after the springboard title. She virtually cinched the gold medal with her third dive—a brilliant one and one-half reverse somersault with a tuck. It earned her 18.92 points, the highest rating in two days of competition.

When the event was over, the 5' 4", 125-pounder was well ahead of the silver medalist, Mady Moreau of France, with a combined total of 147.30 points. Then, McCormick attempted the highboard.

Spectators observed that Pat McCormick repeatedly touched her wedding ring before each dive. It was her one superstition. Apparently, it worked. She led a 1-2-3 United States sweep for her second gold medal. Only America's Vicki Draves in 1948 had won a diving double.

Pat turned down offers to turn professional and cash in on her Olympic success. "My plans are to raise a family, compete in the 1956 Olympics, and then retire."

McCormick returned to the daily schedule of 80 to 100 dives a day, six days a week. Her program was interrupted only when she had a child.

Her husband was with her in Melbourne in 1956, giving her more than moral support. He was the United States Olympic women's diving coach.

Pat won the springboard event with a point total of 142.36—16.47 points more than the runner-up, Jeanne Stunyo of the United States. On her final dive she executed a superb one and one-half backward somersault with a one and one-half twist.

When all the points were totaled in the highboard championship, Pat had 84.85, leading another American sweep. Juno Irwin had 81.64 and Paula Jean Myers, the bronze medalist, had 81.58.

"That was my last competitive dive," Pat McCormick said. "Now I plan to attend to the business of being a housewife."

In the 100-meter backstroke Australian David Thiele's Olympic record and the times of his silver-medal teammate, John Monckton, and Frank McKinney (USA) were all better than the 1952 gold medal time.

Japanese placed 1-2 in the 200-meter breaststroke, and the bronze went to Soviet Charis Yunitschev.

The United States finished second to Australia in both relays. Kevin O'Halloran, Devitt, Rose, and Henricks swam to a world record of 8 minutes, 23.6 seconds in the men's 800-meter freestyle. The Soviet team was third. Fraser, Leech, Sandra Morgan, and Crapp raced to a world record of 4 minutes, 17.1 seconds in the women's 400-meter freestyle relay. South Africa's team came in third.

Australia took the gold and silver in the 400-meter freestyle. Lorraine Crapp set a new Olympic record with a time of 4 minutes, 54.6 seconds, 6.9 seconds ahead of Dawn Fraser and 12.5 seconds faster than Sylvia Ruuska (USA).

The 100-meter backstroke gave British Judith Grinham a gold for her Olympic record 1 minute, 12.9 seconds performance. Carin Cone of the United States had the same time, and British Margaret Edwards was third at 1 minute, 13.1 seconds.

Pat McCormick of the United States swept the two women's diving events and became the first ever to defend both titles successfully. She led Juno Irwin and Paula Jean Myers in a 1-2-3 sweep of the highboard event. Teammate Jeanne Stunyo took the springboard silver, and Canada's Irene MacDonald the bronze.

Robert Clotworthy and Donald Harper of the United States were first and second on the springboard, with Mexico's Joaquin Capilla Pérez the runner-up. Pérez reversed things in the highboard event, taking top honors, with Americans Gary Tobian and Richard Connor second and third.

Water polo brought the Hungarians' hatred of the Soviets into the open. In the semifinals the two teams met, and the passions of the Budapest conflict flared anew. Hungarian partisans shouted insults from the stands, and applauded Hungarian players, however rough. In a rush for the ball Soviet Valentin Prokopov butted Ervin Zádor, opening a cut over Zádor's eye. At the sight of their bloody compatriot, Hungarian spectators surged forward to do battle. Police restored order; Hungary won the match. In the finals Hungary took the gold medal, Yugoslavia the silver, and the Soviet team the bronze.

Another, and legitimate, Hungarian battler was 30-year-old László Papp, in his third Olympics and boxing for the second time as a light middleweight. He outpointed José Torres (USA) to retain his gold standing in the final. Torres eventually became world professional light heavyweight champ. Britain's John McCormack was the bronze winner in the light middleweight class.

In the other boxing classes there were no title defenders—new men took the medals. British boxers won the flyweight (Terence Spinks) and lightweight (Richard McTaggart) contests. Soviet contenders had the golds for featherweight (Vladimir Safronov), light welterweight (Vladimir Yengibaryan), and middleweight (Gennady Schatkov) categories. Germany's Wolfgang Behrendt was bantamweight victor, and Rumanian Nicolae Linca bore away the welterweight laurels. James Felton Boyd and T. Peter Rademacher of the United States were light heavyweight and heavyweight gold medalists, respectively.

Australia's Murray Rose (right, rear) swam the 1,500-meter freestyle in a winning 17 minutes, 58.9 seconds. Japan's Tsuyoshi Yamanaka (right, front) was second. George Breen (left, front) of the United States and Australia's Murray Garretty (left, rear) followed.

Nine months after his Melbourne victory Rademacher fought for the world title in his first professional bout. In the sixth round he was knocked out by the defending champion, Floyd Patterson, the 1952 Olympic middleweight champion.

The weightlifting events were won by either American or Soviet athletes. Records were broken in every case. The American gold medalists were Charles Vinci, setting a world record for bantamweight class; Isaac Berger, ditto, for featherweight and Thomas Kono for light heavyweight; and Paul Anderson, with an Olympic record for heavyweight. The Soviet lifters were lightweight Igor Rybak, who established a new Olympic record, and world record writers Fyodor Bogdanovsky (middleweight) and Arkady Vorobyov (middle heavyweight).

Weight watching helped Anderson defeat Argentina's Humberto Selvetti for the gold medal. Both lifted the same combined total, but the American took the title because of his lighter body weight. Anderson weighed a mere 304 pounds to Selvetti's 317!

Greco-Roman wrestling proved a winning game for Soviet contestants. They took the gold medals in the light flyweight, bantamweight, middleweight, light heavyweight, and heavyweight classes. Finnish wrestlers were featherweight and lightweight champions, and Turkey won the welterweight championship.

The freestyle wrestling awards were more widely distributed. No US wrestler did better than silver medalist middleweight Daniel Hodge. The light flyweight gold was a Soviet gain. Turkish wrestlers took the bantamweight and heavyweight honors; Japanese, the featherweight and welterweight; Iranian, the lightweight and light heavyweight; and a Bulgarian, the middleweight.

Except for 1904, when Cubans won the individual men's foils, French or Italian fencers took off the top awards. In 1956, it was French Christian d'Oriola's victory, the successful defense of his 1952 position. Italian fencers shone in the team foil, individual épée and team épée events, and Hungarian sabre fencers, not very surprisingly, were tops in both individual and team contests. The individual event had been a Hungarian triumph every Olympics from 1924, and the team event, from 1928.

The ladies' foil was won by Gillian Sheen of Great Britain.

Lars Hall (Sweden) repeated as gold medalist in the modern pentathlon, the only athlete ever to win the event in consecutive Games. Finnish Olavi Mannonen, fifth in 1952, moved into second place, and Gábor Benedek (Hungary), who had had the silver in 1952, was sixth. Finland's Väinö Korhonen won the bronze medal. The Soviet pentathlon team finished first, ahead of the American and the Finnish teams.

In canoeing, the gold medal harvest was European. Sweden got the 1,000-meter kayak singles and Germany the doubles. Rumanians won the 1,000-meter Canadian singles and doubles, and the 500-meter ladies' kayak singles was a Soviet triumph. The sculls, both single and doubles, were taken by Soviet men. Vyatscheslav Ivanov, a 19-year-old sculler with less than a year's experience, began a remarkable string of three consecutive victories in the single sculls. Ivanov shattered the gold medal hopes of John Kelly, Jr., whose father had won the single sculls in 1920. Kelly, in his third consecutive Olympic, finally earned a medal—but it was a bronze.

U.S. rowers were best in both coxed and coxless pairs events, and in the fours, Canada took the coxless and Italy the coxed races.

At Melbourne, Hungary's László Papp received his third gold medal, a record for boxing. The 30-year-old light-middleweight boxer defeated José Torres (left) of the United States in the final.

The United States made it eight consecutive victories in the eight-oared crew race. After being beaten in its opening race, the Yale University crew gained a berth in the final by winning the "repechage"—second chance for losers. They placed first in that race and then became the first crew in 36 years to win a gold medal after losing in the opening round.

In the yacht races, the Star class was won by an American crew, and both Dragon and 5.5-meter races by Swedes.

The fastest cycling was done, with one exception, by either Frenchmen or Italians. Italy's Ercole Baldini won the individual road race and Leandro Faggin broke the Olympic record in the 1,000-meter time trial. The Italian team won the 4,000-meter pursuit, as their countrymen had done five times in the past. Michel Rousseau (France) took the 1,000-meter sprint and a French team wheeled home first in the road race. The exception was the Australian victory, a repeat of 1952, in the 2,000-meter tandem race.

Except in the free pistol contest, which was won by Pentti Linnosvuo of Finland, records were broken in every shooting event. With the free rifle Soviet Vassily Borissov shot an Olympic record 1138, a single point above his teammate, Allan Erdman. In the prone position Canadian Gerald Ouellette fired 600, a new world record, ahead of Borissov by one point.

In the three-position rifle firing Anatoly Bogdanov (USSR) and Otakar Horinek (Czechoslovakia) shot identical Olympic record scores. Rumania's Stefan Petrescu set a new Olympic record with the rapid-firing pistol, and Italian Galliano Rossini broke the Olympic record in the clay pigeon event.

Thirty-nine medals were awarded for proficiency in men's gymnastics; the bulk of them went to either Soviet (17) or Japanese (14) athletes. Viktor Tschukarin (USSR) added 3 golds and 1 bronze to his total, and Japan's Takashi Ono accumulated 1 gold, 3 silver, and 1 bronze of his lifetime total of 13 medals. The only gold-medal winner not Soviet or Japanese was German Helmut Bantz, the long horse champion.

The women's gymnastic events were evenly divided between Hungarian and Soviet contestants. Gold medals went to Soviet women for the combined exercises, individual and team, and the horse vault. The laurels for the asymmetrical bars, floor exercises, and balance beam went to Hungarians. Each group had a star performer. Thirty-five-year-old Agnes Keleti of Hungary won 3 gold and 2 silver medals, increasing her career total to 10 Olympic medals—5 gold, 3 silver, and 2 bronze.

Keleti's chief rival was 22-year-old Larissa Latynina of the Soviet Union, whose 4 golds and 1 silver in 1956 gave an inkling of what was to come. During three consecutive Games Latynina would gather more medals than any athlete in Olympic history—18.

Bill Russell and K.C. Jones led the United States team to the basketball championship. The Americans beat the runner-up Russians, 89-55, in the championship game. Russell and Jones subsequently helped build the dynasty of the professional Boston Celtics.

The Soviet Union took the soccer championship, beating second-place Yugoslavia, 1–0, in the final game.

India was at the fore, however, on the hockey field, winning over Pakistan, 1–0. It was the sixth straight win for India.

The Games finished on December 8 without any of the trouble that high emotion had threatened at the start.

FINAL MEDAL STANDINGS			
Nation	G	S	B
Soviet	37	29	32
United States	32	25	17
Australia	13	8	14
Hungary	9	10	7
Italy	8	8	9
Sweden	8	5	6
Germany	6	13	7
Great Britain	6	7	11
Rumania	5	3	5
Japan	4	10	5
France	4	4	6
Turkey	3	2	2
Finland	3	1	11
Iran	2	2	1
Canada	2	1	3
New Zealand	2	–	–
Poland	1	4	4
Czechoslovakia	1	4	1
Bulgaria	1	3	1
Denmark	1	2	1
Ireland	1	1	3
Norway	1	–	2
Mexico	1	–	1
Brazil	1	–	–
India	1	–	–
Yugoslavia	–	3	–
Chile	–	2	2
Belgium	–	2	–
Argentina	–	1	1
Korea	–	1	1
Iceland	–	1	–
Pakistan	–	1	–
South Africa	–	–	4
Austria	–	–	2
Bahamas	–	–	1
Greece	–	–	1
Switzerland	–	–	1
Uruguay	–	–	1

1960

Winter Games
Squaw Valley, California

Squaw Valley, California, located on the Eastern slopes of the Sierra Nevada, near Lake Tahoe, 200 miles east of San Francisco, is a testimony to the tenacity of Alexander Cochran Cushing. The 6' 6" New York socialite first went to the remote region of northeastern California in 1946, arriving on foot because there was no road leading into the valley. Cushing and a group of friends, including Laurence Rockefeller, purchased 50 acres of land there. They also bought cabins from the United States Air Force and launched a winter resort by installing a single chair lift.

Cushing pursued a dream of having the virtually unknown and inaccessible valley play host to the Winter Olympics. He enlisted the support of Goodwin Knight, governor of California (1955–59), and William Knowland and Thomas Kuchel, U.S. senators from California during the mid/late 1950's. Then, he approached the state legislature and succeeded in raising the first $1 million for Squaw Valley. When the United States Olympic Committee gave its support to Cushing's ambition, the resort contained only a few wooden cabins, the chair lift, and a restaurant.

Nominations for the role of host city were considered at a Paris meeting of the International Olympic Committee between June 13 and June 18, 1955. Cushing, recognizing the inadequacies of his resort compared with the posh playgrounds of Europe, stressed the slogan: "Return to the Olympic ideal in its Spartan sense—away from the fashionable hotels!" In a secret ballot to determine the host city, Squaw Valley and Innsbruck, Austria, received 31 votes each. The Austrians were stunned. The next day, a second ballot was taken. The vote was 32 for Squaw Valley and 30 for Innsbruck. Since 36 of the 62 IOC voting members were Europeans, the vote astonished many.

Following considerable preparation the Games were held in Squaw Valley from February 18 through February 28 at an estimated cost of more than $9 million. A total of 693 athletes, from 30 nations, participated. The Games were a competitive and artistic success and attracted unusually large crowds. The American Institute of Architects presented a First Honors Award to the Blyth Arena at Squaw Valley, scene of the ice hockey competition. Although there were no facilities for bobsledding and the sport was not contested, two new events were introduced—women's speed skating and the men's biathlon. At the time the biathlon was a combination of a 20-kilometer cross-country ski race and marksmanship with a rifle. Each competitor had to stop four times during the race to shoot at a target.

For the first time, the United States saw the Winter Games on television. Walt Disney supervised an impressive opening ceremony. Skier Andrea Mead Lawrence, who won two gold medals in 1952, carried the Olympic torch into the stadium and handed it to speed skater Ken Henry, the 1952 Olympic 500-meter gold medalist. Figure skater Carol Heiss recited the oath for all athletes. Speed skater Don McDermott, the 1952 silver medalist in the 500 meters, carried the Stars and Stripes. The Games were formally opened by Vice President Richard M. Nixon in the absence of President Dwight D. Eisenhower.

Prior to the opening, the lack of snow had the organizers in such a quandary that they hired a tribe of Paiute Indians to perform a ceremonial dance designed to cause a snowfall. But it didn't snow. It rained. There was a downpour accompanied by hurricane-strength winds. With the slopes in their worst possible condition, a sudden drop in temperature turned the rain into snow and saved the Games. Before the opening ceremonies ended, the sun appeared.

The U.S. State Department refused to grant entry visas to East German journalists. State charged that the newsmen were propaganda agents of the East German regime.

The nationally televised hockey game between the United States and the Soviet Union on February 27 was particularly memorable. The Americans won, 3–2, and went on to capture their lone gold medal in the sport.

The United States was not considered a serious contender when the hockey tournament opened. Rated ahead were the USSR, the defending Olympic champion; Canada, the 1959 world champion, seeking to regain the crown it lost to the Soviets in Cortina d'Ampezzo; and an experienced team from Czechoslovakia. The Soviet Union opened defense of its title in the final round by beating Czechoslovakia, 8–5. After playing a 2–2 tie with Sweden, the Soviets routed Germany, 7–1. Canada, led by Harry Sinden, who became coach and general manager of a Stanley Cup-winning Boston Bruins' team, won its first two games by shutouts—12–0 over Germany and 4–0 over Czechoslovakia.

The United States, coached by Jack Riley of the United States Military Academy and a 1948 Olympian, defeated Sweden, 6–3, and Germany, 9–1, in its first two games. Roger Christian scored three goals in the opening game and Bill Cleary had four in the victory over the Germans. On February 25, the Americans faced a Canadian team determined to avenge its first loss to the United States four years earlier. However, the United States scored a major upset with a 2–1 victory on goals by Bob Cleary and Paul Johnson

American figure skater Carol Heiss, soon to thrill capacity crowds with her dazzling artistry, recited the oath in behalf of the 693 athletes at the 1960 Winter Games.

and the superb goaltending of Jack McCartan, who made 38 saves. The Americans were outshot, 39–25.

Two days later, the United States trailed the Soviet Union, 2–1, after the first period with Bill Cleary scoring the lone American goal on an assist from his brother, Bob. At 11:01 of the second period, William Christian tied the score, 2–2, on an assist from his brother, Roger. As American television audiences watched, the United States upset the heavily favored Soviets on Bill Christian's second goal of the game at 14:59 of the third period. Roger Christian and Tommy Williams received assists. McCartan made a number of sparkling saves late in the game to preserve the triumph.

Entering the final day of the tournament on the closing day of the Olympics, the standings of the medal contenders were: United States, 4 victories, 0 defeats, 0 ties; Canada 3-1-0; the USSR 2-1-1; Czechoslovakia 2-2-0. The game pairings for the medal contenders that day were Canada—USSR and the United States—Czechoslovakia. A victory by the United States meant the gold medal. An American loss coupled with a Canadian victory raised the possibility of a Canadian gold medal on a goals-for and goals-against basis.

After two periods, the Czechs led the United States, 4–3. As they rested in their dressing room, awaiting the final 20 minutes of the game, the Americans had an unexpected visitor. He was defenseman Nikolai Sologubov, captain of the Soviet team. Sologubov suggested that the Americans inhale from a tank of oxygen. He pointed out that the Russians routinely used it to revitalize tired muscles. It worked for the Americans, too. The United States outscored Czechoslovakia, 6–0, in the third period for a 9–4 triumph. Roger Christian tied the score at 5:59 of the final period on a pass from his brother. At 7:40, Bob Cleary put the Americans in front, 5–4, on an assist by John Mayasich. Roger Christian scored two more goals for a total of four in the game, and the Cleary brothers scored one each before the game ended.

Canada cinched the silver medal by defeating the USSR, 8–5. The Soviets placed third, ahead of Czechoslovakia. There was speculation about the reason for Sologubov's visit to the American dressing room. Some maintained it was a friendly gesture toward the Americans. Others insisted that Sologubov did not want Czechoslovakia, a Soviet bloc nation, to finish ahead of the Soviet Union.

Bill Cleary was the Americans' leading scorer in the tournament's final round, with 12 points on 6 goals and 6 assists. Roger Christian was the runner-up, with 7 goals and 2 assists. McCartan, generally regarded as the star of the "Team of Destiny," led the goalies with 150 saves and 11 goals allowed. Other members of the U.S. team were: Eugene Grazia, John Kirrane, Robert McVey, Richard Meredith, Weldon Olson, Edwyn Owen, Rodney Paavola, Laurence Palmer, and Richard Rodenheiser. McCartan subsequently played professionally in the National Hockey League and in the World Hockey Association. Bill Cleary became the Harvard coach.

The United States also became the first nation to win consecutive men's and women's individual figure skating championships in the 1960 Winter Games. Carol Heiss succeeded Tenley Albright as the women's gold medalist and David Jenkins took the men's crown won four years earlier by his brother, Hayes Alan.

Heiss competed in the 1956 Olympics as a 16-year-old and promised her terminally ill mother she would win the gold medal. She had to settle for a silver. Mrs. Heiss died of cancer later in the

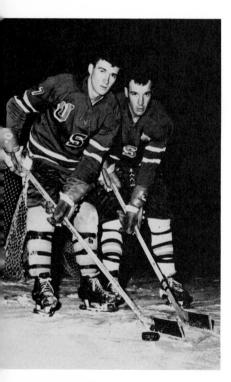

Bill Christian (left) and his brother Roger, of tiny Warroad, in northernmost Minnesota, were key members of the gold-winning U.S. hockey team.

year. Carol pledged to win the gold in 1960 in her mother's memory. And she did. The beautiful New York University sophomore, a four-time world champion, was as proficient in the compulsory figures as she was in free skating.

The official report of the United States Olympic Committee said Carol's "magnificent exhibition in the free skating stirred a capacity crowd of 8,500 to tears and cheers. Clad in crimson costume, embellished with spangles and a tiara in her blonde hair, she bedazzled the judges, her opposition, and the spectators with her sheer artistry."

Sjoukje Dijkstra of The Netherlands, 12th in Cortina, won the silver medal. Barbara Ann Roles of the United States was third.

Then Jenkins, the bronze medalist four years earlier, came from behind to overtake Karol Divin of Czechoslovakia for the men's gold medal. Jenkins, a 23-year-old medical student from Western Reserve University, trailed Divin by 22 points after the compulsory figures. Then he showed why he was regarded as the world's greatest free skater. He put on an electrifying display in his specialty, with triple loops and a triple Salchow, to win the competition.

"I think it was the best I've done under pressure," Jenkins said later. Donald Jackson of Canada won the bronze medal and, for the second consecutive time, Alain Giletti of France finished fourth.

The 1960 figure skating champions became in-laws on April 30, 1960, when Miss Heiss married Hayes Alan Jenkins.

Canada gave North America its first sweep of the figure skating events when Barbara Wagner and Robert Paul took the pairs title. They had finished sixth four years earlier. Germany's Marika Kilius and Hans Jurgen Bäumler placed second, ahead of Nancy and Ron Ludington of the United States.

The biathlon, a combination of cross-country skiing and rifle shooting, was added to the Olympic program in 1960. The sport had been popular with European, especially Scandinavian, military personnel since the early 1900's. In addition to the standing-position target shooting represented by the artist, the biathlete must fire in kneeling and prone positions, doffing and donning his skis between targets.

The Soviet Union won 3 of the 4 gold medals and 6 of the overall total of 12 medals in women's speed skating. Lidia Skoblikova was a double winner, capturing the 1,500- and 3,000-meter events.

Skoblikova, a 21-year-old blue-eyed blond psychology student from the Ural Mountains, shattered the world 1,500-meter mark with a time of 2 minutes, 25.2 seconds and came within a half second of the world 3,000-meter record with a clocking of 5:14.3. Poland's Elwira Seroczynska and Helena Pilejczyk were second and third, respectively, in the 1,500. Another Soviet, Valentina Stenina, was the runner-up in the 3,000, finishing ahead of Finland's Eevi Huttunen.

Germany's Helga Haase, a 25-year-old housewife and mother, upset the favored Soviets to win the 500 meters. She also placed second in the 1,000. Natalia Dontschenko of the USSR was the runner-up in the 500, one tenth of a second ahead of Jeanne Ashworth, America's 21-year-old bronze medalist. Klara Guseva and Tamara Rylova of the USSR won the gold and bronze medals in the 1,000 meters.

American men broke national records in all four speed skating events either during the trials or in the Olympics, yet only Bill Disney managed to win a medal as the USSR again won 3 of the 4 gold medals and 6 of the 12 overall. Yevgeni Grishin equaled his world record of 40.2 seconds in the 500 meters and tied Roald Aas of Norway for first place in the 1,500 meters. Viktor Kosichkin, a 21-year-old Moscow engineer, won the 5,000 meters. Norway's Knut Johannesen, the 5,000-meter runner-up, reversed positions with Kosichkin in the 10,000 meters. They were the first skaters to break 16 minutes for the event. Johannesen, a 26-year-old carpenter,

David Jenkins succeeded his brother as figure skating champ. Speed skater Lidia Skoblikova took the 1,500 and 3,000 (below).

lowered the world record in the 10,000 by an incredible 46 seconds as the first five finishers bettered the former mark. Johannesen's time was 15 minutes, 46.6 seconds. The bronze medal winner was Kjell Bäckman of Sweden. America's Ross Zucco finished 10th in the 10,000, establishing an American record of 16:37.6. He was killed in an automobile accident on September 28, 1960.

Disney, a 27-year-old rug cleaner, finished one tenth of a second behind Grishin in the 500 to take the silver medal. Soviet Rafael Gratsch, the silver medalist in 1956, was third.

No silver medal was awarded in the 1,500 because of the first place tie. Boris Stenin (USSR) captured the bronze medal. Jan Pesman of The Netherlands was the bronze medalist in the 5,000.

The leading American Alpine skier was Penelope "Penny" Pitou, a 21-year-old blonde, from Gilford, New Hampshire, who took home two silver medals. Pitou, the favorite in the downhill, was the first down the hill on February 20. She skidded and almost fell on a treacherous turn, but recorded a time of 1 minute, 38.6 seconds. Several others fell and could not continue, including America's Betsy Snite.

Heidi Biebl, a 19-year-old German, finished exactly one second ahead of Pitou for the gold medal. Traudl Hecher, a 16-year-old from Austria, was three tenths of a second behind the American for the bronze medal.

Biebl was favored in the women's giant slalom on February 23 because of her number 5 starting position. However, she hit a bump, went off the track, returned, and finished 37th. Pitou, suffering from a bad cold, started 11th and posted a time of 1 minute, 40.0 seconds. Yvonne Ruegg of Switzerland, who placed ninth in the downhill, finished one tenth of a second faster than the American on the

Part of the specially-built, award-winning Olympic complex was the background for the ski-jumping competition. Germany's Helmut Recknagel won the event. Jean Vuarnet (left) became the second Frenchman to take the Alpine downhill. His time was 2 minutes, 6 seconds. Unevennesses in the course, which caused the skiers to become airborne, put their control to the severest test.

Switzerland's Roger Staub was first in the men's 1⅛-mile giant slalom.

55-gate course to win the gold medal. Italy's Giuliana Chenal-Minuzzo was two tenths of a second behind Pitou, to take third place and cap a comeback. She was the mother of two at the time.

Pitou's last chance to win a gold medal was in the slalom. Her first run time of 58.5 seconds put her in contention although Canada's 21-year-old Anne Heggtveit, an Ottawa secretary, completed the course in an incredible 54.0 seconds. Pitou, expected to improve on her second run, fell and clocked 1 minute, 21.3 seconds. Her combined time of 2:19.8 gave her a 33rd place finish. Meanwhile, Snite, with runs of 57.4 and 55.5 for 1:52.9, cinched the silver medal behind the 1:49.6 posted by Heggtveit. Germany's Barbi Henneberger was third.

Austria, competing without its 1956 star, Toni Sailer, captured four medals, including one gold, in the men's Alpine skiing. The Games marked the first appearance of metallic skis in the Olympics and 10 percent of the men's downhill competitors used them instead of the wooden skis. Frenchmen, using the French-pioneered metallic skis developed by Emile Allais, captured three medals. Jean Vuarnet, a hotel owner, won the downhill. The event was postponed for three days because of the pre-Games blizzard. Vuarnet's countryman, Guy Perillat, placed third behind Germany's Hanspeter Lanig. The third medal won by a Frenchman on metallic skis went to Charles Bozon, who placed third in the slalom behind Austrians Ernst Hinterseer and Mathias Leitner.

Roger Staub of Switzerland, a 23-year-old sporting goods store owner, upset the giant slalom field with a gold medal time of 1:48.3. It was four tenths of a second faster than Austria's Josef "Pepi" Stiegler and eight tenths of a second faster than Hinterseer, who took the bronze medal.

The major upset in Nordic skiing was the victory by 22-year-old Georg Thoma of Germany in the Nordic combined. He was the first non-Scandinavian winner of the event. Norway's Tormod Knutsen was second and Nikolai Gussakov (USSR) was third. Another German, Helmut Recknagel, became the first non-Scandinavian to win the ski jumping. Recknagel outdistanced silver medalist Niilo Halonen of Finland and Otto Leodolter of Austria, the bronze medalist.

The most exciting Nordic event was the men's 40-kilometer cross-country relay in which Finland's 35-year-old Veikko Hakulinen made up 20 seconds on the fourth and final leg and overhauled Hakon Brusveen of Norway to win the gold medal by eight tenths of a second. The USSR was third. Hakulinen's relay finish earned him his third gold medal in three Olympics. He also won a silver in the 50-kilometer cross-country and a bronze in the 15-kilometer. Finland's Kalevi Hämäläinen and Sweden's Rolf Rämgård were the gold and bronze medalists in the 50 kilometers. Brusveen and Sweden's Sixten Jernberg placed 1-2 in the 15 kilometers. Jernberg captured the 30-kilometer race with Rämgård second and Nikolai Anikin (USSR) third.

The Soviets swept the first three places in the women's 10-kilometer cross-country. The gold medal went to Maria Gusakova, followed by Luibov Baranowa and Radya Jeroschina. The Soviet trio combined to place second to Sweden in the 15-kilometer relay. Finland was third.

A Swede became the first Olympic biathlon champion. Klas Lestander finished ahead of Antti Tyrväinen of Finland. The bronze medal went to Aleksander Privalov (USSR).

FINAL MEDAL STANDINGS			
Nation	G	S	B
Soviet Union	7	5	9
Germany	4	3	1
United States	3	4	3
Norway	3	3	–
Sweden	3	2	2
Finland	2	3	3
Canada	2	1	1
Switzerland	2	–	–
Austria	1	2	3
France	1	–	2
The Netherlands	–	1	1
Poland	–	1	1
Czechoslovakia	–	1	–
Italy	–	–	1

1960

Summer Games

Rome, Italy

In 393 A.D. Emperor Theodosius sent out from Rome the order that abolished the ancient Olympics. Varazdetes, a boxer from Armenia, was the final champion to be recorded. Almost 16 centuries later, when the Modern Games were held for the first time in the capital of the extinct Roman Empire, a boxer with an imperial-sounding name was entered in the list of champions. He would become so famous a professional athlete that his Olympic standing would be all but forgotten.

He was Cassius Marcellus Clay.

Olympic boxing tournaments helped to launch the professional careers of such champions as Floyd Patterson, Ingemar Johansson, José Torres, Frankie Genaro, Fidel LaBarba, and Jackie Fields. A championship was on the mind of Clay, an 18-year-old light heavyweight, when he arrived in broiling Rome for the 1960 Summer Games. The Olympic crown was secondary to the schoolboy. His target was a professional title.

Clay had lost only eight of 170 amateur fights and wanted to turn professional before the Games. He would have, if his coach, Louisville policeman Joe Martin, had not convinced him that an Olympic gold medal would serve as a springboard to a professional career.

Clay was known as the "Louisville Lip" because of his nonstop talking. He was a gregarious, engaging personality, easy to know and to like. And he was an unusually gifted boxer. En route to the final of the 178-pound tournament, Clay stopped Jan Becaus, a Belgian, in the second round, outpointed Gennady Schatkov (USSR), the 1956 middleweight titleholder, and won a close decision over Tony Madigan, an American-trained Australian. Clay's opponent in the championship match was Poland's three-time European titlist, Zbigniew Pietrzykowski.

Castel Sant'Angelo, Rome.

Clay dazzled the 25-year-old Polish boxer with his dancing footwork and quick hands during the first two rounds. Then, he bloodied and battered his opponent in the final round to win the decision on the scorecards of all five judges. They had Clay the winner by 59–57 points, 59–58, 60–56, 59–57, and 60–57. The new champion was so proud of his gold medal that he did not take it off for 48 hours.

Less than two months after the Olympics, on October 29, 1960, Clay outpointed Tunney Hunsaker in his first professional fight. He became the youngest man in history to win the heavyweight championship when he knocked out Charles "Sonny" Liston in the seventh round on February 25, 1964. He was 22 years old at the time. Clay later became a Muslim and changed his name to Muhammad Ali.

Another professional boxing champion emerged from the Rome Olympics. Giovanni "Nino" Benvenuti of Italy, the welterweight gold medalist, became the world middleweight champion on April 17, 1967, when he outpointed the titleholder, Emile Griffith.

Two other American boxers won gold medals in Rome—light middleweight Wilbert McClure and middleweight Edward Crook. Britain's Richard McTaggart lost his lightweight Olympic crown to Polish Kazimierz Pazdzior. McTaggart went away with the bronze medal. In the five other classes, Italian boxers gained two golds and Czech, Soviet, and Hungarian boxers one each.

Of all the athletes who competed in sweltering Rome between August 25 and September 11 the most captivating was 28-year-old Abebe Bikila, a member of the palace guard of Emperor Haile Selassie of Ethiopia.

Bikila, who won the fastest and most unusual marathon up to that time, ushered in the era of the standout African distance runners. He was the first Ethiopian to win a gold medal, the first marathoner to win while running barefoot, and the first neither to start nor finish in the Olympic stadium.

Cassius Clay was only too pleased to have the ladies along Rome's Via Veneto inspect his gold medal. The future Muhammad Ali received his prize for defeating Poland's Zbigniew Pietrzykowski, a veteran of 231 bouts and a 1956 light middleweight bronze medalist.

The field of 69 began the marathon beneath the Capitoline Hill, the religious center of the ancient Roman Empire. Sixty-odd runners raced by moonlight over the cobblestoned Appian Way. The finish line of the race was almost beneath the Arch of Constantine, within a javelin throw of the Colosseum and the Roman Forum.

It was only the third marathon for the 5' 9", 135-pound Bikila. He was unknown, but he had prepared himself with long runs at high altitude. Bikila ran in Rome without shoes, according to a plan developed by his Swedish coach, Onni Niskanen.

Bikila was in a group of four that led over the first eight miles. Soon after they reached the 10-mile mark, all of which was run uphill, Rhadi Ben Abdesselem of Morocco and Bikila began to pull away. The pace was torrid, and the experts predicted they would run themselves into exhaustion.

It didn't happen. Bikila increased his pace and finished nearly 200 meters ahead of the Moroccan in 2 hours, 15 minutes, 16.2 seconds.

Ben Abdesselem finished 25.4 seconds behind the wiry Ethiopian. Barry Magee of New Zealand won the bronze medal. All of the first 15 finishers shattered Emil Zátopek's Olympic record, set in 1952.

Bikila's 26-mile, 385-yard journey was made without the usual refreshments, which he refused to accept. "We are a poor people, and not used to mechanized transport," he said. "We run everywhere. Twenty-six miles is nothing to me. Of course I could have kept going for a long time."

His self-confidence was well-founded; Ray Norton's proved not to be. The Californian went to Rome favored to win a double sprint and had predicted he would win three golds on the track. In his first event, the 100-meter dash, he ran faster than any medal-winner had in Melbourne, but so did five others. Germany's Armin Hary, at 10.2 seconds, had the gold and a new Olympic record. David Sime (USA) had the same time, and 3 sprinters clocked 10.3—Peter Radford (Great Britain), Enrique Figuerola (Cuba), and Frank Budd (USA).

Norton chugged in sixth in the 200 meters, too. "His" second race was Italian Livio Berruti's gold triumph in a world record time of 20.5 seconds. Lester Carney (USA) got the silver and Abdoulaye Seye (France) the bronze. It was the second "U.S." event lost after five straight Olympics.

Otis Davis (USA) and Brooklyn-born Carl Kaufmann (Germany) set the same new world record of 44.9 seconds in the 400 meters. The photo timer gave Davis the gold for 44.91 and Kaufmann the silver for 44.93, and the bronze went to South African Malcolm Spence, who was six tenths of a second longer in the run.

Peter Snell had traveled from New Zealand to Rome in the expectation of getting some experience and the hope of possibly a bronze medal. He experienced the triumph of outrunning Belgium's world-record-holding Roger Moens in the 800 meters, setting a new Olympic record at the same time. George Kerr (Antilles) came in third.

Within an hour of Snell's achievement New Zealand's team cheered another victor. At twenty-seven, with the handicap of a withered arm, Murray Halberg did not look like the best bet for the 5,000 meters. But he had trained up through the shorter distances, and had developed speed. He used it in the last stretch to move out

Otis Davis of Los Angeles became a gold medalist after a photo finish with Germany's Carl Kaufmann in the 400 meters. During an agonizing delay before the photos could tell the winner, Kaufmann lay where he crashed as he hit the tape at the finish line.

Abebe Bikila

We train in shoes, but it's much more comfortable to run without them. The marathon distance is nothing for me. I could have kept going and gone around the course again.

—ABEBE BIKILA

A polite and gracious athlete who ran barefoot, Abebe Bikila became the first Olympic champion from Ethiopia when he won the marathon at Rome in 1960. He was also the first athlete to win consecutive marathon gold medals when he repeated his triumph in the event in Tokyo four years later. It was appropriate for a man whose name means "Budding Flower" in Amharic, his native tongue.

From his little-known starting point of Mout in Ethiopia, where he was born on August 7, 1932, he was projected into a society that was completely alien. But, with his feet and his smile, he bridged the gap and became a world-class athlete.

The son of peasants, Abebe Bikila began to run as a child. He chased pheasant for the family table. Running at unusually high altitude increased Bikila's lung capacity and as a result he developed extraordinary endurance. He loped long distances, yet his pulse beat barely faster at the finish than it did at the start.

"One day I run 10 miles, resting in the afternoon," Bikila said. "The next morning I do only physical training and gymnastics. The day after I run another 10 to 15 miles. I play basketball, volleyball, and tennis. I play these sports about two hours, then run some more," he said.

Under the lights of Rome's Colosseum he defeated the best distance runners in the world. His time was 2 hours, 15 minutes, 16.2 seconds. It was 7 minutes and 50 seconds faster than the Olympic record set by Emil Zátopek of Czechoslovakia in 1952.

When Bikila returned to Ethiopia he was promoted from private to corporal in the Imperial Guard. During preparations for the 1964 Olympics, he reached the rank of sergeant.

Bikila had an appendectomy on September 16, 1964. He resumed training on September 27, and won his second consecutive marathon gold medal on October 21. He ran just as fluidly and effortlessly as he had in Rome, and bettered his Olympic record with a time of 2 hours, 12 minutes, 11.2 seconds. He beat the runner-up by 4 minutes and 8 seconds. The entire length of the marathon course was manned by television cameras.

Immediately after Bikila crossed the finish line in the Olympic Stadium, he performed a series of strenuous exercises which he completed before the silver medalist, Basil Heatley of Great Britain, reached the finish line. The Japanese were impressed with Bikila's performance. Ethiopia was overwhelmed. He was promoted to lieutenant by Emperor Haile Selassie. Resplendent in plumed helmet and beribboned red coat of the Imperial Guard, Bikila was recognized and cheered by all citizens of Addis Ababa, Ethiopia's capital.

He remained, however, as obedient to his mother as he was as a small child. He maintained many family traditions—he didn't sit or smoke in his mother's presence without her permission and he didn't enter her room unless she invited him. Bikila lived with his wife and his four children in a cottage on the outskirts of the capital. Shabby huts surrounded his house, which was set off by a seven-foot corrugated iron fence. Only the bright red uniform and the cottage were outward signs that he was a celebrity. But he drove a private car and was welcomed in Ethiopian society.

Abebe Bikila attempted a third straight Olympic marathon victory in 1968. However, a leg injury forced him to quit the race after ten miles.

A year later Bikila was seriously injured in an automobile accident near Addis Ababa. He was flown immediately to Stoke Mandeville Hospital in England for special treatment. Even Haile Selassie saw him there.

Though Bikila was paralyzed from the waist down, the emperor insisted that he should maintain his rank in the Imperial Guard, which had been upgraded to captain after Mexico City. Youngsters, fellow soldiers, and even the emperor himself visited the national hero's home.

Bikila's feet had been stilled, but he trained his arms and hands to handle a bow and arrow. He became a proficient archer and competed in the Wheelchair Olympics. He remained active until he died on October 25, 1973. An estimated 65,000 persons attended Bikila's funeral.

front. With eight yards between him and Germany's big Hans Grodotzki, the frail New Zealander took the tape and collapsed. Tough little Kazimierz Zimny (Poland), who had set the opening pace, came in third.

The Southern Hemisphere had still more good news four days later. At the head of a group of six runners, every one of whom bettered the Olympic record, Australia's Herb Elliott whirled home in 3 minutes, 35.6 seconds, setting a new world record for the 1,500 meters. He had spent more than half the race in fourth place. Then, on a prearranged signal from his coach, the 22-year-old took off, covering the final 400 meters in 55.6 seconds. Michel Jazy (France) was 2.8 seconds behind him, and Hungary's István Rózsavölgyi 3.6 seconds.

For the fourth time in succession, the running of the 10,000-meter race saw the Olympic record broken. Zátopek did it in London and Helsinki, Kuts did it in Melbourne, and in Rome another Soviet, Pyotr Bolotnikov, chopped 23.4 seconds off the record. The silver (Hans Grodotzki of Germany), bronze (David Power of Australia), and fourth place runners also bettered the former record.

Lee Calhoun led Willie May and Hayes Jones to an American sweep in the 110-meter high hurdles, with the winner and runner-up caught in the identical time of 13.8 seconds. Glenn Davis defended his 400-meter hurdles title with an Olympic record 49.3 seconds. He led Clifton Cushman and Richard Howard in a second successive American sweep. Jack Yerman, Earl Young, Glenn Davis, and Otis Davis combined to set a world record of 3 minutes, 2.2 seconds in the 1,600-meter relay. The German team was second and the Antillean third.

It was a different tale for the Americans in "their" 400-meter relay, however. From 1920 on it had been won by a U.S. team. No one expected a change, least of all Ray Norton. Once again, however, his confidence was presumptuous. In taking the baton from Frank Budd, Norton was outside the legal passing zone. The American team finished in world record time, only to be disqualified. The medals went to the German, Soviet, and British teams.

For the first time a Polish athlete placed in the steeplechase. Zdzislaw Krzyszkowiak shaved the old Olympic record by seven seconds, beating Soviet Nikolay Sokolov and Semyon Rshischtschin (who had placed fifth in 1956).

A Soviet walker, Vladimir Golubnitschy, kept the gold for the 20-kilometer walk in his nation's hands, but the sweep of 1956 couldn't be repeated. Australian Noel Freeman gave the victor only 9.2 seconds to spare, and Britain's Stanley Vickers, the bronze medalist, was 40 seconds behind Freeman.

Britain's Donald Thompson walked 50 kilometers in the Olympic record time of 4 hours, 25 minutes, 30 seconds. Both John Ljunggren (Sweden) and Abdon Pamich (Italy) bettered the old record, as well. They had been third and fourth, respectively, in Melbourne.

Misplaced confidence undid another American "sure thing." Nineteen-year-old John Thomas of Boston University held the world high jump record—7' 3¾". But in Rome, where he was sure he had "psyched" the Soviet jumpers into failure by his repeated practice jumps of seven feet, he could not exceed 7' 0¼". Robert Schavlakadze, 28, and Valery Brumel, 18, of the Soviet Union, both jumped an Olympic record 7' 1". Thomas had bronze where he expected gold. Charles Dumas, the defender, placed sixth.

Australia's Herb Elliott turned on the speed near the end of the 1,500 meters, establishing a world record.

Donald Bragg of the U.S. Army, called Tarzan because he yearned to play the movie part, dueled with his teammate, Ronald Morris, for the pole vault honors. Finally, with the bar at 15′ 5⅛″, Morris failed to clear, and Bragg took the gold with an Olympic record almost six inches higher than Bob Richards had set in Melbourne.

Roman heat in no way hurt Ralph Boston's effort. He covered an Olympic record 26′ 7¾″ in his winning long jump, one-half inch better than his American teammate, Irvin Roberson. Soviet Igor Ter-Ovanesyan could not exceed 26′ 4½″ and took third place. Boston's record shattered the one Jesse Owens achieved in 1936, and without the following wind that had prevented Owens' mark from being official.

Józef Schmidt (Poland) bettered the Olympic record by 1′ 6″ in the triple jump, and both runners-up—Soviets Vladimir Goryayev and Vitold Kreyer—beat the old record, as well.

The shot put was an American sweep, which had happened before, and Parry O'Brien and William Nieder were participants, which also had happened before. But this time the rivalry between them was bitter, and O'Brien did not end with the gold. Nieder got that with a toss of 64′ 6¾″ to O'Brien's 62′ 8¼″. Dallas Long, with 62′ 4¼″, was the bronze medalist.

Al Oerter did again in Rome what he had done in Melbourne: he threw the discus farther than the man favored to win, set a new Olympic record, and led an American sweep of the event. Like Oerter, Richard Babka (silver) and Richard Cochran bettered the 1956 winning distance.

The same could not be said for Harold Connolly or his wife, the former Olga Fikotová of Czechoslovakia. After their gold medal victories and widely publicized romance in the 1956 Games, both represented the United States in the Rome Olympics. Harold Con-

Pole vaulter Donald Bragg of Pennsville, New Jersey, took the gold and set an Olympic record. Photo right: Irvin Roberson (left) of Fort Lee, Virginia, Ralph Boston of Laurel, Mississippi, and Igor Ter-Ovanesyan of the Soviet Union were the silver, gold, and bronze medalists in the long jump.

With fine performances in the throwing events, especially the shot put, decathlete Rafer Johnson was able to edge Taiwan's Chuan-Kwang Yang. Shotputter Bill Nieder keenly observed his competition. In spite of a heavily bandaged knee, the American finished in the top spot.

nolly, the world record holder and defending champion in the hammer throw, finished eighth. The gold medal went to Russia's Vasily Rudenkov, with an Olympic record of 220′ 1¾″, a remarkable 12′ 10¼″ farther than the Melbourne record. Olga Connolly, who had established an Olympic record in the discus four years earlier, saw her mark broken by Nina Ponomaryeva (USSR), whose 1952 record *she* had broken. Olga finished seventh in Rome.

Viktor Tsybulenko, in his third Olympics, reached gold rank with his javelin throw of 277′ 8″. He had climbed from fourth in 1952 to third in 1956.

In training, back at the University of California at Los Angeles, the two principal contestants for the decathlon were close friends. In Rome they were head-and-head rivals, Rafer Johnson for the USA and Chuan-Kwang Yang for Taiwan. Yang, 15 pounds lighter, had bested Johnson in six running and jumping events, but Johnson's lead in three throwing phases had been so superior he had a tiny lead when they came to the final, deciding 1,500-meter race. To win, Yang needed a 10-second win and he took the lead, in high hopes. But Johnson dogged his heels unshakably, and crossed the finish line only 1.2 seconds after Yang. It was Johnson, Yang, and Vassily Kuznyetsov (USSR), in that order. Johnson's total performance wrote a new Olympic record. Yang's was only 58 points lower.

The women's track and field program gave the spectators one of the never-to-be-forgotten experiences: multiple successes by an athlete of rare elegance whose childhood years promised the exact opposite. Wilma Rudolph, who was less than five pounds at birth, in early childhood had double pneumonia and scarlet fever, and survived, but as an invalid with a crippled leg. With unremitting family care she got back the use of her leg, learned basics of running

in high school, and came under the coaching of Ed Temple at Tennessee State University. He called her "Skeeter," but the European correspondents wrote about "La Gazelle." They did not exaggerate. She won the 100-meter dash in 11 seconds, a world record that was not allowed because of strong following wind. Three days later she took the 200 meters in 24 seconds, and then anchored the winning 400-meter relay team. Three times before the same girl had won both dashes, but it was the first time an American did it *and* took another gold medal besides.

The 800-meter run, on the program once before (1928), was revived in Rome, an opportunity for Lyudmila Schevtsova (USSR) to set a new world record time of 2 minutes, 4.3 seconds. Her teammate, Irina Press, took the 80-meter hurdles, ahead of Carol Quinton (Great Britain) and Germany's Gisela Birkemeyer-Köhler, the 1956 silver medalist.

An Olympic record was set in the high jump by Rumanian Iolanda Balas, who cleared 6' 0¾". She had placed fifth in Melbourne.

Soviet athletes won the remaining events. Irina's sister, Tamara Press, put the shot an Olympic record 56' 10", Vyera Krepkina jumped an Olympic record length of 20' 10¾", and Elvira Ozolina tossed the javelin an Olympic record distance of 183' 8".

Soviet weightlifters were victors in five of the seven classes, and every one wrote a new world record in achieving his gold. Featherweights Yevgeny Minayev and Isaac Berger (USA) reversed their 1956 positions. Middle heavyweight Arkady Vorobyov successfully defended his 1956 standing, as did American bantamweight Charles Vinci, who also set a new world record. Viktor Buschuyev took the lightweight honors, Aleksandr Kurynov the middleweight, and Poland's Ireneusz Palinski the light heavyweight.

Rumania and Bulgaria each had a victorious Greco-Roman wrestler; the Soviet Union and Turkey each had three. Turks triumphed in half of the freestyle contests, as well (light fly-, feather-, middle-,

Wilma Rudolph, victor in the 100- and 200-meter races, was a delightful surprise of the 1960 Rome Games. Two Soviet sisters, Irina and Tamara Press, were dominant in other of the women's track and field events. Irina captured the 80-meter hurdles, breaking the Olympic record twice in the semifinals.

Rafer Johnson

The whole decathlon is ridiculous, but the 1,500 meters is insanity.

—RAFER JOHNSON

Rome's Olympic Stadium was awash in artificial light on the evening of September 6, 1960, as Rafer Johnson and his close friend and rival, Chuan-Kwang Yang (C.K. Yang) of Taiwan, prepared for the final of the decathlon.

Rafer Johnson was 6' 3" and weighed 200 pounds, with a sharply shaped physique that triangulated from a 35" waist to a 46" chest. Johnson dreaded the 1,500-meter run, considered by many as the most agonizing phase of the ten-event competition.

In the most dramatic head-to-head 1,500 in Olympic decathlon history, Johnson clocked 4 minutes, 49.7 seconds—1.2 seconds slower than Yang. And in running that little bit slower, Johnson won the Olympic championship. He set an Olympic record of 8,392 points, beating Yang by 58. Vassily Kuznyetsov (USSR) won his second straight bronze medal.

Rafer Johnson was born in Hillsboro, Texas, on August 18, 1935. When Rafer was 10, the Johnson family moved from Texas to Kingsburg, California. For a time, home was a railroad boxcar near a cannery. Rafer Johnson was an all-around athlete at Kingsburg High School. He averaged nine yards a carry as a football halfback, 17 points a game in basketball, and hit over .400 in baseball. He was even better in track and field.

During Rafer's junior year in 1952, his coach, Murl Dodson, drove the 16-year-old 25 miles to Tulare, California, to watch Bob Mathias, the 1948 and 1952 Olympic decathlon champion, perform. Johnson was impressed. "On the way back, it struck me," Johnson said. "I could have beaten most of the guys in the meet. That's when I decided to be a decathlon man."

After Rafer was graduated from Kingsburg High School he enrolled at UCLA. He competed in his first decathlon in 1954. After winning a gold medal at the 1955 Pan-American Games he became the gold medal favorite for the 1956 Melbourne Olympics. However, when his event took place he had an injured knee and a ripped stomach muscle, and finished second to teammate Milt Campbell.

Between Melbourne and Rome, Johnson, Kuznyetsov, and Yang rewrote the record book for the decathlon. The Soviet set a world mark in May 1958. Several months later, Johnson regained the world record, only to have an automobile accident sideline him for the 1959 season. Kuznyetsov recaptured the world record that year.

When Rafer returned to the practice field at UCLA in 1960, he worked out daily with Yang, a schoolmate. The rivalry sharpened their skills as the Summer Olympics approached. On July 8–9, 1960, in Eugene, Oregon, both Johnson and Yang eclipsed the world mark held by Kuznyetsov. In Rome, Yang won four of the first five Olympic decathlon events, yet trailed Johnson by 55 points. Johnson's superiority in the shot put was responsible for his lead. With only the 1,500 remaining, Yang had outscored Johnson in all six of the running and jumping events. Johnson had dominated the three throwing events and led by 67 points.

Johnson's margin represented a 10-second advantage as the final event started. If Yang beat Johnson by more than 10 seconds in the 1,500, he would become the Olympic champion; if not, the American would become the gold medalist. Rafer's strategy was to stay close to his rival.

Yang lunged across the finish line in 4 minutes, 48.5 seconds. Johnson crossed 1.2 seconds later. The scoreboard told the story—Johnson had won by just 58 points. Both athletes bettered the Olympic record. Yang collapsed into the arms of his Taiwanese coach. "I beat Johnson in seven events, yet lost to him," Yang said in the dressing room. "I had to get far in front of him in our last race to win, and I tried, but I couldn't do it."

After receiving the 1960 Sullivan Award as the nation's outstanding amateur athlete, Rafer Johnson retired from competitive sports. He subsequently served as a sports commentator and appeared in several motion pictures. Johnson was active in the 1968 presidential campaign of Sen. Robert F. Kennedy. He was also a member of the President's Commission on Olympic Sports (1975–77).

and light heavy-weight), but the Soviets were shut out. Three Oklahomans made the best American showing in 28 years: Terrence McCann got the bantamweight gold, Douglas Blubaugh the welterweight, and Shelby Wilson the lightweight. Wilfried Dietrich (Germany) was heavyweight champion.

Only once before, in 1912, were no French fencers in the honors lists. Soviet fencers took the men's individual and team foils events, and the women's team foils, which was a new addition to the Games. Germany's Heidi Schmid, winner of the individual foil, was a new face, but the men's épée and sabre, individual and team, brought back old acquaintances. Giuseppe Delfino (Italy), second in 1956 épée, won in 1960. His winning team included veteran Edoardo Mangiarotti, back for his fifth and last Games. Rudolf Kárpáti succeeded in keeping his 1956 winning position and kept the Hungarian hold on the event for the eighth time. The Hungarian sabre team followed suit, making it seven victories in a row. Albert Axelrod, who won a bronze with the foil, was only the fourth American to place in fencing.

Hungarians Ferenc Németh and Imre Nagy were 1-2 in the modern pentathlon, with Robert Beck (USA) in third position.

It would be a long time before spectators at the 1960 Rome Olympics would forget America's powerhouse, gold-medal-winning basketball team. The United States, which never had lost an Olympic basketball game, protected that record with a string of eight straight one-sided victories. The silver-medal-winning Russians came closest

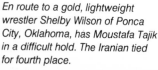

En route to a gold, lightweight wrestler Shelby Wilson of Ponca City, Oklahoma, has Moustafa Tajik in a difficult hold. The Iranian tied for fourth place.

Germany's Armin Hary (center) extended congratulations to the 100-meter runners-up, David Sime (USA) and Britain's Peter Radford, right. Hary and Sime clocked identical times; Radford was a second behind. Not only the rebounding but also the scoring of Ohio State's Jerry Lucas (11) helped the United States remain undefeated in basketball. Purdue's Terry Dischinger (6) was also a member of the strong U.S. team.

to defeating the star-studded American squad, and they were beaten by 24 points, 81–57. The American team, coached by Pete Newell, scored a total of 815 points in its eight games and had only 476 scored against it.

Oscar Robertson and Jerry Lucas tied for scoring honors with a tournament average of 17 points. Other members of the winning team were Jerry West, Terry Dischinger, Walt Bellamy, Bob Boozer, Darrall Imhoff, Jay Arnette, Allen Kelley, Lester Lane, Adrian Smith, and Burdette Haldorson. Haldorson was the only returning member of the 1956 champions.

The Roman Games were happily free of political stress, but not of sadness. The August heat wave was fierce on the twenty-sixth, the day scheduled for both the 100-kilometer team time and the 1,000-meter time cycling trials. Seven miles from the finish of the 100 kilometer, two Danish riders collapsed. Shortly afterward, one of them, 23-year-old Knut Jensen, died in a hospital from apparent sunstroke. Italian police later attributed his death to an overdose of Ronicol, a blood circulation stimulant which had been administered under doctor's orders to four riders by the trainer of Denmark's cycling team.

The other Danish cyclists withdrew from the remainder of the cycling program following Jensen's death. Italy won the event, which was new in 1960.

On the same day in the 1,000-meter time trial, Sante Gaiardoni (Italy) achieved a world record, the heat notwithstanding. The next day he won the 1,000-meter sprint. Italian teams took the 2,000-meter tandem and the 4,000-meter team pursuit. Soviet cyclist Viktor Kapitonov won the gold for the individual road race.

Wilma Rudolph

I'm just naturally lazy. . . . I could get much better times if I wasn't so lazy. . . . After I'm underway, I don't have much trouble.

—WILMA RUDOLPH

Blanche Rudolph, a domestic, and her husband, Ed, a retired porter, raised 19 children in a red-frame cottage in Clarksville, Tennessee. One of the youngest, Wilma, could not walk without braces until she was 11. At 16, she ran to an Olympic bronze medal as a member of America's 400-meter relay team. Four years later in the Rome Olympics Wilma became the first American woman to win a sprint double. She also anchored the winning American 400-meter relay team. She is the only woman from the United States to win three gold medals in Olympic track and field.

Wilma was born on June 23, 1940, in St. Bethlehem, Tennessee; she weighed only 4½ pounds. She was stricken with scarlet fever and double pneumonia when she was four. Blanche Rudolph was told that daily therapeutic massage might restore the use of Wilma's paralyzed leg. For the next two years, the Rudolph family took turns massaging the little girl's leg. Weekly, Mrs. Rudolph and Wilma rode a bus to Nashville where the youngster received heat and water therapy. It was a 90-mile round trip. Wilma was confined to a chair or bed for two years.

When Wilma was eight, she could walk with the aid of a leg brace. Soon after, she was fitted with a special high-top shoe for the brace, and was able to attend school. After classes, Wilma could usually be found shooting a basketball at the peach basket her brother, Wesley, had mounted in the backyard. By age 11, Wilma no longer needed the brace and, at 13, she entered Clarksville High School and made the basketball team. She was all-state at 15, averaging 32.1 points per game.

Wilma's athletic excellence prompted high school officials to establish a track team. She soon was the sensation of the state high school meet, winning the girls' 50-, 75-, and 100-yard dashes. Ed Temple, women's track coach at Tennessee A&I State University, was impressed but not surprised.

Wilma's mother was at the state meet, urging her on. "You're the first one in my house that ever had a chance to go to college," her mother said. "If running's going to do that, I want you to set your mind to be the best."

After less than a year of high school competition, Wilma ran the third leg for the United States team that placed third in the 400-meter relay in the 1956 Olympics. Following the Olympics, Wilma went to Tennessee A&I as Ed Temple had planned.

In the national AAU championships on July 9, 1960, she set a world record of 22.9 seconds for the 200 meters, lowering the mark by three tenths of a second. She won the 100 and 200 and anchored the winning Tennessee A&I relay team.

Wilma Rudolph did the 100 meters in the Rome Olympics in 11.0 seconds to win the gold medal. However, the time was not accepted as a world mark because it was wind-assisted.

The 200 meters was expected to be more difficult because of the presence of Germany's Jutta Heine. Wilma bettered the Olympic record in a heat with a time of 23.2 seconds and then raced to a second gold medal with a time of 24.0 against a strong wind in the final. Wilma's double ended Australia's eight-year reign in the sprints.

The American women's 400-meter relay team was composed of Wilma and three Tennessee A&I teammates—Martha Hudson, Lucinda Williams, and Barbara Jones. They set a world record of 44.4 seconds in a heat. Hudson, Williams, and Jones opened up a two-yard lead in the final. But it was quickly lost because of a poor baton pass between Jones and Rudolph. Heine, the German anchor, raced into the lead. It didn't take long for the long-striding Wilma to outrun her and finish three yards in front in the Olympic record-equaling time of 44.5 seconds.

At Rome, Wilma was America's goodwill ambassador, without portfolio and without equal.

"She's done more for her country than the United States could pay her for," said Ed Temple. After touring Europe, Wilma returned to Clarksville. Every school and every business in her hometown shut down in celebration of "Welcome Wilma Day."

She was named The Associated Press Female Athlete of the Year in 1960 and 1961 and the Sullivan Award winner in 1961.

For three Olympics in a row a Yugoslav soccer team had reached silver rank. In 1960 that was the Danes' position: the Yugoslavs had the gold. Runners-up were the bronze Hungarian and the fourth-ranking Italian teams.

In field hockey there was another change at the top. After six times in first place the team fielded by India was beaten by a Pakistani team, half of whom had taken second rank in 1956.

Of the two golds earned by Soviet marksmen, Aleksey Guscht-schin's was for an Olympic record in the free pistol event. Austrian (Hubert Hammerer—free rifle), German (Peter Kohnke—prone rifle), American (William McMillan—rapid-fire pistol), and Rumanian (Ion Dumitrescu—clay pigeon) contestants each earned golds.

Australian equestrians took both individual and team 3-day events and the individual dressage gold went to a Soviet rider. Individual jumping was an Italian success story, and team jumping gave German Hans-Günter Winkler his third gold medal for horsemanship.

For the third consecutive time Gert Fredriksson (Sweden) took the gold for the 1,000-meter kayak singles event. In Rome, his rival, Erik Hansen, displaced him, but there was another gold in store when Fredriksson took part in the kayak doubles. Hungary took the Canadian singles and the Soviet Union the doubles. For the first time a 2,000-meter kayak relay was run, which German boatmen won. Women had been competing in single kayaks—in Rome, Antonina Seredina (USSR) was the victor—but kayak doubles was a new event, won by a Soviet team which included Seredina.

Following Olympic record-breaking time in the 400-meter freestyle, Chris Von Saltza, the star of the American swim team in 1960, was embraced by Holland's Catharina Lagerberg, the bronze medalist.

The United States' string of successes in the eight-oared rowing competition was terminated when Germany took the gold medal, beating Canada and Czechoslovakia in that order. The Americans placed fifth. German oarsmen were equally proficient in the coxed pairs and fours events. The United States rowers won the coxless fours, the coxless pairs was taken by Soviet oarsmen, and the double sculls by Czech. Vyatscheslav Ivanov (USSR) again won the single sculls. Crown Prince Constantine of Greece skippered the winning yacht in the Dragon-class yachting competition. The 20-year-old prince had only six months' experience in the Dragon class when he entered the event.

America's J. David Gillanders and Mike Troy captured the bronze and gold medals, respectively, in the 200-meter butterfly, an event on the program for the second time.

America's Carolyn Schuler (right) and Janice Andrew of Australia were first and third in the 100-meter butterfly. The Californian lowered the Olympic record to 1:09.5.

For the fourth time Paul Elvström (Denmark) won the dinghy event. Star boating was a Soviet triumph, the first time that nation's sailors had placed. The new Flying Dutchman class was won by Norwegians and the 5.5-meter event by Americans.

Soviet gymnasts, men and women, outshone everyone else. Boris Schakhlin alone took gold honors for individual combined exercises, parallel bars, long horse vault, and pommeled horse events. He had a silver in team combined exercise and in rings, and a bronze in horizontal bar. Albert Azaryan again won the rings contest. Japan's Nobuyuki Aihara repeated his 1956 gold-winning performance of floor exercises and his teammate, Takashi Ono, in the last of his three Olympics, won the horizontal bar competition. Japan took the team combined exercise gold.

In the women's events Soviet gymnasts won every event except the balance beam, which went to Czechoslovakia. Larissa Latynina garnered the gold (again) for individual combined exercises, and for floor exercises and team combined exercises, and silvers for asymmetrical bars and balance beam.

American males regained some of the swimming and diving prestige lost in Australia. Winners of only two gold medals in Melbourne, they won six in Rome plus four silver and three bronze as every Olympic and three world records were smashed. The United States accounted for all three world marks.

Mike Troy, a 17-year-old, lowered his own global standard in the 200-meter butterfly with a time of 2 minutes, 12.8 seconds. Jeff Farrell, who underwent an emergency appendectomy only six days before qualifying for the American team, anchored the winning

800-meter freestyle relay and 400-meter medley relay teams to world records of 8:10.2 and 4:05.4, respectively. The 400 meters was a new event. The United States won the 800 meters by 3 seconds over Japan and the medley by 6.6 seconds from runner-up Australia.

The other American winners were William Mulliken in the 200-meter breaststroke, Gary Tobian in the springboard diving, and Robert Webster in highboard diving. Tobian was the runner-up in the highboard for the second straight time.

The 1,500-meter freestyle saw a 1-2 Australian finish, with Jon Konrads defeating defending champion Murray Rose. George Breen of the United States was the bronze medalist for the second time in a row.

Rose took the 400-meter freestyle as Konrads settled for third behind Japan's Tsuyoshi Yamanaka, who had finished second in Melbourne. Dave Thiele, another Australian, successfully defended his 100-meter backstroke championship.

The 100-meter freestyle event was a close race hotly disputed by John Devitt (Australia) and Lance Larson (U.S.). Both were credited with the same Olympic record time of 55.2 seconds. However, there was a disagreement about the order of finish between first and second place judges. After a long delay, Devitt was declared champion, although electronic devices timed Larson one tenth of a second faster than his Australian rival. Two American protests were rejected by the swimming jury and the International Swimming Federation (FINA). The chief judge eventually decided the issue by naming Devitt the winner.

Chris Von Saltza, with three gold medals and one silver for her reward, led American women to their best showing in the water since 1932. As in the men's competition, every Olympic mark was broken. Three world records were established, two by the United States, and four Olympic records. Americans won five gold and three silver medals overall.

The 16-year-old Von Saltza won the 400-meter freestyle and anchored the world record-setting United States 400-meter freestyle and 400-meter medley relay teams. She placed second in the 100-meter freestyle won by defending champion Dawn Fraser, who gave Australia its only gold medal. Fraser, the first woman to repeat as the 100-meter champion, also captured a pair of silver medals in the relays.

The individual 100-meter backstroke event went to Lynn Burke, who set a world record for the distance on the leadoff leg for the United States in the medley relay. Another world record was established by Britain's Anita Lonsbrough in the 200-meter breaststroke. Carolyn Schuler of the United States took the 100-meter butterfly.

Ingrid Kramer swept the diving gold medals, with America's Paula Jean Pope-Myers winning the silver medal in both events.

The host Italians were victorious in water polo, finishing ahead of the Soviet Union and third-place Hungary.

The Rome Olympics drew a record 5,348 athletes from 83 nations. The Games produced 17 world and 43 Olympic marks. More countries won medals than ever before.

Avery Brundage wrote afterward: "When the Olympic flame, lit by the sun's rays at Olympia, Greece, finally flickered out in Rome there was general agreement that the 1960 Olympic Games—both winter and summer—had been the finest in history."

FINAL MEDAL STANDINGS			
Nation	G	S	B
Soviet Union	43	29	31
United States	34	21	16
Italy	13	10	13
Germany	12	19	11
Australia	8	8	6
Turkey	7	2	–
Hungary	6	8	7
Japan	4	7	7
Poland	4	6	11
Czechoslovakia	3	2	3
Rumania	3	1	6
Great Britain	2	6	12
Denmark	2	3	1
New Zealand	2	–	1
Bulgaria	1	3	3
Sweden	1	2	3
Finland	1	1	3
Austria	1	1	–
Yugoslavia	1	1	–
Pakistan	1	–	1
Ethiopia	1	–	–
Greece	1	–	–
Norway	1	–	–
Switzerland	–	3	3
France	–	2	3
Belgium	–	2	2
Iran	–	1	3
South Africa	–	1	2
The Netherlands	–	1	2
Argentina	–	1	1
United Arab Republic	–	1	1
Canada	–	1	–
Ghana	–	1	–
India	–	1	–
Morocco	–	1	–
Portugal	–	1	–
Singapore	–	1	–
Taiwan	–	1	–
Brazil	–	–	2
Jamaica	–	–	2
Iraq	–	–	1
Mexico	–	–	1
Spain	–	–	1
Venezuela	–	–	1

1964

Winter Games
Innsbruck, Austria

A record 1,332 athletes from 36 nations participated in the ceremonies opening the Games of the IX Winter Olympics, held in Innsbruck, Austria, January 29 through February 9. For the first time, the ceremony was not held in an ice rink. The bowl of the Berg Isel ski jump enabled more than 60,000 persons to view the festivities.

A lack of snow threatened Alpine and Nordic events. There was no snowfall for almost a month before the Games and 3,000 Austrian soldiers hauled 40,000 cubic meters of snow to the ski courses. Another 20,000 cubic meters were hand carried to the Olympic sites and set aside for emergencies. Six snowmaking machines, imported from the United States, worked day and night on the bobsled and luge runs. Except for an occasional flurry there was no snow on the streets of Innsbruck as the Tyrolean city experienced its mildest first week of February in 58 years.

Death cast its shadow over the Games. Kazimierz Kay-Skrzypeski, a 50-year-old British luge athlete, who fled his Polish homeland after the Nazi occupation in 1940, died in a crash on a practice run less than a week before the Games began. Three days later, Ross Milne, a 19-year-old Australian skier, died after he smashed into a tree during a practice downhill run. A black mourning ribbon was placed on the five-ring Olympic flag in memory of the deceased athletes. Shortly after the Games two skiers, Barbi Henneberger (Germany) and Wallace "Bud" Werner (USA) were killed in a Swiss avalanche while making a motion picture.

Once the competition began, Innsbruck became a donnybrook. Jackbooted Austrian police arrested three American athletes for driving a car the wrong way down a one-way street. Austrian troopers were also accused of roughing up women spectators and the French ski coach, and of arresting newsmen merely because they asked questions.

Mongolia and India competed in the Winter Games for the first time. India was represented by one athlete, Gerry Bujakowski, who was injured and did not finish in the men's downhill ski race. North and South Korea also appeared in the Winter Games for the initial time, with the North sharing a silver medal. Prince Karim, the Aga Khan, skied for Iran. He placed 53rd among the 80 finishers in the giant slalom and was 59th among the 77 who completed the men's downhill.

Luge, a new entry on the Olympic schedule, encompassed men's and women's singles competition and a men's doubles event. Ski jumping was separated into two events—70 meters (229′ 8″) and 90 meters (295′ 3¼″). A women's 5-kilometer cross-country ski race also appeared on the program for the first time. Bobsledding returned to the program after an absence of four years. The IX Winter Olympics were the occasion of the first official use of computers as judging aids.

The Soviet Union won the most gold medals. Lidia Skoblikova, a 24-year-old Siberian school teacher, in four consecutive days won all four women's speed skating events. Her career total of six, including two at Squaw Valley, made her the most bemedaled athlete to appear in the Winter Games. Skoblikova's sweep in 1964 had made her the first athlete to win four individual gold medals in a single Olympics—Winter or Summer. Shortly after her victories she was notified by Soviet Premier Nikita Khrushchev of her appointment to full membership in the Communist Party.

Skoblikova led a Soviet sweep in the 500 meters with an Olympic record time of 45 seconds flat, almost a full second under the record

A lack of snow posed a serious problem for the organizers of the 1964 Winter Games. Austrian soldiers were employed to carry imported snow in pack baskets to the barren ski slopes.

set in 1960 by Germany's Helga Haase, who finished eighth in Innsbruck. Two Soviets, Irina Jegorowa and Tatyana Sidorova, placed second and third.

Skoblikova was timed in 2 minutes, 22.6 seconds in the 1,500 meters, lowering her own Olympic mark by 2.6 seconds. Finland's Kaija Mustonen and the USSR's Berta Kolokolzewa trailed in that order. Lidia's victory in the 1,000 meters, her third gold, produced a third Olympic record. The Soviet star was clocked in 1:33.2, nine tenths of a second faster than Klara Guseva's 1960 time. Jegorowa and Mustonen were the silver and bronze medalists.

The women's speed skating concluded on February 2 on slushy ice that left puddles on the course. Skoblikova completed her sweep in the 3,000 but skating conditions prevented her from establishing a fourth Olympic record of the Games. Her time of 5:14.9 was six tenths of a second slower than the mark she posted in 1960. However, she skated 3.6 seconds faster than teammate Valentina Stenina and North Korea's Pil Hwa Han, who tied for the silver medal. No bronze medal was awarded.

Richard "Terry" McDermott, a 23-year-old barber, was the only American gold medal winner in the 1964 Winter Olympics. He captured the men's 500-meter speed skating event, defeating Yevgeni Grishin, the USSR's two-time defending champion. McDermott clocked an Olympic record of 40.1 seconds, one tenth of a second faster than the mark set by Grishin in 1956 and tied by him in 1960. There was a three-way tie for second among Grishin, his countryman Vladimir Orlov, and Norway's Alv Gjestvang. The trio clocked 40.6.

McDermott had finished seventh in the 500 meters in Squaw Valley. Determined to improve, he took afternoons off from his position as an apprentice barber to run and to work with weights. In 1962 he also went to a hypnotist, who put him to sleep and asked him what it would take to win an Olympic gold medal. After McDermott described his make-believe winning race, the hypnotist told him, "For the next two years, you can skate that race every day, and it will be in your subconscious so deep that when you skate in a big race, anywhere, it will be automatic."

That is precisely what happened on a pair of borrowed skates on the morning of February 4, 1964. McDermott obtained the skates from his coach, Leo Freisinger, after discovering they had longer tips than his own.

Men's speed skating competition in 1964 produced champions from four different countries. Ants Antson (USSR) was an upset winner in the 1,500 meters, 30-year-old Knut Johannesen led a Norwegian sweep in the 5,000, and Jonny Nilsson of Sweden, the world record holder, won the 10,000. He was the only competitor to better 16 minutes.

Johannesen, the 10,000-meter champion in 1960, set an Olympic record of 7 minutes, 38.4 seconds in leading teammates Per Ivar Moe and Fred Anton Maier across the 5,000-meter finish line. Johannesen took 10.3 seconds off the former mark. Maier, who would win the event four years later, and Johannesen placed 2–3 behind Nilsson in the 10,000.

Cornelis "Kees" Verkerk of The Netherlands and Villey Haugen of Norway were the silver and bronze medalists in the 1,500 meters.

American chances in Olympic figure skating had been adversely affected by an air disaster. On February 15, 1961, 72 persons aboard

An overflow crowd watched intently as speed skater Terry McDermott of Essexville, Michigan, became the lone American gold medalist. His victory was the more surprising because, as one correspondent put it, speed skating ranked on a par with cricket as a U. S. sport.

a plane bound for the world figure skating championships in Prague, Czechoslovakia, including 18 members of the U.S. figure skating team, were killed when the jetliner crashed at Berg, near Brussels, Belgium. Five of the skaters had participated in the 1960 Games at Squaw Valley. They were Laurence Owen in women's singles, and the pairs teams of Maribel Owen and Dudley Richards and Ila and Ray Hadley. Another victim was Maribel Vinson Owen, mother of Laurence and Maribel and the 1932 Olympic singles bronze medalist.

The United States won only one medal in figure skating in 1964. Scott Allen took the bronze in the men's singles and became the youngest athlete to capture a medal in the Winter Olympics. Three days before his 15th birthday, he was on the victory podium along with winner Manfred Schnelldorfer of Germany and second-place Alain Calmat of France.

The 20-year-old Schnelldorfer, a Munich architectural student, had placed eighth in Squaw Valley, where Calmat was sixth. Many spectators in Innsbruck screamed "foul" when the Frenchman was given unusually high marks for his free skating program, even though he fell twice and burst into tears after his routine was completed. Four years later, Dr. Calmat lit the Olympic caldron to open the Grenoble Games.

The women's title in 1964 went to 22-year-old Sjoukje Dijkstra of The Netherlands, the second-place finisher in Squaw Valley. She built an insurmountable lead in the compulsory figures to finish ahead of Austrian runner-up Regine Heitzer and bronze-winner Petra Burka of Canada. Queen Juliana of The Netherlands was among the spectators when Dijkstra won her country's first gold medal in any sport since the 1948 Summer Games which featured the track triumphs of Fanny Blankers-Koen.

The first gold medals to be awarded in Innsbruck went to 28-year-old Ludmilla Beloussova and 31-year-old Oleg Protopopov in the pairs figure skating competition. The husband and wife team, who repeated in 1968, upset the favored world-championship German tandem of Marika Kilius and Hans Juergen Bäumler. Debbie Wilkes and Guy Revell of Canada were awarded the bronze medal.

The Soviets' margin of victory was less than one point—104.4 to 103.6. The difference was the score awarded the Germans by Canadian judge Dr. Suzanne Morrow, a pairs bronze medalist in 1948. Dr. Morrow had placed the Germans third behind the Russians and the Canadian duo. German fans reacted violently. They booed so strongly that Morrow left rinkside in tears. There was a postscript to the pairs competition. More than a year after the Innsbruck Games Kilius and Bäumler had their silver medals taken away because it was discovered that they were professionals during the Olympic competition.

The Protopopovs, called "the most classical ice skating pair the world has known," were the first Soviets to achieve international superiority in figure skating. Ludmilla was inspired to pursue a skating career after viewing a Sonja Henie motion picture.

Britain's *World Sports Magazine* said, "The graceful calculated movements of the Protopopovs made their difficult overhead lifts look deceptively simple. Their best remembered gimmick always will be Ludmilla's daring ability to caress the ice with her blonde hair during their smoothly slow death spirals, with even her waist swinging only inches above the frozen surface."

Jimmy Heuga, a 20-year-old from Tahoe City, California, shared with Bill Kidd of Stowe, Vermont, the distinction of being the first American men to take medals in skiing. Heuga (below) captured the bronze in the slalom.

Billy Kidd and Jimmy Heuga became the first American men to win medals in Alpine skiing. Kidd took the silver and Heuga the bronze in the two-run slalom behind Austria's 26-year-old Josef "Pepi" Stiegler. Stiegler had the fastest first run and was eighth in the second, for a combined time of 2 minutes, 11.13 seconds. Kidd was sixth and second. He finished just 14/100ths of a second behind Stiegler! Buddy Werner, an American who missed the Squaw Valley Games because of a broken leg, placed eighth.

Stiegler won the slalom gold after he came close to being removed from the Austrian team. A few days before the Olympic competition began, Sepp Sulzberger, the Austrian coach, said Stiegler would have to race against Egon Zimmermann, eventual winner of the downhill, for a berth in the event. Stiegler agreed. He had the best time in the first heat but fell in the second. His performance did not merit a position on the team. However, other Austrian coaches threatened to quit unless "Pepi" was allowed to race in the slalom.

Stiegler also took a bronze medal in the giant slalom. François Bonlieu of France and Austria's Karl Schranz were 1–2 in the event. Bonlieu became the center of controversy when it was discovered that he had been using skis manufactured in the United States during the pre-Olympic Trials. Bonlieu switched to French-made skis for the Games, but it took his victory to make his countrymen forget his indiscretion.

A heavy, Soviet-styled fur coat and hat are the order of dress for gold medalist Claudia Boyarskikh. Called the "best woman skier of the mid-1960's," Miss Boyarskikh was victorious in the 5-kilometer (right) and 10-kilometer races and was a member of the winning relay team.

The runner-up to Zimmermann in the downhill was Leo Lacroix of France, with Wolfgang Bartels of Germany third. Zimmermann's margin of victory was 74/100ths of a second. Hidden in the downhill field was France's Jean Claude Killy, who finished 42nd. He also was disqualified in the first run of the slalom and finished fifth in the giant slalom.

A unique women's Alpine double was scored by the French sisters, Christine and Marielle Goitschel of Val d'Isère. Marielle, 18, was considered a better skier than her 19-year-old sister. However, Christine surprised skiing enthusiasts by winning the gold medal in the slalom, finishing almost a second in front of Marielle, with Jean Saubert of the United States the bronze medalist.

Marielle won the giant slalom; Christine and Saubert were second and third. Austria, led by Christl Haas, swept the downhill. Edith Zimmermann and Traudl Hecher placed second and third.

A 24-year-old Soviet physical education teacher, Claudia Boyarskikh, was the individual star of the women's Nordic competition. She won three gold medals. Her individual victories were in the 5- and 10-kilometer races. She also anchored the winning 15-kilometer relay team which finished ahead of Sweden and Finland.

Mirja Lehtonen (Finland) and Alevtina Koltschina (USSR) were the silver and bronze medalists in the 5 kilometers. Eudokia Mekschilo and Maria Gusakova finished behind Boyarskikh, to give the Soviet Union a sweep in the 10 kilometers.

The 1964 Olympic ski jumping competition was held at Berg Isel. Finland's Veikko Kankkonen and Norway's Toralf Engan were the stars. So close to built-up Innsbruck is the jump that a skier in mid-flight looks like a certain casualty.

Luge, a form of sled racing, made its Olympic debut in 1964. Luge is a French word meaning a low, stubby child's sled with two runners and no steering device. Although not particularly popular in the United States, luge racing, which originated in Switzerland in the 19th century, is a favorite sport in Europe. There are one- and two-man sleds; women compete only on single sleds. The artist shows how a single luge racer maintains a supine position by holding a cord. Some body English is achieved by the protruding feet as the sled careers down a chute made of artificial snow.

American women did not participate in the Nordic events.

Eero Mäntyranta, a 26-year-old Finnish customs officer, and Sweden's Sixten Jernberg were the big winners in the men's events. Jernberg won the 50 kilometers just hours before his 35th birthday. Sweden's Assar Rönnlund and Finland's Arto Tiainen followed across the finish line. Jernberg captured a second gold medal as a member of his country's victorious 40-kilometer relay team, and he was the bronze medalist behind winner Mäntyranta and runner-up Harald Grönningen of Norway in the 15-kilometer race.

Mäntyranta and Grönningen placed 1–2 in the 30-kilometer race, ahead of Igor Worontschichin (USSR). Mäntyranta anchored Finland to the silver medal in the relay, with the Soviets taking the bronze.

Mäntyranta and Grönningen closed out their Olympic victories four years later. Mäntyranta finished with 7 medals—3 gold, 2 silver, and 2 bronze. Grönningen totaled 5 medals—2 gold and 3 silver.

Tormod Knutsen of Norway captured the Nordic combined. Nikolai Kiselev of the Soviet Union was second, ahead of Germany's defending champion, Georg Thoma. It was Norway's seventh victory in the nine times the event was held.

Veikko Kankkonen of Finland and Norway's Toralf Engan placed 1–2 in the 70-meter ski jump and then reversed their order of finish in the 90 meters nine days later. Torgeir Brandtzäg of Norway was the bronze medalist in both events.

Veikko Hakulinen, the greatest Finnish cross-country skier of the 1950's, was unsuccessful in his bid to win a biathlon medal. He placed 15th, as Soviets Vladimir Melanin and Alexander Privalov finished 1–2. The bronze medal went to Olav Jordet of Norway.

Germans took all the men's luge singles medals. Thomas Koehler won the gold medal with a four-run clocking of 3 minutes, 26.77 seconds. Runner-up Klaus Bonsack was 27/100ths of a second behind him. Hans Plenk was the bronze medalist.

Austria finished 1–2 in the men's luge doubles, with Josef Feistmantl and Manfred Stengl aboard the winning two-seater. Italy was third.

Germany's Ortrun Enderlein and Ilse Geisler placed first and second in the women's luge. Helena Thurner of Austria was the bronze medalist.

The American hockey team won only two of seven games and tied for fifth after its gold medal victory in Squaw Valley. The USSR regained the championship, beating Canada, 3–2, while Sweden defeated Czechoslovakia, 8–3, both on the final day of the tournament. Had Canada won the last game, the Canadians and Soviets would have tied in points. Under Olympic rules the gold medal would have gone to the Canadian team because of its triumph over the Soviets.

Sweden, Czechoslovakia, and Canada tied with records of 5–2–0 behind the Soviets' 7–0–0. Sweden was awarded the silver medal and Czechoslovakia the bronze on the basis of goals for and goals against. En route to its gold medal, the USSR defeated the United States, 5–1, and then overwhelmed Germany. The beleaguered German goalie made an incredible 95 saves, yet his team lost, 10–0!

The Canadians almost lost their clergyman coach, Father David Bauer, when Sweden's Carl Oberg hit him with a hockey stick during a game won by Canada, 3–1. Canadian players attempted to retaliate, but were restrained by Father Bauer, a brother of former Boston Bruins' star, Bobby Bauer. Oberg was suspended for one game and the referee, who failed to give the Swede a misconduct penalty, received a two-game suspension.

Neither Canada nor Britain has a bobsled run. Yet Canada won the four-man race and Britain the two-man event. The Canadian victory was more surprising, inasmuch as it marked Canada's debut in Olympic bobsled competition. Stan Benham, the United States coach, called the Canadian triumph "the biggest upset in bobsled history." Vic Emery drove the winning four-man sled that carried Peter Kirby, Douglas Anakin, and John Emery. An Austrian sled was second, while Italians finished third and fourth. The bronze-medal sled was driven by Eugenio Monti.

FINAL MEDAL STANDINGS			
Nation	G	S	B
Soviet Union	11	8	6
Austria	4	5	3
Norway	3	6	6
Finland	3	4	3
France	3	4	–
Sweden	3	3	1
Germany	3	2	3
United States	1	1	4
The Netherlands	1	1	–
Canada	1	–	2
Great Britain	1	–	–
Italy	–	1	3
North Korea	–	1	–
Czechoslovakia	–	–	1

The two-man bobsled team of Anthony Nash (right) and Robin Dixon led Britain to its first Winter Olympic medal since 1952. After a bolt supporting the runners on the British sled broke, Italy's Eugenio Monti repaired it with a bolt he removed from his own bob. In 1965 Monti received the Pierre de Coubertin Fair Play Trophy.

1964

Summer Games

Tokyo, Japan

Tokyo was awarded the 1940 Summer Olympic Games to celebrate the 2,600th anniversary of the Japanese Empire. However, because of World War II, it wasn't until 1964 that the Japanese capital played host to the mammoth international sports festival.

It marked the first time that an Olympics was held in Asia and the Japanese made certain that the spectacle would be staged with all the splendor the Orient could provide. Emperor Hirohito opened the Games in a ceremony that was telecast

live via satellite to the United States. Because of the time difference, the telecast was received late at night, and most viewers actually saw reruns.

So precise were the Japanese in planning for the Games that they held five rehearsals of the opening ceremony, all designed to enhance television coverage. The final rehearsal was staged with the exact number of athletes who would march in the parade of nations.

The Japanese spent more on the Olympic Games than any other nation before them—$3 billion. In three years of preparatory construction they rebuilt central Tokyo; tripled the available hotel space; erected an eight-mile monorail, a 72,000-seat stadium, a new equestrian park, and a prize-winning swimming arena/gymnasium; and built miles of superhighways. The chairman of the committee planning for the Games, Dr. Ryotaro Azuma, said that Japan deliberately used the Games to thrust the nation into the front ranks of the industrial world. "Without the magic of the Olympic name we might not have gotten the investment we needed to rise as a world trade power. . . . It was a governmental policy to make the Olympics our announcement to the world that Japan was no longer a beaten nation," Azuma declared.

The smiling Japanese went out of their way to please the visitors. The entire nation seemed to have adopted the Games, and in even the most drenching rainstorms continued to fill the stadium seats to show their support.

A crowd of 80,000 spectators attended the October 10 opening ceremony. The final bearer of the Olympic torch was Yoshinori Sakai, who was born in Hiroshima during the destruction of that city by an atomic bomb in 1945.

More than 5,500 athletes from 94 nations participated in more events than ever before. World and Olympic marks were broken in almost every sport throughout the 13 days of competition.

The assault was led by America's Don Schollander, the first swimmer to win four gold medals in the same Games. Number one came in the 100-meter freestyle. Although he was not a sprinter, the powerful blond set an Olympic record of 53.4 seconds. Schollander's margin of victory over Britain's Robert McGregor was one tenth of a second.

Electrical timing prevented a major controversy in determining the bronze winner. Germany's Hans-Joachim Klein and America's Gary Ilman both recorded 54.0 seconds. But the bronze went to the German because timing devices showed that he was 1/1,000th of a second faster than the American.

Gold number two came in the 400-meter freestyle relay. His anchor leg following Steve Clark, Mike Austin, and Gary Ilman helped the United States to a world record of 3 minutes, 33.2 seconds. The Americans finished four seconds ahead of runner-up Germany, with Australia third.

Gold number three came when Schollander swam to a world record of 4:12.2 in the 400-meter freestyle, finishing 2.7 seconds ahead of Germany's Frank Wiegand and 2.9 seconds ahead of Allan Wood (Australia).

Schollander's fourth gold was earned in the 800-meter freestyle relay. He swam a 1:55.6 anchor leg, fastest for the American team, which set a world record of 7:52.1 and finished an astonishing 7.2 seconds ahead of runner-up Germany. Clark, Roy Saari, and Ilman were the other members of the world record quartet.

Clark's haul in Tokyo was three relay gold medals. He clocked 52.9 seconds, to equal the world record on the first leg of the 400-meter freestyle relay event. He was given a split of 52.4 on the anchor leg of the 400-meter medley relay team that established a world record of 3:58.4. He was preceded by H. Thompson Mann, Bill Craig, and Fred Schmidt. Clark got his third gold in the 800-meter relay.

United States swimmers captured two other events. Jed Graef led a sweep and set a world record of 2:10.3 in winning the 200-meter backstroke. Gary Dilley finished 2/10ths of a second back, with Robert Bennett the bronze medalist. Dick Roth, who complained of stomach pains, and Roy Saari placed 1-2 in the new 400-meter individual medley event. Roth's time of 4:45.4 was a world record. After the exciting race, the 17-year-old Roth had his appendix removed.

Australia won three swimming gold medals. Robert Windle clocked an Olympic record 17 minutes, 1.7 seconds in the 1,500 meters to give his country its third straight championship in the event. John Nelson (USA) and Allan Wood (Australia) were second and third.

Following the Olympic Trials at Astoria Pool in New York City, Don Schollander (right) of Santa Clara and Roy Saari of El Segundo, California, and John Nelson (left) of Pompano Beach, Florida, became members of the U.S. Olympic swim team. At Tokyo, Schollander became the first swimmer to win four gold medals in the same games, Saari took a gold and a silver and Nelson won a bronze.

Don Schollander

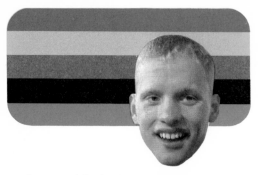

I am a social animal but prefer privacy to being a public figure. I won medals, but I don't want to become one myself.

—DON SCHOLLANDER

When he was 18 he became the first swimmer to win four gold medals in a single Olympics. He was voted The Associated Press Male Athlete of the Year and given the Sullivan Award. At 19 he was a member of the Swimming Hall of Fame and was designated by a group of American sportswriters as the world's greatest athlete. His credentials included 22 world records and 37 American marks.

The blond, 5' 11", 175-pounder was not only a talented athlete but also an intelligent and sensitive young man. At age 22, considered an athlete's prime, Donald Arthur Schollander retired from competitive swimming. He said that he could stand no more of the hypocrisy he found in sports. He was bitter and disillusioned with the direction the Olympic movement had taken. He was aghast at what passed for amateurism, and "the erosion in sports as they became the pawn of internal power struggles and of international power politics."

In his life story Schollander said, "The fault lies with nearly everyone—officials, national leaders, the athletes themselves who, too often, are concerned only with winning. I, too, have wanted to win. And I still have respect for excellence. I think athletes are less to blame than anyone else. . . . They are at least trying, and this is what the Olympics are all about."

Don Schollander was born April 30, 1946, in Charlotte, North Carolina. Martha, his mother, was also a superb swimmer and appeared in several *Tarzan* films with Johnny Weissmuller. Wendell, his father, was a high school all-state football player.

Don learned to swim in Lake Oswego, a suburb of Portland, Oregon. He was taught the basics of swimming at Portland's Aero Club. By the time he was 10 he owned a national age group backstroke record.

During his freshman year in high school he was faced with the choice of trying out for the football or swimming teams. His father suggested that Don try swimming—where he might achieve quicker success. Don made the varsity and swam against boys four years his senior. He went to the state finals as a freshman and won two events. As a sophomore, he was beating everyone throughout the state.

Don then left Lake Oswego and "went to Santa Clara, California, to become a professional amateur." There he swam for the Santa Clara Swim Club, coached by George Haines.

Schollander's first taste of world class competition came at 16. He didn't win, but his competitors included Australia's Olympic champion Murray Rose. During 1962 Don established several new swimming records. On July 27, 1963, he became the first swimmer to break two minutes in the 200-meter freestyle. He also won two national titles and continued to enter his name in the record books.

During 1964, Don had two things on his mind—the Olympics and his impending enrollment at Yale. He studied hard and also won three individual events at the AAU outdoor championships in July-August 1964.

At Tokyo, Don won the 100-meter freestyle by one tenth of a second over Britain's Robert McGregor. His time was 53.4 seconds, an Olympic record. He also won the 400-meter freestyle with a world record 4 minutes 12.2 seconds. Schollander completed his Olympic performance by anchoring the winning gold medal freestyle relay teams, both in world record time. Don's split in the 800 was 1:55.6. It was faster than any of the 31 other swimmers in the race.

When Schollander returned home he plunged into his studies at Yale. Although he broke many records in the years between 1964 and 1968, Don was unable to qualify for the right to defend his 100- and 400-meter freestyle championships. Instead, he earned a trip to Mexico City in his specialty, the 200-meter freestyle. The final brought Schollander together with Australia's Mike Wenden. But first Schollander and Wenden squared off on the anchor leg in the 800-meter freestyle relay. The United States won with Australia second. It was Schollander's final gold medal. Wenden won the 200-meter freestyle the following day. Schollander ended his Olympic career with the silver medal.

A second Australian gold medalist in Tokyo was Ian O'Brien. He won the 200-meter breaststroke with a world record of 2:27.8. Another world record fell to Australia's Kevin Berry in the 200-meter butterfly. He posted a time of 2:06.6 to beat Americans Carl Robie and Fred Schmidt.

United States male divers won five of the six medals in the two events. Ken Sitzberger, Frank Gorman, and Larry Andreasen placed 1-2-3 in the springboard. Bob Webster successfully defended his highboard title. Klaus Dibiasi of Italy finished second, ahead of America's Tom Gompf. Four years later, Dibiasi would win the highboard and place second behind Bernie Wrightson of the United States in the springboard.

American mermaids, led by 15-year-old Sharon Stouder, won six of eight swimming events. Stouder recorded the major upset in the pool by beating favored Ada Kok of The Netherlands in the 100-meter butterfly. She won by nine tenths of a second in the world record time of 1 minute, 4.7 seconds, eclipsing Kok's mark by four tenths of a second.

Stouder came close to another upset when she chased Australia's Dawn Fraser in the 100-meter freestyle. Fraser clocked her third consecutive victory in the event with an Olympic record of 59.5 seconds. Stouder, four tenths of a second behind the Australian, became only the second woman to dip below one minute in the event. Kathleen Ellis of the United States was the bronze medalist.

Stouder increased her haul to three gold medals and one silver in the relays, both won by the Americans by identical 3.1-second

Terri Lee Stickles, Virginia Duenkel, and Marilyn Ramenofsky face the scoreboard that shows not only an American sweep in the women's 400-meter freestyle swim but also a new Olympic record. The old record was bettered by the four first placers.

margins in world record times. The lineup for the winning 400-medley relay team, which defeated the runner-up Dutch quartet, was Cathy Ferguson, Cynthia Goyette, Stouder, and Ellis. Their time was 4:33.9. The Soviet team was 2.2 seconds behind the Dutch.

The victorious 400-meter freestyle team included Stouder, Donna de Varona, Lillian "Pokey" Watson, and Ellis; they clocked 4:03.8. The silver-medal Australian team was anchored by Fraser. The medal brought Fraser's total for three Olympics to a record eight for women swimmers—four gold and four silver.

There were American sweeps in the 400-meter freestyle and the new 400-meter individual medley. Virginia Duenkel, Marilyn Ramenofsky, and Terri Lee Stickles placed 1-2-3 in the freestyle, in which Duenkel set an Olympic mark of 4:43.3. De Varona finished ahead of Sharon Finneran and Martha Randall in the individual medley.

Cathy Ferguson captured the 100-meter backstroke in a world record 1 minute, 7.7 seconds. Christine Caron of France finished ahead of Duenkel in winning the silver medal.

Galina Prozumenschikova became the first Soviet, man or woman, to win a gold medal in swimming or diving. She captured the 200-meter breaststroke in the Olympic record time of 2:46.4. Fourteen-year-old Claudia Kolb (USA) was second and another Soviet, Svetlana Babanina, was third.

The springboard star of the Tokyo Games was Germany's Ingrid Engel-Krämer, the 1960 double gold medalist. She finished ahead of Americans Jeanne Collier and Mary Willard, and was the runner-up to Lesley Bush (USA) in the highboard competition.

Hungary, Yugoslavia, and the Soviet Union finished 1-2-3 in water polo. György Kárpáti and Dezsö Gyarmati of Hungary won their third gold medals in the competition.

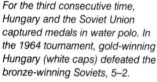

For the third consecutive time, Hungary and the Soviet Union captured medals in water polo. In the 1964 tournament, gold-winning Hungary (white caps) defeated the bronze-winning Soviets, 5–2.

Three other athletes, all British, captured three career water polo gold medals. They were George Wilkinson (1900, 1908, 1912); and Paul Radmilovic and Charles Smith (1908, 1912, 1920). Radmilovic also was a member of Britain's 1908 gold-medal-winning 800-meter freestyle relay swimming team.

Volleyball for men and women and judo were introduced in the Tokyo Games. The USSR and Japan shared the gold medals in volleyball. The Soviets finished ahead of Czechoslovakia and Japan in the men's competition, and the Japanese took the women's championship, with the Soviet Union second and Poland third.

Inna Ryskal (USSR) is the only player to win four medals in volleyball. In addition to her silver medal in 1964, she would capture golds in 1968, 1972, 1976. Another Soviet, Yury Poyarkov, holds the record for medals in men's volleyball. To his gold medal in 1964 he would add another in 1968 and a bronze in 1972.

The host Japanese won three of the four judo gold medals: light-, middle-, and heavy-weight classes. The one that escaped them went to Antonius Geesink, a giant Dutchman, who took the Open competition. Geesink, a 6' 6", 260-pounder, defeated the Japanese champion, Akio Kaminaga, in a long-awaited match that was televised nationally. The outcome shocked Japanese viewers.

James Bregman gave the United States its only medal in the judo competition. He tied for the bronze in the middleweight division. Bregman had gone to Tokyo several years before to study at Sophia University and to learn the sport.

Judo, literally "soft way" in Japanese, made its first Olympic appearance in 1964. Judo was developed from jujitsu, a system of weaponless combat that was known in Japan at least as far back as the 8th century. In 1882 Jigoro Kano, a master of jujitsu, founded a school to reform the old martial concepts and make a competitive sport. In show matches judo fighters wear a pajamalike costume called a judogi. The painting illustrates the object of judo: to use an opponent's own moves to overbalance and throw him.

Lones Wigger and Gary Anderson, two Americans proficient in shooting, took home gold medals in 1964. Anderson, a rare left-handed shooter, won the free rifle event. In 1968, he became the first American to win the event in consecutive Olympics since Morris Fisher in 1920 and 1924. Wigger, a career officer in the United States Army, won the three-position small bore rifle with a world record and placed second to László Hammerl (Hungary) in the small bore rifle, prone position. Both shot the same world record score. Olympic records were broken in both the rapid pistol event, won by Finland's Pentti Linnosvuo, and the clay pigeon shooting, which Italy's Ennio Mattarelli won. The free pistol was another Finnish success, with Väinö Markkanen the gold medalist.

Hungary's Imre Polyak was a persistent Greco-Roman wrestler. After winning silver medals in the featherweight division in 1952, 1956, and 1960, Polyak finally struck gold in Tokyo. His total of four medals is the most ever won by an Olympic wrestler. His countryman, István Kozma, won the gold in the heavyweight class. Japanese wrestlers were conquerors in the light flyweight and bantamweight classes. The lightweight was a Turkish, the welterweight a Soviet, the middleweight a Yugoslav, and the light heavyweight a Bulgarian victory.

Aleksandr Medved of the Soviet Union launched a freestyle wrestling career that made him the first wrestler to win gold medals in three successive Olympics. He was the light heavyweight king in 1964, the heavyweight titlist in 1968, and the super heavyweight champion in 1972. His teammate, Aleksandr Ivanitsky, had the 1964 gold medal for the heavyweight class. Japanese wrestlers excelled in the light flyweight, bantamweight, and featherweight classes. Bulgarians won the lightweight and middleweight contests, and Turkey's Ismail Ogan moved from the 1960 silver to the 1964 gold rank in welterweight class.

The gymnastics reign of Larissa Latynina ended in Tokyo.

Soviet gymnast Larissa Latynina (shown competing at her first Olympics in 1956) won a total of 9 gold, 5 silver, and 4 bronze medals during her Olympic career—the greatest number of medals ever won by an individual athlete. Latynina's accomplishments established a tradition of Soviet supremacy in women's gymnastics. The intricacy and technical proficiency of her routines revolutionized the sport between 1956 and 1964. After retiring from formal competition, Mrs. Latynina became a coach of the Soviet national team.

Dawn Fraser

I love beer. . . . I don't worry about staying up late. I don't watch my diet. I am crazy about sweets and things like that. I have my fun—and I think I am a better swimmer because of it.

—DAWN FRASER

The 1964 Tokyo Olympics were over. Dawn Fraser, the 27-year-old "Granny" of the Australian swimming team who had won an unprecedented third consecutive Olympic 100-meter freestyle gold medal, went to the Imperial Hotel to celebrate. Two teammates persuaded Dawn to go to the gardens of the Imperial Palace. Their target was a souvenir, an Olympic flag. When they made off with their prize and the police intervened, Fraser tried to escape on a policeman's bicycle. But a moat 50 yards wide proved a greater barrier than the swimming champion expected, and she landed in custody. After her arrest (the other pranksters were never identified) and her identity was discovered, the police gave her the flag.

When Fraser returned home, she was named Australian Athlete of the Year. However, her nation's swimming officials suspended her for ten years—at her age, a lifetime ban on competing. She was disciplined for the flag-stealing prank and for her disregard of orders not to march in the opening ceremony at Tokyo. Australian officials wanted the swim team members to conserve their strength for the events scheduled early in the program. Dawn Fraser sued, and the suspension was lifted the following year.

Dawn Fraser was so free-spirited and so outspoken that she and Australian swimming officials had been on a collision course for several years. "I am outspoken and frank about things with which I disagree and some people don't like it," Fraser said. "If this makes me a rebel, then I am a rebel."

Fraser attributed her success as a swimmer to her iconoclasm. She established 39 world records and was the first to better one minute in the 100-meter freestyle. She lowered the world record in the 100 nine successive times. But her most enduring accomplishment was three consecutive Olympic gold medals in the event.

Fraser, one of eight children, was born in Balmain, New South Wales, on September 4, 1937. She began to swim at the age of six in a tidal basin on the Parramatta River in Sydney. When she was 14, coach Harry Gallagher, whom she described as "my Professor Higgins," began to work with her. She did not compete until she was 16. At 18, Fraser starred in the New South Wales championships.

In the 1956 Melbourne Games, she won the 100 meters in the world record time of 1 minute, 2.0 seconds, beating teammate Lorraine Crapp. She also led off the gold-medal-winning 400-meter freestyle relay team. Four years later in Rome, Fraser successfully defended her 100-meter freestyle championship. The 5′ 8½″, 150-pounder lowered her Olympic record to 1:01.2. She also won two silver medals—leading off the 400-meter freestyle team and anchoring the 400-meter medley relay team.

Dawn Fraser was in trouble in the 1964 Tokyo Olympics even before she put on her swimsuit. First, she thumbed her nose at the Australian Olympic Committee when she marched in the opening parade. Then, after her swimsuit chafed her, she changed into another suit whose design was not regulation. Fraser and officials argued. She relented and swam to her third gold medal in the 100-meter freestyle, and another silver in the 400-meter freestyle relay. Fraser's 100-meter time was an Olympic record 59.5 seconds.

Dawn Fraser also swam in three consecutive Olympic 400-meter freestyle finals and bettered her time in each. She placed second in 5 minutes, 2.5 seconds in 1956, fifth in 4:58.5 in 1960, and fourth in 4:47.6 in 1964.

That she performed so well at the age of 27, well beyond the peak of world class female competitors, was a proof of her resilience. Without it, she would never have reached Tokyo. A few months before the Games she was seriously injured in an automobile accident that claimed the life of her mother, and depressed her for months with a sense of guilt.

By order of Queen Elizabeth II, Dawn Fraser became a member of the Order of the British Empire on January 1, 1967.

At the Tokyo Olympics, Boris Schakhlin, 32-year-old Soviet gymnast, received a gold medal in the horizontal bar (above), silvers for individual combined exercises and as a member of the runner-up combined exercises team, and a bronze for his rings performance.

Čáslavská was judged best on the balance beam and the horse vault. She had a silver for her part of the Czech team exercises.

Polina Astakhova defended her crown for asymmetrical bars. It was her misfortune to be on the Soviet team at the same time as Latynina, who generally put her in the shade. Even so, in the three sets of Games from Melbourne to Tokyo, Astakhova acquired 5 gold, 2 silver, and 2 bronze medals.

Japanese gymnasts were acclaimed best in five of the eight men's events. Yukio Endo excelled in the individual and team combined exercises and on the parallel bars, and took a bronze for his floor exercises. That event gave Italy's Franco Menichelli a gold reward; he also got a silver for his rings performance. The pommeled horse was Miroslav Cerar's event and gave Yugoslavia its single gold in gymnastics. Cerar took the bronze for his horizontal bar work; the winner there was long-time gymnast Boris Schakhlin, who accumulated a total of 13 medals in three successive Games.

Joe Frazier, a 20-year-old slaughterhouse employee from Philadelphia, was the only American to go home with a gold medal for boxing. He took the most glamorous of the events—the heavyweight class—and later became the world professional champion.

His victory in Tokyo was the result of a second chance. Frazier scored six straight knockouts in the Olympic Trials before meeting 300-pound Buster Mathis in the final. Mathis won a close decision and a berth on the squad.

Frazier was depressed until it was suggested that he accompany the U.S. boxing team to Tokyo as a sparring partner. Influential Philadelphians obtained a promise from Frazier's employers that if he went to Tokyo he would not lose the job with which he supported his family.

Frazier joined the boxing squad in San Francisco where the fighters entertained servicemen. Frazier was selected to box against Mathis. One of Mathis' punches, a stunning right to Frazier's head, fractured Mathis' index finger. A physician said it would not mend in time for the first Olympic bout in Tokyo.

Frazier took Mathis' place, scored two consecutive knockouts, and advanced to the semifinals where he was opposed by a huge Soviet boxer, Vadim Yemelyanov. The fast-punching American flattened Yemelyanov in 1 minute, 59 seconds of the second round but in doing it broke his left thumb. He refused to let the U.S. team physician X-ray his swollen hand.

"I got to get this gold medal," he said. "It's the only way I can get out of the slaughterhouse."

Frazier won the final in his characteristic manner. Despite the pain in his left hand, he fired blows without letup. He was named the victor over Hans Huber of Germany by a split decision, three votes to two.

Starting in 1952, four medals have been awarded in each boxing class: a gold, a silver, and two bronzes. The bronze awards go to both of the losing semifinalists in each class. In Tokyo, three bronzes went to American boxers: Robert Carmody, flyweight, Charles Brown, featherweight, and Ronald Harris, lightweight. Harris would be the gold medalist in 1968.

The flyweight and light heavyweight gold medals were won by Italian boxers. Feather-, light middle-, and middle-weight crowns went to Soviet contestants, and lightweight, light welterweight, and welterweight to Polish. Japan took the bantamweight event.

American heavyweight boxer Joe Frazier first made the sports headlines by winning a gold medal at Tokyo. He defeated Germany's Hans Huber (right) in the final.

Hungary won the soccer championship, finishing ahead of Czechoslovak, German, and Egyptian teams. India regained the field hockey title from Pakistan, which placed second. The United States continued its unbeaten basketball record, and scored an easy 73-59 victory over the runner-up Soviet squad. With Brazil in third place, all three medal teams repeated their 1960 standings.

Among the American court stars were Larry Brown, Joe Caldwell, Mel Counts, Walt Hazzard, Lucius Jackson, and William "Bill" Bradley, who would become a Rhodes scholar, a star with the professional New York Knickerbockers, and a United States senator. Bradley, the team captain, averaged 10.1 points for nine games, and scored 10 against the Soviets. The top scorer against the Soviets was Jackson, with 17 points.

Germany's Wilhelm Kuhweide won the dinghy class title in yachting. He succeeded Paul Elvström of Denmark, who had been the gold medalist in the event in 1948, 1952, 1956, and 1960. Bahamian sailors proved most adept with Star class yachts, beating U.S. and Swedish boats. New Zealanders won the honors in the Flying Dutchman class, and Danes outsailed German and American crews in the Dragon class.

Ludmila Khvedosyuk (USSR) took the women's kayak singles crown in 1964, the first of three conquests in the events. The kayak doubles was a German triumph, with U.S. and Rumanian teams following. Swedish canoers won the 1,000-meter kayak singles and doubles events. In the new kayak fours, over a 1,000-meter course, Soviet canoers were swiftest, followed by German and Rumanian quartets. Soviet boatmen were first, as well, in the Canadian doubles, but in the singles both German and Rumanian contestants were ahead of them.

Peter Snell scored a double win in track—the 800 and 1,500 meters. The 25-year-old New Zealander won the 1,500 by only 1.5 seconds, but in repeating as 800-meter champion he lowered his Olympic record by 1.2 seconds. The German equestrian team took the bronze, behind gold-winning Italy and the United States.

The United States and the Soviet Union each won two rowing events. The American eight-oared shell came from the Vesper Boat Club of Philadelphia. It beat Germany, the defending champ, by more than five seconds, with Czechoslovakia third. The other American gold came in the pairs with coxswain. The winning shell carried Edward Ferry, Conn Findlay, and Henry Mitchell ahead of the French and Dutch crews.

The Soviet victories were gained in the sculls events. Vyatscheslav Ivanov took his third successive gold for the singles, followed by Germany's Achim Hill, as in 1960. In the double sculls the winning team was only 2.1 seconds ahead of the U.S. pair and 3.17 seconds faster than the Czechs.

Canadian oarsmen beat both Dutch and German crews in the coxless pairs rowing, Denmark led Great Britain and the United States to the finish line in the coxless fours event, and in the coxed fours the final winning lineup was Germany, Italy, and The Netherlands.

Six consecutive victories by Italians in fencing's individual épée event were interrupted by Grigory Kriss (USSR), but Hungarian teamwork won the other épée contest. Foils were Poland's (individual) and the Soviets' (team) victories, and the Soviet team was first with the sabre. Tibor Pézsa of Hungary won the individual sabre, and his countrywoman, Ildikó Njlaki-Rejtö, won the ladies' individual foils. Her team took that foils contest from the Soviet team.

The 3-day individual equestrian gold medal was Mauro Checcoli's, and with his Italian teammates he won a second in the team event, in which the U.S. team took the silver. Swiss, German, and Soviet horsemen had the individual dressage medals; in the team event the order changed to German, Swiss, and Soviet. The U.S. dressage team was all female for the first time. Pierre Jonquières d'Oriola (France), in his fourth Olympics, won the individual jumping, but his team was bested by the German jumping team.

Italian cyclists won three gold and five silver medals. Mario Zanin was the first in the individual road race, Giovanni Pettenella in the 1,000-meter sprint, and Sergio Bianchetto and Angelo Damiano in the 2,000-meter tandem. Jiří Daler (Czechoslovakia) won the new 4,000-meter individual pursuit race, and German cyclists beat back the Italian and Dutch quartets in the team event. A Dutch team took the 100-kilometer team contest and Belgium won the 1,000-meter time race.

Ferenc Török kept the Hungarian gold standing in the modern pentathlon. Second to him was Igor Novikov (USSR), placing among the medalists for the first time in four Olympics. His teammate, Albert Mokeyev, was the bronze man. The team title went to the Soviets, the silver to the U.S. team, and the bronze to the Hungarian.

Every weightlifting category registered a new record in 1964, five of them new world records and two new Olympic records. In the doing, the Soviet lifters won four gold medals and Japan, Poland, and Czechoslovakia each one. In the lightweight class, Polish Waldemar Baszanowski and Soviet Vladimir Kaplunov lifted the same world record weight. The gold went to the Pole on the basis of his lower body weight. Isaac Berger, the 1956 world record setter and gold medalist in the featherweight class, was the silver winner, as he had been in 1960.

To the general surprise, Billy Mills (on the far left), 26-year-old part-Sioux Indian, emerged from the pack and came in first in the 10,000 meters. He later worked for the U.S. Bureau of Indian Affairs.

Billy Mills

I knew all along that I had the ability. But I just couldn't produce on the track. I kept telling myself I could do better.

—BILLY MILLS

In what is considered the upset of the 1964 Olympics, William M. "Billy" Mills, a 26-year-old Marine first lieutenant who is seven sixteenths Sioux Indian, won the 10,000-meters race. No American ever had won the gold medal in the 10,000. The only American even to crack the top six was another Indian, Louis Tewanima, who won the silver medal in 1912, the first Olympics in which the event was contested.

After the memorable and dramatic race, reporters asked Australia's Ron Clarke, the 10,000-meter world record holder, if in planning for the race he had worried about Mills. "Worry about him?" the bronze medalist asked. "I never heard of him."

If it hadn't been for his wife, Patricia, Billy Mills might never have been in Tokyo. In 1962 he had quit track, ending two decades of running. He had run on the Indian reservation in Pine Ridge, South Dakota, where he was born on June 6, 1938. He had competed for the Haskell Indian School in Lawrence, Kansas. He had represented the University of Kansas. And he had been a member of the Marine Corps team in Camp Pendleton, California.

"During my retirement was the only time Pat and I ever got into fights," Mills said. "She was a track fan and wanted to go to watch a meet. But it would tear me apart to attend one."

But Mrs. Mills knew if she kept dragging Billy to meets, he would return to track competition. "Deep down inside I felt I'd failed in sports," Mills said. "I knew I had to run again."

Billy Mills began to work out. He pushed his 5′ 11″, 160-pound body through strenuous practice. During those workouts, he would sight a tree in the distance. That, he'd say to himself, is the finish line of the 10,000-meters race in the Olympics. When he had finished his sprint, he'd pull out a small notebook. "I'd write little paragraphs in my workout book," he said. " 'God has given me the ability. The rest is up to me. Believe. Believe. Believe. . . .' "

During the Olympic Trials, Mills placed second in the 10,000 meters, behind Gerry Lindgren. He also qualified for the marathon, in which he would finish fourteenth.

When the U.S. team arrived in Tokyo, the world record for the 10,000 was 28 minutes, 15.6 seconds. Mills' personal best was almost a minute slower. The day before the 10,000 was run, Mills went to an Olympic Village store where track shoes were distributed by manufacturers at no charge to outstanding distance runners. Mills had to purchase his shoes.

On October 14, the opening day of the Tokyo track and field competition, the track was wet from a morning rain. At 5,000 meters, Mills was the leader in 14 minutes, 4.6 seconds—less than a second slower than his personal best for that distance. With one lap remaining, the race narrowed down to a battle among Clarke, Tunisia's Mohamed Gammoudi, and Mills. Clarke wanted to launch his sprint in the bell lap. But he was boxed in, trapped by Mills and a lapped runner. Clarke moved out and he and Mills accidentally collided. Gammoudi saw his chance and made his move on the final curve. He drove between Clarke and Mills and brushed both off stride.

The American went spinning off to the right, on the outside. The Australian stumbled to the left, on the inside. Gammoudi was in the lead, and the apparent winner. But Mills and Clarke were not through. First Clarke made a run at Gammoudi and passed him. Then Mills streaked past both rivals on the outside, with 50 meters left in the race, and the tape was his. Mills crossed three yards and four tenths of a second in front of Gammoudi, with Clarke third. Mills' time was an Olympic record 28 minutes, 24.4 seconds.

"It was my moment," Mills said. "I stood on the Olympic stand knowing that at least on one occasion, for one moment—one fleeting moment—I was the best in the world."

"I went back to my hometown," he said, "and they gave me a gold ring and they dedicated a building in my name. And they also gave me an Indian name that means 'He Thinks Very Good of His Country'."

American men worked their way back to the top in track, winning five of eight running events on the flat—four more than in Rome. In addition to sprints, their successes included two distance races never before won by Americans, the 5,000- and 10,000-meters.

Billy Mills, a Marine lieutenant, captured the 10,000 on October 14. Running on a wet track, the little-known part-Sioux outran the field in the home stretch, to set an Olympic record of 28 minutes, 24.4 seconds. Mohamed Gammoudi of Tunisia was second, four tenths of a second off the pace. World record holder Ron Clarke of Australia placed third.

Clarke, the greatest distance runner of his time, came back for the 5,000-meter race four days later and again ran into an inspired American, 27-year-old Bob Schul. Gammoudi was scratched. Bill Dellinger (USA) sprinted from the back of the pack to take the lead with a lap to go. On the next-to-the-last turn, Michel Jazy of France moved to the front and opened a 10-yard lead over Schul, in second place. Schul then unleashed his kick and went past Jazy, who had begun to tire. Running the final lap in 54.8 seconds, Schul won the race in 13 minutes, 48.8 seconds. Harald Norpoth of Germany finished second and Dellinger third. Jazy was fourth, ahead of Kenya's Kipchoge Keino. Clarke placed ninth.

On October 21, Clarke made his third try for a gold in the Tokyo Games, but he could do no better than ninth in the marathon. It was won by Ethiopia's Abebe Bikila, running this time in shoes. He became the first repeat winner of the event in Olympic history. Bikila's time was an Olympic record of 2 hours, 12 minutes, 11.2 seconds. Britain's Basil Heatley was second and Kokichi Tsuburaya of Japan third. Bikila's margin of victory, more than four minutes, was the largest since 1924.

The only man to score an individual double in track and field in 1964 was New Zealand's Peter Snell, winner of the 800 meters in Rome. Snell, the world record holder in the 800 meters and mile, prepared for the 1964 Games by running 100 miles a week. It paid off in Tokyo, where he became the first runner since Britain's Albert George Hill in 1920 to win the 800- and 1,500- meter races in the same Olympics.

Snell's primary target in the '64 Games was the metric mile. But the Olympic program offered him the opportunity to attempt the difficult double because the races were scheduled five days apart.

Snell was sixth in the field at the midway mark of the 800-meter final on October 16. But the powerful New Zealander moved into the lead at the 600-meter mark and then raced home to an Olympic record of 1 minute, 45.1 seconds. His time was the second fastest in history, with splits of 52.9 and 52.2. Bill Crothers of Canada won the silver medal, finishing five tenths of a second behind Snell. Kenya's Wilson Kiprugut and George Kerr of Jamaica both clocked 1:45.9, but the bronze medal went to the Kenyan.

On October 21, Snell raced to an easy victory in the 1,500 meters, after running no better than fourth during the first half of the race. He took the lead with 200 meters remaining and coasted to a 3:38.1 victory. His final 400-meter split was 52.7. Josef Odložil of Czechoslovakia and New Zealand's John Davies were timed in 3:39.6, but Odložil was awarded the silver medal. Counting heats and finals, Snell ran a total of six races in six days.

Two future professional football players, Bob Hayes and Henry Carr, regained the sprint championships for the United States. Hayes

Bob Hayes acknowledges the applause of the crowd after receiving his gold medal for the 100 meters. Cuba's Enrique Figuerola and Canada's Harry Jerome were second and third. The American sprinter later played professional football for the Dallas Cowboys.

Dallas Long edged out Randy Matson to win the gold medal in the shot put. For the eighth consecutive time, the winning throw established a new Olympic record.

won the 100 meters in a world record 10 seconds flat. Before that he had run a 9.9 heat that was wind-aided and thus ineligible for record consideration. The pigeon-toed Hayes also anchored the winning United States 400-meter relay team to a world record 39.0 seconds. In that contest Hayes, who was preceded by Otis Paul Drayton, Gerald Ashworth, and Richard Stebbins, found himself in fifth place, three meters behind the leading French team. When he crossed the finish line, he had rearranged the field, giving the United States a three-meter victory over Poland and France. His split was an unbelievable 8.6 seconds!

Carr won the 200 meters with an Olympic record 20.3 seconds. Drayton was second and Edwin Roberts (Trinidad) was third. The Italian defender, Livio Berruti, was fifth.

Mike Larrabee won the 400 meters in 45.1 seconds, a tenth of a second faster than Wendell Mottley of Trinidad and five tenths ahead of Poland's Andrzej Badenski.

Ollan Cassell, Larrabee, Ulis Williams, and Carr ran to a world record of 3:00.7 in the 1,600-meter relay. Great Britain was second and Trinidad third.

Hayes Jones gave the United States a seventh consecutive victory in the 110-meter hurdles, and "Rex" Cawley made it six in a row for America in the 400-meter hurdles.

Gaston Roelants of Belgium, fourth in the steeplechase in Rome, won the event in Tokyo in an Olympic record 8 minutes, 30.8 seconds, 1.6 seconds ahead of Maurice Herriott of Great Britain, and 3 seconds faster than Soviet Yvan Belyayev.

Defending champion walker Vladimir Golubnitschy (USSR) couldn't do better than third place in Tokyo, where Kenneth Matthews (Great Britain) set an Olympic record of 1 hour, 29 minutes, 34 seconds for 20 kilometers. Dieter Lindner (Germany) was second and got the silver.

The 50-kilometer walk was also accomplished in Olympic record time. Abdon Pamich of Italy clipped 14 minutes, 17.6 seconds off the Rome time of Donald Thompson. Pamich had been third in 1960 and fourth in 1956.

Al Oerter, taped together after he tore cartilage in his rib cage,

Competitors in the 20-kilometer walk are on each other's heels as they circle the stadium track.

won his third straight discus gold medal and set an Olympic record of 200′ 1½″. Since Martin Sheridan's three straight discus victories in 1904, 1906, and 1908, no one had won the event in three consecutive Games.

The United States increased to 12 its consecutive triumphs in the pole vault. Using a new fiberglass pole, Fred Hansen took the event with an Olympic record 16′ 8¾″. It demolished Don Bragg's previous record of 15′ 5″.

Dallas Long made it five in a row for U.S. golds for putting the shot. Long's throw of 66′ 8½″ and his teammate Randy Matson's of 66′ 3¼″ both shattered the former Olympic record. Parry O'Brien, winner of the event in 1952 and 1956 and a silver medalist in 1960, finished fourth.

In the high jump competition Valery Brumel (USSR) moved up from second in 1960 to first in 1964. Again his runner-up was John Thomas (USA). In Tokyo both cleared 7′ 1¾″. On the basis of fewer misses the gold was awarded to Brumel.

Defending champion Ralph Boston of the United States was upset in the long jump by Britain's Lynn Davies in cold, windy, and rainy weather. With a leap of 26′ 5¾″ Davies went 1½″ beyond Boston's best distance. Igor Ter-Ovanesyan (USSR) repeated as the bronze medalist.

Jozef Schmidt of Poland successfully defended his triple jump championship, bettering his former Olympic record by 1¾″. As in Rome, he finished ahead of two Soviet jumpers.

Pauli Nevala of Finland won the javelin in Tokyo. The silver medal went to Hungary's Gergely Kulcsár, the 1960 bronze medalist. Romuald Klim (USSR) took the hammer throw with an Olympic record toss of 228′ 10″. Runners-up Gyula Zsivótzky of Hungary and Uwe Beyere of Germany also exceeded the former Olympic record. Although Harold Connolly, the American gold medal winner of 1956, threw farther in Tokyo than he had in Melbourne and Rome, he had to settle for sixth place.

The decathlon produced the closest competition in the history of the event. The crown went to Germany's Willi Holdorf, who ended a U.S. string of 6 victories in the event. Holdorf won by only

In the women's 400-meter relay, Polish sprinters (inside lane) passed the baton in perfect form and streaked to victory in world-record time. The U.S. foursome finished a close second, with Great Britain third.

FINAL MEDAL STANDINGS			
Nation	G	S	B
United States	36	26	28
Soviet Union	30	31	35
Japan	16	5	8
Germany	10	22	18
Italy	10	10	7
Hungary	10	7	5
Poland	7	6	10
Australia	6	2	10
Czechoslovakia	5	6	3
Great Britain	4	12	2
Bulgaria	3	5	2
Finland	3	–	2
New Zealand	3	–	2
Rumania	2	4	6
The Netherlands	2	4	4
Turkey	2	3	1
Sweden	2	2	4
Denmark	2	1	3
Yugoslavia	2	1	2
Belgium	2	–	1
France	1	8	6
Canada	1	2	1
Switzerland	1	2	1
Bahamas	1	–	–
Ethiopia	1	–	–
India	1	–	–
Korea	–	2	1
Trinidad and Tobago	–	1	2
Tunisia	–	1	1
Argentina	–	1	–
Cuba	–	1	–
Pakistan	–	1	–
Philippines	–	1	–
Iran	–	–	2
Brazil	–	–	1
Ghana	–	–	1
Ireland	–	–	1
Kenya	–	–	1
Mexico	–	–	1
Niger	–	–	1
Uruguay	–	–	1

Irena Kirszenstein (Poland), Mary Rand (Great Britain), and Tatyana Schtschelkanova (USSR) wear their silver, gold, and bronze long jump medals.

45 points from Rein Aun (USSR), with Germany's Hans-Joachim Walde in third place, 78 points behind the winner. C.K. Yang of Taiwan, the Rome silver medalist, placed fifth.

America's Wyomia Tyus and Edith McGuire placed 1-2 in the women's 100-meter sprint, with Poland's Ewa Klobukowska third. Tyus tied the world record of 11.2 seconds in a heat and won the final in 11.4. McGuire captured the 200 meters, shattering Wilma Rudolph's Olympic record with a time of 23 seconds flat. She finished ahead of Poland's Irena Kirszenstein, who later would be known as Irena Szewinska. Kirszenstein was a member of Poland's world record 400-meter relay team which clocked 43.6 seconds. It was three tenths of a second faster than the time recorded by the U.S. team of Willye White, Tyus, Marilyn White, and McGuire.

Kirszenstein-Szewinska would become the only woman to win track and field medals in four successive Olympics, a total of seven in five events. Her 3 gold, 2 silver, and 2 bronze tied Australia's Betty Cuthbert for the most track medals won by a woman.

Cuthbert won her seventh medal in Tokyo with a victory in the new 400-meter run. She beat Ann Packer of Britain by two tenths of a second. Packer's consolation came in the 800 meters in which she won the gold medal with a world record 2 minutes, 1.1 seconds.

The Soviet Union's powerful Press sisters, Tamara and Irina, earned three gold medals between them. Tamara successfully defended her shot put title and won the discus, setting Olympic records in both events.

Irina Press won a new event on the Tokyo program, the women's pentathlon, a combination of the 80-meter hurdles, shot put, high jump, long jump, and 200-meter dash. Irina piled up a world record 5,246 points. Britain's Mary Rand was the runner-up.

Rand won the long jump with a world record of 22' 2¼", beating Kirszenstein by 6½". It was Britain's first gold medal in women's track and field. Rand also won a bronze medal as a member of Britain's 400-meter relay team. She later won the heart and became the wife of Bill Toomey, the American decathlon star.

Germany's Karin Balzer, Poland's Tereza Ciepla, and Australia's Pamela Kilborn all equaled the world record of 10.5 seconds in the 80-meter hurdles, but the mark was nullified because of an assisting wind. Judges determined that they finished in that order, with defending champion Irina Press fourth in 10.6.

Rumania captured the two remaining gold medals. Iolanda Balaş won the high jump, raising her Olympic record to 6' 2¾". Mihaela Peneş won the javelin gold medal, placing ahead of Hungary's Márta Rudas and Yelena Gortschakova of the Soviet Union, who set a world record of 204' 8¼" in the qualifying round. That erased the former mark held by defending champion Elvira Ozolina (USSR), who finished fifth. Ozolina was so annoyed with herself after losing that she had her head shaved, and that annoyed her even more.

Three nations were barred from competing in Tokyo—South Africa, because of its apartheid policies; and Indonesia and North Korea, whose track and field and swimming athletes were ruled ineligible because they competed in non-sanctioned pre-Olympic competition.

The International Olympic Committee ordered that no national point totals be kept during the Games. When the Olympics were over, the Olympic scoreboard flashed—SAYONARA.

1968

Winter Games

Grenoble, France

The novelist Stendhal referred to Grenoble, his birthplace, as "a mediocre town in an exceptional location." In the century and a half since that description was written, the city tucked in a narrow valley at the meeting point of the Drac and Isère rivers has grown into the economic, intellectual, and tourist capital of the French Alps. It is a modern city whose every street seems to end in a view of mountains.

If one had been touring France in search of a site for the 1968 winter Olympic Games, it is unlikely that Grenoble would have been a first choice. The city is primarily industrial. Its thick winter fogs are notorious, regularly causing transportation and communication headaches. Nevertheless the selection committee settled on Grenoble. In accepting the Games, the city also accepted the task of adapting its geography to the needs of the Olympics. The result was the most sprawling set of competitions in the history of the Winter Games. The bobsled run at L'Alpe d'Huez was 38 miles from Grenoble. The downhill ski run at Chamrousse was 18 miles away. Except for the 90-meter jump, the Nordic ski events at Autrans and the luge at Villard-de-Lans also were located long distances from town. The events were so spread out that instead of one central Olympic Village to house the athletes, several minivillages were constructed.

The French did not stint in building facilities to accommodate the Games. In the heart of the city, a new stadium seating 60,000 people was constructed solely for the purpose of holding the colorful opening ceremonies of the Olympics. The day after the ceremonies ended, the stadium was turned over to workmen who began its demolition. That helps to explain why the bill for the X Winter Games soared to approximately $240 million. But the French government entertained no complaints about spending that sum because President Charles de Gaulle, a proud man, wanted Grenoble's show to have the proper élan.

Unfortunately, organizers haven't figured out a way to control the weather. And the capricious Alpine weather supplied more than its share of problems for the 1968 Winter Games. In the days before the opening ceremonies, heavy rains inundated the area. In the Alps it snowed so hard that the skiers had to cancel their practice runs. Later, warm temperatures thawed the frozen luge course and heavy fog almost totally enveloped skiers as they raced down the mountains.

However, the opening ceremonies on February 6 went off with precision. The interlocking Olympic rings were traced on the stadium infield

Parachutists (below) landed inside the Olympic rings in the stadium at Grenoble, France, and the 1968 Winter Games began. Favorite Karl Schranz of Austria was denied a gold in the giant slalom event.

and, overhead, skywriters in jet airplanes repeated the pattern that has become the sign of the Games. As part of the spectacular ceremonies, five parachutists, each wearing a chute the color of one of the five Olympic rings, dropped into the stadium, landing inside the correspondingly-colored rings on the field. It was all properly breathtaking.

While the ceremonies opening the 1968 Winter Games were held in near perfect weather, the start of formal competition a day later was all but wiped out by stormy conditions. Only one final could be held.

A major upset was posted in the 30-kilometer cross country ski race. The winner was Franco Nones, a 27-year-old Italian who not only won the 18.6-mile race but finished a substantial 49.7 seconds ahead of his nearest challenger, favored Odd Martinsen of Norway. It marked the first time in Olympic history that a Nordic individual men's race was won by a non-Scandinavian, and the northerners' chagrin at being bested at their special sport was not greatly lessened by knowing that the Italians' coach, Bengt-Herman Nilsson, had trained the Italian team in his native Sweden.

The windy, blizzard-like weather forced the downhill race to be postponed, but not before a dozen skiers who challenged the conditions had been hospitalized. The men's downhill was the first test in the Alpine program and the local fans were pulling for their countryman, handsome Jean-Claude Killy. Preparation was no problem for Killy, who at 24 was shooting for a triple gold medal sweep like Austria's Toni Sailer in 1956—the downhill, giant slalom, and slalom.

The world's best Alpine skiers agreed that the downhill was the toughest test for them. Why did they single out that race as the most grueling?

"Because," said Killy, "the downhill tests character and courage."

"Because," said Guy Perillat, another French skier, "the downhill does not leave room for compromise. You're either in front, or you perish."

Austria's Karl Schranz considered the question and then said: "The downhill demands everything a skier is able to give. No coward will ever win."

If Killy was to achieve his gold medal sweep, he would have to start with the difficult downhill on February 9. The two-mile course included a drop of almost a half mile, a perilous path to glory. Perillat completed the treacherous descent in 1:59.93. It was good enough for first place until Killy's run of 1:59.85 gave him the gold by a few hundredths of a second.

Next came the giant slalom. Again Killy prevailed, this time by a more comfortable margin of better than two seconds—a far from insignificant edge in a sport where winners are often separated from losers by no more than a blink. With two down and one to go, Killy advanced to the slalom, his final Alpine target.

The fickle weather turned foggy for the slalom. Mist shrouded the course, turning skiers and race officials into shadowy images barely discernible even at short range. Each skier had to make two runs down the course, weaving through 62 gates on the first run, and 69 on the second. Killy completed his runs with a combined clocking of 99.73 seconds and watched as the other skiers made their runs at his lead.

The best shot belonged to Schranz, the Austrian, who had finished third in the first heat. Shortly after starting the second run, Schranz pulled up, claiming that a spectator or policeman had wandered onto the course in the fog and interfered with him. He was

We may achieve climate, but weather is thrust upon us.

—O. HENRY

In a major upset, Italy's Franco Nones captured the men's 30-kilometer cross country skiing event. Jean-Claude Killy (14) and teammate Guy Perillat were the gold and silver medalists in the downhill ski competition.

permitted to restart his run and when he completed it his time was 99.22. It seemed that Killy had been beaten. But then word came from the officials that Schranz had missed two gates on his original second run before the interference and restart. Those misses made him ineligible for the rerun and the gold went to Killy. Why the mistake was pointed out after the race and why Schranz was permitted his extra run were never quite explained.

While Killy, Schranz, and the other skiers battled the perverse weather, the figure skating and hockey competition drew crowds to the comfortable confines of the Stade de Glace—the ice stadium.

Skating effortlessly to the strains of Tchaikovsky and Verdi, Peggy Fleming awed the audience with her poise and agility. When she finished, there was no suspense—just a general sigh of admiration. She had brought the United States its only gold medal of the 1968 Winter Games.

The men's competition was an upset, with Wolfgang Schwarz of Austria capturing the gold and his countryman, world champion Emmerich Danzer, finishing no better than fourth. Actually, Tim Wood of the United States went back to the dressing room after his freestyle performance under the impression that *he* had won the gold medal. Other skaters, including 1964 silver medalist Alain Calmat of France, dropped by to congratulate him.

Then, 17 minutes later, after Schwarz, the 27th starter in the 28-man field, finished, Wood learned that Schwarz had won the gold medal and he had earned the silver.

While Fleming and Schwarz dazzled the Olympic audiences with the intricate figures they traced with their slim, short blades, speedskaters on long racing blades dashed around the outdoor rink at Parc Paul Mistral, totally unconcerned with form and design, worried only about the clock. Four world records fell during the competition but the race that is best remembered was the women's 500-meters. Three Americans, Jenny Fish, Dianne Holum and Mary Meyers, finished in a dead heat for second place. Each skater was timed in at 46.3 seconds, two tenths of a second behind the Soviet world champion, Ludmila Titova.

Miss Titova received the gold she had earned and to each of the American skaters went a silver medal. The trio who had hoped that one of them would win a silver prize, returned to the United States with three of them! No bronze medal was awarded in this most unusual of Olympic races.

Soviet world champion Ludmila Titova won the women's 500-meter speed skating event, narrowly defeating three Americans in a unique race.

"We didn't raise her to be a champion. It was all a surprise— and therefore that much more delightful."   Mrs. Doris Fleming

Figure skater Peggy Fleming captured the United States' only gold medal in the 1968 Winter Games with a score of 1,970.5 points. Earlier, Peggy had won her fifth consecutive national championship and three weeks after the Olympics she took her third consecutive international title. Former champion Dick Button called her "a unique combination of athletic ability, technical control, great style, and immense musicality."

Peggy Gale Fleming was born July 27, 1948, in San Jose, Calif. She began skating at the age of nine and "took to it right away." She won her first title in 1960. In 1968, Peggy signed a television contract.

Jean-Claude Killy

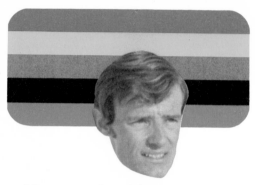

I have never slowed down in my entire life. And I never will. I can't do it.

—JEAN-CLAUDE KILLY

When World War II was over Robert Killy found he had no more interest in staying in the small Paris suburb of St. Cloud. Having packed up all his movables, he set off with his young son, Jean-Claude, for Val d'Isère, a small village in the French Alps.

There, in the pristine air of the tiny tourist town, he established himself as a hotel-keeper and sports shop owner. And there he presented three-year-old Jean-Claude with his first pair of skis.

"He was born to ski," Robert Killy said after Jean-Claude had become king of every hill. "When we moved to Val d'Isère I gave him his first skis and he loved them as some babies love Teddy bears. Even then, he would disappear for hours with them.

"When he was six, he could ski faster than I. I never saw him after that."

If skiing was his love, speed was his obsession. The French came to call him Casse-cou—Breakneck. "I take all the risks," he said. "That is my style. I love the feeling of danger. Skiing is my life. I can not be afraid of it."

He accomplished his greatest achievement under the gaze of thousands of the countrymen who adored him when, at Grenoble, France, in the 1968 Winter Olympics, he completed the Alpine triple by winning gold medals in the downhill, giant slalom, and slalom. The preparatory years might have disheartened a less single-minded youth. Besides broken leg and ankle bones, whose mending kept him off the slopes, he had had to put in two years in a sanatorium, healing an infected lung, and then another two years of Army service, in Algeria, where he contracted debilitating hepatitis.

But his eye was on skiing, and nothing else.

"There is," Killy explained, "no other sensation quite like skiing. It is a rare wine, a beautiful woman . . . unforgettable. I can remember races from 8 or 10 years ago so vividly I can picture in my mind every gate, every turn, every good run.

"Skiing, for me, was a way of expressing myself. You search always for the perfect run. It is so tantalizing. You come close, but you look back up when you have reached the bottom and you know you could have done better.

"It is a sport where you cannot know before if you will have a bad day or a good day. You know *that* when you are in the middle of two gates, but by then there is no time to stop and go back up and start all over.

"I have raced cars, and you are on the same edge. But the track, it does not change. The mountain does. You can never beat the mountain and you know it, but you want to keep trying. Maybe that is what makes us go back up."

Killy acknowledged that his concentration had exacted a toll.

"I am incredibly shy. I know it is ridiculous that I should still be so shy but when I am cut away from the French ski team, my gang, I just don't open my mouth. It's terribly difficult for me to be with people I don't know.

"This shyness has made me push harder in skiing," Killy explained.

He pushed so hard that, on the eve of the Grenoble Olympics, there was no doubt that he was a good bet to achieve the Alpine triple—which had been accomplished only once before, by Toni Sailer of Austria in 1956.

But while the 5-foot-11, 165-pounder with the gray-green eyes and the thin scar cutting across his left cheek and lips was the favorite, he faced the challenge of two other great skiers—Guy Perillat of France in the downhill and Karl Schranz of Austria in the slalom.

The first event on the schedule was the downhill, the most coveted gold because it requires the most daring.

Perillat was the first man down the course, almost two miles long with a vertical drop of almost half a mile. He was timed at 1:59.93. None of the next dozen hopefuls could break two minutes. Killy, starting 14th, knew he would have to go all out, and take every risk. At the signal he hurtled out of the starting gate and rocketed down the slopes. Thousands of Frenchmen lining the course called his name, willing him success. Killy *went* all out, all the way.

When he crossed the finish line, he remained apart from the other skiers while his time was posted. It was 1:59.85—eight hundredths of a second better than Perillat! He broke into a wide grin, joined Perillat, and the two embraced.

Three days later, in the giant slalom, Killy collected his second gold medal with unusual ease, finishing more than two seconds ahead of the field.

But if his skill wasn't fully tested in the giant slalom as it was in the downhill, the slalom would more than make up for it. The weather was atrocious, shrouding the course in deep fog. Schranz, having failed to win a gold, would be at his best, and the course would be dotted with 62 gates for the first run, 69 for the second.

When the two runs had been completed and results computed, Grenoble was stunned. Schranz hadn't beaten Killy, Haakon Mjoen of Norway had. But wait! The judges were in a huddle: gate judges reported Mjoen had missed two gates. Mjoen was disqualified. Stunned Grenoble was ecstatic.

Seconds later, the judges handed down a second ruling and ecstatic Grenoble was flattened again. Schranz, who had been forced to abort his second run at gate 22, was entitled, the judges decreed, to try his second run again. Back to the top of the hill he went, to flash down with a faster combined time than Killy's. To him, then, the gold.

But once more the judges convened.

Then they handed down one of the most incredible rulings in Olympic history. Schranz, they said, had missed gates 17 and 18 on his original second run—both of them before he had been interferred with at gate 22. He therefore had not been entitled to a second try.

Killy had his triple. He was a national hero who, in the making, had gained considerable self-insight. Looking back on his years of preparation he said, "I thought I would be a superman. But nothing happened at all. I was exactly the same as before. I learned that success is like a big ghost—you catch it and there is nothing there."

Following the 1968 triumph he retired from competitive skiing.

"It is my firm belief," he said, "that an athlete should retire from sports at the climax of his career. What can I expect more to win than an Olympic gold medal? It's the climax of my career, and that's the end of it."

As satisfying as those three silver medals were to the United States speedskaters, they could not have been any more gratifying than his 1968 performance was to Italian bobsledder Eugenio Monti, who ended a string of frustrations going back to the 1956 Games. Monti, now 40, had accumulated nine world championships, two Olympic silver medals and two Olympic bronze medals. But in Grenoble he finally struck gold—twice! First he captured the two-man bobsled race and then he piloted Italy's four-man sled to victory.

"I'm done now," Monti said afterward. "I'm satisfied. I'll retire peacefully."

The Games were not without dissensions. For the first time in history, organizers had ordered female competitors to take a sex test, a requirement that some objected to. (The 20 percent of the female athletes who were tested all passed.) Then Avery Brundage, president of the International Olympic Committee, threatened to cancel all skiing events because competitors were exhibiting manufacturers' labels on their skis. Brundage retreated from his hard-line stand but he did insist that skiers not be photographed with their equipment.

Controversy flared anew as the Games ended. This time, it involved an International Olympic Committee report which recommended the reinstatement of South Africa for the 1968 Summer Games at Mexico City. The South Africans had been banned from the 1964 Games in Tokyo because of their racial policy at home. Brundage and the other IOC officers accepted the report. One by one angry nations notified the IOC that if South Africa were allowed to appear in the 1968 Summer Games, they would withdraw. Three months after reinstating South Africa, the IOC, faced with a developing major boycott, reversed its stand and barred South Africa. The turnabout probably saved the Summer Games.

FINAL MEDAL STANDINGS			
Nation	G	S	B
Norway	6	6	2
Soviet Union	5	5	3
France	4	3	2
Italy	4	–	–
Austria	3	4	4
The Netherlands	3	3	3
Sweden	3	2	3
West Germany	2	2	3
United States	1	5	1
Finland	1	2	2
East Germany	1	2	2
Czechoslovakia	1	2	1
Canada	1	1	1
Switzerland	–	2	4
Rumania	–	–	1

Jenny Fish, left, Dianne Holum, and Mary Meyers finished the 500-meter speed skating event with identical times, just behind Ludmila Titova. The three Americans were awarded silver medals.

1968

Summer Games
Mexico City, Mexico

To comprehend the 1968 Summer Games, one must consider the tenor of the times. An unpopular war in Southeast Asia had fomented widespread student protest. Campuses everywhere—from Japan in the east to Europe and America in the west—had become battlegrounds between the establishment and its increasingly strident critics. In the United States the assassinations of Martin Luther King and Robert Kennedy and the withdrawal of President Lyndon Johnson from politics were registered as body blows across the troubled country.

Mexico City itself was a mariachi band in discord. From the start, the choice of Mexico City, with its one and one-half mile altitude, as a site for the Games was widely criticized. The thin air so far above sea level was a matter of much concern for many national Olympic committees. Their unhappiness was compounded 10 days before the start of the Games when simmering unrest on the campus at Mexico City's university spilled over into full-fledged violence.

There are any number of versions of what started the trouble. They range from a fight between two students over a girl, to long-term distress over the plight of Mexico's poor. Whatever the cause, the result was disastrous. More than 30 students were killed in riots. More than 100 were injured and more than 300 were jailed.

The Olympic Games began on time on October 12 with little show of concern for the turmoil that had preceded them. After all, Gustavo Diaz Ordaz, president of Mexico, had said: "We aspire to the friendship of all the nations of the world." The opening ceremonies, as colorful as ever, altered an old custom. For the first time in the history of the Modern Games, the Olympic flame was ignited by a woman. The honor was given to 20-year-old Norma Enriqueta Basilio, a hurdler representing the host Mexican team.

Four days after the start of the Games, the medal presentation ceremony after the 200-meter dash dispelled all complacency. Three of the eight finalists were Americans. Two of them won medals. Tommie Smith finished first in world record time and John Carlos took third. Both were blacks from San Jose State College in California, where Harry Edwards, an instructor in sociology and anthropology, attempted to organize a black boycott of the Games. Smith and Carlos had planned to participate in Edwards' boycott, and they were determined to make their own protest.

Both came out of the semifinals hurting, Carlos with a sore back, and Smith with a pulled groin muscle. The muscle pull was so painful that Smith lay with his leg packed in ice for two hours, waiting for the finals. Tightly taped, he went to the mark for the medal race and flashed over the distance in 19.8 seconds. Carlos finished third, just behind Peter Norman of Australia. Both clocked 20.0 seconds.

At the medal ceremony the two Americans made their move. Shoeless, they mounted the victory stand, with their sweat pants rolled up to reveal long black socks, familiar in ghetto neighborhoods. Each wore a black glove. As the "Star Spangled Banner" was played, saluting the American gold medal victory, Smith and Carlos bowed their heads and defiantly thrust their gloved fists skyward in a black power salute.

Payton Jordan, the American track coach, said, "They'll regret this for the rest of their lives." But Smith and Carlos showed no remorse.

"This was a victory for black people everywhere," said Smith,

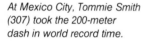

At Mexico City, Tommie Smith (307) took the 200-meter dash in world record time.

who once held 11 world records. "We are proud we did it," added Carlos.

The United States Olympic Committee reprimanded the two athletes and issued an official apology. That did not satisfy the International Olympic Committee which warned about drastic sanctions against the United States team, including possible expulsion from the Games, unless stronger action were taken against Smith and Carlos. Under pressure, the USOC suspended the two athletes from the American team and ordered them expelled from the Olympic Village.

The expulsion was academic because Smith and Carlos had moved out anyway. But it was symbolic and it created an immediate split in the American team. Many athletes supported the stand of their teammates. Others defended the USOC action.

A decade later, Smith, a track coach at Santa Monica College, said, "I did what I did because I felt it, not because someone told me to do it. I felt it was my contribution not only to all people but especially to athletes to let them know they do have a place in life."

When three other black Americans, Lee Evans, Larry James, and Ron Freeman, scored a 1-2-3 medal sweep in the 400-meter run, they were watched carefully for signs of further protest. But there were none, unless one counted the black berets they wore to the victory stand.

Evans, who broke Tommie Smith's world record with a time of 43.8, was asked if the berets had any particular significance. "I won my gold medal for all black people of the world," he replied. "And for my white friends, too."

Australia's Peter Norman stood at attention as Tommie Smith and John Carlos, both of the United States, gave the black power salute during the medal presentation ceremonies. Norman was second; Smith and Carlos were first and third, respectively.

Bob Beamon

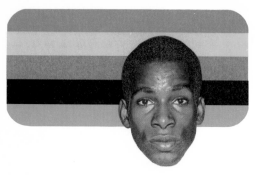

But, then, come to think of it, I was in the air a long time.

—BOB BEAMON

Of all Olympic records, the most impressive single achievement was Bob Beamon's long jump in the XIX Olympiad in the Estadio Olimpico at Mexico City, Oct. 18, 1968. In one fantastic effort, unmatched in the recorded history of track and field, Bob Beamon soared an incredible and incomprehensible 29′ 2½″. The jump totally eclipsed the world record—by almost two feet—and shattered the mythical barrier of 28 feet. Beamon's jump was so long that it eluded the range of the specially installed electronic measuring device. Track historians tried to translate the record into more meaningful terms. They calculated that Beamon's jump was the equivalent of feats that remained unaccomplished more than a decade later—running the mile in 3:43, high jumping 8′, putting the shot 76′ 7″.

Instead of receiving praise for his achievement, Beamon encountered detractors wherever he went. They challenged what he had accomplished, questioned how he had done it, attached so many asterisks that the argument over the record obliterated the record itself. There is no doubt it preyed on Beamon's mind. "Some people said I made a lucky jump in the Olympics," he said. "After a while, that kind of talk gets into your mind."

The controversy centered on several factors—a following wind of 2.0 meters per second (the maximum allowable velocity for a record), a lightning fast runway that had enabled five triple jump finalists to break the world record, and the thin air of Mexico City. The most vocal detractors concluded that Mexico City's altitude was mother to the achievement.

The facts, however, prove that the biggest factor of all was Bob Beamon. The competition included the world-record coholders, Ralph Boston of the United States and Igor Ter-Ovanesyan of the Soviet Union. All three competed under the same circumstances of wind, runway, and altitude and neither Boston nor Ter-Ovanesyan was able to break the world record that day. That leaves little doubt that Beamon was THE factor. In support of Beamon, Bert Nelson, publisher of *Track & Field News*, wrote that "Bob's amazing jump was a combination of the greatest talent ever [in the field], his firing up for the ultimate in competition, a perfect step, fast runway, the altitude, the maximum assisting wind, and excellent form."

Earlier Bob Beamon had made an even bigger leap—out of the ghetto. "My high school (Jamaica in New York City) was a jungle," Beamon explained. Beamon took refuge in basketball. The stringy, 6-foot-3 basketball player was so good that the Harlem Magicians offered him a contract after he had graduated from high school. Some colleges were just as impressed, but the sensitive Beamon settled on North Carolina A.T. to be near his ailing grandmother. His high school coach, Lawrence Ellis, had also convinced him that he should concentrate more on jumping than basketball. And, when his grandmother died, he moved to Texas-El Paso, where he came under the skilled track guidance of Wayne Vandenberg.

Beamon, meanwhile, worked on his speed and perfecting a technique in which the jumper does not so much jump as walk in the air while sailing over the pit. By 1968, he was undefeated outdoors.

After Mexico City he had great fame and little else. He was so broke that he could not even pay his telephone bill. His wife lost her job. After the marriage ended in divorce, Beamon decided to return to college at Texas-El Paso. He got so far behind in his studies that he had to drop three courses. When he refused to compete in a meet against Brigham Young University in a protest over Mormon racial policies, he was stripped of his track scholarship.

At the urging of promoters trying to capitalize on his record, Beamon competed even while he was injured. He changed his takeoff to compensate, and had difficulty reaching 25 feet.

Ignorant of the truth, but no less ready to pronounce judgment, the belittlers cited their "facts" to prove that the wonderful jump was only a fluke. They pretty well broke Beamon's spirit.

He turned professional in 1973. He was named to the National Track and Field Hall of Fame (1977).

Most of the militance and protest in the 1968 Games was concentrated on the track and field team. Two black Americans, Jim Hines—who equaled his 9.9-second world record—and Charlie Greene, finished first and third in the 100-meter dash. But they refused to accept their medals from Avery Brundage, who was the most visible of the IOC officials whose conciliatory attitude to South Africa had angered blacks. To avoid further problems and embarrassment, the medal presentations to Hines and Greene were made by Lord Burghley of Great Britain.

When black American boxer George Foreman was asked what he thought about the racial turmoil, he shrugged it off, saying, "That stuff's for college kids. They live in a different world."

Foreman's world was the boxing ring. And he made the 1968 Games memorable in that ring. Traditionally, the Olympics have been the last amateur stop for some of the world's top boxers. They were for Foreman in 1968.

A husky 19-year-old who came out of the slums of Houston, Foreman had only 21 amateur bouts before the Olympics. He wiped out every opponent he faced in the Games and in the finals he stopped Iones Chepulis of the USSR in the second round, to capture the gold medal in the heavyweight division.

Foreman was immediately mobbed by his teammates, who presented him with a bouquet of roses. He turned the flowers over to the Russian in a sportsmanlike gesture and then acknowledged the cheers of the crowd by marching around the ring, waving a small American flag.

Jim Hines anchored the U.S. 400-meter relay team to victory in world record time. In contrast to the outbreaks of racial protest, frequent among black Americans in 1968, George Foreman waved an American flag after capturing a gold in heavyweight boxing competition.

With an unorthodox style that came to be known as "The Fosbury Flop," Dick Fosbury of Medford, Oregon, won a gold medal with a 7' 4½" high jump. Bob Beamon (right) took the long jump with an incredible leap of 29' 2½".

Several individual performances made track and field history. There was the world record of Bob Beamon. The spindly youngster soared through the thin atmosphere as if propelled by a rocket to win the long jump with an unbelievable leap of 29′ 2½″.

On the day before his record leap, Beamon barely qualified for the finals, earning it on his last jump of the day. Once qualified, he stunned the track world on his first medal jump. From a sprinting start, Beamon took off from his right foot and flew skyward, seeming for a moment to be walking on air. When he landed, he had almost over-jumped the pit.

Beamon leaned over and kissed the ground. "I was thanking that Man up there for letting me hit the ground where He did," Beamon said.

Beamon's jump left other competitors flabbergasted. No one was close to him. Great Britain's Lynn Davies, the 1964 Olympic champion, was so awestruck that his own performance was affected. "I was so shocked," he said, "I ceased to be a competitor and became a spectator."

There was Bill Toomey, who spent four years preparing for the competition and captured the punishing 10-event decathlon by a margin of only 82 points. "I couldn't miss," Toomey joked after winning his gold medal. "Ten's my favorite number. Ten letters in my name, born on January 10th, always wore number 10 as a ball player. It had to be the decathlon."

There was Oregon's Dick Fosbury, whose unorthodox high jump form was frowned upon by track purists—until it earned him a gold medal. The traditional high jump technique sent competitors leaping off their inside foot, lifting the outside foot over the bar first, and then following it in a sort of rolling motion with the rest of the body. Fosbury, however, propelled off his outside foot, turned his back to the bar and went over in a head-first, backward motion. The style was called "The Fosbury Flop" and even its inventor found it difficult to explain.

Bill Toomey, caught in the middle of his long jump, won that phase of the decathlon with a distance of 25′ 9¾″. He was first, as well, in putting the shot (left). His 82-point margin of victory was enough to set a new Olympic record.

"It's the only way I know how to do it," he said. "I don't care what they call it, as long as it gets me across. Sometimes, I see movies and I wonder how I do it."

There was Bob Seagren, who won the pole vault on the eve of his 22nd birthday in the closest competition of the Games. It took seven hours to settle the battle. When it was over the young American's 17' 8½" vault, the same as those of two Germans, earned him the gold on the basis of fewer misses. It marked a world record and the first time the 17' height had been bettered in the Olympics. But Seagren had not even started to vault until the bar was raised to 17 feet!

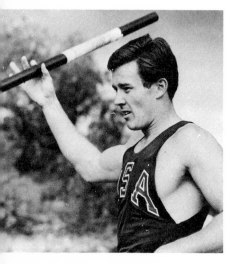

Pole vaulter Bob Seagren was awarded a gold medal on the basis of fewer misses after the American and two Germans went over the bar at 17' 8½".

Bill Toomey

In the decathlon, you have 10 mistresses instead of one, all keeping you busy. It's more work—but more fun, too.

—BILL TOOMEY

It took Bill Toomey until he was 24 years old to recognize the full significance of the decathlon. He had tried the event in 1959 with moderate success and again in 1962 with a more promising performance that persuaded him to pursue it seriously. In 1968, at the age of 29, he won the Olympic gold medal.

Bill Toomey began his track career as a quarter-miler. But there were many who could run the distance in much faster time, and Bill Toomey never liked being in the middle of the pack. "All of a sudden," he explained, "I realized I was just another quarter-miler in a world of stinking quarter-milers." When he looked at other events to try he decided that, rather than attempt one, he would be happier with ten. It was as simple a decision as that.

There were those who laughed out loud when he began to work at the decathlon. After all, he weighed only 168 pounds, and a high school accident had left his right hand partially paralyzed.

"You know what it takes to become a decathlon man?" he asked. "It takes the upper body of a weight man, the lower body of a sprinter, and the brain of an idiot."

Toomey began serious training in 1963 and just missed qualifying for the 1964 Olympic team.

Over the next four years he continued to build his body and perfect his techniques. By 1968, the junior high school teacher from Santa Barbara, Calif., was ready. He now weighed 190, and had conquered the techniques of the throwing events well enough to be competitive, although the pole vault was still capable of mastering him.

So were his chief competitors—Kurt Bendlin and Hans-Joachim Walde of West Germany. Toomey had spent time training with them two years before, but when they arrived in Mexico City they went their separate ways.

It was almost over after the first day of competition on October 18. Toomey used his quarter-miler's speed to clock 45.6 seconds in the 400-meters, an astounding time for a decathlete. His long jump of 25' 9¾" gave him an almost insurmountable lead. His 4,499 points were the best-ever first day score.

But the second day of competition was totally different. It was so hot Toomey drank several gallons of water. He suffered a touch of diarrhea. And Mexican officials lost his vaulting pole. Although the pole eventually was found, its temporary loss seemed to have a psychological effect on Toomey. The event had always given him trouble, and he was so unsettled that he missed his first two attempts at 11' 9¾".

High up in the stands of the Olympic stadium, Toomey's parents, his two brothers, and thousands of American rooters watched with concern as he prepared for his final try. "My mother could not look," said Jim Toomey, Bill's younger brother. "I was so nervous, I walked out of the stands."

Bill started his approach, hit full stride—and pulled up. "I don't know why I stopped," he said. "I was just prolonging the agony. For the first time in my life, I felt, 'The country is expecting something from you.' Suddenly I realized the clock was running. I had only 30 seconds to jump. I said, 'The heck with it,' and started again."

He sped down the runway once more, planted the pole and sailed upward. The cheer that followed told Toomey's mother he had made it. She took her hands away from her eyes. Jim Toomey raced back into the stands.

Before the final event, the 1,500 meters, Toomey worried that the West Germans would work together to beat him by enough time to overtake his point total. But there was no collusion, and the heat and altitude had taken their toll of the West Germans as much as they had of the American. It was Toomey's race all the way, and as he crossed the finish line he flashed victory signs with both hands. His time of 4:57.1 gave him a total of 8,193 points for the decathlon, an Olympic record.

In the stands, West Germany's famed decathlon coach, Friedel Schirmer, greeted Toomey's mother:

"Your boy is the greatest in the world."

In Mexican waters, Debbie Meyer (above, foreground) became the first swimmer to take three individual golds; the United States, Denmark, and East Germany finished first, second, and third in the Dragon class yacht race at Acapulco; the United States team (dark caps) faced Cuba in the water polo tournament. Neither team won a medal.

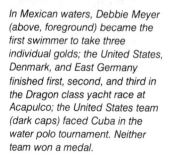

Debbie Meyer

I wasn't a very good swimmer.

—DEBBIE MEYER

The gifts Deborah Meyer received on Christmas Day 1964 stunned her. Number 1 was the news that her family was moving from Haddonfield, N.J., to Sacramento, Calif. Number 2 was a stopwatch with the inscription: "Mexico City, 1968."

"I wasn't sure if I liked the idea of moving," she explained. "As for the stopwatch, I thought the inscription was funny. I wasn't a very good swimmer. And I didn't have any thoughts of making the Olympic team in 1968."

Less than four years later, in Mexico City, 16-year-old Debbie Meyer became the first swimmer in history to win three individual gold medals in a single Olympics. Her time of 4:31.8 for the 400-meter freestyle established a new Olympic record. The 200- and 800-meter freestyle events were on the women's program for the first time, so her respective times of 2:10.5 and 9:24.0 also set Olympic standards. Her superlative performance in Mexico City earned her the Sullivan Award as the outstanding amateur athlete of the year.

Debbie first hit the water at age five when she began swimming in the Severn River at Annapolis, Md., where she was visiting her mother's parents. At eight she started swimming competitively in Haddonfield. She was never considered anything but average, and her clockings didn't even warrant the purchase of a stopwatch.

When she joined the Arden Hills Swim Club in Sacramento, Debbie came under the tutelage of coach Sherman Chavoor. In his drills, Chavoor stressed obedience, punctuality, and above all, endurance. "Coaching swimmers," he said, "is 90 percent conditioning." Chavoor called it condition-

ing. His swimmers called it surviving. Anyone late for practice had to pull weeds for hours.

When Debbie was introduced to Chavoor, his first words were: "Okay, Debbie, let's see you do a fast 20 laps." Debbie immediately jumped into the pool but had to be pulled out after eight. If Chavoor was not pushing her to do more laps, he was yelling at her to produce faster times. He saw Debbie's raw talent, her natural stroke and cross-legged kick, and recognized that if he drilled her unsparingly the Olympics could be a realistic goal.

By the time she was 15, Debbie was 5-foot-7, 115 pounds, strong enough to swim the Arden Hills pool several hundred times each day, and successful enough to have the unique status of being selected Sportswoman of the Year 1967 by TASS, the Soviet news agency.

But Chavoor continued to yell at Debbie, even in Mexico City. Rival coaches could not believe how hard he was driving his star. "Now show some guts," he shouted. "Get moving in that water."

But on the morning of the 200-meter finals, while warming up for her heat in the 800-meters, Debbie was afflicted with dysentery. The pain and discomfort roiled her insides. When she got out of the pool, tears were streaming down her face. She was not sure whether she would be able to continue. But when it was time for her heat, Debbie got back on the starting blocks and turned in the fastest qualifying time.

That night she faced her greatest test in the finals of the 200-meters. She was swimming against Jan Henne, the gold medalist in the 100-meters, and she was still fighting a queasy stomach.

Meyer got off to a bad start, and it was obvious that she wasn't at her best. At the first turn she led Henne by only a head. Chavoor was worried. "She's holding back," he said. "She's not going to make it that way." But Debbie did what she had to. Head to head with Henne with just five meters to go, Debbie surged ahead with her last half-dozen strokes and won by a mere 0.5 seconds.

After that there was no stopping Debbie. She flashed off the starting blocks in the 800-meter finals, pulled to an early lead, and swam home a full 10 seconds ahead of the field.

Prior to the Olympics, Debbie Meyer had decided that if she won one gold medal it would be for her parents. If she won two, the second would go to Chavoor. Only if she won three would she keep a medal for herself.

It went nicely with her stopwatch.

There was Al Oerter, the 32-year-old discus thrower, who had won three straight Olympic gold medals but was considered a long shot in the 1968 Games because of his age. Nevertheless, Oerter responded to the Olympic challenge and pressure, becoming the first athlete to win gold medals in the same event in four consecutive Games. His winning throw was 212′ 6½″—five feet farther than his best previous effort.

For Ron Clarke of Australia the victory podium remained elusive. He was 31 and had set 17 world records during his running career. He never won an Olympic gold medal. The dream was over as well for Ethiopia's Abebe Bikila, who was seeking a third straight marathon victory, and for world mile record-holder Jim Ryun of the United States, who finished a distant second to Kenya's Kipchoge Keino in the 1,500-meter run.

In swimming and diving, the United States won 23 of the 33 events, with 16-year-old Debbie Meyer becoming the first swimmer to take three individual events in a single Olympics: the 200-, the 400-, and the 800-meter freestyle. The star of the men's swimming competition was Roland Matthes of East Germany, who won both individual backstroke races and broke his own 100-meter world record on the opening leg of the medley relay.

The perfect gold medal streak of the United States in basketball was in jeopardy in 1968. Several American collegiate stars had chosen to pass up the Olympics. Among the missing was Lew Alcindor, the nation's dominant undergraduate player, whose 7-foot presence would have been a boon to the Americans. Coach Hank Iba compensated for the missing players by using his squad to maximum effect. Led by Spencer Haywood and Jo Jo White, the young Americans swept nine straight games and won another basketball gold medal.

Czechoslovakia's Vera Caslavska (above) was the star women's gymnast and became the first woman to win four golds in a summer games. She took the uneven bars, the long horse, individual all-around, and the floor exercise. Spencer Haywood (8) of the United States attempts to block the shot of Yugoslavia's Peter Skansi. The United States remained undefeated in Olympic basketball as the 1968 team won nine consecutive games. Yugoslavia was runner-up.

FINAL MEDAL STANDINGS			
Nation	G	S	B
United States	45	28	34
Soviet Union	29	32	30
Japan	11	7	7
Hungary	10	10	12
East Germany	9	9	7
France	7	3	5
Czechoslovakia	7	2	4
West Germany	5	10	10
Australia	5	7	5
Great Britain	5	5	3
Poland	5	2	11
Rumania	4	6	5
Italy	3	4	9
Kenya	3	4	2
Mexico	3	3	3
Yugoslavia	3	3	2
The Netherlands	3	3	1
Bulgaria	2	4	3
Iran	2	1	2
Sweden	2	1	1
Turkey	2	–	–
Denmark	1	4	3
Canada	1	3	1
Finland	1	2	1
Ethiopia	1	1	–
Norway	1	1	–
New Zealand	1	–	2
Tunisia	1	–	1
Pakistan	1	–	–
Venezuela	1	–	–
Cuba	–	4	–
Austria	–	2	2
Switzerland	–	1	4
Mongolia	–	1	3
Brazil	–	1	2
Belgium	–	1	1
South Korea	–	1	1
Uganda	–	1	1
Cameroon	–	1	–
Jamaica	–	1	–
Argentina	–	–	2
Greece	–	–	1
India	–	–	1
Taiwan	–	–	1

Vera Caslavska, who had won three gold medals in Tokyo, dominated the gymnastics events, becoming the first woman to win four individual gold medals in a summer Games. At Mexico City, Vera was also the symbol of Czech resistance to Soviet dominance. In fact, she presented her gold medals to the leaders of the Czech independence movement, Alexander Dubcek, Ludvik Svoboda, and Oldrich Cernik. However, when a hard-line regime returned to power in Czechoslovakia, the gymnast and her husband, runner Josef Odlozil, whom she had married in Mexico City, were harassed and humiliated. Both were repeatedly denied employment.

The oldest competitor in the Games, 67-year-old Louis Noverraz, yachtsman in the 5.5 meter class, took a silver medal home with him to Switzerland.

Other athletes who performed memorably at Mexico City included Mohammad Nassiri, who won Iran's first gold medal in weightlifting; 44-year-old Bill Steinkraus of the United States, who took a gold medal in the Grand Prix equestrian jumping event; Czechoslovakia's Miroslava Rezkova, who captured the gold for high jump on her third try; Milena Duchkova, also of Czechoslovakia, who received a gold for platform diving; Britain's Robert Braithwaite, who tied a world record in clay pigeon shooting; France's Daniel Morelon and Pierre Trentin, who won duplicate golds in cycling competition; Bjorn Ferm of Sweden, gold medalist in the modern pentathlon event; Viorica Viscopoleanu of Rumania and Margitta Gummel of East Germany, who established world records in the women's long jump and shot put, respectively; and Britain's David Hemery, triumphant in the 400-meter hurdles.

Canada's only gold medal was captured in the equestrian team Grand Prix jumping event. In other team competition, Pakistan achieved the gold in field hockey; Hungary was the recipient of the gold medal for soccer; the USSR won both the women's and the men's volleyball events; and Yugoslavia was victorious in water polo. The United States qualified for all seven rowing finals but failed to win a single gold medal.

During the closing ceremonies on October 27, with the massed athletes of 100-odd nations marching arm in arm around Estadio Olimpico, fiesta-style, the scoreboard signaled the call to the next Olympiad with a simple message: "Munich '72."

Riding "Snowbound," Bill Steinkraus, a 44-year-old from Noroton, Connecticut, was awarded a gold medal in Grand Prix equestrian jumping.

1972

Winter Games

Sapporo, Japan

Austria's 33-year-old skier Karl Schranz was the center of the most heated controversy of the 1972 Winter Olympics in Sapporo, Japan. Three days before the opening ceremonies, Schranz, a favorite in the men's Alpine events, was barred from competing in the Games. His exclusion was the result of a feud between the International Olympic Committee (IOC) and the International Skiing Federation (FIS). The central issue was commercialism.

FIS was sympathetic to skiers and therefore indirectly to manufacturers of ski equipment. Leading skiers were subsidized by manufacturers in return for exposure of their products in international competition. Schranz was reputed to have earned upward of $60,000 a year prior to the Sapporo Games. Avery Brundage, the 84-year-old president of the IOC and the autocratic protector of amateurism, led the opposition.

When Brundage arrived in Sapporo, he was determined to put an end to ski "shamateurism." He said he had a black list of 40 names. All were skiers who, according to Brundage, had violated IOC regulations. Brundage said they would not be allowed to flaunt the rules, and that punitive action would be taken.

When Schranz was asked about Brundage's threats, the Austrian said, "This thing of amateur purity is something that dates back to the 19th century when amateur sportsmen were regarded as gentlemen and everyone else was an outcast. The Olympics should be a competition of skill and strength and speed—and no more."

One day after Schranz' remarks were printed, the IOC executive met to study the question of amateur eligibility. When the meeting ended, Schranz was barred from the Games. He was the only skier of the 40 on Brundage's black list to be punished. The vote was 28–14. What doomed

In a dispute with Avery Brundage, Austria's star skier Karl Schranz, a veteran of 18 seasons of world class meets, was excluded from the 1972 Winter Games for commercialism. Although Italy's World Cup champion Gustavo Thoeni (below) won the men's giant slalom, his performance in the slalom, which earned him a silver medal, was a personal disappointment.

Schranz was allowing his name and picture to be used in commercial advertising. That made him the most serious offender.

Schranz said, "The Russians are subsidized by their government and all international athletes get help from one source or another."

Jean-Claude Killy of France, the 1968 Alpine triple gold medalist, said, "There are no amateurs anymore. To be good, a skier must literally devote from four to six years of his life to the sport. You don't have time for school or a job, and you must travel the world. That's hard to do without compensation."

Karl Heinz Klee, president of the Austrian Ski Federation, threatened to withdraw his team from the Winter Olympics. "Schranz is being sacrificed in a highly unethical manner," Klee said. "Under the circumstances, there is one road open to us—the road home." However, at Schranz' urging, the Austrians did not withdraw.

Subsequently, the FIS suspended French skier Annie Famose because of her involvement with a European television network.

There were 1,125 athletes from 35 nations who competed in Sapporo, the largest city and the first in Asia ever to host a Winter Games. (The city was scheduled to hold the 1940 Winter Games but war intervened.) Sapporo, with a population of more than 1 million, is on Japan's northernmost main island of Hokkaido. It is located 400 miles west of Vladivostok, USSR, and is approximately on the same latitude as Milwaukee, Wisconsin, Buffalo, New York, and Marseilles, France. Wherever one went in Sapporo in early 1972, there was no escaping signs saying YOKOSO, meaning WELCOME.

Male Alpine skiers from Spain, Italy, and Switzerland welcomed the absence of Schranz and went on to win gold medals. Francisco Fernández-Ochoa took the slalom for Spain's first-ever Winter

Olympics championship. He finished just ahead of the Italians Gustavo and Rolando Thoeni. Ochoa had trained with the French and was advised by France's world champion Jean-Noël Augert. However, in the two-run slalom, Augert was severely handicapped by bruised ribs suffered in a classification race. He placed fifth in the event, although only Ochoa was faster on the first run. Gustavo Thoeni was 32/100ths of a second faster than Ochoa on the second run, but the Spaniard's combined time of 1 minute, 49.27 seconds earned him the gold medal. Gustavo clocked 1:50.28, 2/100ths of a second faster than his cousin, Rolando.

Gustavo Thoeni, the 1971 and 1972 World Cup champion, won the two-run giant slalom which officials called the steepest in history. Thoeni was third fastest on the first run and second fastest on the second. Switzerland's Edmund Bruggmann and Werner Mattle finished second and third. The Swiss rallied after finishing the first run in 10th and 11th places. Bruggmann had the fastest second run and Mattle the third fastest. Only 24/100ths of a second separated the silver and bronze medalists.

Only in the downhill on Mount Eniwa did Austrian men win a medal. Heinrich Messner took the bronze, although handicapped by the flu. The co-favorites were France's Henri Duvillard and Switzerland's Bernhard Russi. Russi placed first as the Swiss occupied four of the first six positions, including the runner-up Roland Collombin, who was only 64/100ths of a second behind the gold medalist. Duvillard finished 19th.

The failure of Duvillard and Augert was indicative of the eclipse of French success in the men's Alpine events in which Killy had scored a triple four years earlier.

By finishing first in the men's slalom, Francisco Fernández-Ochoa became the first Spaniard to capture a gold in Winter Olympic competition. The victory was considered an indication of the increasingly wider appeal of winter sports.

During the women's downhill presentation ceremonies, Switzerland's gold medalist Marie-Thérèse Nadig (center) appeared to feel the cold more than Austria's silver medalist Annemarie Proell (left) and bronze winner Susan Corrock of the United States. Combatting thick clouds and a major snowstorm on Mount Teine, Barbara Cochran (below), 21-year-old member of a competitive skiing family from Richmond, Vermont, scored an upset victory in the women's slalom.

Austria, disappointed by the banning of Schranz, was also disappointed by the performance of 18-year-old Annemarie Proell, a strong favorite in the women's Alpine events. Annemarie, a freckle-faced, 150-pounder, was the 1971 and 1972 World Cup champion. However, in Sapporo, she twice finished second to Switzerland's Marie-Thérèse Nadig, a 17-year-old. Nadig started the downhill in the number 13 position and recorded a time of 1 minute, 36.68 seconds. Proell, the 15th starter, was 32/100ths of a second slower. Susan Corrock stunned the Alpine world by placing third, giving the United States its first skiing medal since 1964.

Three days after the downhill, Nadig made it two in a row over Proell in the giant slalom, with another Austrian, Wiltrud Drexel, third. Drexel was 13/100ths of a second faster than Canada's Laurie Kreiner.

The gold medal in the slalom went to Barbara Cochran, a 21-year-old member of America's foremost skiing family. Her two-run combined total of 1 minute, 31.24 seconds was only 2/100ths of a second faster than the runs of 17-year-old Danièle Debernard of France—the smallest margin in Olympic skiing history. Florence Steurer of France was third. Proell was fifth and Nadig fell during the first run. Marilyn Cochran, a sister of the gold medalist, missed a gate on the first run and was disqualified.

Barbara Cochran's victory in the slalom was the first for an American in an Alpine event since Andrea Mead Lawrence's (1952). "Until today I felt that the highest award in skiing would be winning the World Cup," she said. "However, now I am just beginning to understand the importance of winning a gold medal in the Olympic Games."

Barbara's unexpected triumph was the result of delicate psychology as well as smooth skiing. When Barbara arrived in Sapporo, ski coach Hank Tauber permitted her to practice alone. "That way, I could think things out for myself," she said. At times, Barbara worked out with her younger brother, Bob, and her boyfriend, Rick Chaffee, both slalom specialists. It was the two of them who lifted Barbara overhead to signal her triumph at the foot of Mount Teine on February 11th, 1972.

While there was no triple gold medalist such as Killy in Alpine skiing in 1972, Ard Schenk of The Netherlands, who was nicknamed The Flying Dutchman, became the third male speed skater and the first in 20 years to win three individual events in a single Olympics.

Schenk, a handsome, blond, blue-eyed 200-pound powerhouse, began his collection in the Makomanai Stadium in the 5,000 meters on February 4. He had an unfavorable starting position, skating in the first pair. During the race, he battled a heavy snowstorm. This accounted for his comparatively slow winning time of 7 minutes, 23.61 seconds. His own world record was 7:12.00, and the Olympic mark was 7:22.40 set by Fred Anton Maier of Norway in 1968. Nevertheless, Schenk beat runner-up Roar Grönvold of Norway by 4.57 seconds. Sten Stensen, another Norwegian, took the bronze medal, almost 10 seconds behind the winner.

For one day, February 5, Schenk was not king as Erhard Keller, a West German dental student, retained his 500-meter title with an Olympic record 39.44 seconds, finishing ahead of Sweden's former world record holder Hasse Börjes and the Soviet Union's Valeri Mouratov. World record holder Leo Linkovesi of Finland placed sixth. Keller won despite three nerve-racking false starts, two of them his fault. Schenk placed 34th among the 37 starters.

Schenk, a physiotherapist from Amsterdam, regained his confidence the following day and won the 1,500-meter event with an Olympic record 2:02.96. Grönvold placed second, ahead of Sweden's Goran Claesson. This was a particularly satisfying victory for Schenk because he had won the silver medal in this event in 1968.

The 10,000-meter race was skated under sunny skies on February 7. Soviet Valeri Lavroushkin, starting in the first pair, shattered the Olympic record of 15 minutes, 23.60 seconds set by Sweden's Jonny Hoeglin in 1968. Stensen, in the second pair, and Verkerk, in the fourth pair, lowered the mark even further. Verkerk then waited three hours until Schenk went to the starting line in the 12th and final pair. The 6' 3½" Dutch ace used his giant and rhythmic strides to glide over the ice in 15:01.35, eclipsing Hoglin's record by an astonishing 22.25 seconds! Verkerk and Stensen were awarded the silver and bronze prizes.

The few Dutch attending the Games began immediately to celebrate Schenk's victories, singing *Ard Is Always World Champion*.

In 1972 Northbrook, Illinois, which calls itself the "Speed Skating Capital of America," produced the first American women gold medalists in the sport—16-year-old Anne Henning and 20-year-old Dianne Holum. Henning, a curly-haired blonde who traveled with her lucky Snoopy button and a generous supply of peanut butter, won the gold medal in the 500-meter race and a bronze in the 1,000. Holum, who worked as a waitress the previous year to finance a three-month training period in The Netherlands, captured the 1,500-meter race and placed second in the 3,000. Holum had narrowly missed winning a gold medal in Grenoble, tying for second in the 500 and taking the bronze in the 1,000.

Skating in the fifth pair with Nina Statkevich (USSR), the 1971 world champion, in the Sapporo 1,500-meter event, Holum trailed in the early part of the race, and then streaked to a 38.9-second final

Displaying grace and strength, Dianne Holum became the first American to take a gold in women's Olympic speed skating. The 20-year-old from Northbrook, Illinois, won the 1,500 in Olympic record time and finished second in the 3,000-meter race.

lap to win in the Olympic record time of 2:20.85. Statkevich was sixth. World record holder Christina "Stien" Baas-Kaiser of The Netherlands took the silver medal, and finished ahead of another Dutch girl, Atje Keulen-Deelstra. Holum broke the mark of 2:22.40 set by Kaija Mustonen of Finland in 1968.

Henning twice broke the Olympic record in winning the Sapporo 500 meters. Paired with Sylvia Burka, the American's progress was impeded by the Canadian as the skaters changed lanes. Despite a near collision, Henning posted a time of 43.73 seconds that shattered the Olympic mark set by Lidia Skoblikova (USSR) in 1964. Burka was disqualified for blocking Henning, a development that prompted the United States coach, Ed Rudolph of Northbrook, Illinois, to lodge a protest that was upheld. After all of the skaters completed the race, Henning was permitted a solo run and the choice of selecting her best time.

Henning accepted the challenge because she wanted a shot at her own world record under ideal race conditions. With an enthusiastic crowd supporting her, Henning lowered her own Olympic record to 43.33. However, her world mark of 42.75 stood.

Soviets placed second and third in the 500. Vera Krasnova took the silver medal, while defending champion, Ludmila Titova, captured the bronze. Sheila Young of the United States was fourth.

Henning's extra race proved costly a day later when she finished third in the 1,000 meters. Monika Pflug, a 17-year-old bookbinding apprentice from West Germany, scored the upset of women's speed skating by winning the gold medal. After two false starts, she clocked an Olympic record 1:31.40, breaking the mark set by Caroline Geijssen of The Netherlands in 1968. "I didn't have it. I woke up feeling like I'd been hit by a truck," said Henning. Keulen-Deelstra won the silver medal, finishing 1/100th of a second better than Henning. Titova, the world record holder, was fourth and Holum placed sixth.

A fall in the 500 prevented Ard Schenk from winning four golds in speed skating. Czechoslovakia's Ondrej Nepela took the gold in figure skating.

Holum took an early lead in the 3,000 meters that held up until she was overtaken by world record holder Baas-Kaiser. Skating in the next-to-last pair, the Dutch woman clocked 4 minutes, 52.14 seconds. That was good enough for the gold medal and bettered the Olympic record set by Johanna "Ans" Schut, also of The Netherlands, in Grenoble. Silver medalist Holum was more than six seconds behind Baas-Kaiser. Keulen-Deelstra was third.

When competition moved into the indoor Makomanai Ice Palace for the figure skating, a major controversy developed. Many of the world's leading skaters were dissatisfied with the scoring and judging system. The dispute had come to a head during the 1971 world championship. The compulsory figures and the free skating program each counted 50 percent toward the total score at the time. At the 1971 championships, Austria's stocky and methodical Beatrix "Trixi" Schuba built such a commanding lead in the relatively dull and seldom-watched compulsory figures that she captured the title. However, 21 of the 22 contestants were judged higher in the freestyle skating.

Although Trixi was no better than seventh in the free skating at Sapporo, which was dominated by Janet Lynn of the United States and Karen Magnussen of Canada, she won the Olympic gold. Schuba's precise perfection in the compulsory figures enabled her to enter the free skating with an insurmountable lead.

Lynn, a pixy in pink, whirled through her program with grace despite a fall, to place first in the freestyle. However, she ended up with a bronze medal, and Magnussen took the silver. The 1972 Games marked the last Olympics in which the 50–50 percent scoring system was used.

The men's figure skating champion was Ondrej Nepela of Czechoslovakia. He won although he fell for the first time in four years of major competition. The Czech was first in the compulsory figures and fourth in the free skating. Sergei Chetveroukhin (USSR) and France's Patrick Pera placed second and third, ahead of two Americans, Ken Shelley and John Misha Petkevich.

Irina Rodnina and Aleksei Ulanov of the Soviet Union succeeded the Protopopovs as the pairs champions. Ludmilla Smirnova and Andrei Suraikin won the silver medal. But the talk of Sapporo was the romantic involvement of Aleksei and Ludmilla. After the Games, Smirnova and Ulanov became partners on and off the ice.

An East German tandem, Manuela Gross and Uwe Kagelmann, won the bronze medal. The Americans—Kenneth Shelley and Alicia "JoJo" Starbuck, who later married football's Terry Bradshaw—placed fourth.

The frustration with the scoring system was emphasized by seventh-place finishers Melissa and Mark Militano. The American couple apparently lost points for wearing unorthodox costumes. "Skating is creative," Mark complained. "We have no intention of bowing to the traditions that say we can't express ourselves on the ice in our own way."

West Germany placed 1–2 in the two-man bobsled event with Wolfgang Zimmerer driving the gold-medal boblet. Jean Wicki drove the bronze-medal Swiss sled and also piloted the winning four-man sled. Italy was second in the four-man, while Zimmerer also collected his second medal of the Games, steering the bronze-medal sled. Only 85/100ths of a second separated the first three sleds over the four runs.

The highly regarded Soviet teams of Irina Rodnina and Aleksei Ulanov (center) and Ludmilla Smirnova and Andrei Suraikin (left) were first and second in the pairs figure skating. Manuela Gross and Uwe Kagelmann of East Germany were the bronze medalists.

The United States did not place a sled in the top-ten finishers in either event for the first time in the post-World War II era. The shutdown of the only United States bobsled facility in Lake Placid, New York, was given as the excuse.

East Germany captured eight of the nine medals in the luge competition. Wolfgang Scheidel, Harald Ehrig, and Wolfram Fiedler finished 1–2–3 in the men's singles. The East German team of Horst Hornlein-Reinhard Bredow and the Italian tandem of Paul Hildgartner-Walter Plaikner tied for the gold medal in the men's doubles. The teams had a two-run combined time of 1 minute, 28.35 seconds. There was no silver medal awarded. Klaus Bonsack-Wolfram Fiedler (East Germany) received the bronze.

In the women's singles, Anna Maria Muller won the gold medal by 31/100ths of a second over Ute Ruhrold. Margit Schumann was another 5/100ths of a second behind. The sweep was sweet revenge for the East Germans. Four years earlier, Muller, Angela Knoesel, and Otrun Enderlein, the 1964 champion, captured the top three places, but were disqualified for allegedly warming the runners of their sleds to increase speed.

The outstanding Nordic skier of the Games was Galina Kulakova of the Soviet Union. She won the 5- and 10-kilometer races and anchored the winning 15-kilometer relay team. Kulakova, a physical education teacher, had won a silver medal in the 5 kilometers and a bronze in the relay in 1968.

Finland's Marjatta Kajosmaa was the 1972 runner-up in the 5 kilometers, the bronze medalist in the 10 kilometers, and anchor in the silver-medal relay team that finished ahead of third-place Norway. Helena Sikolova of Czechoslovakia was the 5-kilometer bronze medalist. Alevtina Olunina (USSR) was the silver medalist in the 10 kilometers.

Sven-Ake Lundback, a 24-year-old Swede, won the men's 15-kilometer race. Soviet Fedor Simaschov was second. Norway's 20-year-old Ivar Formo won the bronze medal, finishing 6/100ths of a second ahead of Juha Mieto of Finland.

A 31-year-old Soviet, Vyacheslav Vedenin, won the 30-kilometer event. Norway's Paal Tyldum and Johs Harviken were second and third. At the age of 37, Walter Demel (West Germany) finished fifth.

Werner Geeser, a 24-year-old Swiss electromechanic, shocked the favored Scandinavians and Soviets by holding a 35-second lead at the 40-kilometer mark of the 50-kilometer race. But he slowed down in the final 10 meters and finished sixth. Norway, with Tyldum and Magne Myrmo, took the first two places.

Vedenin, with the fastest lap ever skied up to that time, anchored the Soviet Union to a narrow victory over Norway in the 40-kilometer relay. Switzerland was a surprise third as an unknown, Eduard Hauser, outraced Sweden's Lundback, the individual 15-kilometer gold medalist, on the final leg.

For the second consecutive time a German won the Nordic combined. The gold medal went to East Germany's Ulrich Wehling. Rauno Miettinen of Finland was second, while another East German, Karl-Heinz Luck, was third. Franz Keller (West Germany), the 1968 gold medalist, was 33rd.

The Japanese swept the 70-meter ski jump. The medalists in order of finish were Yukio Kasaya, Akitsugu Konno, and Seiji Aochi. Defending champion Jiri Raska of Czechoslovakia was fifth.

A Soviet team, anchored by Galina Kulakova, was number one in the 15-kilometer cross-country relay. A Finnish team and a Norwegian team were runners-up—33.22 seconds and 1 minute 5.34 seconds behind.

Five days later, the Japanese were as chagrined about the 90-meter jump as they were elated after the 70-meter jump. Kasaya's seventh place was their highest finish in the 90 meters. Wojciech Fortuna took the first gold medal ever won by Poland in ski jumping. Walter Steiner of Switzerland was the silver medalist and Rainer Schmidt of East Germany was third.

Magnar Solberg of Norway became the only man to win two gold medals in the biathlon, repeating his 1968 triumph. Finishing behind Solberg in Sapporo were Hansjorg Knauthe of East Germany and Lars Arwidson of Sweden, in third place.

The Soviet Union repeated its victory in the biathlon relay although the host Japanese surprisingly led after the first lap. Finland won the silver medal and East Germany the bronze.

Canada, a bronze medalist in ice hockey in 1968 and a six-time winner of the competition, was absent from the ice hockey tournament in Sapporo. The Canadians had withdrawn from international amateur play in 1970 in a dispute over the use of professional players. The Canadians felt playing professionals was the only way to equalize competition against the Soviets, whom they considered to be of dubious amateur status.

At Sapporo the Soviet team won its third straight gold medal with a record of 4 wins, 0 losses, and 1 tie, including a 7–2 triumph over the United States. The Soviets were led by Valeri Kharlamov, the tournament's top scorer with 15 points on 9 goals and 6 assists, and the goaltending of Vladislav Tretiak, who played while wearing a revolutionary bird-cage face mask.

The Soviets cinched their gold medal on the last day of the tournament by defeating Czechoslovakia, 5–2. The surprising United States team, which averaged only 22 years of age, tied the Czechs for second place with a 3–2–0 record, but took the silver medal because of its 5–1 triumph over Czechoslovakia. American goalie Mike Curran stopped 51 shots during that game and emerged as the leading netminder of the tournament. Craig Sarner was the top American scorer with 9 points on 4 goals and 5 assists. Mark Howe, 16-year-old son of Gordie Howe, was also a member of the U.S. squad.

The Japanese spent a record sum to stage the 1972 Winter Olympics. The Games left the city of Sapporo with new government-built expressways, a subway system, and large apartment complexes. As for the Games themselves, they were classified as "beautiful and perfect." In spite of the quarrel concerning commercialism which clouded the future of the Winter Olympics, the Japanese could be justly proud of the 1972 Winter Games. They had done a commendable job as host nation, offering excellent facilities and a friendly spirit.

More than 2½ years after the Olympic flame was extinguished in Sapporo, a 50-year-old Winter Olympics mistake was corrected. On September 13, 1974, Anders Haugen, an 86-year-old Norwegian-born American, was officially awarded the 1924 bronze medal in ski jumping. That made him the first American to win a medal in Nordic skiing. For a 50th anniversary reunion of the 1924 Norwegian Olympic team a former athlete brought a copy of the official 1924 Olympic results. He noted that Haugen, who placed fourth in the competition, had made the longest jump of the day, that his scores had been totaled incorrectly, and that he was entitled to third place, ahead of Norway's Thorleif Haug.

Soviet athletes, winners of a total of 16 medals at the XI Winter Games, march in the closing ceremonies at Sapporo. The Soviets were particularly strong in Nordic skiing.

FINAL MEDAL STANDINGS			
NATION	G	S	B
Soviet Union	8	5	3
East Germany	4	3	7
Switzerland	4	3	3
The Netherlands	4	3	2
United States	3	2	3
West Germany	3	1	1
Norway	2	5	5
Italy	2	2	1
Austria	1	2	2
Sweden	1	1	2
Japan	1	1	1
Czechoslovakia	1	–	2
Poland	1	–	–
Spain	1	–	–
Finland	–	4	1
France	–	1	2
Canada	–	1	–

1972

Summer Games
Munich, West Germany

Who will live and who will die. . . . Who by fire, who by the sword. . . ."

The words of the ancient Rosh Hashanah prayer, offered at sundown on September 8, 1972, to usher in the Hebrew year 5733, had a special poignancy.

Rosh Hashanah is always a solemn occasion. This one was doubly so, as Jews everywhere mourned the slaughter in Munich two days earlier of 11 Israeli Olympic athletes and officials by Arab terrorists.

At four in the morning of September 5, eight men in athletic sweat suits scaled the fence sur-

rounding the men's quarters of the Olympic Village in Munich. In their athletes' bags they carried automatic weapons and hand grenades.

In the dawn hush they made their way to 31 Connollystrasse, where the Israeli team of 28 was housed. At approximately 4:25, the door of the apartment where seven Israelis were sleeping was opened with a key. The sound aroused huge Yosef Gottfreund, a wrestling referee. As he rushed at the door, trying to hold off the intruders, he shouted the alarm: "Terroristen! Hevreh, sakanah!" (Danger, guys! Terrorists!)

Gunfire and muffled screams shattered the morning stillness. Several Israelis escaped through windows, but two were already dead, and nine others were hostages of the militant Arabs who called themselves Black September terrorists, sworn to destroy Israel. News of the assault spread first through the Olympic complex and then through the world. For the next 23 hours millions of television watchers shared the excruciating drama in Munich. It would be all that many of them would remember of the Games there, where the hosts had lavished energy and fortune to prepare a splendid setting for their celebration.

While German officials, from Chancellor Willy Brandt down, tried to negotiate the release of the hostages, a lesser struggle took place within the Olympic circles between those who demanded that the Games be stopped— and, like Norway and The Netherlands, withdrew their athletes to demonstrate their distress—and those who felt with Avery Brundage, officiating in his final Olympics, that there should be no yielding to criminal pressure. The argument ceased when the schedule was suspended in the evening of September 5.

The following morning 80,000 people gathered in the Olympic Stadium for an unscheduled ceremony. They were there to mourn the 11 Israelis killed by the Black Septembrists: the 2 in the dawn raid and the 9 hostages, all slain when German police tried to pick off their captors as they boarded an escape plane.

Swimmer Mark Spitz, an American Jew, had won a record seventh gold medal in Munich on September 4. The following morning, he went to a scheduled 9 A.M. press conference to discuss his achievement. He learned of the siege at 31 Connollystrasse shortly before he faced newsmen.

"I don't want to get up at that microphone," he told a United States swimming coach. "I'd be a perfect target for someone with a gun." Spitz, shielded by three American swimming officials, responded to questions while seated, then said to a coach, "Let's get the hell out of here."

As Spitz left the press conference, a West German official said that as Spitz, a Jew and famous, would be an object for any other Arab terrorists who might have penetrated the Olympic Village, the German government wanted him out of Munich immediately. Spitz left for England that day from Fürstenfeldbruck airfield where Black Septembrists killed the Israeli hostages early the next morning.

Before his departure, Spitz won four individual and three relay gold medals. Every race in which he was involved produced a world record. In Munich he wanted to do what he had failed to do four years before in Mexico City. There he had been touted to win six gold medals and had had to settle for two relay gold medals, a silver in the 100-meter butterfly, and a bronze in the 100-meter freestyle.

Peter Daland, head coach of the United States men's swimming team in Munich, said Mark would be tough. He was. He began in the 200-meter butterfly on August 28. He had finished last in that event in Mexico City. This time he won easily, more than two seconds ahead of teammates Gary Hall and Robin Backhaus.

Staged as the "Games of Joy" in an effort to erase the memory of the 1936 Berlin Games, the 1972 Munich Games experienced terror and death when masked Palestinian guerrillas stormed the Israeli living quarters, killing two Israeli athletes and taking nine others as hostages. German police dressed as athletes (above) climbed the complex in an unsuccessful attempt to attain vantage points from which to confront the terrorists. Later the nine Israeli hostages, five guerrillas, and a German policeman were killed in an airport shootout. Following the horror, a memorial service was held and flags flew at half-staff at the Olympic stadium (page 302).

Mark Spitz

It's tremendous, the pressure of not losing. . . . It's reached a point where my self-esteem comes into it. I just don't want to lose.

—MARK SPITZ

Mark Spitz won 2 gold medals on August 28, 1972, 1 on August 29, and 2 on August 31, one for each swimming race he entered. Psychologically, the hardest test for him had been the first race, the 200-meter butterfly, which he had been favored to win in Mexico City and had finished in 8th place. When he wiped out that failure by winning in Munich the pressure on him might have been expected to diminish; in fact, it increased. He faced the prospect of being called a failure even if he took a record six gold medals. That was because there were seven events he could enter and seven possible golds.

Mark Spitz knew what it was to lose.

Prior to the 1968 Olympics in Mexico City, George Haines, his coach at the Santa Clara Swim Club and the 1968 men's Olympic coach, predicted that Spitz would win five or six gold medals. The boast was attributed to the swimmer. When he won only two gold medals, both in relay events, he was ridiculed for talking and not performing.

Four years later, in Munich, Spitz was fully aware of the challenge that confronted him.

"I'm making no predictions," he said. "I'll just swim my best."

His best proved to be a perfect record. He entered 7 events and won 7 gold medals. Whether he was alone or part of a team, every event set a world record.

The 7 gold medals won by Spitz is a record for a single Olympics. His career total of 11 medals— 9 gold (8 of them for world record swims), 1 silver, and 1 bronze—is a record for swimmers. His 4

individual gold medals in a single Olympics is unmatched in men's competition.

Mark Andrew Spitz was born February 10, 1950, in Modesto, California. He spent his early years in Hawaii and began to swim competitively at the age of nine when the family returned to California and settled in Sacramento. He made his international debut when he was 15 in the World Maccabean Games in Israel, where he won four gold medals.

Mark's most enthusiastic fan, his father, Arnold, once told *Sports Illustrated*, "I've got my life tied up in this kid. . . . He's beautiful, he's exceptional. . . . If people don't like it, the hell with them. Swimming isn't everything, *winning* is. I told him I didn't care about winning age groups. I care about world records."

Affected by that attitude, Mark won no popularity contests in Mexico City and, on the whole, he found it a jolting experience.

Between Mexico City and Munich, Spitz went to the University of Indiana. There, the handsome 6-foot, 170-pound swimmer led the school to three NCAA championships.

It was Sherman Chavoor, coach of the Arden Hills Swim Club, who helped Spitz prepare for the Munich Olympics.

"This guy has worked every day, 3-4-5 hours, for 12–13 years," Chavoor said. He wants to accomplish something. He would like to surpass any other swimmer." His whippet-slim body and extremely powerful kick made that seem a good bet.

In Munich he had won the 100-meter butterfly, 200-meter butterfly, and 200-meter freestyle, and anchored the 400- and 800-meter freestyle relays when the pressure began to reach him. He wanted to drop out of the 100-meter freestyle.

"Six medals is enough," he said. "I've already won five. The sixth is a cinch—the medley relay. All I wanted to do was beat All-America golden boy Don Schollander's record of four gold medals—and I've done it. Leave me alone."

But Chavoor wouldn't. "If he drops out of one, I'll break his damn neck," said Chavoor. Spitz swam the 100, leading from start to finish. The medley relay proved to be the cinch that Mark had predicted. The United States won by 2.2 seconds and Spitz had it all—a perfect 7-for-7.

After Mark Spitz retired from swimming, following the 1972 Olympics, Paul Zimmerman, a New York sports columnist, observed, "There are those who feel he is not enjoying his invasion of the history books, that he is having trouble coping with the mantle of destiny."

Within an hour, Spitz joined America's 400-meter freestyle relay team of Dave Edgar, John Murphy, and Jerry Heidenreich to beat the Soviet and East German teams with a clocking of 3:26.42.

The following night, Mark overhauled teammate Steve Genter on the last lap to win the 200-meter freestyle in 1:52.78. Werner Lampe of West Germany took the bronze medal, with Australia's defending champion, Mike Wenden, fourth.

Spitz won his fourth and fifth gold medals on August 31. He beat Bruce Robertson of Canada and third-place finisher Heidenreich in the 100-meter butterfly in the time of 54.27 seconds, bettering his own world mark. Roland Matthes of East Germany was fourth. Spitz then anchored the winning 800-meter freestyle relay team of John Kinsella, Fred Tyler, and Genter to an easy triumph over the West German and Soviet swimmers. The time was 7:35.78. The world record set by Spitz in the 100-meter butterfly on August 31, 1972, was not broken until August 27, 1977, when Joe Bottom, a 22-year-old University of Southern California graduate, lowered the mark of 54.27 seconds to 54.18.

Spitz trailed Wenden, the defending champion, in the heats and semifinals of the 100-meter freestyle. But he destroyed Wenden in the final on September 3 when he clocked 51.22 seconds. Heidenreich was second, finishing ahead of Soviet Vladimir Bure. Spitz became the first modern athlete to win seven gold medals in a single Olympics when he took part on the final day of the swimming program in the 400-meter medley relay. The American team of Mike Stamm, Tom Bruce, Spitz swimming the butterfly, and Heidenreich anchoring, scored a victory over East Germany and Canada in 3:48.16.

On the day Spitz won his seventh gold, Rick DeMont, a 16-year-old high school student from San Rafael, California, had his heart broken. Minutes before the race he was prohibited from swimming in the final of the 1,500-meter freestyle. He was barred because his doping test had turned up positive following his September 1 victory in the 400-meter freestyle. He won that race by one-hundredth of a second from Australia's Bradford Cooper.

At Munich, Mark Spitz, 22-year-old predental student, made Olympic history by winning seven gold medals, including the 200-meter butterfly (above). Jerry Heidenreich (extreme left) Mike Stamm (partly hidden), and Tom Bruce carried Spitz after their team captured the 400-meter medley relay. Spitz swam the butterfly leg of the medley and turned a close race with the East Germans into a four-yard lead for anchorman Heidenreich.

Australia's Graham Windeatt congratulates Rick DeMont (left) of San Rafael, California, after the latter's victory in the 400-meter freestyle. DeMont was stripped of his gold medal after a post race urinalysis revealed traces of a banned ephedrine in his system. DeMont had been taking the drug for an asthmatic condition. Australia's Shane Gould (below) was the women's swimming star at Munich—picking up three golds, one silver, and one bronze.

DeMont had told the USOC that he was using a drug to combat bronchial asthma, but the U.S. officials did not so inform the IOC medical examiners. DeMont had to give back his gold medal, the first winner in 60 years to have to do so. When DeMont was disqualified as the 400-meter champion the gold medal was awarded to Cooper. Genter and Tom McBreen, both of the United States, moved up into second and third places.

The 1,500-meter freestyle championship was retained by Mike Burton (USA) with a world record 15 minutes, 52.58 seconds. Graham Windeatt (Australia) and Douglas Northway (USA) placed second and third.

Another repeat winner was East Germany's Roland Matthes, unbeaten in the backstroke for six years. He duplicated his Mexico City double in the 100- and 200-meter events. Mike Stamm of the United States was the silver medalist in both backstroke events. His teammates, John Murphy and Mitchell Ivey, placed third in the 100 and 200, respectively.

Nobutaka Taguchi gave Japan its second breaststroke swimming medal in the 100 meters. He set a world record of 1 minute, 4.94 seconds, to finish ahead of Americans Tom Bruce and John Hencken.

Hencken won the 200-meter breaststroke in a world record 2:21.55. Britain's David Wilkie was second and Taguchi third.

Gunnar Larsson of Sweden took both the 200- and 400-meter individual medley events. Larsson posted an Olympic record of 2:07.17 in beating Americans Tim McKee and Steve Furniss in the 200. Larsson and McKee clocked identical times of 4:31.98 in the 400, but electrical timing equipment indicated the Swede won by 2/1,000ths of a second. Andras Hargitay of Hungary was third.

Vladimir Vasin (USSR) captured the springboard, finishing ahead of Italy's Franco Cagnotto and America's Craig Lincoln. Klaus Dibiasi (Italy) successfully defended his platform championship; Richard Rydze of the United States placed second and Cagnotto third.

Australia's 15-year-old Shane Gould was the queen of the pool. She waved a toy kangaroo after winning each of her three gold medals in world record time. The 5′ 7″, 132-pounder was a freestyler, who was the pre-Olympic world record holder in all distances from 100 to 1,500 meters. It was a surprise, therefore, when Gould's first victory was in the 200-meter individual medley. With a time of 2:23.07, she finished ahead of 13-year-old Kornelia Ender of East Germany and the Mexico City silver medalist, Lynn Vidali of the United States.

Two days later, Gould returned to her specialty and won the 400-meter freestyle, beating Italy's Novella Calligaris by more than three seconds, with a 4:19.04 clocking. Gudrun Wegner of East Germany took the bronze medal. Gould's third gold medal came in the 200-meter freestyle, in which she was timed in 2:03.56 and finished in front of Americans Shirley Babashoff and Keena Rothhammer. The Australian was upset in the 100- and 800-meter freestyle races, in which she placed third and second, respectively. When she had completed her events, Gould had appeared in 12 heats and final races, more than any other female swimmer in Olympic history.

Rothhammer won the 800-meter freestyle with a world record 8:53.68. Calligaris was third. Sandra Neilson of the United States won the 100-meter freestyle, with Babashoff second.

Neilson and teammate Melissa Belote also took home three gold medals. Neilson's other two were earned by America's world record-setting relay teams. She swam the leadoff leg in the 400-meter freestyle relay and anchored the 400-meter medley relay. Her teammates in the freestyle were Jennifer Kemp, Jane Barkman, and Babashoff. The winning time was 3:55.19, with East Germany a close second and West Germany third. Belote led off the medley relay and was followed by Cathy Carr, Deena Deardruff, and Neilson. They clocked 4:20.75. East and West Germany again placed second and third.

Belote won both backstroke events, setting a world record of 2:19.19 in the 200 meters. Teammate Susie Atwood was second in the 200 and Canada's Donna Marie Gurr was third. The silver medalist in the 100 was Andrea Gyarmati of Hungary, whose parents Eve Székely and Dezsö Gyarmati, had won gold medals in swimming and water polo, respectively. Atwood took the bronze medal in the 100.

An American and an Australian split the breaststroke races. Cathy Carr of the United States set a world record of 1:13.58 in the 100 to beat Galina Stepanova (USSR) and Beverley Whitfield (Australia). Whitfield won the 200 meters, with Dana Schoenfield (USA) second and Stepanova third. Stepanova, as Prozumenschikova, had been the bronze medalist in Mexico City and the gold medalist in Tokyo.

Japan's 19-year-old Mayumi Aoki established a world record of 1:03.34 in the 100-meter butterfly. Roswitha Beier of East Germany was second and Gyarmati third.

Karen Moe, Lynn Collela, and Ellie Daniel gave the United States a sweep of medals in the 200-meter butterfly. Moe's time of 2:15.57 was a world mark. Another world record, 5:02.97, was set by Gail Neall of Australia in the 400-meter individual medley. Leslie Cliff of Canada was second and Calligaris third.

With three dives remaining in the springboard event Maxine "Micki" King, a 29-year-old U.S. Air Force captain, was in third place. Four years earlier, King had the gold medal within her grasp. But, on her next-to-last dive, she hit the board and broke an arm.

In a highly controversial game, Aleksander Belov scored a layout, enabling the Soviets to hand the United States its first defeat in Olympic basketball. After protesting to no avail judges' rulings that were contrary to international rules, the USA declined the silver medal.

In an extremely tight race, Valery Borzov (right) emerged as the winner of the 100-meter sprint. (From left) Jobst Hirscht of West Germany, Alexander Korneliuk of the USSR, and Robert Taylor of the United States finished sixth, fourth, and second, respectively.

Although she executed her final dive, Micki dropped to fourth place. Seeking to erase those bitter memories she performed spectacularly, and won the gold medal. Sweden's Ulrika Knape was second and Marina Janicke of East Germany was third.

Knape won the Munich highboard diving event, with Milena Duchkova of Czechoslovakia second and Janicke again third.

The Soviet Union and Hungary each had three victories and two ties in the final round of the water polo tournament. The Soviets were awarded the gold medal because they outscored opponents by six goals, one more than silver medalist Hungary. The surprising United States team took the bronze medal.

The United States had won 63 consecutive games and seven consecutive gold medals as it faced the Soviet Union in the championship basketball game in Munich. With 10 minutes left to play the Soviets led by 10 points. American coach Hank Iba ordered his team to employ an all-court press. The tactic worked and the Soviets' lead dwindled to one point, 49-48, with 10 seconds remaining. Doug Collins stole the ball and was fouled when he drove to the basket. The clock showed three seconds left in the game.

Collins sank both free throws, putting the United States ahead, 50-49, for the first time in the game. On the Soviets' inbound pass, the ball was deflected and the crowd, thinking the game was over, flowed onto the court. However, the clock still showed one second left and officials cleared the court to give the USSR team another inbounds chance. The Soviets failed to score the basket and the game again seemed to be over. However, Dr. R. William Jones of Great Britain, secretary general of the International Amateur Basketball Federation (FIBA), ruled that play had been improperly resumed at one second and the Soviets should have had three seconds to play the ball.

So the clock was reset at three seconds. Ivan Edeshko, given the ball to throw inbounds, made a court-length pass. His target was Aleksander Belov, who was under the basket, guarded by Kevin Joyce and Jim Forbes. Belov, a 6' 8" forward, jumped for the ball. He collided with the two Americans, who fell to the floor. Belov came down with the ball, leaped again, and dropped it through the basket for the two points that gave the USSR a 51-50 victory.

The United States filed several protests over the strange rulings in the final few seconds—rulings that included a timeout called by the Soviet coach while the ball was in play, which was contrary to international rules. The protest was unavailing; the Soviet team was declared Olympic champion. The United States team declined to accept the silver medal.

In the tournament Tom Henderson and Dwight Jones each scored 83 points; Mike Bantom had 69, one more than Jim Brewer and three more than Collins; Tom McMillen had 61.

Belov, the Soviet star who scored the controversial final basket in the championship game, died of cancer at the age of 26 on October 4, 1978.

Besides Rick DeMont and the basketball team, other Americans had bruising experiences in Munich. Eddie Hart and Rey Robinson, co-world record holders in the 100-meter dash, were disqualified when they missed second round heats because of a mix-up about the starting times. Stan Wright, an assistant men's track coach, had read the starting time for the heats, 1615 hours, as 6:15 P.M. instead of translating the time to 4:15. Hart and Robinson, to whom the heats schedule was also accessible, realized they were late while they were relaxing in the Olympic Village. On television they saw the sprinters lining up for the heats. They raced to the stadium but arrived too late to compete.

Running in the city of his birth, slender and mustashioed Frank Shorter, 24, became the first American since John Hayes in 1908 to win the marathon.

However, another American sprinter, Robert Taylor, in the stadium in time for his heat, eventually won a silver medal in the final. He finished behind blond powerhouse Valery Borzov, who became the first Soviet sprinter to win the 100.

Borzov's time of 10.14 seconds was two tenths of a second slower than the world record shared by Hart and Robinson. When Borzov also won the 200 in 20.00 seconds, he became the first man to win an Olympic sprint double since Bobby Morrow (USA) in 1956. Larry Black (USA) was the 1972 silver medalist in the 200 in 20.19.

Memories of the John Carlos-Tommie Smith Mexico City protest were renewed after Vince Matthews and Wayne Collett of the United States finished 1-2 in the 400 meters. The two allegedly made a black power protest during the victory ceremony. They talked and fidgeted on the podium and looked away during the playing of the *Star Spangled Banner*. Both denied it was a protest, but the IOC called their behavior "disgusting," and barred them from future Olympic competition. That meant that the United States had to withdraw from the 1,600-meter relay race. It was won by Kenya, with Great Britain second and France third.

However, it was a different story in the 400-meter relay in which Hart, the anchor man, held off Borzov and gave the United States the gold in 38.19 seconds, equal to the world record. West Germany was third. Hart's teammates were Larry Black, Robert Taylor, and Black's first cousin, Gerald Tinker, who went on to a career in the National Football League.

Other American track gold medals went to David Wottle, Rodney Milburn, and Frank Shorter. Wottle, a bridegroom of two months, captured the imagination of the Olympic crowd by running the 800-meter race while wearing a golf cap. He came from far off the pace to score an upset victory over Evgeny Arzhanov (USSR), although both were clocked in 1:45.9. Mike Boit of Kenya was the bronze medalist, 1/10th of a second behind.

The 22-year-old Wottle was so excited about giving the United States its first victory in the event since 1956 that he forgot to take his cap off while on the victory podium during the playing of the national anthem. "I am very embarrassed," said a tearful Wottle later. "I just forgot. I didn't realize it was on my head. What will the millions of television watchers think of me? I'm going to apologize to the American people. Right now, and again, and again."

Milburn gave the United States its ninth consecutive victory in the 110-meter hurdles. He equaled the world record with a time of 13.24 seconds in beating Guy Drut of France and fellow American Tom Hill. Willie Davenport of the United States, the defending champion, was fourth.

Shorter's was the first American triumph in the marathon in 64 years. Shorter, a Yale graduate and University of Florida law student, had been born in 1948 in Munich while his father served there in the United States army. He took the lead at nine miles and won by more than two minutes from Karel Lismont of Belgium. Mamo Wolde of Ethiopia, the defending champion, was third. Shorter's time—2 hours, 12 minutes, 19.8 seconds—was 8.6 seconds off the Olympic mark set by Abebe Bikila of Ethiopia in 1964.

Finland won its first distance races in 36 years as Lasse Viren, a 23-year-old policeman, captured the 5,000- and 10,000-meter races. It was the fourth such double in Olympic history. Hannes Kolehmainen of Finland was the youngest to do it in 1912 when he was 22. The others were Czechoslovakia's Emil Zátopek in 1952 and Vladimir Kuts (USSR) in 1956.

Viren won the 5,000 in an Olympic record 13 minutes, 26.4 seconds. He finished one full second ahead of defending champion Mohamed Gammoudi of Tunisia. Ian Stewart of Great Britain was third.

Viren took the 10,000 in a world record 27:38.4, despite falling midway during the race. Emiel Puttemans of Belgium was second, followed by Miruts Yifter of Ethiopia. Shorter was fifth.

Finland won its third running gold medal in Munich when 24-year-old Pekka Vasala, with the fastest final 800-meters up to that point (1:49.0), took the 1,500-meter championship. His winning time of 3:36.3 was half a second faster than that of Kenya's defending titleholder, Kip Keino. Rod Dixon of New Zealand was third.

Lasse Viren (301) was the fourth man in Olympic history to take both the 5,000- and 10,000-meter races. In spite of a fall, the Finn established a world record in the 10,000 meters (below)—an event that he was not expected to win. The following day he qualified for the 5,000-meter finals. Running very intelligently, he set an Olympic record in the event.

Jim Ryun of the United States, one of the world's great middle distance runners, failed in his third attempt to win a 1,500-meter gold medal. With his wife watching in the stands, Ryun did not qualify for the final. He hobbled home ninth in the fourth heat in the time of 3:51.5 after a collision. With 550 meters left in the race, Pakistan's Mohamed Younis swung wide and made contact with Ryun who stumbled backward into Ghana's Billy Fordjour. Ryun and Fordjour fell and the American was stunned and injured. With absolutely no chance of catching the field, Ryun nevertheless picked himself up, and resumed running. At the finish line Keino tried to solace him for the loss of his hopes.

Keino won the 3,000-meter steeplechase, beating his fellow Kenyan, Benjamin Jipcho, with an Olympic record 8 minutes, 23.6 seconds. Tapio Kahtanen of Finland was third. The defending titlist, Kenya's Amos Biwott, had led for most of the race, but he faded to sixth.

Uganda won its first Olympic gold medal ever when John Akii-Bua, a superb performer, took the 400-meter hurdles. Running in the inside lane, Akii-Bua overpowered the field and raced to a world record 47.82 seconds. Ralph Mann of the United States was second, 1/100th of a second ahead of Britain's defending champion, David Hemery.

Germans swept the walking competition. Bernd Kannenberg of West Germany won the 50-kilometer race. Larry Young of the United States took his second consecutive bronze medal in the event.

Peter Frenkel of East Germany won the 20-kilometer event, with Russia's defending champion Vladimir Golubnitschy the runner-up.

Rodney Milburn of Opelousas, Louisiana, equaled the world record in the 110-meter hurdles.

With a leap of 27' ½", Randy Williams (USA) received the gold in the long jump, an event in which the United States has enjoyed particular success.

It was the Soviet walker's fourth medal, the same number Ugo Frigerio accumulated, although all the Italian's medals were gold. Golubnitschy had won golds in the 20 kilometers in 1960 and 1968 and a bronze in 1964.

The only man successfully to defend his title in track and field was Viktor Saneyev (USSR). Despite an injured Achilles tendon, Saneyev won the triple jump on the first of his six tries in the final.

His teammate, Yuri Tarmak, won the high jump at 7' 3¾". Stefan Junge of East Germany and 18-year-old Dwight Stones of the United States, in his first major international meet, tied at 7' 3", but Junge was awarded the silver medal because he cleared the height on his second attempt while the youngest member of the American track and field team made it on his third and final attempt.

For the first time since 1956 someone other than Al Oerter took the discus title, and for the first time since 1896, a non-American won the pole vault.

Wolfgang Nordwig of East Germany, who had equaled Bob Seagren's winning vault in Mexico City, soared an Olympic record 18' 0½" in the pole vault. His margin of victory over Seagren was 4", and over Jan Johnson (USA), 6". Both American vaulters had their poles confiscated the night before the qualifying round by the Technical Committee of the Games, following a dispute over their flexibility and weight. Seagren and Johnson therefore went into the competition using poles with which they were not comfortable.

Ludvik Danek of Czechoslovakia, the silver medalist in Tokyo and bronze medalist in Mexico City, finally won the gold medal in the discus in Munich with a heave of 211' 3". Jay Silvester of the United States, the world record holder, was second, followed by Ricky Bruch of Sweden.

A string of six consecutive victories by the United States in the shot put was ended by Poland's bearded 32-year-old Wladyslaw Komar. The 6' 5", 270-pound giant, sixth in Mexico City, established an Olympic record of 69' 6". George Woods of the United States repeated as silver medalist, finishing one-half inch behind the winner.

The Soviet Union's 33-year-old Janis Lusis, the defending title-holder in the javelin throw, came within an inch of Klaus Wolfermann of West Germany in what was called the upset of Munich's track and field competition. Wolfermann tossed the javelin an Olympic record 296′ 10″. Bill Schmidt of the United States was third, the first American medalist in the event in 20 years.

Anatoli Bondarchuk (USSR) threw the hammer an Olympic record 247′ 8″. Hungary's defending champion Gyula Zsivótzky, in his fourth Olympics, was fifth.

Randy Williams gave the United States its only gold medal in the field events when he won the long jump. The 19-year-old University of Southern California student outdistanced Hans Baumgärtner (West Germany). Arnie Robinson (USA) was third. The event marked the Olympic farewell of Igor Ter-Ovanesyan (USSR). He was a bronze medalist in 1960 and 1964 and placed fourth in Mexico City in 1968.

His teammates placed 1-2 in the decathlon. Nikolai Avilov set a world record of 8,454 points. He won by 419 points more than Leonid Lutvinyenko's total and 470 more than Ryszard Katus' (Poland).

It was the first time since women's track and field events were introduced in 1928 that the United States failed to win an individual title. Kathy Schmidt placed third in the javelin in which East Germany's Ruth Fuchs and Jacqueline Todten finished 1-2. Kathy Hammond finished third in the 400-meter run, Rita Wilden of West Germany was the silver medalist, and the winner was Monika Zehrt of East Germany. Zehrt anchored the winning team in the new 1,600-meter relay race. The silver medal went to the U.S. team and the bronze to the West German.

Renate Stecher of East Germany won a sprint double. She clocked 11.07 seconds in the 100 meters and an Olympic record 22.40 seconds in the 200 meters. Raelene Boyle of Australia was second in both dashes. Silvia Chivas of Cuba finished 1/100th of a second behind Boyle in the 100. Defending champion Irena Szewinska of Poland was third in the 200.

Soviet Evgeny Arzhanov slipped and fell at the finish line in a desperate effort to defeat David Wottle in the 800 meters. The American winner delighted the crowd by wearing a golf cap and by waiting until near the end of the race to turn on the speed.

Olga Korbut

I can't believe that girl who won the medals is really me. I can't understand how it all happened. I did not intentionally set out to be a star.

—OLGA KORBUT

Olga Korbut wasn't sure she knew the girl whose picture kept appearing on magazine covers.

The impish face, the infectious smile, and the pigtails gave her a feeling of familiarity—and a sense of unreality.

"Sometimes I look at a picture of myself in a magazine and I actually envy that girl in the picture," Korbut said.

Olga was born on May 16, 1955, in Grodno, Byelorussia, the youngest of four daughters of an industrial engineer and a restaurant cook.

At the age of 10, Olga entered the gymnastics program in school. She frequently invited the boys she played with to watch her perform some of her acrobatic and tumbling maneuvers.

Olga was made a member of the Soviet national team in 1970. She was selected by Larissa Latynina, the chief national coach, winner of the most Olympics medals in gymnastics. Olga was not unknown in the gymnastics world, but how well she would perform under the pressure of Olympic competition was a question mark.

Olga emerged from the 1972 Games as an international celebrity after winning one silver and three gold medals. The electronic beam of television transmitted her elfin grace around the world and gave an immeasurable lift to the sport of gymnastics.

Ironically, it was failure rather than success that made her the darling of Olympic television viewers. The cameras zoomed in on Olga as she fell off the uneven parallel bars, and lost a chance to win a gold medal. The embarrassed 4' 11", 85-pound teenager burst into tears, and exposed to the world a shattering moment of vulnerability.

What the camera saw, the world felt.

"She came back the next night and won a gold medal and it was the old story of triumph over tragedy," said Richard Appleman, an official of the United States Gymnastics Federation.

Olga deliberately reached out to her audience. "If I establish contact with the spectators, then I am sure of success. I am not interested in medals and titles. I don't need them. I need the love of the public and I fight for it."

The applause may have been more pleasing than medals, but she collected golds in the floor exercises, balance beam, and team combined exercises.

Following the Olympic Games, the interest in gymnastics generated by television prompted the Soviet Union to send Olga and her teammates on international tours. As gymnastics clubs opened in cities and towns, popular Olga became an embarrassment to the Soviets who insist that the individual be subordinate to the state.

"Olga represented a breakdown of the system," said Appleman. "There was a worldwide adulation of this girl that the Soviets couldn't stop."

Friction developed between the star and the state. Prior to the 1976 Olympics in Montreal her coach, Renald Knish, criticized Olga.

Olga did not win an individual gold medal in 1976. But she took a silver medal in her specialty, the balance beam. The event was won by Rumania's 14-year-old Nadia Comaneci, who emerged as the Gymnastics Queen of the Games.

At 21, Olga Korbut was not what she was at 17, neither so enthusiastic, nor so engaging. She made her final tour of the United States late in 1976, purchased a $177 white wedding gown while shopping in St. Louis, and explained that she was retiring from competition.

"It is out of my character to be a fifth or sixth-ranking member of a team," Olga said. "Young and fearless girls will advance gymnastics further. I'm a little worried about the adjustment. I can't even imagine what it will be like to no longer appear in a hall before a big crowd of people, never again to present the spectators with a smile."

In January 1978, Olga married Leonid Bortkevich, a folk rock singer, in the Minsk Wedding Palace.

Olga remained in gymnastics. She worked in Minsk as a coach for the Department of Gymnastics at the Byelorussian State Sport Committee.

On March 10, 1979, Olga gave birth to a son.

Stecher also anchored the silver medal 400-meter relay team that finished behind a West German team anchored by Heidemarie Rosendahl. Cuba was third.

Rosendahl won a second gold medal in the long jump and added a silver in the five-event pentathlon, captured by Mary Peters of Great Britain with a world record of 4,801 points.

West Germany's Ulrike Meyfarth cleared 6′ 3½″, a world record in the high jump. Meyfarth, who was three months past her 16th birthday, became the youngest person in the history of track and field to hold a world record. Her best pre-Olympic height was 5′ 11¾″.

Soviet athletes took the shot put, the discus, and a new event, the 1,500 meters. Nadyeschda Tschischova set a world record of 69 feet in the shot put. Faina Melnik took the discus with an Olympic record of 218′ 7″. Ludmila Bragina won the 1,500-meter race in 4 minutes, 1.4 seconds.

The 800 meters went to Hildegard Falck of West Germany, who ran an Olympic record 1:58.6, one tenth of a second faster than Niele Sabaite (USSR).

The 80-meter hurdles was changed to 100 meters. The first Olympic champion at the new distance was Annelie Ehrhardt of East Germany. Another new event, the 1,600-meter relay, was won by East Germany in the world record time of 3:23.0. The United States team won the silver medal, finishing ahead of West Germany.

The most appealing athlete in Munich was one of the smallest. Soviet gymnast Olga Korbut was an apostle for her sport. Watching her via television a worldwide audience suddenly became aware of the artistry and beauty of gymnastics maneuvers. Before the Games were over Korbut was an international celebrity. She won gold medals in the floor exercises, balance beam, and team combined exercises, and a silver in the uneven parallel bars. She appeared headed for the all-around championship until the uneven parallel bars segment of the event. In that, she started poorly, stopped, and began her routine again. The restart cost her valuable points and she

The ingratiating personality and outstanding performances of Olga Korbut, a 17-year-old Soviet, held world television audiences spellbound and greatly increased the popularity of the Olympic gymnastic program.

Sugar Ray Seales (left) of Tacoma, Washington, outpointed Bulgaria's Anghel Anghelov in the final of the light welterweight boxing match. Boxers from Yugoslavia and Nigeria shared the bronze medal.

dropped out of contention. Korbut's moment of imperfection, and her obvious distress at failing, only endeared her the more to an enchanted viewing public. She overshadowed her teammate, Ludmila Turischeva, who won the event, and Karin Janz (East Germany) who was second.

Janz, a 20-year-old medical student and a private in the People's Police, also won gold medals in the long horse and uneven parallel bars, a silver in the team combined exercises, and a bronze in the balance beam. That brought her Olympic total for 1968 and 1972 to 7 medals—2 gold, 3 silver, and 2 bronze.

Japan dominated the men's competition for the second consecutive Olympics, winning 12 out of a possible 18 medals. Sawao Kato repeated as all-around champion and increased his two-Olympics medal aggregate to 6 gold, 2 silver, and 1 bronze. Kato's teammate, 29-year-old Akinori Nakayama, won 2 gold medals and boosted his 1968–1972 haul to 6 gold, 2 silver, and 2 bronze medals.

Archery returned to the Olympic program after an absence of 52 years. Americans John Williams and Doreen Wilber won the men's and women's titles.

The domination of field hockey by India and Pakistan came to an end when West Germany took the championship game.

Poland, Hungary, and East Germany placed 1-2-3 in soccer. Japan won the men's volleyball crown, followed by East Germany and the Soviet Union, while the women's title went to the Soviet Union, with Japan second. North Korea shut out South Korea for the bronze medal.

Although an outdoor team handball tournament was played in 1936, indoor team handball joined the Olympic program in 1972. Yugoslavia, Czechoslovakia, and Rumania were the medalists.

Teofilo Stevenson, Cuba's handsome heavyweight, was the most impressive fighter in the boxing competition. En route to his gold medal, he overwhelmed American hope Duane Bobick so completely in a second round match that the referee stopped the bout. Stevenson was one of three Cuban boxers to win gold medals. The Cubans also won one silver and one bronze medal.

The lone United States gold medalist was light welterweight Sugar Ray Seales. America also had three bronze medalists—bantamweight Ricardo Carreras, welterweight Jesse Valdez, and middleweight Marvin Johnson. Mate Parlov of Yugoslavia, the light heavyweight champion, later became the professional champion in that division, and was dethroned by Johnson.

Hungary's András Balczó won the individual modern pentathlon title after placing second in 1968. His total of three gold medals for the sport is an Olympic record. In the team event, Hungary was bested by the Soviet squad. Finland's team was third.

East Germany did best in rowing, with victories in the coxed and coxless pairs, and in the coxless fours. Soviet oarsmen took both single and double sculls. West Germany's coxed fours crew triumphed, and New Zealand's tough, fast eights crew was more than two seconds ahead of the runner-up U.S. men.

The shooting events included firing at moving targets at 55 yards, an event suggestive of the 1900 running boar event. Soviet, Colombian, and British marksmen were the winners. Skeet, added in 1968, was won by a score of 195, and curiously, all three medalists shot that same score. The judges gave the gold to Konrad Wirnhier (West Germany), the silver to Yevgeny Petrov (USSR), and the bronze to Michael Buchheim (East Germany).

U.S. Major Lones Wigger won the free rifle event. His teammate, John Writer, took the three-position, small bore rifle title. With 598 out of a possible 600 points Victor Auer (USA) was declared winner of the small bore rifle (prone) event. After a recount, the gold medal was given to Ho Jun Li of North Korea, whose score was 599.

Italy's Angelo Scalzone won the trapshooting with a world record. Jozef Zapedzski (Poland) repeated his 1968 success with the rapid fire pistol, and Ragnar Shanaker was the free pistol champion.

The Soviet double sculls team (background) of Aleksandr Timoshinin and Gennadi Korshikov narrowly defeated the Norwegians for the first-place award.

Although weightlifter Vasili Alekseyev (right) dropped the bar and fell during his first attempt, the Soviet took the gold in the super heavyweight category. Popular American wrestler Chris Taylor (below, left) overwhelmed West Germany's Wilfried Dietrich, 1960 heavyweight gold medalist, in a super heavyweight wrestling match. Aleksandr Medved (USSR), who had defeated Taylor, won the gold in the super heavyweight division, new to the program in 1972. Taylor died in 1979.

Liselott Linsenhoff of West Germany became the first woman to win the individual dressage in the equestrian events. She also was a member of the defending dressage champion team that placed second behind the Soviets. When Linsenhoff, Hannelore Weygand, and Anneliese Küppers won the team dressage silver medal in 1956, it was the first Olympic equestrian event in which medals were won by a team composed entirely of women. Linsenhoff ended her Olympic career in Munich with 5 medals—2 gold, 2 silver, and 1 bronze.

British riders took both the 3-day individual and team events. Individual jumping honors were won by Graziano Mancinelli (Italy), Ann Moore (Britain), and Neal Shapiro (USA). West Germany took the team jumping, ahead of the U.S. and Italian teams.

The oldest athlete to participate in Munich was Mrs. Hilda Lorna Johnstone, a member of the British riding team. She had placed 21st in 1956 and 13th in 1968. In her 70th year, she placed 12th in Munich.

When judo made its Olympic debut in 1964, a Dutchman, Antonius Geesink, was the surprise winner. After an absence in Mexico City, the sport returned to the program in Munich, and another giant from The Netherlands was the star of the competition. Japan won three individual gold medals in its national sport, but 242-pound Willem Ruska, so fast that he ran the 100 meters in 11.0 seconds, won gold medals in both the heavyweight and open divisions.

United States yachtsmen won three medals. Harry Melges skippered a three-man crew to the gold medal in the Soling class, as long-time champion Paul Elvström (Denmark), finished a surprising 16th. Glen Foster and Donald Cohan received bronze medals in the Tempest and Dragon classes. Valentin Mankin (USSR) won the Tempest class; he had placed first in the Finn class in Mexico City. Rodney Pattison repeated his victory in the Flying Dutchman, and became the first Briton to win consecutive gold medals in yachting. John Cueno (Australia) won the Dragon class.

Canoeing presented four new events, all slalom: men's and women's kayak singles and men's Canadian singles and pairs. East German canoeists won every one. To Rumania went the Canadian singles event, and Soviet paddlers, men and women, took every remaining contest.

Hungary's Imre Foldi won the bantamweight championship in weightlifting on his third try. He had placed second in 1964 and 1968. Yan Talts gave the Soviet Union its fourth straight victory in the heavyweight division, while Vasili Alekseyev took the super heavyweight title.

Bulgarian lifters were victorious in the feather-, middle-, and middle heavy-weight classes. Poland claimed the flyweight gold, the Soviet Union the lightweight, and Norway the light heavyweight.

Greco-Roman wrestlers from the Soviet Union won four of the contests; Rumanian and Bulgarian each won two; and Czechoslovakian and Hungarian one apiece. Freestyle wrestling champions in 4 categories were Soviet, in 2, Japanese, and in 3, American. Dan Gable won the lightweight, Wayne Wells the welterweight, and Ben Peterson the light heavyweight.

Chris Taylor, a 400-pound American super heavyweight, outweighed Aleksandr Medved, a Soviet two-time Olympic gold medalist, by more than 150 pounds in their match on the opening day of wrestling competition. The decision, in favor of Medved, drew such a strong protest that the Turkish referee was barred from officiating for the remainder of the tournament. Medved went on to win the championship and became the third triple Olympic wrestling gold medalist.

Polish fencers won the foils contests; the team success was Poland's first in that event. Hungarian épée fencers took both individual and team honors. Gyözö Kulcsar, the defending épée titlist, was dropped to bronze standing as Csaba Fenyvei took the gold. The individual saber gold medal went to a Soviet fencer for the first time. Italy won the team event.

Among the cyclists only Daniel Morelon (France) retained his 1968 title, for the 1,000-meter sprint. Soviet cyclists were first home in the tandem and the 100-kilometer team races. The road race honors went to The Netherlands, the 1,000-meter time trial to Denmark, the individual pursuit to Norway, and the team pursuit to West Germany.

A total of 7,147 athletes from a record 122 nations participated in the XX Olympiad, which opened on August 26 and closed on September 11. The final, somber ceremony paused for a brief period of silent meditation for the slain Israelis. Things hadn't gone the way the organizers had planned. With imagination and open-handed expenditure they had turned the site where rubble from World War II bomb damage was dumped into a stunning complex of 80,000-seat stadium, 8,000-seat swimming hall, 12,000-seat gym, and commodious Olympic Village. Over much of the site they had erected an enormous acrylic canopy, which alone cost $61 million. Almost from the time the last of the 5,976 relay runners appeared with the flame from Olympia, the "Games of Joy" had belied their name. In its flaw, the final message flashed on the electric scoreboard was consistent with the plans that went awry. It read: THANK YOU, AVERY BRANDAGE.

FINAL MEDAL STANDINGS			
Nation	G	S	B
Soviet Union	50	27	22
United States	33	30	30
East Germany	20	23	23
West Germany	13	11	16
Japan	13	8	8
Australia	8	7	2
Poland	7	5	9
Hungary	6	13	16
Bulgaria	6	10	5
Italy	5	3	10
Sweden	4	6	6
Great Britain	4	5	9
Rumania	3	6	7
Cuba	3	1	4
Finland	3	1	4
The Netherlands	3	1	1
France	2	4	7
Czechoslovakia	2	4	2
Kenya	2	3	4
Yugoslavia	2	1	2
Norway	2	1	1
North Korea	1	1	3
New Zealand	1	1	1
Uganda	1	1	–
Denmark	1	–	–
Switzerland	–	3	–
Canada	–	2	3
Iran	–	2	1
Belgium	–	2	–
Greece	–	2	–
Mongolia	–	2	–
Austria	–	1	2
Colombia	–	1	2
Argentina	–	1	–
Lebanon	–	1	–
Mexico	–	1	–
Pakistan	–	1	–
South Korea	–	1	–
Tunisia	–	1	–
Turkey	–	1	–
Brazil	–	–	2
Ethiopia	–	–	2
Spain	–	–	2
Ghana	–	–	1
India	–	–	1
Jamaica	–	–	1
Niger	–	–	1
Nigeria	–	–	1

1976

Winter Games
Innsbruck, Austria

In May 1970 the International Olympic Committee (IOC) awarded the 1976 Winter Games to Denver, Colorado. Following an extensive campaign by environmentalists who feared the damage the Games might cause, Colorado voters in November 1972 rejected a $5 million bond issue for financing the venture. The city immediately withdrew its bid to host the Games. Three months later the IOC selected Innsbruck as the locale. The Austrian city, site of the 1964 Winter Games, was chosen because it already had the necessary facilities.

The Games were held in Innsbruck February 4 through February 15 with 1,054 athletes, representing 37 nations, participating. The opening ceremony was unusual inasmuch as the Austrian Organizing Committee erected two torches, commemorating the two Olympics held in Innsbruck, to light the flame. Josef Feistmantl, Austria's 1964 Olympic luge cochampion, lit one caldron and then helped Austria's Christl Haas, the 1964 downhill winner, to light the other.

Following the 1972 massacre at Munich, security precautions were extensive. An estimated 5,000 specially-trained soldiers and police were employed to guard against possible terrorist attacks.

The 1976 Winter Games marked the official debut of a new IOC president. Michael Morris, 3rd Baron Killanin, had succeeded Avery Brundage following the Munich Games. Brundage, who as IOC president from 1952 to 1972 was a severe critic of the Winter Games, had died on May 8, 1975, in Garmisch-Partenkirchen, West Germany. Lord Killanin, a 61-year-old, pipe-smoking Irish peer, did much to create the overall friendly atmosphere of the XII Winter Games.

Lord Killanin was involved in a major controversy, however. Pressure from the Communist

Hands aloft in victory. Women's downhill silver and bronze medalists, Austria's Brigitte Totschnig (left) and Cindy Nelson of Lutsen, Minnesota, are delighted not only for themselves but particularly for "Granny," Rosi Mittermaier (center), winner of the gold. Before a mountainside crowd of 60,000, Austria's prime skier Franz Klammer (below) took the downhill in a dangerous crouch. He established a new course record.

states caused the IOC to withdraw the press accreditation of the staff of Radio Free Europe. After U.S. Secretary of State Henry Kissinger protested the IOC decision, Lord Killanin stated that the commission simply wanted the Games to be free of all propaganda and the decision stood.

A 25-year-old Fräulein from West Germany, who had been on the international skiing circuit for ten years, was the unexpected outstanding athlete at Innsbruck. Her name was Rosi Mittermaier, but other skiers affectionately called her "Omi" (Granny). Rosi had competed in the 1968 and 1972 Olympics and was disappointed that she had not won a medal. Yet, she always had a smile.

On February 13, Rosi came within 12/100ths of a second of being the first woman to win all three Alpine events—the downhill, the slalom, and the giant slalom. Mittermaier was fourth down the course in the giant slalom, an event in which she placed 12th in Sapporo and 20th in Grenoble. Kathy Kreiner of Canada, who skied first, was given relatively little chance of winning. Yet she zigzagged down the 49-gate course and crossed the finish line in the gold medal time of 1 minute, 29.13 seconds. Rosi was 54/100ths of a second ahead of Kreiner's time at the intermediate mark. However, when she completed her descent Rosi's time on the scoreboard read 1:29.25.

Danièle Debernard of France won the bronze medal in the giant slalom with a time of 1:29.95. Defending champion Marie-Thérèse Nadig of Switzerland was fifth and Rosi's sister, Evi Mittermaier, eighth.

Rosi Mittermaier began her quest for the downhill triple crown on February 8. Her work was eased when Austria's Annemarie Proell, the multiple World Cup champion, retired and Nadig, the 1972 Olympic titleholder, was so ill with the flu that she could not compete. The vivacious, popular Rosi, a hotel and restaurant waitress during the off-season in her hometown of Reit im Winkl, near the Austrian border, had been sixth in the downhill in Sapporo and 25th in Grenoble. The pre-race favorite in 1976 was Austria's Brigitte Totschnig. Mittermaier posted a time of 1:46.16 to beat Totschnig by 52/100ths of a second. It was Rosi's first major downhill victory.

Cindy Nelson won the bronze medal in the downhill and received cabled congratulations from President Gerald Ford. The 20-year-old American went to Innsbruck an underdog because of inconsistency in pre-Olympic races. "I decided not to talk to anyone before the Olympics because all they would do would be to ask me about my bad results, and I didn't want to be reminded of them," she said.

On February 11, with almost everyone from her hometown on the slopes watching, Mittermaier won her second gold medal by racing to a two-run triumph in the slalom. She finished only 33/-100ths of a second in front of Italy's Claudia Giordani. Hanni Wenzel of Liechtenstein, sixth after the first run, was the bronze medalist.

In Rosi's first Olympic appearance in the slalom in 1968, she had been disqualified on the second run. She placed 17th in 1972. Linda Cochran, the younger sister of Barbara Cochran, the 1972 slalom gold medalist, was the top American finisher in 1976, placing sixth.

The day following the opening, February 5, 22-year-old Franz Klammer of the host nation was under tremendous pressure to win the dangerous downhill, the showcase event of the Alpine ski program. Klammer, a farmboy from the province of Carinthia, who had been earning about $150,000 annually from ski manufacturers, started in 15th position. Already posted on the scoreboard were the times of defending champion Bernhard Russi of Switzerland (1:46.06) and of Italy's Herbert Plank (1:46.59).

All of Austria expected Klammer, the 1975 downhill World Cup champion, to win the gold medal. Klammer went into a dangerous deep crouch late in his descent in an effort to overcome early difficulties and a poor intermediate time in which he trailed Russi. His "frog style" was the most dangerous because it limited his control over his skis. When Klammer crossed the finish line the scoreboard showed his time to be 1:45.73.

The Soviets continued to enjoy success in Nordic skiing. Sergei Saveliev (above) was first in the 30-kilometer cross-country race. Heini Hemmi and Ernst Good (right) were awarded medals and bouquets for leading Switzerland to first- and second-place finishes in the giant slalom.

"I let the skis go," Klammer said, meaning he went all out, forgetting danger. "I had a lot of trouble along the whole course. I thought I was going to crash all along the way."

Klammer took 10 seconds off the course record he set the previous year. Russi finished second and Plank was third.

Major surprises were produced by two Swiss bricklayers in the giant slalom. Heini Hemmi and Ernst Good placed 1-2, as the 27-year-old Hemmi won his first major international race in eight years of competition. Sweden's Ingemar Stenmark was third, ahead of Italy's defending champion Gustavo Thoeni. The success of the Swiss skiers sent Thoeni, a four-time World Cup champion, storming off the slope. Thoeni missed the bronze medal by 62/100ths of a second.

The men's slalom on February 14 was Thoeni's last chance to win a gold medal in Innsbruck. He hoped thereby to become the only male skier in history to win championships in two Olympics. However, Thoeni placed second to countryman Piero Gros, finishing 44/100ths of a second behind the gold medalist in the two-run event. Willy Frommelt of Liechtenstein was third, giving the tiny nation two bronze medals in the Games.

After the race a disappointed Thoeni said, "Everything is all right as long as an Italian skier wins. I made technical errors at the top of my second run. Otherwise I feel I had two good performances."

Scandinavia was shut out for the first time in the Nordic 30-kilometer cross-country race. Two Soviets, Sergei Saveliev and Ivan Garanin, finished first and third. It was Bill Koch, however, a 20-year-old from Guilford, Vermont, who stole the show by winning the silver medal. It was the first medal won by the United States in cross-country skiing.

Koch was unknown to the American public. Foreign competitors knew of him because of his third-place finish in a pre-Olympic race

Billy Koch (above) was the American surprise at Innsbruck, taking the silver in the 30-kilometer cross-country. He crossed the finish line seconds behind gold medalist Saveliev. With his brother, Fritz, watching, Bill Koch lifted their mother into his arms after his U.S. team finished sixth in the 40-kilometer cross-country relay. A Finnish team won the event.

Seefeld, located about 10 miles northwest of Innsbruck, was the site of the Nordic skiing competition in 1976. The high-altitude health resort and winter-sports center is also famous for its church architecture and sulfur thermal baths. Visitors can enjoy open-air swimming in the midst of winter sports.

in Rosi Mittermaier's hometown. That was only his second race at the 30-kilometer distance. It made his finish of less than 29 seconds behind Saveliev even more remarkable.

Very few people knew that Koch competed under the handicap of exercise-induced asthma, which made it difficult for him to breathe. To counter the asthma, Koch took a drug called chromyl sodium. Months before he went to Innsbruck, U.S. officials informed Olympic executives about the American's condition, to make certain there would be no dispute over the use of the drug.

Following Koch's silver medal performance, trustees at Marlboro College, where his father was president, collected money to send his mother and his brother to Austria to see the remainder of the events. They saw Bill place sixth in the 15-kilometer race three days later. Nikolai Bajukov and Evgeni Beliaev, both of the USSR, placed 1-2. Finland's Arto Koivisto was third. Koch was in 12th place after two thirds of the race, but skied the fastest final five kilometers of any competitor. The race was marred by unruly spectators and amateur skiers. Koivisto lurched off the trail and into a snowbank to avoid colliding with a fan who cut across his path. The Finn claimed the incident cost him the silver medal and possibly the gold. The Soviet's Garanin, the bronze medalist in the 30 kilometers, fell over a tourist skier, took a spill, and finished fourth.

Koch displayed his grit by persisting in the grueling 50-kilometer race to its end. It was only the second time he had competed in such a race. He led at the halfway point and then faded, to finish 13th. Norway's Ivar Formo won the gold medal. Gert-Dietmar Klause of East Germany was second and Sweden's Benny Soedergren third. Finland, Norway, and the Soviet Union placed 1-2-3 in the 40-kilometer relay.

East Germany's Ulrich Wehling, a 23-year-old physical education student, became the first repeat winner in the Nordic combined since Norway's Johan Gröttumsbraaten scored consecutive victories in 1928 and 1932. Urban Hettich of West Germany took the silver despite an 11th place finish in the jumping. Konrad Winkler of East Germany won the bronze medal.

Nikolai Kruglov and Aleksandr Elizarov, both of the USSR, placed 1–3 in the biathlon. The silver medal went to Heikki Ikola of Finland. The Soviet Union also captured the biathlon relay, finishing ahead of Finland and East Germany.

Austria's hopes of winning the 70-meter ski jump rested on the skills of 17-year-old Anton "Toni" Innauer, who had been in a pre-Olympic slump. During practice he had shown flashes of brilliance, but in the competition he tied for seventh with another Austrian, Rudolf Wanner. Both finished just behind countryman Reinhold Bachler. East Germany, in Hans-Georg Aschenbach and Jochen Danneberg, produced the gold and silver medalists. Austria's Karl Schnabl was third.

It was an amazing comeback for Aschenbach, who had undergone knee surgery in August 1975. After his victory, he was asked when he regained his form. "A couple of hours ago," was the reply.

From Klammer's triumph in the downhill on the opening day of competition until the closing day of the Games Austrians waited impatiently for their second gold medal. It came in the 90-meter ski jump. Schnabl came from behind to edge Innauer for the championship. Henry Glass of East Germany was third.

East Germany took all the gold in bobsledding and luge. The team of Meinhard Nehmer, Jochen Babcok, Bernhard Germeshausen, and Bernhard Lehmann won the four-man bobsled race. Detlef Guenther (below) surpassed Joseph Fendt (West Germany) and teammate Hans Rinn to capture the men's luge singles.

Soviet Galina Kulakova anchored the winning team in the women's cross-country relay and became the first woman to win four Nordic gold medals. Finland was second and East Germany was third. The relay had been changed in 1973 from 15 kilometers and 3 competitors to 20 kilometers and 4 racers.

Kulakova, the defending champion, was stripped of a bronze medal in the individual 5-kilometer event because she took nose drops containing a banned drug. The drops, which she used without advising the Russian team physician, contained ephedrine, the same drug which caused the disqualification of American swimmer Rick DeMont during the Munich Olympics. Galina's bronze medal went to fourth-place finisher Nina Baldicheva, another Soviet. The gold medalist was Finland's Helena Takalo. Second place went to Raisa Smetanina (USSR).

Smetanina and Takalo reversed positions in the 10-kilometer event, with Kulakova capturing the bronze this time.

East Germany ruled the chutes, sweeping all five gold medals in bobsledding and luge. Meinhard Nehmer piloted the victorious two-man and four-man bobsleds. His four-run time in the boblet was 57/100ths of a second faster than that of a West German sled steered by Wolfgang Zimmerer. A Swiss sled driven by Erich Schaerer was third.

Nehmer's was 46/100ths of a second faster than Schaerer's runner-up sled in the four-man race. Zimmerer piloted West Germany to the bronze medal.

Detlef Guenther won the men's luge singles. Josef Fendt of West Germany was second, while another East German, Hans Rinn, was the bronze medalist. Rinn came back to team with Norbert Hahn for the luge doubles gold medal. West Germany's Hans Brandner and Balthasar Schwarm placed second, ahead of Austria's Rudolf Schmid and Franz Schashner.

Margit Schumann, the bronze medalist in an East German sweep in Sapporo, took the gold medal in the women's luge singles in Innsbruck. She was followed closely by teammate Ute Ruehrold. Elisabeth Demleitner of West Germany was third.

Sheila Young became the most successful American speed skater since Irving Jaffee and John Shea each captured two gold medals in Lake Placid in 1932. Young, the world sprint champion, won gold, silver, and bronze medals. The 25-year-old from Detroit raced through Innsbruck's morning fog on February 6 and clocked an Olympic record 42.76 seconds for 500 meters on what was described as "slow ice." She erased the mark of 43.33, set by America's Anne Henning in 1972, but did not come close to her own world record of 40.91 seconds set in Switzerland the week before the Olympics.

The first five finishers smashed the Olympic record, with Cathy Priestner of Canada placing second in 43.12. Tatiana Averina (USSR) was third. Fourth-place finisher Leah Poulos of the United States was only 4/100ths of a second behind Averina.

Young's victory gave the United States its first gold medal of the Games. Sheila had sold her racing bicycle for $250 to enable her fiancé, James Ochowicz, also a cyclist, to travel to Innsbruck. After her triumph, Young left the rink on the arm of Ochowicz and said, "As I came around the first turn I could hear Jim screaming 'fight, fight, fight.' "

Young's silver medal came in the opening 1,500-meter race in which ten skaters bettered the Olympic record. It was an unexpected medal for Young, who finished behind Soviet Galina Stepanskaya. The winner clocked 2 minutes, 16.58 seconds. Averina was third.

Averina won the 1,000 meters, with Poulos second and Young third. The winner was timed in an Olympic record 1:28.43. Poulos, from Northbrook, Illinois, was 14/100ths of a second behind the gold medalist.

Averina took her second gold medal with an Olympic record 4:45.19 in the 3,000 meters. She finished 4/100ths of a second ahead of East Germany's Andrea Mitscherlich and 5/100ths of a second in front of Lisbeth Korsmo, the bronze medalist from Norway.

In three consecutive days, American speed skater Sheila Young gained a gold, a silver, and a bronze. Of her honors, Sheila said, "I wouldn't trade four silvers for one gold." Speed skater Leah Poulos (right) of Northbrook, Illinois, herself a silver medalist in the 1,000 meters, was proud to display the gold medal won by fiancé Peter Mueller of Madison, Wisconsin, in the men's 1,000-meter speed skating race.

A controversy erupted when American speed skating coach Dianne Holum, winner of the 1,500-meter gold medal in 1972, accused United States Olympic Committee President Phil Krumm of tampering with her team and influencing the selection of racers. She specifically accused Krumm of forcing U.S. speed skating officials to reverse themselves on a plan to hold skate-offs to select the third starter for the 1,000- and 3,000-meter women's races and the 1,500-meter men's race.

The only American men's gold medalist in speed skating was Peter Mueller in the 1,000 meters, a new race on the Olympic program. He beat Jorn Didriksen of Norway and Valery Muratov of the USSR. The 21-year-old Mueller was engaged to Leah Poulos, the runner-up in the women's 1,000. "I am glad Peter won the gold instead of me," she said. "I couldn't have lived with him if I had upstaged him."

Dan Immerfall was the only other American to win a speed skating medal. He placed third in the 500, behind the USSR's Yevgeni Kulikov, the world record holder, and Muratov. Kulikov's time of 39.17 seconds was an Olympic record. Immerfall, a 20-year-old from Madison, Wisconsin, dedicated his bronze medal to his widowed mother.

The 1,500-meter race went to Norway's Jan Egil Storholt in the Olympic record time of 1 minute, 59.38 seconds. Yuri Kondakov (USSR) placed second, ahead of Hans Van Helden of The Netherlands. Another Norwegian, Sten Stensen, took the 5,000 meters, followed by Piet Kleine and Van Helden of The Netherlands. Kleine, Stensen, and Van Helden were 1-2-3 in the 10,000 meters, Kleine establishing an Olympic record of 14 minutes, 50.59 seconds.

A new scoring system was instituted in figure skating. Competitors in 1976 were judged on a basis of 40 percent for compulsory figures, 20 percent for a short program, and 40 percent for free skating. Previously, compulsory figures and free skating were scored on an equal 50-50 basis.

When the judges reached their decisions in Innsbruck, America's Dorothy Hamill and Britain's John Curry emerged as the figure skating champions. Both were coached by Carlo Fassi, who had also guided Peggy Fleming to an Olympic gold medal in 1968.

Hamill, a 19-year-old from Riverside, Connecticut, beat Dianne de Leeuw, a California resident who competed for The Netherlands, her mother's country. Christine Errath of East Germany was third. Hamill's program included an innovative spin dubbed the Hamill Camel. The free skating portion of the competition was scheduled for Friday, the 13th, an ominous date for someone as nervous and superstitious as Dorothy. She wore a tiny four-leaf clover on the left shoulder of her skating outfit. Hamill was almost flawless, receiving a 5.8 out of a possible 6.0 rating on technical excellence from eight of the nine judges. The American judge rated her 5.9. All the judges rated Hamill 5.9 on the artistic part of her program.

Curry, a 25-year-old who lived in New York and trained in Denver, cinched Britain's only gold medal of the Games with a superb five-minute free skating program complete with triple jumps and spins. Vladimir Kovalev of the USSR and Toller Cranston of Canada were the silver and bronze medalists.

Irina Rodnina, 26, and Aleksandr Zaitsev, 23, a newly married Soviet couple and winner of three consecutive world titles, captured the pairs gold medal. Rodnina had won the Olympic championship

Soviet speed skater Tatiana Averina received the gold in the 1,000 and 3,000 meters, with Olympic records in both.

Dorothy Hamill

I was so keyed up I never wanted to go to bed.

—DOROTHY HAMILL

Moments before she was to begin her free skating performance in Innsbruck's Olympic rink, high-strung Dorothy Hamill glimpsed a sign that read "Dorothy, wicked witch of the West." It was an effort of her well-wishers to encourage her, but she thought it was disparagement. "I started to cry as soon as I saw the sign those people were holding up," the attractive 19-year-old said. "Then I realized they were all friends, trying to make me relax. I felt better and all the nervousness was gone. Everything was okay."

It was more than okay. It was dazzling, and the crowd of 9,000 showed her they knew it. They expressed their thrill by applauding ten times, and tossed her so many flowers that she needed three girls to help her gather them up. When she left the ice, she had won the most glamorous and possibly the most dramatic event of the Winter Games. She was the women's figure skating champion of the 1976 Olympics. It culminated 11 years of dedication.

Dorothy first stepped onto the ice on Binney Pond in Riverside, Connecticut, where she was born on July 26, 1956. She wore a pair of $5.95 skates given to her as a Christmas present.

Dorothy quickly learned to go forward, but it was difficult to maneuver in other directions. "I went home that day and told my mom that I wanted to take skating lessons. I wanted to learn to skate backward," she said.

Dorothy soon evidenced strong potential. She arranged her school schedule so she could practice uninterrupted hours, beginning at 5 o'clock in the morning. As she improved she went to Denver, to train under renowned Carlo Fassi at the Colorado Ice Arena.

"I knew from the moment I started working with Dorothy in 1971 that she had a good chance to go all the way," Fassi said. "Dorothy had the technical skills and a special quality that cannot be taught."

She also had poor vision. "I am terribly nearsighted," she said. "I can't see the scoreboard without glasses. I don't like contacts. I wear glasses in doing my compulsory figures, but I leave them in the dressing room for the free skating."

Fassi devised a rigid schedule to improve Dorothy's technical skills. He demanded that she practice compulsory figures, the weakest part of her repertoire, four hours a day, and free skating two hours a day. The schedule was adhered to 6 days a week, 11 months a year, for 5 years.

When Hamill arrived in Innsbruck, she was a two-time United States champion and considered to be the best woman free skater in the world, but the Innsbruck favorite was Dianne de Leeuw of the Netherlands.

When the initial phase of the compulsory exercises was completed, Hamill wasn't first, but neither was de Leeuw. The American was second, with de Leeuw third. First place was held by Isabel De Navarre of West Germany.

Dorothy finished first in the short program. De Leeuw was fourth and De Navarre 11th. As the free-skating portion of the program approached, the gold medal was within Hamill's grasp.

Dorothy's mother couldn't stand the suspense of watching her, but those who did saw an athlete of assurance and musicality, who never showed preparation for a leap.

De Leeuw, skating last, and facing the virtually impossible task of catching Dorothy, gave a daring exhibition. But she stumbled on a double Lutz and on a double Axel. Hers was the silver.

Dorothy and her family were joined by Fassi and his wife for a celebration. "I was so keyed up I never wanted to go to bed," Dorothy said.

A month later, Dorothy Hamill won figure skating's Triple Crown when she added the 1976 world championship to her Olympic and American titles. Then she turned professional, joining the Ice Capades. She also became a familiar face on television.

In January 1982 she married Dean Paul Martin, the son of entertainer Dean Martin.

in 1972 with a different partner, Aleksei Ulanov. East Germany placed second and third in the pairs in Innsbruck. The tandem of Romy Kermer and Rolf Oesterreich took the silver medal, while the duo of Manuela Gross and Uwe Kagelmann repeated as bronze medalists.

Ice dancing was a new addition to the Olympic program. An American couple, Colleen O'Connor and James Millns, won the bronze medal. They finished behind two Soviet pairs—Ludmila Pakhomova and Aleksandr Gorshkov, and silver medalists Irina Moiseeva and Andrey Minenkov.

The mighty Soviet hockey team won its fourth straight gold medal by defeating an emotional Czechoslovakian team, 4–3, in the championship game. The United States lost to West Germany, 4–1, on the final day, ruining its chances of winning the bronze medal.

A 7–1 victory by the Czechs over Poland in an earlier match was nullified. It was discovered that the Czech captain, Frantisek Pospisil, a defenseman, had taken codeine, a banned substance, to combat the flu which was rampant in Innsbruck. Pospisil was allowed to continue playing, but Dr. Otto Trefny, the Czech team physician, was banned from the Olympics for life.

The Soviet team finished with a record of five victories and no losses. Czechoslovakia won two and lost two for the silver medal, while West Germany took the bronze with a record of two victories and three defeats. Canada again did not compete.

John Curry and Dorothy Hamill reigned on the ice. Twenty-five-year-old John Curry became the first Briton to take the gold in the men's competition. With expertly disciplined performances in rigid school figures and a dazzling program in free skating, pixieish Dorothy Hamill of Riverside, Connecticut, captured the gold.

FINAL MEDAL STANDINGS			
Nation	G	S	B
Soviet Union	13	6	8
East Germany	7	5	7
United States	3	3	4
Norway	3	3	1
West Germany	2	5	3
Finland	2	4	1
Austria	2	2	2
Switzerland	1	3	1
The Netherlands	1	2	3
Italy	1	2	1
Canada	1	1	1
Great Britain	1	–	–
Czechoslovakia	–	1	–
Liechtenstein	–	–	2
Sweden	–	–	2
France	–	–	1

1976

Summer Games
Montreal, Quebec

The 1976 Summer Olympics, held in Montreal, were the first Games—winter or summer—in which the host nation failed to win a gold medal.

It was one of many embarrassments for Canada, whose Olympics, scarred by political wrangling, were a financial disaster.

In 1970, when Mayor Jean Drapeau made his successful bid on behalf of Montreal, he expected the Games to be self-financing and to cost $310 million. However, inflation, labor disputes, and cost over-runs increased the bill to an estimated $1.5 billion.

In the wake of the Munich disaster, security cost some $100 million, one third of the total anticipated expenditure for the Games. A 16,000-man militia protected athletes, members of the national delegations, the International Olympic Committee members, and visiting dignitaries, including Britain's Queen Elizabeth II, who officially opened the Games on July 17th.

Soldiers patrolled the competition sites, the Olympic Village with its twin 19-story pyramid-shaped buildings that housed the athletes, the airports, and hotels of VIPs. Buses to be used by athletes were searched. Helicopters hovered overhead. Everyone who entered the Olympic Village, which was surrounded by a 10-foot fence, went through an electronic gate equipped with a metal detector. All hand parcels were screened. For their own protection, the athletes were virtual prisoners.

Many athletes who went to Montreal returned home without participating in the Games.

Thirty-two nations, the majority from black Africa, withdrew after the IOC refused to ban New Zealand from the Games because its rugby team was playing in racially-segregated South Africa. The walkout removed track and field potential stars from Ethiopia, Nigeria, Kenya, Tanzania, and Uganda, among them Filbert Bayi, of

Tanzania, the world record holder at 1,500 meters, John Akii-Bua of Uganda, the defending champion in the 400-meter hurdles, Mike Boit and Sam Kipkurkat of Kenya, favorites in the 800 meters, and Ethiopia's distance specialist, Miruts Yifter. Jean-Claude Ganga, the IOC member from Congo and secretary-general of the Supreme Council for Sport in Africa, led the pullout.

Canada refused to permit Taiwan's 43-member Olympic delegation to enter the country under the banner of the Republic of China, its official International Olympic Committee designation. The action was taken because the Canadian government recognized The People's Republic of China. The IOC invited the Taiwanese to call themselves "Taiwan" and march with their national flag in the opening ceremony. The Taiwanese refused to abandon the name Republic of China and withdrew before the start of the Games.

The disputes over the New Zealand and Taiwanese issues caused a reduction in the number of participating nations from a record 122 in Munich to 88 in Montreal. However, a record 7,356 athletes competed.

The lighting of the Olympic caldron during the opening ceremony was performed by 15-year-old Stephane Prefontaine of Montreal and 16-year-old Sandra Henderson of Toronto, representing Canada's French and English heritages.

The parade of nations included an Israeli team, on which hurdler Esther Roth was the only returnee from the Munich Games. A somber memorial service for the 11 Israelis killed during the 1972 Olympics was held before the opening of the Games.

It took a small girl from Rumania to let the sunshine in on the 1976 Summer Games. She was 14-year-old Nadia Comaneci, 4' 11" and 88 pounds in weight.

Her opening day victory in the uneven parallel bars gained her a score of ten—the first perfect mark in Olympic gymnastics history.

Nadia Comaneci (Miss Perfection) succeeded Olga Korbut as the Olympics gymnastics queen. The 14-year-old Rumanian registered seven perfect scores, in obtaining 3 gold medals, 1 silver, and 1 bronze.

Nadia Comaneci

I think so much of what I must do, I do not hear the crowd.

—NADIA COMANECI

Gymnastics coach Bela Karolyi spotted a couple of six-year-old girls in a school playground pretending to be gymnasts. The bell rang, and they disappeared into the school. Twice he visited the school, but he could not find them.

"I went a third time and I asked, 'Who likes gymnastics?' In one of the classrooms, two girls sprang up. One became a very promising ballerina. The other is Nadia," Karolyi said.

Comaneci was born in Gheorghe Gheorghiu-Dej, Rumania, on Nov. 12, 1961. Less than 15 years later, in Montreal, she awed a worldwide television audience with her daring gymnastics.

She was so brilliant that she completely overshadowed Olga Korbut, the darling of 1972. What's more, the performance of the 4′ 11″, 86-pound perfectionist created havoc with the scoreboards. They had not been programmed to register the perfect scores that brought her 5 medals—3 gold, 1 silver, and 1 bronze.

A perfect gymnastics score is 10. No one had ever achieved a 10 in Olympic competition. So, when Nadia recorded a perfect score in the individual uneven parallel bars event on July 18th, the scoreboard could not register it. Before the competition was over, Nadia had seven perfect scores.

In her first gymnastics meet, held in 1967, she had finished 13th. "I gave her a Canadian doll, an Eskimo, made of seal skin," Bela said. "It was for good luck. I didn't want her to be superstitious. I told her, 'You must never finish 13th again.'"

During the next seven years, she was unbeaten. The doll collection started by Karolyi had increased to more than 200 in that time, but it was the worn seal-skin Eskimo doll that accompanied her to the Olympics.

The little girl who collected dolls had been thoroughly schooled in her responsibility.

"I don't come here to smile," Nadia said when she arrived in Montreal. "I come here to do a job. I leave the smiling to Olga."

Olga was there, but she never had a chance. The television cameras that had magnified her into a world figure in Munich, to the exclusion of winners like Ludmila Turischeva, were riveted on Nadia, turning her into the 1976 superstar.

The two met as the winning Soviet team greeted the runner-up Rumanian squad after the team competition. Korbut stood with five other Russians on the victory platform and extended her hand down to Nadia.

"I feel we are friends," Nadia said later.

Comaneci was embarrassed by all the attention, and homesick. "It was fun when I first was picked for special instruction," Nadia said. "Now it is work. I must practice three to four hours a day. Of course, I enjoy the sport but I must work very hard. I think so much of what I must do, I do not hear the crowd."

Her success in Montreal made her a Rumanian "Hero of Socialist Labor." Perhaps inevitably, the success came to seem a burden. Gymnastics enthusiasts expected more perfect scores. Karolyi, never forgetful of his role as mentor and of the years invested in his star, pressed for improvement. "We want to develop perfection," he said, "until she gets only tens."

Karolyi, who inevitably brings to mind Offenbach's Hoffman, with his clockwork doll Olympia, could not freeze Nadia in time. At 16, she had changed. She was four inches taller and twenty pounds heavier. The boyish body had become a young woman's. Her interests were broadening.

During a meet in West Germany in 1978, Comaneci was beaten by teammate Emilia Eberle, 14. Nadia's highest mark in four events was 9.7. Reports circulated that she had tired of practice, that she had fallen in love, that she had left the special sports school. Nadia seemed disinclined to help the stories along. In May 1979, slim and poised, the champion won the all-around event and two single-apparatus titles in the European championships.

At the Moscow Olympics in 1980, she was the center of a scoring controversy but still picked up two more gold medals (beam and floor exercises) and two more silver medals (team and all-around).

Nelli Kim (USSR) followed just behind Nadia Comaneci as the gymnastics star. She too scored perfectly (twice). Her medal total was four.

With daring somersaults and ballet-like routines Nadia scored six additional tens, totally enchanting the millions of television viewers around the world. When she completed her performances, Nadia had won three gold medals—for the uneven parallel bars, the balance beam, and the all-around events. She also won a silver medal in team competition and a bronze in the floor exercises.

Comaneci's chief competition came from the Soviet Union's 19-year-old Nelli Kim, from the central Asian city of Chimkent. Nelli also won three gold medals—in the horse vault, floor exercises, and team exercises—plus a silver in the all-around. She achieved two perfect tens.

Kim, like Comaneci, was a wisp of a girl who attacked the bars and beams with a determination reminiscent of another Soviet gymnastics star, Olga Korbut, who reigned in Munich. In Montreal, Korbut at 21 managed only one gold and one silver medal, sharing first place in the team exercises and placing second in the balance beam. She was fifth in both the uneven parallel bars and the all-around events.

Ludmila Turischeva (USSR), defending all-around champion, placed third in the event, took second place in both the horse vault and floor exercises, and won a gold medal in the team exercises. She announced her retirement after the competition.

American women kept intact an unenviable streak of never having won a gymnastics medal. However, for the first time in 44 years, an American male won a medal. Peter Kormann, a junior at Southern Connecticut State College, took a bronze in the floor exercises won by Nikolai Andrianov (USSR). Andrianov, the star of the men's competition, won seven medals—four golds, two silvers, and a bronze. The 24-year-old blond student dethroned Japan's two-time all-around champion, 29-year-old Sawao Kato, who finished second. Kato won two gold medals, to bring his three Olympic aggregate to 8 gold, 2 silver, and 1 bronze medal.

Another Japanese, Shun Fujimoto, was probably the most courageous athlete to perform in Montreal. He led his country to a fifth consecutive gold medal in the team event while competing with a broken kneecap and torn ligaments in his right leg.

A Soviet judge and a Bulgarian coach were charged by American gymnastics officials with using illegal influence to try to help their athletes in the men's events.

A Soviet contestant was caught cheating in modern pentathlon. Boris Onischenko, a member of the Soviet's 1972 team champions, was disqualified on the second day of the five-day competition when officials discovered a device in his dueling sword. The weapon was wired so that it would score a winning hit without making contact. Fencers are wired so that when a weapon makes contact a light over the judges' desk blinks when a hit is registered. Onischenko was dropped from the Soviet team and flown home. His departure enabled Great Britain to win the team gold medal, with Czechoslovakia second and Hungary third. Poland's Janusz Pyciak-Peciak, Pavel Lednev (USSR), and Jan Bartu of Czechoslovakia finished 1-2-3 in the individual event.

In the women's fencing Idiko Schwarczenberger of Hungary won the gold, and the Soviet team proved best.

East German women, led by Kornelia Ender, and the American men, paced by John Naber, shared honors in swimming. The deep-voiced, muscular East German mermaids captured 11 of 13 races, while the United States took 12 of 13 gold medals in the men's events.

Ender, the strapping 5' 10" daughter of an army officer from the town of Halle, won four gold medals and a silver. Seventeen-year-old Ender captured the 100- and 200-meter freestyles in the world record times of 55.65 seconds and 1:59.26. She also equaled the world mark of 1:00.13 in the 100-meter butterfly and anchored the team of Ulrike Richter, Hannelore Anke, and Andrea Pollack to a world record of 4:07.95 in the 400-meter medley relay. The United States placed second in the medley.

Other East German gold medalists were Ulrike Richter, with Olympic records in the 100- and 200-meter backstroke, Petra Thuemer, with world records of 4:09.89 and 8:37.14 in the 400- and 800-meter freestyle events, Anke in the 100-meter breaststroke, Pollack with an Olympic record of 2:11.41 in the 200-meter butterfly, and Ulrike Tauber, with another world mark of 4:42.77 in the 400-meter individual medley.

Boris Onischenko (above), a member of the USSR's modern pentathlon squad, reacts glumly to the Jury of Appeals decision banning him from the Olympics on the grounds that his foil had been rigged to cheat. Under the knowledgeable eye of an official, Kornelia Ender dives into the pool at the start of a heat of the 100-meter butterfly, an event she went on to win. The East German not only captured 3 individual and 1 relay gold medals but also established 2 individual world records and equaled 1 world mark.

An American Bicentennial flag aloft, U.S. swimmers march around the pool area. With the exception of the 200-meter breaststroke, U.S. men swimmers were first in all events. John Naber (left) of Southern California broke two individual world records and received the gold in the 100- and 200-meter backstroke and in two relay events.

Marina Koshevaia, with a world record 2:33.35, led a Soviet sweep in the 200-meter breaststroke.

The only gold medal won by a disappointing American team came in the 400-meter freestyle relay, and prevented the first shutout of United States women since 1952. Kim Peyton, Wendy Boglioli, Jill Sterkel, and Shirley Babashoff swam to an Olympic record of 3:44.82, defeating an East German quartet.

David Wilkie, in the 200-meter breaststroke, was the only non-American winner in the men's swimming competition in which only the 100-meter butterfly did not produce a world record. Wilkie, who finished ahead of Americans John Hencken and Rick Colella, gave Great Britain its first men's swimming gold medal since 1908. First and second places were reversed in the 100-meter breaststroke with Hencken's time 1:03.11.

The golds won by 20-year-old John Naber, 6' 6" and 195 pounds, came in the 100-meter backstroke (55.49), the 200-meter backstroke (1:59.19), and in the two relays. Naber, Hencken, Matt Vogel, and Jim Montgomery made up the 400-meter medley relay team (3:42.22) that finished in front of Canada and West Germany. The quartet of Mike Bruner, Bruce Furniss, Naber, and Montgomery captured the 800-meter freestyle relay (7:23.22), with the Soviet Union second and Great Britain third.

Peter Rocca of the United States won silver medals in both backstroke events as Roland Matthes of East Germany, the defending gold medalist, could manage only a bronze in the 100. Dan Harrigan's third place finish in the 200 gave the United States a sweep.

Other American 1-2-3 finishes were in the 200-meter freestyle, and the 100- and 200-meter butterfly events. Furniss (1:50.29) turned back Naber and Montgomery in the 200-meter freestyle. Vogel touched before Joe Bottom and Gary Hall in the 100-meter butterfly. Bruner (1:59.23) bested Steve Gregg and Bill Forrester in the 200-meter butterfly. The first of Mark Spitz's Munich Olympic records was shattered by Gregg in a heat of the 200.

Brian Goodell scored a double. He won the 400-meter freestyle (3:51.93), with countryman Tim Shaw second. He also captured the 1,500-meter freestyle (15:02.40), with Bobby Hackett of the United States the silver medalist.

There were two other races in which Americans placed first and second. Montgomery won the 100-meter freestyle (49.99); Jack

Capt. Phil Boggs, 26, of the U.S. Air Force Academy, took the men's springboard diving title with a most impressive score. A fine effort from North Carolina's Phil Ford (right, passing the ball) helped the United States to regain supremacy in basketball. The Americans easily defeated Yugoslavia (dark shirts) in the finals, 95–74.

Babashoff, Shirley's brother, was the runner-up. Rod Strachen was the gold medalist in the 400-meter individual medley (4:23.68), with Tim McKee taking the silver.

The diving competition provided its own special drama. American coach Tom Gompf reported that the Soviets proposed a deal by which they would receive voting support for their women's springboard diver, Irina Kalinina, in exchange for a promise to have Soviet judges back Phil Boggs of the United States in the men's event. Gompf said he made it clear a deal was unacceptable.

Kalinina placed seventh in the springboard competition, which was won by Jennifer Chandler of the United States. Christa Kohler (East Germany) was the silver medalist and American Cynthia McIngvale, the bronze medalist. Boggs took the men's event, ahead of Franco Cagnotto (Italy) and Alexander Kosenkov (USSR).

Italy's Klaus Dibiasi captured the highboard title and became the first diver in Olympic history to win the same event in three successive Games. He increased his Olympic medal total to five—three gold and two silver.

Elena Vaytsekhovskaia (USSR) took the women's highboard championship, with Ulrika Knape of Sweden second and America's Deborah Wilson placing third.

A threat of Soviet withdrawal from the Games was precipitated by a diver, 17-year-old Sergei Nemtsanov. A ninth-place finisher in the men's highboard, Nemtsanov disappeared from the Olympic Village three days before the Games' closing on August 1. The Soviets, who held that Nemtsanov had been "brainwashed" or kidnapped, demanded his immediate return, and threatened to break off all sports relationships with Canada if the youth were permitted to remain in Canada. Canadian officials did not scare, and the Soviets did not leave. Later Nemtsanov surfaced at the Soviet consulate in Montreal, said he had changed his mind about defecting, and wanted to return home.

The defending champion Soviet water polo team also was embroiled in a controversy. After losing to The Netherlands and being

held to a tie by Rumania, the Soviets forfeited a game to Cuba because they apparently had lost all hope of winning a medal. Only under pressure from the International Swimming Federation, which threatened possible disciplinary action, did the Soviet team continue to compete. Hungary won its sixth gold medal in the sport, with Italy second and The Netherlands third.

The United States regained the men's basketball championship it lost in Munich. The Americans were nearly upset in the second round by a Puerto Rican team, led by Butch Lee of Marquette University, who scored 35 points. The Americans trailed through much of the second half and then went ahead, 91–90, on a splurge by Phil Ford of North Carolina and Quinn Buckner of Indiana. After Naftali Rivera's basket put Puerto Rico back in the lead, Adrian Dantley of Notre Dame scored for the United States. Two free throws by Ford cinched the United States' 95–94 victory.

A 95–74 one-sided win over Yugoslavia in the championship game gave the Americans the gold medal. The Soviet team, upset by Yugoslavia in an earlier game, had to settle for the bronze medal.

Women's basketball was introduced in Montreal. The Soviet squad won the gold medal. The United States was second and Bulgaria third. The United States team lost the first women's Olympic basketball game ever played, 84–71, to underdog Japan.

The massive Soviets, unbeaten in six years, assured the championship with a 112–77 rout of the United States. Iuliana Semenova, a 7' 2" center, paced the Soviets with 32 points and 19 rebounds. Ann Meyers was the American high scorer with 17 points. Lucy Harris was the top American scorer in the tournament, with 76 points.

Long played on the local-school level, women's basketball was introduced to Olympic audiences at Montreal. Since 1936 when the court was divided into two sections, and the women players were classified as guards and forwards, the game has steadily become more similar to the men's version. Except for high-necked jerseys, even the women's uniforms resemble the men's.

Lasse Viren

I just wanted to run. Running is fun. I enjoy competing. That is it. I'll probably always run.

—LASSE VIREN

During the six Olympics held from 1912 through 1936, distance runners from Finland won a total of 41 medals. In the next six Olympics, Finnish distance runners were able to win only one, a bronze medal in the 1956 marathon.

Lasse Artturi Viren helped his country regain preeminence in distance running. Viren, a policeman, won the 5,000- and 10,000-meter runs in the 1972 Munich Olympics and duplicated the feat in Montreal in 1976—achieving this "double double" for the first time in Olympic history.

Hannes Kolehmainen (1912), Emil Zátopek of Czechoslovakia (1952), and Soviet Vladimir Kuts (1956) all had won the 5,000 and 10,000 in the same Olympics. None repeated.

In Montreal, Viren found himself not only the leader of a Finnish resurgence, but also the center of a controversy over what has been called "blood-doping."

Blood-doping is a technique by which blood is withdrawn from an athlete and its oxygen-carrying hemoglobin stored. When the athlete's system has replenished the red blood cells, the stored hemoglobin is returned to his body, allowing him, supposedly, to perform better because of this greater oxygen-carrying capacity. If an individual's hemoglobin count were far below the optimum, there might be reason to seek an increase in oxygen-carrying capacity. However, for anyone with an optimum level of hemoglobin, increasing the hemoglobin could lead to congestive heart failure.

Some Finns and Swedes have acknowledged experimenting with the blood-doping technique, but there is neither evidence that Lasse Viren used it, nor, says his doctor, any sense in the suggestion—his hemoglobin count is normally close to the optimum. Although runners whom he has beaten have impugned Viren, Chris Brasher, the 1956 British gold medalist in the 3,000-meter steeplechase who became a track and field writer for a London newspaper, dismissed the critics.

"I look at the character of the man and those who are close to him," said Brasher. "He's utterly marvelous, completely self-sufficient. Blood-doping has been done by others, but not by Viren, I'm sure."

Viren was born on July 22, 1949, in Myrskylä, a town of 2,300 about 65 miles northeast of Helsinki. Lasse's mother, Elvi, remembered he ran whenever he could, even after a full day helping his father, Johann, a truck driver.

Viren began his Olympic career in a heat of the 10,000-meter run in Munich on August 31, 1972. It was only his ninth race over the distance. Halfway through the September 3 final, which resulted in a dramatic victory, the 5' 11", 134-pounder stumbled and crashed to the track.

He was down for at least three seconds, got up, and ran on. With an unparalleled final 800 meters of 1 minute, 56.4 seconds, Viren ran down the field, to win the gold medal and set a world record of 27:38.4.

On September 10, Viren trailed Steve Prefontaine of the United States and Mohamed Gammoudi of Tunisia on the last lap of the 5,000 meters. Then he ran the concluding four laps in 3:59.8 and the final 400 meters in 55.8 seconds, to win in the Olympic record time of 13:26.4.

Viren wasn't so fast in the Montreal 10,000 on July 26, 1976, as he had been in Munich. His gold medal time was 27:40.4, with a second half 13:31.5.

In the 5,000 on July 30, Viren's major competition was expected to be New Zealand's Rod Dixon and Dick Quax. They, plus Klaus-Peter Hildenbrand of West Germany and Brendan Foster of Great Britain, were bunched on the last lap with Viren in front. They went to the tape with fractions of seconds separation. Viren won in 13:24.8, breaking his own Olympic record. Quax was second in 13:25.2, followed by Hildenbrand (13:25.4.), Dixon (13:25.5.), and Foster (13:26.2).

Four years after Montreal, the Finn hero competed in the Moscow Games, finishing fifth in the 10,000 meters.

The East German women were decisive in track and field, just as they were in swimming. They won nine of 14 events, placed second in four others, and third in six more. They captured 19 of the 38 medals available. The only event in which East Germany did not win a medal was the shot put, won by Ivanka Christova of Bulgaria.

The pentathlon was an East German sweep, with Siegrun Siegel, Christine Laser, and Burglinde Pollak finishing in that order. Other East German winners were Baerbel Eckert in the 200 meters, Johanna Schaller in the 100-meter hurdles, Rosemarie Ackermann in the high jump, Angela Voigt in the long jump, Evelin Schlaak in the discus, and Ruth Fuchs in the javelin. The East German team of Marlis Oelsner, Renate Stecher, Carla Bodendorf, and Eckert won the 400-meter relay, defeating West Germany and the Soviet Union. A quartet of Doris Maletzki, Brigitte Rohde, Ellen Streidt, and Christina Brehmer raced to a world record of 3 minutes, 19.23 seconds in the 1,600-meter relay. The United States team of Debra Sapenter, Sheila Ingram, Pam Jiles, and Rosalyn Bryant finished second, with the Soviet Union team third.

Annegret Richter of West Germany won the 100 meters and took a silver in the 200. Stecher, East Germany's defending double sprint champion, was second in the 100 and third in the 200.

Irena Szewinska of Poland, competing in her fourth consecutive Olympics, ran a world record 49.29 in the 400 meters. It was her seventh Olympic career medal and made the 30-year-old economist the first woman to win medals in the 100-, 200-, and 400-meter runs.

The only other women's world record was established by Tatyana Kazankina (USSR), who clocked 1:54.94 for 800 meters, and then completed a double in the 1,500 meters.

American women won only three medals. In addition to a silver in the 1,600-meter relay, Kathy McMillan won a silver in the long jump and Kathy Schmidt repeated her Munich bronze medal finish in the javelin.

Finland's Lasse Viren became the first runner in Olympic history to win the 5,000- and 10,000-meter races in successive Olympics. He began his "double double" on July 26th with an easy victory in the 10,000. His last lap was run in 61.3 seconds and brought him home ahead of Portugal's Carlos Lopes and Brendan Foster of Great Britain.

Tatyana Kazankina (USSR) narrowly defeated East Germany's Gunhilde Hoffmeister (above, right) in the 1,500 meters. Another East German, Baerbel Eckert, established an Olympic record in leading the field in the 200-meter race. West Germany's Annegret Richter (181) followed in second place.

Four days later, Viren won the 5,000 meters, with Dick Quax of New Zealand second, followed by Klaus-Peter Hildenbrand of West Germany.

On July 31, Viren attempted to duplicate the 1952 feat of Emil Zátopek of Czechoslovakia by tripling in the marathon. However, he could do no better than fifth. East Germany's Waldemar Cierpinski, a former steeplechaser, ran the fastest marathon in Olympic history, with a time of 2 hours, 9 minutes and 55 seconds. Defending champion Frank Shorter of the United States was second in 2:10.46. Karel Lismont of Belgium was third.

Bearded 24-year-old Alberto Juantorena became the first Cuban ever to win a gold medal in track and field and the first to capture the 400- and 800-meter runs in the same Olympics. The 6′ 2″, 185-pound runner won the 800 meters on July 25th with a world record clocking of 1 minute, 43.50 seconds in his first major competition over the distance. Ivo Vandamme of Belgium was second in 1:43.86, with America's Rick Wohlhuter the bronze medalist in 1:44.12. The world record holder for the mile, John Walker of New Zealand, was eliminated in a heat.

On July 29th, Jauntorena, who switched from Cuba's basketball team to its track team, won his specialty, clocking 44.26 seconds in the 400 to beat a pair of Americans.

Hernan Frazier, Ben Brown, Fred Newhouse, and Maxie Parks won the gold medal in the 1,600-meter relay, placing ahead of Poland and West Germany. The 400-meter relay went to the United States team of Harvey Glance, John Jones, Millard Hampton, and Steve Riddick. East Germany was the runner-up, and the Soviet team, anchored by Valery Borzov, the bronze-medal winner.

Borzov, the defending sprint double gold medalist, managed only a bronze medal in the 100 meters in which Hasely Crawford, with a 10.06 clocking, became Trinidad's first gold medalist in history. Don Quarrie of Jamaica was second.

Following his third-place finish in the 100, Borzov dropped out of the 200, won by Quarrie in 20.23. Hampton and Dwayne Evans (USA) won the silver and bronze medals.

John Walker won the 1,500 meters in the disappointing time of 3 minutes, 39.17 seconds, the slowest time since Ron Delany's Melbourne run. His margin of victory over the Belgian Vandamme was only 10/100ths of a second. Paul-Heinz Wellmann of West Germany was third in 3:39.33.

In taking the marathon in world record time, East Germany's Waldemar Cierpinski (above) had to endure a Montreal downpour. Cierpinski, the first German to win a marathon gold medal, was a former steeplechase runner. Hungary's Miklos Nemeth, son of the 1948 hammer champion, broke the world mark in the javelin.

Guy Drut gave France its first gold medal in men's track and field in 20 years with his victory in the 110-meter hurdles. It ended a streak of American gold medals in the event dating back to 1932. Drut defeated Alejandro Casanas of Cuba by 3/100ths of a second and 33-year-old Willie Davenport of the United States by 5/100ths of a second. Davenport, who made his first Olympic appearance in 1964, did remarkably well in Montreal after returning from a crippling knee injury in 1975.

Edwin Moses won the 400-meter hurdles for the United States, setting a world record of 47.64. Mike Shine, his teammate, was a surprising second, ahead of Evgeni Gavrilenko (USSR). Moses, a long-striding Morehouse College student, erased the mark of 47.82 set by John Akii-Bua of Uganda in the Munich Games.

Anders Garderud won Sweden's first track and field gold medal since 1952 by taking the 3,000-meter steeplechase with a world record of 8 minutes, 8.02 seconds, after Frank Baumgartl of East Germany, with whom he was running neck and neck, tripped over the final hurdle and fell. Baumgartl got up and finished third, behind Poland's Bronislaw Malinowski.

Mac Wilkins, an outspoken maverick, won the discus after severely criticizing the USOC and the American system of building sports teams. His winning toss of 221' 5.4" erased Al Oerter's 1968 Olympic record. East Germany's Wolfgang Schmidt was second, followed by John Powell (USA).

Wilkins and Al Feuerbach, a shot putter, created a stir among American track and field officials when they left their quarters to train with the West Germans about 50 miles east of Montreal.

Feuerbach could do no better than fourth in the shot put, won by 20-year-old Udo Beyer of East Germany. Evgeni Mironov and Aleksandr Barishnikov (USSR) were second and third. It was the first time in 40 years that the United States failed to win a medal in the event.

Viktor Saneyev (USSR) kept his gold medal streak intact. The 31-year-old became the first in Olympic history to win the triple jump in three consecutive Games. James Butts of the United States was second, followed by Brazil's Joao de Oliveira.

The Soviet Union swept the hammer throw, with winner Yuri Sedykh placing ahead of Alexei Spiridonov and Anatoli Bondarchuk. Hungary's Miklos Németh joined his father, Imre, as an Olympic gold medalist. Imre was the 1948 champion in the hammer. Miklos

Trinidad's Hasely Crawford jubilantly accepted his gold medal for the 100 meters. Soviet Valery Borzov, (right), first in the event in 1972, took the bronze and Jamaica's Don Quarrie was awarded the silver. In the 1,500, New Zealand's John Walker crossed the finish line 1/10th of a second ahead of Belgium's Ivo Vandamme (103). Regarding his particularly slow time, the winner said, "Time is not important. Winning the gold medal is, because even the world record is here today, gone tomorrow."

won the javelin contest in Montreal with a world record throw of 310' 4½".

Poland's Tadeusz Slusarski was the unexpected winner in the pole vault. Finland's Antti Kalliomaki and Dave Roberts (USA), the world record holder, placed second and third. All three medalists equaled the Olympic record of 18' 0½" and final placings were determined on the basis of fewer misses.

Arnie Robinson, a bronze medalist in Munich, won the 1976 gold medal in the long jump, with another American, Randy Williams, placing second. Frank Wartenberg of East Germany was third.

It rained in Montreal on July 31, the day of the high jump final. Dwight Stones, the American favorite and world record holder, had a history of not performing well in wet conditions. He finished third. The gold medal went to Poland's 19-year-old Jacek Wszola, the youngest individual winner in the men's track and field competition. Greg Joy of Canada was the silver medalist.

Mexico won its first-ever gold medal in track and field when Daniel Bautista came in first in the 20-kilometer walk, ahead of East Germans Hans Reimann and Peter Frenkel.

The most dramatic triumph by an American was that of decathlon champion Bruce Jenner. On July 29 and 30, Jenner displayed his athletic versatility and dethroned Nikolai Avilov (USSR) as decathlon titleholder. Jenner set a world record of 8,618 points, far outdistancing runner-up Guido Kratschmer of West Germany. Avilov, who set the former world mark in the Munich Games, was the bronze medalist.

The rowing events were increased by the addition of quadruple sculls for men; and for women single, double, and quadruple sculls, coxless pairs, and coxed fours and eights. In the eight men's events Soviet rowers won the coxed fours, Finland the single sculls, and Norway the double. East Germans won the five other events. Of the six women's events, four went to East German women, and two to Bulgarian.

The yachting program added two new classes of boats: the Tornado (won by Great Britain) and the 470 (won by West Germany).

There were nine canoeing events for men and two for women in the Montreal Games, and with the exception of the gold-medal performance in the 1,000-meter Canadian singles by Yugoslavia's Matija Ljubek, the events went to Iron Curtain country contestants. The Soviet Union won 6, East Germany 3, and Rumania 1.

In the boxing tournament U.S. fighters won 5 gold medals, 1 silver, and 1 bronze, for their best showing since sweeping all seven championships in the 1904 Games in St. Louis.

The United States winners were Leon and Michael Spinks, Leon in the light heavyweight and Michael in the middleweight division; light welterweight Sugar Ray Leonard, lightweight Howard Davis, and flyweight Leo Randolph. Bantamweight Charles Mooney took a silver medal and heavyweight John Tate a bronze. The Spinks boys were the first brothers in history to win Olympic boxing gold medals.

A 6′ 5″, 225-pound Cuban, Teofilo Stevenson, became the first heavyweight to win consecutive gold medals. The 24-year-old Stevenson, whom Fidel Castro would not permit to turn professional, entered the Montreal tournament with a background of 130 fights, 118 of which he won, 90 by knockouts.

Leon Spinks' opponent in the light heavyweight gold medal bout was knockout artist Sixto Soria of Cuba. Despite undisguised attempts by the Soviet referee to aid the battered Soria, the Marine Corps corporal punished the Cuban. He dropped Soria twice and forced the official to stop the contest in the third round.

Nineteen months later Leon Spinks became the world heavyweight champion. He beat Muhammad Ali on a 15-round split decision in Las Vegas, on February 15, 1978, for the World Boxing Association's version of the title. But his reign was short. Ali regained the crown seven months later to the day, by outpointing Spinks in New Orleans.

Edmund "Tad" Coffin gave the United States its first gold medal ever in the individual three-day equestrian event. Teammate John Michael Plumb placed second. The two then combined with Bruce Davidson and Marie Anne Tauskey to capture the three-day team competition.

Alwin Schockemoehle of West Germany outpointed Michel Vaillancourt (Canada) and François Mathy (Belgium) in the individual jumping. France took the team event. Individual dressage gold was Christine Stuckelberger's (Switzerland). German riders won the team event, ahead of Swiss and American teams. Among the interested spectators during the equestrian events were Queen Elizabeth and Prince Philip, whose daughter, Princess Anne, was the first member of Britain's Royal Family to participate in the Olympics. When her horse fell during the three-day competition she was thrown, but she remounted and finished the event.

Americans again swept the individual archery contests. Darrell Pace, the 19-year-old world champion, won the men's championship. The women's gold medal went to 23-year-old Luann Ryon.

Margaret Murdock (USA), so nearsighted that she could not read the top line of an eye chart unassisted, became the first woman ever to win an Olympic shooting medal. In a bizarre sequence of reversals in the judging, the 33-year-old Murdock was first called the winner of the three position small-bore rifle title, then was one of a tie for it, and finally denied it. A magnifying device determined that one of the bullets fired by her teammate, Lanny Bassham, was

Clearing 15′ 9″ in the pole vault, Bruce Jenner went into the lead in the race to the decathlon gold. The versatile 26-year-old, who was 10th in the decathlon in 1972 and who had spent the four intervening years in dedicated self-improvement, amassed a world record number of points in the ten-event competition.

Bruce Jenner

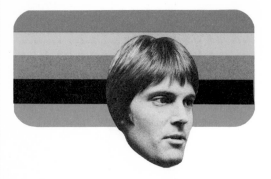

Everything in my whole life pointed me toward winning the gold medal.

—BRUCE JENNER

Bruce Jenner was a decathlete for six years, before he hit the headlines. An injury in 1970 that ended a football career placed him on the path that led to the decathlon gold medal. In the 1976 Montreal Olympics, he established a world record of 8,618 points.

When it was over, his wife, Chrystie, said she was going to bronze his socks. "He's worn them every meet for the last six years. His college coach, L. D. Weldon, gave them to him. The elastic's gone. There's practically nothing left to them." They were a talisman to Jenner in his climb to fame. On the pinnacle of the athletic world, he was clear-minded about the awesome power of television to make instant heroes of successful athletes.

"What other heroes do we have left in the United States?" the 26-year-old Jenner asked. "We're not at war, so we don't have war heroes. Politicians aren't on top right now. And actors are only acting the roles of heroes.

"Men see me as someone who went to the Olympics, took on everybody and conquered the world. That's a manly image. On the other hand, when the decathlon was over, I went over, as I always did, to kiss Chrystie. It was on television and from the women's point of view, I came across as sensitive," he said.

The handsome, 6' 2", 195-pound All-American man was born in Mt. Kisco, New York, on Oct. 28, 1949. He attended high school in Newtown, Connecticut, and went to Graceland College in Iowa, from which he was graduated in 1973. It was there that Jenner turned from football to the decathlon. He had been a schoolboy champion in the pole vault and the high jump, and he had the personal encouragement of Graceland coach L. D. Weldon.

Jenner qualified as the third American decathlete on the 1972 United States Olympic team. He finished 10th in Munich, where Nikolai Avilov of the Soviet Union won the championship with a world record 8,454 points.

After Munich, Jenner set a 1976 goal of 8,600 points for himself. "I made a slogan," he said. "Eighty-five in '75, eighty-six in '76."

Chrystie Jenner became a stewardess to support them and Bruce trained with such thoroughness that when he reached Montreal, he felt he could beat both Avilov and 8,600 points.

"When I walked onto the track I felt it was sort of my destiny to win," he said. "Everything in my whole life pointed me toward winning the gold medal.

"But I felt there was a lot of pressure on me. Pole vaulter Dave Roberts was my roommate. I sat in my room and watched TV and saw the rain come down and I saw him lose although he was by far the best vaulter. I was very nervous," the future gold medalist said.

At the end of the first day of the two-day event, Guido Kratschmer of West Germany was first, with 4,333 points, Avilov was second with 4,315, and Jenner third with 4,298. However, the American was much stronger than either of the leaders in the final five events. He felt confident about his chances. "All I had to do was come near my best in each event," he said.

He did, and entered the final event—the 1,500-meter run—with 7,904 of his slogan's 8,600 points. It proved to be the fastest 1,500 of his life, and with it he broke Avilov's world record.

"I started going down the backstretch and the more I picked it up, the better I felt," Jenner said. "Down the last straight, I knew I was close to 8,600 and I couldn't slow down. I kept driving, driving, driving. I leaned at the tape, and looked at the clock." He had 8,618 points!

After that, sports telecasting, product endorsements, and special interviewing kept Bruce in the public eye and increased his bank account.

Shortly after the birth of their first child, Burt, in 1978, the Jenners began to have marriage difficulties. After an attempt at reconciliation and the birth of a daughter, Casey, in 1980, the couple were divorced. In January 1981, Bruce married Linda Thompson, a performer on the television show *Hee Haw*.

less than 1/25th of an inch nearer the center of the target than first believed. Bassham, a 29-year-old Army captain, was declared the gold medal winner while Murdock, who wore thick glasses, had to settle for a silver, although both finished with 1,162 points.

Japan regained the women's volleyball title with a 3–0 victory over the Soviet Union. South Korea was third. The men's crown went to Poland, followed by the Soviet Union.

East Germany was the soccer gold medalist, finishing ahead of Poland and the Soviet Union. New Zealand defeated Australia, 1–0, for the field hockey championship. Australia took the silver, and Pakistan won the bronze with a 3–2 victory over The Netherlands. The Soviet Union won both the men's and women's team handball gold medals.

Japan captured 3 of the 6 judo titles, the Soviet Union took 2, and Cuba 1. The major surprise for the Americans was the heavyweight bronze medal won by Al Coage, a 33-year-old nightclub bouncer.

Soviet wrestlers won 7 of the 10 gold medals in Greco-Roman and 5 of the 10 in freestyle wrestling. Finland, Poland, and Yugoslavia each claimed a Greco-Roman triumph. In the freestyle, Japanese wrestlers won two events and Bulgarian, South Korean, and United States contestants were successful in one event each.

In the finals, Soviets won 6 gold medals, Bulgarians 2, and East Germans 1 in the nine-event weightlifting program which underwent a drastic rules change. The press lift was dropped, reducing the

With 25 seconds left in the third and final round, Cuba's Teofilo Stevenson (right) knocked out Rumania's Mircea Simon, becoming the first heavyweight boxer to receive consecutive gold medals. Princess Anne, the first member of the British royal family to appear in the Olympics and the only royal competitor at Montreal, was thrown by her temperamental mount, Goodwill. She was 24th in a field of 28.

Nation	G	S	B
Soviet Union	47	43	35
East Germany	40	25	25
United States	34	35	25
West Germany	10	12	17
Japan	9	6	10
Poland	8	6	11
Bulgaria	7	8	9
Cuba	6	4	3
Rumania	4	9	14
Hungary	4	5	12
Finland	4	2	–
Sweden	4	1	–
Great Britain	3	5	5
Italy	2	7	4
Yugoslavia	2	3	3
France	2	2	5
Czechoslovakia	2	2	4
New Zealand	2	1	1
South Korea	1	1	4
Switzerland	1	1	2
Jamaica	1	1	–
North Korea	1	1	–
Norway	1	1	–
Denmark	1	–	2
Mexico	1	–	1
Trinidad and Tobago	1	–	–
Canada	–	5	6
Belgium	–	3	3
The Netherlands	–	2	3
Portugal	–	2	–
Spain	–	2	–
Australia	–	1	4
Iran	–	1	1
Mongolia	–	1	–
Venezuela	–	1	–
Brazil	–	–	2
Austria	–	–	1
Bermuda	–	–	1
Pakistan	–	–	1
Puerto Rico	–	–	1
Thailand	–	–	1

As the XXI Summer Games came to a close, thoughts turned to Moscow and the 1980 Olympics. Of the Games, Montreal Major Jean Drapeau said, "The spirit of the Olympics will stay with us, stay with Montreal, stay with Quebec, stay with Canada."

number of lifts to two. Vasili Alekseyev (USSR) repeated as super heavyweight champion. Bulgaria's Norair Nurikyan, the 1972 featherweight gold medalist, dropped to the bantamweight class and again placed first.

Two weightlifters were among three athletes who were disqualified for using banned anabolic steroids during the Games. They were Mark Cameron, a 23-year-old American heavyweight; Peter Pavlasek, a Czechoslovakian super heavyweight lifter; and Danuta Rosuni of Poland, a woman discus thrower.

Ten weeks after urine tests were analyzed, the IOC Executive Board stripped three weightlifters of their medals. Bulgarian heavyweight champion Valentin Khristov and Poland's lightweight titlist Zbigniew Kaczmarek, as well as silver medalist Blagoi Blagoev of Bulgaria, a light heavyweight, were found guilty of taking anabolic steroids. Also disqualified were weightlifters Phil Grippaldi of the United States and Arne Norback of Sweden. Neither Grippaldi nor Norback was a medalist, however.

When it came time to say "Adieu, Jeux de la XXI Olympiade Montréal" the so-called East German Sports Factory had produced the biggest surprise of the Games. The nation of 17 million had produced winners of 40 gold medals—6 more than the United States and only 7 fewer than the Soviet Union.

The success of the East Germans was the result of years of scientific planning and programming the lives of athletes. It had done what the planners wanted, but whether such planning was desirable was an open question. Many sports officials and athletes from Western nations insisted that the broad-shouldered East German women had taken body-building steroids, with the result that they seemed more masculine than feminine.

For the first time it was possible to plan to transmit the flame from Olympia with magical swiftness. By laser beam it could go from Olympia to Ottawa in 1/20th of a second. The ease of passing on the flame served to underline the difficulty of conveying and preserving the spirit of the ancient pursuit of excellence.

1980

Winter Games

Lake Placid, New York

In the years following the 1932 Winter Games in Lake Placid, local officials continually lobbied the sports federations to bring the competition back to the little fairy-tale town in New York's Adirondack Mountains. Finally, on Oct. 23, 1974, the International Olympic Committee (IOC) announced that Lake Placid had been selected as host for the XIII Winter Games. Advances in snow-making and refrigeration had negated the argument regarding undependable snow conditions.

Between 1932 and 1980 the town itself had not changed much, not even in population. It remained a tourist hamlet, as well as the scene of numerous world championship winter events. In fact, Lake Placid had put more local residents on Olympic teams than any other community regardless of size. Immediately following the IOC announcement of 1974, Lake Placid residents—including the Rev. Bernard Fell, a former policeman who became president of the Lake Placid Olympic Organization Committee (LPOOC)—began preparing for the Games. New hotels, guest houses, and restaurants were built, and the requisite sports facilities were either constructed or remodeled. Some $200 million in local, state, and federal funds was spent. The total was $50 million above "final" budget.

In spite of the construction, the 1980 Winter Games were billed as the "Olympics in Perspective." With the rising cost of each festival of Games threatening the very life of the institution, organizers and promoters of the Lake Placid Olympics promised a no-frills operation that

Lake Placid, a small resort town in New York's Adirondack Mountains that had hosted the 1932 Winter Games, underwent extensive construction prior to the 1980 winter events.

would "return the Games to the athletes." Emphasis would be placed on constructing the best possible sports facilities and seeing to it that the events were run smoothly and efficiently. The masses of spectators and the media, who would bring important revenues to the entire area, would have to be properly managed, but they would take second place to the competitions themselves.

The events that took place between Tuesday, Feb. 12, and Sunday, Feb. 24, 1980, did put the emphasis on athletes rather than on extravagant showmanship, and in an odd way the Olympic ideal was served. The "glory of sport and honor of our teams," commemorated in the Olympic Oath, prevailed. For the home crowd there was euphoria over the victory of the U.S. hockey team and pride in the five gold medals won by Eric Heiden. For everyone there were surprises, disappointments, and thrills that helped them forget the ordeals of being in Lake Placid.

Although the LPOOC carried off the athletic competitions smoothly, there were hitches in almost every other area. The Games were only a few days old before people began calling them the "Olympics in Chaos." A mismanaged bus system left thousands of spectators stranded in the bitter cold and ultimately caused New York Gov. Hugh Carey to declare a partial emergency. Massive traffic jams in and around Lake Placid further prevented transportation to and from the various sites. The ticket-selling and telephone systems were overloaded. And IOC indulged in a public reprimand to the LPOOC for its bungling of the first medal ceremony on frozen Mirror Lake.

As far as the shopkeepers on Main Street were concerned, Lake Placid was a ghost town. What was supposed to be a bonanza for the tiny Adirondack community had turned into a boondoggle in the early days of the contests. Merchants who laid in huge inventories and boosted prices to double or triple their normal level were not drawing customers. With all private vehicular travel forbidden, only an occasional state trooper's car was seen cruising the main business thoroughfare. There was only a smattering of pedestrians, except during breaks in activities at the nearby Fieldhouse and skating rink.

The owner of a corner restaurant near the main Olympic center, advertising "Buffet Breakfast $5.95, Lunch $7.95, Dinner $12.95," felt that midtown business was suffering from a psychological effect. Although a few stores posted half-price signs as the events went on, the gouge continued. A cup of coffee was going for up to $1.50. One restaurant advertised a steak sandwich for $18.50. An Italian place offered a plate of spaghetti for $10.00. Hotel room prices were exorbitant. A centrally located motel jumped its rooms from $28.50 a day to $91.00 a day during the Games. Souvenirs also were bringing outrageous prices. One man bought three T-shirts for his kids. Price: $28.00. To the complaints about transportation, tickets, and the overall disorganization were added cries of "rip-off!"

A political issue that caused headaches for the Olympic Committee was a familiar one: whether to allow Taiwan to take part under the name of the Republic of China. In 1976, Taiwan's 43-member Olympic delegation was barred from competing in the Montreal Summer Games under the banner of the Republic of China, its official IOC designation. The action was taken because the Canadian government had recognized the People's Republic of China. The Taiwanese were invited to participate under the name of

Early in the Games, a mismanaged bus system caused many fans to wait unduly in the cold.

Taiwan and to march in the opening ceremony with their national flag, but they refused to abandon the designation of Republic of China and withdrew before the start of the Games. In 1979 the IOC ruled that China could participate in the Lake Placid Games and that Taiwan could take part only if it changed its name, flag, and national anthem. The Taiwanese again refused but still sent a 27-member delegation to Lake Placid. Seeking a revocation of the IOC rules, they filed suit in the New York state supreme court in Plattsburgh and in a court in Switzerland, home of the IOC. On Thursday, February 7, Justice Norman Harvey struck down the IOC regulation and declared the Taiwanese eligible to participate under their own name. But the LPOOC filed an appeal; on February 11 a state appellate court reversed the decision, and on February 12 the state's highest court also held against Taiwan. With not enough time to appeal to the U.S. Supreme Court, the delegation went home.

Political tensions, including a possible boycott of the Summer Games in Moscow by the United States and others, the memory of the terrorist attack at the 1972 Summer Games in Munich, and the last-minute threat of arson made security a primary concern in Lake Placid. At the III Winter Games in 1932, it took 53 state troopers and four horses to keep the peace. In 1980 an army of almost 1,000 security personnel was mobilized. Among them were some 800 New York state troopers, 75 FBI agents, and law-enforcement officers of the U.S. Secret Service and State Department.

Even though, at about 10:00 A.M. on Tuesday, February 19, a power failure briefly knocked out electricity at several competition sites, the power loss did not delay any of the scheduled events. The medal award ceremonies were going without a hitch, and ticket sales were brisk. Most importantly, the bus system showed signs of improvement early in the week, and by Wednesday it was running almost as smoothly as the LPOOC had planned. Newly arriving spectators were pleasantly surprised at the efficiency with which they were moved. Temperatures and spirits rose markedly. On Main

X rays and television monitors were utilized to check all luggage entering the Olympic Village.

The U.S. hockey team was the surprise of Lake Placid. Its victory over the Soviet team was considered one of the biggest upsets in Olympic history. Goalie Jim Craig, above, a former baseball catcher, played without relief and allowed an average of only 2.14 goals per game.

Street business was booming even with prices high. A major reason for the turnaround was the emergence of the U.S. hockey team as perhaps the most exciting group of athletes ever to perform in the Winter Games.

There was no reason to expect the American hockey team to finish any better than fifth or sixth in the Olympic tournament. The class of the contest was the Soviet team, which featured the world's finest passing attack, depth at virtually every position, and a seemingly limitless reserve of determination. The Soviets had won the last four Olympic gold medals in hockey, and as a warm-up for the 1980 Winter Olympics had polished off some of the best teams of the National Hockey League (NHL). Among the players were such standouts as Vladislav Tretiak, considered by many the best goalie in the world; veteran captain Boris Mikhailov; forward Helmut Balderis; defenseman Valeri Vasiliev; and Viacheslav Fetisov, billed as "the Bobby Orr of Russia."

The twelve 20-man teams in the tournament were divided into two divisions—Red and Blue. Every team played its division's rivals one time, and the top two teams from each division played the top two teams from the other division in the medal round. The Blue Division comprised the United States, Czechoslovakia, Sweden, West Germany, Norway, and Rumania. The Red Division was made up of the Soviet Union, Finland, Canada, the Netherlands, Poland, and Japan.

Following a series of dramatic, come-from-behind victories, the U.S. team won the right to play in the medal round. The other finalists were the USSR, as expected; Sweden, which had stayed away from the 1976 contest to protest the loss of its star players to North American professional clubs; and Finland, a solid, hard-checking team. In the early evening hours of Friday, February 22, the U.S. team, now classified as "the Boys of Winter," scored a 4–3 upset over the Soviets. Superb play by goalie Jim Craig and a 25-foot score by Mike Eruzione highlighted the contest. Wild rejoicing by the partisan American crowd followed into the night and the next day. The win led Coach Herb Brooks to utter another Brooksism: "Boys, we went to the well again, and the water was colder and the water was deeper."

There were shouts of "We beat the Russians!" and "Stuff the bear!" coming from the streets of Lake Placid, when Sweden and

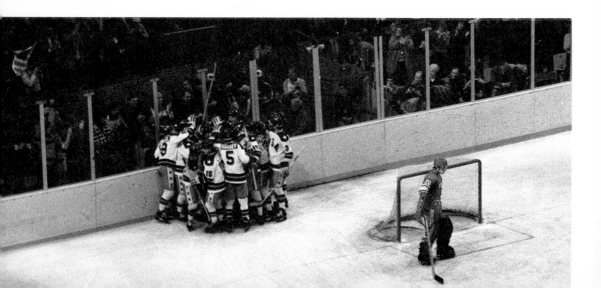

Finland took the ice at 8:30 for the second matchup of the medal round. The favored Swedes outshot their opponents 30 to 25 but needed two goals in the last period to come away with a 3–3 tie. With the United States playing Finland next and Sweden taking on the Soviet Union, the possibilities for gold, silver, and bronze still boggled the mind. However, if the Americans could beat the Finns in their Sunday matchup, the gold would be theirs.

In the game against Finland, the United States trailed 2–1 after two periods and looked sluggish in the first moments of the last session. The crowd took time out from its flag-waving and foot stamping to sit and be worried. Perhaps the team finally had met an obstacle—pressure—that it could not surmount. It was a fear shared by everyone in the arena, except the Boys of Winter. "We were behind," said left wing Rob McClanahan, "but we played the third period with great confidence." With McClanahan scoring the go-ahead goal, the U.S. team went on to a 4–2 win and the gold medal. When the buzzer sounded, the Boys of Winter threw their sticks and gloves into the crowd, and flag-waving fans rushed onto the ice. Their hands upraised, Mike Eruzione and Rob McClanahan took one of the flags and displayed it proudly. Shortly thereafter the Soviet Union took out its frustration against Sweden, clinching the silver medal with a 9–2 victory. Sweden received the bronze.

Although Americans, many of whom had never seen an ice hockey game, delighted in the play of the U.S. hockey team, they also took great pleasure and pride in the Olympic performance of speed skater Eric Heiden. His five gold medals and complete domination of the sport were awesome. The 21-year-old from Madison, Wisconsin, established new Olympic records in all five events and a world mark in the 10,000 meters. Canada's Gaetan Boucher was second to Heiden in the 1,000-meter event, and Norway's Kai Arne Stenshjemmet was runner-up in the 1,500 and 5,000. In the wom-

In the spirit of camaraderie that characterized the U.S. hockey team throughout the competition, "the Boys of Winter" celebrated atop the winners' podium. Captain Mike Eruzione had invited his teammates to join him on the podium after the team received their gold medals.

Eric Heiden

It really doesn't matter whether I win or lose, just so long as I do my best.

—ERIC HEIDEN

By the noon of Saturday, Feb. 23, 1980, Eric Heiden had rewritten the Olympic record book and shown himself the absolute master of speed skating. He not only had won five gold medals but also had set five Olympic records and a world mark. At 6′1″ and 185 pounds, with a boyish grin and gentle, engaging manner, the 21-year-old from Madison, Wisconsin, conveyed an impression of amiable strength. On the ice, sleeked into his skating skin and poised for the skating gun, his 29″ thighs suggesting immense frog legs, he was a figure of truly formidable power. Enormous strides moved him in seconds from standing to speeds close to those of Thoroughbreds, speeds that his superb physique permitted him to maintain.

Heiden's interest in sports was shared by his family. He was born and grew up in Madison, where his grandfather was the University of Wisconsin ice hockey coach. His father, Jack, an orthopedic surgeon, was a champion senior cyclist and his mother, Nancy, played competition tennis and enjoyed skiing and skating. His younger sister Beth was a bronze medalist at the 1980 Winter Games.

Training, at which he was relentless, was a principal reason for his success. While he is obviously an excellent athlete, it was hard work and perseverance rather than sheer natural ability that made the difference, said his coach, Dianne Holum.

Eric was a child of the work ethic. In preparation for Lake Placid, Heiden began his regime in May 1979. He worked out 3–4 hours a day, five days a week through June. Thereafter, it was two workouts six days a week and one on the seventh day. The exercise involved running, cycling, simulated skating, jogging, duck walking, and weightlifting. He has said, "I guess I'm kind of weird, but I enjoy being tired."

Somehow along the route, he also had learned self-control so nearly total that when the pressure seemed greatest, he seemed coolest. He also had acquired considerable practice with the down-home one-liners and good-humored rebuffs that reporters love.

Lake Placid and nonstop television had the effect of making the athletes larger than life. None more so than Eric Heiden, which was an irony not lost on him. A few weeks earlier, very few of his countrymen knew him or what he did. Speed skating ranks near the bottom of the U.S. sports spectrum in terms of participation and fan interest. Whereas there were 11 Olympic standard 400-meter rinks in the Netherlands and nine in Japan in 1980, there were only two refrigerated rinks in North America—one built in 1965 in suburban West Allis, Wisconsin, and one in Lake Placid, New York, made for the 1980 Winter Olympics.

In Norway, where speed skating has an intense following, a biography of Heiden was published when he became the first American world champion in the 20th century. The acclaim helped to accustom him to public attention. Between the time he began skating, at 13, and the XIII Winter Olympic Games, Eric had learned how to keep his balance in the glare of adulation. At 17 it had been a great lark to enter the 1976 Olympics, and creditable enough when he finished 7th in the 1,500- and 19th in the 5,000-meter races. He was competing against men who had years more competitive experience. Then, to general disbelief, including his own, the very next year he won the all-around world championship. And the proof that it was no fluke came the next year, when he again took the championship. He repeated again in 1979 and added the world sprint championship. In March 1980, however, he was defeated in his bid to retain the world championship. He finished second in the overall standings.

Unlike many past Olympic heroes, Eric Heiden refused to allow his success at Lake Placid to be exploited commercially. Instead he began devoting himself to cycling, hockey, and a future career in sports medicine.

en's speed-skating contests, East Germany's Karin Enke captured the 500 meters; the USSR's Natalia Petruseva was first in the 1,000 meters; Annie Borckink of the Netherlands took the 1,500; and Bjoerg Eva Jensen of Norway earned a gold in the 3,000 meters. Leah Poulos Mueller, the American who won a silver in the 1,000 meters in 1976, earned two more silver medals, and Beth Heiden, Eric's younger sister, of whom much was expected, received a bronze in the 3,000 meters. Following the 1,000-meter race, Ms. Heiden observed: "If I could have, I would have changed my name last spring when both Heidens became well known in this country. The pressure has been really good for my brother. He really knows how to handle it. It's a new experience for me. It kind of bothers me, but what can I say? There's nothing I can do about it."

For those who had expected victories for American figure skaters Linda Fratianne and Charlie Tickner, silver and bronze medals, respectively, were disappointments. Those who could appreciate their hard work and gritty perseverance were proud. The most shocking disappointment for the United States, however, was the sudden withdrawal from the pairs figure-skating competition of Tai Babilonia and Randy Gardner due to his groin and abdomen injury.

Speed skater Natalia Petruseva, right, a 24-year-old Soviet graduate student, captured the gold medal in the 1,000 meters and a bronze medal in the 500.

Eric Heiden, a 21-year-old Wisconsinite, entered his name in the record book by taking all the gold in the men's speed skating.

The singles figure-skating competition belonged to Britain's Robin Cousins and East Germany's Anett Poetzsch. Cousins skated a spectacular free-skating program to outscore Jan Hoffmann and Charlie Tickner. Poetzsch earned the gold by skating brilliantly to music from "Funny Girl."

The pairs figure skating was expected to be a dramatic contest between the young American pair, winners of the 1979 World Championships, and the veteran Soviet pair of Irina Rodnina and Aleksandr Zaitsev, the 1976 gold medalists. According to Gardner, the Soviets' strength was "in their speed and power." The Americans' strength was in their "style, power, and choreography. So it balances out." The Lake Placid pairs event consisted of the short program, two minutes of prescribed elements, and the free-skating program, five minutes for the skaters to show off to their best advantage. Once the American team was forced to withdraw during the short program, there was little question of the eventual outcome. When their turn came, the Soviet pair were welcomed by applause from the dispirited crowd and went on to give a near flawless performance that earned several 5.9 marks. In the free-skating program, two days later on February 17, Rodnina and Zaitsev performed as powerfully as ever and won the gold. Their teammates, Marina Cherkosova and Sergei Shakrai, were awarded silver medals, and bronze medals were hung on East Germany's Manuela Mager and Uwe Bewersdorff. In fifth place, to the noisy joy of the packed house, was the American sister and brother team of Caitlin and Peter Carruthers.

In the men's figure-skating singles, Robin Cousins, a 22-year-old Briton who had spent the previous two years training in Denver, Colorado, fulfilled a three-year timetable by carrying off a gold medal. Cousins, coached by Carlo Fassi, the man who had groomed gold medalists Peggy Fleming, Dorothy Hamill, and John Curry, was a delight to watch in free skating. Jan Hoffmann, a 24-year-old East German medical student, was the star of the compulsory program and took the silver. Charlie Tickner was pleased to receive the bronze. The new gold medalist commented: "I think with technical standards so high, you have to look for something extra. It's far too easy to go around and jump, jump, jump."

The long program was the final phase of the women's events, and the top two contenders, Ms. Fratianne and Anett Poetzsch, a 19-year-old East German, staged a battle. Fratianne, who skated first, performed a highly athletic program to the strains of music from *Carmen*. She had the house roaring and clapping when she hit two triple jumps in the first 30 seconds of her four-minute program and received a standing ovation at the finish. Her scores did not belie the crowd's enthusiasm. The five 5.8's for technical merit and five 5.9's for artistic impression seemed to guarantee her the gold. But despite her best efforts and the fervent hopes of the American crowd, Fratianne could not beat Poetzsch. The East German skated brilliantly to music from *Funny Girl,* collecting enough points to maintain her overall lead. Fratianne had to settle for the silver medal, even though she defeated Poetzsch in the free skate. Dagmar Lurz of West Germany managed to fight off the challenge of sensational Swiss free skater Denise Biellmann to win the bronze medal. An uninspiring free skater, Lurz won on the basis of her second-place standing in the compulsories.

The gold medal in ice dancing was captured by Natalia Linichuk and Gennadi Karponosov, the two-time world champions from the USSR. The Hungarian pair, Krisztina Regoczy and Andras Sallay, performed an upbeat program that earned them the silver medal. "Min and Mo," Andrey Minenkov and Irina Moiseeva, an attractive Soviet couple who were the silver medalists in 1976, were third.

Waving to the crowd was a pleasure for the medalists in the pairs figure skating—Cherkosova-Shakrai (left, silver), Rodnina-Zaitsev (gold), and Mager-Bewersdorff (bronze). Soviet dancers Natalia Linichuk and Gennadi Karponosov could not be denied a gold medal.

Ingemar Stenmark

Speed, speed, just speed, that's all I think about.

—INGEMAR STENMARK

Ingemar Stenmark, the 23-year-old Swedish slalom specialist who many say has revolutionized Alpine skiing, had never worked out so little before a season as he did in 1980.

"It's more important for me to feel the joy of skiing when it comes to the big, important championships. I don't want to get bored with skiing. That's the reason why I cut my training schedule," Stenmark said.

In spite of the late start, Stenmark continued his domination of World Cup competition during the early part of the 1980 season. He finished first in two of five slalom events and did not lose at all in his specialty, the giant slalom. Stenmark had won the overall World Cup championship in 1976, 1977, and 1978, and would have won again in 1979 had it not been for a change in the scoring system that penalized a skier not participating in all three Alpine events. (Stenmark does not ski in downhill competition.) He finished as the overall runner-up in 1980, a spot he would hold during the following three years.

But with all his successes, the single most important skiing title—an Olympic gold medal—had eluded him prior to 1980. Going into the 1976 Games at Innsbruck, young Stenmark was considered a favorite but managed only a bronze medal.

Stenmark's triumphs after the 1976 Games elevated him almost to the level of a god in his home country. When Stenmark races, the schools in Stockholm close down for one or two hours, the factories close, and the streets are all but empty. Everyone is at home watching the race on television. But Stenmark's enormous popularity also created intense pressure to bring home gold from Lake Placid.

The pressure grew even heavier on his 6', 170-pound frame after placing third in the first run of the giant slalom. But he did not disappoint. The next day he charged down the course in his characteristically rhythmic, fluid turns and contentedly won the event. With some of the pressure off, Stenmark went out three days later and won the gold medal in the special slalom, again with an impeccable second run.

The son of a bulldozer driver, Ingemar Stenmark was born and reared in the village of Tarnaby (pop. 500) in Swedish Lapland. It is located about 100 miles south of the Arctic Circle, and in the long winters there are only two hours of daylight. Stenmark began skiing at the age of five on a small hill in back of his house. Stenmark's father explained that he must either use his natural talent as a skier or become a bulldozer driver. Ingemar decided to be a skier.

At age 13 he was discovered by coach Hermann Nogler, who immediately recognized his ability. At age 17 he participated in World Cup competition, and it was not long before he won his first giant slalom. His fluid style and enormous leg strength—he can high jump almost five feet from a standing position—made him the king of Alpine skiing in a few short years. Elan, the Yugoslavian-based company that makes his skis, is said to pay more than $250,000 a season to the Swedish ski association for the use of Stenmark's name. Olympic rules allow much of it to be returned to him.

Very much a loner—rarely participating in the ski-circuit social life—Stenmark spends a great deal of time in the reaches of Lapland, running through the forest alone or with his dog. His other training methods (when he does work out before the season) include gymnastic exercises, walking a tightrope, and riding a unicycle. In addition to Swedish, he speaks English, French, German, Italian, and Serbo-Croatian. His comments to the press are usually brief.

Before the 1980 Games, however, Stenmark talked at length about the pressures of being the best. "To win the Olympics—two golds—is going to be hard, more difficult mentally." Not surprisingly, after the competition, his attitude changed. "I have nothing more to achieve," he said. "I ski just for fun now," he added.

Sweden's Ingemar Stenmark became king of the men's Alpine skiing with two gold medals. Hanni Wenzel won the first-ever gold medals for the tiny principality of Liechtenstein; all told, Wenzel won two golds (the slalom and giant slalom) and a silver in the downhill. At 5'4", 125 pounds, Hanni was at the time one of the tiniest skiers on the women's international circuit. Andreas Wenzel also took a silver (giant slalom), making them the first brother and sister to win Alpine medals in the same Games. Annemarie Moser-Proell of Austria, the 1972 silver medalist in the downhill and giant slalom, received a gold medal this time (the downhill). During a 12-year-career, the 26-year-old restaurateur had won 61 World Cup races and six overall World Cup trophies. The downhill was her first Olympic gold. Leonhard Stock, who went to Lake Placid as an alternate, was the surprise winner in the men's downhill. Phil Mahre's silver medal in the men's slalom coming less than a year after a serious injury, was a testimony to the American's courage. He missed becoming the first American Alpine skier to capture an Olympic gold medal by half a second. Stephen Podborski's bronze medal in the downhill was a favorite with the nearby Canadians. Podborski was one of the ''Kamikaze Kanadians,'' so called because of their reckless, breakneck style.

Bobsled driver Erich Schaerer, a 34-year-old businessman from Zurich, Switzerland, got a powerful assist from brakeman Josef Benz and overpowered the two-man bobsled field. The Swiss team's combined time of 4:09.36 beat by more than 1.5 seconds East Germany's Bernhard Germeshausen and Hans Jurgen Gerhardt. Another East German sled, driven by Meinhard Nehmer, finished third. In the four-man event, Nehmer drove the gold-medal-winning sled. A Swiss sled, driven by Schaerer, was second and East Germany's No. 2 sled was just behind and was awarded the bronze. The U.S. four-man team, which included former Olympic medal-winning hurdler Willie Davenport, finished in 12th place. A crowd estimated at 17,000 watched the final bobsled runs.

The bobsled run at Mount Van Hoevenberg, 6.5 miles from the center of Lake Placid, was built originally for the 1932 Olympics. For the 1980 Games, the walkway, spectator galleries, timing installations, refrigerated piping, and lighting were added.

Sweden's Ingemar Stenmark, a 1976 bronze medalist, took the gold in both slalom events in 1980.

Hanni Wenzel

You can't just count on the Lake Placid Olympics. In just one race, anything can happen. You can't build up your season for just one event.

—HANNI WENZEL

In her comment prior to the Lake Placid Games, Hanni Wenzel did not mean to imply that she was not planning to do well. She was, but she was not going to consider the world off its axis if her hopes were jolted in one event. As it turned out, Hanni was right: anything can happen. Counting on it or not, Wenzel won big—and not just in one event. Her two gold and one silver medals matched the record performance of Rosi Mittermaier in the 1976 Winter Games. Wenzel replaced the old pro Annemarie Moser-Proell as the queen of Alpine skiing.

The 23-year-old "Liechtenstein dumpling," as the diminutive (5′4″) Wenzel has been called, comes from a family of skiers. All seven of Liechtenstein's athletes at the 1980 Winter Games were Alpine skiers, and three of them were Wenzels. For the first time in the history of the Winter Olympics, a brother and sister won Alpine medals in the same Games. Andreas Wenzel, 21, took the silver medal in the men's giant slalom. The total of four medals won by Hanni and Andreas equaled about one for every 6,000 residents of Liechtenstein. The third member of the Wenzel trio, 18-year-old Petra, finished 19th in the women's giant slalom.

As Hanni stood on the victory rostrum to collect her first gold medal—for the giant slalom—25,000 pairs of eyes were glued to the television in a tiny, mountainous corner of central Europe.

The normally staid principality of Liechtenstein was ga-ga. Hundreds of blue-and-red flags draped windows and lined the streets in the capital city of Vaduz, which resounded with the noisy tributes to the blonde-haired, brown-eyed "Golden Hanni." Every restaurant and bar was jammed, and the celebration went on into the early hours of the morning. Prince Franz Joseph II sent a telegram of congratulations. A group of Vaduz businessmen set off for Lake Placid just to shake her hand. Lore Wenzel, Hanni's mother, who had been too nervous to watch the second run, was invited to a special dinner in one of Vaduz's most exclusive restaurants. Her husband, Hubert, was in Lake Placid as the manager of the Liechtenstein team.

Hanni was born on Dec. 14, 1956, in West Germany but has lived in Liechtenstein since she was a year old. Like all great skiers, she took to the slopes almost as soon as she could stand. Andreas and Petra were not far behind. "She helped me until I was 15 or 16," says Andreas. "Then I got too strong. Do I help her now? No. She is the best in the world."

Indeed, Hanni was already becoming a world-class skier when Andreas was 16. At the age of 19 she won the slalom title at St. Moritz. At the 1976 Innsbruck Olympics, she took a bronze medal in the slalom. And in 1978 she won her first overall World Cup championship, a feat the Olympian repeated in 1980. She was second in the standings in 1979.

At Lake Placid, Hanni was the fastest, most elegant, and technically best competitor on the slopes. "She has such great technique," said West Germany's Irene Epple, runner-up in the giant slalom. "She really gets her edges into the snow, and she has the ability to change weight from one ski to the other so quickly." Hanni Wenzel loves high speeds—not only on the slopes. She has a passion for motorbikes. Brother Andreas, on his part, is fanatical about fast cars. Speeding down the steep, winding roads of their native countryside is a favorite pastime for two of the world's most exciting ski racers.

Hanni spent many years of her training with the Swiss teams and said that was "a very big advantage." The national character of her own people, she says, also is a factor in her success. "We're individualists, very strong-willed."

Hanni, who continued to ski competitively after Lake Placid, finished third in the overall World Cup standings in 1981 and was runner-up two years later.

Hanni Wenzel, the 23-year-old "Liechtenstein dumpling," brought glory to her tiny nation by winning gold medals in both slaloms and a silver in the downhill. Her brother, Andreas, was the silver medalist in the men's giant slalom. They were the first brother and sister to take Alpine medals in the same Winter Olympics.

Soviet skier Nikolai Zimyatov completed the 50-kilometer cross-country event in Olympic record time for his third gold medal. He also finished first in the 30 kilometers and was a member of the gold-winning relay team.

In Nordic skiing the stars were Nikolai Zimyatov of the Soviet Union, who won three gold medals, and Ulrich Wehling of East Germany, who became the first male athlete to win a gold medal in three different Winter Games. In winning the 30-kilometer race, the first Olympic or world championship run on artificial snow, Zimyatov, a 24-year-old student at the Institute of Physical Culture in Moscow, took the first gold medal of the XIII Winter Games and put the Soviets into the all-time Winter Olympics lead in number of gold medals won. Six days later, on February 20, he picked up a second gold as the anchor of the victorious relay team, and three days after that he set a new Olympic record in the 50-kilometer cross-country. Wehling, a 27-year-old physical education student who suffered a serious knee injury in 1978, won his third consecutive gold in the Nordic combined. Finland's Jouko Karjalainen was second, and East Germany's Konrad Winkler won his second consecutive Olympic bronze. On Sunday, February 17, Thomas Wassberg of Sweden nipped Finland's Juha Mieto, the "Scandinavian Giant," by one-hundredth of a second for the gold medal in the men's 15-kilometer cross-country race. Mieto, a member of the 1976 gold-medal-winning relay team, also took the silver in the 50-kilometer cross-country.

Among the Nordic skiing women, 24-year-old East German Barbara Petzold won the 10 kilometers and anchored East Germany's quartet to another gold in the relay. Raisa Smetanina of the USSR was first in the 5 kilometers. Finland's Hilkka Riihivouri was runner-up in both the 5 and 10 kilometers.

As a teenager at the 1976 Winter Games, Austria's Anton Innauer had flown to a silver medal in the 90-meter jump. With a total

Ski jumping continued to draw large crowds of spectators. East Germany's Manfred Deckert, above, tied for the silver medal in the 70 kilometers. Finland's Jouko Tormanen, below, enjoyed "very good winds and good luck" as he flew to an Olympic gold in the 90 kilometers.

of 266.3 points in the 70-meter jump at Lake Placid, the 21-year-old vegetarian soldier was the gold medalist beyond all doubt. Manfred Deckert of East Germany and Hirokazu Yagi of Japan each had 249.2 total points and received silver medals. A bronze was not awarded. Finland's Jouko Tormanen rode the winds of the 90-meter jump to an Olympic gold medal and a future as a national hero. Hubert Neuper of Austria and Jari Puikkonen, another Finn, were second and third respectively.

Although Vera Zozulia became the first Russian to win a gold medal in luge, namely in the women's singles, East German lugers dominated the sport. Hans Rinn and Norbert Hahn, who had shared a sled since 1968, became the first athletes to win consecutive gold medals in the men's doubles luge. Bernhard Glass came through to win the gold in the men's singles. Another East German, Melitta Sollmann, was second in the women's event.

A 10-kilometer sprint for biathletes was added to the Olympic program in 1980. Frank Ullrich of East Germany won the event, took a silver in the 20 kilometers, and was a member of the silver-medal relay team. Anatoli Aljabiev, a 29-year-old lieutenant in the Soviet Army, finished first in the 20 kilometers, was third in the 10 kilometers, and was a member of the gold-medal-winning relay team.

In the race among nations for medals, East Germany won a total of 23 (9 gold, 7 silver, and 7 bronze), but the Soviet Union took the most gold (10), as well as 6 silver and 6 bronze, for 22 overall. The United States was a distant third, with 6 gold, 4 silver, and 2 bronze.

Not all of the outstanding performers received official Olympic medals. There were many athletes whose best efforts were not recognized only because they didn't happen to win. To help rectify that injustice, The Associated Press awarded medals of "extraordinary merit" to some of the lesser lights who exemplified the Olympic spirit as much as such champions as Eric Heiden, Ingemar Stenmark, Hanni Wenzel, and Nikolai Zimyatov. The gold medal for extraordinary merit went to Arturo Kinch of Costa Rica, who was his team's only competitor, doubling also as flagbearer, trainer, counselor, and national delegate. The 23-year-old skier, 145 pounds of grit, took a nasty spill in the men's downhill, injuring a leg. He tried again in the giant slalom, tipped a gate, and tumbled into the snow. On crutches, Kinch had to be restrained from tackling the hill again in the slalom. The silver and bronze medals for extraordinary merit went to Faride Rahme of Lebanon and Guizhen Wong of China, who finished 34th and 35th (next-to-last and last) in the women's giant slalom. Their claim to immortality: they didn't beat the mountain, but the mountain didn't beat them.

Other names that made Olympic headlines included Terry McDermott, a former gold-medal-winning speed skater, who took the oath for all judges and officials; Jim McKay, who remained the one constant during more than 50 hours of telecasting by ABC; Chuck Mangione who composed the Olympic theme; Art Devlin, a Lake Placid native and promoter, who served as vice president of the organizing committee; and Scott Hamilton, a 21-year-old figure skater who was "really proud" to carry the American flag during the opening ceremonies.

The main attraction at the Olympic Village—the hit of Lake Placid, as far as most were concerned—was the game room. Full of blinking electronic video games, Foosbol tables, and row upon row of pinball machines, the game room provided relaxed and pleasurable competition after the day's skiing, skating, and sledding were over.

In terms of camaraderie and pure excitement of competition— and those, after all, are what the Olympics are really about—the 1980 Winter Games in Lake Placid, N.Y., were both enormously successful and not soon to be forgotten. Petr Spurney, the general manager of the LPOOC, summed up well: "When you go to a once-in-a-lifetime experience," he said, "the wait in line is part of the experience."

FINAL MEDAL STANDINGS			
Nation	G	S	B
Soviet Union	10	6	6
East Germany	9	7	7
United States	6	4	2
Austria	3	2	2
Sweden	3	0	1
Liechtenstein	2	2	0
Finland	1	5	3
Norway	1	3	6
The Netherlands	1	2	1
Switzerland	1	1	3
Great Britain	1	0	0
West Germany	0	2	3
Italy	0	2	0
Canada	0	1	1
Hungary	0	1	0
Japan	0	1	0
Bulgaria	0	0	1
Czechoslovakia	0	0	1
France	0	0	1

In the biathlon, Anatoli Aljabiev (13), a 29-year-old lieutenant in the Soviet Army, earned a gold in his specialty, the 20 kilometers, and a bronze in the 10 kilometers. He also anchored his relay team to victory. East Germany's Eberhard Rosch (11) was third in the 20 kilometers and a mainstay of the silver-winning relay team.

Soviet policy in Afghanistan adversely affected the Olympics. Above, Afghan rebels face Soviet troops.

Athletes and fans expressed strongly their views regarding holding the Games in Moscow.

1980
Summer Games
Moscow, USSR

On Dec. 27, 1979, President Hafizullah Amin of Afghanistan was ousted from power, executed, and replaced by exiled former Deputy Premier Babrak Karmal. The overthrow was engineered by the Soviet Union, which had airlifted thousands of troops into Afghanistan in the preceding days. In early 1980 protests were expressed throughout the world against the brazen Soviet maneuver.

U.S. President Jimmy Carter denounced the Soviet intervention as "an extremely serious threat to peace. . . ." Carter then announced several retaliatory measures against the Kremlin. He also said that if the "aggressive action" continued, the United States would consider boycotting the 1980 Summer Olympic Games, to be held in Moscow on July 19–August 3. On January 20, Carter formally proposed that the Games be moved from Moscow, post-

poned, or canceled unless all Soviet troops were removed from Afghanistan in one month. In a letter to United States Olympic Committee (USOC) President Robert Kane, Carter said that if none of these changes were effected an international boycott should be organized.

Sympathy with the U.S. proposal was not long in coming. Canadian Prime Minister Joe Clark publicly called for moving the Games from the Soviet capital. British Prime Minister Margaret Thatcher also declared her government's support for moving the Games from Moscow. Although participation in an actual boycott would have to be determined by the National Olympic Committee of each country, the U.S. position found growing support. Whatever the reaction of the rest of the world, President Carter was firm.

In spite of a boycott by the United States and other Western nations, the Games of the XXII Olympiad began on schedule in Lenin Central Stadium before 100,000 persons. Misha the Bear, the official mascot, was a celebrity.

Bill Bradley Argues for a Permanent Olympic Site

The 1980 Summer Olympics, which were boycotted by more than 60 countries in protest against the Soviet Union's invasion of Afghanistan, drew attention to the urgent need for major changes to make the modern Olympics more consistent with the ideals that inspired the original Greek festivals.

One immediate reform should be the establishment of a permanent site in Greece for the Summer Olympics, as well as an appropriate home for the Winter Games. Such action has been considered by the International Olympic Committee (IOC) as an alternative to the current system of moving the events to a different location every four years.

Putting the Summer Olympics permanently in Greece and the Winter Games in their own home would help the Olympics become a strong institution rather than short-lived spectacles vulnerable to political or economic exploitation by temporary host countries and other nations. Given a stable, enduring setting, the Games could take on a special identity of their own, much like the celebrations of old.

A permanent site for the Olympics also could be coupled with an extension of the Games from two weeks to perhaps two or even three months. That would allow participants to know one another better and to share experiences that generally are impossible in the often politically charged competitive environment of contemporary Olympiads.

In addition, the normal functions of the Olympic Village might be expanded to include cultural and artistic expressions from various parts of the world. Though the emphasis on sports would continue, the introduction of other activities would recognize the value of the whole person.

Naturally, important questions would have to be answered. How would the financial burden be borne? If financial benefits accrued from the Games, how would they be shared? What governing body would control the Olympic site?

The government of Greece has suggested some ways to proceed. It has proposed the formation of a politically neutral and militarily inviolable "Olympic State" in the area of the original site at Olympia. Under the Greek plan, this state would be under IOC jurisdiction, although sovereign territorial rights would remain with Greece. The Olympic Committee would install and own all facilities at the site. It also would be permitted to administer the Olympic area and to determine the terms of and conditions for entry. Greek law would apply within the area, but Greek military forces would not be allowed to enter under any circumstances.

The members of the IOC should study the Greek plan and any other proposals that demonstrate a serious commitment to preserving the Olympic ideals.

In the future, other actions to make the Olympics less political should be considered. It might help to eliminate team sports, which can be tantamount to war games. Team competition could take place apart from the Olympics. Another improvement would be a revision of the rules on eligibility, making skill the only standard, with no artificial distinctions such as amateurism. A third useful change might be to award a medal to all competitors and reserve gold medals only for those athletes who break Olympic records.

Above all, the reforms should be designed to reduce the causes of and opportunities for political conflict at the Games and to maximize attention on the participants.

If the right steps are taken soon enough, the modern Olympics still can achieve the goals that their founder, Pierre de Coubertin, set: To create "international respect and good will" and "construct a better and more peaceful world."

Editor's Note: Bill Bradley, now a U.S. senator from New Jersey, was a member of the U.S. Olympic basketball team in 1964.

Carter and the U.S. State Department realized full well that a disruption of the Moscow Games would also have a devastating political and social effect on the Soviet Union. It was perhaps the most damaging weapon in Carter's diplomatic arsenal. In his January 20 letter to Kane, President Carter noted "the desirability of keeping government policy out of the Olympics," but argued that "the Soviet government attaches enormous political importance to holding the 1980 Olympic Games in Moscow."

For the first time a socialist country would play host to the Olympics, and Moscow organizers predicted that the Games would be nothing less than "a major event in human history." The 1980 Olympics would be the culmination of a long political and social process, giving a stamp of legitimacy to the Soviet system. Soviet citizenry would be at the center of global attention, its way of life showcased in all the pomp and glamour of the Olympic Games.

The high place accorded to sports and physical education in the Soviet way of life would make the plaudits of the world ever more rewarding—and legitimizing—to the Russian people. The Communist leadership had long recognized the value of athletics as a political instrument and had made it one of its highest national priorities. Unlike the United States and other Western nations, where an athlete's development depends primarily on his or her own initiative and where the benefit of professional coaching does not become available until the athlete is relatively accomplished, the Soviet Union begins formal training for promising athletes as soon as they begin school. The education is intensive and for the most part restricted to sports. The best prospects are winnowed out in regional competitions, and the elite are guaranteed a life of comfort and privilege. It is a no-nonsense, production-line approach, which many Westerners consider grim. To the Soviets, however, every gold medal is a vindication of socialist ideology. More than a year before the 1980 Games were to open, Viktor Grishin, the head of the Moscow party committee and a member of the nation's ruling Politburo, said: "It is necessary to ensure that, in relations with foreigners, residents of the capital show cordiality and hospitality,

Much of Moscow was refurbished for the Games. The opening and closing ceremonies as well as several athletic events were held in Lenin Central Stadium (above), which was built in the mid-1950's. Soviet security forces were everywhere throughout the contests.

East Germans dominated the women's swimming events, setting several world and Olympic marks. Vladimir Salnikov (below) made history by breaking the 15-minute barrier in the 1,500-meter freestyle. He took three gold medals overall.

stress the advantages of the Soviet way of life and the achievements of our society, and at the same time repulse the propaganda of alien ideas and principles, and the onslaughts on our country and on the ideas of communism and socialism.''

Preparations for the Olympics were a major concern of the state. A reported $350 million was taken from government coffers for the Games. Eleven new athletic centers were built and an equal number refurbished or expanded. In addition there were a spacious new Olympic Village, a television broadcast center, press headquarters, 35-story hotel, international post office, computer center, and other facilities. Roads were repaved, buildings cleaned, and historic church domes gilded. Olympic cakes appeared in bakery windows, posters were put up all over town, and taxi drivers were given crash courses in foreign languages. It was decreed that, just prior to the Games, the streets would be cleared of indigents and drunks. So that they would not be exposed to Western influence, children would be removed to camps, outside the city. All in all, it was one massive effort to make the city, its people, and the entire nation ready for a glorious occasion.

The U.S. House of Representatives and Senate overwhelmingly approved resolutions supporting Carter's stand. At a meeting of the IOC in Lake Placid on February 9, U.S. Secretary of State Cyrus Vance reiterated to the committee that his government would oppose sending a team to the Olympic Games ''in the capital of an invading nation.'' Days later, USOC President Kane announced that his organization would ''accept any decision concerning U.S. participation in the Games the president makes. . . .''

February 20, the deadline set by President Carter for the Soviet Union to pull out its troops from Afghanistan, passed with no change in the status quo, and the boycott was officially on. On April 12 in Colorado Springs, the USOC House of Delegates voted in favor of the boycott by a 2-to-1 margin. The resolution did contain a provision to send a team ''if the president of the United States advises the USOC on or before May 20 that international events have become compatible with the national interest and the national security is no longer threatened.'' It was hoping against hope.

Earlier, on March 25, the British Olympic Association disregarded the wishes of the Margaret Thatcher government and voted to participate in the Moscow Games. On April 26, however, the Canadian Olympic Association agreed to back the boycott. Other National Olympic Committees also supported the U.S. stand.

For the boycotters, there was a price to pay. A variety of U.S. concerns lost millions. The National Broadcasting Company (NBC), which was to have televised the Games in the United States, sacrificed a reported $22 million in outlays not covered by insurance, as well as untold millions in advertising revenue. American suppliers of uniforms, souvenirs, athletic equipment, and technology had to cancel important business.

The biggest losers, of course, were the athletes. They were, understandably, intensely disappointed. For many it was the loss of a once-in-a-lifetime opportunity. Years of single-minded dedication and forward-looking enthusiasm were being brought to nothing. Swimmers and gymnasts, for example, many of whom peak in the early teens, would easily be past their prime by 1984. And others might not be able to muster the hope that would sustain them through four more years of preparation.

Some American athletes simply did not understand the rationale of a boycott. Politics should not interfere with the Olympics, they argued, and what difference would a boycott make, anyway? Some felt as if they were being used as pawns. "Why us?" they asked. Although most Olympic aspirants remained opposed to any boycott, a surprising number spoke out against going to Moscow. Some U.S. athletes proposed that they be allowed to participate in the Moscow Games but not take part in the opening or closing ceremonies or the presentation of medals. The National Olympic Committees of several European countries suggested that the Games be held in Moscow but without the usual political trappings. All nations would march in under the Olympic flag; all athletes would wear similar uniforms; no national anthems would be played; and no flags would be raised at the award ceremonies. The IOC decided to allow teams the option of not using their national flags or anthems at Olympic ceremonies, but further depoliticization was ruled out.

The Games were officially opened by Soviet President Leonid Brezhnev at 4 P.M. on July 19. A crowd of more than 100,000 packed Lenin Central Stadium. The Opening Ceremonies were lavish and featured goose-stepping Soviet soldiers carrying doves of peace, a dramatic card-flashing routine, and a calisthenics exhibition. Misha the Bear, the official mascot, was seen widely. Soviet basketball captain Sergei Belov carried the torch and lighted the flame. Soviet police, dressed in white hats and gloves, and soldiers completely sealed off not only the stadium but the city itself. Security was extremely tight and would remain so throughout the competition. Checkpoints were established at the Olympic Village, all hotels, and every transportation center. When a Frenchman asked why a French athlete was "searched for 30 minutes at customs," he was told by a Soviet official that he "was cleared in 30 minutes." The Frenchman was encouraged to "look at the positive."

In the opening remarks Lord Killanin, outgoing president of the IOC, welcomed the athletes, especially those "who showed their complete independence to travel and compete despite the pressures placed on them." Sixteen of the participating nations refused to carry their national flags during the ceremonies. Olympic or National Olympic Committee flags were displayed by some instead. Several national teams simply remained in the Olympic Village and were represented at the ceremonies by officials of their national committees. Dick Palmer, secretary of the British Olympic Association, carried the Olympic flag and was the sole Briton to march

Barbara Krause, a 21-year-old official in the East German state police, stood on the victory platform following the 100- and 200-meter freestyle swimming events and the 400-meter freestyle relay.

Michelle Ford's stuffed koala shared the moment as the Australian won a gold medal in the 800-meter freestyle.

Ethiopia's Miruts Yifter (191) became a hero by winning the 5,000- and 10,000-meter runs. The 800 and 1,500 runs featured the Steve Ovett (279)-Sebastian Coe (254) rivalry.

during the opening. In addition, throughout the Games, athletes from various Western nations accepted their medals under the Olympic banner and with the Olympic, not their national, anthem playing. These actions were meant as protests against the Soviet action in Afghanistan. On the other hand, two Americans, one of whom had attended every modern Olympic except 1936 and 1964, unveiled an American flag in the stadium shortly before the opening festivities. One of them commented that they "wanted to show" they were "proud of being Americans" and "were sorry the athletes couldn't come." Although the boycott by such athletic powers as the United States, West Germany, and Japan caused the Games to be primarily a meet between Communist nations, "a picnic for Warsaw Pact athletes," the XXII Olympic Games provided enough excitement on the field to interest even the keenest sports enthusiast. In fact, numerous world and Olympic records were established in Moscow. In terms of number, 5,687 athletes from 81 nations took part in the Games; some 55 countries stayed away because of the Afghanistan situation; and less than half of the anticipated number of visitors traveled to the USSR to witness "The Olympics in the Name of Peace for the Glory of Sport."

The Soviet Union, which had never won a gold medal in men's swimming, took the Olympic gold in 7 of 13 events in 1980. In declaring themselves a new force in men's international swimming, the Soviets also captured 7 silver and 3 bronze medals. Sergei

Fesenko had the honor of becoming the first Soviet male swimmer to wear Olympic gold. He did so by winning in the 200-meter butterfly on the first day of the events. The 21-year-old went on to be awarded a silver in the 400-meter individual medley. Vladimir Salnikov, a 20-year-old student at the Leningrad Institute for Physical Culture, broke the 15-minute barrier in the 1,500-meter freestyle. His world record time was 14:58.27. Swimmers equate the achievement with breaking the 4-minute mile in track. Salnikov, who had been named 1979 swimmer of the year by *Swimming World* magazine, also won a gold medal in the 400-meter freestyle in Olympic record time of 3:51.31 and was a member of the gold-medal-winning 800-meter freestyle relay team. The 6′6″, 157-pound son of a sea captain had spent time training in the United States. Other Soviet swimmers to earn gold medals were Robertas Zulpa (200-meter breaststroke), Sergei Kopliakov (200-meter freestyle), and Aleksandr Sidorenko (400-meter individual medley). Duncan Goodhew, a 23-year-old Briton who swam competitively for North Carolina State, captured the 100-meter breaststroke; Sweden's Par Arvidsson, a 20-year-old student at the University of California at Berkeley, won the 100-meter butterfly; and Bengt Baron, also of Sweden, took the gold in the 100-meter backstroke. Hungarians Sandor Wladar and Zoltan Verraszto were first and second in the 200-meter backstroke. The Australian team finished first in the 400-meter relay, followed by the USSR and Britain.

With the Americans absent, East Germany completely dominated the women's swimming events, capturing 26 of a possible 39 medals. Rica Reinisch, a 15-year-old student, set world records in the 100- and 200-meter backstroke and was a member of the gold-medal-winning, world-record-setting (4:06.67) 400-meter medley relay team. Barbara Krause, a 21-year-old official in the East German state police, established a world record in the 100-meter freestyle and an Olympic record in the 200-meter freestyle. Petra Schneider broke her own world mark in the 400-meter individual medley. Ute Geweniger, Ines Geissler, and Ines Diers established Olympic records in the 100-meter breaststroke, the 200-meter butterfly, and the 400-meter freestyle, respectively. Caren Metschuck edged out fellow East Germans Andrea Pollack and Christiane Knacke in the 100-meter butterfly. Only the victories of Michelle Ford of Australia in the 800-meter freestyle and Lina Kachushite of the USSR in the 200-meter breaststroke, both in Olympic record time, prevented a sweep of the gold by East Germany, whose freestyle relay team also was victorious.

Soviet men took three of the six medals in the diving competition, and the awards for the women divers were divided equally between the USSR and East Germany. The Soviet Union's Irina Kalinina was first in the springboard with 725.91 points, and Martina Jaschke of East Germany outshone Servard Emirzyan and Liana Tsotadze, both of the USSR, in the platform. A major controversy over the officiating developed during the men's springboard competition. Loud applause from a crowd at a nearby pool caused Aleksandr Portnov to turn a two-and-a-half reverse somersault into a belly flop. He complained about the noise. Later a camera flash-bulb distracted East Germany's Falk Hoffmann during a dive. He too complained to the officials. The Soviet contestant was permitted to dive again; the East German was not. Portnov won the gold; Hoffmann lost a possible bronze. Although the award ceremony

Italy's high jumper Sara Simeoni (above) set a new Olympic record. East Germany's Lutz Dombrowski earned a gold by long jumping an impressive 28′1¼″.

The 50-kilometer walk got underway with the eventual bronze medalist, Yevgeny Ivchenko (704) of the Soviet Union, in a central spot. East Germany's Hartwig Gauder and Spain's Jorge Liopart crossed the finish line in the first and second positions.

was delayed two days, the International Swimming Federation refused to honor a protest. Hoffmann, however, did take the gold in the platform event.

In the track-and-field events the match-up between Britain's two prime middle-distance runners, Steve Ovett and Sebastian Coe, was anticipated eagerly. In Oslo on July 1, Coe, who already had won honors in the 800 meters (1:42.33), the 1,500 meters (3:32.1), and the mile (3:49), added a fourth world record to his collection—2:13.4 in the 1,000 meters. However, 45 minutes after setting the new 1,000-meter mark, Ovett took two tenths of a second off Coe's mile record. Two weeks later, at another Oslo meet, Ovett tied Coe's mark in the 1,500 meters. Although the two runners had not raced against each other in two years, the stage was set for some high Olympic drama. Just deciding to ignore his prime minister's wishes and compete in Moscow was a difficult decision for the articulate Coe, the recipient of two bachelor of arts degrees. After much soul-searching, he concluded that "governments, politicians, are ruled by expediency. Athletes live in a world of natural law."

In the cool Moscow evening air of Saturday, July 26, Ovett zoomed past Nikolai Kirov of the USSR in the final curve and held off Coe in the stretch to win the gold in the 800 meters. His time was a full three seconds slower than Coe's record. Coe, who finished a second ahead of bronze medalist Kirov, acknowledged that he "blew it in the backstretch." Ovett, a quiet, 24-year-old former art student from the seaside resort of Brighton, took his victory in stride. He said: "The 1,500 is the one I'm really prepared for. It's the one I want. Steve Ovett is a miler." Six days later, however, Coe had something to say about Ovett's dream. The 23-year-old stepped on the accelerator near the end of the 1,500, passed East Germany's Jurgen Straub, who would emerge with a silver medal, and won the gold in the relatively slow time of 3:38.4. Coe then knelt and sobbed, shook off a Soviet official to take a victory lap, and was hugged by his rival

Steve Ovett, this time the bronze medalist. It was Steve's first loss in the 1,500 meters since 1977. As the medals were presented by the Marquis of Exeter, David Burghley, the 1928 gold medalist in the 400-meter hurdles, the Britons in the stadium ignored the playing of the Olympic hymn and proudly sang *God Save the Queen* and *Rule Britannia*.

Britons did well in other track-and-field events, too. Daley Thompson and Allan Wells were presented with gold medals following the decathlon and 100-meter dash. Thompson, 22, the son of a Nigerian mother and Scottish father, finished first in three of the five events on the first day of the decathlon competition and then went on to score an impressive victory. Two Soviets, Yuri Kutsenko and Sergei Zhelanov, were second and third. On a jovial note, the gold medalist said that "blue movies" would be part of his future. He then turned serious and commented: "Sure I'd like to earn a million like Bruce Jenner, but I'd like to keep doing this too. I'm an athlete first, and I'll try to get the most out of myself before leaving the sport for anything else." Wells, a 28-year-old Scot who was coached by his wife, took the 100-meter dash over runners-up Silvio Leonard of Cuba and Petar Betrov of Bulgaria. Wells' time was not particularly fast. His time in the 200 meters was fast enough, however, to win a silver medal behind Italy's Pietro Mennea. Another Briton, Gary Oakes, earned a bronze medal in the 400-meter hurdles. He lost out to East Germany's Volker Beck and USSR's Vasily Arkhipenko.

Following in the footsteps of Finland's Lasse Viren, who won the 5,000- and 10,000-meter runs in 1972 and 1976, Miruts Yifter captured the Olympic "distance-double" crown. The 5'3½", 115-pound Ethiopian army officer, who missed the 1976 Montreal Olympics because of the boycott by African nations, would not be denied this time. The lead changed hands some 50 times in the 10,000 before Yifter used his predictable kick and crossed the finish line first. Viren, who led with 700 meters to go, finished fifth. Five days later Yifter, who claimed to be 37 but may have been older, ran the 5,000 in Olympic-record time of 13:21.0, six tenths of a second ahead of Tanzania's Suleiman Nyambui, the silver medalist. Following the event, Ethiopian tribal dancers performed joyously outside Lenin Central Stadium.

World records were set in three men's field events, the pole vault, the hammer throw, and the high jump. An unusually noisy crowd witnessed some exciting pole-vaulting. Three times during the competition, the public-address announcer was forced to request "silence, please." Charges of pro-Soviet officiating also marred the event. To the consternation of the partisan Soviets, Wladyslaw Kozakiewicz, a 26-year-old physical education instructor and one of Poland's most popular athletes, not only won the gold medal but also established a world record of 18'11½". Konstantin Volkov of the USSR and Tadeusz Slusarski of Poland, the 1976 gold medalist, tied for second place.

The Soviet Union swept the medals in the hammer throw, considered the glamour event by the Soviets. In securing his second consecutive Olympic gold, Yuri Sedykh, 25, averaged 265'6" with his five throws. His tosses included a world record 268'5½". Gerd Wessig, a 21-year-old, 6'6" East German cook, cleared 7'8¾" for a world record on his way to the gold medal in

Daley Thompson became the first Briton since Thomas Kiely in 1904 to win the decathlon. Thompson, whose score was a good one, announced that he would continue to compete.

Rumania's Nadia Comaneci, the gymnast queen of 1976, returned to the spotlight in Moscow. The 18-year-old fell from the uneven parallel bars during her optional program and finished by sharing the all-around silver medal. She did, however, take the gold in the balance beam and tied for one in the floor exercises.

the high jump. Wessig, who had trained as a decathlete and made the East German team just before the Games, had never jumped higher than 7'6½". Poland's Jacek Wszola, the 1976 gold medalist in the high jump, received the 1980 silver medal and East Germany's Jorg Freimuth was awarded the bronze.

Waldemar Cierpinski of East Germany ran a slower marathon than he had in Montreal, but his time of 2:11:03.0 earned him a second consecutive gold medal. Culminating 13 years of training, Poland's Bronislaw Malinowski passed Tanzania's Filbert Bayi at the final water jump in the 3,000-meter steeplechase and took the gold. The 28-year-old physical education teacher had been the silver medalist in 1976. Viktor Saneyev disappointed the home folks when he failed to obtain his fourth consecutive Olympic gold in the triple jump. He was outjumped by teammate Jaak Uudmae and had to settle for a silver medal. Lutz Dombrowski of East Germany long jumped an impressive 28'¼" for the gold. It was the second longest jump behind Bob Beamon's 1968 mark.

The women track athletes who performed in Moscow broke several records, both world and Olympic. Nadezhda Tkachenko scored a world record 5,083 points in the pentathlon. Her Soviet teammates Olga Rukavishnikova and Olga Kuragina were the silver and bronze medalists. The Soviets also dominated the women's 800-meter run as Nadezhda Olizarenko broke the world mark with a time of 1:53.5. The world record fell to the East German team in the 400-meter relay. The USSR team was second and the British contingent was third. Baerbel Wockel and Ilona Slupianek, both of East Germany, Maria Colon of Cuba, and Sara Simeoni of Italy established Olympic marks in the 200-meter dash, the shot put, the javelin, and the high jump, respectively.

While precise and dazzling performances by gymnasts Olga Korbut of the USSR and Nadia Comaneci of Rumania were fond memories of the 1972 and 1976 Olympics, the 1980 women's gymnastics program, witnessed by a capacity crowd of 12,000 at the Sports Palace, was marred by controversy. The awarding of the gold in the all-around to Yelena Davydova of the USSR over Comaneci was questioned by Bela Karolyi, the Rumanian coach. Karolyi charged that the chairman of the gymnastics federation reduced Comaneci's score on the balance beam "in an arrangement" to guarantee Soviet victory. A spokesman for the Soviets said that a delay of nearly 30 minutes in posting the score of Comaneci was caused by the refusal of Maria Simionescu, the Rumanian head judge, to accept the score. A jury reviewed the case and disagreed with Mrs. Simionescu. Comaneci, who had fallen from the uneven parallel bars during her optional program, shared the all-around silver medal with East Germany's 15-year-old Maxi Gnauck. After her victory, Davydova, the 19-year-old daughter of a Leningrad autoworker, was tossed in the air by her teammates.

Simionescu was the center of another dispute the following evening when she protested the awarding of a 9.85 score to Natalya Shaposhnikova, a 19-year-old, 4'10" Soviet, for her balance beam routine. Comaneci, now a 5'2", 99-pound 18-year-old, received the gold for the event and the score stood. Shaposhnikova had to settle for the bronze; Davydova took the silver. Ms. Comaneci and Nelli Kim, the 23-year-old Soviet team captain who played second fiddle to Comaneci at Montreal but still captured four medals (three gold and a silver), shared the 1980 first prize in the floor exercises. Natalya Shaposhnikova, the winner of the gold in the vault, and Maxi Gnauck, the winner of the gold in the uneven bars, tied for the silver medal in the floor exercises. The Soviet women easily took their eighth consecutive gold medal for team performance.

Aleksandr Dityatin was dominant in the men's gymnastic competition. The handsome blond Soviet not only was in the medal circle following each event but also became the first male gymnast to score a perfect 10. Dityatin, the 22-year-old world champion, received three gold medals (team, all-around, and rings), four silver medals (horizontal bars, side horse, long horse, and parallel bars), and one bronze medal (floor exercises). No athlete had ever won more medals at a single modern Olympics. Aleksandr Tkachyov, also of the USSR, took two golds (team and parallel bars) and a silver (rings). Their teammate, Nikolai Andrianov, the winner of seven medals at Montreal, added five more to his collection—gold in the team and long horse, silver in the all-around and floor exercises, and bronze in the horizontal bars. Hungary's Zoltan Magyar, Bulgaria's Stoyan Deltchev, and East Germany's Roland Bruckner wore gold following the side horse, horizontal bars, and floor exercise events. Magyar, who was a member of the bronze-winning team, received a 10 in the side horse. The Soviet coach disagreed publicly with the notion that the absence of the American and Japanese gymnasts took away from the caliber of the competition. It was accepted, however, that the male gymnasts were continuing to reach new plateaus of technical excellence.

Cuba was a powerhouse in boxing, winning the gold medal in six of the 11 divisions and a silver in two, and sharing a bronze in two others. According to Col. Don Hull of the International Boxing Federation, the "Cubans were the best prepared I've ever seen them. They were in excellent condition in every class in every way. They were out to win every fight from the start." For the third consecutive time, Téofilo Stevenson, a 29-year-old Cuban heavyweight who had broken the trend and not turned professional, won a gold. However, two of Stevenson's opponents managed to stay in the ring the full three rounds this time, and at least one expert noted that his boxing talents seemed to be

Aleksandr Dityatin, a 22-year-old Soviet, was first not only in the rings but also in the all-around and was a member of the gold-winning team. He did, in fact, take a medal in each gymnastic event.

Yugoslavia's men's basketball team shocked the host Soviets by winning the gold medal. The new champions defeated Brazil in the semifinal round. As at the Montreal Olympics, Finland's rower Pertti Karppinen was first in the single sculls.

declining. Defying the U.S. boycott, a small delegation of Puerto Rican boxers participated at Moscow.

The favored Soviet men's basketball squad, the "UCLA of the East," had to settle for a bronze medal. The aging Soviets were defeated first by the Italian "fun" team and then by the Yugoslavs in overtime. In winning the gold, the Yugoslavs played a Western-style game. Italy, which lost to the Yugoslavs in the final, 86–77, was awarded the silver medal. As in 1976, the Soviets did manage to capture the women's basketball tournament, with Bulgaria and Yugoslavia in the second and third spots, respectively.

Except for two North Koreans, the silver and bronze medalists in the 115-pound group, and two Cubans, the gold medalist in the 123-pound class and the bronze medalist in the 220-pound category, Soviets and East Europeans won all the medals for weightlifting. In the ten classes, one Olympic and five world records were set. The hometown crowd was severely disappointed, however, by the performance of Vasili Alekseyev, the winner of the gold medal in the superheavyweight class at Munich and Montreal. The 6'3", 328-pound Soviet, now 38, was eliminated from the competition and saw the gold medal go to his chief Soviet rival, Sultan Rakhmanov. Rejected by his former fans, Alekseyev insisted that he was an "old and very strong horse" and that he would be back.

Vladimir Parfenovich of the USSR earned three gold medals in canoeing, capturing the 500-meter kayak singles and with Sergei Chukhrai both kayak pairs events. East Germany's Rudiger Helm won his second consecutive gold medal in the 1,000-meter kayak singles and was a member of the gold-medal-winning 1,000-meter kayak fours team. Bulgaria's Lubomir Lubenov and the USSR's Sergei Postrekhin were the leaders in the 1,000-meter and 500-meter Canadian singles, respectively. East Germany was first in both of the women's canoeing events.

Several 1976 gold medalists repeated in the rowing events, in which East Germans were particularly successful. Repeaters included Finland's Pertti Karppinen in the single sculls, East Germany's Bernd and Jorg Landvoight in the coxswainless pairs, and the East German team in the pairs with coxswain. The yachting competition was held at three courses laid out in the Baltic Sea, near Tallinn, Estonia. Brazil won two of the yachting events, the 470 class and the Tornado class; Spain was first in the Flying Dutchman class; Finland's Ekso Rechardt won the Finn Monotype class; Denmark's Poul Jensen, Valdemar Bandolwski, and Erik Hansen received their second consecutive gold medals in the Soling class; and the Soviet Union was awarded gold following the Star class races.

The new African nation of Zimbabwe, formerly Rhodesia, won its first gold medal, as its women field hockey players outdistanced teams from Austria and the USSR. Teams from India, Spain, and the Soviet Union were first, second, and third respectively in men's field hockey. In other team sports, East Germany was the winner of the men's handball competition; the Soviet Union earned gold in the women's division; Czechoslovakia succeeded in the soccer tourney; and host teams in both men's and women's volleyball and in water polo finished with gold medals. Soviets also took the gold in both the individual and the team

Weightlifter Sultan Rakhmanov of the USSR succeeded his teammate Vasili Alekseyev, twice a gold medalist, as number one in the superheavyweight class.

modern pentathlon, as well as in the women's archery event. Tomi Poikolainen of Finland was the leader of the male archers.

The cycling track at Moscow's Olympic complex proved to be one of the world's fastest. Dressed in a tight suit, East Germany's Lothar Thoms set an Olympic record in winning a gold medal in the 1,000-meter time trial. Switzerland's Robert Dill-Bundi outraced France's Alain Bondue and Denmark's Hans-Henrik Orstead in the individual pursuit. Three Olympic flags were raised at the medals ceremony following the pursuit, marking the first time that national flags were not used at such an occasion. Soviet cyclists were victorious in the team pursuit and in the two road races.

In the equestrian events, the Soviet Union captured eight of a possible 18 medals. French fencers followed tradition and won gold medals in two of the six men's events (the team foil and the team épée) and in both of the women's events. Viktor Krovopovskov of the USSR repeated as the gold medalist in the individual sabre and again was a member of the gold-medal sabre team. The French also enjoyed gold-medal victories in judo: Thierry Rey in the 132-pound class and Angelo Parisi in the heavyweight class. Italy's Ezio Gamba, Switzerland's Juerg Roethlisberger, Belgium's Robert Van De Walle, and East Germany's Dietmar Lorenz were first in the 157-pound, the 190-pound, the 209-pound, and the open classes, respectively. Soviets reigned in the other judo classes. Soviet wrestlers dominated in Greco-Roman wrestling but even to a greater degree in the freestyle. Wrestling in the Greco-Roman featherweight division, Stilianos Migiakis was the only Greek to win a gold medal at Moscow. Aleksandr Me-

A fireworks display was part of the ceremonies as the Moscow Games concluded officially on Sunday, August 3, 1980.

FINAL MEDAL STANDINGS			
Nation	G	S	B
Soviet Union	80	70	47
East Germany	47	36	43
Bulgaria	8	16	16
Cuba	8	7	5
Italy	8	3	4
Hungary	7	10	15
Rumania	6	6	13
France	6	5	3
Great Britain	5	7	9
Poland	3	14	14
Sweden	3	3	6
Finland	3	1	4
Yugoslavia	2	3	4
Czechoslovakia	2	2	9
Australia	2	2	5
Denmark	2	1	2
Brazil	2	—	2
Ethiopia	2	—	2
Switzerland	2	—	—
Spain	1	3	2
Austria	1	3	1
Greece	1	—	2
Belgium	1	—	—
India	1	—	—
Venezuela	1	—	—
Zimbabwe	1	—	—
North Korea	—	3	2
Mongolia	—	2	2
Tanzania	—	2	—
Mexico	—	1	3
Netherlands	—	1	3
Ireland	—	1	1
Uganda	—	1	—
Jamaica	—	—	3
Guyana	—	—	1
Lebanon	—	—	1

lentev, Viktor Vlasov, and Igor Sokolov—all of the Soviet Union —established world records in free-pistol shooting, the small-bore rifle (3 positions), and the moving target.

Declaring that the records set in Moscow are "ample proof of the standards set at these Games," and that he only grieves "for those who were not able to participate," Lord Killanin officially closed the 1980 Summer Olympics on Sunday, August 3. Solemnly the flags of Greece, the Soviet Union, and the city of Los Angeles were raised over Lenin Central Stadium. According to the rules, the U.S. flag should have been used and *The Star-Spangled Banner* should have been played. However, in light of the U.S. boycott and its position regarding Soviet troops in Afghanistan, the IOC decided to use the flag of the city of Los Angeles, the scheduled host of the 1984 Summer Games, and play the Olympic hymn instead. The IOC feared that without such action, the U.S. Embassy in Moscow might have protested, and the committee did not "want to embarrass" the Soviet hosts. As the Olympic flag came down and the torch burned for the final moments, fireworks exploded in the sky above the stadium. A gymnastic exhibit, dancing, singing, and performances by marching bands followed. Concluding the ceremony, a huge inflated likeness of the Olympic mascot, Misha, was released from the center of the stadium.

Meanwhile on the Capitol steps in Washington, D.C., on July 30, President Carter presided over an "Olympic Medals Ceremony" and presented congressional gold medals to more than 400 American athletes, coaches, and managers. The president declared that if the U.S. Olympic team "had been in Moscow . . ., with all the pageantry and spectacle, it would have been impossible for the United States "credibly to maintain" its continuing effort to seek freedom in Afghanistan. The ceremony, sponsored by the United States Olympic Committee, was part of a five-day, $950,000 salute to the 1980 U.S. Summer Olympic team.

The Presidents of the IOC

The most influential individual within the Olympic movement, the president of the International Olympic Committee (IOC), is the overseer of the entire Olympic movement. He is assisted by the members of the executive board.

The IOC, a permanent organization created by the Congress of Paris of June 23, 1894, selects such persons as the members see fit to serve as members. All IOC members must speak French or English and be citizens of and reside in a country that has a recognized National Olympic Committee. The basic obligations and responsibilities of IOC members are "to encourage the organization and development of sport and sport competition . . . to inspire and lead sport within the Olympic ideal . . . to ensure the regular celebration of the Olympic Games . . . to make the Olympic Games ever more worthy of their glorious history. . . ." From its members the IOC chooses its president by secret ballot and by an absolute majority of those present. The term of office is eight years, and reelection for successive four-year terms is possible.

Since the revival of the modern Games, seven men have held the post of IOC president. Demetrios Bikelas (1835–1908), a prominent Greek author and historian, was the first IOC president. He was responsible for organizing the 1896 Games, the first modern Olympic competition. Since the 1900 Games were scheduled for Paris and since the rules then stipulated that the president should be a resident of the country organizing the Games, Baron Pierre de Coubertin, the French educator who had done so much to bring about the revival of the Olympic movement and who had been secretary-general of the IOC during the 1896 Games, seemed the obvious person to assume the IOC leadership. Coubertin remained IOC president until 1925 and was an IOC member until his death in 1937. Only briefly, during World War I, did the Baron Godefroy de Blonay, a Swiss, serve in Coubertin's place. Coubertin, who served in the French Army, did not think it proper that a military man lead the IOC.

Comte Henri de Baillet-Latour, a Belgian sportsman, succeeded Coubertin as IOC president in May 1925. A former IOC vice president, he was selected mainly in consequence of his organizing the successful 1920 Games in Antwerp on particularly short notice. Baillet-Latour was born on March 1, 1876. He became an amateur horseback rider of some note and was elected president of the Jockey Club of Brussels. Under his leadership, the IOC developed

Belgium's Count Henri de Baillet-Latour, president of the IOC (1925-42), was responsible for the 1936 Games in Berlin.

the slogan "All Sports for All" as the basic principle of competitive athletes. He played a major role in discussions with German Chancellor Adolf Hitler concerning the 1936 Games and was influential in urging the United States not to withdraw from the controversial Berlin Games to protest the Nazi treatment of the Jews.

Baillet-Latour retained the IOC presidency until his sudden death on January 6, 1942. With attention focused on the war effort, the IOC presidency passed to J. Sigfrid Edström, an IOC member from 1920 and a vice president from 1938. Edström, a Swedish industrialist who had been a first-rate sprinter, did not take over the presidency until September 5, 1946.

Born on November 21, 1870, Edström in time became one of Sweden's leading industrialists. From 1903 to 1933 he was president of the Asea Electric Company. He was a member of the American Institute of Electrical Engineers and of the Institute of Electrical Engineers in London.

A founder of the International Athletic Foundation, Edström served as the organization's president for 34 years (1912–46). He was active in combining the various branches of Swedish sports under a single administration. Edström was a member of the Swedish Olympic Committee (1905–48), and as such, was responsible for organizing the 1912 Games in Stockholm. He gave his support to the IOC's decision to add a "Week of Winter Sports" to the 1924 Games. Edström was particularly disappointed that a truce ending the Korean War was not achieved during the 1952 Games, at the conclusion of which he retired. He died in Stockholm on March 18, 1964.

For twenty of their most trying years, the Olympic Games were in the uncompromising hands of Avery Brundage. A big, crusty, resolute man, he held the presidency of the IOC from 1952 to 1972. During that time no aspect of the international games escaped his influence. He was the unbending champion of amateurism, ready to do battle with anyone who would inject commercialism into the Games. He was as dedicated a foe of intrusive advertisers as he was of individual athletes and politicians or government figures who might endeavor to turn the Olympic Games to their own ends.

Brundage directed the IOC, as he did everything, forcefully. If he did not invariably get his way, he did often enough for the IOC members to be very familiar with his iron will. He was generally respected, sometimes feared, and on occasion hated.

He was born in Detroit, Michigan, on September 28, 1887. His parents, of modest circumstances, separated when he was six, and he went to live with aunts and uncles in Chicago. He studied engineering at the University of Illinois and, after graduation, took a job hauling bricks. He worked his way into construction of large-scale commercial buildings.

After the 1929 stock market crash, he began to buy, for a few cents on the dollar, the depressed stocks of promising companies, and to invest in real estate. When the Depression of the 1930's was past, Brundage was the millionaire owner of a Chicago hotel and of extensive real estate, including a golf course, in Santa Barbara. He maintained homes in both Chicago and Santa Barbara, and eventually in Lausanne, Switzerland, near the IOC headquarters.

Brundage first became interested in the Olympics as a competitor. In the 1912 Games he placed fifth in the pentathlon, 14th in the decathlon, and 22d in the discus.

Swedish industrialist J. Sigfrid Edström, president of the IOC (1946-52), oversaw the 1948 Games, the first Olympics following a 12-year disruption due to world war. He had organized the silken-smooth Stockholm Games.

One of his greatest disappointments was that he failed to win a medal. A teammate, Jim Thorpe, originally finished first in both the pentathlon and decathlon. Thorpe walked away with the honors and returned home a hero. Later it was discovered that he had accepted money for playing baseball. He was stripped of his medals, and all of his marks were erased from the record books. A campaign was waged for many years to restore Thorpe's medals. Brundage's opponents accused him of making no effort on Thorpe's behalf because of personal jealousy. His reply was characteristically pointed: "I do not have the power to change that judgment even if I wished." (Thorpe's medals were restored to him in 1983.)

Brundage served as president of the United States Olympic Association and Committee from 1929 to 1952. He became a member of the IOC in 1936. He served as vice chairman of the IOC from 1945 to 1952, when he was named president.

Conflicts involving Brundage began with the 1936 Games in Berlin. Adolf Hitler's Nazi legions were goose-stepping toward World War II. In spite of a strong move in the United States to boycott the Games, Brundage visited Berlin in his capacity as president of USOA and then announced, "We will compete. Nonparticipation would do more harm than good."

Brundage never had any love for the Winter Games. He harbored a special dislike for Alpine skiing, contending that the glamorous sport was riddled with commercialism and semiprofessionalism. He repeatedly threatened to remove Alpine skiing from the Winter Games. When skiers and manufacturers vehemently objected, he threatened to eliminate the Winter Olympic Games.

Brundage believed that the Olympics were no place for political and ideological confrontations. When a number of African nations threatened to withdraw and Mexico City was threatening not to hold the Games in 1968 if South Africa was permitted to compete, Brundage staunchly defended the South Africans' right to enter athletes: the South African practice of apartheid was not an Olympic matter. The nine-man IOC executive board overruled him, however, and South Africa was barred.

Among the biggest problems the willful IOC president encountered were those dealing with the two Germanys and the two Chinas. After considerable bickering, Brundage persuaded the East and West Germans to compete as one team. Later they competed separately. He had no such success with the two Chinas. Taiwan, or Nationalist China, remained a member of the IOC during his lifetime. But the People's Republic of China, with its 900 million population, refused to join the IOC while Taiwan was a member.

One of the greatest crises of his tenure came in the last Olympics Brundage supervised—the 1972 Games in Munich, Germany. When 11 Israelis, 5 Arab terrorists, and 1 German policeman lay dead following an invasion of Olympic Village, Brundage was urged to cancel the Games out of sympathy for the slain Israelis. "The Games must go on," he decreed. "If we bow to political blackmail, no Olympics ever will be free of such dangers." A memorial service for the Israelis was held in the Olympic stadium, and the Games continued.

Brundage reluctantly turned over the IOC reins to Lord Killanin in 1972. His wife, Elizabeth, had died a year earlier. On June 20, 1973, he married much younger Mariann, Princess Reuss, a mem-

The Olympic career of Avery Brundage spanned 60 years. It began when he appeared as a competitor at the 1912 Olympics (above). It came to an end following the 1972 Games. (Below) Brundage delivers a speech insisting that the 1972 Summer Games continue despite the deaths of 11 Israelis at the hands of Arab terrorists.

In September 1972, Avery Brundage personally introduced his successor as IOC president, Lord Killanin (left), to the press. The Irish peer gave up the post after opposing the U.S.-led boycott of the 1980 Games in Moscow.

Juan Antonio Samaranch, 60-year-old Spanish diplomat, followed Lord Killanin to the IOC presidency in 1980. His first major challenge would be to see that the Games are returned to some sort of normalcy following the boycott.

ber of one of Germany's titled families. Less than two years later, on May 8, 1975, he died of a heart attack at the age of 87.

Michael Morris, 3d Baron Killanin, became the sixth president of the IOC in September 1972. Killanin was generally considered more liberal and amenable to change than his predecessor. In fact, at the time of his appointment Lord Killanin was quoted as saying that the Olympics were "not my substitute religion. I've got my own religion."

Michael Morris was born on July 30, 1914. He was educated at Eton, the Sorbonne in Paris, and Magdalene College, Cambridge. The future IOC president not only earned bachelor's (1935) and master's (1939) degrees, but also found time to enjoy boxing, rowing, and horseback riding. Upon the death of his uncle in 1927, Michael Morris inherited the title. As Baron Killanin of Galway (County Galway), he is a member of the House of Lords of the United Kingdom.

From 1935 until 1939 he was a member of the editorial staff of the *Daily Express* and the *Daily Mail*. He was a war correspondent for the *Express* during the Sino-Japanese war and later assistant political and diplomatic correspondent in Europe for the *Mail*. During World War II, Killanin served in the King's Royal Rifle Corps, earning the rank of major.

In addition to becoming involved in the IOC during the 1950's, Lord Killanin pursued a variety of other interests. He was associated with the production of several motion pictures, including *The Quiet Man* with John Ford. He coauthored *The Shell Guide to Ireland,* wrote newspaper columns and articles, served on the board of several companies, and was chairman of the Dublin Theatre Festival (1958-70). In addition Killanin contributed to *Four Days,* a summary of the Munich crisis; edited, with John Rodda, *The Olympic Games: 80 Years of People, Events & Records;* and wrote a synopsis of the 1976 Olympics as well as his memoirs.

Lord Killanin became Ireland's representative to the IOC in 1952, chief of protocol for the IOC in 1966, and an IOC vice president in 1968. He was president of the Olympic Council of Ireland (1950–72) and a member of the French Academy of Sport (1974). After strongly opposing the U.S.-led boycott of the 1980 Moscow Games, Lord Killanin departed as IOC president.

Meeting in Moscow in July 1980, the 83d session of the IOC elected Juan Antonio Samaranch, Spain's ambassador to Moscow and Mongolia, to succeed Lord Killanin. Born on July 17, 1920, the future IOC dignitary was graduated from the Higher Institute of Business Studies in Barcelona. He subsequently served as the municipal councillor responsible for sport for the city of Barcelona, national delegate for physical education and sports, and president of the Barcelona Diputacion (prefecture).

A member of the Spanish Olympic Committee since 1953 and its president (1967–70), Samaranch became a member of the IOC in 1966. He was its chief of protocol (1968–75, 1979), a member of the commission for press and public relations (1967–72), and a member of the executive board (1970–78, 1979–   ). Although the IOC president has participated in such sports as golf, boxing, soccer, and horseback riding, his reputation is greater as a sports administrator than as an athlete. In addition to his IOC positions, he was president of the Spanish Federation of Roller Skating and of the International Boat Show. His hobby is stamp collecting.

GOLD MEDALISTS 1896-1980

Included in this section are all Olympic gold medal winners (1896-1980). The list is arranged alphabetically by sport with the Summer Olympics given first, then the Winter Games. Sports that were once, but are not now, part of the Summer Olympic program are listed as Discontinued Sports at the end of the Summer Games. Discontinued events of a particular sport that remain part of the Olympic competition are included at the end of the particular sport. If no gold medal is given for a particular year, the event was not held that time. Official abbreviations for the nations participating in the Games precede the listing.

AFG	Afghanistan	GHA	Ghana	NOR	Norway
AHO	Netherlands Antilles	GRE	Greece	NZL	New Zealand
ALB	Albania	GUA	Guatemala	PAK	Pakistan
ALG	Algeria	GUI	Guinea	PAN	Panama
AND	Andorra	GUY	Guyana	PAR	Paraguay
ANG	Angola	HAI	Haiti	PER	Peru
ANT	Antilles	HBR	British Honduras	PHI	Philippines
ARG	Argentina	HKG	Hong Kong	POL	Poland
ARS	Saudi Arabia	HOL	Netherlands	POR	Portugal
AUS	Australia[1]	HON	Honduras	PRK	North Korea
AUT	Austria	HUN	Hungary	PUR	Puerto Rico
BAH	Bahamas	INA	Indonesia	RHO	Rhodesia
BAR	Barbados	IND	India	ROM	Rumania
BEL	Belgium	IRL	Ireland	RUS	Russia
BEN	Benin (Dahomey)	IRN	Iran	SAF	South Africa
BER	Bermuda	IRQ	Iraq	SAL	El Salvador
BIR	Burma	ISL	Iceland	SCO	Scotland
BOH	Bohemia	ISR	Israel	SEN	Senegal
BOL	Bolivia	ISV	Virgin Islands	SEY	Seychelles
BOT	Botswana	ITA	Italy	SIN	Singapore
BRA	Brazil	JAM	Jamaica	SLE	Sierra Leone
BUL	Bulgaria	JOR	Jordan	SMR	San Marino
CAF	Central Africa Republic	JPN	Japan	SOM	Somali Republic
CAN	Canada	KEN	Kenya	SRI	Sri Lanka
CEY	Ceylon	KHM	Cambodia	SUD	Sudan
CGO	Congo Republic	KOR	South Korea	SUI	Switzerland
CHA	Chad	KUW	Kuwait	SUR	Surinam
CHI	Chile	LAO	Laos	SWE	Sweden
CIV	Ivory Coast	LAT	Latvia	SWZ	Swaziland
CMR	Cameroon Republic	LBA	Libya	SYR	Syria
COK	Congo (Kinshasa)	LBR	Liberia	TAN	Tanzania
COL	Colombia	LES	Lesotho	TCH	Czechoslovakia
CRC	Costa Rica	LIB	Lebanon	THA	Thailand
CUB	Cuba	LIE	Liechtenstein	TOG	Togo
CYP	Cyprus	LIT	Lithuania	TRI	Trinidad and Tobago
DAH	Dahomey (Benin)	LUX	Luxembourg	TUN	Tunisia
DEN	Denmark	MAD	Madagascar	TUR	Turkey
DOM	Dominican Republic	MAL	Malaysia	UGA	Uganda
ECU	Ecuador	MAR	Morocco	URS	USSR
EGY	Egypt	MAW	Malawi	URU	Uruguay
ENG	England	MEX	Mexico	USA	United States of America
ESP	Spain	MGL	Mongolia	VEN	Venezuela
EST	Estonia	MLI	Mali	VIE	Vietnam
ETH	Ethiopia	MLT	Malta	VOL	Upper Volta
FIJ	Fiji	MON	Monaco	WAL	Wales
FIN	Finland	MOZ	Mozambique	YUG	Yugoslavia
FRA	France	MRI	Mauritius	ZAI	Zaire
GAB	Gabon	NCA	Nicaragua	ZAM	Zambia
GBR	Great Britain	NEP	Nepal	ZIM	Zimbabwe
GDR	German Democratic Republic	NGR	Nigeria		
GER	German Federal Republic	NIG	Niger		

[1]or Australasia, representing a combined team from Australia and New Zealand, in the years up to and including 1912

Summer Games

Archery

MEN

1900   Au chapelet—33 m, Hubert van Innis, BEL
     Au cordon doré—33 m, Hubert van Innis, BEL
     Au chapelet—50 m, Eugène Mougin, FRA
     Au cordon doré—50 m, Henri Herouin, FRA
     Sur la perche à la herse, Emmanuel Foulon, FRA
     Sur la perche à la pyramide, Emile Grumiaux, FRA
1904   Double American Round, Phillip Bryant, USA
     Double York Round, Phillip Bryant, USA
     Team Round, Potomac Archers, Washington, D.C. (William Thompson, Robert Williams, Louis Maxon, G. C. Spencer)
1908   Continental Style, E. G. Grisot, FRA
     York Round, W. Dod, GBR
1920   Fixed bird target
      Small birds, Edmond van Moer, BEL
      Large birds, Edouard Cloetens, BEL
      Team, BEL (Louis van de Perck, Edouard Cloetens, Edmond van Moer, Firmin Flamand, Joseph Hermans, Auguste van de Verre)
     Moving bird target
      28 m, Hubert van Innis, BEL
      33 m, Hubert van Innis, BEL
      50 m, Julien Louis Brulé, FRA
      Team, 28 m, HOL (Adrianus Cornelis Theeuwes, Hendrikus van Bussel, Jan Joseph Packbiers, Adrianus van Merrienboer, Jan Babtiest Josef van Gestel, Theodorus B. Willems, Petrus Godefridus de Brouwer, Johannes Jacobus van Gestel)
      Team, 33 m, BEL (Hubert van Innis, Alphonse Allaert, Edmond de Knibber, Louis Delcon, Jérome de Mayer, Louis van Beeck, Pierre van Thielt, Louis Fierens)
      Team, 50 m, BEL (Hubert van Innis, Alphonse Allaert, Edmond de Knibber, Louis Delcon, Jérome de Mayer, Louis van Beeck, Pierre van Thielt, Louis Fierens)
1972   John Williams, USA
1976   Darrell Pace, USA
1980   Tomi Poikolainen, FIN

WOMEN

1904   Double Columbia Round, M. C. Howell, USA
     Double National Round, M. C. Howell, USA
     Team Round, Cincinnati A. C.

      (M. C. Howell, H. C. Pollock, L. Woodruff, L. Taylor)
1908   National Round. Q. F. Newall, GBR
1972   Doreen Wilber, USA
1976   Luann Ryon, USA
1980   Keto Losaberidze, URS

Athletics
Track and Field

MEN

100-Meter Dash

1896	Thomas Burke, USA
1900	Francis Jarvis, USA
1904	Archie Hahn, USA
1906	Archie Hahn, USA
1908	Reginald Walker, SAF
1912	Ralph Craig, USA
1920	Charles Paddock, USA
1924	Harold Abrahams, GBR
1928	Percy Williams, CAN
1932	Eddie Tolan, USA
1936	Jesse Owens, USA
1948	Harrison Dillard, USA
1952	Lindy Remigino, USA
1956	Robert Morrow, USA
1960	Armin Hary, GER
1964	Robert Hayes, USA
1968	Jim Hines, USA
1972	Valery Borzov, URS
1976	Hasely Crawford, TRI
1980	Allan Wells, GBR

200-Meter Dash

1900	Walter Tewksbury, USA
1904	Archie Hahn, USA
1908	Robert Kerr, CAN
1912	Ralph Craig, USA
1920	Allen Woodring, USA
1924	Jackson Scholz, USA
1928	Percy Williams, CAN
1932	Eddie Tolan, USA
1936	Jesse Owens, USA
1948	Melvin Patton, USA
1952	Andrew Stanfield, USA
1956	Robert Morrow, USA
1960	Livio Berruti, ITA
1964	Henry Carr, USA
1968	Tommie Smith, USA
1972	Valery Borzov, URS
1976	Don Quarrie, JAM
1980	Pietro Mennea, ITA

400-Meter Run

1896	Thomas Burke, USA
1900	Maxey Long, USA
1904	Harry Hillman, USA
1906	Paul Pilgrim, USA
1908	Wyndham Halswell, GBR
1912	Charles Reidpath, USA
1920	Bevil Rudd, SAF
1924	Eric Liddell, GBR
1928	Raymond Barbuti, USA
1932	William Carr, USA
1936	Archie Williams, USA

1948	Arthur Wint, JAM
1952	George Rhoden, JAM
1956	Charles Jenkins, USA
1960	Otis Davis, USA
1964	Michael Larrabee, USA
1968	Lee Evans, USA
1972	Vince Matthews, USA
1976	Alberto Juantorena, CUB
1980	Viktor Markin, URS

800-Meter Run

1896	Edwin Flack, AUS
1900	Alfred Tysoe, GBR
1904	James Lightbody, USA
1906	Paul Pilgrim, USA
1908	Melvin Sheppard, USA
1912	James Meredith, USA
1920	Albert Hill, GBR
1924	Douglas Lowe, GBR
1928	Douglas Lowe, GBR
1932	Thomas Hampson, GBR
1936	John Woodruff, USA
1948	Malvin Whitfield, USA
1952	Malvin Whitfield, USA
1956	Thomas Courtney, USA
1960	Peter Snell, NZL
1964	Peter Snell, NZL
1968	Ralph Doubell, AUS
1972	Dave Wottle, USA
1976	Alberto Juantorena, CUB
1980	Steve Ovett, GBR

1,500-Meter Run

1896	Edwin Flack, AUS
1900	Charles Bennett, GBR
1904	James Lightbody, USA
1906	James Lightbody, USA
1908	Melvin Sheppard, USA
1912	Arnold Jackson, GBR
1920	Albert Hill, GBR
1924	Paavo Nurmi, FIN
1928	Harri Larva, FIN
1932	Luigi Beccali, ITA
1936	John Lovelock, NZL
1948	Henry Eriksson, SWE
1952	Josef Barthel, LUX
1956	Ron Delany, IRL
1960	Herbert Elliott, AUS
1964	Peter Snell, NZL
1968	Kipchoge Keino, KEN
1972	Pekka Vasala, FIN
1976	John Walker, NZL
1980	Sebastian Coe, GBR

5,000-Meter Run

1912	Hannes Kolehmainen, FIN
1920	Joseph Guillemot, FRA
1924	Paavo Nurmi, FIN
1928	Ville Ritola, FIN
1932	Lauri Lehtinen, FIN
1936	Gunnar Höckert, FIN
1948	Gaston Reiff, BEL
1952	Emil Zátopek, TCH
1956	Vladimir Kuts, URS
1960	Murray Halberg, NZL
1964	Bob Schul, USA
1968	Mohamed Gammoudi, TUN
1972	Lasse Viren, FIN
1976	Lasse Viren, FIN
1980	Miruts Yifter, ETH

10,000-Meter Run

1912	Hannes Kolehmainen, FIN
1920	Paavo Nurmi, FIN
1924	Ville Ritola, FIN
1928	Paavo Nurmi, FIN
1932	Janusz Kusocinski, POL
1936	Ilmari Salminen, FIN
1948	Emil Zátopek, TCH
1952	Emil Zátopek, TCH
1956	Vladimir Kuts, URS
1960	Pyotr Bolotnikov, URS
1964	William Mills, USA
1968	Naftali Temu, KEN
1972	Lasse Viren, FIN
1976	Lasse Viren, FIN
1980	Miruts Yifter, ETH

Marathon

1896	Spyridon Louis, GRE
1900	Michel Theato, FRA
1904	Thomas Hicks, USA
1906	William Sherring, CAN
1908	John Hayes, USA
1912	Kenneth MacArthur, SAF
1920	Hannes Kolehmainen, FIN
1924	Albin Stenroos, FIN
1928	Mohamed El Ouafi, FRA
1932	Juan Zabala, ARG
1936	Kitei Son, JPN
1948	Delfo Cabrera, ARG
1952	Emil Zátopek, TCH
1956	Alain Mimoun, FRA
1960	Abebe Bikila, ETH
1964	Abebe Bikila, ETH
1968	Mamo Wolde, ETH
1972	Frank Shorter, USA
1976	Waldemar Cierpinski, GDR
1980	Waldemar Cierpinski, GDR

110-Meter Hurdles

1896	Thomas Curtis, USA
1900	Alvin Kraenzlien, USA
1904	Frederick Schule, USA
1906	R. G. Leavitt, USA
1908	Forrest Smithson, USA
1912	Frederick Kelly, USA
1920	Earl Thomson, CAN
1924	Daniel Kinsey, USA
1928	Sidney Atkinson, SAF
1932	George Saling, USA
1936	Forrest Towns, USA
1948	William Porter, USA
1952	Harrison Dillard, USA
1956	Lee Calhoun, USA
1960	Lee Calhoun, USA
1964	Hayes Jones, USA
1968	Willie Davenport, USA
1972	Rod Milburn, USA
1976	Guy Drut, FRA
1980	Thomas Munkelt, GDR

400-Meter Hurdles

1900	Walter Tewksbury, USA
1904	Harry Hillman, USA
1908	Charles Bacon, USA
1920	Frank Loomis, USA
1924	F. Morgan Taylor, USA
1928	David Burghley, GBR
1932	Robert Tisdall, IRL
1936	Glenn Hardin, USA
1948	Roy Cochran, USA
1952	Charles Moore, USA
1956	Glenn Davis, USA
1960	Glenn Davis, USA
1964	Rex Cawley, USA
1968	David Hemery, GBR
1972	John Akii-Bua, UGA
1976	Edwin Moses, USA
1980	Volker Beck, GDR

3,000-Meter Steeplechase

1900	George Orton, CAN (2,500 m)
1904	James Lightbody, USA (2,500 m)
1908	Arthur Russell, GBR (3,200 m)
1920	Percy Hodge, GBR
1924	Ville Ritola, FIN
1928	Toivo Loukola, FIN
1932	Volmari Isohollo, FIN
1936	Volmari Isohollo, FIN
1948	Thore Sjöstrand, SWE
1952	Horace Ashenfelter, USA
1956	Christopher Brasher, GBR
1960	Zdzislaw Krzyszkowiak, POL
1964	Gaston Roelants, BEL
1968	Amos Biwott, KEN
1972	Kipchoge Keino, KEN
1976	Anders Gärderud, SWE
1980	Bronislaw Malinowski, POL

400-Meter Relay

1912	GBR (David Jacobs, Harold Macintosh, Victor d'Arcy, William Applegarth)
1920	USA (Charles Paddock, Jackson Scholz, Loren Murchison, Morris Kirksey)
1924	USA (Francis Hussey, Louis Clarke, Loren Murchison, Alfred Leconey)
1928	USA (Frank Wykoff, James Quinn, Charles Borah, Henry Russell)
1932	USA (Robert Kiesel, Emmett Toppino, Hector Dyer, Frank Wykoff)
1936	USA (Jesse Owens, Ralph Metcalfe, Foy Draper, Frank Wykoff)
1948	USA (Norwood Ewell, Lorenzo Wright, Harrison Dillard, Melvin Patton)
1952	USA (Dean Smith, Harrison Dillard, Lindy Remigino, Andrew Stanfield)
1956	USA (Ira Murchison, Leamon King, Thane Baker, Robert Morrow)
1960	GER (Bernd Cullmann, Armin Hary, Walter Mahlendorf, Martin Lauer)
1964	USA (Otis P. Drayton, Gerald Ashworth, Richard Stebbins, Robert Hayes)
1968	USA (Charles Greene, Melvin Pender, Ronnie-Ray Smith, Jim Hines)
1972	USA (Larry Black, Robert Taylor, Gerald Tinker, Eddie Hart)
1976	USA (Harvey Glance, John Jones, Millard Hampton, Steve Riddick)
1980	URS (Vladimir Muravyov, Nikolai Sidorov, Aleksandr Aksinin, Andrei Prokofev)

1,600-Meter Relay

1908	USA (William Hamilton, Nathaniel Cartmell, John Taylor, Melvin Sheppard)
1912	USA (Melvin Sheppard, Edward Lindberg, James Meredith, Charles Reidpath)
1920	GBR (Cecil Griffiths, Robert Lindsay, John Ainsworth-Davis, Guy Butler)
1924	USA (Con Cochrane, Alan Helffrich, Olivier McDonald, William Stevenson)
1928	USA (George Baird, Emerson Spencer, Fred Alderman, Raymond Barbuti)
1932	USA (Ivan Fuqua, Edgar Ablowich, Carl Warner, William Carr)
1936	GBR (Frederick Wolff, Godfrey Rampling, William Roberts, Arthur Godfrey Brown)
1948	USA (Arthur Harnden, Clifford Bourland, Roy Cochran, Malvin Whitfield)
1952	JAM (Arthur Wint, Leslie Laing, Herbert McKenley, George Rhoden)
1956	USA (Louis Jones, Jesse Mashburn, Charles Jenkins, Thomas Courtney)
1960	USA (Jack Yerman, Earl Young, Glenn Davis, Otis Davis)
1964	USA (Ollan Cassell, Michael Larrabee, Ulis Williams, Henry Carr)
1968	USA (Vincent Matthews, Ronald Freeman, Larry James, Lee Evans)
1972	KEN (Charles Asati, Hezahiah Nyamau, Robert Ouko, Julius Sang)
1976	USA (Herman Frazier, Ben Brown, Fred Newhouse, Maxie Parks)
1980	URS (Remigius Vallutis, Mikhail Linge, Nikolai Chernetsky, Viktor Markin)

20-Kilometer Walk

1956	Leonid Spirin, URS
1960	Vladimir Golubnitschy, URS
1964	Kenneth Matthews, GBR
1968	Vladimir Golubnitschy, URS
1972	Peter Frenkel, GDR
1976	Daniel Bautista, MEX
1980	Maurizio Damilano, ITA

50-Kilometer Walk

1932	Thomas Green, GBR
1936	Harold Whitlock, GBR
1948	John Ljunggren, SWE
1952	Giuseppe Dordoni, ITA
1956	Norman Read, NZL
1960	Donald Thompson, GBR
1964	Abdon Pamich, ITA
1968	Christoph Höhne, GDR
1972	Bernd Kannenberg, GER
1980	Hartwig Gauder, GDR

Pole Vault

1896	William Hoyt, USA
1900	Irving K. Baxter, USA
1904	Charles E. Dvorak, USA
1906	Fernand Gonder, FRA
1908	E. Cooke, Jr., A. Gilbert (tie), USA
1912	Harry S. Babcock, USA
1920	Frank K. Foss, USA
1924	Lee S. Barnes, USA
1928	Sabin W. Carr, USA
1932	William Miller, USA
1936	Earle Meadows, USA
1948	Guinn Smith, USA
1952	Robert Richards, USA
1956	Robert Richards, USA
1960	Donald Bragg, USA
1964	Fred Hansen, USA
1968	Bob Seagren, USA
1972	Wolfgang Nordwig, GDR
1976	Tadeusz Slusarski, POL
1980	Wladyslaw Kozakiewicz, POL

High Jump

1896	Ellery Clark, USA
1900	Irving Baxter, USA
1904	Samuel Jones, USA
1906	Con Leahy, GBR/IRL
1908	Harry Porter, USA
1912	Alma Richards, USA
1920	Richmond Landon, USA
1924	Harold Osborn, USA
1928	Robert W. King, USA
1932	Duncan McNaughton, CAN
1936	Cornelius Johnson, USA
1948	John Winter, AUS
1952	Walter Davis, USA
1956	Charles Dumas, USA
1960	Robert Schavlakadze, URS
1964	Valery Brumel, URS
1968	Dick Fosbury, USA
1972	Yuri Tarmak, URS
1976	Jacek Wszola, POL
1980	Gerd Wessig, GDR

Long Jump

1896	Ellery Clark, USA
1900	Alvin Kraenzlein, USA
1904	Myer Prinstein, USA
1906	Myer Prinstein, USA
1908	Francis Irons, USA
1912	Albert Gutterson, USA
1920	William Pettersson, SWE
1924	William De Hart Hubbard, USA
1928	Edward Hamm, USA
1932	Edward Gordon, USA
1936	Jesse Owens, USA
1948	Willie Steele, USA
1952	Jerome Biffle, USA
1956	Gregory Bell, USA
1960	Ralph Boston, USA
1964	Lynn Davies, GBR
1968	Bob Beamon, USA
1972	Randy Williams, USA
1976	Arnie Robinson, USA
1980	Lutz Dombrowski, GDR

Triple Jump

1896	James Connolly, USA
1900	Myer Prinstein, USA
1904	Myer Prinstein, USA
1906	Peter O'Connor, GBR/IRL
1908	Timothy Ahearne, GBR/IRL
1912	Gustaf Lindblom, SWE
1920	Vilho Tuulos, FIN
1924	Anthony Winter, AUS
1928	Mikio Oda, JPN
1932	Chuhei Nambu, JPN
1936	Naoto Tajima, JPN
1948	Arne Åhman, SWE
1952	Adhemar Ferreira Da Silva, BRA
1956	Adhemar Ferreira Da Silva, BRA
1960	József Schmidt, POL
1964	József Schmidt, POL
1968	Viktor Saneyev, URS
1972	Viktor Saneyev, URS
1976	Viktor Saneyev, URS
1980	Jaak Uudmae, URS

Shot Put

1896	Robert Garrett, USA
1900	Richard Sheldon, USA
1904	Ralph Rose, USA
1906	Martin Sheridan, USA
1908	Ralph Rose, USA
1912	Patrick McDonald, USA
1920	Ville Pörhölä, FIN
1924	Clarence Houser, USA
1928	John Kuck, USA
1932	Leo Sexton, USA
1936	Hans Woellke, GER
1948	Wilbur Thompson, USA
1952	Parry O'Brien, Jr., USA
1956	Parry O'Brien, Jr., USA
1960	William Nieder, USA
1964	Dallas Long, USA
1968	Randy Matson, USA
1972	Wladyslaw Komar, POL
1976	Udo Beyer, GDR
1980	Vladimir Kiselyov, URS

Discus Throw

1896	Robert Garrett, USA
1900	Rudolf Bauer, HUN
1904	Martin Sheridan, USA
1906	Martin Sheridan, USA
1908	Martin Sheridan, USA
1912	Armas Taipale, FIN
1920	Elmer Niklander, FIN
1924	Clarence Houser, USA
1928	Clarence Houser, USA
1932	John Anderson, USA
1936	Kenneth Carpenter, USA
1948	Adolfo Consolini, ITA
1952	Sim Iness, USA
1956	Alfred Oerter, USA
1960	Alfred Oerter, USA
1964	Alfred Oerter, USA
1968	Alfred Oerter, USA
1972	Ludwik Danek, TCH
1976	Mac Wilkins, USA
1980	Viktor Rashchupkin, URS

Hammer Throw

1900	John Flanagan, USA
1904	John Flanagan, USA
1908	John Flanagan, USA
1912	Matthew McGrath, USA
1920	Patrick Ryan, USA
1924	Frederick Tootell, USA
1928	Patrick O'Callaghan, IRL
1932	Patrick O'Callaghan, IRL
1936	Karl Hein, GER
1948	Imre Németh, HUN
1952	József Csermák, HUN
1956	Harold Connolly, USA
1960	Vasily Rudenkov, URS
1964	Romuald Klim, URS
1968	Gyula Zsivótzky, HUN
1972	Anatoli Bondarchuk, URS
1976	Yuri Sedykh, URS
1980	Yuri Sedykh, URS

Javelin Throw

1906	Erik Lemming, SWE
1908	Erik Lemming, SWE
1912	Erik Lemming, SWE
1920	Jonni Myyrá, FIN
1924	Jonni Myyrá, FIN
1928	Erik Lundkvist, SWE
1932	Matti Järvinen, FIN
1936	Gerhard Stöck, GER
1948	Tapio Rautavaara, FIN
1952	Cyrus Young, USA
1956	Egil Danielsen, NOR
1960	Viktor Tsybulenko, URS
1964	Pauli Nevala, FIN
1968	Janis Lusis, URS
1972	Klaus Wolfermann, GER
1976	Miklos Németh, HUN
1980	Dainis Kula, URS

Decathlon

1904	Thomas Kiely, GBR/IRL
1912	Jim Thorpe, USA, Hugo Wieslander, SWE (cowinners)
1920	Helge Lövland, NOR
1924	Harold Osborn, USA
1928	Paavo Yrjölä, FIN
1932	James Bausch, USA
1936	Glenn Morris, USA
1948	Robert Mathias, USA
1952	Robert Mathias, USA
1956	Milton Campbell, USA
1960	Rafer Johnson, USA
1964	Willi Holdorf, GER
1968	Bill Toomey, USA
1972	Nikolai Avilov, URS
1976	Bruce Jenner, USA
1980	Daley Thompson, GBR

DISCONTINUED EVENTS

60 Meters

1900	Alvin Kraenzlein, USA
1904	Archie Hahn, USA

5 Miles

1906	Henry Courtenay Hawtrey, GBR
1908	Emil Voigt, GBR

200-Meter Hurdles

1900	Alvin Kraenzlein, USA
1904	Harry Hillman, USA

4,000-Meter Steeplechase

1900	John Rimmer, GBR

3,000 Meters, Team

1912	USA (Tell Berna, Norman Taber, George Bonhag)
1920	USA (Horace Brown, Arlie Alfred Schardt, Ivan Dresser)
1924	FIN (Paavo Nurmi, Ville Ritola, Elias Katz)

3 Miles, Team

1908	GBR (Joseph Deakin, Arthur Robertson, William Coales)

5,000 Meters, Team

1900	GBR (Charles Bennett, John Rimmer, Sidney Robinson, Alfred Tysoe, Stanley Rowley)

Cross-Country, Individual

1912	Hannes Kolehmainen, FIN
1920	Paavo Nurmi, FIN
1924	Paavo Nurmi, FIN

Cross-Country, Team

1904	USA (Arthur Newton, George Underwood, Paul Pilgrim, Howard Valentine, D. C. Munson)
1912	SWE (Hjalmar Andersson, John Eke, Josef Ternström)
1920	FIN (Paavo Nurmi, Heikki Liimatainen, Teodor Koskenniemi)
1924	FIN (Paavo Nurmi, Ville Ritola, Heikki Liimatainen)

Standing High Jump

1900	Ray Ewry, USA
1904	Ray Ewry, USA
1906	Ray Ewry, USA
1908	Ray Ewry, USA
1912	Platt Adams, USA

Standing Long Jump

1900	Ray Ewry, USA
1904	Ray Ewry, USA
1906	Ray Ewry, USA
1908	Ray Ewry, USA
1912	Konstantin Tsiklitiras, GRE

Standing Triple Jump

1900	Ray Ewry, USA
1904	Ray Ewry, USA

56-Lb. Weight Throw

1904	Etienne Desmarteau, CAN
1920	Patrick McDonald, USA

Stone Put

1906	Nicolaos Georgantas, GRE

Discus, Ancient Style

1906	Werner Järvinen, FIN
1908	Martin Sheridan, USA

Javelin, Free Style

1908	Erik Lemming, SWE

Shot Put, Both Hands

1912	Ralph Rose, USA

Discus, Both Hands

1912	Armas Taipale, FIN

Javelin, Both Hands

1912	Julius Saaristo, FIN

Pentathlon

1906	Hjalmar Mellander, SWE
1912	Jim Thorpe, USA, Ferdinand Bie, NOR (cowinners)
1920	Eero Lehtonen, FIN
1924	Eero Lehtonen, FIN

Tug-of-War

1900	SWE/DEN (Gustaf Söderström, Karl Staaf, August Nilsson, Eugen Schmidt, Edgar Aabye, Charles Winckler)
1904	USA (O. G. Olson, S. B. Johnson, H. Sicling, C. Magnussen, Pat Flanagan)
1906	GER (Heinrich Schneidereit, Heinrich Rondi, Wilhelm Born, Willy Dörr, Karl Kaltenbach, Wilhelm Ritzenhof, Joseph Krämer, Julius Wagner)
1908	GBR (William Hirons, F. W. Goodfellow, Edmond Barrett, James Shepherd, Frederick Humphreys, Edwin Mills, Albert Ireton, Frederick Merriman)
1912	SWE (Adolf Bergman, Arvid Andersson, John Edman, Erik Frederiksson, Carl Jonsson, Erik Larsson, August Gustafsson, Carl H. Lindström)
1920	GBR (G. Canning, F. Holmes, Edwin Mills, James Shepherd, H. Stiff, John Sewell, Frederick Humphreys, E. Thorn)

1,500-Meter Walk

1906	George Bonhag, USA

3,000-Meter Walk

1906	György Sztantics, HUN
1920	Ugo Frigerio, ITA

3,500-Meter Walk

1908	George Larner, GBR

10,000-Meter Walk

1912	George Goulding, CAN
1920	Ugo Frigerio, ITA
1924	Ugo Frigerio, ITA
1948	John Mikaelsson, SWE
1952	John Mikaelsson, SWE

10-Mile Walk

1908	George Larner, GBR

WOMEN

100-Meter Dash

1928	Elizabeth Robinson, USA
1932	Stanislawa Walasiewicz, POL
1936	Helen Stephens, USA
1948	Francina Blankers-Koen, HOL
1952	Marjorie Jackson, AUS
1956	Betty Cuthbert, AUS
1960	Wilma Rudolph, USA
1964	Wyomia Tyus, USA
1968	Wyomia Tyus, USA
1972	Renate Stecher, GDR
1976	Annegret Richter, GER
1980	Lyudmila Kondratyeva, URS

200-Meter Dash

1948	Francina Blankers-Koen, HOL
1952	Marjorie Jackson, AUS
1956	Betty Cuthbert, AUS
1960	Wilma Rudolph, USA
1964	Edith McGuire, USA
1968	Irena Szewinska, POL
1972	Renate Stecher, GDR
1976	Baerbel Eckert, GDR
1980	Baerbel Eckert Wockel, GDR

400-Meter Run

1964	Betty Cuthbert, AUS
1968	Colette Besson, FRA
1972	Monika Zehrt, GDR
1976	Irena Szewinska, POL
1980	Marita Koch, GDR

800-Meter Run

1928	Lina Radke, GER
1960	Lyudmila Schevtsova, URS
1964	Ann Packer, GBR
1968	Madeline Manning, USA
1972	Hildegard Falck, GER
1976	Tatyana Kazankina, URS
1980	Nadezhda Olizarenko, URS

1,500-Meter Run

1972	Ludmila Bragina, URS
1976	Tatyana Kazankina, URS
1980	Tatyana Kazankina, URS

400-Meter Relay

1928	CAN (Fanny Rosenfeld, Ethel Smith, Florence Bell, Myrtle Cook)
1932	USA (Mary Carew, Evelyn Frutsch, Annette Rogers, Wilhelmina Von Bremen)
1936	USA (Harriet Bland, Annette Rogers, Elizabeth Robinson, Helen Stephens)
1948	HOL (Xenia Stad de Jong, Jeanette Witziers-Timmer, Gerda van der Kade-Koudijs, Francina Blankers-Koen)
1952	USA (Mae Faggs, Barbara Jones, Janet Moreau, Catherine Hardy)
1956	AUS (Shirley de la Hunty, Norma Croker, Fleur Mellor, Betty Cuthbert)
1960	USA (Martha Hudson, Lucinda Williams, Barbara Jones, Wilma Rudolph)
1964	POL (Tereza Ciepla-Wieczorek, Irena Kirszenstein, Halina Górecka-Richter, Ewa Klobukowska)
1968	USA (Barbara Ferrell, Margaret Bailes, Mildrette Netter, Wyomia Tyus)
1972	GER (Christiane Krause, Ingred Mickler, Annegret Richter, Heidemarie Rosendahl)
1976	GDR (Marlis Oelsner, Renate Stecher, Carla Bodendorf, Baerbel Eckert)
1980	GDR (Romy Muller, Baerbel Eckert Wockel, Ingrid Auerswald, Marlies Gohr)

1,600-Meter Relay

1972	GDR (Dagmar Kaesling, Rita Kuehne, Helga Seidler, Monika Zehrt)
1976	GDR (Ellen Streidt, Christina Brehmer, Brigitte Rohde, Doris Maletzki)
1980	URS (Tatyana Prorochenko, Tatyana Gopstchik, Nina Zyuskova, Irina Nazarova)

80-Meter Hurdles[1]

1932	Mildred Didrikson, USA
1936	Trebisonda Valla, ITA
1948	Francina Blankers-Koen, HOL
1952	Shirley de la Hunty-Strickland, AUS
1956	Shirley de la Hunty, AUS
1960	Irina Press, URS
1964	Karin Balzer, GER
1968	Maureen Caird, AUS
1972[1]	became 100 meters

100-Meter Hurdles

1972	Annelie Ehrhardt, GDR
1976	Johanna Schaller, GDR
1980	Vera Komisova, URS

High Jump

1928	Ethel Catherwood, CAN
1932	Jean Shiley, USA
1936	Ibolya Csák, HUN
1948	Alice Coachman, USA
1952	Esther Brand, SAF
1956	Mildred McDaniel, USA
1960	Iolanda Balaş, ROM
1964	Iolanda Balaş, ROM
1968	Miloslava Rezková. TCH
1972	Ulrika Meyfarth, GER
1976	Rosemarie Ackerman, GDR
1980	Sara Simeoni, ITA

Long Jump

1948	Olga Gyamati, HUN
1952	Yvette Williams, NZL
1956	Elzbieta Krzesinska, POL
1960	Vyera Krepkina, URS
1964	Mary Rand, GBR
1968	Viorica Viscopoleanu, ROM
1972	Heidemarie Rosendahl, GER
1976	Angela Voigt, GDR
1980	Tatyana Kolpakova, URS

Shot Put

1948	Micheline Ostermeyer, FRA
1952	Galina Zybina, URS
1956	Tamara Tyschkevitsch, URS
1960	Tamara Press, URS
1964	Tamara Press, URS
1968	Margitta Gummel-Helmboldt, GDR
1972	Nadezhda Chizova, URS
1976	Ivanka Christova, BUL
1980	Ilona Slupianek, GDR

Discus Throw

1928	Halina Konopacka, POL
1932	Lillian Copeland, USA
1936	Gisela Mauermayer, GER
1948	Micheline Ostermeyer, FRA
1952	Nina Romaschkova, URS
1956	Olga Fikotová, TCH
1960	Nina Ponomaryeva, URS
1964	Tamara Press, URS
1968	Lia Manoliu, ROM
1972	Faina Melnik, URS
1976	Evelin Schlaak, GDR
1980	Evelin Jahl, GDR

Javelin Throw

1932	Mildred Didrikson, USA
1936	Tilly Fleischer, GER
1948	Herma Bauma, AUT
1952	Dana Zátopková, TCH
1956	Inese Yaunzeme, URS
1960	Elvira Ozolina, URS
1964	Mihaela Peneş, ROM
1968	Angéla Németh, HUN
1972	Ruth Fuchs, GDR
1976	Ruth Fuchs, GDR
1980	Maria Colon, CUB

Pentathlon

1964	Irina Press, URS
1968	Ingrid Becker, GER
1972	Mary Peters, GBR
1976	Siegrun Siegl, GDR
1980	Nadezhda Tkachenko, URS

Basketball

MEN

1904	USA (A. W. Manweiler, A. A. Heerdt, G. L. Redlein, William Rhode, Ed Miller, Charles Monahan)
1936	USA (Ralph Bishop, Joe Fortenberry, Carl Stanley Knowles, Jack William Ragland, Carl Shy, William Wheatly, Francis Johnson, Sam Balter, John Haskell Gibbons, Frank John Lubin, Arthur Owen Mollner, Donald Arthur Piper, Duane Alex Swanson, Willard Schmidt)

1948	USA (Clifford Barker, Donald Barksdale, Ralph Beard, Lewis Beck, Vincent Boryla, Gordon Carpenter, Alex Groza, Wallace Jones, Robert Kurland, Raymond Lumpp, Robert Pitts, Jesse Renick, Robert Robinson, Kenneth Rollins)
1952	USA (Charles Hoag, William Hougland, Melvin Dean Kelley, Robert Kenney, Clyde Lovellette, Marcus Freiberger, Victor Wayne Glasgow, Frank McCabe, Daniel Pippin, Howard Williams, Ronald Bontemps, Robert Kurland, William Lienhard, John Keller)
1956	USA (Carl Cecil Cain, William Hougland, K. C. Jones, William Russell, James Patrick Walsh, William Evans, Burdette Haldorson, Ronald Tomsic, Richard James Boushka, Gilbert Ford, Robert Eugene Jeangerard, Charles Frick Darling)
1960	USA (Jay Arnette, Walter Bellamy, Robert Boozer, Terry Dischinger, Burdette Haldorson, Darrall Imhoff, Allen Kelley, Lester Lane, Jerry Lucas, Oscar Robertson, Adrian Smith, Jerry West)
1964	USA (Jim Barnes, William Bradley, Lawrence Brown, Joe Caldwell, Mel Counts, Richard Davies, Walter Hazzard, Lucius Jackson, John McCaffrey, Jeffrey Mullins, Jerry Shipp, George Wilson)
1968	USA (John Clawson, Ken Spain, Joseph White, Michael Barrett, Spencer Haywood, Charles Scott, Bill Hoskett, Calvin Fowler, Michael Silliman, Glynn Saulters, James King, Donald Dee)
1972	URS (A. Belov, S. Belov, A. Boloshev, I. Dvorny, M. Korkia, S. Kovalenko, M. Paulauskas, A. Polivoda, S. Sakandelidze, G. Volnov, I. Yedeshko, A. Zharmukhammedov)
1976	USA (Michael Armstrong, Quinn Buckner, Kenny Carr, Adrian Dantley, Walt Davis, Phil Ford, Ernie Grunfeld, Phil Hubbard, Mitch Kupchak, Tom LaGarde, Scott May, Steven Sheppard)
1980	YUG (Andro Knego, Dragan Kicanovic, Rajko Zizic, Mihovil Nakic, Zeljko Jerkov, Branko Skroce, Zoran Slavnic, Kresimir Cosic, Ratko Radovanovic, Duje Krstulovic, Drazen Dalipagic, Mirza Delibasic)

Women

1976	URS (Iuliana Semenova, Angele Rupshene, Tatyana Zakharova, Raisa Kurvyakova, Olga Barisheva, Tatyana Ovetchkina, Nadezhda Zakharova, Nelli Feryabnikova, Olga Sukharnova, Tamara Daunene, Natalia Klimova)
1980	URS (Angele Rupshene, Lubov Sharmay, Vida Besselene, Olga Korosteleva, Tatyania Ovetchkina, Nadezhda Olkhova, Iuliana Semenova, Ludmila Rogozina, Nelli Feryabnikova, Olga Sukharnova, Tatyana Nadyrova, Tatyana Ivinskaya)

Boxing

Light Flyweight

1968	Francisco Rodriguez, VEN
1972	Gyoergy Gedo, HUN
1976	Jorge Hernandez, CUB
1980	Shamil Sabyrov, URS

Flyweight

1904	George Finnegan, USA
1920	Frank Genaro, USA
1924	Fidel La Barba, USA
1928	Antal Kocsis, HUN
1932	István Énekes, HUN
1936	Willy Kaiser, GER
1948	Pascual Perez, ARG
1952	Nathan Brooks, USA
1956	Terence Spinks, GBR
1960	Gyula Török, HUN
1964	Fernando Atzori, ITA
1968	Ricardo Delgado, MEX
1972	Gheorghi Kostadinov, BUL
1976	Leo Randolph, USA
1980	Petar Lessov, BUL

Bantamweight

1904	Oliver Kirk, USA
1908	A. H. Thomas, GBR
1920	Clarence Walker, SAF
1924	William Smith, SAF
1928	Vittorio Tamagnini, ITA
1932	Horace Gwynne, CAN
1936	Ulderico Sergo, ITA
1948	Tibor Csik, HUN
1952	Pentti Hämäläinen, FIN
1956	Wolfgang Behrendt, GER
1960	Oleg Grigoryev, URS
1964	Takao Sakurai, JPN
1968	Valery Sokolov, URS
1972	Orlando Martínez, CUB
1976	Yong Jo Gu, PRK
1980	Juan Hernandez, CUB

Featherweight

1904	Oliver Kirk, USA
1908	Richard Gunn, GBR
1920	Paul Fritsch, FRA
1924	John "Jackie" Fields, USA
1928	Lambertus van Klaveren, HOL
1932	Carmelo Robledo, ARG
1936	Oscar Casanovas, ARG
1948	Ernesto Formenti, ITA
1952	Jan Zachara, TCH
1956	Vladimir Safronov, URS
1960	Francesco Musso, ITA
1964	Stanislav Stepaschkin, URS
1968	Antonio Roldan, MEX
1972	Boris Kousnetsov, URS
1976	Angel Herrera, CUB
1980	Rudi Fink, GDR

Lightweight

1904	Harry Spanger, USA
1908	Frederick Grace, GBR
1920	Samuel Mosberg, USA
1924	Hans Nielsen, DEN
1928	Carlo Orlandi, ITA
1932	Lawrence Stevens, SAF

1936	Imre Harangi, HUN
1948	Gerald Dreyer, SAF
1952	Aureliano Bolognesi, ITA
1956	Richard McTaggart, GBR
1960	Kazimierz Pazdzior, POL
1964	Józef Grudzien, POL
1968	Ronald Harris, USA
1972	Jon Szczepanski, POL
1976	Howard Davis, USA
1980	Angel Herrera, CUB

Light Welterweight

1952	Charles Adkins, USA
1956	Vladimir Yengibaryan, URS
1960	Bohumil Nemeček, TCH
1964	Jerzy Kulej, POL
1968	Jerzy Kulej, POL
1972	Ray Seales, USA
1976	Ray Leonard, USA
1980	Patrizio Oliva, ITA

Welterweight

1904	Albert Young, USA
1920	Albert Schneider, CAN
1924	Jean Delarge, BEL
1928	Edward Morgan, NZL
1932	Edward Flynn, USA
1936	Sten Suvio, FIN
1948	Julius Torma, TCH
1952	Zygmunt Chychia, POL
1956	Nicolae Linca, ROM
1960	Giovanni Benvenuti, ITA
1964	Marian Kasprzyk, POL
1968	Manfred Wolke, GDR
1972	Emilio Correa, CUB
1976	Jochen Bachfed, GDR
1980	Andres Aldama, CUB

Light Middleweight

1952	László Papp, HUN
1956	László Papp, HUN
1960	Wilbert McClure, USA
1964	Boris Lagutin, URS
1968	Boris Lagutin, URS
1972	Dieter Kottysch, GER
1976	Jerzy Rybicki, POL
1980	Armando Martinez, CUB

Middleweight

1904	Charles Mayer, USA
1908	John Douglas, GBR
1920	Harry Mallin, GBR
1924	Harry Mallin, GBR
1928	Piero Toscani, ITA
1932	Carmen Barth, USA
1936	Jean Despeaux, FRA
1948	László Papp, HUN
1952	Floyd Patterson, USA
1956	Gennady Schatkov, URS
1960	Edward Crook, USA
1964	Valery Popentschenko, URS
1968	Christopher Finnegan, GBR
1972	V. Lemechev, URS
1976	Michael Spinks, USA
1980	José Gomez, CUB

Light Heavyweight

1920	Edward Eagan, USA
1924	Harry Mitchell, GBR
1928	Victor Avendaño, ARG
1932	David Carstens, SAF
1936	Roger Michelot, FRA
1948	George Hunter, SAF
1952	Norvel Lee, USA
1956	James F. Boyd, USA
1960	Cassius Clay, USA
1964	Cosimo Pinto, ITA

1968	Dan Poznyak, URS
1972	Mate Parlov, YUG
1976	Leon Spinks, USA
1980	Slobodan Kacar, YUG

Heavyweight

1904	Samuel Berger, USA
1908	A. L. Oldham, GBR
1920	Ronald Rawson, GBR
1924	Otto von Porat, NOR
1928	Arturo Jurado, ARG
1932	Santiago Lovell, ARG
1936	Herbert Runge, GER
1948	Rafael Iglesias, ARG
1952	Hayes Edward Sanders, USA
1956	T. Peter Rademacher, USA
1960	Franco De Piccoli, ITA
1964	Joseph Frazier, USA
1968	George Foreman, USA
1972	Téofilo Stevenson, CUB
1976	Téofilo Stevenson, CUB
1980	Téofilo Stevenson, CUB

Canoeing

MEN

Kayak Singles—500 Meters

| 1976 | Vasile Diba, ROM |
| 1980 | Vladimir Parfenovich, URS |

Kayak Singles—1,000 Meters

1936	Gregor Hradetzky, AUT
1948	Gert Fredriksson, SWE
1952	Gert Fredriksson, SWE
1956	Gert Fredriksson, SWE
1960	Erik Hansen, DEN
1964	Rolf Peterson, SWE
1968	Mihály Hesz, HUN
1972	Aleksandr Shaparenko, URS
1976	Rudiger Helm, GDR
1980	Rudiger Helm, GDR

Kayak Pairs—500 Meters

| 1976 | GDR (Joachim Mattern, Bernd Olbricht) |
| 1980 | URS (Vladimir Parfenovich, Sergei Chukhrai) |

Kayak Pairs—1,000 Meters

1936	AUT (Adolf Kainz, Alfons Dorfner)
1948	SWE (Hans Berglund, Lennart Kingström)
1952	FIN (Kurt Wires, Yrjö Hietanen)
1956	GER (Michel Scheuer, Meinrad Miltenberger)
1960	SWE (Gert Fredriksson, Sven-Olov Sjödelius)
1964	SWE (Sven-Olov Sjödelius, Nils Utterberg)
1968	URS (Aleksandr Schaparenko, Vladimir Morozov)
1972	URS (Nikolai Gorbachev, Viktor Kratassyuk)
1976	URS (Sergei Nagorny, Vladimir Romanovsky)
1980	URS (Vladimir Parfenovich, Sergei Chukhrai

Kayak Fours—1,000 Meters

| 1964 | URS (Nikolay Tschuschikov, Anatoly Grischin, Vyatscheslav Ionov, Vladimir Morozov) |

1968	NOR (Steinar Amundsen, Egil Söby, Tore Berger, Jan Johansen)
1972	URS (Yuri Filatov, Yuri Stezenko, Vladimir Morozov, Valery Didenko)
1976	URS (Yuri Filatov, Vladimir Morozov, Sergei Chukhrai, Aleksandr Degtiarev)
1980	GDR (Rudiger Helm, Bernd Olbricht, Harald Marg, Bernd Duvigneau)

Canadian Singles—500 Meters

| 1976 | Aleksandr Rogov, URS |
| 1980 | Sergei Postrekhin, URS |

Canadian Singles—1,000 Meters

1936	Francis Amyot, CAN
1948	Josef Holeček, TCH
1952	Josef Holeček, TCH
1956	Leon Rotman, ROM
1960	János Parti, HUN
1964	Jürgen Eschert, GER
1968	Tibor Tatai, HUN
1972	Ivan Patzaichin, ROM
1976	Matija Ljubek, YUG
1980	Lubomir Lubenov, BUL

Canadian Pairs—500 Meters

| 1976 | URS (Sergei Petrenko, Aleksandr Vinogradov) |
| 1980 | HUN (Laszio Folton, Istvan Vaskuti) |

Canadian Pairs—1,000 Meters

1936	TCH (Vladimir Syrovátka, Jan-Felix Brzák)
1948	TCH (Jan-Felix Brzák, Bohumil Kudrna)
1952	DEN (Bent Peder Rasch, Finn Haunstoft)
1956	ROM (Alexe Dumitru, Simion Ismailciuc)
1960	URS (Leonid Geischtor, Sergey Makarenko)
1964	URS (Andrey Khimitsch, Styepan Oschtschepkov)
1968	ROM (Ivan Patzaichin, Serghei Covaliov)
1972	URS (Vladas Chessyunas, Yuri Lobanov)
1976	URS (Sergei Petrenko, Aleksandr Vinogradov)
1980	ROM (Ivan Potzaichin, Toma Simionov)

Canadian Slalom

| 1972 | Reinhard Eiben, GDR |

Canadian Two-Man Slalom

| 1972 | GDR (Walter Hofmann, Rolf-Dieter Amend) |

Kayak Slalom

| 1972 | Siegbert Horn, GDR |

DISCONTINUED EVENTS

Kayak Singles—10,000 Meters

| 1936 | Ernst Krebs, GER |
| 1948 | Gert Fredriksson, SWE |

Kayak Singles—10,000 Meters (Con't.)

1952	Thorvald Strömberg, FIN
1956	Gert Fredriksson, SWE

Kayak Pairs—10,000 Meters

1936	GER (Paul Wevers, Ludwig Landen)
1948	SWE (Gunnar Åkerlund, Hans Wetterström)
1952	FIN (Kurt Wires, Yrjö Hietanen)
1956	HUN (János Urányi, László Fábián)

Kayak Singles—2,000-Meter Relay

1960	GER (Paul Lange, Günter Perleberg, Friedhelm Wentzke, Dieter Krause)

Canadian Singles—10,000 Meters

1948	František Čapek, TCH
1952	Frank Havens, USA
1956	Leon Rotman, ROM

Canadian Pairs—10,000 Meters

1936	TCH (Václav Mottl, Zdenek Škrdiant)
1948	USA (Stephen Lysack, Stephan Macknowski)
1952	FRA (Georges Turlier, Jean Laudet)
1956	URS (Pavel Kharin, Gratsian Botev)

Folding Kayak Singles—10,000 Meters

1936	Gregor Hradetzky, AUT

Folding Kayak Pairs—10,000 Meters

1936	SWE (Sven Johansson, Eric Bladström)

WOMEN

Kayak Singles—500 Meters

1948	Karen Hoff, DEN
1952	Sylvi Saimo, FIN
1956	Yelisaveta Dementyeva, URS
1960	Antonina Seredina, URS
1964	Lyudmila Khvedosyuk, URS
1968	Lyudmila Pinayeva-Khvedosyuk, URS
1972	Yulia Ryabchinskaya, URS
1976	Carol Zirzow, GDR
1980	Birgit Fischer, GDR

Kayak Pairs—500 Meters

1960	URS (Maria Schubina, Antonina Seredina)
1964	GER (Roswitha Esser, Annemarie Zimmermann)
1968	GER (Roswitha Esser, Annemarie Zimmermann)
1972	URS (Lyudmila Pinayeva-Khvedosyuk, Ekaterina Kuryshko)
1976	URS (Nina Gopova, Galina Kreft)
1980	GDR (Carste Genauss, Martina Dischof)

Canoe Slalom

1972	Angelika Bahmann, GDR

Cycling

Road Race Individual

1896	A. Konstantinidis (87 km), GRE
1906	B. Vast (84 km), FRA
1912	Rudolph Lewis (320 km), SAF
1920	Harry Stenqvist (175 km), SWE
1924	Armand Blanchonnet (188 km), FRA
1928	Henry Hansen (168 km), DEN
1932	Attilio Pavesi (100 km), ITA
1936	Robert Charpentier (100 km), FRA
1948	José Beyaert (194.63 km), FRA
1952	André Noyelle (190.4 km), BEL
1956	Ercole Baldini (187.73 km), ITA
1960	Viktor Kapitonov (175.38 km), URS
1964	Mario Zanin (194.83 km), ITA
1968	Pierfranco Vianelli (196.2 km), ITA
1972	Hennie Kuiper (200 km), HOL
1976	Bernt Johansson (180 km), SWE
1980	S. Soukhoroutchenkov (189 km), URS

4,000-Meter Individual Pursuit

1964	Jiři Daler, TCH
1968	Daniel Rebillard, FRA
1972	Knut Knudsen, NOR
1976	Gregor Braun, GER
1980	Robert Dill-Bundi, SUI

2,000-Meter Tandem

1906	GBR (J. Matthews, Arthur Rushen)
1908	FRA (Maurice Schilles, André Auffray)
1920	GBR (Harry Ryan, Thomas Lance)
1924	FRA (Lucien Choury, Jean Cugnot)
1928	HOL (Bernhard Leene, Daan van Dijk)
1932	FRA (Maurice Perrin, Louis Chaillot)
1936	GER (Ernst Ihbe, Carl Lorenz)
1948	ITA (Ferdinando Teruzzi, Renato Perona)
1952	AUS (Lionel Cox, Russel Mockridge)
1956	AUS (Ian Browne, Anthony Marchant)
1960	ITA (Giuseppe Beghetto, Sergio Bianchetto)
1964	ITA (Angelo Damiano, Sergio Bianchetto)
1968	FRA (Daniel Morelon, Pierre Trentin)
1972	URS (Vladimir Semenets, Igor Tselovainkov)

4,000-Meter Team Pursuit

1908	GBR (Leonard Meredith, Benjamin Jones, Ernest Payne, Charles Kingsbury)
1920	ITA (Franco Giorgetti, Ruggero Ferrario, Arnaldo Carli, Primo Magnani)
1924	ITA (Angelo De Martino, Alfredo Dinale, Aleardo Menegazzi, Francesco Zucchetti)
1928	ITA (Luigi Tasselli, Giacomo Gaioni, Cesare Facciani, Mario Lusiani)
1932	ITA (Marco Cimatti, Paolo Pedretti, Alberto Ghilardi, Nino Borsari)

1936	FRA (Robert Charpentier, Jean Goujon, Guy Lapébie, Roger Le Nizerhy)
1948	FRA (Charles Coste, Serge Blusson, Ferdinand Decanali, Pierre Adam)
1952	ITA (Marino Morettini, Guido Messina, Mino De Rossi, Loris Campana)
1956	ITA (Leandro Faggin, Valentino Gasparella, Antonio Domenicali, Franco Gandini)
1960	ITA (Luigi Arienti, Franco Testa, Mario Vallotto, Marino Vigna)
1964	GER (Lothar Claesges, Karlheinz Henrichs, Karl Link, Ernst Streng)
1968	DEN (Gunnar Asmussen, Per Pedersen Lyngemark, Reno B. Olsen, Mogens Frey Jensen)
1972	GER (Jürgen Colombo, Guenther Haritz, Udo Hempel, Guenther Schumacher)
1976	GER (Gregor Braun, Guenther Schumacher, Hans Lutz, Peter Vonhot)
1980	URS (Viktor Manakov, Valery Movchan, Vladimir Osokin, Vitaly Petrakov)

1,000-Meter Scratch (Sprint)

1896	Paul Masson (2,000 m), FRA
1900	Georges Taillandier (2,000 m), FRA
1906	Francesco Verri, ITA
1908	(Void, time limit exceeded)
1920	Maurice Peeters, HOL
1924	Lucien Michard, FRA
1928	René Beaufrand, FRA
1932	Jacobus van Egmond, HOL
1936	Toni Merkens, GER
1948	Mario Ghella, ITA
1952	Enzo Sacchi, ITA
1956	Michel Rousseau, FRA
1960	Sante Gaiardoni, ITA
1964	Giovanni Pettenella, ITA
1968	Daniel Morelon, FRA
1972	Daniel Morelon, FRA
1976	Anton Tkac, TCH
1980	Lutz Hesslich, GDR

1,000-Meter Time Trial

1896	Paul Masson (333.33 m), FRA
1906	Francesco Verri (333.33 m), ITA
1928	Willy Falck Hansen, DEN
1932	Edgar Gray, AUS
1936	Arie van Vliet, HOL
1948	Jacques Dupont, FRA
1952	Russel Mockridge, AUS
1956	Leandro Faggin, ITA
1960	Sante Gaiardoni, ITA
1964	Patrick Sercu, BEL
1968	Pierre Trentin, FRA
1972	Niels Fredborg, DEN
1976	Klaus-Jürgen Grunke, GDR
1980	Lothar Thoms, GDR

100-Kilometer Team Time Trial

1960	ITA (Antoni Bailetti, Ottavio Cogliati, Giacomo Fornoni, Livio Trapè)
1964	HOL (Evert Gerardus Dolman, Gerben Karstens, Johannes Pieterse, Hubertus Zoet)
1968	HOL (Fedor den Hertog, Jan Krekels, Marinus Pijnen, Henk Zoetemelk)
1972	URS (Boris Chouhov, Valery

Lardy, Gennadi Komnatov, Valery Likhachev)
1976 URS (Anatoly Chukanov, Valery Chaplygin, Vladimir Kaminsky, Aavo Pikkuu)
1980 URS (Y. Kashirin, O. Logvin, S. Shelpakov, A. Yarkin)

DISCONTINUED EVENTS

One-Lap Race

1908 Victor L. Johnson, GBR

5,000-Meter Track Race

1906 Francesco Verri, ITA
1908 Benjamin Jones, GBR

10,000-Meter Track Race

1896 Paul Masson, FRA

20-Kilometer Track Race

1906 William Pett, GBR
1908 Charles B. Kingsbury, GBR

50-Kilometer Track Race

1920 Henry George, BEL
1924 Jacobus Willems, HOL

100-Kilometer Track Race

1896 Léon Flameng, FRA
1908 Charles H. Bartlett, GBR

12-Hour Race

1896 Adolf Schmal, AUT

Road Race—Team

1912 SWE (Eric Friborg, Ragnar Malm, Axel Persson, Algot Lönn)
1920 FRA (Fernand Canteloube, Georges Detreille, Achille Souchard, Marcel Gobillot)
1924 FRA (Armand Blanchonnet, René Hamel, Georges Wambst)
1928 DEN (Henry Hansen, Leo Nielsen, Orla Jörgensen)
1932 ITA (Attilio Pavesi, Guglielmo Segato, Giuseppe Olmo)
1936 FRA (Robert Charpentier, Guy Lapébie, Robert Dorgebray)
1948 BEL (Lode Wouters, Léon Delathouwer, Eugène van Roosbroeck)
1952 BEL (André Noyelle, Robert Grondelaers, Lucien Victor)
1956 FRA (Arnaud Geyre, Maurice Moucheraud, Michel Vermeulin)

Equestrian

Three-Day Event—Individual

1912 Axel Nordlander, SWE
1920 Helmer Mörner, SWE
1924 Adolph D. C. van der Voort van Zijp, HOL
1928 Charles F. Pahud de Mortanges, HOL

1932 Charles F. Pahud de Mortanges, HOL
1936 Ludwig Stubbendorf, GER
1948 Bernard Chevallier, FRA
1952 Hans von Blixen-Finecke, SWE
1956 Petrus Kastenman, SWE
1960 Lawrence Morgan, AUS
1964 Mauro Checcoli, ITA
1968 Jean-Jacques Guyon, FRA
1972 Richard Meade, GBR
1976 Edmund Coffin, USA
1980 Federico Euro Roman, ITA

Three-Day Event—Team

1912 SWE (Axel Nordlander, Nils Adlercreutz, Ernst Casparsson)
1920 SWE (Helmer Mörner, Åge Lundström, Georg von Braun)
1924 HOL (Adolph D. C. van der Voort van Zijp, Charles F. Pahud de Mortanges, Gerard P. C. de Kruijff)
1928 HOL (Charles F. Pahud de Mortanges, Gerard P. C. de Kruijff, Adolph D. C. van der Voort van Zijp)
1932 USA (Earl Thomson, Harry Chamberlin, Edwin Argo)
1936 GER (Ludwig Stubbendorff, Rudolf Lippert, Konrad von Wangenheim)
1948 USA (Frank Henry, Charles Anderson, Earl Thomson)
1952 SWE (Hans von Blixen-Finecke, Nils Olof Stahre, Karl Folke Frölén)
1956 GBR (Frank Weldon, Arthur Laurence Rook, Albert Edwin Hill)
1960 AUS (Lawrence Morgan, Neale Lavis, William Roycroft)
1964 ITA (Mauro Checcoli, Paolo Angioni, Giuseppe Ravano)
1968 GBR (Derek Allhusen, Richard Meade, Reuben Jones)
1972 GBR (Mark Phillips, Mary Gordon-Watson, Bridget Parker, Richard Mead)
1976 USA (Tad Coffin, Bruce Davidson, J. Michael Plumb, Mary Anne Tauskey)
1980 URS (Aleksandr Blinov, Yuri Salnikov, Valery Vulkov)

Grand Prix Jumping—Individual

1900 Aimé Haegeman, BEL
1912 Jean Cariou, FRA
1920 Tommaso Lequio, ITA
1924 Alphonse Gemuseus, SUI
1928 František Ventura, TCH
1932 Takeichi Nishi, JPN
1936 Kurt Hasse, GER
1948 Humberto Mariles Cortés, MEX
1952 Pierre Jonquères d'Oriola, FRA
1956 Hans-Günter Winkler, GER
1960 Raimondo D'Inzeo, ITA
1964 Pierre Jonquères d'Oriola, FRA
1968 William Steinkraus, USA
1972 Graziano Mancinelli, ITA
1976 Alwin Schokemoehle, GER
1980 Jan Kowalczyk, POL

Dressage—Team

1928 GER (Carl Friedrich Frhr. von Langen, Hermann Linkenbach, Eugen Frhr. von Lotzbeck)
1932 FRA (Xavier Lesage, Charles Marion, André Jousseaume)

1936 GER (Heinz Pollay, Friedrich Gerhard, Hermann von Oppeln-Bronikowski)
1948 FRA (André Jousseaume, Jean Saint Fort Paillard, Maurice Buret)
1952 SWE (Henri Saint Cyr, Gustaf-Adolf Boltenstern, Jr., Gehnäll Persson)
1956 SWE (Henri Saint Cyr, Gehnäll Persson, Gustaf-Adolf Boltenstern, Jr.)
1964 GER (Harry Boldt, Reiner Klimke, Josef Neckermann)
1968 GER (Josef Neckermann, Reiner Klimke, Liselott Linsenhoff)
1972 URS (Elena Petushkova, Ivan Kizimov, Ivan Kalita)
1976 GER (Harry Boldt, Reiner Klimke, Gabriela Grillo)
1980 USR (Yuri Kovshov, Viktor Ugryomov, Vera Misevich)

Grand Prix Jumping—Team

1912 SWE (C. Gustaf Lewenhaupt, Gustaf Kilman, Hans von Rosen)
1920 SWE (Hans von Rosen, Claes König, Daniel Norling)
1924 SWE (Åke Thelning, Axel Ståhle, Åge Lundström)
1928 SPA (José Navarro Morenés, José Alvarez de los Trujillos, Julio Garcia Fernández)
1932 (all teams disqualified)
1936 GER (Kurt Hasse, Marten von Barnekow, Heinz Brandt)
1948 MEX (Humberto Mariles Cortés, Rubén Uriza, Alberto Valdés)
1952 GBR (Wilfred Harry White, Douglas Stewart, Harry Llewellyn)
1956 GER (Hans-Günter Winkler, Fritz Thiedemann, Alfons Lütke-Westhues)
1960 GER (Hans-Günter Winkler, Fritz Thiedemann, Alwin Schockemöhle)
1964 GER (Hermann Schridde, Kurt Jarasinski, Hans-Günter Winkler)
1968 CAN (Jim Elder, Jim Day, Tom Gayford)
1972 GER (Fritz Liggs, Gerhard Wiltfang, Hartwig Steenken, Hans-Günter Winkler)
1976 FRA (Marcel Rozier, Hubert Parot, Marc Roquet, Michel Roche)
1980 URS (Vyacheslav Chukanov, Viktor Poganovsky, Viktor Asmaev, Nikolai Korolkov)

Dressage—Individual

1912 Carl Bonde, SWE
1920 Janne Lundblad, SWE
1924 Ernst Linder, SWE
1928 Carl von Langen, GER
1932 Xavier Lesage, FRA
1936 Heinz Pollay, GER
1948 Hans Moser, SUI
1952 Henri St. Cyr, SWE
1956 Henri St. Cyr, SWE
1960 Sergey Filatov, URS
1964 Henri Chammartin, SUI
1968 Ivan Kizimov, URS
1972 Liselott Linsenhoff, GER
1976 Christine Stueckelberger, SUI
1980 Elisabeth Theurer, AUT

DISCONTINUED EVENTS

High Jump

1900   Dominique Maximien Gardères, FRA

Long Jump

1900   Constant van Langhendonck, BEL

Figure Riding

1920   Bouckaert, BEL
       Team, BEL

Fencing

MEN

Foil—Individual

1896   Emile Gravelotte, FRA
1900   E. Coste, FRA
1904   Ramón Fonst, CUB
1906   Georges Dillon-Kavanagh, FRA
1912   Nedo Nadi, ITA
1920   Nedo Nadi, ITA
1924   Roger Ducret, FRA
1928   Lucien Gaudin, FRA
1932   Gustavo Marzi, ITA
1936   Giulio Gaudini, ITA
1948   Jehan Buhan, FRA
1952   Christian d'Oriola, FRA
1956   Christian d'Oriola, FRA
1960   Viktor Schdanovitsch, URS
1964   Egon Franke, POL
1968   Ion Drimba, ROM
1972   Witold Woyda, POL
1976   Fabio Dal Zotto, ITA
1980   Vladimir Smirnov, URS

Foil—Team

1904   CUB (Ramón Fonst, Albertson Van Zo Post, Manuel Diaz)
1920   ITA (Baldo Baldi, Tommaso Costantino, Aldo Nadi, Nedo Nadi, Abelardo Olivier, Oreste Puliti, Pietro Speciale, Rodolfo Terlizzi)
1924   FRA (Lucien Gaudin, Philippe Cattiau, Jacques Coutrot, Roger Ducret, Henri Jobier, André Labatut, Guy de Luget, Joseph Peroteaux)
1928   ITA (Ugo Pignotti, Oreste Puliti, Giulio Gaudini, Giorgio Pessina, Giorgio Chiavacci, Gioacchino Guaragna)
1932   FRA (Philippe Cattiau, Edward Gardère, René Lemoine, René Bondoux, Jean Piot, René Bougnol)
1936   ITA (Giulio Gaudini, Gioacchino Guaragna, Gustavo Marzi, Giorgio Bocchino, Manlio Di Rosa, Ciro Verratti)
1948   FRA (André Bonin, René Bougnol, Jehan Buhan, Jacques Lataste, Christian d'Oriola, Adrien Rommel)
1952   FRA (Jehan Buhan, Christian d'Oriola, Adrien Rommel, Claude Netter, Jacques Noël, Jacques Lataste)
1956   ITA (Edoardo Mangiarotti, Giancarlo Bergamini, Antonio Spallino, Luigi Carpaneda, Manlio Di Rosa, Vittorio Lucarelli)
1960   URS (Viktor Schdanovitsch, Mark Midler, Yury Sissikin, German Sveschnikov, Yury Rudov)
1964   URS (German Sveschnikov, Yury Sissikin, Mark Midler, Viktor Schdanovitsch, Yury Scharov)
1968   FRA (Daniel Revenu, Gilles Berolatti, Christian Noël, Jean-Claude Magnan, Jacques Dimont)
1972   POL (Witold Woyda, Lech Koziejowski, Jerzy Kaczmarek, Marek Dabrowski)
1976   GER (Matthias Behr, Thomas Bach, H. Hein, K. Reichart)
1980   FRA (Didier Flament, Paskal Jolyot, Bruno Boscherie, Phillippe Bonnin)

Épée—Individual

1900   Ramón Fonst, CUB
1904   Ramón Fonst, CUB
1906   Georges de la Falaise, FRA
1908   Gaston Alibert, FRA
1912   Paul Anspach, BEL
1920   Armand Massard, FRA
1924   Charles Delporte, BEL
1928   Lucien Gaudin, FRA
1932   Giancarlo Cornaggia-Medici, ITA
1936   Franco Riccardi, ITA
1948   Luigi Cantone, ITA
1952   Edoardo Mangiarotti, ITA
1956   Carlo Pavesi, ITA
1960   Giuseppe Delfino, ITA
1964   Grigory Kriss, URS
1968   Gyözö Kulcsár, HUN
1972   Csaba Fenyvei, HUN
1976   Alexander Pusch, GER
1980   Johan Harmenberg, SWE

Épée—Team

1906   FRA (Pierre d'Hugues, Georges Killon-Kavanagh, Mohr, Georges de la Falaise)
1908   FRA (Gaston Alibert, Bernard Gravier, Alexandre Lippmann, Eugène Olivier, Henri-Georges Berger, Charles Collignon, Jean Stern)
1912   BEL (Paul Anspach, Henri Anspach, Robert Hennet, Fernand de Montigny, Jacques Ochs, Francis Rom, Gaston Salmon, Victor Willems)
1920   ITA (Nedo Nadi, Aldo Nadi, Abelardo Olivier, Tullio Bozza, Giovanni Canova, Andrea Marrazzi, Dino Urbani, Antonio Allocchio, Tommaso Costantino, Paolo Thaon di Revel)
1924   FRA (Lucien Gaudin, Georges Buchard, Roger Ducret, André Labatut, Lionel Liottel, Alexandre Lippmann, Georges Tainturier)
1928   ITA (Carlo Agostoni, Marcello Bertinetti, Giancarlo Cornaggia-Medici, Renzo Minoli, Giulio Basletta, Franco Riccardi)
1932   FRA (Philippe Cattiau, Georges Buchard, Bernard Schmetz, Jean Piot, Fernand Jourdant, Georges Tainturier)
1936   ITA (Saveiro Ragno, Alfredo Pezzana, Giancarlo Cornaggia-Medici, Edoardo Mangiarotti, Franco Riccardi, Giancarlo Brusati)
1948   FRA (Henti Guérin, Henri Lepage, Marcel Desprets, Michel Pécheux, Edouard Artigas, Maurice Huet)
1952   ITA (Dario Mangiarotti, Edoardo Mangiarotti, Franco Bertinetti, Carlo Pavesi, Giuseppe Delfino, Roberto Battaglia)
1956   ITA (Giuseppe Delfino, Alberto Pellegrino, Edoardo Mangiarotti, Carlo Pavesi, Giorgio Anglesio, Franco Bertinetti)
1960   ITA (Giuseppe Delfino, Alberto Pellegrino, Carlo Pavesi, Edoardo Mangiarotti, Fiorenzo Marini, Gian-Luigi Saccaro)
1964   HUN (Gyözö Kulcsár, Zoltán Nemere, Tamás Gábor, István Kausz, Arpád Bárány)
1968   HUN (Csaba Fenyvesi, Zoltán Nemere, Pál Schmitt, Gyözö Kulcsár, Pál Nagy)
1972   HUN (Sandor Erdoes, Gyözö Kulcsár, Csaba Fenyvesi, Pal Schmitt)
1976   SWE (Carl Von Essen, Hans Jacobson, Rolf Edling, Leif Hogstrom)
1980   FRA (Phillippe Riboud, Patrick Picot, Hubert Gardas, Phillippe Boisee)

Sabre—Individual

1896   Jean Georgiadis, GRE
1900   Georges de la Falaise, FRA
1904   Manuel Diaz, CUB
1906   Jean Georgiadis, GRE
1908   Jenö Fuchs, HUN
1912   Jenö Fuchs, HUN
1920   Nedo Nadi, ITA
1924   Sándor Posta, HUN
1928   Ödön Tersztyánszky, HUN
1932   György Piller, HUN
1936   Endre Kabos, HUN
1948   Aladár Gerevich, HUN
1952   Pál Kovács, HUN
1956   Rudolf Kárpáti, HUN
1960   Rudolf Kárpáti, HUN
1964   Tibor Pézsa, HUN
1968   Jerzy Pawlowski, POL
1972   Viktor Sidiak, URS
1976   Viktor Krovopovskov, URS
1980   Viktor Krovopovskov, URS

Sabre—Team

1906   GER (Gustav Casmir, Jacob Erckrath de Bary, August Petri, Emil Schön)
1908   HUN (Jenö Fuchs, Oszkár Gerde, Péter Tóth, Lajos Werkner, Dezsö Földes)
1912   HUN (Jenö Fuchs, László Berti, Ervin Mészáros, Dezsö Földes, Oszkár Gerde, Zoltan Schenker, Péter Tóth, Lajos Werkner)
1920   ITA (Nedo Nadi, Aldo Nadi, Oreste Puliti, Baldo Baldi, Francesco Gargano, Giorgio Santelli, Dino Urbani)
1924   ITA (Renato Anselmi, Guido Balzarini, Marcello Bertinetti, Bino Bini, Vincenzo Cuccia, Oreste Morrica, Oreste Puliti, Giulio Sarrocchi)

1928	HUN (Odön Tersztyánszky, Sándor Gombos, Atilla Petschauer, János Garay, József Rády, Gyula Glykais)
1932	HUN (György Piller, Endre Kabos, Attila Petschauer, Ernö Nagy, Gyula Glykais, Aldár Gerevich)
1936	HUN (Endre Kabos, Aladár Gerevich, Tibor Berczelly, Pal Kovács, László Rajcsányi, Imre Rayczy)
1948	HUN (Aladár Gerevich, Rudolf Kárpáti, Pál Kovács, Tibor Berczelly, László Rajcsányi, Bertalan Papp)
1952	HUN (Pál Kovács, Aladár Gerevich, Tibor Berczelly, Rudolf Kárpáti, László Rajcsányi, Bertalan Papp)
1956	HUN (Rudolf Kárpáti, Aladár Gerevich, Pál Kovács, Attila Keresztes, Jenö Hámori, Dániel Magay)
1960	HUN (Zoltán Horváth, Rudolf Kárpáti, Tamás Mendelényi, Pál Kovács, Gábor Delneky, Aladár Gerevich)
1964	URS (Yakov Rylsky, Nugzar Asatiani, Mark Rakita, Umar Mavlikhanov, Boris Melnikov)
1968	URS (Vladimir Nazlymov, Eduard Vinokurov, Viktor Sidyak, Mark Rakita, Umar Mavlikhanov)
1972	ITA (Michele Maffei, Mario Aldo Montano, Rolando Rigoli, Mario Tullio Mantano)
1976	URS (Viktor Krovopovskov, Eduard Vinokurov, Viktor Sidyak, Vladimir Nazlymov)
1980	URS (Mikhail Burtsev, Viktor Krovopovskov, Viktor Sidyak, Vladimir Nazlymov)

DISCONTINUED EVENTS

Foil for Fencing Masters

1896	Léon Pyrgos, GRE
1900	Lucien Mérignac, FRA

Épée for Fencing Masters

1900	Albert Ayat, FRA
1906	Cyrille Verbrugge, BEL

Épée for Amateurs and Fencing Masters

1900	Albert Ayat, FRA

Sabre for Fencing Masters

1900	Antonio Conte, ITA
1906	Cyrille Verbrugge, BEL

Three-Cornered Sabre

1906	Gustav Casmir, GER

Single Sticks

1904	Albertson Van Zo Post, CUB

WOMEN

Foil—Individual

1924	Ellen Osiier, DEN
1928	Helene Mayer, GER
1932	Ellen Preis, AUT
1936	Ilona Elek, HUN
1948	Ilona Elek, HUN
1952	Irene Camber, ITA
1956	Gillian Sheen, GBR
1960	Heidi Schmid, GER
1964	Ildikó Ujlaki-Rejtö, HUN
1968	Yelena Novikova, URS
1972	Antonella Lonzo Rogno, ITA
1976	I. Schwarczenberger, HUN
1980	Pascale Trinquet, FRA

Foil—Team

1960	URS (Tatyana Petrenko, Valentina Rastvorova, Lyudmila Schischova, Valentina Prudskova, Aleksandra Zabelina, Galina Gorokhova)
1964	HUN (Ildikó Ujlaki-Rejtö, Katalin Juhász-Nagy, Lidia Sákovics-Dömölky, Judit Mendelényi-Ágoston, Paula Földessy-Marosi)
1968	URS (Aleksandra Zabelina, Yelena Novikova, Galina Gorokhova, Tatyana Samusenko, Svetlana Tschirkova)
1972	URS (Elena Belova, Aleksandra Zabelina, Galina Gorokhova, Tatyana Samusenko)
1976	URS (Elena Belova, Olga Kniazeva, Valentina Disorova, Nailia Guiliazova)
1980	FRA (Brigitte Latri-Gaudin, Pascale Trinquet, Isabelle Boeri-Bebard, Veronique Brouquier)

Field Hockey

1908	GBR (H. I. Wood, Harry Scott Freeman, L. C. Baillon, John Robinson, Edgar Page, Alan Noble, Percy Rees, Gerald Logan, Stanley Shoveller, Reginald Pridmore, Eric Green)
1920	GBR (Harry Haslam, John Bennett, Charles Atkin, Harold Cooke, Eric Crockford, Cyril Wilkinson, William Smith, George McGrath, John McBryan, Stanley Shoveller, Rex Crummack, Arthur Leighton, H. K. Cassels, Colin Campbell, Charles Marcom)
1928	IND (Richard James Allen, Leslie Charles Hammond, Michael E. Rocque, Sayed M. Yusuf, Broome Eric Pinniger, Rex A. Norris, Ernest John Cullen, Frederic S. Seaman, Dhyan Chand, George E. Marthins, Maurice A. Gateley, Jaipal Singh, Shaukat Ali, Feroze Khan)
1932	IND (Arthur Charles Hind, Carlyle Carrol Tapsell, Leslie Charles Hammond, Masud Minhas, Broome Eric Pinniger, Lal Shah Bokhari, Richard John Carr, Gurmit Singh, Dhyan Chand, Roop Singh, Sayed Mohomed Jaffar)
1936	IND (Richard James Allen, Carlyle Carrol Tapsell, Mohomed Hussain, Baboo Narsoo Nimal, Ernest John

	Cullen, Joseph Galibardy, Shabban Shahab ud Din, Dara Singh, Dhyan Chand, Roop Singh, Sayed Mohomed Jaffar, Cyril James Michie, Fernandes Paul Peter, Joseph Phillip, Garewal Gurcharan Singh, Ahsan Mohomed Khan, Ahmed Sher Khan, Lionel C. Emmett, Mirza Nasir ud Din Masood)
1948	IND (Leo Pinto, Trilochan Singh, Randhir Singh Gentle, Keshava Datt, Amir Kumar, Maxie Vaz, Kishan Lal, Kunwar Digvijai Singh, Grahanandan Singh, Patrick Jansen, Lawrie Fernandes, Ranganandhan Francis, Akhtar Hussain, Leslie Claudius, Jaswant Raiput, Reginald Rodrigues, Latifur Rehman, Balbir Singh, Walter D'Souza, Gerry Glacken)
1952	IND (Ranganandhan Francis, Dharam Singh, Randhir Singh Gentle, Leslie Claudius, Keshava Datt, Govind Perumal, Raghbir Lal, Kunwar Digvijai Singh, Balbir Singh, Udham Singh, Muniswamy Rajgopal, Chinadorai Deshmutu, Meldric St. Clair Daluz, Granhanandan Singh)
1956	IND (Shankar Laxman, Bakshish Singh, Randhir Singh Gentle, Leslie Walter Claudius, Amir Kumar, Govind Perumal, Raghbir Lal, Gurdev Singh, Balbir Singh, Udham Singh, Raghbir Singh Bhola, Charles Stephen, Ranganandhan Francis, Balkishan Singh, Amit Singh Bakshi, Kaushik Haripal, Hardyal Singh)
1960	PAK (Abdul Rashid, Bashir Ahmad, Manzur Hussain Atif, Ghulam Rasul, Anwar Ahmad Khan, Habib Ali Kiddi, Noor Alam, Abdul Hamid, Abdul Waheed, Nasir Ahmad, Mutih Ullah, Mushtaq Ahmad, Munir Ahmad Dar, Kurshid Aslam)
1964	IND (Shankar Laxman, Prithipal Singh, Dharam Singh, Mohinder Lal, Charanjit Singh, Gurbux Singh, Joginder Singh, John V. Peter, Harbinder Singh, Kaushik Haripal, Darshan Singh, Jagjit Singh, Bandu Patil, Udham Singh, Ali Sayeed)
1968	PAK (Zakir Hussain, Tanvir Ahmad Dar, Tariq Aziz, Saeed Anwar, Riaz Ahmed, Gulrez Akhtar, Khalid Mahmood Hussain, Mohammad Ashfaq, Abdul Rashid, Mohammad Asad Malik, Jahangir Ahmad Butt, Riaz-ud-Din, Tariq Niazi)
1972	GER (Peter Kraus, Michael Peter, Dieter Freise, Michael Krause, Eduard Thelen, Horst Droese, Catsen Keller, Ulrich Klaes, Wolfgang Baumgart, Uli Vos, Peter Trump)
1976	NZL (P. D. Ackerley, J. V. Archibald, A. Borren, A. M. Chesney, J. H. Christensen, G. J. Dayman, A. Ineson, A. L. McIntyre, N. McLeod, B. J. Maister, S. G. Maister, T. W. Manning, W. A. Parkin, M. M. Patel, R. U. Patel, E. L. Wilson)

Field Hockey (Con't.)

1980   IND (Schofield Allan, Chettri Bir
Bhadur, Dung Dung Sylvanus,
Rajinder Singh, Deavinder
Singh, Gurmail Singh,
Ravinder Pal Singh, Baskaran
Vasudevan, Somaya
Maneypanda, Maharaj Krishon
Kaushik, Charanjit Kumar,
Mervyn Fernandis, Amarjit
Rana Singh, Shahid Mohamed,
Zafar Iqbal, Surinder Singh)

WOMEN

1980   ZIM (Sarah English, Anne Mary
Grant, Brenda Jones Phillips,
Patricia Jean McKillop, Sonia
Robertson, Patricia Joan
Davies, Maureen Jean George,
Linda Margaret Watson, Susan
Huggett, Gillian Margaret
Cowley, Elizabeth Murial
Chase, Sandra Chick, Helen
Volk, Christine Prinsloo,
Arlene Nadine Boxhall, Anthea
Doreen Stewart)

Gymnastics

MEN

**All-Around (Combined Exercises,
Individual)**

1900	Gustave Sandras, FRA
1904	Julius Lenhart, AUT
1906	Pierre Payssé, FRA
1908	Alberto Braglia, ITA
1912	Alberto Braglia, ITA
1920	Giorgio Zampori, ITA
1924	Leon Štukelj, YUG
1928	Georges Miez, SUI
1932	Romeo Neri, ITA
1936	Alfred Schwarzmann, GER
1948	Veikko Huhtanen, FIN
1952	Viktor Tschukarin, URS
1956	Viktor Tschukarin, URS
1960	Boris Schakhlin, URS
1964	Yukio Endo, JPN
1968	Sawao Kato, JPN
1972	Sawao Kato, JPN
1976	Nikolai Andrianov, URS
1980	Aleksandr Dityatin, URS

Team

1904	USA	1948	FIN
1906	NOR	1952	URS
1908	SWE	1956	URS
1912	ITA	1960	JPN
1920	ITA	1964	JPN
1924	ITA	1968	JPN
1928	SUI	1972	JPN
1932	ITA	1976	JPN
1936	GER	1980	URS

Floor Exercise (Free Exercise)

1932	István Pelle, HUN
1936	Georges Miez, SUI
1948	Ferenc Pataki, HUN
1952	William Thoresson, SWE
1956	Valentin Muratov, URS
1960	Nobuyuki Aihara, JPN
1964	Franco Menichelli, ITA
1968	Sawao Kato, JPN
1972	Nikolai Andrianov, URS
1976	Nikolai Andrianov, URS
1980	Roland Bruckner, GDR

Flying Rings

1896	Ioannis Mitropoulos, GRE
1904	Hermann Glass, USA
1924	Franco Martino, ITA
1928	Leon Štukelj, YUG
1932	George Gulack, USA
1936	Alois Hudec, TCH
1948	Karl Frei, SUI
1952	Grant Schaginyan, URS
1956	Albert Azaryan, URS
1960	Albert Azaryan, URS
1964	Takuji Hayata, JPN
1968	Akinori Nakayama, JPN
1972	Akinori Nakayama, JPN
1976	Nikolai Andrianov, URS
1980	Aleksandr Dityatin, URS

Horizontal Bar

1896	Hermann Weingätner, GER
1904	Anton Heida, Edward Hennig, USA (tie)
1924	Leon Štukelj, YUG
1928	Georges Miez, SUI
1932	Dallas Bixler, USA
1936	Aleksanteri Saarvala, FIN
1948	Josef Stalder, SUI
1952	Jack Günthard, SUI
1956	Takashi Ono, JPN
1960	Takashi Ono, JPN
1964	Boris Schakhlin, URS
1968	Mikhail Voronin, URS, Akinori Nakayama, JPN (tie)
1972	Mitsuo Tsukahara, JPN
1976	Mitsuo Tsukahara, JPN
1980	Stoyan Deltchev, BUL

Long Horse (Vaults)

1896	Carl Schuhmann, GER
1904	Anton Heida, George Eyser, USA (tie)
1924	Frank Kriz, USA
1928	Eugen Mack, SUI
1932	Savino Guglielmetti, ITA
1936	Alfred Schwarzmann, GER
1948	Paavo Aaltonen, FIN
1952	Viktor Tschukarin, URS
1956	Helmut Bantz, GER, Valentin Muratov, URS (tie)
1960	Boris Schakhlin, URS, Takashi Ono, JPN (tie)
1964	Haruhiro Yamashita, JPN
1968	Mikhail Voronin, URS
1972	Klaus Koeste, GDR
1976	Nikolai Andrianov, URS
1980	Nikolai Andrianov, URS

Parallel Bars

1896	Alfred Flatow, GER
1904	George Eyser, USA
1924	August Güttinger, SUI
1928	Ladislav Vácha, TCH
1932	Romeo Neri, ITA
1936	Konrad Frey, GER
1948	Michael Reusch, SUI
1952	Hans Eugster, SUI
1956	Viktor Tschukarin, URS
1960	Boris Schakhlin, URS
1964	Yukio Endo, JPN
1968	Akinori Nakayama, JPN
1972	Sawao Kato, JPN
1976	Sawao Kato, JPN
1980	Aleksandr Tkachyov, URS

Side (Pommeled) Horse

1896	Jules Alexis Zutter, SUI
1904	Anton Heida, USA
1924	Josef Wilhelm, SUI

1928	Hermann Hänggi, SUI
1932	István Pelle, HUN
1936	Konrad Frey, GER
1948	Huhtanen, Aaltonen, Savolainen, FIN (tie)
1952	Viktor Tschukarin, URS
1956	Boris Schakhlin, URS
1960	Boris Schakhlin, URS, Eugen Ekman, FIN (tie)
1964	Miroslav Cerar, YUG
1968	Miroslav Cerar, YUG
1972	Viktor Klimenko, URS
1976	Zoltan Magyar, HUN
1980	Zoltan Magyar, HUN

DISCONTINUED EVENTS

Club Swinging

1904	Edward Hennig, USA
1932	George Roth, USA

Combined Competition (7 Apparatus)

1904	Anton Heida, USA

Combined Competition (9 Events)

1904	Adolf Spinnier, SUI

Free System—Team

1912	NOR
1920	DEN

Horizontal Bar—Team

1896	GER

Parallel Bars—Team

1896	GER

Rope Climbing

1896	Nicolaos Andriakopoulos, GRE
1904	George Eyser, USA
1906	Georgios Aliprantis, GRE
1924	Bedřich Šupčik, TCH
1932	Raymond Bass, USA

Sidehorse Vault

1924	Albert Seguin, FRA

Swedish System—Team

1912	SWE
1920	SWE

Triathlon

1904	Max Emmerich, USA

Tumbling

1932	Rowland Wolfe, USA

WOMEN

**All-Around (Combined Exercises,
Individual)**

1952	Maria Gorokhovskaya, URS
1956	Larissa Latynina, URS
1960	Larissa Latynina, URS
1964	Vera Čáslavská, TCH
1968	Vera Čáslavská, TCH
1972	Ludmila Turischeva, URS

1976	Nadia Comaneci, ROM	
1980	Yelena Davydova, URS	

Team

1928	HOL
1936	GER
1948	TCH
1952	URS
1956	URS
1960	URS
1964	URS
1968	URS
1972	URS
1976	URS
1980	URS

Beam

1952	Nina Botscharova, URS
1956	Ágnes Keleti, HUN
1960	Eva Bosáková, TCH
1964	Vera Čáslavská, TCH
1968	Natalya Kutschinskaya, URS
1972	Olga Korbut, URS
1976	Nadia Comaneci, ROM
1980	Nadia Comaneci, ROM

Floor Exercise (Free Exercise)

1952	Ágnes Keleti, HUN
1956	Ágnes Keleti, HUN, Larissa Latynina, URS (tie)
1960	Larissa Latynina, URS
1964	Larissa Latynina, URS
1968	Larissa Petrik, URS; Vera Čáslavská, TCH (tie)
1972	Olga Korbut, URS
1976	Nelli Kim, URS
1980	Nelli Kim, URS; Nadia Comaneci, ROM (tie)

Long Horse (Vaults)

1952	Yekaterina Kalintschuk, URS
1956	Larissa Latynina, URS
1960	Margarita Nikolayeva, URS
1964	Vera Čáslavská, TCH
1968	Vera Čáslavská, TCH
1972	Karin Janz, GDR
1976	Nelli Kim, URS
1980	Natalya Shaposhnikova, URS

Uneven Parallel Bars

1952	Margit Korondi, HUN
1956	Ágnes Keleti, HUN
1960	Polina Astakhova, URS
1964	Polina Astakhova, URS
1968	Vera Čáslavská, TCH
1972	Karin Janz, GDR
1976	Nadia Comaneci, ROM
1980	Maxi Gnauck, GDR

DISCONTINUED EVENTS

Team Exercise with Portable Apparatus

1952	SWE
1956	HUN

Handball

MEN

1972	YUG (Zoran Zivkovic, Abaz Arslanagic, Miroslav Pribanic,

Petar Fajfric, Milorad Karalic, Djoko Lavrnic, Slobodan Miskovic, Hrvoje Horvat, Branislav Pokrajac, Zdravko Miljak, Milan Lazarevic, Nebojsa Popovic)

1976	URS (Mikhail Istchenko, Anatoli Fedjukin, Vladimir Maximov, Sergei Kushnirjuk, Vasily Iljin, Vladimir Krazov, Yuri Klimov, Yuri Lagutin, Alexandr Anpilogov, Evgeni Tchernyshov, Valery Gassiy, Anatoli Tomin, Yuri Kidjaev, Alexandr Rezanov)
1980	GDR (Siegfried Voigt, Gunter Dreibrodt, Peter Rost, Klaus Gruner, Hans-Georg Beyer, Dietmar Schmidt, Hartmut Kruger, Lothar Doering, Ernst Gerlach, Frank Wahl, Ingolf Wiegert, Wieland Schmidt, Rainer Hoft, Georg Jaunich)

WOMEN

1976	URS (Natlia Sherstjuk, Rafiga Shabanova, Lubov Berezhnaja, Zinaida Turchina, Tatjana Glustchenko, Maria Litoshenko, Ludmila Shubina, Galina Zakharova, Aldona Chesaitite, Nina Lobova, Ludmila Pantchuk, Larisa Karlova, Igor Turchin)
1980	URS (Natalia Timoshkina, Larisa Karlova, Irina Palchikova, Tatiana Kochergina, Ludmila Poradnik, Larisa Savkina, Aldona Nenenene, Yulia Safina, Olga Zubareva, Valentina Lutaeva, Lubov Odinokova, Sigita Strechen, Natalia Lukianenko, Zinaida Turchina)

Judo

60 kg	**(132 lbs 4 oz)**
1980	Thierry Rey, FRA
65 kg	**(143 lbs 5 oz)**
1980	Nikolai Solodukhin, URS
71 kg	**(156 lbs 8 oz)**
1980	Ezio Gamba, ITA
78 kg	**(171 lbs 15 oz)**
1980	Shota Khabareli, URS
86 kg	**(189 lbs 10 oz)**
1980	Juerg Roethlisberger, SUI
95 kg	**(209 lbs 7 oz)**
1980	Robert Van De Walle, BEL
Over	**95 kg**
1980	Angelo Parisi, FRA
Open	
1980	Dietmar Lorenz, GDR

Classification Prior to 1980

Lightweight

1964	Takehide Nakatani, JPN
1972	Takao Kawaguchi, JPN
1976	Hector Rodriguez, CUB

Welterweight

1972	Toyokazu Nomura, JPN

Light Middleweight

1976	Vladimir Nevzorov, URS

Middleweight

1964	Isao Okano, JPN
1972	Shinobu Sekine, JPN
1976	Isamu Sonoda, JPN

Light Heavyweight

1972	Shota Chochoshvili, URS
1976	Kazuhiro Ninomiya, JPN

Heavyweight

1964	Isao Inokuma, JPN
1972	Willem Ruska, HOL
1976	Sergei Novikov, URS

Open

1964	Antonius Geesink, HOL
1972	Willem Ruska, HOL
1976	Haruki Uemura, JPN

Modern Pentathlon

Individual

1912	Gustaf Lilliehöök, SWE
1920	Gustav Dyrssen, SWE
1924	Bo Lindman, SWE
1928	Sven Thofelt, SWE
1932	Johan Oxenstierna, SWE
1936	Gotthard Handrick, GER
1948	William Grut, SWE
1952	Lars Hall, SWE
1956	Lars Hall, SWE
1960	Ferenc Németh, HUN
1964	Ferenc Török, HUN
1968	Björn Ferm, SWE
1972	Andras Balczo, HUN
1976	Janusz Pyciak-Peciak, POL
1980	Anatoly Starostin, URS

Team

1952	HUN (Gábor Benedek, István Szondy, Aladár Kovácsi)
1956	URS (Igor Novikov, Aleksandr Tarassov, Ivan Deryugin)
1960	HUN (Ferenc Németh, Imre Nagy, András Balczó)
1964	URS (Igor Novikov, Albert Mokeyev, Viktor Mineyev)
1968	HUN (András Balczó, István Móna, Ferenc Török)
1972	URS (Boris Onischenko, Pavel Lednev, Vladimir Shemelov)
1976	GBR (Adrian Parker, Robert Nightingale, Jeremy Fox)
1980	URS (Anatoly Starostin, Pavel Lednev, Evgeny Lipeev)

Rowing

MEN

Single Sculls

1900	Henri Barrelet, FRA
1904	Frank Greer, USA
1906	Gaston Delaplane, FRA
1908	Harry Blackstaffe, GBR
1912	William Kinnear, GBR

Single Sculls (Con't.)

1920	John Kelly, Sr., USA
1924	Jack Beresford, Jr., GBR
1928	Henry Pearce, AUS
1932	Henry Pearce, AUS
1936	Gustav Schäfer, GER
1948	Mervyn Wood, AUS
1952	Yury Tyukalov, URS
1956	Vyatscheslav Ivanov, URS
1960	Vyatscheslav Ivanov, URS
1964	Vyatscheslav Ivanov, URS
1968	Henri Jan Wienese, HOL
1972	Yuri Malishev, URS
1976	Pertti Karppinen, FIN
1980	Pertti Karppinen, FIN

Double Sculls

1904	USA (John Mulcahy, William Varley)
1920	USA (John Kelly, Sr., Paul Costello)
1924	USA (Paul Costello, John Kelly, Sr.)
1928	USA (Paul Costello, Charles McIlvaine)
1932	USA (Kenneth Myers, William E. Garrett Gilmore)
1936	GBR (Jack Beresford, Jr., Leslie Southwood)
1948	GBR (Richard Burnell, Bertram Bushnell)
1952	ARG (Tranquilo Cappozzo, Eduardo Guerrero)
1956	URS (Aleksandr Berkutov, Yury Tyukalov)
1960	TCH (Václav Kozák, Pavel Schmidt)
1964	URS (Oleg Tyurin, Boris Dubrovsky)
1968	URS (Anatoly Sass, Aleksandr Timoschinin)
1972	URS (Aleksandr Timoschinin, Gennadi Korshikov)
1976	NOR (Frank and Alf Hansen)
1980	GDR (Joachim Drelfke, Klaus Kroppellen)

Coxswainless Pairs

1908	GBR (J. R. K. Fenning, Gordon Thomson)
1924	HOL (Antonie C. Beijnen, Wilhelm H. Rösingh)
1928	GER (Bruno Müller, Kurt Möschter)
1932	GBR (Hugh Robert Arthur Edwards, Lewis Clive)
1936	GER (Willi Eichhorn, Hugo Strauss)
1948	GBR (John Wilson, William George Laurie)
1952	USA (Charles Logg, Thomas Price)
1956	USA (James Fifer, Duvall Hecht)
1960	URS (Valentin Boreyko, Oleg Golovanov)
1964	CAN (George Hungerford, Roger Charles Jackson)
1968	GDR (Jörg Lucke, Hans-Jürgen Bothe)
1972	GDR (Siegfried Brietzek, Wolfgang Mager)
1976	GDR (Jorg Landvoigt, Bernd Landvoigt)
1980	GDR (Bernd Landvoigt, Jorg Landvoigt)

Coxswainless Fours

1904	USA (George Dietz, August Erker, Albert Nasse, Arthur Stockhoff)
1908	GBR (Collier Robert Cudmore, James Angus Gillan, Duncan McKinnon, John Robert Somers-Smith)
1924	GBR (Charles R. M. Eley, James A. MacNabb, Robert E. Morrison, Terrence Robert B. Sanders)
1928	GBR (John G. H. Lander, Michael Henry Warriner, Richard Beesly, Edward Vaughan Bevan)
1932	GBR (John C. Babcock, Hugh R. A. Edwards, Jack Beresford, Jr., Rowland D. George)
1936	GER (Rudolf Eckstein, Anton Rom, Martin Karl, Wilhelm Menne)
1948	ITA (Giuseppe Moioli, Elio Morille, Giovanni Invernizzi, Franco Faggi)
1952	YUG (Duje Bonačič, Velimir Valenta, Mate Trojanovič, Petar Šegvič)
1956	CAN (Archibald McKinnon, Lorne Loomer, I. Walter D'Hondt, Donald Arnold)
1960	USA (Arthur Ayrault, Ted Nash, John Sayre, Richard Wailes)
1964	DEN (John Hansen, Björn Haslöv, Erik Petersen, Kurt Helmudt)
1968	GDR (Frank Forberger, Dieter Grahn, Frank Rühle, Dieter Schubert)
1972	GDR (Frank Forberger, Frank Rühle, Dieter Schubert, Dieter Grahn)
1976	GDR (Siegfried Brietzke, Andreas Decker, Stefan Semmler, Wolfgang Mager)
1980	GDR (Jurgen Thiele, Andreas Decker, Stefan Semmier, Siegfried Brietzke)

Pairs with Coxswain

1900	HOL (François Antoine Brandt, Roelof Klein, Hermanus Brockmann)
1906	ITA (Enrico Bruna, Emilio Fontanella, Giorgio Cesana) (1,000 m)
	ITA (Enrico Bruna, Emilio Fontanella, Giorgio Cesana) (1,600 m)
1920	ITA (Ercole Olgeni, Giovanni Scatturin, Guido De Filip)
1924	SUI (Edouard Candeveau, Alfred Felber, Emile Lachapelle)
1928	SUI (Hans Schöchlin, Karl Schöchlin, Hans Bourquin)
1932	USA (Joseph Schauers, Charles Kieffer, Edward Jennings)
1936	GER (Gerhard Gustmann, Herbert Adamski, Dieter Arend)
1948	DEN (Fin Pedersen, Tage Henriksen, Carl Ebbe Andersen)
1952	FRA (Raymond Salles, Gaston Mercier, Bernard Malivoire)
1956	USA (Arthur Ayrault, Jr., Conn Findlay, Armin Kurt Seiffert)
1960	GER (Bernhard Knubel, Heinz Renneberg, Klaus Zerta)
1964	USA (Edward Ferry, Conn Findlay, Henry Kent Mitchell)
1968	ITA (Primo Baran, Renzo Sambo, Bruno Cipolla)
1972	GDR (Wolfgang Gunkel, Jorge Lucke, Klaus-Dieter Neubert)
1976	GDR (Harald Jahrling, Friedrich Ulrich, Georg Spohr)
1980	GDR (Harald Jahrling, Friedrich Ulrich, Georg Spohr)

Fours with Coxswain

1900	FRA (Emile Delchambre, Jean Cau, Henri Bouckaert, Henri Hazebrouck, Charlot)
1906	ITA (Enrico Bruna, Emilio Fontanella, Riccardo Jandinoni, Giorgio Cesana, Giuseppe Poli)
1912	GER (Albert Arnheiter, Otto Fickeisen, Rudolf Fickeisen, Hermann Wilker, Otto Maier)
1920	SUI (Willy Brüderlin, Max Rudolf, Paul Rudolf, Hans Walter, Paul Staub)
1924	SUI (Emile Albrecht, Alfred Probst, Eugen Sigg, Hans Walter, Walter Loosli)
1928	ITA (Valerio Perentin, Giliante D'Este, Nicolo Vittori, Giovanni Delise, Renato Petronio)
1932	GER (Hans Eller, Horst Hoeck, Walter Meyer, Joachim Spremberg, Karlheinz Neumann)
1936	GER (Hans Maier, Walter Volle, Ernst Gaber, Paul Söllner, Fritz Bauer)
1948	USA (Warren Westlund, Robert Martin, Robert Will, Gordon Giovanelli, Allen Morgan)
1952	TCH (Karel Mejta, Jiři Havlis, Jan Jindra, Stanislav Lusk, Miroslav Koranda)
1956	ITA (Alberto Winkler, Romano Sgheiz, Angelo Vanzin, Franco Trincavelli, Ivo Stefanoni)
1960	GER (Gerd Cintl, Horst Effertz, Klaus Riekemann, Jürgen Litz, Michael Obst)
1964	GER (Peter Neusel, Bernhard Britting, Joachim Werner, Egbert Hirschfelder, Jürgen Oelke)
1968	NZL (Richard John Joyce, Dudley Leonard Storey, Ross Hounsell Collinge, Warren J. Cole, Simon Ch. Dickie)
1972	GER (Peter Berger, Hans-Johann Faerber, Gerhard Auer, Alois Bierl, Uwe Benter)
1976	URS (Vladimir Eshinov, Nikolai Ivanow, Mikhail Kuznetsov, Alexandr Klepikov, Alexandr Lukianov)
1980	GDR (Dieter Wendisch, Ullrich Diessner, Walter Diessner, Gottfried Dohn, Andreas Gregor)

Eight-Oared Shell

1900	USA
1904	USA
1908	GBR
1912	GBR
1920	USA
1924	USA
1928	USA
1932	USA
1936	USA
1948	USA
1952	USA
1956	USA
1960	GER

1964	USA
1968	GER
1972	NZL
1976	GDR
1980	GDR

Quadruple Sculls

1976	GDR (Wolfgang Gueldenpfennig Rudiger Reiche, K. Heinz Bussert, Michael Wolfgramm)
1980	GDR (Frank Dundr, Karsten Bunk, Uwe Heppner, Martin Winter)

DISCONTINUED EVENTS

Naval Rowing Boats

1906	ITA (Varese)

16 Man—Naval Rowing Boats

1906	GRE

Coxed Fours, Inriggers

1912	DEN (Ejlert Allert, Jörgen Hansen, Carl Möller, Carl Petersen, Poul Hartmann)

WOMEN

Single Sculls

1976	Christine Scheiblich, GDR
1980	Sanda Toma, ROM

Double Sculls

1976	BUL (Svetla Ozetova, Zdravka Yordanova)
1980	URS (Yelena Khloptseva, Larisa Popova)

Quadruple Sculls

1976	GDR (Anke Borchmann, Jutta Lau, Viola Poley, Roswietha Zobelt, Liane Weigelt)
1980	GDR (Sybille Reinhardt, Jutta Ploch, Jutta Lau, Roswietha Zobelt, Liane Buhr)

Eights

1976	GDR
1980	GDR

Coxswainless Pairs

1976	BUL (Siika Kelbecheva, Stoyanka Grouicheva)
1980	GDR (Ute Steindorf, Cornelia Klier)

Fours with Coxswain

1976	GDR (Karin Metze, Bianka Schwede, Gabriele Lohs, Andrea Kurth, Sabine Hess)
1980	GDR (Ramona Kapheim, Silvia Frohlich, Angelika Noack, Romy Saalfield, Kirsten Wenzel)

Shooting

Clay Pigeon (Trench)—Individual

1900	Roger de Barbarin, FRA
1906	Gerald Merlin, GBR (Single Shot)

1908	Walter Ewing, CAN
1912	James Graham, USA
1920	Mark Arie, USA
1924	Gyula Halasy, HUN
1952	George Genereux, CAN
1956	Galliano Rossini, ITA
1960	Ion Dumitrescu, ROM
1964	Ennio Mattarelli, ITA
1968	John Robert Braithwaite, GBR
1972	Angelo Scalzone, ITA
1976	Donald Haldeman, USA
1980	Luciano Giovannetti, ITA

Pistol—Rapid-Fire Pistol, 25 Meters

1896	Jean Phrangoudis, GRE
1900	Maurice Larrouy, FRA
1906	Maurice Lecoq, FRA
1908	Paul van Asbroeck, BEL
1912	Alfred Lane, USA
1920	Guilherme Paraense, BRA
1924	H. M. Bailey, USA
1932	Renzo Morigi, ITA
1936	Cornelius van Oyen, GER
1948	Károly Takács, HUN
1952	Károly Takács, HUN
1956	Stefan Petrescu, ROM
1960	William McMillan, USA
1964	Pentti Linnosvuo, FIN
1968	Josef Zapedzki, POL
1972	Josef Zapedzki, POL
1976	Norbert Klaar, GDR
1980	Corneliu Ion, ROM

Pistol—Sport (Free) Pistol, 50 Meters

1896	Sumner Paine, USA
1900	Karl Röderer, SUI
1906	Georgios Orphanidis, GRE
1912	Alfred Lane, USA
1920	Carl Frederick, USA
1936	Torsten Ullman, SWE
1948	Edwin V. Cam, PER
1952	Huelet Benner, USA
1956	Pentti Linnosvuo, FIN
1960	Aleksey Guschtschin, URS
1964	Väinö Markkanen, FIN
1968	Grigory Kossykh, URS
1972	Ragnar Skanaker, SWE
1976	Uwe Potteck, GDR
1980	Aleksandr Melentev, URS

Rifle—Small-Bore Rifle, 50 Meters, Prone

1908	A. A. Carnell, GBR
1912	Frederick Hird, USA
1920	Lawrence Nuesslein, USA
1924	Pierre de Lisle, FRA
1932	Bertil Rönnmark, SWE
1936	Willy Rögeberg, NOR
1948	Arthur Cook, USA
1952	Iosif Sirbu, ROM
1956	Gerald Ouellette, CAN
1960	Peter Kohnke, GER
1964	László Hammerl, HUN
1968	Jan Kurka, TCH
1972	Ho Jun Li, PRK
1976	Karlheinz Smieszek, GER
1980	Karoly Varga, HUN

Rifle—Small-Bore Rifle, Combined, 3 Positions

1952	Erling Kongshaug, NOR
1956	Anatoly Bogdanov, URS
1960	Viktor Schamburkin, URS
1964	Lones Wigger, USA
1968	Bernd Klingner, GER
1972	John Writer, USA
1976	Lanny Bassham, USA
1980	Viktor Vlasov, URS

Skeet

1968	Yevgeny Petrov, URS
1972	Konrad Wirnhier, GER
1976	Josef Panacek, TCH
1980	Hans Kjeld Rasmussen, DEN

Moving Target

1972	Lakov Zhelezniak, URS
1976	Aleksandr Gazov, URS
1980	Igor Sokolov, URS

DISCONTINUED EVENTS

Free Rifle

1896	Pantelis Karasevdas, GRE
1906	3 Positions, Gudbrand G. Skatteboe, NOR
	Prone, Gudbrand G. Skatteboe, NOR
	Kneeling, Konrad Stäheli, SUI
	Standing, Gudbrand G. Skatteboe, NOR
	Any Position, Marcel Meyer de Stadelhofen, SUI
1908	Jerry Millner, GBR

Rifle—Full-Bore Rifle, 300 Meters, 3 Positions

1896	Georgios Orphanidis, GRE
1906	Gudbrand Skatteboe, NOR
1908	Albert Helgerud, NOR
1912	Paul Colas, FRA
1920	Morris Fisher, USA
1924	Morris Fisher, USA
1948	Emil Grünig, SUI
1952	Anatoly Bogdanov, URS
1956	Vassily Borissov, URS
1960	Hubert Hammerer, AUT
1964	Gary Anderson, USA
1968	Gary Anderson, USA
1972	Lones Wigger, USA

Team

1906	SUI (Konrad Stäheli, Jean Reich, Louis Richardet, Marcel Meyer de Stadelhofen, Alfred Grütter)
1908	NOR (Albert Helgerud, Ole Saether, Gudbrand G. Skatteboe, Olaf Saether, Einar Liberg, Julius Braathe)
1912	SWE (Mauritz Eriksson, C. Hugo Johansson, Erik Blomqvist, Carl Björkman, Bernhard Larsson, G. Adolf Jonsson)
1920	USA (Morris Fisher, Carl Osburn, Dennis Fenton, Lloyd Spooner, Willis Lee)
1924	USA (Morris Fisher, Walter Stokes, Joseph Crockett, Chan Coulter, Sidney Hinds)

Military Rifle

1900	3 Positions, Emil Kellenberger, SUI
	Kneeling, Konrad Stäheli, SUI
	Prone, Achille Paroche, FRA
	Standing, Lars Jörgen Madsen, DEN
1906	Léon Moreaux, FRA (200 m)
	Louis Richardet, SUI (300 m)
1912	3 Positions, Sándor Prokopp, HUN
	Any Position, Paul Colas, FRA

Military Rifle (Con't.)

1920   Prone, Otto M. Olsen, NOR (300 m)
      Prone, C. Hugo Johansson, SWE (600 m)
      Standing, Carl Osburn, USA

Team

1900   SUI (Emil Kellenberger, Franz Böckli, Konrad Stäheli, Louis Richardet, Alfred Grütter)
1908   USA (William Leushner, W. B. Martin, C. B. Winder, Kellogg K. V. Casey, Albert Eastman, C. S. Benedict)
1912   USA (Charles Burdette, Allan Briggs, Harry Adams, Joseph Jackson, Carl Osburn, Warren Sprout)
1920   (Standing) DEN (Lars Jörgen Madsen, Niels H. D. Larsen, Anders Marius Petersen, Erik Saetter-Lassen, Anders Peter Nielsen)
      (Prone-300 m) USA (Carl Osburn, Joseph Jackson, Lloyd Spooner, Morris Fisher, Willis Lee)
      (Prone-600 m) USA (Dennis Fenton, Ollie Schriver, Willis Lee, Lloyd Spooner, Joseph Jackson)
      (Prone-300 + 600 m) USA (Joseph Jackson, Willis Lee, Ollie Schriver, Carl Osburn, Lloyd Spooner)

Small Bore Rifle

1908   Moving Target, A. F. Fleming, GBR
      Disappearing Target, William Kensett Styles, GBR
1912   Disappearing Target, Wilhelm Carlberg, SWE

Team

1908   GBR (M. K. Matthews, Harry R. Humby, William E. Pimm, E. J. Amoore)
1912   (25 m) SWE (Johan Hübner von Holst, Eric Carlberg, Wilhelm Carlberg, Gustaf Boivie)
      (50 m) GBR (William Edwin Pimm, Edward John Lessimore, Joseph Pepé, Robert Cook Murray)
1920   USA (Lawrence Nuesslein, Arthur Rothrock, Dennis Fenton, Willis Lee, Ollie Schriver)

Running Deer Shooting, Single Shot

1908   Oscar Swahn, SWE
1912   Alfred Swahn, SWE
1920   Otto M. Olsen, NOR
1924   John K. Boles, USA

Team

1908   SWE (Alfred Swahn, Arvid Knöppel, Oscar Swahn, E. O. Rosell)
1912   SWE (Alfred Swahn, Oscar Swahn, Åke Lundeberg, Olof Arvidsson)
1920   NOR (Harald Natvig, Otto M. Olsen, Ole Andreas Lilloe-

      Olsen, Einar Liberg, Hans Nordvik)
1924   NOR (Ole Andreas Lilloe-Olsen, Einar Liberg, Harald Natvig, Otto M. Olsen)

Running Deer Shooting, Double Shot

1908   Walter Winans, USA
1912   Åke Lundeberg, SWE
1920   Ole Andreas Lilloe-Olsen, NOR
1924   Ole Andreas Lilloe-Olsen, NOR

Team

1920   NOR (Ole Andreas Lilloe-Olsen, Thorstein Johansen, Harald Natvig, Hans Nordvik, Einar Liberg)
1924   GBR (C. W. Mackworth-Praed, A. Whitty, H. S. Perry, P. Neame)

Running Deer Shooting, Single and Double Shot

1952   John Larsen, NOR
1956   Vitaly Romanenko, URS

Running Wild Boar Shooting

1900   Louis Debray, FRA

Live Pigeon Shooting

1900   Leon de Lunden, BEL

Clay Pigeon Shooting—Team

1908   GBR (Alexander Maunder, J. F. Pike, Charles Palmer, J. M. Postans, F. W. Moore, P. Easte)
1912   USA (Charles Billings, Ralph Spotts, John Hendrickson, James Graham, Edward Gleason, Frank Hall)
1920   USA (Mark Arie, Frank Troeh, Frank Wright, Frederick Plum, Horace Bonser, Forest McNeir)
1924   USA (Frank Hughes, S. H. Sharman, William Silkworth, Fred Etchen)

Military Revolver

1896   John Paine, USA
1906   Louis Richardet, SUI (20 m)
      Jean Fouconnier, FRA (20 m— Model 1873)

Team

1900   SUI (Karl Röderer, Konrad Stäheli, Louis Richardet, Friedrich Lüthi, Paul Probst)
1908   USA (James Edward Gorman, Ira Calkins, John Dietz, Charles Axtell)
1912   (30 m) SWE (Wilhelm Carlberg, Eric Carlberg, Johan Hübner von Holst, Paul Pálen)
      (50 m) USA (Alfred Lane, Henry Sears, Peter Dolfen, John Dietz)
1920   (30 m) USA (Louis Harant, Alfred Lane, Carl Frederick, James Snook, Michael Kelly)
      (50 m) USA (Carl Frederick, Alfred Lane, James Snook, Michael Kelly, Raymond Bracken)

Duelling Pistol

1906   Léon Moreaux, FRA (20 m)
      Konstantinos Skarlatos, GRE (25 m)

Soccer

1900	GBR	1948	SWE
1904	CAN	1952	HUN
1906	DEN	1956	URS
1908	GBR	1960	YUG
1912	GBR	1964	HUN
1920	BEL	1968	HUN
1924	URU	1972	POL
1928	URU	1976	GDR
1936	ITA	1980	TCH

Swimming and Diving

MEN

100-Meter Freestyle

1896   Alfréd Hajós, HUN
1904   Zoltán von Halmay (100 yds), HUN
1906   Charles Daniels, USA
1908   Charles Daniels, USA
1912   Duke Kahanamoku, USA
1920   Duke Kahanamoku, USA
1924   John Weissmuller, USA
1928   John Weissmuller, USA
1932   Yasuji Miyazaki, JPN
1936   Ferenc Csik, HUN
1948   Walter Ris, USA
1952   Clarke Scholes, USA
1956   Jon Henricks, AUS
1960   John Devitt, AUS
1964   Donald Schollander, USA
1968   Michael Wenden, AUS
1972   Mark Spitz, USA
1976   Jim Montgomery, USA
1980   Jorg Woithe, GDR

200-Meter Freestyle

1900   Frederick Lane, AUS
1904   Charles Daniels, USA
1968   Michael Wenden, AUS
1972   Mark Spitz, USA
1976   Bruce Furniss, USA
1980   Sergei Kopliakov, URS

400-Meter Freestyle

1896   Paul Neumann (500 m), AUT
1904   Charles Daniels (400 yds), USA
1906   Otto Scheff, AUT
1908   Henry Taylor, GBR
1912   George Hodgson, CAN
1920   Norman Ross, USA
1924   John Weissmuller, USA
1928   Alberto Zorilla, ARG
1932   Clarence Crabbe, USA
1936   Jack Medica, USA
1948   William Smith, USA
1952   Jean Boiteux, FRA
1956   Murray Rose, AUS
1960   Murray Rose, AUS

1964   Donald Schollander, USA
1968   Michael Burton, USA
1972   Bradford Cooper, AUS
1976   Brian Goodell, USA
1980   Vladimir Salnikov, URS

1,500-Meter Freestyle

1896   Alfréd Hajós (1,200 m), HUN
1900   John Jarvis (1,000 m), GBR
1904   Emil Rausch (1 mile), GER
1906   Henry Taylor, GBR
1908   Henry Taylor, GBR
1912   George Hodgson, CAN
1920   Norman Ross, USA
1924   Andrew Charlton, AUS
1928   Arne Borg, SWE
1932   Kusuo Kitamura, JPN
1936   Noboru Terada, JPN
1948   James McLane, USA
1952   Ford Konno, USA
1956   Murray Rose, AUS
1960   John Konrads, AUS
1964   Robert Windle, AUS
1968   Michael Burton, USA
1972   Michael Burton, USA
1976   Brian Goodell, USA
1980   Vladimir Salnikov, URS

100-Meter Backstroke

1904   Walter Brack (100 yds), GER
1908   Arno Bieberstein, GER
1912   Harry Hebner, USA
1920   Warren Kealoha, USA
1924   Warren Kealoha, USA
1928   George Kojac, USA
1932   Masaji Kiyokawa, JPN
1936   Adolf Kiefer, USA
1948   Allen Stack, USA
1952   Yoshinobu Oyakawa, USA
1956   David Theile, AUS
1960   David Theile, AUS
1968   Roland Matthes, GDR
1972   Roland Matthes, GDR
1976   John Naber, USA
1980   Bengt Baron, SWE

200-Meter Backstroke

1900   Ernst Hoppenberg, GER
1964   Jed Graef, USA
1968   Roland Matthes, GDR
1972   Roland Matthes, GDR
1976   John Naber, USA
1980   Sandor Wladar, HUN

100-Meter Breaststroke

1968   Donald McKenzie, USA
1972   Nobutaka Taguchi, JPN
1976   John Hencken, USA
1980   Duncan Goodhew, GBR

200-Meter Breaststroke

1908   Frederick Holman, GBR
1912   Walter Bathe, GER
1920   Häkan Malmroth, SWE
1924   Robert Skelton, USA
1928   Yoshiyuki Tsuruta, JPN
1932   Yoshiyuki Tsuruta, JPN
1936   Tetsuo Hamuro, JPN
1948   Joseph Verdeur, USA
1952   John Davies, AUS
1956   Masaru Furukawa, JPN
1960   William Mulliken, USA
1964   Ian O'Brien, AUS
1968   Felipe Muñoz, MEX
1972   John Hencken, USA
1976   David Wilkie, GBR
1980   Robertas Zulpa, URS

100-Meter Butterfly

1968   Douglas Russell, USA
1972   Mark Spitz, USA
1976   Matt Vogel, USA
1980   Par Arvidsson, SWE

200-Meter Butterfly

1956   William Yorzik, USA
1960   Michael Troy, USA
1964   Kevin Berry, AUS
1968   Carl Robie, USA
1972   Mark Spitz, USA
1976   Mike Bruner, USA
1980   Sergei Fesenko, URS

400-Meter Individual Medley

1964   Richard Roth, USA
1968   Charles Hickcox, USA
1972   Gunnar Larsson, SWE
1976   Rod Strachan, USA
1980   Aleksandr Sidorenko, URS

800-Meter Freestyle Relay

1906   HUN (József Onódy, Henrik Hajós, Géza Kiss, Zoltán von Halmay)
1908   GBR (John Henry Derbyshire, Paul Radmilovic, William Foster, Henry Taylor)
1912   AUS (Cecil Healy, Malcolm Champion, Leslie Boardman, Harold Hardwick)
1920   USA (Perry McGillivray, Pua Kela Kealoha, Norman Ross, Duke Paoa Kahanamoku)
1924   USA (Wallace O'Connor, Harry Glancy, Ralph Breyer, John Weissmuller)
1928   USA (Austin Clapp, Walter Laufer, George Kojac, John Weissmuller)
1932   JPN (Yasuji Miyazaki, Masanori Yusa, Takashi Yokoyama, Hisakichi Toyoda)
1936   JPN (Masanori Yusa, Shigeo Sugiura, Masaharu Taguchi, Shigeo Arai)
1948   USA (Walter Ris, James McLane, Wallace Wolf, William Smith)
1952   USA (Wayne Moore, William Woolsey, Ford Konno, James McLane)
1956   AUS (Kevin O'Halloran, John Devitt, Murray Rose, Jon Henricks)
1960   USA (George Harrison, Richard Blick, Michael Troy, F. Jeffrey Farrell)
1964   USA (Stephen Clark, Roy Saari, Gary Ilman, Donald Schollander)
1968   USA (John Nelson, Stephen Rerych, Mark Spitz, Donald Schollander)
1972   USA (John Kinsella, Frederick Tyler, Steven Genter, Mark Spitz)
1976   USA (Mike Bruner, Bruce Furniss, John Naber, Jim Montgomery)
1980   URS (Sergei Kopilakov, Vladimir Salnikov, Ivar Stukolkin, Andrei Krylov)

400-Meter Medley Relay

1960   USA (Frank McKinney, Paul Hait, Lance Larson, F. Jeffrey Farrell)

1964   USA (H. Thompson Mann, William Craig, Fred Schmidt, Stephen Clark)
1968   USA (Charles Hickcox, Donald McKenzie, Douglas Russell, Kenneth Walsh)
1972   USA (Mike Stamm, Tom Bruce, Mark Spitz, Jerry Heidenreich)
1976   USA (John Naber, John Hencken, Matt Vogel, Jim Montgomery)
1980   AUS (Mark Kerry, Peter Evans, Mark Tonelli, Neil Brooks)

Springboard Diving

1908   Albert Zürner, GER
1912   Paul Günther, GER
1920   Louis Kuehn, USA
1924   Albert White, USA
1928   Peter Desjardins, USA
1932   Michael Galitzen, USA
1936   Richard Degener, USA
1948   Bruce Harlan, USA
1952   David Browning, USA
1956   Robert Clotworthy, USA
1960   Gary Tobian, USA
1964   Kenneth Sitzberger, USA
1968   Bernie Wrightson, USA
1972   Vladimir Vasin, URS
1976   Phil Boggs, USA
1980   Aleksandr Portnov, URS

High Diving

1904   George Sheldon, USA
1906   Gottlob Walz, GER
1908   Hjalmar Johansson, SWE
1912   Erik Adlerz, SWE
1920   Clarence Pinkston, USA
1924   Albert White, USA
1928   Peter Desjardins, USA
1932   Harold Smith, USA
1936   Marshall Wayne, USA
1948   Samuel Lee, USA
1952   Samuel Lee, USA
1956   Joaquin Capilla Pérez, MEX
1960   Robert Webster, USA
1964   Robert Webster, USA
1968   Klaus Dibiasi, ITA
1972   Klaus Dibiasi, ITA
1976   Klaus Dibiasi, ITA
1980   Falk Hoffmann, GDR

DISCONTINUED EVENTS

50-Yard Freestyle

1904   Zoltán von Halmay, HUN

100-Meter Freestyle (Sailors)

1896   Ioannis Malokinis, GRE

Obstacle Event

1900   Frederick Lane, AUS

400-Meter Breaststroke

1904   Georg Zacharias, GER
1912   Walter Bathe, GER
1920   Häkan Malmroth, SWE

880-Yard Freestyle

1904   Emil Rausch, GER

4,000-Meter Freestyle

1900   John Jarvis, GBR

Underwater Swimming

| 1900 | Charles de Vendeville, FRA |

Plunge for Distance

| 1904 | W. E. Dickey, USA |

Plain High Diving

1912	Erik Adlerz, SWE
1920	Arvid Wallman, SWE
1924	Richmond Eve, AUS

200-Meter Team Swimming

| 1900 | GER (Ernst Hoppenberg, Max Hainle, Max Schöne, Julius Frey, Herbert von Petersdorff) |

200-Yard Relay

| 1904 | USA (Joseph Ruddy, Leo Goodwin, Louis Handley, Charles Daniels) |

200-Meter Individual Medley

| 1968 | Charles Hickcox, USA |
| 1972 | Gunnar Larsson, SWE |

400-Meter Freestyle Relay

1964	USA (Stephen Clark, Michael Austin, Gary Ilman, Donald Schollander)
1968	USA (Zachary Zorn, Stephen Rerych, Mark Spitz, Kenneth Walsh)
1972	USA (David Edgar, Mark Spitz, J. Murphy, J. Heidenreich)

WOMEN

100-Meter Freestyle

1912	Fanny Durack, AUS
1920	Ethelda Bleibtrey, USA
1924	Ethel Lackie, USA
1928	Albina Osipowich, USA
1932	Helene Madison, USA
1936	Hendrika Mastenbroek, HOL
1948	Greta Andersen, DEN
1952	Katalin Szöke, HUN
1956	Dawn Fraser, AUS
1960	Dawn Fraser, AUS
1964	Dawn Fraser, AUS
1968	Jan Henne, USA
1972	Sandra Neilson, USA
1976	Kornelia Ender, GDR
1980	Barbara Krause, GDR

200-Meter Freestyle

1968	Debbie Meyer, USA
1972	Shane Gould, AUS
1976	Kornelia Ender, GDR
1980	Barbara Krause, GDR

400-Meter Freestyle

1920	Ethelda Bleibtrey (300 m), USA
1924	Martha Norelius, USA
1928	Martha Norelius, USA
1932	Helene Madison, USA
1936	Hendrika Mastenbroek, HOL
1948	Ann Curtis, USA
1952	Valéria Gyenge, HUN
1956	Lorraine Crapp, AUS
1960	Susan Christine Von Saltza, USA
1964	Virginia Duenkel, USA

1968	Debbie Meyer, USA
1972	Shane Gould, AUS
1976	Petra Thuemer, GDR
1980	Ines Diers, GDR

800-Meter Freestyle

1968	Debbie Meyer, USA
1972	Keena Rothhammer, USA
1976	Petra Thuemer, GDR
1980	Michelle Ford, AUS

100-Meter Backstroke

1924	Sybil Bauer, USA
1928	Maria Johanna Braun, HOL
1932	Eleanor Holm, USA
1936	Dina Wilhelmina Senff, HOL
1948	Karen Margrete Harup, DEN
1952	Joan Harrison, SAF
1956	Judy Grinham, GBR
1960	Lynn Burke, USA
1964	Cathy Ferguson, USA
1968	Kaye Hall, USA
1972	Melissa Belote, USA
1976	Ulrike Richter, GDR
1980	Rica Reinisch, GDR

200-Meter Backstroke

1968	Lillian (Pokey) Watson, USA
1972	Melissa Belote, USA
1976	Ulrike Richter, GDR
1980	Rica Reinisch, GDR

100-Meter Breaststroke

1968	Djurdjica Bjedov, YUG
1972	Cathy Carr, USA
1976	Hannelore Anke, GDR
1980	Ute Geweniger, GDR

200-Meter Breaststroke

1924	Lucy Morton, GBR
1928	Hilde Schrader, GER
1932	Claire Dennis, AUS
1936	Hideko Maehata, JPN
1948	Petronella van Vliet, HOL
1952	Éva Székely, HUN
1956	Ursula Happe, GER
1960	Anita Lonsbrough, GBR
1964	Galina Prozumenschtschikova, URS
1968	Sharon Wichman, USA
1972	Beverly Whitfield, AUS
1976	Marina Koshevaia, URS
1980	Lina Kachushite, URS

100-Meter Butterfly

1956	Shelley Mann, USA
1960	Carolyn Schuler, USA
1964	Sharon Stouder, USA
1968	Lynette McClements, AUS
1972	Mayumi Aoki, JPN
1976	Kornelia Ender, GDR
1980	Caren Metschuck, GDR

200-Meter Butterfly

1968	Ada Kok, HOL
1972	Karen Moe, USA
1976	Andrea Pollack, GDR
1980	Ines Geissler, GDR

400-Meter Individual Medley

1964	Donna De Varona, USA
1968	Claudia Kolb, USA
1972	Gail Neall, AUS
1976	Ulrike Tauber, GDR
1980	Petra Schneider, GDR

400-Meter Freestyle Relay

1912	GBR (Bella Moore, Jennie Fletcher, Annie Spiers, Irene Steer)
1920	USA (Margaret Woodbridge, Frances Schroth, Irene Guest, Ethelda Bleibtrey)
1924	USA (Gertrude Ederle, Euphrasia Donnelly, Ethel Lackie, Mariechen Wehselau)
1928	USA (Adelaide Lambert, Eleonora Garatti, Albina Osipowich, Martha Norelius)
1932	USA (Josephine McKim, Helen Johns, Eleanor Saville-Garatti, Helene Madison)
1936	HOL (Johanna Selbach, Catherina Wagner, Willemijntje den Ouden, Hendrika Mastenbroeck)
1948	USA (Marie Corridon, Thelma Kalama, Brenda Helser, Ann Curtis)
1952	HUN (Ilona Novák, Judit Temes, Éva Novák, Katalin Szöke)
1956	AUS (Dawn Fraser, Faith Leech, Sandra Morgan, Lorraine Crapp)
1960	USA (Joan Spillane, Shirley Stobs, Carolyn Wood, Susan Christine Von Saltza)
1964	USA (Sharon Stouder, Donna De Varona, Lillian "Pokey" Watson, Kathleen Ellis)
1968	USA (Jane Barkman, Linda Gustavson, Susan Pedersen, Jan Henne)
1972	USA (Sandra Neilson, Jennifer Kemp, Jane Barkman, Shirley Babashoff)
1976	USA (Kim Peyton, Wendy Boglioli, Jill Sterkel, Shirley Babashoff)
1980	GDR (Barbara Krause, Caren Metschuck, Ines Diers, Sarina Hulsenbeck)

400-Meter Medley Relay

1960	USA (Lynn Burke, Patty Kempner, Carolyn Schuler, Susan Christine Von Saltza)
1964	USA (Cathy Ferguson, Cynthia Goyette, Sharon Stouder, Kathleen Ellis)
1968	USA (Kaye Hall, Catie Ball, Ellie Daniel, Susan Pedersen)
1972	USA (Melissa Belote, Catherine Carr, Deena Deardruff, Sandra Neilson)
1976	GDR (Ulrike Richter, Hannelore Anke, Andrea Pollack, Kornelia Ender)
1980	GDR (Rica Reinisch, Ute Geweniger, Andrea Pollack, Caren Metschuck)

Springboard Diving

1920	Aileen Riggin, USA
1924	Elizabeth Becker, USA
1928	Helen Meany, USA
1932	Georgia Coleman, USA
1936	Marjorie Gestring, USA
1948	Victoria Draves, USA
1952	Patricia McCormick, USA
1956	Patricia McCormick, USA
1960	Ingrid Krämer, GER
1964	Ingrid Engel-Krämer, GER
1968	Sue Gossick, USA
1972	Micki King, USA

| 1976 | Jennifer Chandler, USA |
| 1980 | Irina Kalinina, URS |

High Diving

1912	Greta Johansson, SWE
1920	Stefani Fryland-Clausen, DEN
1924	Caroline Smith, USA
1928	Elizabeth Pinkston-Becker, USA
1932	Dorothy Poynton, USA
1936	Dorothy Hill-Poynton, USA
1948	Victoria Draves, USA
1952	Patricia McCormick, USA
1956	Patricia McCormick, USA
1960	Ingrid Krämer, GER
1964	Lesley Bush, USA
1968	Milena Duchková, TCH
1972	Ulrika Knape, SWE
1976	Elena Vaytsekhovskaia, URS
1980	Martina Jaschke, GDR

DISCONTINUED EVENTS

200-Meter Individual Medley

| 1968 | Claudia Kolb, USA |
| 1972 | Shane Gould, AUS |

Volleyball

MEN

1964	URS	1976	POL
1968	URS	1980	URS
1972	JPN		

WOMEN

1964	JPN	1976	JPN
1968	URS	1980	URS
1972	URS		

Water Polo

1900	GBR	1948	ITA
1904	USA	1952	HUN
1908	GBR	1956	HUN
1912	GBR	1960	ITA
1920	GBR	1964	HUN
1924	FRA	1968	YUG
1928	GER	1972	URS
1932	HUN	1976	HUN
1936	HUN	1980	URS

Weightlifting

Flyweight
(52 kg, 114 lbs 10 oz)

1972	Zygmunt Smalcerz, POL
1976	Aleksandr Voronin, URS
1980	Kanibek Osmanoliev, URS

Bantamweight
(56 kg, 123 lbs 7 oz)

1948	Joseph N. De Pietro, USA
1952	Ivan Udodov, URS
1956	Charles Vinci, USA
1960	Charles Vinci, USA
1964	Aleksey Vakhonin, URS
1968	Mohammad Nasiri, IRN
1972	Imre Foeldi, HUN
1976	Norair Nurikyan, BUL
1980	Daniel Nunez, CUB

Featherweight
(60 kg, 132 lbs 4 oz)

1920	Frans de Haes, BEL
1924	Pierino Gabetti, ITA
1928	Franz Andrysek, AUT
1932	Raymond Suvigny, FRA
1936	Anthony Terlazzo, USA
1948	Mahmoud Fayad, EGY
1952	Rafael Tschimischkyan, URS
1956	Isaac Berger, USA
1960	Yevgeny Minayev, URS
1964	Yoshinobu Miyake, JPN
1968	Yoshinobu Miyake, JPN
1972	Norair Nurikan, BUL
1976	Nikolai Kolesnikov, URS
1980	Viktor Mazin, URS

Lightweight
(67.5 kg, 148 lbs 13 oz)

1920	Alfred Neuland, EST
1924	Edmond Decottignies, FRA
1928	Kurt Helbig, GER, Hans Haas, AUT (tie)
1932	René Duverger, FRA
1936	Anwar Mohammad Mesbah, EGY, Robert Fein, AUT (tie)
1948	Ibrahim Shams, EGY
1952	Thomas Kono, USA
1956	Igor Rybak, URS
1960	Viktor Buschuyev, URS
1964	Waldemar Baszanowski, POL
1968	Waldemar Baszanowski, POL
1972	Mukharbi Kirzhinov, URS
1976	Piotr Koroi, URS
1980	Yanko Roussev, BUL

Middleweight
(75 kg, 165 lbs 6 oz)

1920	Henri Gance, FRA
1924	Carlo Galimberti, ITA
1928	Roger François, FRA
1932	Rudolf Ismayr, GER
1936	Khadr el Touni, EGY
1948	Frank Spellman, USA
1952	Peter George, USA
1956	Fyodor Bogdanovsky, URS
1960	Aleksandr Kurynov, URS
1964	Hans Zdražila, TCH
1968	Viktor Kurentsov, URS
1972	Yordan Bikov, BUL
1976	Yordan Mitkov, BUL
1980	Assen Zlatev, BUL

Light Heavyweight
(82.5 kg, 181 lbs 14 oz)

1920	Ernest Cadine, FRA
1924	Charles Rigoulot, FRA
1928	Sayed Nosseir, EGY
1932	Louis Hostin, FRA
1936	Louis Hostin, FRA
1948	Stanley Stanczyk, USA
1952	Trofim Lomakin, URS
1956	Thomas Kono, USA
1960	Ireneusz Palinski, POL
1964	Rudolf Plukfelder, URS
1968	Boris Selitsky, URS
1972	Leif Jenssen, NOR
1976	Valeri Shary, URS
1980	Yurik Vardanyan, URS

Middle Heavyweight
(90 kg, 198 lbs 7 oz)

1952	Norbert Schemansky, USA
1956	Arkady Vorobyov, URS
1960	Arkady Vorobyov, URS
1964	Vladimir Golovanov, URS
1968	Kaarlo Kangasniemi, FIN

1972	Andon Nikolov, BUL
1976	David Rigert, URS
1980	Peter Baczako, HUN

First Heavyweight
(100 kg, 220 lbs 7 oz)

| 1980 | Ota Zaremba, TCH |

Second Heavyweight[1]

1896	Launceston Elliott, GBR (one-hand lift)
	Viggo Jensen, DEN (two-hand lift)
1904	Oscar Paul Osthoff, USA (dumbbell competition)
	Perikles Kakousis, GRE (two-hand lift)
1906	Josef Steinbach, AUT (one-hand lift)
	Dimitrios Tofalos, GRE (two-hand lift)
1920	Filippo Bottino, ITA
1924	Giuseppe Tonani, ITA
1928	Josef Strassberger, GER
1932	Jaroslav Skobla, TCH
1936	Josef Manger, GER
1948	John Davis, USA
1952	John Davis, USA
1956	Paul E. Anderson, USA
1960	Yury Vlassov, URS
1964	Leonid Schabotinsky, URS
1968	Leonid Schabotinsky, URS
1972	Yan Talts, URS
1976	Yuri Zaitsev, URS
1980	Leonid Taranenko, URS

Super Heavyweight
(above 110 kg, 242 lbs 8 oz)

1972	Vasili Alekseyev, URS
1976	Vasili Alekseyev, URS
1980	Sultan Rakhmanov, URS

[1] 1896–1906: open; 1920–1952: above 82.5 kg (181 lbs 14 oz); 1956–1968: above 90 kg (198 lbs 7 oz); 1972–1980: 110 kg (242 lbs 8 oz)

Wrestling

FREESTYLE

Light Flyweight (Paperweight)

1904	Robert Curry, USA
1972	Roman Dmitriev, URS
1976	Khassan Issaev, BUL
1980	Claudio Pollio, ITA

Flyweight

1904	George Mehnert, USA
1948	Lennart Viitala, FIN
1952	Hasan Gemici, TUR
1956	Mirian Tsalkalamanidze, URS
1960	Ahmet Bilek, TUR
1964	Yoshikatsu Yoshida, JPN
1968	Shigeo Nakata, JPN
1972	Kymomi Kato, JPN
1976	Yuji Takada, JPN
1980	Anatoly Beloglazov, URS

Bantamweight

1904	Isaac Niflot, USA
1908	George N. Mehnert, USA
1924	Kustaa Pihlajamäki, FIN
1928	Kaarlo Mäkinen, FIN

Bantamweight (Con't.)

1932	Robert E. Pearce, USA
1936	Ödön Zombori, HUN
1948	Nasuh Akar, TUR
1952	Shohachi Ishii, JPN
1956	Mustafa Dagistanli, TUR
1960	Terrence McCann, USA
1964	Yojiro Uetake, JPN
1968	Yojiro Uetake, JPN
1972	Hideaki Yanagida, JPN
1976	Vladimir Yumin, URS
1980	Sergei Beloglazov, URS

Featherweight

1904	Benjamin Bradshaw, USA
1908	George S. Dole, USA
1920	Charles E. Ackerly, USA
1924	Robin Reed, USA
1928	Allie Morrison, USA
1932	Hermanni Pihlajamäki, FIN
1936	Kustaa Pihlajamäki, FIN
1948	Gazenfer Bilge, TUR
1952	Bayram Şit, TUR
1956	Shozo Sasahara, JPN
1960	Mustafa Dagistanli, TUR
1964	Osamu Watanabe, JPN
1968	Masaaki Kaneko, JPN
1972	Zaga Abdulbekov, URS
1976	Jung-Mo Yang, KOR
1980	Magomedgasan Abushev, URS

Lightweight

1904	Otto Roehm, USA
1908	George de Relwyskow, GBF
1920	Kalle Anttila, FIN
1924	Russell Vis, USA
1928	Osvald Käpp, EST
1932	Charles Pacôme, FRA
1936	Károly Kárpáti, HUN
1948	Celal Atik, TUR
1952	Olle Anderberg, SWE
1956	Emamali Habibi, IRN
1960	Shelby Wilson, USA
1964	Enyu Valtschev (Dimov), BUL
1968	Abdollah Movahed Ardabili, IRN
1972	Dan Gable, USA
1976	Pavel Pinigin, URS
1980	Saipulla Absaidov, URS

Welterweight

1904	Charles Ericksen, USA
1924	Hermann Gehri, SUI
1928	Arvo Haavisto, FIN
1932	Jack F. Van Bebber, USA
1936	Frank Lewis, USA
1948	Yaşar Dogu, TUR
1952	William Smith, USA
1956	Mitsuo Ikeda, JPN
1960	Douglas Blubaugh, USA
1964	Ismail Ogan, TUR
1968	Mahmut Atalay, TUR
1972	Wayne Wells, USA
1976	Jiichiro Date, JPN
1980	Valentin Raitchev, BUL

Middleweight

1908	Stanley Bacon, GBR
1920	Eino Leino, FIN
1924	Fritz Hagmann, SUI
1928	Ernst Kyburz, SUI
1932	Ivar Johansson, SWE
1936	Emile Poilvé, FRA
1948	Glen Brand, USA
1952	David Tsimakuridze, URS
1956	Nikola Stantschev, BUL
1960	Hasan Güngör, TUR
1964	Prodan Gardschev, BUL
1968	Boris Gurevitsch, URS

1972	Levan Tediashvili, URS
1976	John Peterson, USA
1980	Ismail Abilov, BUL

Light Heightweight

1920	Anders Larsson, SWE
1924	John Spellman, USA
1928	Thure Sjöstedt, SWE
1932	Peter J. Mehringer, USA
1936	Knut Fridell, SWE
1948	Henry Wittenberg, USA
1952	Wiking Palm, SWE
1956	Gholam-Reza Takhti, IRN
1960	Ismet Atli, TUR
1964	Aleksandr Medved, URS
1968	Ahmet Ayik, TUR
1972	Ben Peterson, USA
1976	Levan Tediashvili, URS
1980	Sanasar Oganesyan, URS

Heavyweight

1904	B. Hansen, USA
1908	George C. O'Kelly, GBR/IRL
1920	Robert Roth, SUI
1924	Harry Steele, USA
1928	Johan C. Richthoff, SWE
1932	Johan C. Richthoff, SWE
1936	Kristjan Palusalu, EST
1948	Gyula Bóbis, HUN
1952	Arsen Mekokischvili, URS
1956	Hamit Kaplan, TUR
1960	Wilfried Dietrich, GER
1964	Aleksandr Ivanitsky, URS
1968	Aleksandr Medved, URS
1972	Ivan Yarygin, URS
1976	Ivan Yarygin, URS
1980	Ilya Mate, URS

Super Heavyweight

1972	Aleksandr Medved, URS
1976	Soslan Andiyev, URS
1980	Soslan Andiyev, URS

GRECO-ROMAN STYLE

Light Flyweight (Paperweight)

1972	Gheorghe Berceanu, ROM
1976	Alexei Shumakov, URS
1980	Zaksylik Ushkempirov, URS

Flyweight

1948	Pietro Lombardi, ITA
1952	Boris Gurevitsch, URS
1956	Nikolay Solovyov, URS
1960	Dumitru Privulescu, ROM
1964	Tsutomu Hanahara, JPN
1968	Petar Kirov, BUL
1972	Petar Kirov, BUL
1976	Vitaly Konstantinov, URS
1980	Vakhtang Blagidze, URS

Bantamweight

1924	Eduard Pütsep, EST
1928	Kurt Leucht, GER
1932	Jakob Brendel, GER
1936	Márton Lörincz, HUN
1948	Kurt Pettersén, SWE
1952	Imre Hódos, HUN
1956	Konstantin Vyrupayev, URS
1960	Oleg Karavayev, URS
1964	Masamitsu Ichiguchi, JAP
1968	János Varga, HUN
1972	Rustem Kazakov, USR
1976	Pertti Ukkola, FIN
1980	Shamil Serikov, USR

Featherweight

1912	Kaarlo Koskelo, FIN
1920	Oskari Friman, FIN
1924	Kalle Anttila, FIN
1928	Voldemar Väli, EST
1932	Giovanni Gozzi, ITA
1936	Yasar Erkan, TUR
1948	Mehmet Oktav, TUR
1952	Yakov Punkin, URS
1956	Rauno Mäkinen, FIN
1960	Müzahir Sille, TUR
1964	Imre Polyák, HUN
1968	Roman Rurua, URS
1972	Gheorghi Markov, BUL
1976	Kazimier Lipien, POL
1980	Stilianos Migiakis, GRE

Lightweight

1906	Rudolf Watzl, AUT
1908	Enrico Porro, ITA
1912	Eemil Väre, FIN
1920	Eemil Väre, FIN
1924	Oskani Friman, FIN
1928	Lajos Keresztes, HUN
1932	Erik Malmberg, SWE
1936	Lauri Koskela, FIN
1948	Gustaf Freij, SWE
1952	Schazam Safin, URS
1956	Kyösti Lehtonen, FIN
1960	Avtandil Koridze, URS
1964	Kazim Ayvaz, TUR
1968	Munji Mumemura, JPN
1972	Shamil Khisamutdinov, URS
1976	Suren Nalbandyan, URS
1980	Stefan Rusu, ROM

Welterweight

1932	Ivar Johansson, SWE
1936	Rudolf Svedberg, SWE
1948	Gösta Andersson, SWE
1952	Miklós Szilvási, HUN
1956	Mithat Bayrak, TUR
1960	Mithat Bayrak, TUR
1964	Anatoly Kolesov, URS
1968	Rudolf Vesper, GDR
1972	Vitezslav Macha, TCH
1976	Anatoli Bykov, USR
1980	Ferenc Kocsis, HUN

Middleweight

1906	Verner Weckman, FIN
1908	Frithiof Märtensson, SWE
1912	Claes Johansson, SWE
1920	Carl Westergren, SWE
1924	Edvard Vesterlund, FIN
1928	Väinö A. Kokkinen, FIN
1932	Väinö A. Kokkinen, FIN
1936	Ivar Johansson, SWE
1948	Axel Grönberg, SWE
1952	Axel Grönberg, SWE
1956	Givy Kartoziya, URS
1960	Dimiter Dobrev, BUL
1964	Branislav Simič, YUG
1968	Lothar Metz, GDR
1972	Csaba Hegedus, HUN
1976	Momir Petkovic, YUG
1980	Gennady Korban, URS

Light Heavyweight

1908	Verner Weckman, FIN
1912	No gold medalist
1920	Claes Johansson, SWE
1924	Carl Westergren, SWE
1928	Ibrahim Moustafa, EGY
1932	Rudolf Svensson, SWE
1936	Axel Cadier, SWE
1948	Karl-Erik Nilsson, SWE

1952	Kaelpo Gröndahl, FIN
1956	Valentin Nikolayev, URS
1960	Tevfik Kis, TUR
1964	Boyan Radev, BUL
1968	Boyan Radev, BUL
1972	Valeri Rezantsev, URS
1976	Valeri Rezantsev, URS
1980	Norbert Nottny, HUN

Heavyweight

1896	Carl Schuhmann, GER
1906	Sören Marius Jensen, DEN
1908	Richárd Weisz, HUN
1912	Yrjö Saarela, FIN
1920	Adolf Lindfors, FIN
1924	Henri Deglane, FRA
1928	Rudolf Svensson, SWE
1932	Carl Westergren, SWE
1936	Kristjan Palusalu, EST
1948	Ahmet Kireçci, TUR
1952	Johannes Kotkas, URS
1956	Anatoly Parfenov, URS
1960	Ivan Bogdan, URS
1964	István Kozma, HUN
1968	István Kozma, HUN
1972	Nikolae Martinescu, ROM
1976	Nikolai Bolboshin, URS
1980	Gheorghi Raikov, BUL

Super Heavyweight

1972	Anatoly Roshin, URS
1976	Aleksandr Kolchinski, URS
1980	Aleksandr Kolchinski, URS

Yachting

Dragon Class

1948	NOR (Thor Thorvaldsen, Sigve Lie, Haakon Barfod)
1952	NOR (Thor Thorvaldsen, Sigve Lie, Haakon Barfod)
1956	SWE (Folke Bohlin, Bengt Palmquist, Leif Wikström)
1960	GRE (Crown Prince Constantine, Odysseus Eskidjoglou, Georgios Zaimis)
1964	DEN (Ole Berntsen, Christian von Bülow, Ole Poulsen)
1968	USA (George Friedrichs, Barton Jahncke, Gerald Schreck)
1972	AUS (John Bruce Cueno, Thomas Anderson, John Shaw)

Finn Monotype Class (Dinghy)

1920	HOL (Johannes Joseph Antonius Hin, Franciscus Fidelis J. Hin) —12-foot dinghy
	GBR (F. A. Richards, T. Hedberg) —18-foot dinghy
1924	Léon Huybrechts, BEL
1928	Sven Thorell, SWE
1932	Jacques Lebrun, FRA
1936	Daniel Marinus J. Kagchelland, HOL
1948	Paul Elvström, DEN
1952	Paul Elvström, DEN
1956	Paul Elvström, DEN
1960	Paul Elvström, DEN
1964	Wilhelm Kuhweide, GER
1968	Valentin Mankin, URS
1972	Serge Maury, FRA
1976	Jocken Schumann, GDR
1980	Ekso Rechardt, FIN

Flying Dutchman Class

1960	NOR (Peder Lunde, Jr., Björn Bergvall)
1964	NZL (Helmer Pedersen, Earle Welles)
1968	GBR (Rodney Pattison, Iain S. MacDonald-Smith)
1972	GBR (Rodney Pattison, Christopher Davies)
1976	GER (Eckart Diesch, Joerg Diesch)
1980	ESP (Alesandro Abascal, Miguel Noguer)

470 Class

1976	GER (Frank Huebner, Harro Bode)
1980	BRA (Marcos Soares, Eduardo Penido)

Soling Class

1972	USA (Harry Melges)
1976	DEN (Poul Jensen, Valdemar Bandolowski, Erik Hansen)
1980	DEN (Poul Jensen, Valdemar Bandolowski, Erik Hansen)

Star Class

1932	USA (Gilbert Gray, Andrew Libano, Jr.)
1936	GER (Peter Bischoff, Hans-Joachim Weise)
1948	USA (Hilary Smart, Paul Smart)
1952	ITA (Agostino Straulino, Nicolo Rode)
1956	USA (Herbert Williams, Lawrence Low)
1960	URS (Timir Pinegin, Fyodor Schutkov)
1964	BAH (Durward Knowles, Cecil Cooke)
1968	USA (Lowell North, Peter Barrett)
1972	AUS (David Forbes)
1980	URS (Valentin Mankin, Alexander Muzyschenko)

Tempest Class

1972	URS (Valentin Mankin)
1976	SWE (John Albrechtson, Inguar Hansson)

Tornado Class

1976	GBR (Reginald White, John Osborn)
1980	BRA (Alexander Welter, Lars Sigurd Bjorkstrom)

DISCONTINUED EVENTS

5.5-Meter Class

1952	USA (Britton Chance, Sumner White, Edgar White, Michael Schoettle)
1956	SWE (Lars Thörn, Hjalmar Karlsson, Sture Stork)
1960	USA (George O'Day, James Hunt, David Smith)
1964	AUS (William Northam, James Sargeant, Peter O'Donnel)
1968	SWE (Ulf Sundelin, Jörgen Sundelin, Peter Sundelin)

6-Meter Class

1908	GBR (G. U. Laws, T. D. McMeekin, Charles W. H. Crichton)
1912	FRA (Amédée Thubé, Gaston Thubé, Jacques Thubé)
1920	NOR (Andreas Brecke, Paal Kaasen, Ingolf Röd)
1924	NOR (Eugen Lunde, Christopher Dahl, Anders Lundgren)
1928	NOR (Crown Prince Olav, Johan Anker, Erik Anker, Haakon Bryhn)
1932	SWE (Tore Holm, Martin Hindorff, Olle Åkerlund, Ake Bergqvist)
1936	GBR (Charles Leaf, Christopher Boardman, Miles Belville, Russell Harmer, Leonard Martin)
1948	USA (Herman Whiton, Alfred Loomis, James Weekes, James Smith, Michael Mooney)
1952	USA (Herman Whiton, Eric Ridder, Julian Roosevelt, John Morgan, Everard Endt, Emelyn Whiton)

1907 Rating

1920	BEL (Emile Cornellie, Florimond Cornellie, Fréderic-Albert Bruynseels)

6.5-Meter Class

1920	HOL (Johan Carp, Petrus Wernink, Bernard Carp)

7-Meter Class

1908	GBR (Charles Rivett-Carnac, Norman Bingley, R. T. Dixon, Frances Clytie Rivett-Carnac)
1920	GBR (Cyril Macey Wright, Dorothy Winifred Wright, R. H. Coleman, W. J. Maddison)

8-Meter Class

1908	GBR (Blair Cochrane, A. N. L. Wood, Hugh Sutton, J. E. Rhodes, C. R. Campbell)
1912	NOR (Thoralf Glad, Th. Valentin Aas, Andreas Brecke, Torleiv Corneliussen, Christian Jebe)
1920	NOR (Magnus Konow, Reidar Marthiniussen, Ragnar Vig, Thorleif Christoffersen)
1924	NOR (August Ringvold, Sr., Rick Bockelie, Harald Hagen, Ingar Nielsen, August Ringvold, Jr.)
1928	FRA (Donatien Bouché, André Lesauvage, Jean Lesieur, Virginie Hériot, Charles de la Sablière, André Derrien)
1932	USA (Owen Churchill, John Biby, Jr., William Cooper, Carl Dorsey, Robert Sutton, Alan Morgan, Pierpont Davis, Alphonse Burnand, Jr., Thomas Webster, John Huettner, Richard Moore, Kenneth Carey)
1936	ITA (Giovanni Leone Reggio, Bruno Bianchi, Luigi De Manincor, Domenico Mordini, Luigi Mino Poggi, Enrico Massimo Poggi)

1907 Rating

1920 NOR (August Ringvold, Sr., Th. Holbye, Tell Wagie, Kristoffer Olsen, A. Bruun Jacobsen)

10-Meter Class

1912 SWE (Carl Hellström, Jr., Erik Wallerius, Harald Wallerius, Humbert Lundén, Herman Nyberg, Harry Rosenwärd, Paul Isberg, Filip Ericsson)

1919 Rating

1920 NOR (Archer Arentz, Willy Gilbert, Robert Gjertsen, Arne Sejersted, Halfdan Schjött, Trygve Schjött, Otto Falkenberg)

1907 Rating

1920 NOR (Erik Herseth, Sigurd Holter, Ingar Nielsen, Ole Sörensen, Gunnar Jamvold, Petter Jamvold, Claus Juell)

12-Meter Class

1908 GBR (Thomas Glen-Coats, J. H. Downes, John Buchanan, J. C. Bunten, A. D. Downes, David Dunlop, John Mackenzie, Albert Martin, Gerald Tait, J. S. Aspin)
1912 NOR (Johan Anker, Alfred Larsen, Nils Bertelsen, Halfdan Hansen, Magnus Konow, Petter Larsen, Eilert Falch Lund, Fritz Staib, Arnfinn Heje, Gustav Thaulow)

1907 Rating

1920 NOR (Henrik Östervold, Jan Östervold, Ole Östervold, Hans Stoermann Naess, Lauritz Christiansen, Halvor Mögster, Rasmus Birkeland, Halvor Birkeland, Kristen Östervold)

1919 Rating

1920 NOR (Johan Friele, Olav Örvig, Arthur Allers, Christen Wiese, Martin Borthen, Egil Reimers, Kaspar Hassel, Thor Örvig, Erik Örvig)

Sharpie

1956 NZL (Peter Mander, John Cropp)

30 m²

1920 SWE (Gösta Lundqvist, Rolf Steffenburg, Gunnar Bengtsson, Axel Calvert)

40 m²

1920 SWE (Tore Holm, Yngve Holm, Axel Rydin, Georg Tengvall)

Swallow

1948 GBR (Stewart Morris, David Bond)

Open Class

1900 GBR (Lorne C. Currie, J. H. Gretton, Linton Hope)

.5-Ton Class

1900 Texier, FRA

.5-1.0-Ton Class

1900 GBR (Lorne C. Currie, J. H. Gretton, Linton Hope)

1-2-Ton Class

1900 GER (Martin Wiesner, Heinrich Peters, Ottokar Weise, Georg Naue)

2-3-Ton Class

1900 E. Shaw, GBR

3-10-Ton Class

1900 Howard Taylor, USA

10-20-Ton Class

1900 FRA (E. Billard, P. Perquer)

Discontinued Sports

CRICKET

1900 FRA (T. H. Jordan, A. J. Schneidau, R. Horne, H. Terry, F. Roques, W. Anderson, D. Robinson, W. T. Attrill, W. Browning, A. McEvoy, P. H. Tomalin, J. Braid)

CROQUET

1900 Aumoitte, FRA—Singles, 1 ball
Waydelick, FRA—Singles, 2 balls
FRA (Johin, Aumoitte)—Doubles

FIELD HANDBALL[1]

1936 GER (Heinz Körvers, Arthur Knautz, Willy Bandholz, Hans Keiter, Wilhelm Brinkmann, Georg Dascher, Erich Herrmann, Hans Theilig, Helmut Berthold, Alfred Klingler, Fritz Fromm, Karl Kreutzberg, Heinrich Keimig, Wilhelm Muller, Kurt Dossin, Rudolf Stahl, Hermann Hansen, Fritz Spengler, Edgar Reinhardt, Günther Ortmann, Wilhelm Baumann, Helmut Braselmann)

[1] Indoor Team Handball was introduced in 1972. See page 393.

GOLF

Men

1900 Charles E. Sands, USA
1904 George Seymour Lyon, CAN

Team

1904 USA (Charles C. Egan, R. E. Hunter, Kenneth Edwards, C. E. Smoot, Walter Egan, Ned Sawyer, Ned Cummins, Mason E. Phelps, Nathan Moore, Warren Wood)

Women

1900 Margaret Abbott, USA

JEU DE PAUME

1908 Jay Gould, USA

LACROSSE

1904 CAN (George Cloutier, George Cattanach, Benjamin Jamieson, Jack Flett, George Bretz, Eli Blanchard, Hilliard Laidlaw, H. Lyle, W. Brennaugh, L. H. Pentland, Sandy Cowan, William Laurie Burns, William F. L. Orris)
1908 CAN (Frank J. Dixon, "Doc" George Campbell, Angus Dillon, Richard Louis Duckett, George H. Rennie, Clarence McKerrow, Alexander T. Turnbull, Henry Hoobin, Ernest Hamilton, John Broderick, Thomas Gorman, Patrick "Paddy" Brennan)

LAWN TENNIS

Men's Singles

1896 John Pius Boland, GBR/IRL
1900 Hugh Lawrence Doherty, GBR
1904 Beals C. Wright, USA
1906 Max Decugis, FRA
1908 Josiah George Ritchie, GBR, Arthur Wentworth Gore, GBR —Indoor Courts
1912 Charles Lyndhurst Winslow, SAF, André H. Gobert, FRA— Indoor Courts
1920 Louis Raymond, SAF
1924 Vincent Richards, USA

Men's Doubles

1896 GBR-IRL/GER (John Pius Boland, Fritz Traun)
1900 GBR (Reginald Frank Doherty, Hugh Lawrence Doherty)
1904 USA (Edgar W. Leonard, Beals C. Wright)
1906 FRA (Max Decugis, Maurice Germot)
1908 GBR (George W. Hillyard, Reginald Frank Doherty)
GBR (Arthur Wentworth Gore, Herbert Roper Barrett)— Indoor Courts
1912 SAF (Charles Lyndhurst Winslow, Harold Austin Kitson)
FRA (André H. Gobert, Maurice Germot)—Indoor Courts
1920 GBR (O. G. Noel Turnbull, Max Woosnam)
1924 USA (Vincent Richards, Frank Hunter)

Women's Singles

1900 Charlotte Cooper, GBR
1906 Esmee Simiriotou, GRE

1908 Dorothy Chambers, GBR
Gwendoline Eastlake-Smith, GBR—Indoor Courts
1912 Marguerite Broquedis, FRA
Edith M. Hannam, GBR—Indoor Courts
1920 Suzanne Lenglen, FRA
1924 Helen Wills, USA

Women's Doubles

1920 GBR (Winifred Margaret McNair, Kitty McKane)
1924 USA (Hazel Wightman, Helen Wills)

Mixed Doubles

1900 GBR (Charlotte Cooper, Reginald Frank Doherty)
1906 FRA (Marie Decugis, Max Decugis)
1912 GER (Dora Köring, Heinrich Schomburgk)
GBR (Edith M. Hannam, Charles Percy Dixon)—Indoor Courts

1920 FRA (Suzanne Lenglen, Max Decugis)
1924 USA (Hazel Wightman, R. Norris Williams)

MOTOR BOATING

1908 A-Class, E. B. Thubron, FRA
B-Class, Thornycroft, Redwood, GBR
C-Class, Thornycroft, Redwood, GBR

POLO

1900 GBR (A. Rawlinson, Frank J. MacKey, Foxhall Keene, Dennis Daly)
1908 GBR (Charles D. Miller, Patrick W. Nickalls, George A. Miller, Herbert H. Wilson)
1920 GBR (Tim P. Melville Frederick W. Barrett, John Wodehouse, Vivian N. Lockett)
1924 ARG (Arturo J. Kenny, Juan D. Nelson, Enrique Padilla, Juan

B. Miles, Guillermo Brooke Naylor)
1936 ARG (Luis J. Duggan, Roberto Cavanagh, Andrès Gazzotti, Manuel Andrada)

RACKETS

1908 Evan B. Noel, GBR—Men's singles
GBR (Vane H. Pennel, John J. Astor)—Men's doubles

ROQUE

1904 Charles Jacobus, USA

RUGBY

1900	FRA	1920	USA
1908	AUS	1924	USA

Winter Games

BIATHLON

10-Kilometer Individual

1980 Frank Ullrich, GDR

20-Kilometer Individual

1960 Klas Lestander, SWE
1964 Vladimir Melanin, URS
1968 Magnar Solberg, NOR
1972 Magnar Solberg, NOR
1976 Nikolai Kruglov, URS
1980 Anatoli Aljabiev, URS

Relay

1968 URS
1972 URS
1976 URS
1980 URS

BOBSLED

2-Man

1932	USA	1964	GBR
1936	USA	1968	ITA
1948	SUI	1972	GER
1952	GER	1976	GDR
1956	ITA	1980	SUI

4-Man

1924	SUI	1956	SUI
1928	USA	1964	CAN
1932	USA	1968	ITA
1936	SUI	1972	SUI
1948	USA	1976	GDR
1952	GER	1980	GDR

FIGURE SKATING

Pairs

1908 GER (Anna Hübler, Heinrich Burger)
1920 FIN (Ludowika and Walter Jakobsson-Eilers)
1924 AUT (Helene Engelmann, Alfred Berger)
1928 FRA (Andrée Joly, Pierre Brunet)
1932 FRA (Andrée and Pierre Brunet)
1936 GER (Maxie Herber, Ernst Baier)
1948 BEL (Micheline Lannoy, Pierre Baugniet)
1952 GER (Ria and Paul Falk)
1956 AUT (Elisabeth Schwarz, Kurt Oppelt)
1960 CAN (Barbara Wagner, Robert Paul)
1964 URS (Ludmilla Beloussova, O. Protopopov)
1968 URS (Ludmilla Beloussova, O. Protopopov)
1972 URS (Irina Rodnina, Aleksei Ulanov)
1976 URS (Irina Rodnina, Aleksandr Zaitsev)
1980 URS (Irina Rodnina, Aleksandr Zaitsev)

Men's Singles

1908 Ulrich Salchow, SWE
1920 Gillis Grafström, SWE
1924 Gillis Grafström, SWE
1928 Gillis Grafström, SWE
1932 Karl Schaefer, AUT
1936 Karl Schaefer, AUT
1948 Richard Button, USA
1952 Richard Button, USA
1956 Hayes Alan Jenkins, USA
1960 David Jenkins, USA

1964 Manfred Schnelldorfer, GER
1968 Wolfgang Schwarz, AUT
1972 Ondrej Nepela, TCH
1976 John Curry, GBR
1980 Robin Cousins, GBR

Women's Singles

1908 Madge Syers, GBR
1920 Magda Julin-Mauroy, SWE
1924 Herma Planck-Szabó, AUT
1928 Sonja Henie, NOR
1932 Sonja Henie, NOR
1936 Sonja Henie, NOR
1948 Barbara Ann Scott, CAN
1952 Jeannette Altwegg, GBR
1956 Tenley Albright, USA
1960 Carol Heiss, USA
1964 Sjoukje Dijkstra, HOL
1968 Peggy Fleming, USA
1972 Beatrix Schuba, AUT
1976 Dorothy Hamill, USA
1980 Anett Poetzsch, GDR

ICE DANCING

1976 URS (Ludmila Pakhomova, Aleksandr Gorshkov)
1980 URS (Natalia Linichuk, Gennadi Karponosov)

ICE HOCKEY

1920	CAN	1956	URS
1924	CAN	1960	USA
1928	CAN	1964	URS
1932	CAN	1968	URS
1936	GBR	1972	URS
1948	CAN	1976	URS
1952	CAN	1980	USA

LUGE

Men's Singles

1964	Thomas Koehler, GER
1968	Manfred Schmid, AUT
1972	Wolfgang Scheidel, GDR
1976	Detlef Guenther, GDR
1980	Bernhard Glass, GDR

Men's Doubles

1964	AUT (Josef Feistmantl, Manfred Stengl)
1968	GDR (Klaus Bonsack, Thomas Koehler)
1972	ITA (Paul Hildgartner, Walter Plaikner), GDR (Horst Hornlein, Heinhard Bredow) (tie)
1976	GDR (Hans Rinn, Norbert Hahn)
1980	GDR (Hans Rinn, Norbert Hahn)

Women's Singles

1964	Ortrun Enderlein, GER
1968	Erica Lechner, ITA
1972	Anna Marie Müller, GDR
1976	Margit Schumann, GDR
1980	Vera Zozulia, URS

SKIING, ALPINE

MEN

Downhill

1948	Henry Oreiller, FRA
1952	Zeno Colò, ITA
1956	Anton Sailer, AUT
1960	Jean Vuarnet, FRA
1964	Egon Zimmermann II, AUT
1968	Jean-Claude Killy, FRA
1972	Bernhard Russi, SUI
1976	Franz Klammer, AUT
1980	Leonhard Stock, AUT

Giant Slalom

1952	Stein Eriksen, NOR
1956	Anton Sailer, AUT
1960	Roger Staub, SUI
1964	François Bonlieu, FRA
1968	Jean-Claude Killy, FRA
1972	Gustavo Thoeni, ITA
1976	Heini Hemmi, SUI
1980	Ingemar Stenmark, SWE

Slalom

1948	Edi Reinalter, SUI
1952	Othmar Schneider, AUT
1956	Anton Sailer, AUT
1960	Ernst Hinterseer, AUT
1964	Josef Stiegler, AUT
1968	Jean-Claude Killy, FRA
1972	Francisco Fernández-Ochoa ESP
1976	Piero Gros, ITA
1980	Ingemar Stenmark, SWE

WOMEN

Downhill

1948	Hedy Schlunegger, SUI
1952	Trude Jochum-Beiser, AUT
1956	Madeleine Berthod, SUI
1960	Heidi Biebl, GER
1964	Christl Haas, AUT
1968	Olga Pall, AUT
1972	Marie Thérèse Nadig, SUI
1976	Rosi Mittermaier, GER
1980	Annemarie Moser-Proell, AUT

Giant Slalom

1952	Andrea Mead Lawrence, USA
1956	Ossi Reichert, GER
1960	Yvonne Ruegg, SUI
1964	Marielle Goitschel, FRA
1968	Nancy Greene, CAN
1972	Marie Thérèse Nadig, SUI
1976	Kathy Kreiner, CAN
1980	Hanni Wenzel, LIE

Slalom

1948	Gretchen Fraser, USA
1952	Andrea Mead Lawrence, USA
1956	Renée Colliard, SUI
1960	Anne Heggtveit, CAN
1964	Christine Goitschel, FRA
1968	Marielle Goitschel, FRA
1972	Barbara Cochran, USA
1976	Rosi Mittermaier, GER
1980	Hanni Wenzel, LIE

DISCONTINUED EVENTS

Men's Combined Alpine

1936	Franz Pfnür, GER
1948	Henri Oreiller, FRA

Women's Combined Alpine

1936	Christi Cranz, GER
1948	Trude Beiser, AUT

SKIING, NORDIC

MEN

15-Kilometer Cross-Country

1924	Thorleif Haug, NOR
1928	Johan Gröttumsbraaten, NOR
1932	Sven Utterström, SWE
1936	Erik-August Larsson, SWE
1948	Martin Lundström, SWE
1952	Hallgeir Brenden, NOR
1956	Hallgeir Brenden, NOR
1960	Haakon Brusveen, NOR
1964	Eero Mäntyranta, FIN
1968	Harald Grönningen, NOR
1972	Sven-Ake Lundback, SWE
1976	Nikolai Bajukov, URS
1980	Thomas Wassberg, SWE

30-Kilometer Cross-Country

1956	Veikko Hakulinen, FIN
1960	Sixten Jernberg, SWE
1964	Eero Mäntyranta, FIN
1968	Franco Nones, ITA
1972	Vyacheslav Vedenin, URS
1976	Sergei Saveliev, URS
1980	Nikolai Zimyatov, URS

50-Kilometer Cross-Country

1924	Thorleif Haug, NOR
1928	Per Erik Hedlund, SWE
1932	Veli Saarinen, FIN
1936	Elis Viklund, SWE
1948	Nils Karlsson, SWE
1952	Veikko Hakulinen, FIN
1956	Sixten Jernberg, SWE

(continued)

1960	Kalevi Hämäläinen, FIN
1964	Sixten Jernberg, SWE
1968	Ole Ellefsaeter, NOR
1972	Paal Tyldum, NOR
1976	Ivar Formo, NOR
1980	Nikolai Zimyatov, URS

Combined (Cross-Country and Jump)

1924	Thorleif Haug, NOR
1928	Johan Gröttumsbraaten, NOR
1932	Johan Gröttumsbraaten, NOR
1936	Oddbjörn Hagen, NOR
1948	Heikki Hasu, FIN
1952	Simon Slåttvik, NOR
1956	Sverre Stenersen, NOR
1960	Georg Thoma, GER
1964	Tormod Knutsen, NOR
1968	Franz Keller, GER
1972	Ulrich Wehling, GDR
1976	Ulrich Wehling, GDR
1980	Ulrich Wehling, GDR

40-Kilometer Cross-Country Relay

1936	FIN
1948	SWE
1952	FIN
1956	URS
1960	FIN
1964	SWE
1968	NOR
1972	URS
1976	FIN
1980	URS

Ski Jumping (70 Meter)

1924	Jacob T. Thams, NOR
1928	Alfred Andersen, NOR
1932	Birger Ruud, NOR
1936	Birger Ruud, NOR
1948	Petter Hugsted, NOR
1952	Arnfinn Bergmann, NOR
1956	Antti Hyvärinen, FIN
1960	Helmut Recknagel, GER
1964	Veikko Kankkonen, FIN
1968	Jiri Raska, TCH
1972	Yukio Kasaya, JPN
1976	Hans-Georg Aschenbach, GDR
1980	Anton Innauer, AUT

Ski Jumping (90 Meter)

1964	Toralf Engan, NOR
1968	Vladimir Beloussov, URS
1972	Wojciech Fortuna, POL
1976	Karl Schnabl, AUT
1980	Jouko Tormanen, FIN

WOMEN

5-Kilometer Cross-Country

1964	Claudia Boyarskikh, URS
1968	Toini Gustafsson, SWE
1972	Galina Kulakova, URS
1976	Helena Takalo, FIN
1980	Raisa Smetanina, URS

10-Kilometer Cross-Country

1952	Lydia Wideman, FIN
1956	Ljubovj Kozyreva, URS
1960	Maria Gusakova, URS
1964	Claudia Boyarskikh, URS
1968	Toini Gustafsson, SWE
1972	Galina Kulakova, URS
1976	Raisa Smetanina, URS
1980	Barbara Petzold, GDR

Cross-Country Relay

1956	FIN
1960	SWE
1964	URS
1968	NOR
1972	URS
1976	URS
1980	GDR

SPEED SKATING

MEN

500 Meters

1924	Charles Jewtraw, USA
1928	Clas Thunberg, FIN, Bernt Evensen, NOR (tie)
1932	John A. Shea, USA
1936	Ivar Ballangrud, NOR
1948	Finn Helgesen, NOR
1952	Kenneth Henry, USA
1956	Yevgeni Grishin, URS
1960	Yevgeni Grishin, URS
1964	Richard McDermott, USA
1968	Erhard Keller, GER
1972	Erhard Keller, GER
1976	Yevgeni Kulikov, URS
1980	Eric Heiden, USA

1,000 Meters

1976	Peter Mueller, USA
1980	Eric Heiden, USA

1,500 Meters

1924	Clas Thunberg, FIN
1928	Clas Thunberg, FIN
1932	John A. Shea, USA

1936	Charles Mathisen, NOR
1948	Sverre Farstad, NOR
1952	Hjalmar Andersen, NOR
1956	Y. Grishin, Y. Mikhailov (tie), URS
1960	Y. Grishin, URS, Roald Edgar Aas, NOR (tie)
1964	Ants Antson, URS
1968	Cornelis Verkerk, HOL
1972	Ard Schenk, HOL
1976	Jan Egil Storholt, NOR
1980	Eric Heiden, USA

5,000 Meters

1924	Clas Thunberg, FIN
1928	Ivar Ballangrud, NOR
1932	Irving Jaffee, USA
1936	Ivar Ballangrud, NOR
1948	Reidar Liaklev, NOR
1952	Hjalmar Andersen, NOR
1956	Boris Shilkov, URS
1960	Viktor Kosichkin, URS
1964	Knut Johannesen, NOR
1968	F. Anton Maier, NOR
1972	Ard Schenk, HOL
1976	Sten Stensen, NOR
1980	Eric Heiden, USA

10,000 Meters

1924	Julius Skutnabb, FIN
1932	Irving Jaffee, USA
1936	Ivar Ballangrud, NOR
1948	Ake Seyffarth, SWE
1952	Hjalmar Andersen, NOR
1956	Sigvard Ericsson, SWE
1960	Knut Johannesen, NOR
1964	Jonny Nilsson, SWE
1968	Jonny Hoeglin, SWE
1972	Ard Schenk, HOL
1976	Piet Kleine, HOL
1980	Eric Heiden, USA

WOMEN

500 Meters

1960	Helga Haase, GER
1964	Lidia Skoblikova, URS
1968	Ludmila Titova, URS
1972	Anne Henning, USA
1976	Sheila Young, USA
1980	Karin Enke, GDR

1,000 Meters

1960	Klara Guseva, URS
1964	Lidia Skoblikova, URS
1968	Carolina Geijssen, HOL
1972	Monika Pflug, GER
1976	Tatiana Averina, URS
1980	Natalia Petruseva, URS

1,500 Meters

1960	Lidia Skoblikova, URS
1964	Lidia Skoblikova, URS
1968	Kaija Mustonen, FIN
1972	Dianne Holum, USA
1976	Galina Stepanskaya, URS
1980	Annie Borckink, HOL

3,000 Meters

1960	Lidia Skoblikova, URS
1964	Lidia Skoblikova, URS
1968	Johanna Schut, HOL
1972	Christina Baas-Kaiser, HOL
1976	Tatiana Averina, URS
1980	Bjoerg Eva Jensen, NOR

PHOTO CREDITS

Unless otherwise acknowledged below, all photographs included in this volume were supplied by The Associated Press.

Page(s) 8—FPG (left), Alpha; 9—DiMaggio Kalish, Peter Arnold (left), FPG; 14–15—Ernst Haas, Magnum; 16—Abbie Carroll Wilson; 17—National Museum of Athens (top right), Hugh Stern, Monkmeyer; 18–19—The Metropolitan Museum of Art; 20–21—Raymond V. Schoder, S.J.; 22—National Museum, Rome, European Art Color (top), Shostal; 23—Shostal; 24—Rene Burri, Magnum; 24–25, 26—Bettmann Archive, Inc.; 27—Brown Brothers; 28—The Mansell Collection; 35—George Zolandaikas; 36—Bettmann Archive, Inc.; 37—Monkmeyer; 40—Photo Researchers; 41—International Tennis Hall of Fame and Tennis Museum; 42, 44, 47—United States Olympic Committee (USOC); 48—USOC (program), Missouri Historical Society; 50—Missouri Historical Society; 51–54, 56–57—USOC; 58–Canadian Public Archives; 59—Photo Researchers; 60, 62–64—USOC; 65—Alpha; 66–69—USOC; 71—USOC (bottom right); 72—USOC; 73—Monkmeyer; 74—© G.D. Hackett, N.Y.; 75—Belgian National Tourist Office; 76—USOC; 78—USOC (bottom); 80–82—USOC; 83—Culver Pictures, Inc.; 84—USOC; 85—French Tourist Office; 86—USOC; 87—USOC, National Ski Hall of Fame (bottom right); 89–93—USOC; 95—Brown Brothers; 96–98—USOC; 99—USOC (top right); 100–101—Culver Pictures, Inc.; 103—Culver Pictures, Inc.; 104—USOC; 105—Alpha; 106–07, 110–11—USOC; 112—Photo Researchers; 113—USOC; 114—USOC (left); 115—USOC (left); 118—USOC; 119—USOC (right); 121—Photo Researchers; 139—Keystone (top); 143—Alpha; 146—Press Photo; 148—FPG (top); 158–FPG; 161—Bettmann Archive, Inc.; 169—Central Picture Services, Grolier; 172—Olympic Photo Association (bottom); 184—Lise Dermist, Image Bank; 191—Finnish Tourist Office; 204—Photo Researchers; 211—Image Bank; 224—Squaw Valley Ski Association; 231—John G. Ross, Photo Researchers; 239—USOC; 291—Jerry Cooke; 347—Paul Sutton, Duomo; 353 (top)—Zimmerman/FPG; 365—Lehtikuva/Photoreporters; 366 (both)—Tony Duffy/Duomo; 367 (top)—Tony Duffy/Duomo; 368 (top)—Lehtikuva/Photoreporters; 370—Photoreporters; 371—Don Morely/Duomo; 373—Don Morely/Duomo; 374 (top)—Don Morely/Duomo, Photoreporters; 376—Francolon/Simon, Gamma.
Cover Photo: J. Zimmerman/FPG

INDEX